Designing and Implementing Computer Workgroups

ISBN 0-13-082709-6

90000

9 780130 827098

Hewlett-Packard® Professional Books

Atchison	Object-Oriented Test & Measurement Software Development in C++
Blinn	Portable Shell Programming
Blommers	Architecting Enterprise Solutions with UNIX Networking
Blommers	Practical Planning for Network Growth
Caruso	Power Programming in HP OpenView
Chew	The Java/C++ Cross-Reference Handbook
Cook	Building Enterprise Information Architectures
Costa	Planning and Designing High Speed Networks
Crane	A Simplified Approach to Image Processing
Day	The Color Scanning Handbook
Derickson	Fiber Optic Test and Measurement
Eisenmann and Eisenmann	Machinery Malfunction Diagnosis and Correction
Fernandez	Configuring the Common Desktop Environment
Fristrup	USENET: Netnews for Everyone
Fristrup	The Essential Web Surfer Survival Guide
Gann	Desktop Scanners: Image Quality
Grady	Practical Software Metrics for Project Management and Process Improvement
Greenberg	A Methodology for Developing and Deploying Internet and Intranet Solutions
Grosvenor, Ichiro, O'Brien	Mainframe Downsizing to Upsize Your Business: IT-Preneuring
Gunn	A Guide to NetWare® for UNIX®
Helsel	Graphical Programming: A Tutorial for HP VEE
Helsel	Visual Programming with HP VEE, Third Edition
Holman, Lund	Instant JavaScript
Kane	PA-RISC 2.0 Architecture
Knouse	Practical DCE Programming
Lee	The ISDN Consultant
Lewis	The Art & Science of Smalltalk
Lichtenbelt, Crane, Naqvi	Introduction to Volume Rendering
Loomis	Object Databases in Practice
Lucke	Designing and Implementing Computer Workgroups
Lund	Integrating UNIX® and PC Network Operating Systems
Madell	Disk and File Management Tasks on HP-UX
Mahoney	High-Mix Low-Volume Manufacturing
Malan, Letsinger, Coleman	Object-Oriented Development at Work: Fusion in the Real World
McFarland	X Windows on the World
McMinds/Whitty	Writing Your Own OSF/Motif Widgets
Norton, DiPasquale	Thread Time: The Multithreaded Programming Guide
Orzessek, Sommer	ATM & MPEG-2: A Practical Guide to Computer Security
Phaal	LAN Traffic Management
Pipkin	Halting the Hacker: A Practical Guide to Computer Security
Poniatowski	HP-UX 11.x System Administration "How To" Book, Second Edition
Poniatowski	HP NetServer Guide for Windows NT®
Poniatowski	HP-UX System Administration Handbook and Toolkit
Poniatowski	HP-UX 10.x System Administration "How To" Book
Poniatowski	Learning the HP-UX Operating System
Poniatowski	Windows NT® and HP-UX System Administrator's "How To" Book
Ryan	Distributed Object Technology: Concepts and Applications
Simmons	Software Measurement: A Visualization Toolkit
Sperley	Enterprise Data Warehouse, Volume 1: Planning, Building, and Implementation
Thomas	Cable Television Proof-of-Performance
Thomas, Edgington	Digital Basics for Cable Television Systems
Thornburgh	Fibre Channel for Mass Storage
Weygant	Clusters for High Availability: A Primer of HP-UX Solutions
Witte	Electronic Test Instruments
Yawn, Stachnick, Sellars	The Legacy Continues: Using the HP 3000 with HP-UX and Windows NT

Designing and Implementing Computer Workgroups

Robert W. Lucke
Senior Technical Consultant
Hewlett-Packard Company
Portland, Oregon

http://www.hp.com/go/retailbooks

Prentice Hall PTR
Upper Saddle River, NJ 07458
http://www.phptr.com

Library of Congress Cataloging-in-Publication Data

Lucke, Robert W.
Designing and implementing computer workgroups / Robert W. Lucke
p. cm. -- (Hewlett-Packard professional books)
Includes bibliographical references.
ISBN 0-13-082709-6
1. System design. 2. Work groups--Data processing. I. Title.
II. Series.
QA76.9.S88L83 1999
650'.0285'46--dc21 **99-24936**
CIP

Editorial/production supervision: *Vanessa Moore*
Cover production: *Talar Agasyan*
Cover design: *Design Source*
Cover design director: *Jerry Votta*
Manufacturing manager: *Alexis R. Heydt*
Marketing manager: *Lisa Konzelmann*
Acquisitions editor: *Jill Pisoni*
Project coordinator: *Anne Trowbridge*
Manager, Hewlett-Packard Retail Publishing: *Patricia Pekary*
Editor, Hewlett-Packard Retail Publishing: *Susan Wright*

Published by Prentice-Hall, Inc.
A Simon & Schuster Company
Upper Saddle River, New Jersey 07458

Prentice Hall books are widely used by corporations and government agencies for training, marketing, and resale.
The publisher offers discounts on this book when ordered in bulk quantities.
For more information, contact Corporate Sales Department, Phone: 800-382-3419;
Fax: 201-236-7141; E-mail: corpsales@prenhall.com
Or write: Prentice Hall PTR, Corp. Sales Dept., One Lake Street, Upper Saddle River, NJ 07458.

ISBN 0-13-082709-6

Printed in the United States of America

10 9 8 7 6 5 4 3 2

Prentice-Hall International (UK) Limited, *London*
Prentice-Hall of Australia Pty. Limited, *Sydney*
Prentice-Hall Canada Inc., *Toronto*
Prentice-Hall Hispanoamericana, S.A., *Mexico*
Prentice-Hall of India Private Limited, *New Delhi*
Prentice-Hall of Japan, Inc., *Tokyo*
Prentice-Hall (Singapore) Pte. Ltd., *Singapore*
Editora Prentice-Hall do Brasil, Ltda., *Rio de Janeiro*

This book is dedicated to my loving wife,
Teri,
without whose patience and support
I wouldn't be
where I am today.

Contents

List of Figures

Preface

Welcome! This book is aimed squarely at system administrators, systems engineers, network designers, and computer users who want practical, real-world advice to help improve the design of their current computer environments. If you wonder why your file server may not able to serve the number of clients you expected, read on! If you wonder why things come to a grinding halt on Friday afternoon, read on! If you want evolutionary techniques to harness and apply new technology in your computer network, read on! Or, if you are just curious about what it takes to design and implement an enterprise-wide architecture based on client-server workgroups, read on!

Computers and, increasingly, large networks of computers are becoming more important in successfully meeting the challenges faced by today's businesses. A computer network allows individuals to share data and computational resources with other users, while using their own local resources (central processing unit or CPU, graphical user interface or GUI, and mass storage) to avoid the resource shortages that my occur in a more centralized environment. Unfortunately, the potential increase in productivity provided by decentralized computer networks has associated costs: increased complexity, increased system administration effort, and increased vulnerability to failures. This book provides tools for dealing with these issues in your environment.

The structure of the computer network, and the allocation of resources within that network, is crucial to successfully "getting the job done" from an individual user's perspective. Frequently, however, the structure of our networks, and the groups of computers within them, is determined more by uncontrolled evolution and short-term necessity[1] than it should be. Because of this uncontrolled evolutionary approach, the potential of the compute power in the network cannot be fully realized by its users.

Designing and Implementing Computer Workgroups is an attempt to apply systems engineering techniques and the author's over 25 years of real-world experience to simplifying the design, implementation, and controlled evolution[2] of computer workgroups. Some of the methodologies used are borrowed from the software development world, since complexity is something that most software developers deal with on a daily basis. In addition to focusing on methods of reducing complexity, this book deals with some of the challenges related to the interoperability of different computer operating system types (e.g. various "flavors" of Unix® and PC-based workstations running Microsoft® Windows™) within the workgroup.

There are many excellent books that focus on the individual aspects of computer systems: networking, client-server applications development, system administration, OS kernel tuning, etc. This book will focus on systems design using those individual elements along with a practical, vendor and technology neutral approach for the type of real-world, *existing* environments that are encountered every day. The word "existing" is emphasized here, because many environments do not have the luxury of being redesigned from scratch. In the real world, where business needs drive decisions, today's environment must be transformed into tomorrow's solution with minimal interruption to the workgroup's users.

First we will cover theoretical approaches to workgroup design, since we will need a model or framework to guide our choices. After the introduction of the theoretical model, however, we will proceed on to real-world examples of analysis, design, and redesign of networked computer workgroups. Once we have workgroup design principles firmly in hand, we will examine ways of gluing workgroups together across a distributed enterprise. This information is all based on my software development, system administration, and professional consulting experiences with large customers.

Next we will focus on tying the myriad aspects of workgroup design together in enough detail that a high-level design (or transition plan) can be sketched out and basic technology choices can be made. When specifics are necessary, they will usually concentrate on the Unix and Microsoft Windows operating systems, since they are most frequently encountered in today's networks.

So, let us begin. Please read on!

1. Unbolting an airplane's wings for maintenance or redesign while it is flying at 30,000 feet is not generally considered a good idea.

2. In nature, the evolutionary process is known neither for its great speed nor for its optimal solutions. In computer networks, the process is somewhat faster, but still produces less than optimal solutions in the general case.

About the Author

Rob Lucke is a Senior Technical Consultant who works for Hewlett-Packard's Americas Technical Computing Advanced Technology Center. Much of Rob's time is spent performing environmental assessments for large manufacturing companies, focusing on improvements in technical engineering infrastructure. He has also helped implement large software development environments in several HP customers. This book is based on his experiences and observations while working with some of HP's largest technical computing customers.

Rob's professional specialties include: computing architectures, large-scale system administration, software development, system and application performance tuning, and heterogeneous interoperability. He holds a Bachelor's degree in Electrical and Computer Engineering and has over 25 years of computing experience. Rob's perspective truly extends from the chip to the enterprise.

His hobbies include horseback riding (dressage and jumping), large-scale lawn architecture, food, wine, foreign languages, and Monty Python.

Acknowledgments

I would like to acknowledge the following individuals for their contributions to this book: Greg Cagle, Steve Jumonville of 3Com Corporation, Mark Richards of EMC, Michael Wierzbinski of Farragut Consulting, Jaap Kooman of the University of Delft in The Netherlands, Tom Spuhler, John Blommers, Fred Sprague, Bobby Masson, Alan Roberts, and Michael Mahon of Hewlett-Packard, all of whom have helped keep me "honest."

I wish to express my profound thanks to NXA and AORTA teams at Origin B.V. in The Netherlands, Philips Research Laboratories, and Philips Semiconductors, who kindly allowed me to describe the AORTA architecture (See "Case Study: Workgroup Design for Power Users — AORTA" on page 333.) Many of the concepts in this book are a direct result of lessons learned from the AORTA environment. I would also like to thank Ronald van Driel for his contributions to this section.

I am grateful to the entire RAPTOR team at Hewlett-Packard's Spokane Division: Scotty Smith, Dan Krantz, Gary Davis, Joe Giegel, Mike Griffith, Ken Laird, Ken Olsen, Steve McKinsey, TJ Mills, Ed Murrah, Brian Town, Paul Arndt, and John Westerman for allowing me to share their success with my readers. (See "Case Study: Design, Redesign, and Evolution — The RAPTOR Project" on page 349.)

I would like to acknowledge the efforts of Patricia Pekary and Susan Wright at Hewlett-Packard Retail Publishing who encouraged me to write this book. I also wish to thank Jill Pisoni and Vanessa Moore at Prentice Hall, who supported my through the production processs. A special note of thanks goes to my copy editor, Diane Lange, who helped make the book more readable.

Finally, I would like to thank my boss, Bob Vomaske, for supporting this project and showing immense patience.

How to Use This Book

This book is structured so that each successive chapter builds upon the information presented by its predecessors. In the beginning, the information is mainly theoretical, becoming more and more concrete as you progress to two case studies of actual workgroup environments. The general structure of the book is:

- Theoretical groundwork — Chapters 1 through 3.
- High-level workgroup structure — Chapters 4 and 5.
- Workgroup hardware components — Chapters 6 through 8.
- Internal workgroup structure — Chapters 9 through 13.
- Interconnection and interoperability issues — Chapters 14 and 15.
- Case studies of workgroup implementation — Chapters 16 and 17.
- Supporting material — Chapter 18 and Appendices A through D.

For readers that are unfamiliar with the client-server model or object-oriented programming concepts, covering the first three chapters will provide a good basis for later design topics. However, for readers that just want to get to the "meat" of the topic or who are not interested in the theoretical underpinnings, the first three chapters may be skipped or used as reference material. Another approach is to start with the two case studies, note the essentials of a good workgroup design, and then tackle any unfamiliar technical ground by covering material in the other chapters.

CHAPTER 1

At the Beginning: Client-Server Design Concepts

In this first chapter, we will cover some of the basic concepts that later design principles and methodologies are built upon. First we cover the "client-server" architecture, because it is a proven approach to building flexible, scalable environments. Once we introduce the client-server architecture, we will examine some of the ways of allocating resources within the framework provided by that architecture.

1.1 Defining the Client-Server Architecture

While the term "client-server" is encountered frequently in today's computer industry, the meaning is often unclear or ambiguous. We will explore some of the meanings of the term "client-server", along with potential applicability to computer network environments and commonly encountered network resources. Many of today's system administration tools have not caught up with the management requirements necessary to automatically analyze and create a client-server distribution of network resources; manual techniques may be quite successful at this task.

The intent of this section is to identify, as well as clarify, some of the potential meanings of "client-server" and to present a method for manually analyzing, grouping, and managing client-server–based resources in a computer network.

1.2 What Does "Client-Server" Really Mean?

As computer professionals, we all must cope with a never-ending stream of new technology. Along with the introduction of each new technology comes a dizzying array of matching terminology. We use (or abuse) the many technical terms to the point that they begin to take on the quality of a "buzzword", that is, a word or phrase frequently heard but seldom understood.

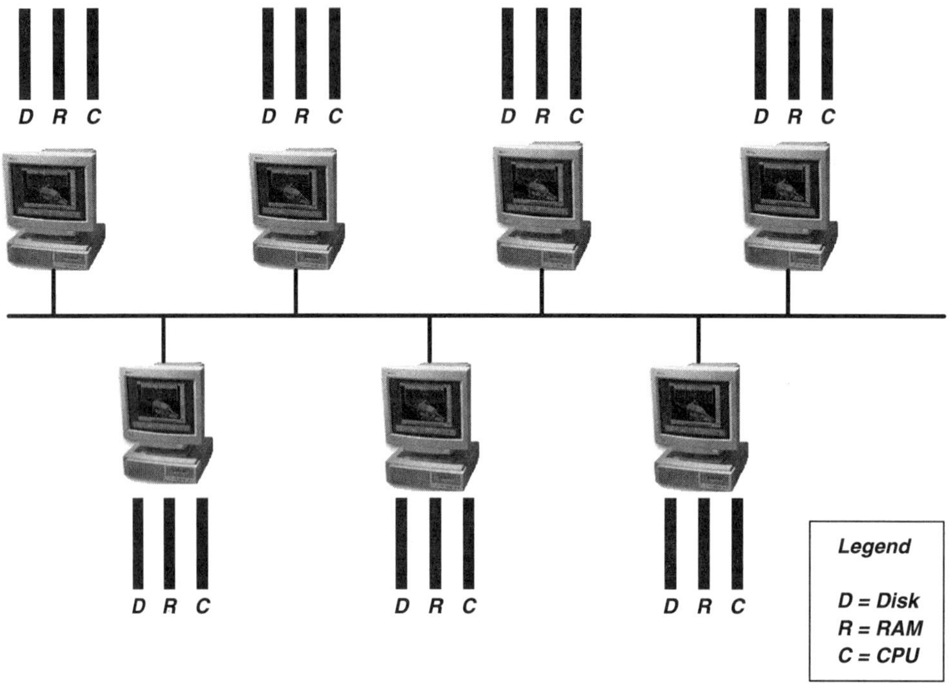

Figure 1-1 Hardware Resources in a Peer-to-Peer Computer Relationship

"Client-server" is one term that has fulfilled its potential for becoming an industry buzzword. This is unfortunate; the term "client-server" has a lot of relevance to today's networks.

Part of the difficulty with getting our arms around the term is that it takes on different meanings or connotations, depending upon who is doing the defining. In a very general sense, the term client-server really denotes a type of relationship between entities. The entities we will discuss, of course, are software applications running on networked computer systems. There are many such types of possible relationships (such as a hierarchy) between multiple entities, but we will only examine two here: "peer-to-peer" and "client-server". Let's take a short look at one of those relationships, "peer-to-peer", that will help us when we look more closely at a client-server relationship.

1.2.1 Examining a "Peer-to-Peer" Relationship

In a peer-to-peer relationship, all entities have equal standing with one another, and all are equally capable of running the same set of services. In many ways, this relationship is the easiest type to recognize, configure, and manage. This does not mean that it is necessarily the most efficient or cost-effective way of allocating computer resources.

In peer-to-peer configuration, all of the individual systems are configured (more or less) alike. They have relatively equal amounts of resources (e.g., disk, memory, and CPU power), and all resources are equally shared among the various systems in the group. Each machine is completely capable of performing any task that a particular user may desire, without the involvement of, or reliance on, another system's resources. For those of you who are familiar with Apollo Computer and the DOMAIN/OS[1], this was by default a peer-to-peer environment when considering system hardware capabilities.

Figure 1-1 depicts a network of computer systems configured in a peer-to-peer manner. Every computer has the same hardware resources—disk, RAM, and CPU—as well as the same software configuration in terms of operating system and applications. Because the machines are all similarly configured, a user who is running a word-processing application uses far less of the local resources than a user that might be doing a thermal analysis of a circuit board. In the first case, there are very probably underutilized resources, such as RAM, CPU cycles, or hardware graphics acceleration. In the second case, the local resources are more likely to be fully utilized, possibly even overutilized.

Underutilization of resources is common in a peer-to-peer network where there are multiple applications types being used. The underutilization of resources on some systems, along with full or overutilization on others can mean that some users are not able to get their tasks completed in the optimum amount of time, while others may have no difficulties. Here is an example of how misallocation of resources in a networked environment can actually cost money.

1.2.2 The Client-Server Relationship

In a client-server relationship, there are at least two types of logical entities involved: the client entity and the server entity. It is important to note at this point that the term client-server may be applied either to hardware (computer system) or to software (applications) running on the hardware. This is one potential point of confusion, as the hardware *may* be configured differently to run the client software or the server software, but does not necessarily have to be[2].

In the case of software entities, it is possible that both client and server may exist on the same computer system or be split across multiple systems in the network. How the actual tasks that an applications performs are split between the client and the server entities will vary, usually determined by the application's designer. There are some commonly encountered configurations of client-server software that we shall discuss later.

1. Legend has it that Apollo Computer's DOMAIN stood for Distributed Object Multiple Access Interactive Network / Operating System.

2. The industry commonly refers to a computer system that runs client software as a "client" and one that runs server software as a "server". We will adopt this convention to avoid causing additional confusion.

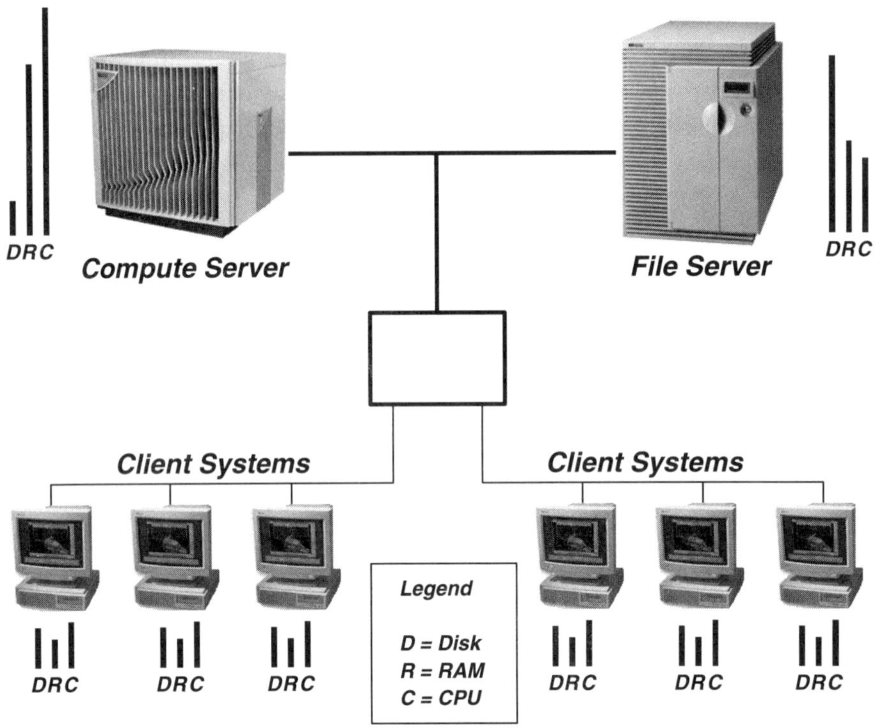

Figure 1-2 Hardware Resources in a Client-Server Computer Relationship

Unlike the peer-to-peer environment, the client-server relationship is not one of equal capability between client and server entities. The server entity "possesses" and manages a well-defined set of resources on behalf of its client or clients. The client-server model may also be characterized as a "request-response" interaction. To use the resource, the clients *must* make requests to the server entity. The server responds to, services, or "serves" its client's requests for the resource that it manages. Since the client-server relationship is a logical[3] one, nothing prevents both the client and the server components of an application from running on the same underlying hardware.

Figure 1-2 shows an environment that has resources unequally distributed between client and server machines. You can think of the system resources as being water in a set of buckets associated with each system; in this example there are buckets for RAM, CPU cycles, and disk storage. Resources are moved from the client system's buckets and reapportioned to the resource bucket belonging to a server or group of servers in the network.

3. That is, not enforced by physical constraints.

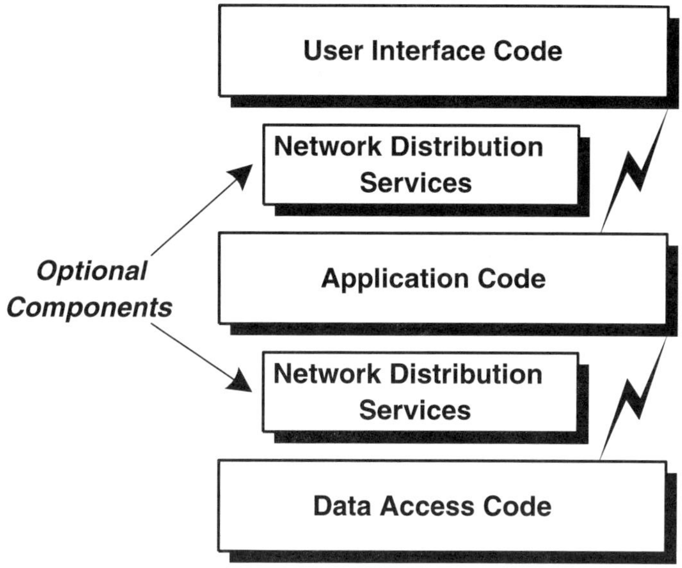

Figure 1-3 Client-Server Application Components

In this type of environment, there are usually *N* clients to each server, with the server providing all of the services associated with its resource to multiple clients. The client-server relationship may be thought of as a many-to-one relationship. The number of clients that a server can handle depends on several factors, including the type of resource being managed, the number of total simultaneous requests, and the request frequency from each client.

One other important performance factor is the type of connection between the client and the server and its relative "health". Obviously a poor network connection can influence clients and servers communicating across the network[4]. Because one of the defining characteristics of today's client-server applications is the presence of a network connection between the client and the server, you will notice that we will focus a lot of our effort on the network portion of the environment.

1.2.3 Client-Server Application Configurations and Components

Within the term client-server, there are many possible application configurations. The configuration of a client-server architecture is determined by where the associated application is broken into separate components. At the most basic level, the application may be split into sev-

4. Other types of client-to-server connections, such as Unix pipes, FIFOs, shared memory, or other interprocess communication mechanisms, have their own characteristics and failure modes.

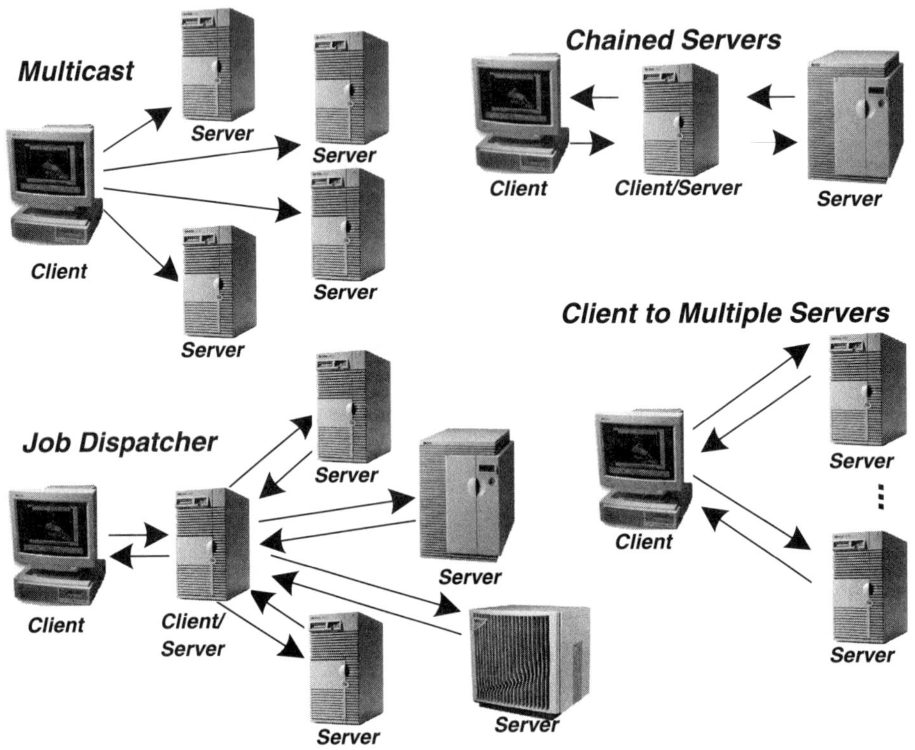

Figure 1-4 Examples of Client-Server Physical Distribution Models

eral different components: the graphical user interface (presentation logic), application logic, and data management logic.

It is possible to insert distribution services between any, all, or none of the three basic components. In the latter case, you end up with the familiar "monolithic" application configuration, running on a single system. With distribution services inserted, the result is a client-server application. This is diagrammed in Figure 1-3.

Sometimes identifying a client-server relationship is difficult because the system being studied is a hybrid design. Under these circumstances, there may be multiple levels of client-server relationships, or a single level where one client may in turn be a server to other clients. There are some commonly encountered client-server configurations which involve more complicated physical distributions of the application components and some more complicated interactions between those components. Some examples are shown in Figure 1-4.

Combinations involving other relationship models are possible, based on the whims of the application designers. For these reasons, and others, there may not be a clean distinction in hybrid system designs or systems that are in transition between the client-server model and other configurations. We will try to stick to the clearly identifiable cases, and you should avoid designing such complicated relationships if at all possible.

1.2.4 Client-Server Distribution Services

While describing the client-server application architecture, we did not venture beyond the conceptual description of the application being split into components and "glued" together with "distribution services". Examining the available distribution services in an environment is an important aspect of both good design and analysis. If the necessary services are not available or reliable, client-server applications may quite literally fall apart.

The term "distribution services" is a very general label. The services used to allow distribution of client-server application components include: remote procedure call facilities (RPC), directory services, system management services, performance measurement services, load balancing, and a whole host of other potential components. These services may be distributed across multiple systems or reside on a single server. When designing an environment, it is easier to separate the services as if they were running on their own computer systems, only collapsing the relationships between services and the physical server system when the final hardware configuration is determined.

Our schematic view of the client-server world, then, is the client logic communicating with servers providing data access, transaction processing, and compute power. Interaction between the client and the rest of the environment takes place through some form of communication facility. A set of infrastructure services provides the glue to hold the application architecture together.

A transaction processing function or database server may, in some cases, differentiate a "commercial" client-server application from a "technical" client-server application. The transaction facility may be viewed as providing the business logic necessary to properly direct client behavior, according to a predefined set of rules used to model data flow in a business. In most technical applications, this particular service is usually absent[5] or may be viewed as part of the data service.

The infrastructure services are common functionality needed by all client-server applications and their users for proper operation. Time synchronization between computers systems, software licensing, electronic mail, directory services, user authentication and access (security), software distribution, and especially environmental management are all examples of services needed by almost every application in the client-server environment. Determining what these

5. Making a distinction between a "technical" application and a "commercial" application is a difficult undertaking, at best. I believe that deep down, the distinction is an artificial one, and mention it only because it is frequently encountered in real customer environments. The technical versus commercial chasm is born of the traditional rift between Information Technology (IT) staff and the Engineering Services, each with their own "special" needs and computer environments to support them. I have noticed lately that both groups are adopting some of the other's best practices and values, so maybe this artificial distinction will finally disappear, as I believe it should.

common services are and ensuring their availability is an important part of the design or assessment of a client-server environment.

1.2.5 A Pause to Catch Our Breath

Whew. So far we have taken a whirlwind tour of the term "client-server". Let's pause and examine some important points. First of all, you should have some idea of the characteristics of a client-server application and its supporting environment by this point. You should also have some feel for just how flexible the client-server architecture is. Now let's put some of this information to good use by introducing some more specific details.

1.2.6 How Do I Recognize a Client-Server Relationship?

For those of us that are used to other relationship models, the client-server model and its many permutations may seem strange at first. The natural tendency is to configure everything in peer-to-peer mode, which is easier to grasp conceptually. This is also the way that environments tend to evolve, starting with one machine, adding another, and another, and so on.

We may ask, "Just how do I recognize a client-server environment when I see one?" This can be easier than it first seems. When confronted by something that purports to use a client-server model, start by asking the following questions:

- What is the resource that is being managed?
- Who is doing the resource management?
- Who is using the resource?

With the answers to these questions in hand, try drawing a picture[6] that represents the relationships among the entities being examined. You should see:

- A clear logical or physical division between the manager and the users of the resource (the server and the clients)
- Usually, one server to multiple clients
- A clear division of "intelligence" or "responsibility" with regards to managing the resource, with the client being the least capable of the two entities

For simplicity, we have only considered a single client to single server relationship up to this point. Figure 1-5 shows a slightly more complicated situation.

The X-windows system, used by Unix™ and other operating systems to provide remote graphical display capabilities, is a good example of a client-server relationship that takes a little

6. Getting into the habit of drawing pictures of the relationships between various entities will make analyzing complex situations easier when we encounter them later. One of the things I always ask for is a diagram of whatever environment I am analyzing.

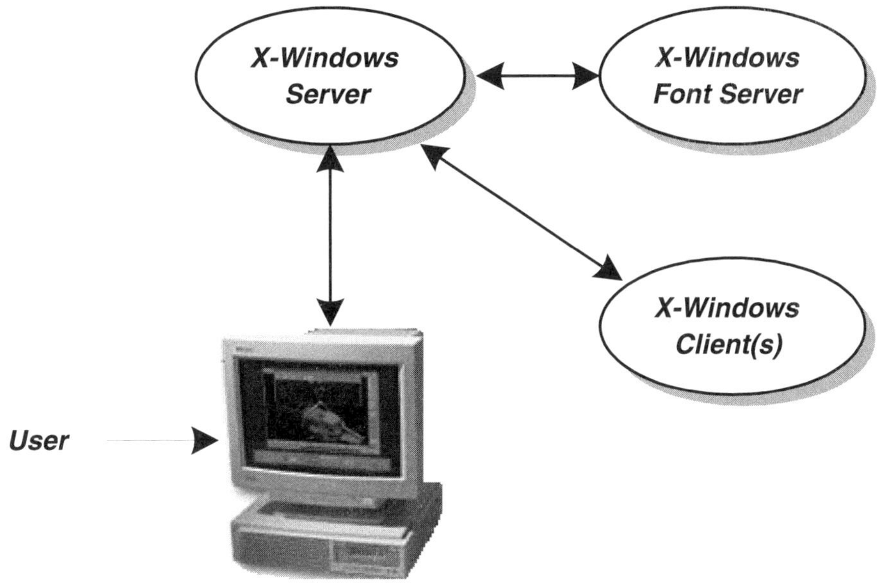

Figure 1-5 Where Is the Client and Where Is the Server?

analysis to understand. Users that are new to the X-windows system frequently ask, "Aren't the programs that are using the X-windows display actually the servers, since they are acting on behalf of the user?"

At first glance, it appears that the client and the server entities are reversed. After identifying the resources being managed, the picture makes a little more sense. It is the user's graphics display and input devices that are being managed by the X-windows server on behalf of the X-windows clients that are using them. So, with regards to the X-windows services, the programs are indeed clients to the X-windows server and not vice versa.

Note also that the X-windows server itself makes use of the X-windows font server. So, as shown in Figure 1-5, there are multiple client-server relationships at work. The X-windows clients are using resources "served" by the X-windows server, and the X-windows server is using resources that are "served" by the X-windows font server.

There is another important point to be made here. Because of the flexibility inherent in the example, a resourceful (no pun intended) system administrator is free to move the components to the physical system in the network that best suits the needs. The X-windows font server and the X-windows client are free to run on any physical machine, but the X-windows server is tied to the physical resource, the graphics display, that it is managing.

1.2.7 What Is Important About the Client-Server Model?

So far, we have talked about what the client-server model is, shown conceptual models of the supporting environment, and discussed how to identify some client-server characteristics in a system. But why is the client-server model important? Why does a large portion of the industry focus on this particular way of designing applications? There are several very good reasons to consider client-server design in your computer environment:

- The per seat cost of a computerized solution may be lower with the client server model.
- Specialized hardware may be used to provide resource-intensive services, improving client performance.
- General-purpose hardware may be specifically tuned to perform the specialized service, improving client performance.
- Measuring (and therefore managing) the usage of a service may be easier if it is localized to specific places in the environment.
- The clients may be insulated from changes in the server environment.
- The client-server model provides better scaling than other usage models.

Remember that in a peer-to-peer relationship every system is equally capable of providing a particular service. For optimal performance, this implies that all systems should be configured with the same hardware and software resources. This can lead to overconfiguration of resources in areas like Random Access Memory (RAM), disk space, CPU power, I/O capability, and system expandability. Due to the overconfiguration, each system may cost more than it should, especially if the local resources are underutilized[7]. By designing the environment so that the clients use services provided by suitably configured servers, the server resources may be better utilized and the clients need not be so heavily configured.

Whenever a server must provide access to a specialized resource, there are two common ways to approach the situation: choose a specialized machine type, if the need warrants it, or choose a general purpose machine that is capable of providing the service if properly tuned. The specialized computer usually provides a unique service, or provides it in a way that no other machine can, often at an extra cost.[8] A general-purpose computer can be moved from place to place and retuned to meet the new service needs.

Providing the proper level of performance to clients of a particular service and measuring the level of that performance can be a challenge. This is especially true if the resources are scattered all over the network as in the peer-to-peer model. With the client-server model, if you know that a particular machine provides only one type of service to its clients, it is far easier to

7. This is a very common situation that I find in my customer environments, peer-to-peer configurations, and resource imbalances.

8. An example of such a specialized machine might be a parallel supercomputer.

measure the total resource utilization and, therefore, the machine's ability to provide the service. If more access to the resource being served is required, then the machine may be upgraded or, if possible, additional servers added.

Under the client-server model, it is possible to insulate a client from implicit knowledge of where the requested service is located in the network. This is desirable for a number of reasons, but the most important is: if a client cares only that the service is provided, not *where* it is provided, then the client can be insulated from changes in the service environment. For example, in a client-server environment designed with this rule in mind, if a system manager noticed that additional capacity was necessary for a given service, he would only need to plug another server into the network to provide the additional capacity. Furthermore, if the need for additional capacity was a temporary situation, when the extra capacity was no longer needed the server could be removed without impacting clients of the service.

1.2.8 Client-Server Model Summary

In summary, the term "client-server" defines a specific type of relationship between two, or possibly more, logical entities. These entities are usually software in nature and may co-exist on the same computer system hardware or be separated by a network connection. The server-to-client ratio is one to many, as opposed to one-to-one-to-one as in a peer-to-peer relationship. There usually is a disparity in capability between the client and server entity, with the client requesting use of a resource from the server, which manages the desired resource.

Client-server applications consist of individual components with distribution services inserted between them. Common client-server application components are the presentation logic, the application logic, and the data management logic. While this model is useful in the initial understanding of client-server principles, real-life applications tend to be more complicated and require more analysis to understand the roles that each component plays in the whole.

There are multiple "styles" of client-server applications. The style of client-server application depends on where the application designers inserted distribution services into the application logic. There are advantages and disadvantages to each of the commonly encountered client-server application styles. Finally, there is a basic choice to be made between using general-purpose and special-purpose computer systems to run server software.

1.3 Architectural Balance with the Client-Server Model

We have seen that the client-server architecture offers us an enormous amount of flexibility in partitioning resources within our computer environment—So much flexibility, in fact, that it is sometimes difficult to know where to begin. Many times we are not actually developing client-server applications from scratch, so we are left as system managers and designers to partition the resources to deal with constraints that are caused by existing applications, legacy systems, and other organizational needs.

This means that to meet user performance expectations we must properly locate the individual pieces of the client-server applications in our network and properly proportion the disk

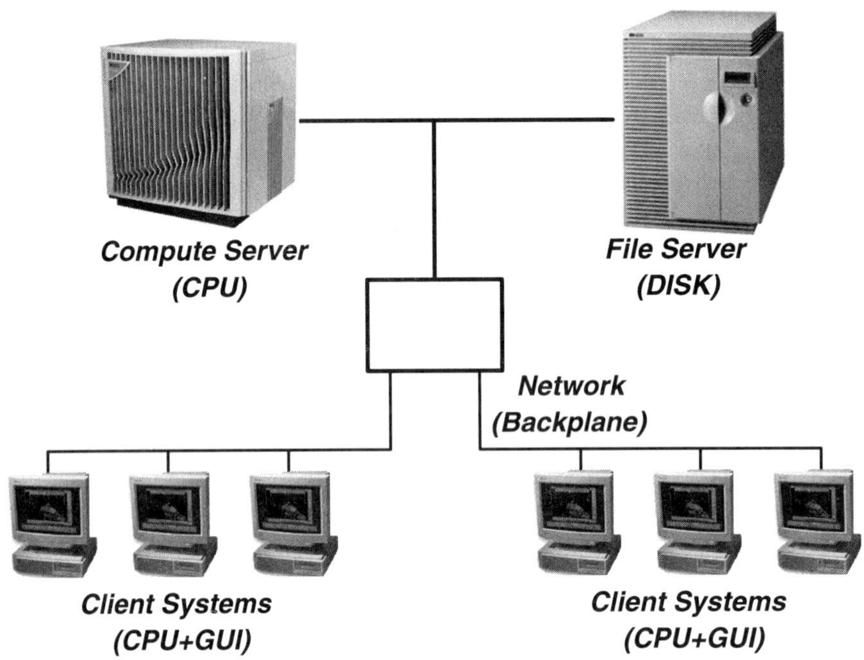

Figure 1-6 The Client-Server Virtual Computer

storage, compute power, network bandwidth, and other resources needed by those applications. This is one of the central themes in the client-server world, and we will return to it again and again.

1.3.1 Introducing the Client-Server Virtual Computer

In complex situations, it helps to have a mental model to help sort out details involved. With that in mind, we introduce the "client-server virtual computer" model, depicted in Figure 1-6.

Imagine a stand-alone computer and its individual components, sitting in its own metal enclosure. This computer has a CPU motherboard, I/O interfaces, peripherals, and a user interface, all tied together by the electrical signals running along a backplane inside the computer's chassis. This stand-alone computer's overall performance depends on the performance balance between its individual components, and one of the central performance determiners is the speed of the bus or backplane that allows communication among those components.

Our client-server networked environment may be thought of as a computer, too. This computer, however, is "virtual", because at any moment its components are scattered throughout the network. Imagine the three hardware components of the virtual computer (client, compute server, and file server) all tied together by a central backplane: the network. A client-server application, instead of running on a stand-alone computer, will run on the client-server virtual computer, using nonlocal resources. We can visualize each user (client) in the network environment having his or her own virtual computer (or computers), with the resource allocation depending on what client-server applications are being run at any given moment in time.

If any one of the components of our virtual computer is not properly balanced, the users will not be able to harness all of the "potential energy" available in the network. In a truly balanced environment, the user may not be aware of the resources being used, their location, or the network that ties them together. A properly designed network environment gives the impression of unlimited capability for getting work done. It is our job as designers and implementors to further this impression to the best of our abilities.

1.3.2 General Resource Allocation in Client-Server Environments

There are as many ways to allocate resources in a client-server environment as there are people attempting to do it. This is one of the negative aspects of the client-server model. Finding and maintaining the proper allocation of resources in a client-server environment is the single hardest endeavor in the client-server world.

Remember that we had some questions to use in *finding* client-server relationships:

- What are the resources being managed?
- Who is doing the resource management?
- Who is using the resource?

To these basic questions, we can add a few more to start helping us choose the location for client-server resources:

- How is the resource currently distributed in my network, if at all?
- What can be gained by managing the resource in a client-server manner?
- Will the cost of consolidation be recovered?
- What is the best way to utilize current hardware and network infrastructure?

There are two general approaches to allocating a client-server resource and making it available to potential clients: one requires manual intervention by the system administrator, and the other uses a layer of software that automatically locates and accesses the proper resources. Both of these methods require system administrative effort to implement. The first "hard codes" a location for the resource, and the second allows flexible management of the resource's location. Both have their place in our "bag of tricks".

1.3.3 Manual Distribution of Client-Server Resources

Many of us do not develop our own client-server application software—it can be a difficult task. The opportunities for us lie in the realm of properly configuring the existing resources in our networks to support the client-server–capable applications that already exist. Most system managers, at one point or another, have decided that managing multiple copies of Unix manual pages, user login information, or common application data is not desirable due to the need to keep multiple copies of the data "in sync".

One approach is to move to single copies of such data, and to make that data available to client systems by "hard-coding" references to it in the environment. The term "hard-coding" refers to Unix symbolic (soft) links across the network[9], common automounter maps, reserved share names, centralized login services[10], or other services that are located "by convention". We will call this type of action "manual creation" of client-server resources. Experienced system managers are familiar with the general approach, but may not think of it as creating a client-server relationship (or an explicit dependency between the client and the server of the resource.)

This procedure may be repeated for each identified resource (usually file or data resources) in the network, and implicitly makes the machines containing the information into servers. The labor-intensive nature of manually creating client-server resources, coupled with its tendency to create hidden dependencies, means that a careful analysis must be done to ensure that the benefits outweigh the disadvantages.

1.3.4 Automatic Location of Client-Server Resources

In the previous section, we dealt with the manual creation of resources that may be located on the disk or in disk-based databases. Another major type of client-server resource involves the allocation of compute resources for specialized portions of a client-server application that may not run to best advantage on a client system. Examples of this type of application are software compiles or "builds", circuit simulators used in Electronic Design Automation (EDA), computational analysis packages used in Mechanical Design Automation (MDA), and programs that are capable of dividing tasks so that they run on multiple computers simultaneously. We will refer to a computer that provides this type of service as a "compute server", and we have already seen a reference to compute servers in our previous discussion of three-tier client-server architecture.

An important point to repeat: the client software should have no knowledge of specific service providers hard-wired into it, if at all possible. If a server providing a service can be located either by a directory service or chosen by a load-balancing[11] service then the client need not have any knowledge of available resources. Using an external service for locating resources

9. Ugh! Please don't do this. Network softlinks are like rabbits, they multiply until they are completely out of control. One of my customers holds the record for successive levels of Unix symbolic links across the network.

10. For example, "Network Information Service (NIS)" from Sun Microsystems, the DCE registry, or the Microsoft® Windows™ "Domain Controller" services all provide centralized management of user login (authentication) information.

11. A load-balancing service has knowledge of task types and the best-suited servers for those tasks. It also is capable of monitoring how busy each server is, to allow selection of the least-busy server for a newly created task.

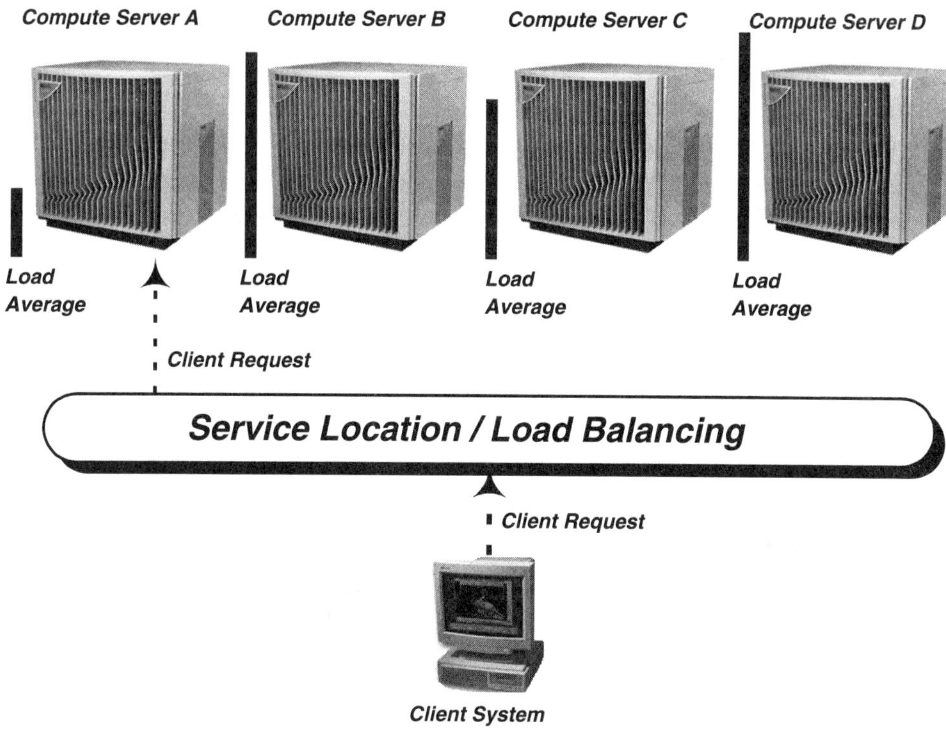

Figure 1-7 Locational Transparency of Client-Server Services

removes an explicit dependency between the client and server, allowing flexibility in moving or adjusting the available resources in the network to meet the client needs. This method of not building in server location information is called "locational transparency" or "service transparency". A high-level diagram of locational transparency is shown in Figure 1-7.

1.3.5 Measurement of Client-Server Resources

If proper allocation of network resources is the key to client-server application performance, the measurement of resource usage is fundamental to maintaining that performance. One way of stating this is: "You can't manage what you don't measure". Because user needs evolve and application usage follows, it is imperative that system administrators closely monitor resource usage trends in their client-server environments to prevent performance problems. Some of the resources that need measuring are the primary components of the three-tier client-server virtual computer, as shown in Figure 1-8.

The ability to measure performance trends in the client-server environment can enable system managers to stay ahead of the user's needs. Capacity planning on the major servers and the network helps maintain the user illusion of unlimited ability to perform work by measuring

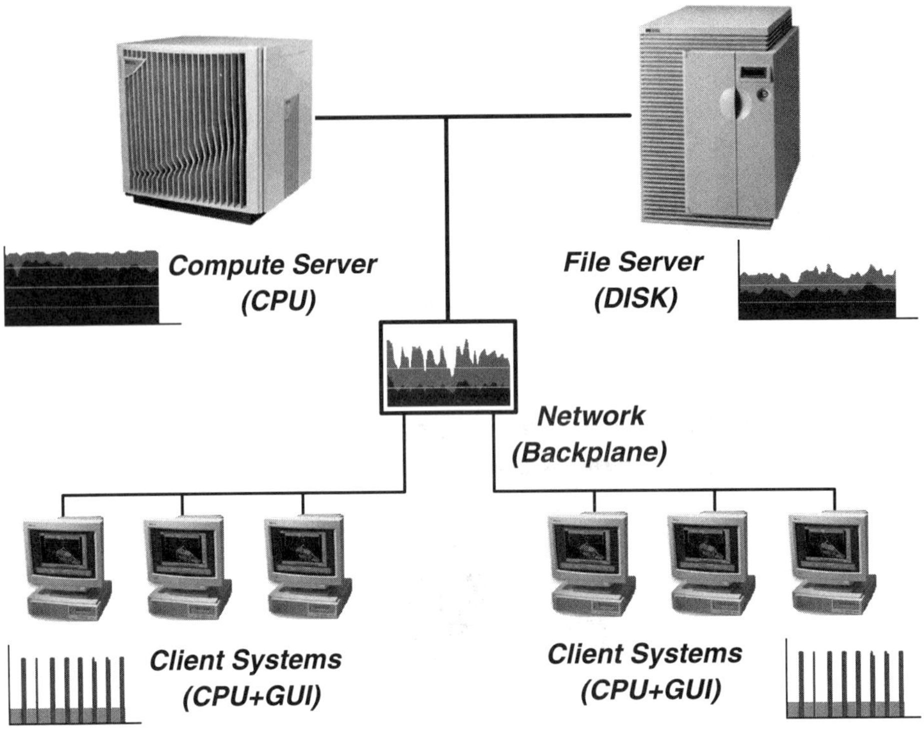

Figure 1-8 Measurement Points for Client-Server Resources

and allowing real-time adjustment of resources to meet needs. Servers that are dedicated to a particular task make measuring the usage of a single service easier, otherwise there must be a clear way to differentiate between usage of the hardware resources by multiple services on the same computer.

1.4 Summary of Client-Server Architecture

We have all encountered the term "client-server" at one point in our computing careers. As we have seen, the client-server architecture is extremely flexible, which is partly responsible for the many different definitions of the phrase. When someone says "client-server", we must carefully understand what *they* mean when they use the term and take care to match it with our definition. I have encountered people who think that a dumb, character-based terminal, connected to a mainframe by a serial cable, is client-server computing. That is certainly one viewpoint. When performing analysis or assessments, such a gap in definitions can lead to mismatched expectations.

the following major design observations that have been made about client-server up to this point:

- Resource management is the primary issue with the client-server model.
- We may view a client-server environment as if it were a virtual computer, which depends on architectural balance to maintain its performance.
- Locational transparency of server resources is a key design goal in client-server environments and shares that characteristic with object-based environments.
- To actively manage client-server resources, the relevant performance parameters must be measured.
- Dedicating server hardware resources to a single service can make measurement of resource usage easier.

Before closing this section, let's take a look at a more formal definition of the term "client-server":

> **Client/server computing (CSC) can be defined as the division of processing and data between one or more front-end client machines that run applications and a single back-end server machine that provides a service to each client. This is often taken to mean that the machines are connected by a network and that the clients are workstations running a graphical user interface. More generally, a client/server system can be defined as one in which some element of the computation, user interface, or database access is performed by an independent application, as a service to another; possibly on the same machine.** ***In this broader sense, all object-oriented systems are client/server systems, though the converse is not true. [emphasis added]***[12]

This definition underlines some key points from our previous discussion and introduces the next level of system abstraction beyond the client-server model, that of an object-oriented nature. We will find the object-oriented approach to systems design useful, as we will see in the next chapter.

1.5 Design Concepts Summary

In this chapter we covered some of the basic foundations for the design and analysis activities to follow. By now you should have a feeling for some of the differences between the client-server model and other configurations. You should be able to recognize the client-server model at work and realize that architectural balance requires proper location of resources in the network. With the groundwork laid, the foundation poured, and several cornerstones in place, we will now proceed to other important architectural elements.

12. Ian Graham, *Migrating to Object Technology*, page 133. © 1994 Benjamin Cummings Publishing Company Inc. Reprinted by permission of Addison Wesley Longman, a division of Pearson Education Limited. See [2].

CHAPTER 2

Object-Oriented Principles: Learning from Software Development

This chapter is an overview of some of the fundamentals of object-oriented software design and analysis. With the architectural foundation poured in the previous chapter, we will take a quick look at applying object-oriented programming methodologies to analyze and reduce the structural complexity that is inherent in networked computer environments.

Our purpose here is to show a connection between some of the object-oriented techniques that software developers use to deal with complexity and our attempts to master the complexity involved with design, analysis, and administration of a complex client-server systems environment. We will hope to borrow techniques and principles from our software brethren, and apply them to the higher level components in the environment that we are accustomed to dealing with. Primarily this is to avoid the necessity of inventing new techniques where the trail may already have been blazed.

2.1 Applying Object-Oriented Principles to Client-Server Design

Before we begin looking at the term "object-oriented", let's agree up front that this will not be a full tutorial on "object-orientedness" or object-oriented (OO) software design. There are a plethora of good books that cover this particular topic in detail[1]. We are only after an understanding of some of the object-oriented concepts that we can put to use in our own design work

1. My favorite book on object-oriented concepts is *Object-Oriented Analysis and Design with Applications*, 2nd edition by Grady Booch. Mr. Booch is Chief Scientist at Rational Software Corporation and is well known in the software engineering world.

with client-server systems. We will briefly explore the meaning of OO design, take a look at the difference in OO analysis, and finally explore some OO principles that we will find useful.

2.1.1 What Is Meant by "Object-Oriented"?

The word "object" is defined as:

> **Something material that may be perceived by the sense… something that when viewed stirs a particular emotion… something mental or physical toward which thought, feeling, or action is directed… the goal or end of an effort or activity… a thing that forms an element of or constitutes the subject matter of an investigation or science.[2] …**

All of these senses of the word "object" might apply in one way or another to the systems design process. The best portion of the definition for our purposes, however, is "a thing that forms an element of or constitutes the subject matter of an investigation. …" Grady Booch defines object orientation, in the software sense as:

> **Object-oriented programming is a method of implementation in which programs are organized as cooperative collections of objects, each of which represents and instance of some class, and whose classes are all members of a hierarchy of classes united via inheritance relationships[3].**

Let's dissect this definition in terms that system administrators, designers, and users can relate to, because after all we are not writing object-oriented software, we are trying to design environments that can run client-server applications. First, there is a specific method for doing object-oriented design and implementation that differs from the traditional software design and implementation methods. Object-oriented programs have a different organization, involving collections of objects which are members of classes, a hierarchical relationship between classes, and something called inheritance.

At this point, my job of describing objects and their relationships would be easier if we had a pictorial way of representing an object. We will put off a complete description of all aspects of an object until later, but a picture to use is immediately useful. Our object symbol is diagrammed in Figure 2-1.

2. By permission. From *Merriam-Webster's Collegiate® Dictionary*, Tenth Edition © 1998 by Merriam-Webster, Incorporated.

3. Grady Booch, *Object-Oriented Analysis and Design with Applications*, page 38, © 1994 Benjamin Cummings Publishing Company Inc. Reprinted by permission of Addison Wesley Longman. See [1].

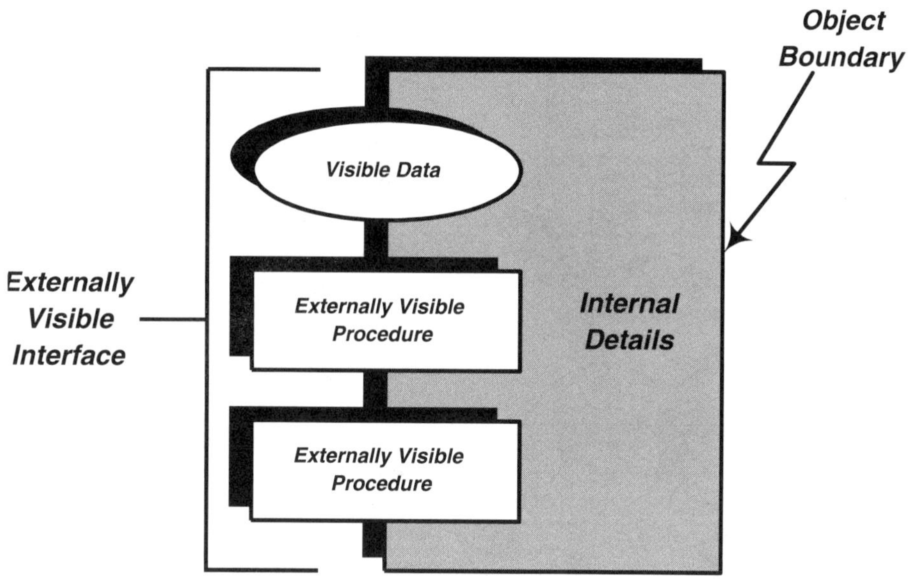

Figure 2-1 A Picture of an Object

Now that we have a symbol to use for an object, we can proceed[4]. If objects are sub-components of complete applications in the OO programming world our objects are the components of a complete client-server environment. There are objects at many levels in the structures that make up our target environment: systems contain application components and operating system components, networks contain groups of clients and servers, data storage contains configuration files and executable files, and so on. Some examples of the objects that we will deal with during design and analysis are: client-server program components, operating systems and subsystems, data stores, and client and server computer systems.

In the OO programming world, classes represent common structures of code (behavior) and data. If you think about it for a minute, you will see that most operating systems or applications may be divided into data (executable files, library files, configuration files, etc.) and a set of system administration procedures or program operations that operate on those data elements. So while the original designers of the applications in our environment may not necessarily have thought in terms of OO design, we are free to group those components into our own objects if it serves our purposes.

4. I must mention here that we are actually using a icon representing a module, borrowed from Grady Booch's object-oriented design (OOD) methodology. I choose this rather than his standard object or class symbol (see Figure 2-6) because of its explicit interface representation. I am hoping that Grady will forgive me for the adaptation.

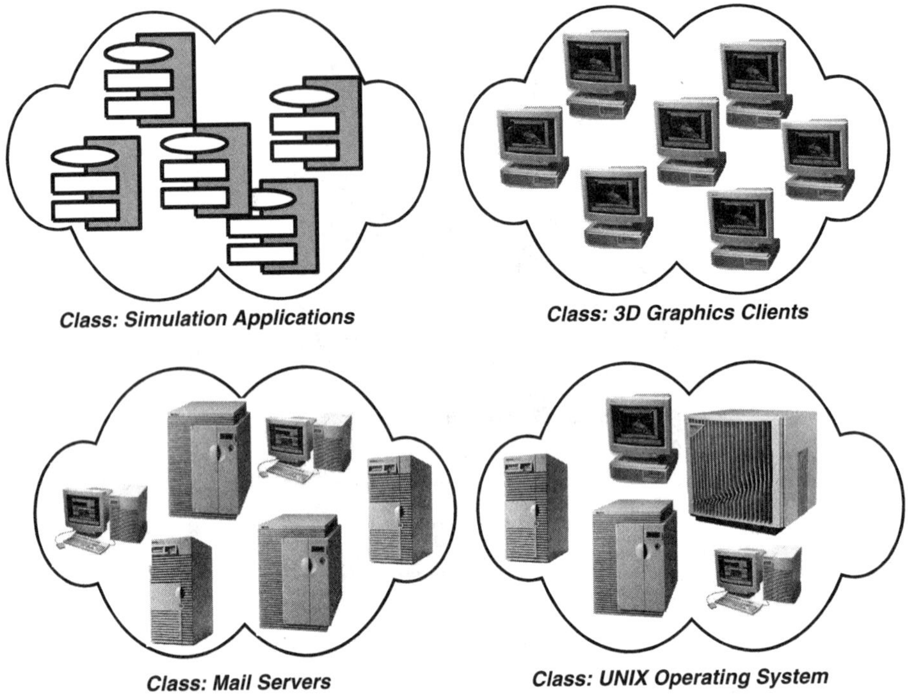

Figure 2-2 Object Class Examples

In our adaptation of the OO model, classes are imaginary groupings of common characteristics, and objects are specific instances of components that possess the characteristics. Some of those common characteristics might be: 3D graphics hardware, Unix operating systems, compute-intensive resource needs, or "runs a particular application component".

Single inheritance in the OO world allows taking an existing class and extending it by adding data and operations (behavior) to the original class definition. OO multiple inheritance involves creating a class from more than one "superclass" or "base class". The actual relationship is a hierarchy, as shown in Figure 2-3.

Rarely is the inheritance hierarchy as orderly as depicted in Figure 2-3, but hopefully you get the idea. We will visualize inheritance as if it were layering of data and procedures from one class on top of others to produce a new class with a combined set of functionality. Now that some of the introductions are out of the way, let's study why OO concepts are something we will use.

2.1.2 Why Are Object-Oriented Principles Useful to Us?

Okay, I can already hear you saying, "But all of that's programming, what does it have to do with the design of client-server computer environments?" Remember when we examined a

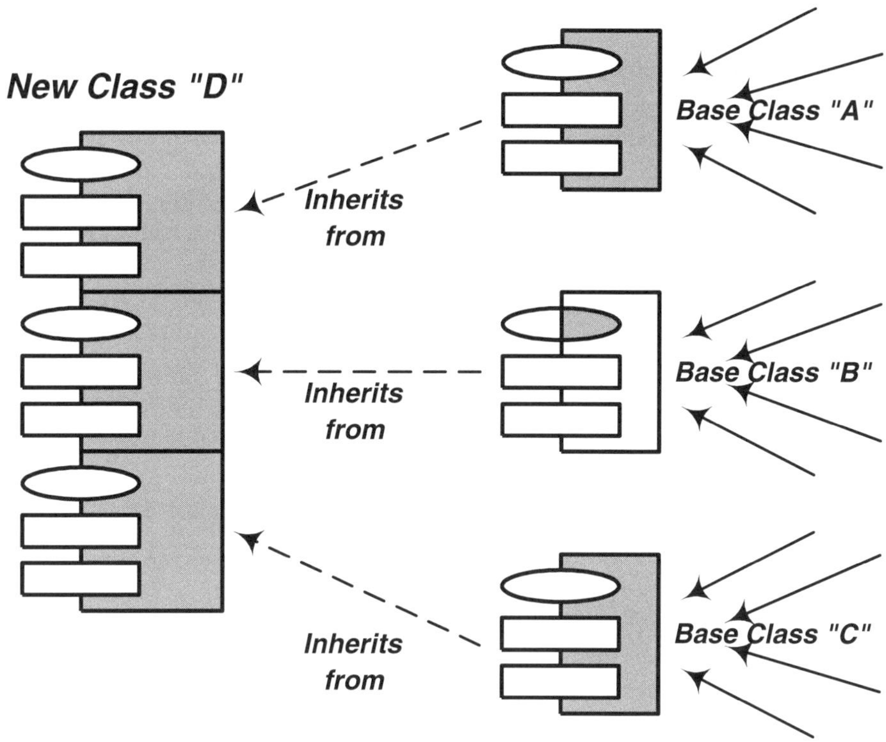

Figure 2-3 Object-Oriented Inheritance

definition of client-server computing? That definition stated, "... *all object-oriented systems are client-server systems, although the converse is not true*", which indicates there may be a useful connection between all of the work that has been put into object-oriented things in the software world and our efforts in the client-server world.

So, the logical argument goes something like this: if an object-oriented approach to software design is a good thing, and we can apply OO techniques to our client-server design and analysis work, then we can expect our client-server implementations to benefit[5]. In the future, we might even get an easier transition to a more object-oriented environment as a side benefit, if that is one of our goals. Remember also the close relationship between the client-server application components and the underlying hardware that runs them. If we structure our client-server resources in an object-oriented way, it is more than likely that the hardware structure will follow.

5. This is about as close to formal logic as you can expect to get in this book.

2.1.3 Object-Oriented Principles We Will Use

Continuing in our adaptations from the OO world, let's take a look at some of the defining attributes of the object model[6]. Hopefully, we can use these attributes later in *our* design and analysis process. We will concentrate on the four major elements of the object model: "abstraction", "encapsulation", "modularity", and "hierarchy". First, a definition of "abstraction":

> **An abstraction denotes the essential characteristics of an object that distinguish it from all other kinds of objects and thus provide crisply defined conceptual boundaries, relative to the perspective of the viewer[7].**

This is a very useful definition, it seems we use this concept all the time, maybe without realizing it. When we ask ourselves, "What makes this object unique?", we are applying abstraction. When we are identifying classes of objects in our target environments, we are applying abstraction. That was relatively painless; what about "encapsulation"? Let's take a look:

> **Encapsulation is the process of hiding all of the details of an object that do not contribute to its essential characteristics[8].**

Visualize taking an object and "pushing" all nonessential pieces of it into a box. The pieces that we choose to "hide" in this manner depend on how we abstract the object's characteristics during analysis and design. This operation produces the "internal details" described in Figure 2-1, which pictures an object. By hiding details, we make the "exterior" of the object (or its visible interface) simpler from the viewpoint of the observer. Next, let's tackle a definition of "modularity":

> **Modularity is the property of a system that has been decomposed into a set of cohesive and loosely coupled modules[9].**

Programmers may use the word "modular" to describe software that is well-written or well-packaged, maybe even reusable for other tasks. In this sense, it is usually a positive measure of the physical characteristics of the application: its design and how its components are grouped. There are also some more esoteric elements to the judgment, however, that have to do

6. Grady Booch, *Object-Oriented Analysis and Design with Applications*, page 34, © 1994 Benjamin Cummings Publishing Company Inc. Reprinted by permission of Addison Wesley Longman. See [1].

7. Ibid., page 41.

8. Ibid., page 49.

9. Ibid., page 54.

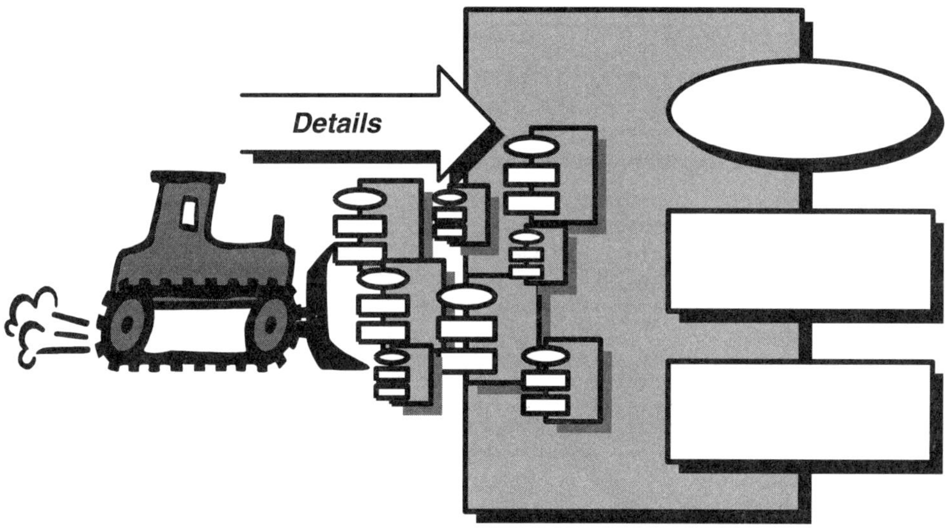

Figure 2-4 Abstraction, Encapsulation, and Modularity at Work

with aesthetic or artistic judgements. We would like to package our client-server applications, and the hardware that runs them, so that the same description applies to them.

The phrase "loosely coupled" in the definition of modularity also bears some examination. When two objects are "tightly coupled", there is usually a dependency of some sort between them, a dependency that causes a failure if one member of the object "team" is not cooperating. A "loosely coupled" relationship implies more independence and possibly a greater immunity to failure (or at least the ability to handle failure gracefully). Let's take a stab at our final principle, "hierarchy":

Hierarchy is a ranking or ordering of abstractions[10].

In object-oriented design, analysis, and programming, hierarchy is used to describe the relational characteristics of a class (Booch's "kind of" relationship[11]), as well as structural characteristics or membership of an object (Booch's "part of" relationship[12]). Both the "kind of" and "part of" relationships are useful to us to describe classes or objects in the environments that we are examining. We will also use specific hierarchies to describe the relative relationships

10. Ibid., page 59

11. Ibid., page 14.

12. Ibid., Page 14

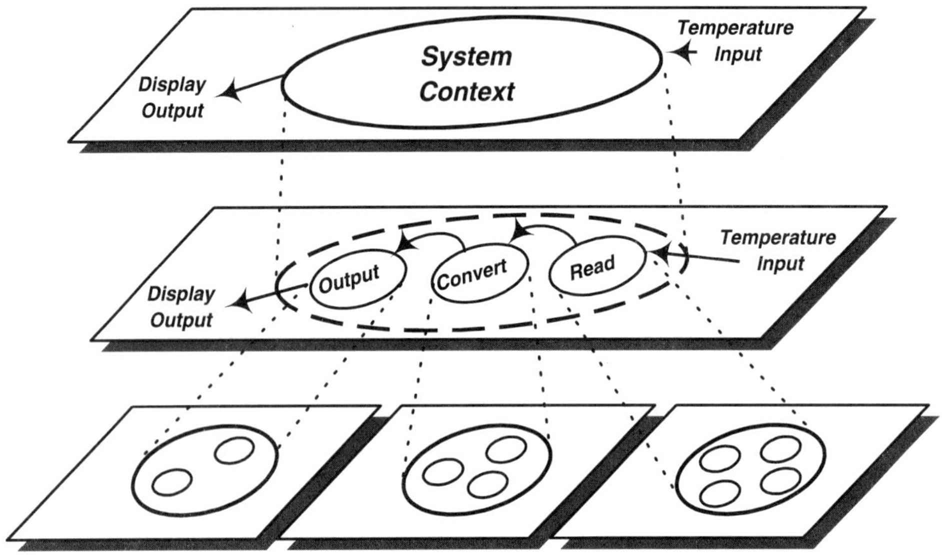

Figure 2-5 Structured Analysis Diagram of Example Problem

between classes or objects in our client-server design and analysis. Examples of more specific class hierarchies in our terminology are: storage classes (registers, processor cache, random access memory, disk storage, and off-line storage), network classes (enterprise, workcenter, workgroup, and system), operating system classes (Unix, Microsoft Windows, and others), and client-server system hardware classes (client, file server, and compute server).

2.1.4 Comparing Design Methodologies

As we have already seen, OO design and analysis are different from what most of us are used to. At one point in our careers, we may have been exposed to traditional structured programming techniques, which are mainly centered around "functional decomposition". The functional decomposition method breaks down complex *algorithms* into smaller, more manageable units or procedures. Of course, the OO method will approach the problem differently, by breaking it into objects and relationships between objects. Let's take an example problem to solve and use both methods to arrive at a solution, then compare the solutions.

Our example is a trivial one, but will exhibit some of the differences in the final system that results from the OO design method and the structured design method:

> **Design a software system that reads an electrical current, proportional to the external temperature and represented as an unsigned 64-bit number, from an external sensor. Convert the integer value to a Fahrenheit temperature and output that value to a liquid-crystal display in ASCII characters. The LCD hardware accepts an ASCII string as the value to display.**

We are leaving out a lot of potential details here and making the job of interfacing to the system hardware easier than it might be in the real world. With a Structured Analysis/Structured Design (SA/SD) approach, we might diagram the problem as indicated in Figure 2-5.

Notice that the analysis is centered around the algorithmic or procedural structure of the problem. It is the processing flow that we are breaking down, until we reach small enough pieces to implement. The structure of the code and data, when they are implemented, will follow the structure that we create during the analysis and design. Because that is centered around an algorithmic partition of the problem, the program structure will also be centered around the algorithms used.

One of the major negative issues to be dealt with is "gluing" the procedures together with global data, which creates implicit dependencies between the code and data elements. As the program becomes more complex, these dependencies may be forgotten, overlooked, or broken by other programmers. The broken dependencies may cause program faults or failures.

In the object-oriented part of our example, we are approaching the problem in a completely different manner. We are looking to divide the problem up into independent objects — entirely self-contained units. The objects will communicate with one another via messages[13]. This is diagrammed in Figure 2-6.

Note that the actual objects in the diagram are derived from generalized classes. We do this to allow for potential re-use of the basic code and data. The "temperature monitor" is a main module that sends messages to the objects that make up our example software system.

Aside from the individual notations that we used to describe the problem, let's examine some differences between the approach:

- We have carefully designed a set of classes that allow us to derive the resulting objects we need, for example a basic "Sensor" class. This is done in a generic way to allow for extension and re-use in the future.
- We have separated the solution into objects that contain all code and data to perform a particular operation, with well-defined boundaries and interfaces.
- The individual objects are independent and could be located on separate systems or execute on separate processors on a multi-processor machine. The messaging service to support remote communication might be different from the method used by the implementation language.

As we shall see, one of the greatest benefits of the object model is the elimination of hidden or

13. While the model for communication between objects might be "messages", some object-oriented languages implement the messages between objects within the same module as procedure calls to object "methods". Remote messaging might use a facility called "Remote Procedure Call" or RPC.

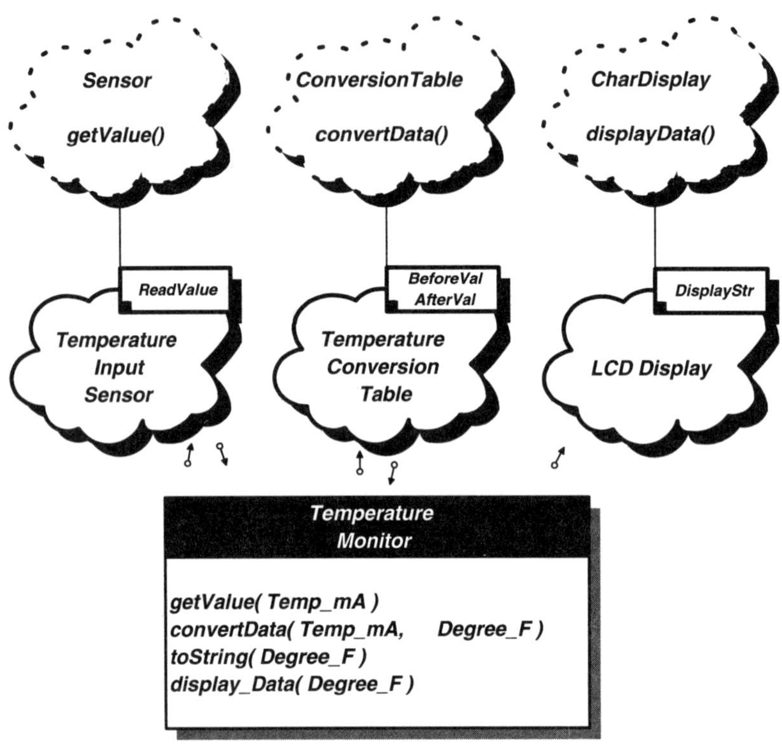

Figure 2-6 Object-Oriented Analysis Diagram of Example Problem

undiscovered dependencies between elements in a software system. This is an important difference resulting from the initial design approach and one that can improve the reliability of a complex system[14]. We should note that OO principles may be implemented with non-OO languages and services, but this is usually harder than using the OO-specific tools to do the job.

2.2 Object-Oriented Design Principle Summary

After introducing some of the basic concepts of object-oriented design and analysis, we showed how object-oriented approaches might differ from structured analysis or structured design methods. You should be able to recognize basic object-oriented characteristics when they appear and apply some of the object-oriented design principles in your own environment.

14. In all fairness, removing dependencies (on data and code elements) is a practice that all good programmers follow, irrespective of the methodology or implementation language. The object-oriented approach and its tools, however, can make this work easier by supporting mechanisms like inheritance.

Many of the techniques used by OO practitioners are useful to us for the simple reason that they help us to grasp complex environments. Because there is a connection between OO software and client-server software, understanding and applying some of the basic OO principles can help us to bring some order to our unruly environments. By using techniques that were pioneered by OO software developers, we can avoid "reinventing the wheel" when dealing with client-server environments. Basic OO principles like abstraction, encapsulation, modularity, and hierarchy can form the basis for our design and reengineering practices.

In our situation, we are actually forced to reverse the preferred object-oriented design process. Normally, if we were designing OO software "from scratch", we would follow object-oriented analysis (OOA) processes to specify the set of classes we need, and then apply object-oriented design (OOD) to the results, using object-oriented programming (OOP) to build classes and objects and group them together into applications. However, because most of the components in our environments are "ready-made" by computer manufacturers and software developers, we have to attempt to reverse the process: examine the finished components and try to impose an OO structure on them.

As with any tool, technique, or approach, there are places where our way of doing things will apply and places where it will not. The quality of the result depends on the underlying flexibility of the operating systems, hardware, and application components we are working with. The more flexibility we are given to relocate, reconfigure, and reengineer the components and their relationships, the more benefits we may see. As you gain experience, you will begin to immediately recognize positive opportunities for applying OO principles in your client-server environment.

CHAPTER 3

Attacking Complexity: Class-Based System Administration

In this chapter, we will discuss the origins and characteristics of complexity as it applies to networked computer systems, why it is our enemy, and how to make attempts at controlling its side effects. We will build on the object-oriented principles of the last chapter by developing a shorthand notation for analyzing client-server environments and introducing "class-based system administration" as a method of discovering and managing common system characteristics and eliminating unwanted dependencies between system elements.

3.1 What Is Complexity and Why Should We Control It?

The word "complex" is defined as:

> **Composed of two or more parts, a composite... hard to separate, analyze or solve... complex suggests the unavoidable result of a necessary combining and does not imply a fault or failure[1]. ...**

This definition certainly applies to today's computer environments, but why is this the case? Surely, no one sets out to create complexity for its own sake! So, why do our systems become complex? A short answer to the question might be "because they can". It is interesting to note that the word complex does not necessarily carry a negative connotation.

We continue to add components to our environments because it is easier than redesigning or reimplementing the whole thing. The system complexity is the necessary result of the complexity of the problems being solved, coupled with the evolution of computer technology, soft-

1. By permission. From *Merriam-Webster's Collegiate® Dictionary, Tenth Edition* © 1998 by Merriam-Webster, Incorporated.

ware applications, and the business structures that they support[2]. Another way of viewing it is that the high levels of complexity result from the sheer number of interrelated hardware and software components in a typical network environment.

We should pause briefly to differentiate between perceived complexity and actual complexity. You may have encountered objects that appear simple on the surface but upon closer examination are actually quite complex "inside". How is this done? Complex objects that appear simple usually are carefully crafted to be that way[3]. The interface to the outside world exposes the absolute minimum number of details necessary to use the object. Both the OO concepts of abstraction and encapsulation are hard at work in such objects. Objects with a lower perceived complexity are easier for us to manage.

If complexity is not necessarily a bad thing, then why worry about it? One reason that we pay attention to complexity is that the more complex a system is, the more open it is to breakdown or catastrophic failure. The more components a system contains and the more computer systems it is distributed across, the more possible "failure modes" exist. One small failure in a complex system can cascade through multiple components into a complete failure of the whole system. If components of the failed system are shared with other systems, which often is the case, a single failure can have wide-reaching consequences. For example, a directory service failure on a networked computer three thousand miles away can cause failures and loss of productivity in the local network.

Another potential result of complexity is unpredictable behavior, or chaos (another way of saying "unpredictable behavior"). In today's computer environments, the word "complexity" appears to have gained a more negative connotation than the dictionary definition might suggest. To the user of computer systems, the word "complex" seems to be associated more and more with the word "failure". This is an association that we want to prevent with our efforts, if possible.

A system may not have been originally designed in a complex way, but it may evolve and gain complexity over time. The evolutionary process tends to happen outside of any controlled analysis or design process. Statements like, "We don't have time for a design, we need to make the change today" are a sure sign of future problems. Our natural tendency is to continue adding components to the existing environment little by little, treating it as a monolithic whole[4], until it is obvious that this approach is no longer working. The end result might be a system that is so unreliable that it no longer meets its user's needs.

2. Nothing ever seems to get simpler, does it?

3. There is a power and elegance to simplicity, but it is not necessarily easy to produce.

4. How many times have you heard an extraordinarily complex group of computer systems described as if it were a monolithic entity called "the network" or "the system" ? This is the ultimate example of humans applying the concept of abstraction.

If we rely on the services of a complex system or set of systems to support our activities, then system failures can place those activities at risk. The news is full of reports of some very complex systems and their very visible failures: communications satellites, stock market exchanges, telephone systems, power distribution grids, and so on. We all have examples of lost productivity due to such system failures. Failures in important systems affect all users of the associated services: businesses and, directly or indirectly, each one of us on a personal level.

3.1.1 Software Complexity

It might be said that complexity is something that all software developers deal with on a daily basis. Most of the software development methodologies that exist today are attempts to deal with the complexity that is inherent in software systems and reduce the problems being solved to manageable, implementable pieces. There apparently are no analogous methodologies for dealing with computer system administration issues. However, one thing that both software development and system administration share is the same enemy: complexity. What causes software complexity?

As the available compute power grows, the size and complexity of problems being solved by applications grows as well. In addition to the application software, the underlying operating system is being called upon to provide more and more basic services. Software subsystems are being added or modified at each new release of the operating system to support the requirement for new functionality. The operating system is also called on to manage *larger* resources: Terabytes of disk and Gigabytes of RAM, amounts unimaginable only five years ago, are now becoming commonplace. The advent of 64-bit computing allows applications to access huge virtual address spaces, enabling even larger applications with even larger problems to be solved.

The power of operating systems like Unix or Microsoft Windows lies in their flexibility and their general ability to run multiple application types. The operating system software, based on all of the possible permutations of the subsystem options, and the interrelations between subsystems may be viewed as being infinitely configurable. Choosing the right configuration for hundreds of machines and maintaining it can be an arduous task. Configuring the operating system for each machine differently is not only undesirable, but virtually impossible[5] in large environments.

3.1.2 System and Subsystem Complexity

Our picture of a computer system's software would be much simpler if the subsystems and the other pieces it comprises were all independent. This, however, is not the case—there are

5. Only a masochist would configure every machine differently, except by accident.

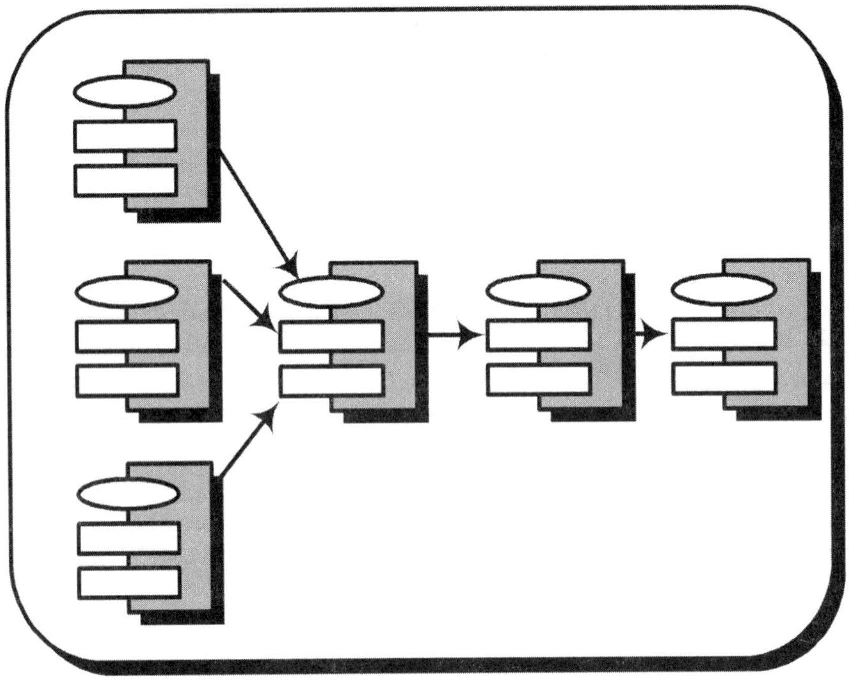

Figure 3-1 Subsystem Objects Within a Computer System

multiple dependencies between the subsystems that exist within the operating system on a given system, let alone the dependencies that exist across subsystems and between application components that use those subsystems. To begin picturing the dependencies, let's put our previously introduced object symbol to work, as in Figure 3-1.

The set of object relationships in Figure 3-1 is a very simplistic representation of what exists in real computer systems on a much larger scale. To visualize this, try looking at the figure from right to left and imagine an Ethernet interface card, its driver, the TCP/IP[6] subsystem, and some of the protocols that are implemented "on top of" TCP/IP, like SMTP[7], SMB[8], or SNMP[9].

6. Transmission Control Protocol / Internet Protocol.

7. Simple Mail Transfer Protocol.

8. Server Message Block, a Microsoft Windows file-sharing protocol.

9. Simple Network Management Protocol.

Realizing that this is only a small example of a single set of relationships in one subsystem out of hundreds is a humbling experience[10]. Each object has its own set of characteristics, operations, and a well-defined interface to other objects that might use it. The dependencies depicted in Figure 3-1 by arrows beg for a little more explanation.

A component that depends on another relies upon it to properly complete its job. This means if something goes wrong and the component that is depended on fails the client component does not get its task completed. Whether the dependency is loosely coupled or tightly coupled and how the client software is written determines how the client component handles the error. In a loosely coupled environment, the client component might be free to seek another source for the required service. In a tightly coupled environment, behavior such as hangs, aborts, or other relatively final "I give up" actions are the possible outcomes.

3.1.3 Why Are Our Computer Networks Complex?

In some of our previous discussion, we mentioned that computer networks and their hardware architecture tend to mimic the structure of the software that runs on them. We should add that the software structure itself tends to mimic the nature of the organizations that use it, as well as the problems that they are attempting to solve. The more complex an organization is and the more complex its business practices, the more complex the underlying computer support structures. This is a great example of "form follows function".

We should not overlook the emergence of single-user workstations as a factor in increasing the overall complexity of computer networks. Where once a system administrator could handle the needs of several hundred users by administering a single multiuser mainframe and its peripherals, introduction of the workstation paradigm means that he must administer several hundred individual machines and associated servers to cover the needs of the same number of users. System administration techniques and tools have not kept pace with the rate of increase in associated complexity.

In the late 1960s and early 1970s, work was done primarily on large multiuser systems that supported hundreds to thousands of users per machine, each with their own character-based terminal[11]. It was very easy for users of these "time-sharing" machines to share resources like disk storage, printers, and applications. Unfortunately, there was one resource being shared that was not desirable to share: a single CPU.

10. Just try completing a map of all dependencies in a particular computer system, including hardware, operating system, and applications. Such diagrams have been called "bedsheets" for a reason. I once did this for the HP-UX version 9.05 operating system, just to prove a point about complexity.

11. This was quite an advance for those of us that were used to teletype machines, punch cards, or paper tape as our primary interface to the computer system.

In the early 1980s, a new approach to computing was born[12]: the workstation. This type of machine had its own CPU, disks, bit-mapped graphics display, mouse, and, more importantly, an integrated network connection. *The primary design center for the workstation was the sharing of data, over an integrated network connection, without sharing a CPU with other users*[13]. There is a consequence to this conscious design choice: the use of workstations to provide unshared compute resources carries with it an implied reliance on client-server principles for allocating shared resources. Most computer vendors provide separate hardware for the separate functionality: for workstations are not servers and servers are not workstations. Unless the peer-to-peer model is used throughout the environment, there is a client-server partitioning of resources, however unconscious it might be.

The trend towards more and more workstations in our networks continues today. Workstations are becoming ever cheaper as technology, manufacturing techniques, and competition enable round after round of price reductions. Personal workstations, now in the under $1000 dollar range, are found in an increasing number of private homes. The result is that our computing environments have many more individual machines than they might if the workstation was not available and affordable. Improvements in networking technology, coupled with the Internet[14] and corporate intranets, are driving the number of interconnected computers in our environments ever higher. Increasing complexity is a consequence of this interconnection.

3.1.4 Network Dependencies

Adding a network connection to a system adds yet another dimension to the possible dependencies and the associated system administration burden. As if the level of within a single system were not enough, we insist on networking hundreds or thousands of individual systems together. This affords us, or our users, a wonderful opportunity to create dependencies on resources that are located across the network, on machines that we may not have any control over. The potential impact to reliability should be obvious, but is frequently overlooked.

With the addition of the network, we now have two primary categories of dependencies to deal with: local dependencies and nonlocal ones. We will define local dependencies as those that exist within the physical confines of a single computer system and its subsystems. Nonlocal dependencies involve resources that are "out there", somewhere in the network, residing on

12. Whether this happened at Xerox PARC (Palo Alto Research Center), Apollo Computer Inc., or Sun Microsystems Inc. is a matter of some debate. The first commercial product, however, was from Apollo Computer.

13. This is a very important point to remember. Standard workstation characteristics include such things as integrated networking, bit-mapped graphics display, pointing device (such as a mouse), and nonshared CPU.

14. The term internet existed in networking terminology before the entity called "The Internet", which refers to part of the worldwide collection of computers also called the "World Wide Web". To avoid confusing the two terms, we will use the capitalized version, "Internet" whenever we are referring to the latter case, and "internet" when referring to the former.

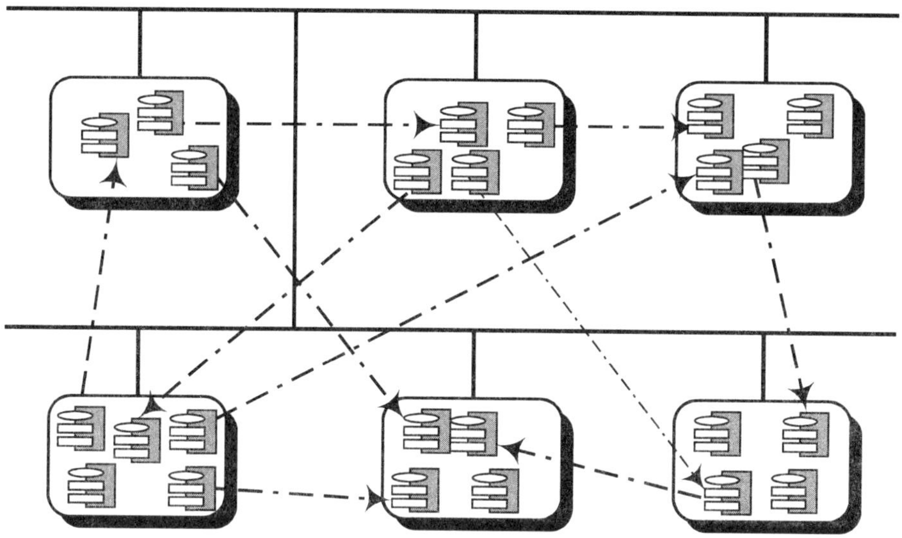

Figure 3-2 Nonlocal System Dependencies

other systems. Figure 3-2 shows a (vastly) simplified diagram of some nonlocal dependencies in a networked environment.

Dependencies may be for services, compute resources, disk (file) resources, as well as between system or application components. A user who relies on a specific network location for his files, and hard-codes that location into scripts or application source code will experience a failure if the location of the files is moved. Because management of client-server resources often involves the adding, subtracting, or movement of those resources, this type of dependency is a large problem, both for users and system administrators.

In addition to local and non-local types of dependencies, we need to make several finer distinctions. A dependency may be recognized or unrecognized. Hidden dependencies, dependencies that exist or are created without knowledge of the consequences, fall into the unrecognized group. Recognized dependencies are well-known relationships between components like the client and server portions of an application in the environment or between other types of resources. One example of such a dependency is that between an NIS master or slave server and

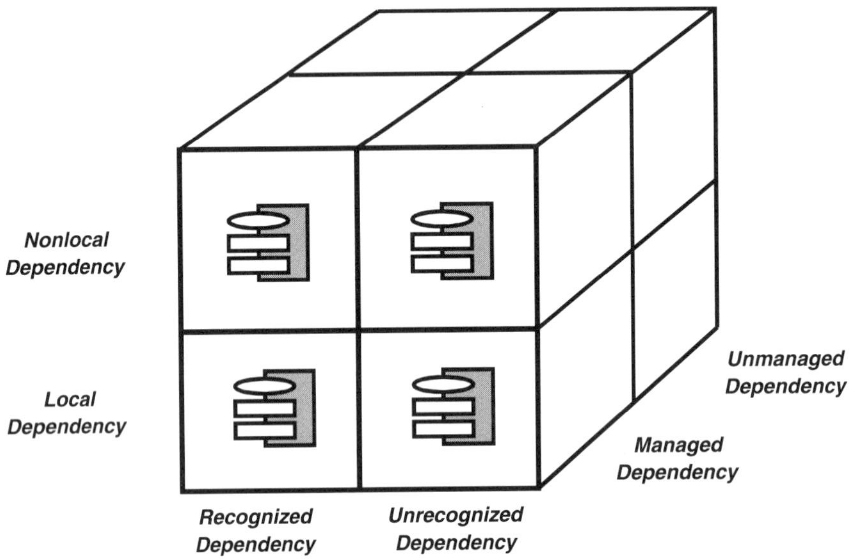

Figure 3-3 Types of Dependencies

an NIS client[15]. This type of dependency may also have been discovered during the course of analysis or by experience with previous failures.

Once a dependency is recognized, it may be managed or unmanaged. There are recognized dependencies that we have no control over and cannot manage because they are designed into an application or service. There are also dependencies that we recognize and choose not to manage. Providing NIS slave servers or multiple Microsoft Windows domain controllers for user authentication is an example of managing a recognized dependency between a service and its clients in a manner that can hide server failures.

The types or categories of dependencies we have discussed are depicted in Figure 3-3. Along with the types of dependencies, we will use a hierarchy to describe the relationships between the dependencies in a client-server environment. At this point we have only described the local portions of the dependency hierarchy; we will leave the nonlocal portion for a later discussion. See "Another Level in the Architectural Hierarchy?" on page 55 for the nonlocal portion of this hierarchy.

The local portion of the dependency hierarchy is represented in Figure 3-4. This diagram gives us a framework to start categorizing the dependencies between objects in our target environment, both for analysis and for design activities. We previously mentioned the "kind of" and

15. NIS allows master servers that have the only read-write version of their database and slave servers that merely replicate the information from the master servers.

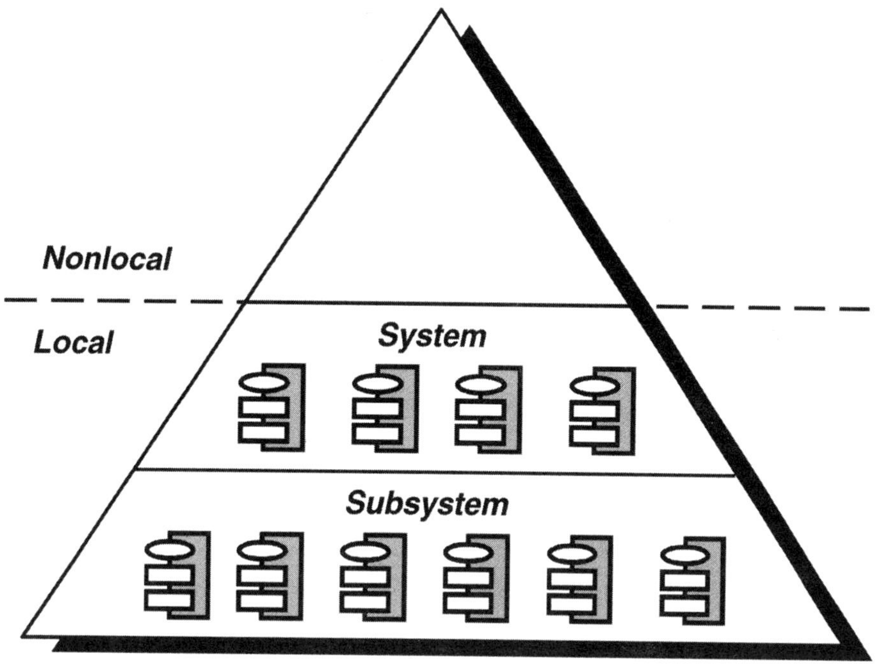

Figure 3-4 Hierarchy of Local Dependencies

"part of" relationships in our previous object-oriented design discussion. The hierarchy depicted in Figure 3-4 is equivalent to the "part of" relationship described by Grady Booch (See Bibliography). The "kind of" relationship involves the classes that the individual components belong to, such as a specific application, operating system, or subsystem.

3.1.5 Effects of Complexity in Networked Computer Environments

Complexity in a computer network is unavoidable due to the large number of interrelated hardware and software components. Additionally, the configuration of most networks is constantly changing (or evolving) as people, hardware, and application components are added, removed, or relocated. The changes in the environment, whether planned or not, increase the probability of unpredictable behavior, or chaos, as dependencies between individual components and locations of services are altered.

Dealing with the complexity of modern computer environments can quickly overwhelm a system administrator, no matter how competent or experienced. The number of systems an individual can manage depends on his or her ability to simultaneously deal with all operating parameters for that system. To make changes to a system's configuration, a system administrator must be knowledgeable about the every configuration variable for a particular operating system "flavor" and its potential dependencies on others. Then he or she must be able to keep track of the

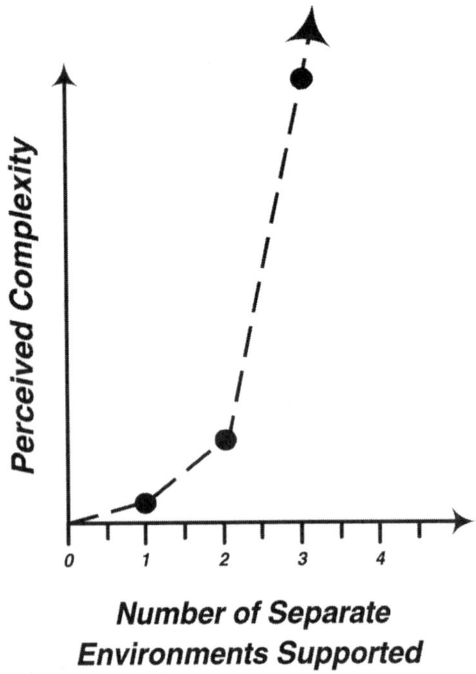

Figure 3-5 Perceived Complexity Versus Number of Supported Environments

actual system's state in his or her head and must be able to do this for every physical system under his or her management[16]. Successful system administrators are masters of dealing with complexity.

Today's networks are typically heterogeneous, comprising several types of operating systems: several Unix variants from several vendors, multiple versions of Microsoft Windows, and legacy systems running older operating systems. I believe that the level of perceived complexity per operating system variant supported by a single system administrator is exponential in the number of different environments supported. In other words, two operating system environments (including multiple versions of the same operating system) are X^2 as complex to manage as one, three are X^3 as complex, and so on. The difficulty, of course, is that a single human is only capable of dealing with a certain level of complexity at once. For this reason, beyond three system types, system administrators usually "specialize" in managing one or two operating system types, and work to a lesser degree with others.

In a typical networked environment, system administrators are forced to cope with constant changes in the number, type, location, and configurations of the computer systems they

16. This is one reason that system administrators become upset when users make unauthorized changes to their systems.

manage. The constant change, coupled with the manual effort necessary to reconfigure each system, conspires to keep system administrators constantly on the run. It is rare, indeed, to find a group of system administrators that is happy with the quality of their lives or the level of service they can provide to their environments. Successful system administrators are masters of complexity, but systems of networked computers present a unique challenge, one that cannot always be easily met.

Complexity has a number of side effects, including potentially unpredictable behavior (chaos) and increased system administration effort. It is the system manager's responsibility to cope with the complexity in the environment being managed, whether or not the existing components are well designed, well documented, or properly distributed. The more complex the environment being managed, the more the possibility exists for system management mistakes that can add to overall unpredictable nature of the environment.

3.2 Applying Object-Oriented Principles to System Administration

In the last several sections, we have talked about complexity as it applies to software, host computer systems, and networks of host computer systems. While complexity in and of itself is not necessarily bad, we have made no secret about the fact that unmanaged complexity is frequently our enemy. If the level of complexity in your environment is not a problem, then you are "home free", and you can stop reading now. Based on my experiences with customer environments, however, this is a rarity. Our next challenge is to put some of the previously discussed principles to work in tackling complexity in our own environments.

First of all, a very general approach to dealing with complexity is stated as follows:

> **The technique of mastering complexity has been known since ancient times: *divide et impera* (divide and rule)[17].**

This gives us a suggestion about *what* to do: break the problems we face down into smaller pieces. In the previous chapter we saw two software design and analysis methodologies for subdividing problems into smaller, more manageable pieces: functional decomposition and object-oriented analysis. The methodology we will use, the *how*, is rooted in the object-oriented analysis and design principles that we have explored previously. Now is the time for us to begin applying the principles of encapsulation, modularity, abstraction, and hierarchy to the elements of our systems, in the hopes of gaining some benefits.

3.2.1 An Object-Oriented Notation for System Design and Analysis

One of the easiest ways to understand relationships between objects is to draw pictures of the objects involved and "connect the dots" with any dependencies. To represent the dependen-

17. E. Dijkstra, 1979, "Programming Considered as a Human Activity" in *Classics in Software Engineering*, edited by Ed Yourdon. See [17]. Also see *WWW.Yourdon.com.*

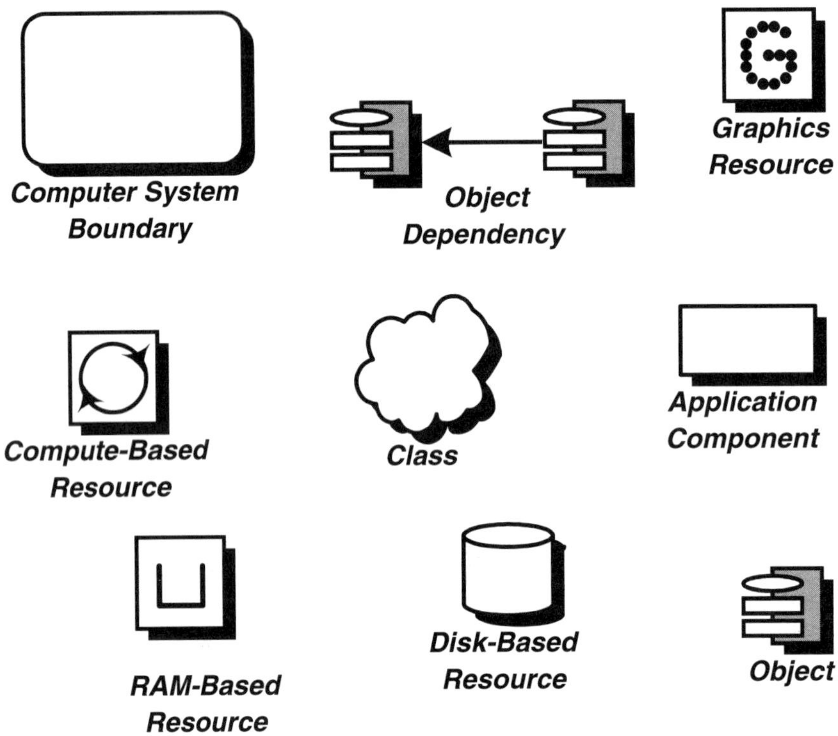

Figure 3-6 Design Elements

cies, objects, and object relationships within our system environments, we will employ a pictorial notation. We do not need a full-blown software analysis and design notation for our purposes, although the level of complexity that we deal with can approach that of a large-scale software application.

We need several different picture, or icons, to represent the components of our target environments. At this point, several of our design objects have not been introduced, so we will to expand our notation as we go. Let's start with simple pictorial representations for the following items:

- A computer system boundary or container, used to physically group components existing on a single computer system together
- A generalized object with its external interface, which we can use when it is necessary to detail the data and procedural interface definition for an object
- An object class, used to represent a unique set of characteristics that may be inherited by a system object

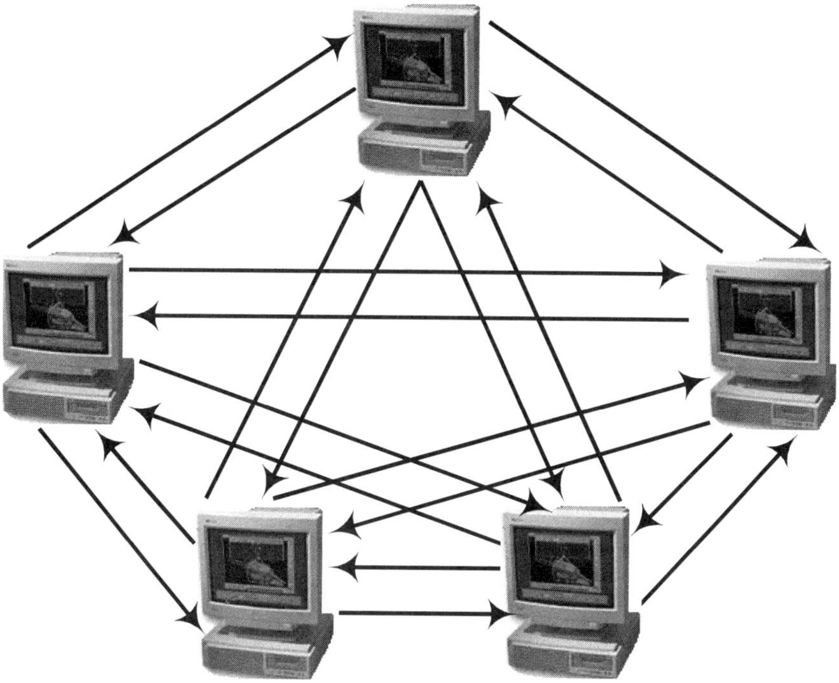

Figure 3-7 Peer-to-Peer Dependencies

- An application component, which is a container used to group all objects belonging to a local application or subsystem together, used in place of the object symbol when we don't care about the interface presented by the object
- Dependencies between objects are represented by a line and arrowhead
- Disk-based resources represented by a standard drum-shaped icon
- RAM-based resources
- Specialized graphics resources
- Compute-based resources depicted with a circle and arrows representing "cycles" of the CPU

We have already introduced some of these elements in the preceding figures, so they should not seem completely unfamiliar. This current set of pictures, shown in Figure 3-6, will get us started with the design drawings we need. The compete set is available in Appendix D.

I have chosen symbols that are readily available from standard software development templates in popular drawing programs, or even software analysis packages, to make our notation easier to use. We should not become entangled in using the exact symbols pictured here—feel free to develop your own notation. The important part is that you begin thinking in terms of

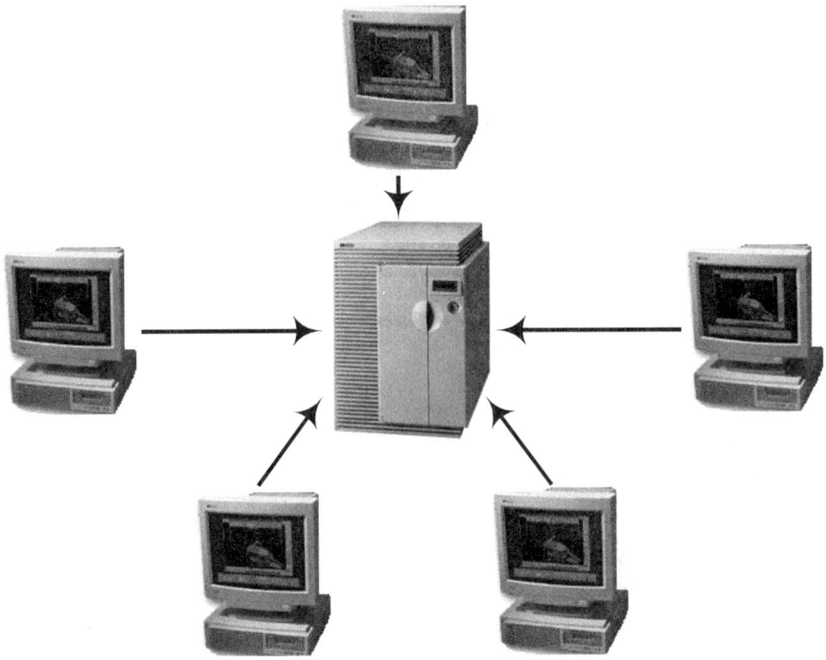

Figure 3-8 Client-Server Dependencies

objects, their interfaces, and the dependencies that exist between them. How you represent the items and their relationships is of secondary importance

In the next section, we will get some practice looking at dependencies in a client-server environment using a network file system (even though we have chosen NFS for the example, the observations hold true for other network file systems, also).

3.2.2 Client-Server Architecture and Dependency Reduction

The client-server model may have an advantage over the peer-to-peer configuration in terms of reducing dependencies or fixed relationships between objects in the environment. A good example of this is with file sharing services between multiple clients. In a completely peer-to-peer file sharing environment, every client system has to mount the disks of every other client system, as illustrated in Figure 3-7.

This amounts to *N*(*N*-1) dependencies for each client. Besides being a system administration problem in terms of keeping the access paths and configuration tables constant, in some net-

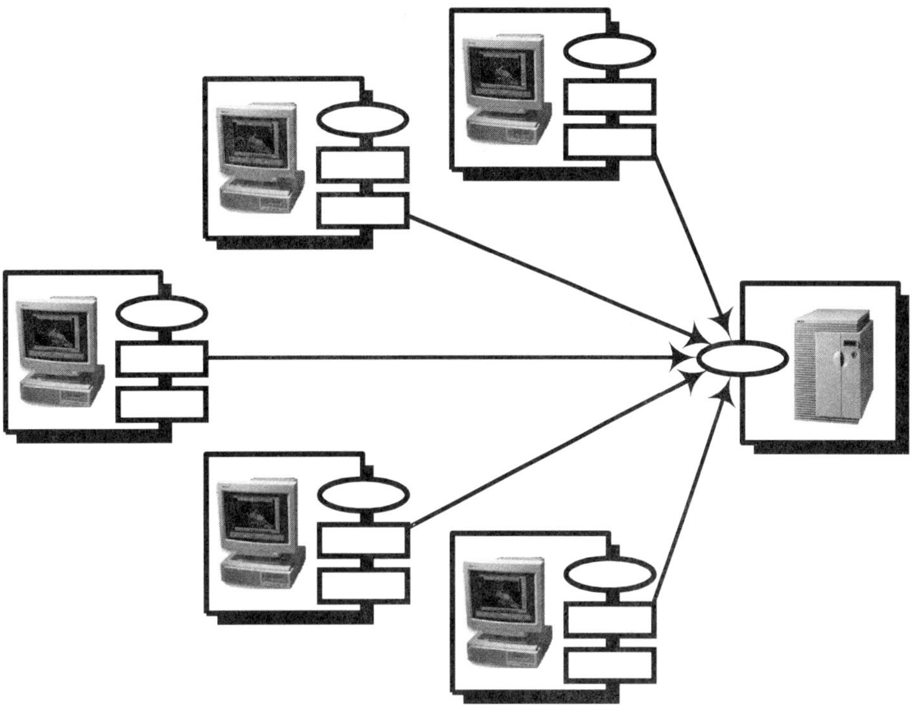

Figure 3-9 Example: Computer Systems as Networked Objects

work file systems, like NFS, the client system may hang if the server becomes unavailable[18]. The more dependencies there are, the more potential for hangs and loss of productivity. The same situation, with a central file server instead of individual file systems, appears in Figure 3-8.

The complexity of the file sharing environment has been reduced from $N(N-1)$ dependencies, as in the peer-to-peer configuration, to N dependencies in the client-server configuration. There is a price to be paid for this reduction in complexity: the file server is now a single point of failure, and we must take measures to prevent loss of its services[19]. The additional cost of the hardware must be weighed against the potential increase in reliability, which results in increased user productivity. Performance may also be increased by off-loading the server function from the client to a separate, dedicated machine.

18. This is because of the "stateless" nature of NFS. If a server becomes unavailable, a client continues to retry its last operation until it gets a response. When the server recovers, the client picks up where it left off.

19. We will cover more on high availability and protection of server hardware resources in Chapter 7.

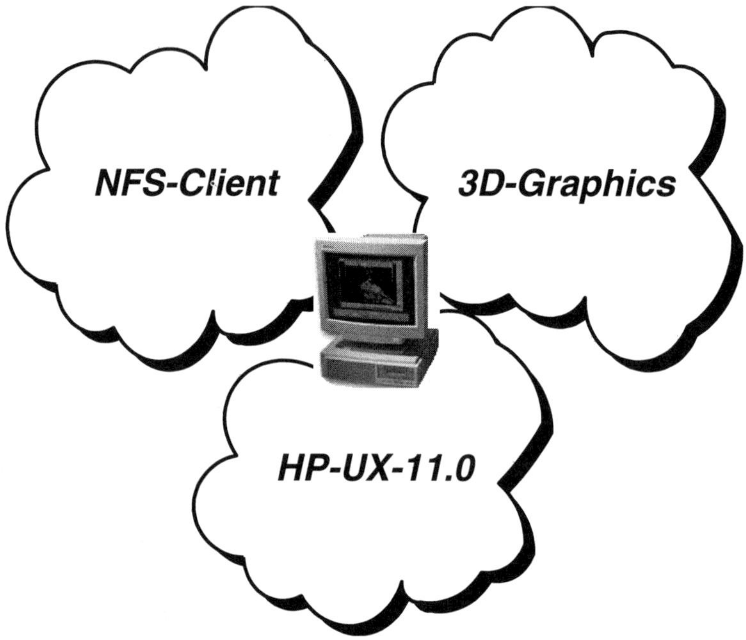

Figure 3-10 System Membership in Multiple Classes

Another way of diagramming the relationships between systems, using our system analysis notation, is represented in Figure 3-9. We are representing the use, by the client systems, of the data provided by the file server. The client systems have arrows drawn from the procedural portion of their interface that represents read, write, and mount (map) operations to the data interface of the file server machine to depict this relationship. The depiction of the interface details is provided as an example to familiarize you with the approach; it is rare that we will need to go to this level of detail.

3.2.3 Identifying System Classes

Since having every system in your environment configured differently from the others is a recipe for system administration chaos, we need to find a way to recognize and manage commonality in the system configurations in our network. Our method is to identify common sets of system characteristics, create system classes from those characteristics, and apply a class name or label to those characteristics. This is a direct application of abstraction to computer and application environments, and I call it "class-based system management". Many experienced system administrators already practice variations of this approach in their day-to-day jobs without applying a specific label to the process.

System class names may be (1) application oriented, such as "Mail-Server", "Mail-Client", "NIS_Master", "NFS_Client", "NIS_Client", or "Software_Development", (2) operating

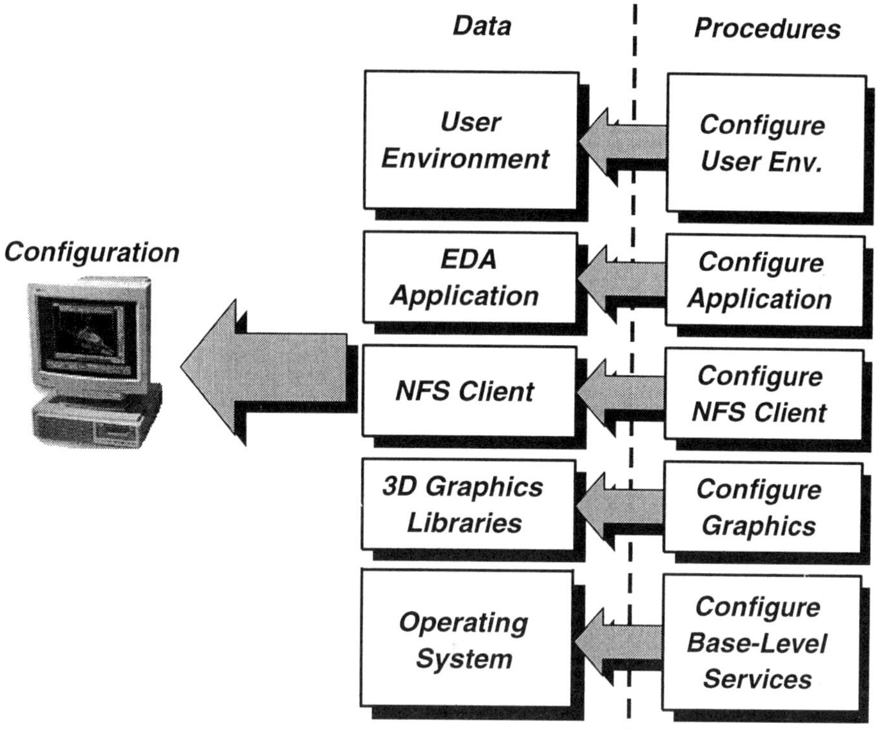

Figure 3-11 System Class Inheritance as a Layering of Data and Procedures

system oriented, for example: "HP-UX-11.0", HP-UX-10.20", "Solaris-2.6", or "WinNT-4.0", (3) hardware oriented, as in "3D-Graphics", "Multiprocessor", or "RAID-Storage" or, (4) resource oriented, like: "File-Server", "Software-Build-Server", "Database-Server", or "Compute-Server." The choices for your class names are important; they describe the unique functionality resident in your environment. Class-based system administration depends upon the proper identification and labeling of your system classes.

Once we have identified common use patterns, common hardware configurations, common software configurations, and common system administration procedures that are shared by groups of systems, we may begin to reuse these patterns to save design and system administration effort. How many different system classes you have in your environment will depend upon how diverse your particular environment is and what level of detail you wish to manage with class-based techniques. We will cover more on this topic in Appendix C, where we will cover environmental assessment methods.

3.2.4 Deriving System Administration Objects

You can picture a system class as a group of system characteristics that could potentially exist in an actual system. All of the classes and their associated characteristics are "theoretical" groupings until they actually are created[20] as part of a physical system. When analyzing a system, you should begin to think in terms of what system classes it does (or will) belong to. Because this approach may be new to you, don't worry if it takes some time for you to feel comfortable with it.

It is important to note that a single system may be, and frequently is, a member of multiple system classes. For example, a server system may be derived from the "HP-UX 11.0", "RAID-Storage", "Multiprocessor", and "File-Server" classes, and a high-performance workstation client might belong to "HP-UX 11.0", "Large-RAM", "3D-Graphics", "Multiprocessor", and "NFS-Client" classes or the "WinNT-4.0", "3D-Graphics", and "NFS-Client" classes. Membership in each one of these classes is based on analyzing any significant[21] differences in system management practices, hardware or software configuration, or application usage patterns that characterize the attributes of the class.

Since we are not working in an object-oriented language and do not have support for inheritance, we need to come up with a mental model that describes inheritance of system class characteristics and may be implemented for system administration. Remember from our previous OO discussion that the definition of an object in an object-oriented programming language involved both definitions of data members and procedural actions on that data. Our system class inheritance model will work in much the same way, with configuration data and configuration actions (commands) substituted for the OO language definitions.

We can use the term "inheritance", in the system administration sense, as a layering of software, configuration, and system administration components from the class definition(s) that a system belongs to. In cases where classes interact, the system administration component responsible for configuration changes to the class must be intelligent enough to recognize the interaction and change its behavior accordingly.

The deriving (layering) of class capabilities may be visualized as in Figure 3-11. In the real world, some of the individual layers and their configuration procedures may be as simple as setting a single environment variable.

3.2.5 Design Goals for Class-Based System Administration

Our design goals throughout all of our system analysis, design, and reengineering efforts will be:

- Simple, clean interface definitions between objects

20. Object-oriented programmers would use the term "instantiated".

21. "Significant" in this sense means "causing differences in system administration procedures".

- Use objects to "contain" underlying complexity
- Reuse of components
- Minimization of dependencies between objects
- Reduction in perceived complexity
- Improved reliability
- Scalability
- Automated system administration procedures

Simple, clean interfaces between objects in our environment allows us to more easily understand the relationship between the objects. Since we are limited by the number of components, interfaces, and dependencies that we can grasp at one time, this goal allows us to:

Lower the perceived complexity, and raise the familiarity.

There are a number of approaches to achieving this: design the interface to meet the criteria from the start, analyze and reorganize components if possible, or encapsulate existing components within an object that provides the desired interface[22].

If we can identify similarities in systems and their components and encapsulate the details in classes, then the procedures for each class may be reused each time a system is derived from the class. Additionally, if different operating system types may have interfaces to their components designed in a similar manner, then differences in procedures may be hidden in a commonly shared class. We would like to be able to say, "Create a 4 Gigabyte disk partition", and obtain the proper result, no matter what operating system class the system belongs to.

Since dependencies between objects are a major source of failures, minimizing the dependencies is a good thing, if possible. While we may not have control over all of the application component dependencies in our environment, sometimes we do have control over some aspects of their behavior and placement. We have already discussed examples of using redundant resources to cover failures where the client component is "smart" enough to locate them. Another area we can control involves the presentation of data located on file servers to our users and their applications. We will discuss this thoroughly in a later chapter.

Automation of system administration procedures allows the hiding of lower-level details of system management and potential reductions in perceived complexity. Investment in automation may free system administrators from highly repetitive, error-prone tasks on multiple systems. The first step in the automation of system administration tasks is to document the manual processes that are currently in use.

Once the processes are documented, they may be generalized to fit multiple system types, tested against actual systems, and refined to remove extraneous operations or errors. Our ulti-

22. There are a number of system administration tools that take this approach, hiding the detailed configuration steps behind a graphical user interface.

mate goal is to shout "System configure thyself!" and obtain the appropriate results. We will cover more on approaches to assessment and automation of current processes in a later chapter.

3.3 Class-Based System Administration Summary

Complexity exists at many levels in today's networked environments. One of the manifestations of this complexity is the dependency between individual network objects like application components. There are different categories of dependency types: recognized versus unrecognized, managed versus unmanaged, and local versus nonlocal.

The environmental complexity may be dealt with by encapsulating details within higher-level "container objects" that lower the overall perceived complexity. Lowering the perceived complexity helps the system administration personnel by allowing them to handle higher-level tasks. The perceived complexity is also tied to the number of distinct operating system variants that are present in the environment.

Part of the job of designing or analyzing a complex network environment is gaining knowledge about the different groups of system configurations or "classes" that exist. The common characteristics of these classes may be used to create common processes for installation and management of the class members. This will be referred to as "class-based system administration."

CHAPTER 4

Divide and Conquer: Justifying a Workgroup Model

Furthering our efforts to understand (and tame) the monolithic entity frequently called "The Network", this chapter examines one of the evolutionary processes, the growth in distance between computing resources, that has contributed to today's monolithic environment. With a little more understanding of how we got to where we are today in terms of monolithic architecture, an argument is presented for subdividing "The Network" into smaller "workgroup" units. Once we have made the arguments for the subdivision, we present our formal definition of the term "workgroup".

4.1 The Evolution of the Monolithic Network Environment

Before we actually make our arguments for formally dividing the network, we will start with what appears to be a minor digression from our stated path. Bear with me—this trip down memory lane will bolster our later arguments by showing the that much of the existing network structure or architecture may have been the result of unplanned evolution, fueled by rapid technological change. The thread we are following involves the growing separation between the resources in a computer environment. Let's start up the "way-back" machine[1] and make a brief journey.

4.1.1 Seven Degrees of Network Separation

As communication and networking technologies have advanced since the 1970s, the distance between the computer user and the resources being used has dramatically increased as well. This increase in user-to-resource distance, along with dramatic increases in the reliability

1. For those of you who remember the cartoon, I apologize to Professor Peabody for the use of his invention.

of intervening communication media, coupled with the separate processing and display capabilities of the workstation, is at least partially responsible for the existence of the client-server architecture. While the distance between users and their resources or system components may be growing, the techniques to deal with the added complexity may not be.

Many early computer systems were commonly located in what we today call the "computer room" or "the glass house", a specially constructed room that has raised floors for hiding bundles of cables, special air conditioning to absorb the heat generated, and special power systems to supply the large number of watts required for the centralized equipment[2]. The types of external connections supported by these systems were primarily serial terminal, card reader, and teletype (TTY) connections over RS-232, with short cable distances and low data rates[3]. The equipment and its users were typically located within tens or hundreds of feet of each other.

At this point in time, the resources were all local to a single machine, and nothing was networked in today's sense of the term. But it did not take long for this picture to change. Today there is a distinct segregation between the technologies used for local-area networking (LAN) and for wide-area networking (WAN) data transmission. We will also segregate our discussion into these two categories and will follow this pattern in the future.

4.1.2 The Evolution of Wide-Area Communications

Advances in data communications and electronics technologies enabled data terminals and, later, other computer systems to communicate over longer distances, via voice telephone lines. Many of the original networking technologies and standards were built upon serial communication methods previously used by the TTY and terminal devices. Acoustic couplers and modems enabled serial communication to take place over phone lines intended for voice traffic, but the data rate available was low enough that the usage was limited to remote terminals. The resources in use were still very much centralized in nature.

Digital transmission of data over specially conditioned leased telephone lines enabled remote terminals and job entry devices to communicate with computer systems over relatively long distances. These connections were shared by large numbers of remote devices to justify the high costs. The ASCII[4] (and EBCDIC) data sent from the remote devices was multiplexed together locally and transmitted via the shared media.

It was not long before newly designed protocols like SDLC and HDLC allowed communication from computer to computer, instead of just between the computer and peripheral devices. The communications were still limited to intracontinental distances, mainly because of the lim-

2. Today the glass house still exists, and specialized computer equipment is still located there. The development of the integrated circuit has allowed air cooling to replace the need for the glass house in all but special cases like servers.

3. Does anyone in the audience remember the blazing 10 characters per second (CPS) available on the old TTYs?

4. American standard code for information interchange.

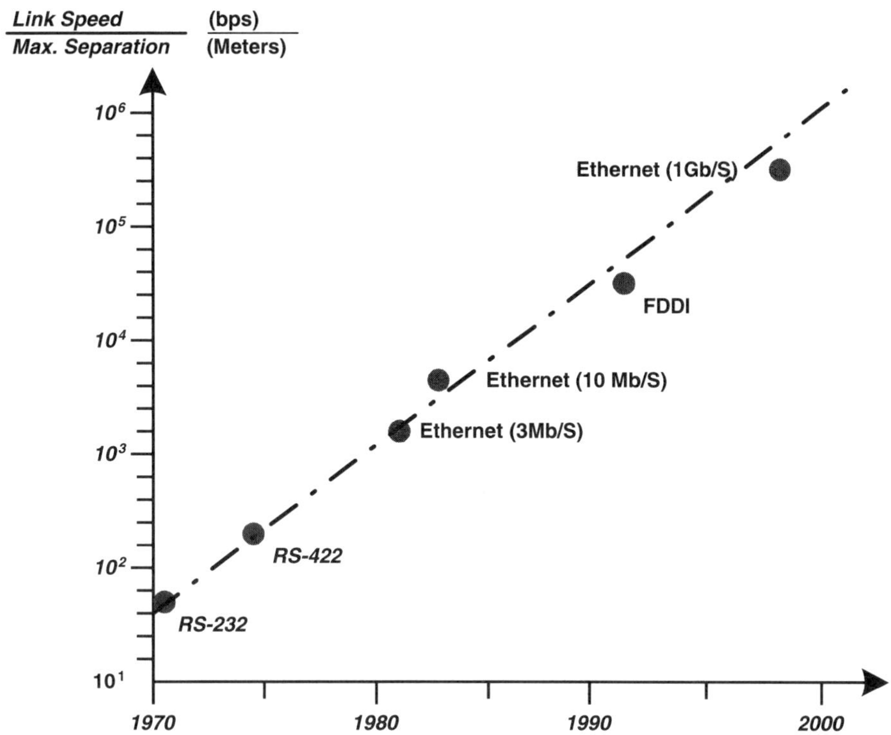

Figure 4-1 Growth in Local Area Network Connection Distances and Data Rates

ited number of underwater cables available to carry traffic and the cost of tying up such a limited resource.

Satellite communications have bridged the gaps between the world's continents, and fiber-optic transmission of data has increased both the number and the reliability of available underwater data connections. It is now possible to transmit data between any two points on the earth's surface via combinations of cellular, land-based, and satellite links. Of course, connections between some points are still cheaper than others. The next generation of satellite technology promises pervasive and inexpensive transmission of data across the entire world, without intervening land-based communication.

4.1.3 From WAN to LAN and Back

In many networks, computers and people that share resources were once required to be located physically adjacent to one another. This was driven primarily by the early characteristics of LAN technologies such as Ethernet and token ring, which had limited ability to span distances due to limitations of the physical media. Thus the distance-spanning characteristics of the local area network actually dictated the physical distribution of the local computer equipment in much the same way that cooling and power requirements dictated the creation of the "glass house".

We are not talking about large distances when discussing the early state of LAN technology. Most Ethernet backbones were strung inside of a single building using coaxial cable that was approximately 0.5 inch in diameter. Connections were made with "vampire" taps, so called because they had "fangs" that tapped into the two conductors inside the coax. Originally Ethernet was only capable of spanning 500 meters in a single physical cable or "segment". This was a great improvement over the limitations of RS-232 and RS-422 connections, however.

The original limitations on Ethernet are now gone, and there is a hierarchy of physical media and multiple transmission rates available, ranging from 10 Megabits per second, up to one Gigabit per second (there is already discussion of 10 Gigabits per second.) The interface to the Ethernet physical media is contained in a single chip, which automatically senses the data rate and whether the operation is full duplex or not. Gigabit Ethernet (abbreviated GbE) is capable of spanning 2-3 kilometers with fiber-optic media, a distance that approaches what would have required a WAN connection in the past.

Because of the developments in networking and communication technologies, the logical grouping of computer systems in modern network environments is much freer to follow the way that local users are actually sharing common resources. The physical necessities dictated by the technologies in our tool kit are being removed from our design criteria. The LAN and WAN are growing in scope and richness of connections, and both are increasing their reliability and data transmission rates to the point where resources may now be placed with much more flexibility than in the past. The WAN now may span the world, with transmission capabilities growing every day, while the LAN is also broadening its connection and bandwidth abilities.

All of the evolution discussed to this point is very relevant to us when we try to understand why existing networks are structured as they are, in our decisions about where to place resources, and how to interconnect the computer systems that provide those resources. Fortunately we have a wide range of tools in our construction kit. With the advent of new technologies, complex organizations, global companies, and decentralized management, physical adjacency for the information systems they use can no longer be the rule.

Other networking technologies, such as "virtual local-area networks" (VLANs), are removing the need for systems on a segment to be physically connected to share information (such as broadcast packets) that was once localized to the LAN. We will cover more of this topic in Chapter 9. The question we must still face is "How do we group the widely distributed systems that are sharing common data in our network into manageable, understandable units?"

4.2 Arguments for a Formal Subdivision of "The Network"

We previously described the tendency to refer to a networked computer environment as if it were a monolithic whole called "The Network". This is a very human attempt to reduce the complexity of a large collection of objects to something that is more manageable, something that can be readily grasped, discussed, or visualized. But it is very difficult to apply design principles

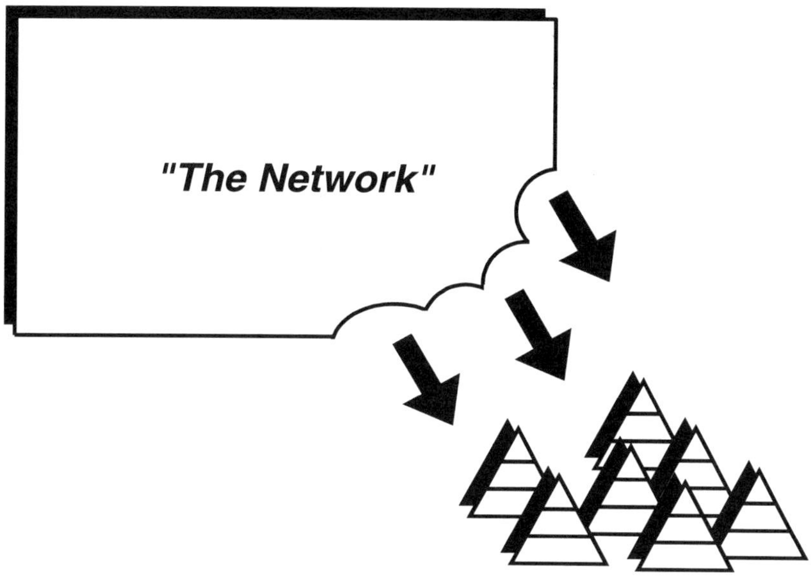

Figure 4-2 Subdividing the Monolithic Network

to something that by nature is monolithic and so complex as to be impossible to grasp. Let us take the informal tendency and examine some arguments for a more formal subdivision of "The Network".

4.2.1 Projects and Groups—The Natural Way People Work

Computer resources naturally tend to group around the people that use them. Part of this is organizational—the people that pay for the services like to have them physically and financially under their control. An additional factor is performance: it is still the case that local resources and services are the quickest and easiest to locate, access, and manage.

4.2.2 Another Level in the Architectural Hierarchy?

The addition of a level of hierarchy above the system level may reduce the perceived complexity of the environment, at the cost of increasing the number of logical objects in the network[5]. This increase in complexity must be offset by some redeeming quality to be of value.

Our hope is that reusable development of system administration and design techniques associated with the new, smaller architectural entity may allow scaling, replication, and the

5. This layer does not add physical entities to "The Network"; we are creating a class of object, called a container class by our object-oriented programming brethren, that is used for regrouping the existing ones. This container helps us identify and control (hide) dependencies.

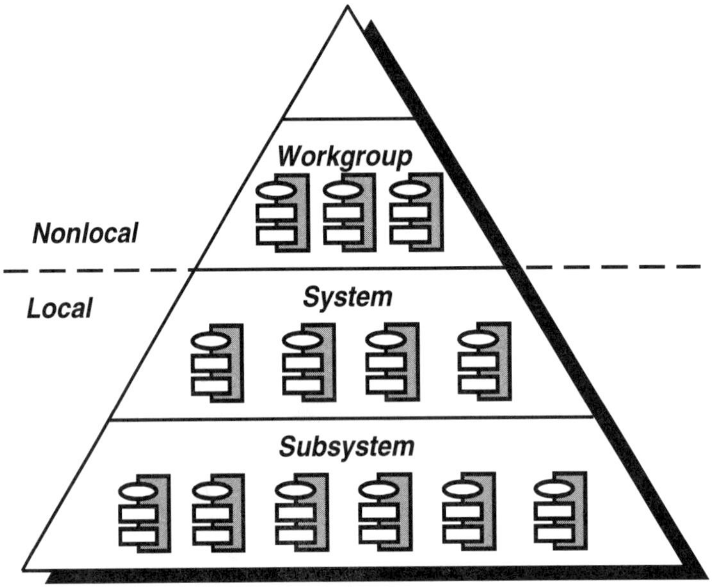

Figure 4-3 Adding the Workgroup to the Network Hierarchy

other desirable traits to be applied to the smaller units, where previously all operations were performed on "The Network" and were difficult at best.

4.2.3 Regularity of Structure: Providing Scaling and Replication

As we have already discussed, regularity in the component structure of a system opens the door to automating the design, creation, and management of the components. We may then scale and replicate the components as if we had an assembly line.

The ability to scale the individual components within a smaller subunit allows the environment to grow until it reaches a "critical mass". This is the point at which additional scaling would cause a drastic increase in system administration effort or a drastic decrease in performance. When this point is reached, the unit may be split or "cloned" into two separate units with resource reapportioned between them.

4.2.4 Coping with Physical Distribution of Resources

As resources become more and more widely distributed, there is the potential for them to appear as a pool of separate components and services, with no apparent unifying structure. This sea of apparently unrelated resources is very difficult for system administrators and user to make sense of. We can apply the term "creeping scope" to describe the growing administration responsibilities, both in terms of physical distribution and additional complexity.

New networking technologies, such as virtual LANs[6] (or VLANs), increase the potential for widely distributed resources. The natural tendency in environments without a regular structure is for the resources to be managed based on their physical location, rather than their class membership or functionality. Systems that are to provide the same functionality should not appear to have different "personalities", depending on where they are located.

4.2.5 A Basis for Common System Administration and Automation

Just as breaking programming problems into smaller, more manageable pieces makes implementation possible, breaking system administration "domains" into smaller units can tend to simplify the management procedures. The additional benefit is that some services are not required to scale as much as would be the case with a larger number of client systems using them.

4.3 At Last — Defining the Term "Workgroup"

We have been dancing around to keep from directly using a specific term for this subdivision of the network for almost three chapters now; it can no longer be avoided. You knew it was coming because of the book's title. Consider this the point at which we first introduce the term we will use to describe the new member of our network hierarchy: the workgroup. The proposition we will address in the next section is how to define the term workgroup in a useful manner.

We should use our new term "workgroup" with care: it may mean different things to different people. This caution is added because there are several areas where the term is already used, for example, the Microsoft Windows environment. Our definition will tend to be a little more flexible than some of the others, however, because we are including room for systems from multiple vendors.

Our definition of the term "workgroup" is:

> **A workgroup is a group of users, systems, and resources centered around a common purpose, forming the basis for local resource allocation, sizing, and management.**

This new entity, the workgroup, takes its place in the previously introduced network hierarchy just above the individual system level as depicted in Figure 4-3. Now that we have added a workgroup object to our design tool kit, let's update our design notation to include a workgroup icon for us to use. To remind ourselves that a workgroup should be built upon three-tier client-server principles, we will use a pyramid with three levels to represent one in our activities. This icon is represented in Figure 4-4, along with the previously introduced symbols.

6. A virtual LAN allows the forwarding of broadcast packets, which would normally be localized to the physical media, to other locations. We will discuss more on this topic in Chapter 9.

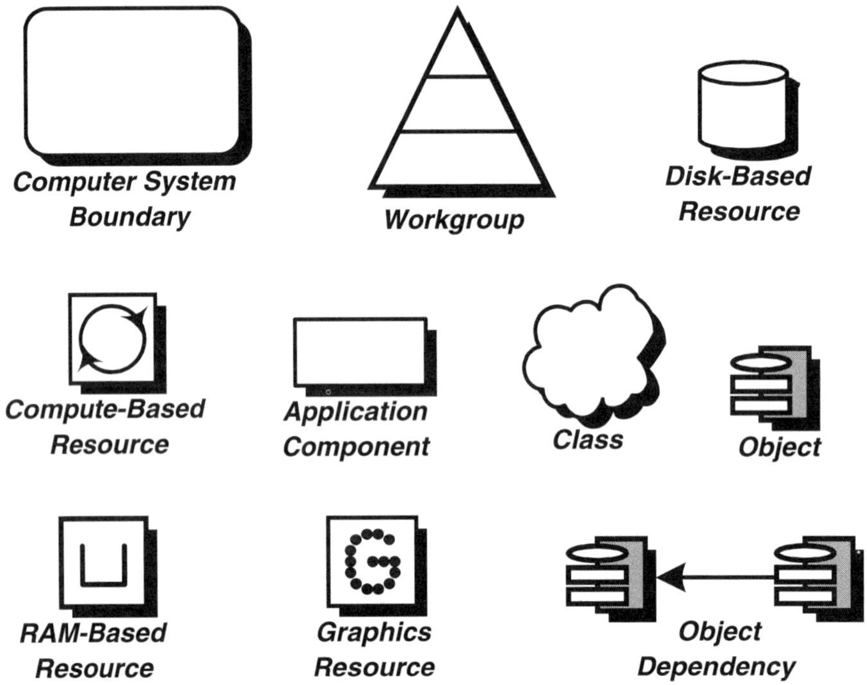

Figure 4-4 Design Icons with Workgroup Added

4.4 The Workcenter

Sometimes, each physical location, office building, or manufacturing facility will have only a single workgroup. In that case, all resources may be viewed as part of the workgroup itself. In larger locations, however, there may be several workgroups in the same physical location. In this situation, there may be resources that are still local but are shared by multiple workgroups across a "campus". We will define this type of shared resource as a "workcenter" resource.

This completes the local resource hierarchy for our workgroup model. All other resources may be viewed as nonlocal, being shared by all workgroups within the particular entity, whether it is a whole company, corporate division, or some other structure. The global resources of this type will be classed as "enterprise" resources. A picture of the complete hierarchy is shown in Figure 4-5.

Today, however, this is not the end of the story (or the hierarchy.) The explosive growth of the Internet or "World Wide Web", which links millions of computers across the world, is changing the way we view and access resources via our computers, both as private and corporate citizens. The "web browser" and associated software technology is making information available in new and exciting ways, breaking down some of the boundaries between the corporate

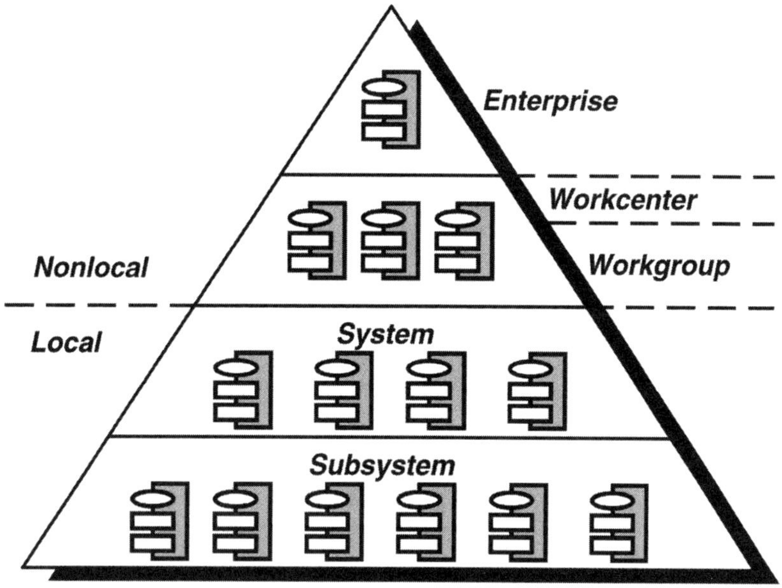

Figure 4-5 Adding Enterprise Resources to the Network Hierarchy

intranets and the outside world. For the time being, we will stop at the corporate intranet boundary, postponing discussion of external resources in the Internet until later.

4.5 Workgroup Summary

The increase in complexity of our computer networks is making the monolithic approach to network design and management intractable. Many environments continue to evolve in a monolithic way until the increasing complexity begins to cause chaotic behavior and associated unpredictability. To contain the local resource dependencies, create well-defined interfaces to external resources, and to allow for scalability, replication, and common administration and automation techniques, a different approach is needed.

Dividing the network environment into smaller subunits called workgroups allows a reduction in overall complexity at the cost of an additional network "entity" or object. In this chapter we have examined some of the characteristics of a workgroup and have identified a resource hierarchy for use in design and analysis of network resources and objects. In addition to workgroup resources, there are other possible levels in the hierarchy: workcenter resources and enterprise resources.

It is important for you to recognize the evolutionary forces at work within a monolithic network and to begin seeing the possible common structure in such an environment. Using the network resource hierarchy as a guide, it is possible to identify and categorize the objects present in a network. This is at the very heart of the design and evaluation process we will use in future chapters.

CHAPTER 5

Primary Structure: Introducing the Three-Tier Client-Server Workgroup

Now that we have covered the defining characteristics of the client-server architecture and have a definition for the term workgroup, we are ready to craft a preferred model of the workgroup style that we will use. This chapter will discuss some of the attributes that we wish our final product to have and how to assemble the architectural pieces into a model that we can use for analysis and design.

5.1 Observations About Networked Computer Environments

In our previous discussion, we made several observations about computer networks and their complexity. Fortunately for our sanity, there are other aspects of computer networks, besides complexity, that deserve our scrutiny. As we begin tackle the job of designing and analyzing computer environments, what are some of the traits that we would hope to apply or encounter?

After quite a few years of looking at other people's computer environments, I have more than a few observations to share about the desirable attributes of a such environments. We will examine the terms "scalability", "interoperability", "performance", "security", "structure", "resiliency", and "manageability". This may not be an exhaustive list, but it is a real good start.

Scalability While various groups in an organization may perform the same function, the computer systems they rely on may require vastly different amounts and distributions of resources. A group of fifteen technical writers has a very different set of file server needs from a group of five hundred technical writers, both in terms of potential storage space and hardware performance levels. A group of fifteen technical writers also has very different file server needs

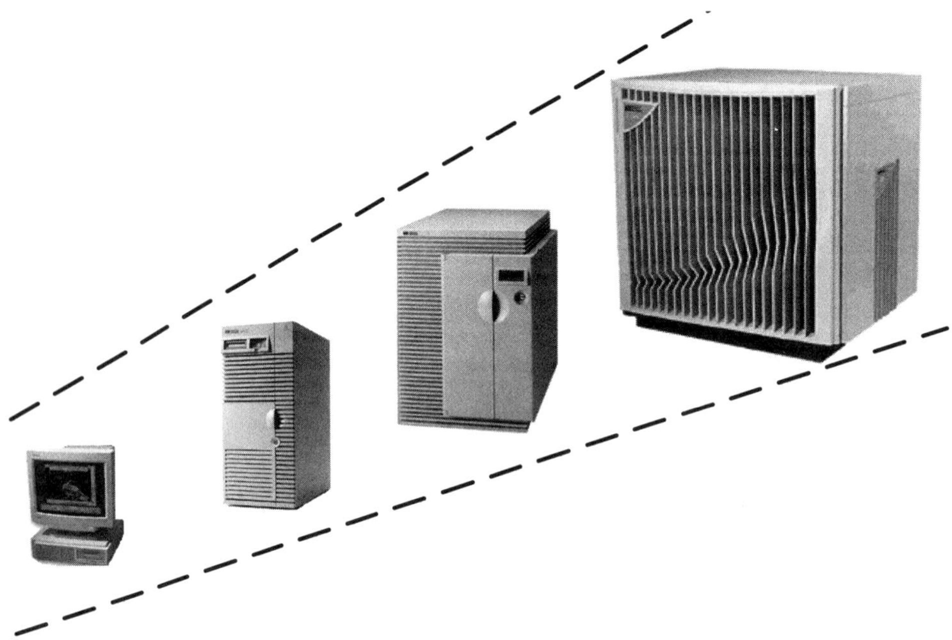

Figure 5-1 Hardware Scalability Based on User Needs

when compared to a group of fifteen mechanical engineers. The hardware configuration of the client systems may be markedly different as well, with different RAM and graphics needs.

To share design and administration characteristics between different groups of computer users performing the same tasks requires defining the relevant resources and *sizing,* or *scaling* them based on resource needs. Rather than reinvent the hardware configurations and system administration procedures, we would like to take all that we know about a particular server type and adjust it based on the number of users and type of service that it provides.

Elements that must be scaled are RAM, I/O capability, CPU power, network interfaces and bandwidth, and local disk storage. How easy it is to scale the environment depends on understanding the application and user behavior and its impact on hardware, software, and network configuration. Most vendors offer a range of capabilities in their server systems, so choosing the proper hardware configuration for a given situation is important. Our goal is to be able to plug the number and type of users in an environment into a spreadsheet and obtain the resource requirements (scaling) necessary for the related servers and network components.

Interoperability Today's networks frequently contain multiple vendor's hardware, and also multiple vendor's operating systems. Because each operating system may have different system administration procedures, networking protocols, file systems, desktop paradigms, or other characteristics, common ground must be found for cooperation between these systems.

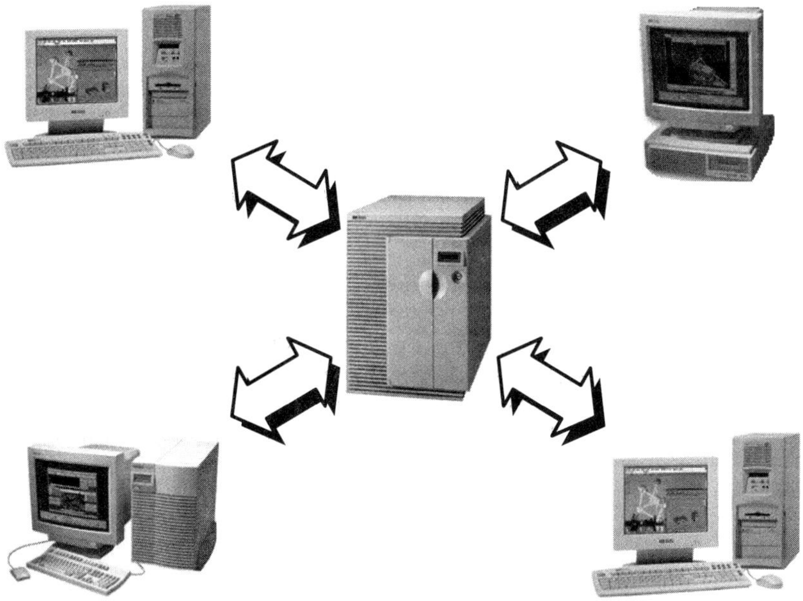

Figure 5-2 Client System Interoperability

Some situations may be easier than others in this regard. The adoption of open standards holds the promise of mutual cooperation between dissimilar operating systems; at the other end of the spectrum is the "one-size-fits-all" approach offered by a homogeneous environment.

Because the sharing of data is the primary reason for the existence of the workstation client, interoperability at the file system level is crucial. Of course, data sharing depends upon the other operating system characteristics like networking protocols, physical (local) file systems, and network file systems. Without the ability to share data, the client systems become isolated islands in the information sea.

In addition to data sharing and system administration issues, we should consider the impact to the system users that is caused by multiple environments, multiple command sets, and multiple "look-and-feel" paradigms presented by the operating systems and their graphical user interfaces or GUIs. Common icons for actions and applications, common menus, and common behaviors (like object selection and drag-and-drop) are all important to user productivity when working with multiple client systems. Designing, implementing, and supporting such an environment can actually decrease the overall system administration burden. while making the user's transition between different system types easier.

We have briefly touched on some of the many issues associated with interoperability. In fact, there are many levels of interoperability required for a healthy, functional computing environment. We will delay further discussion of the details of interoperability until a later time.

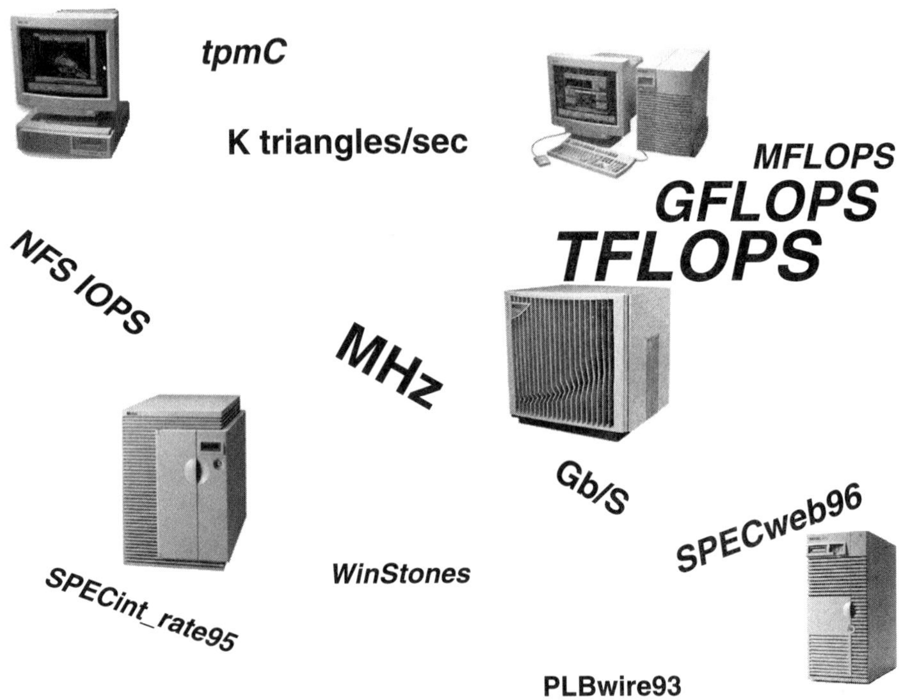

Figure 5-3 How Do We Define Performance?

Performance The term "performance" is loaded with multiple connotations and differing expectations. How much performance is enough performance[1]? What specific aspect of performance is being examined? Should the discussion center around client system performance, server performance, network performance, or application performance[2]? How can application performance be divorced from the overall performance of the environment? How do we determine that our performance requirements are being met? We should ask each of these questions, and more, to ensure that there is a common set of expectations surrounding the performance of our environment.

Networking infrastructure performance is a primary enabling factor for the performance of all nonlocal activities within the environment; remember that it is the connection between the components of our client-server virtual computer (see Figure 1-6, page 12). The proper level of network performance must be sustained even in periods of peak usage. From the user's point of

1. To the "power user", having the latest, greatest, most powerful client system may be as much ego gratification as it is a job requirement. I admit that I belong to this group of users.

2. I believe the answer to this particular question is "yes".

view, the network and its systems should provide an apparently infinite pool of resources at their disposal.

Once again, the key is balance—there needs to be enough power available to perform the required jobs, but no more. Idle resources are wasted resources that could be put to use elsewhere. To preserve the user's magical perspective of the environment as an infinite resource, everything must be designed and tuned to allow maximum possible application performance.

Along with the proper amount of resources, the proper location of those resources is also essential. While running compute-intensive jobs on an inadequately configured local client is guaranteed to frustrate a single user, running compute-intensive jobs on a shared resource such as a file server is guaranteed to provoke a riot[3] (once someone finally figures out what the problem is). Preventing the destructive interference between multiple services on the same server is best accomplished by dedicated hardware.

Security Computer system security is a topic that some people have devoted entire careers to. As you might imagine, an expert in this field must be able to understand the operating system, network protocols, and operation of applications to an infinitesimal level of detail. We do not have space to completely cover this topic in this book, but we will attempt to point out some of the issues that are relevant to security and enterprise security in our environments.

Many organizations today need to share information with other internal or external customers that they may not completely trust. The proper level of security is essential if businesses are to protect vital information and services from competitors. Additionally, the need to connect to the Internet for services introduces security risks from "hacking" that must be properly prevented or contained.

The addition of a network interface or dial-up modem line to a computer system opens up a whole new world of possibilities for security breaches. The possibility of remote attacks over these external connections is eliminated if the computer's user must have physical access to the machine itself. For this very reason, many of the most secure systems in the world have no network connections or modems and are locked away in secure vaults.

For file-based resources, the default protections provided by the operating system may not be adequate for enterprise-wide or external sharing, after all, they were designed to provide protection for users (and resources) that are localized to a single machine[4]. Most systems that allow remote access to files have been augmented by access control lists, or ACLs. An ACL specifies

3. It seems that it is far easier to demonstrate savings in the hardware budget than it is to quantify and attach a price tag to the productivity loss of multiple users when the file server is nonresponsive.

4. An example of this is the Unix file permissions, which allow read, write, and execute permissions for only three groups of users: the file's owner, the file's group, and all other users.

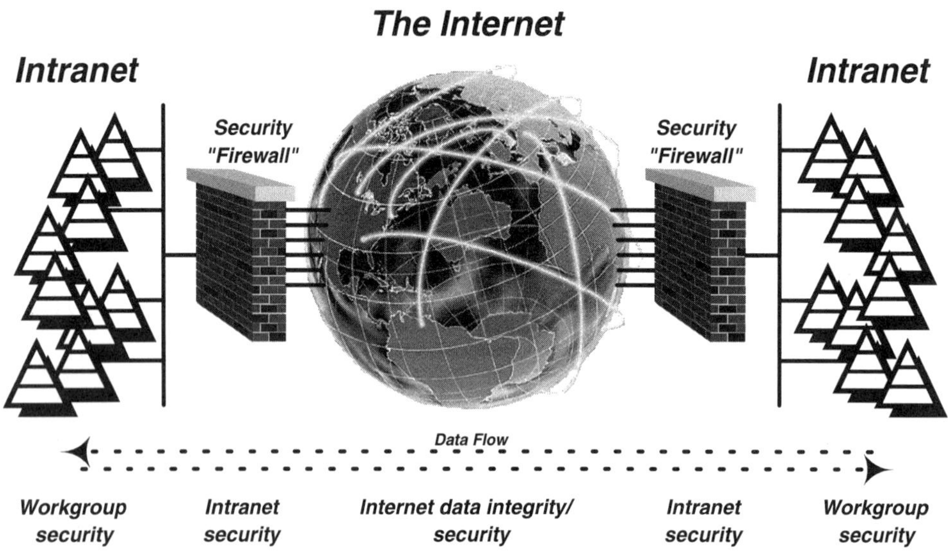

Figure 5-4 Computer Network Security

users, groups of users, or specific entities that are allowed access to file-based resources to a finer level of detail.

In addition to file-based resources, the services that a computer provides must also be protected from unwanted access. The networking interconnection of machines has heightened the need for the protection of system services, and at the same time it has made protecting them more complex. There are a number of approaches to protecting services, including the filtering of service requests by a "firewall" machine or router, the addition of security elements like ACLs to directory services, or even elimination of the service altogether if it is too much of a risk.

As Figure 5-4 shows, there are several zones of security needed for computer networks. It comes as no surprise that once again we are dealing with a hierarchy, in this case a hierarchy of security needs. Individual workgroups need internal security, there are security needs between workgroups in the same intranet, data in transit through the Internet requires security, and finally there must be security for services and data in the remote intranet. We will deal more with some specific security issues later.

Regular Structure We previously mentioned our observation that computer systems tend to mimic the structure and complexity of the organizations that they service. An important factor in this "form-follows-function" observation is that sometimes an important piece of the environment is under someone else's control. Unfortunately we cannot always ignore corporate politics while we are trying to design or improve our computer environments. There are many

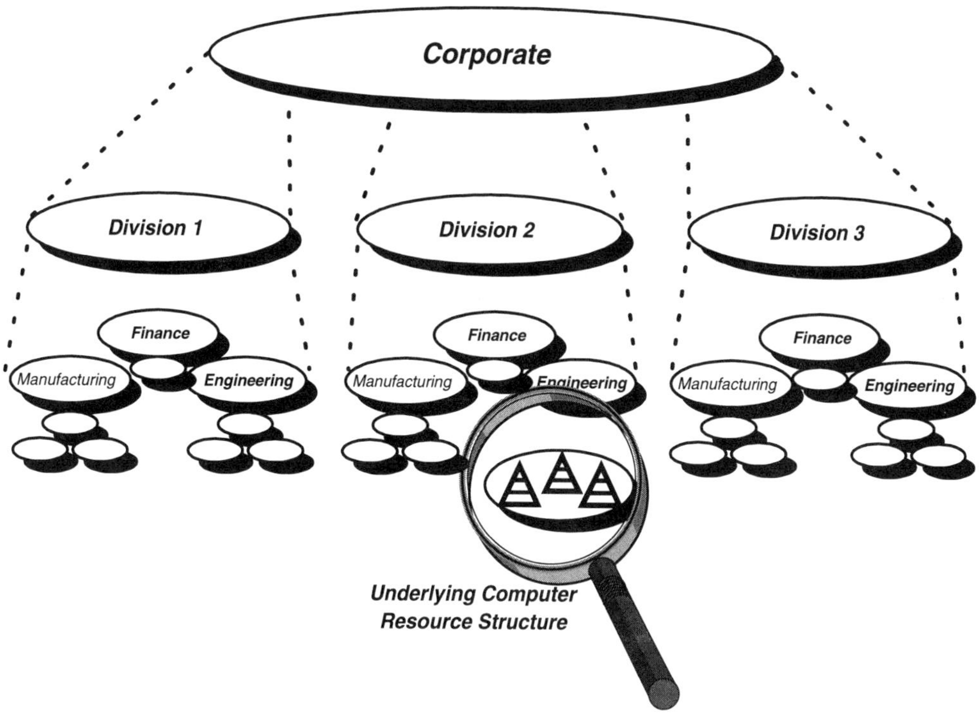

Figure 5-5 Network Structure Mimics Organizational Structure

good books on organizational structure and policy, so we will not cover this topic in this book. The only hope we can have to make changes in an extremely political organization is the strength of our technical arguments and their supporting evidence. Even then, we may have to be satisfied with improving the small areas that we can actually affect.

I very rarely find that customers have a well-defined architecture with even a basic description of the structure and its goals. Having a hardware architecture is important because it provides a standard or set of blueprints for creating consistent environments. Also important is a description of how the computer resource structure maps to the organizational structure. Anyone who thinks that having no plan is a viable option should visit the Winchester Mystery House in San Jose, California.

The owner of the house, Sara Winchester, believing that she would die if construction on it ever stopped, had workmen continuously busy for thirty-eight years. Besides the tremendous expense of building, changing, moving, and rebuilding, there are architectural oddities that are often attributed to her belief in the occult. The house has stairways that lead to nowhere, doors that open onto brick walls, and many other things that are "unexplained".

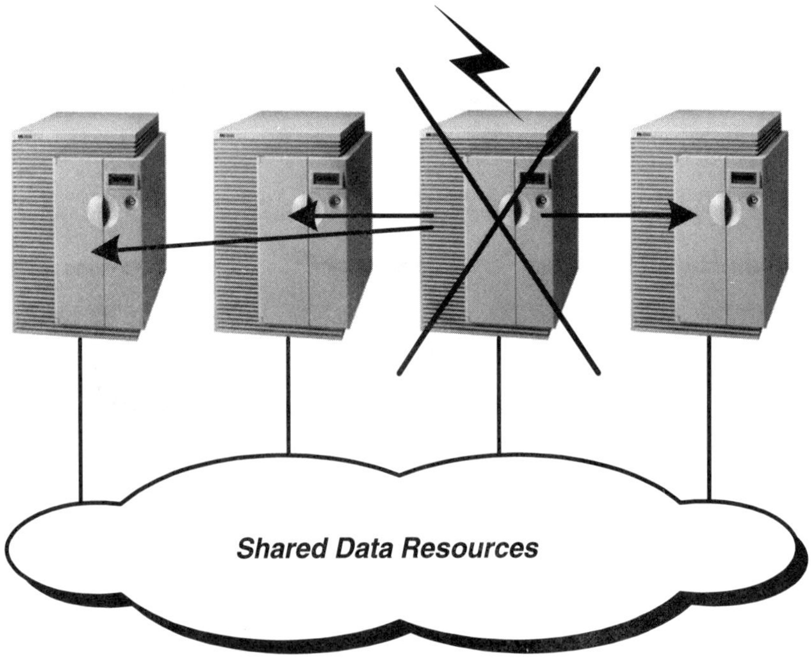

Figure 5-6 Hardware System Resistance to Failure

I have a more believable explanation that has nothing to do with the paranormal: she had no architecture or finished product in mind[5]; the main objective was to maintain continuous construction, never mind the cost. The result was a beautiful oddity, now a tourist attraction, that must be very difficult to maintain (1257 windows, approximately 10,000 window panes, 467 doorways, 40 staircases, and over 20,000 gallons of paint, ...). Any similarities between this example and existing networks or software projects is merely coincidental.

Resiliency The relocation of resources from client systems to networked servers helps in the sharing of those resources and in keeping the utilization factor higher than it would be in a peer-to-peer configuration. The side effect of allocating resources to server machines is that those servers then may represent single points of failure for the resources that they provide. Effective steps must be taken to prevent the loss of services provided by the server systems.

Beyond that, the entire environment must be able to adapt to failures and day-to-day occurrences like routine maintenance. There are a number of approaches to protecting against failure: replication of services, hardware redundancy, recreation of data resources (RAID arrays

5. In all fairness, *WWW.WinchesterMysteryHouse.com* reports that although there were no master blueprints, the owner of the house did sketch new rooms on pieces of paper and tablecloths. Sounds more than a little familiar...

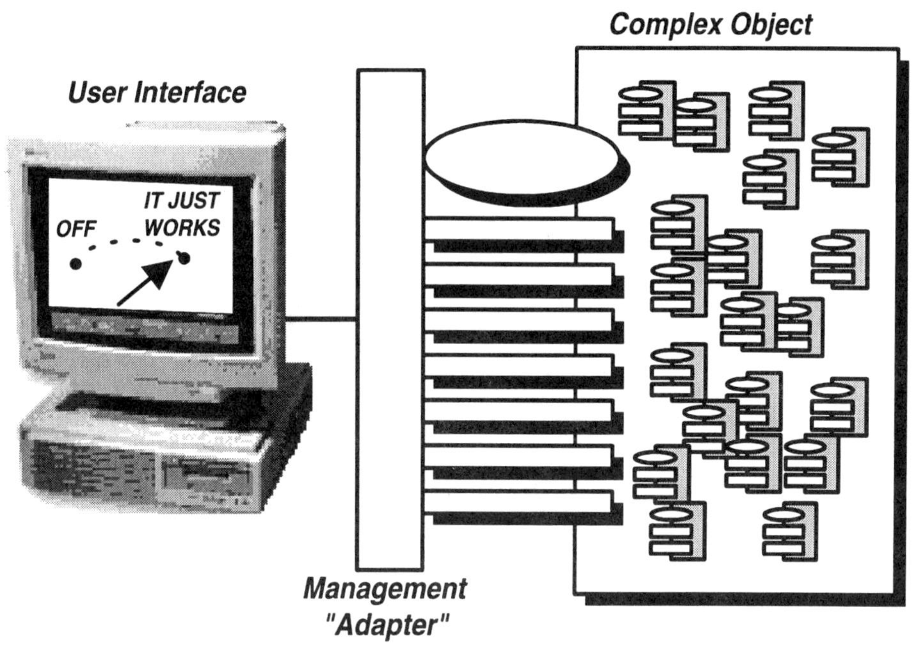

Figure 5-7 Component Manageability

with parity or mirrored data, backup tapes...). Obviously the type of system and its relative importance will dictate the amount of effort that is possible to protect its users from failures. One of the first steps should be to buy reliably engineered hardware and software in the first place.

Even the most reliably engineered hardware is subject to component failures. To deal with those failures, it is possible to configure clusters of separate machines that share a common set of data used by services or applications. In the event of a hardware failure, the service or application will "migrate" to available hardware. This operation is depicted in Figure 5-6. We will cover more on this topic when we discuss the configuration of workgroup servers.

Manageability How manageable a system component is may be decided by the nature of the component itself or how it is used within the network environment. It appears that the primary push in the software world today is to provide as much functionality to the user as possible in as short a time as possible. The manageability of a particular system or application is often not considered a primary design objective.

A measure of the manageability of a particular component is how well it hides its inherent complexity behind an easy to use interface. That interface may be directly used by a system administrator, as in the case of system utilities with a GUI, or used indirectly through another-management tool, such as network management software used to configure and monitor networking equipment. An interface of this type is shown in Figure 5-7.

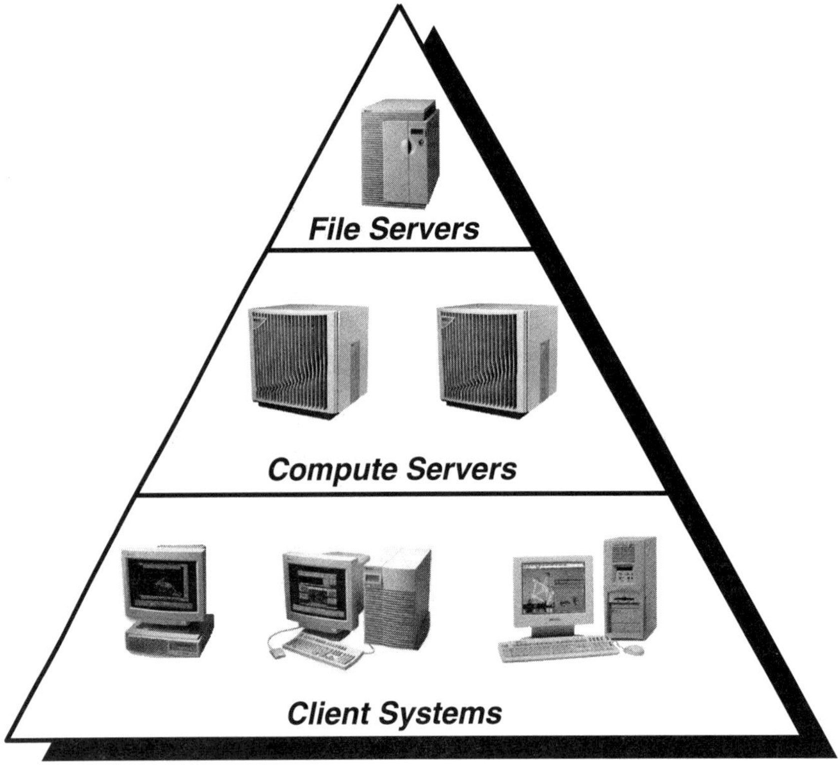

Figure 5-8 Three-Tier Client-Server Workgroup Hardware Elements

While all of these traits are desirable in our environments, it is difficult to apply them to a large and complex object like "The Network". How do we measure the resiliency, scalability, or performance of the whole thing? It is much easier to ensure that these characteristics are present in the smaller pieces of the environment that we call workgroups. The hope is that by engineering the smaller pieces of the environment to have the desired characteristics and recognizing that there are different relational hierarchies and techniques involved, the whole environment will be more stable and reliable.

5.1.1 Elements of the Three-Tier Client-Server Workgroup Architecture

Now that we have defined some of the desirable characteristics of a workgroup, let's take a look at the architecture and hardware components that can be used to implement one. We begin by selecting a particular client-server model as our blueprint, proceeding to describe aspects of the individual elements of that model. At this point we are building upon all of the preliminary discussion of the client-server architecture presented in the first chapter.

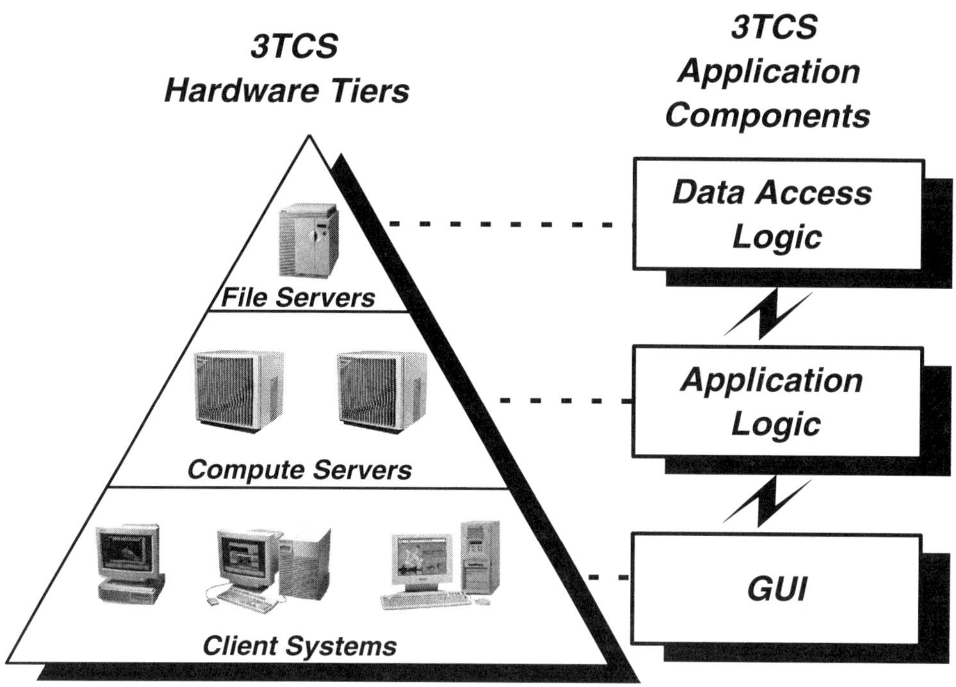

Figure 5-9 Mapping Client-Server Components to the Three Hardware Tiers

5.1.2 The Three-Tier Client-Server Model

The previous discussion about client-server application styles, relationships, and components was meant to get us ready for selecting one particular incarnation of the client-server model, often dubbed the "three-tier client-server model", or just "three-tier client-server". This is the client-server application configuration depicted in Figure 1-3, with all of the optional distribution components present. Recall that the three basic components of this type of client-server application are presentation logic (GUI), application logic, and data access logic.

The three client-server application components may be thought of as running on three "tiers", or layers, of underlying hardware: clients, application (or compute) servers, and data (or database or file) servers. The three-tier client-server (3TCS) model offers us the most flexible framework for dealing with this type of application architecture[6], therefore, we will adopt 3TCS as our model of choice. From this point forward, unless explicitly noted, we will be talking about 3TCS when we say "client-server model".

6. This is because we may designate special compute server resources to run specialized application components on behalf of the client systems. This allows us to include legacy systems as part of the workgroup architecture and incorporate their services into the client system's application.

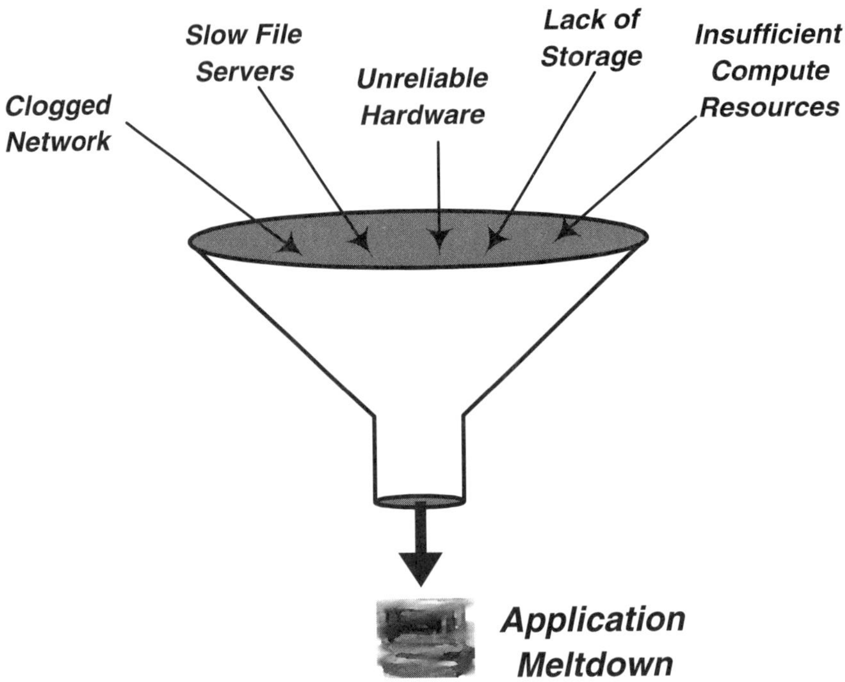

Figure 5-10 Environmental Problems Concentrate on the User's Desktop

The three hardware tiers are depicted in Figure 5-8, their mapping to three-tier client-server application components is shown in Figure 5-9, and each hardware tier is discussed individually in other chapters in this book. A brief note on terminology is needed here to avoid possible confusion. The term compute-server will refer to the machine that hosts the applications when they are executing (requiring CPU resources.)

The executable file, containing the application's code on the disk, will exist in on-line storage on a file server. We will not adopt the (confusing) convention of calling the system that contains the application executable files an application server, because this is just a more specialized definition of a file server.

5.2 Lucke's Law of Proximate Blame

Before we begin with a functional model of the 3TCS workgroup, a brief discussion of a "hierarchy of importance" is in order. When you are designing or evaluating an environment, never lose sight of the fact that the environment exists to serve its users. A user may tend to reverse the hierarchy of system importance that we employ: *my* client system, *your* compute server, and *your* file server. After years of experience with complex systems and observation of their users, I have come to the following conclusion:

> **In any complex system, the naive user will blame whatever physical component is closest to them for any perceived failures.**

As facetious as it may sound, this statement recognizes potentially profound consequences for the system designer or system administrator. It may be hard for users to visualize abstract software concepts[7], a remote procedure call, or a directory service, so the tendency is to blame the desktop computer or the client portion of their applications for perceived problems. This may be simply because things that are visible or physically present are easier targets[8].

The true culprits probably lie "out there" in the network, or might be associated with the network itself. An improperly constructed environment may be viewed as a giant, inverted funnel that channels all problems directly to the user's desktop, as shown in Figure 5-10. We must focus on narrowing the scope of the funnel and constructing reliable, stable, and well-balanced environments for our users.

5.3 A Functional Model of a Three-Tier Client-Server Workgroup

To walk into an existing unstructured network environment, to analyze an existing workgroup, or to design a new workgroup would all be a difficult endeavors without some form of structural reference to guide us. The analogy that I use is one of not having blueprints available when trying to initially build or later modify a building. How are we to recognize or properly locate the structural components used?

Years of analyzing complex environments have taught me that there is a similar structure in all environments of the type we are discussing. After several attempts and more than a little floundering around, I devised a model of workgroup structure that I continue to use in design and analysis work today. It is certainly not the only model, view, or approach, but it has served me well. This workgroup design/analysis structure is shown in Figure 5-11.

This model comprises five interrelated layers of functionality. The model is drawn as a pyramid because each successively higher layer depends on the stability of the lower layers for its support. If the lower level functionality is not performing properly, the higher levels will suffer. This concentration of environmental problems compounds at each successively higher level,

7. See Donald A. Norman, *The Psychology of Everyday Things* [3], for an analysis of user interfaces, mental models, and how users tend to derive one from the other.

8. Then again, there is always the most visible target of all — the local system administrator.

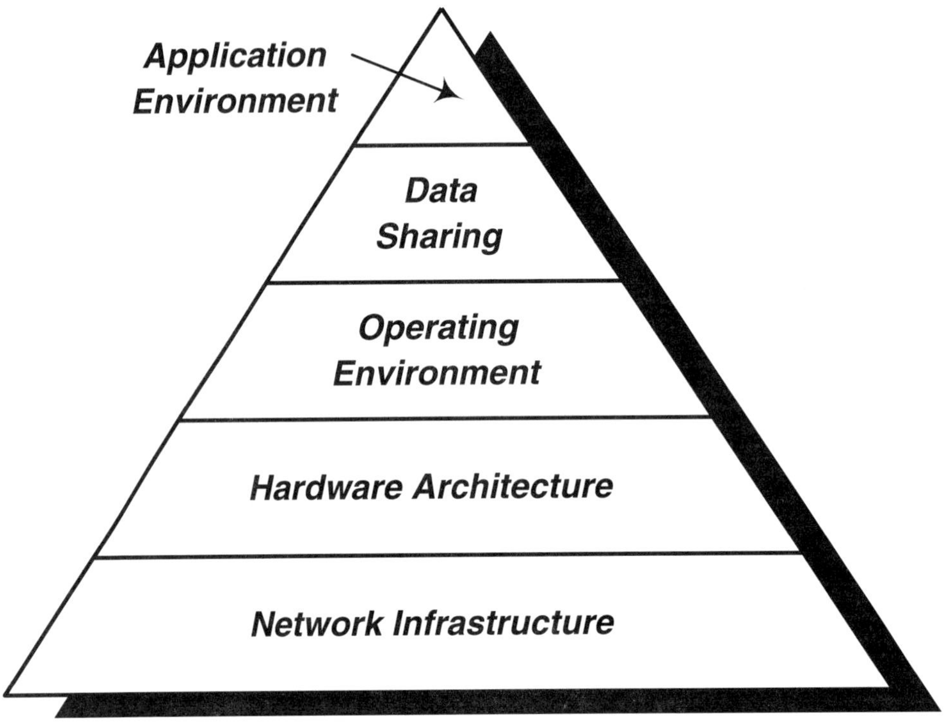

Figure 5-11 A Five-Layer Workgroup Functional Model

culminating in unpredictable behavior for the user. Figure 5-10 shows this process of compounding resulting in "application meltdown" on the user's client system.

While we will devote a chapter to each of the individual layers of the functional model later, a brief description of each layer is in order here.

Network Infrastructure This layer consists of the physical network hardware and management software, including the physical connections between the components of the 3TCS workgroup. We include both the LAN and WAN components of the network, because each works together to maintain communication between workgroups, workgroup components, and networked services required by the higher layers of the model.

Hardware Architecture This layer represents the physical distribution of client-server hardware resources. Merely adopting the 3TCS model is not enough, we must describe the complete allocation and distribution of resources such as CPU cycles, RAM, disk storage, and other hardware resources in the workgroup environment.

Operating Environment The operating environment is the set of operating systems, operating system configurations, system monitoring, and system-management processes. The contents of this layer also provide the services that glue the client-server application components together into cohesive applications.

Data Sharing The data-sharing layer is responsible for distribution of common data between the client systems and the servers in the workgroup. There are one or more data-sharing mechanisms at work in this layer, including distribution of user authentication and security information.

Application Environment The application environment comprises the user's desktop menus, icons, actions, and the set of applications that are provided to support his or her daily activities. As the five-layer diagram implies, this is the absolute pinnacle of the workgroup environment. The application environment possesses the highest level of abstraction with respect to the rest of the pyramid—the user should not know or care about the details that are hidden in the layers below.

The workgroup functional model will serve as a reference for our future design and analysis activities. The workgroup environmental assessment methodology discussed in Appendix C uses this model to structure the data collection process, the technical analysis, and the final report. For more information on the environmental assessment methodology, see Appendix C.

5.4 3TCS Workgroup Structure Summary

At the beginning of this chapter we made several observations about desirable qualities for a workgroup: scalability, interoperability, performance, security, resiliency, manageability, and regularity of structure. This chapter's primary discussion centered around several models that are useful in determining the regularity of structure in the workgroup environment. In following chapters, we will work on ensuring that each individual component, or building block, possesses the desirable characteristics introduced here.

The five-layer functional workgroup model was introduced, along with the "concentration effect" and its effect on user perceptions and productivity. While certainly not the only model available for workgroup design and analysis, this model has been tested in many large customer environmental assessments and is my reference for distributing resources. Using this model for performing environmental assessments is covered in detail elsewhere.

Finally, we have discussed the components of the 3TCS workgroup, clients, file servers, and compute servers and how each of the three tiers in 3TCS applications map to one of the hardware components. The user's virtual computer (or virtual computers if running multiple applications) depends on the reliability and availability of the individual hardware resources. In the next three chapters we will discuss these individual hardware components: the client, the file server, and the compute server. In the following five chapters, we will examine each of the individual layers of the workgroup model in detail.

CHAPTER 6

Windows onto the Workgroup: The Workgroup Client System

In this chapter we will examine some of the essential characteristics of a workgroup client system. We will also examine some of the issues surrounding the proper selection of client system resources.

6.1 The Client System

The most (physically and politically) visible portion of the 3TCS hardware hierarchy is the client system, which usually sits on a user's desk. There are many available technology choices for a client system: high-performance workstations from multiple Unix vendors, Microsoft Windows-based PCs, high-performance Windows NT workstations, X-terminals, and several newer technologies like the network computer (NC). Each of these choices has its own resource and performance characteristics. Which choice is the right one for the client system?

6.2 Selecting the Proper Client System Hardware Configuration

The correct choice for the client system hardware depends[1] on the job type (or class) that its user is expected to perform. Obviously we should not expect a mechanical engineer to perform three-dimensional shaded modeling on an NC device that provides a limited GUI and less computational power than needed. Likewise, we should not expect a documentation specialist to need a client system with graphics that is capable of real-time 3D rotations or a CPU that is capable of over a Giga-FLOP of floating-point computation per second.

The selection of client system type for a particular user or set of users, then, depends on the user's job criteria and the applications being used. A distinction is made between a "thin"

1. This is not an intentional reference to what I call the consultant's universal answer: "It depends".

client like an NC and a "thick" client like a fully configured Unix or Windows NT workstation. Understanding the application mix and their resource personalities is extremely important in the selection process.

The overall set of resources needed by the client, whether it is "thick" or "thin", depends on the needs of the users. The general principle being suggested is: consider the amount each configurable resource on the client system against the potential gains if that resource were centralized, shared, and had a higher utilization factor. Here are several examples of primary selection criteria for client system hardware, based on the user's job class.

Required Graphics Capability The first criterion, graphics capability, is actually one of the primary determining factors for selecting a "thick" client system configuration over a "thin" one. Users whose jobs require manipulation of 3D graphics objects are candidates for fully configured, high-powered 3D workstations. The graphics resources are not typically "sharable" between multiple users, so the only option is to configure them locally.

Display devices, such as X-terminals or PC clients with X-server software, are suitable for users that do not have a need for local high-powered graphics, *provided that the remainder of the workgroup environment is designed to provide adequate resources for their virtual computer(s).*[2] It is ignoring this last point that has given devices such as X-terminals a bad reputation.

One advantage of using low-cost display devices like X-terminals or PC systems with X-windows server software is that there is little need to continuously update the user's hardware to stay current with performance gains. More effort may be concentrated on maintaining the proper level of shared resources in the workgroup to maximize the user's overall performance, instead of supporting desktop client "churn".

Necessary Local CPU Performance The amount of local CPU configured for a given client system may be coupled to the graphics needs as described above, but there are other job classes that may require local compute power. This is usually required if a user is to perform local operations such as small software development compiles or hardware modeling that require some measure of independence.

In general, CPU resources should be configured in globally sharable locations within the workgroup, where the utilization factor may be kept high. A conscious effort is needed to determine a threshold above which CPU-intensive tasks will not be executed locally on the client system. We will discuss more about this when we cover the compute server portion of the workgroup.

2. This is a controversial recommendation. Many users have their egos tied up with having the latest, most powerful workstation sitting on their desk. This is a political problem, not a technical one.

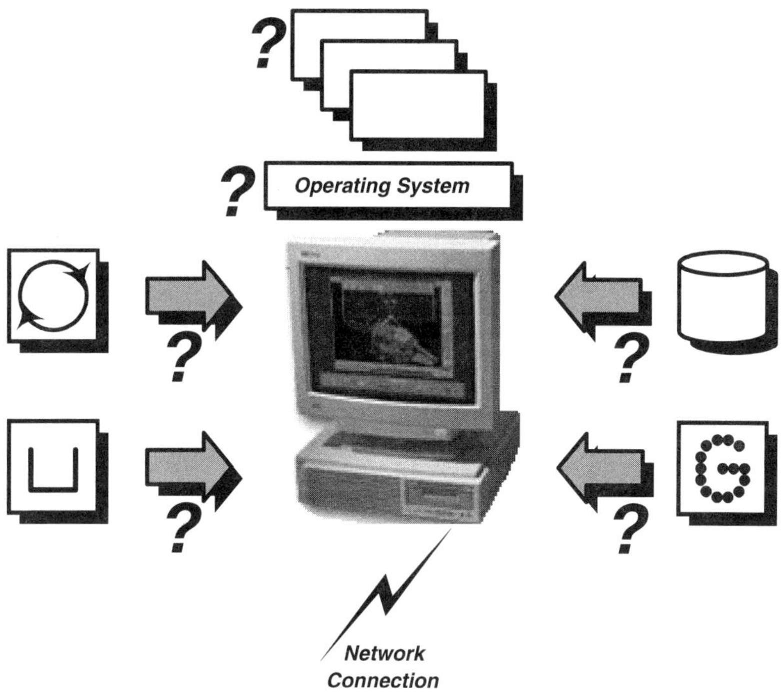

Figure 6-1 Client System Analysis and Configuration Choices

Local I/O and Disk Storage Capabilities Local disk storage is another resource that requires close examination. Thin clients typically have little if any local I/O capabilities, with the exception of a network interface, and there usually is a major distinction between thick client and server hardware in the areas of I/O expansion and performance.

Local storage should be sufficient to hold the operating system components needed for booting the client (such as operating system configuration files and virtual memory paging areas) and containing any performance critical application or system shared library files. These local files can create system-management issues if they need updating.

The thick client system may need space for temporary files resulting from operations like compilation that might impact performance if they were not local to the client. This type of data should be transitory in nature, so that it may be recreated if necessary and requires no backup activities. In general, disk resources should be allocated in globally sharable locations like the file server so that they may be more efficiently managed and utilized.

The thick client system may need space for temporary files resulting from operations like compilation that might impact performance if they were not local to the client. This type of data should be transitory in nature, so that it may be recreated if necessary and requires no backup activities. In general, disk resources should be allocated in globally sharable locations like the file server so that they may be more efficiently managed and utilized. (See page 82 for more discussion on local client data resources and configuration). Specialized I/O capabilities like EPROM burners, PC-compatible disk drives, and CD-ROM devices are also a consideration when users have special needs. It is relatively inefficient to centralize resources like this away from the user's work area.

RAM Configuration System RAM is another resource that may be underutilized at any given time. It is a difficult undertaking, however, to determine exactly just how much RAM is needed for a given client. If the client system begins paging, either to the local disk or over the network, then the amount of RAM in the client needs to be increased to support the local activity. More virtual memory and, in the end, physical RAM may be used in situations where multiple users are running the same set of applications on individual client systems.

Placing multiple users of the same application on a shared compute resource, however, may improve the overall usage of RAM resources across the workgroup. This is because a system's virtual memory "image" of the application code may be shared by multiple users *on the same system*. If those users were running on a multiple CPU server with enough RAM, then the total RAM needed would be less than the previous example.

Network Interface All clients will have a network interface, or they will not be able to participate in the workgroup environment. Specifics of workgroup networking technology are discussed in Chapter 9, so we will mention only the major concern: ensuring that the network interface will support the required client data rates without being overconfigured. Most client systems will have an integrated Ethernet interface; other technologies require the addition of interface cards to the client and may cost additional system management overhead (for adding the card and drivers).

6.3 Selecting the Proper Client System Software

There currently is a choice of several major operating systems available for client hardware: Microsoft Windows and Windows NT, and Unix. Each of these choices has pluses and minuses in areas like manageability, scalability, functionality, and stability. Careful evaluation is necessary to ensure that the operating system choice will meet the needs of the user community without overwhelming the system administration community. The "because it's there" and "because it's new and exciting" approaches to adopting operating system technology have both been disastrous for many organizations. Certainly the maxim "Look before you leap" applies to the selection of client (and server) operating systems.

Application Availability and Compatibility The availability of applications in each of the environments is a key issue, with the ideal being compatible versions across all client system types. There are issues to consider with data compatibility as well: some of the hardware is big-endian and some is little-endian[3], which can result in different data file formats, even from the same application. This fundamental hardware difference can result in different byte orders when data is written to the disk, unless the application is smart enough to deal with the situation. This difference can have profound impact on data-sharing efforts between big-endian and little-endian client systems.

The User Desktop Another important factor in selecting a client system is the "desktop paradigm" used. This is essentially a look and feel that includes menus, window decorations, and icons, as well as behaviors like drag-and-drop and window resizing. Most users are used to a particular desktop environment and cling to it with a near religious fervor. To substitute an unfamiliar environment may cause confusion, training issues, or potential hard feelings.

In addition to the visible components and behaviors, most client desktop environments have a behind-the-scenes messaging facility that allows programs to communicate, schedule one another, and pass data back and forth. This messaging facility also allows integration of programs that may never have been designed to handle such things as drag-and-drop operations. This functionality enables "magic" things to happen on the desktop on behalf of the user and is a good example of hiding internal complexity with a GUI.

The Microsoft Windows and Windows NT platforms provide one set of desktop environments, and each Unix vendor usually has its own proprietary version of a desktop. One desktop environment, called the Common Desktop Environment (CDE), is beginning to gain popularity[4] and is even available across both types of operating systems. We will discuss more about the desktop when we tackle the subject of system interoperability.

Client Data-Sharing Software Because the client must share data with other systems in the network, it usually is running the client portion of a network file system or other data-sharing mechanism. Care must be taken to properly configure the client with enough resources to support simultaneous execution of the user desktop, the application programs, and the data-sharing client software. This configuration might require additional RAM, CPU power, local storage, or all three.

We will discuss some of the specifics of the popular data-sharing mechanisms in Chapter 7. Determining the data-sharing mechanisms present in the workgroup for each client class will determine the necessary client system resources.

3. The terms "big-endian" and "little-endian" refer to which portion of a multiple byte quantity is stored in memory first. A big-endian system stores the most-significant bytes at lower memory addresses, and little-endian hardware stores the most significant bytes at higher memory addresses.

4. CDE is based on the X-windows system and is a standard administered by the OpenGroup. More information on CDE is available at *WWW.OpenGroup.org*.

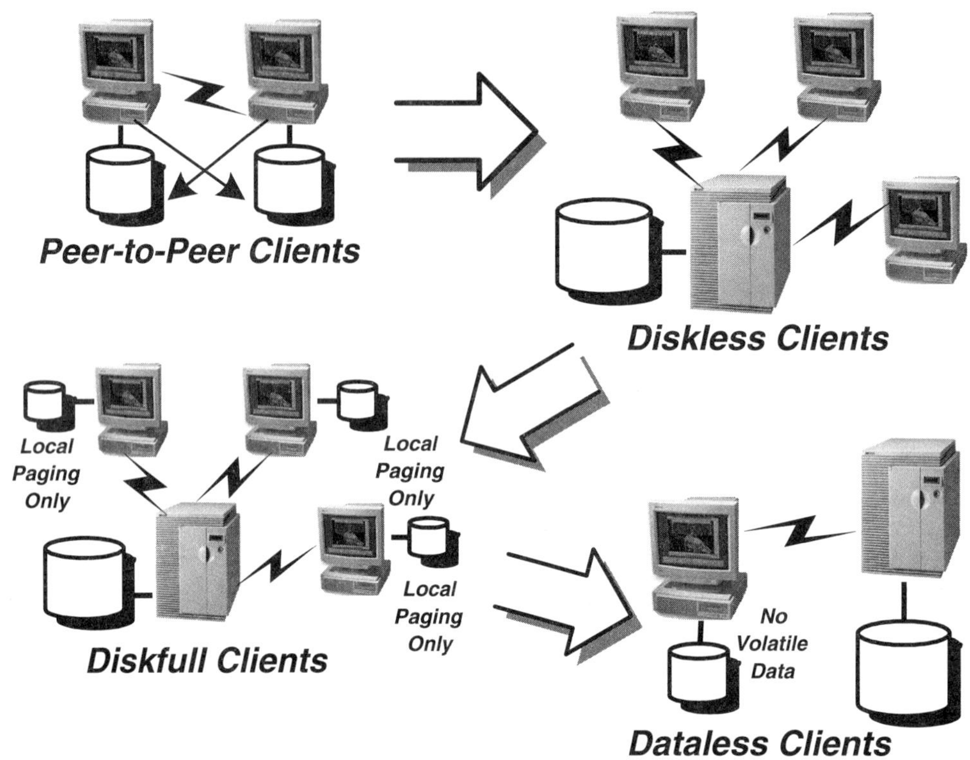

Figure 6-2 Evolution of Unix Client System Configurations

6.4 The "Dataless" Client System

A client system may be easier to manage if all volatile[5] data is located on a central server. When client systems are configured in a peer-to-peer mode, with local user data on each local disk, the dependencies involved, coupled with the need to separately back up the data from hundreds or thousands of clients can be overwhelming. An example of volatile data is the information contained in a user's home directory, project documents, or other data that is changing on a frequent basis. We will call a client system that contains no local, volatile data a "dataless" system.

The Unix world has already been through the progression from peer-to-peer, to "diskless" workstations, to "diskfull" workstations, and is swinging back to the dataless client with central server configuration. The Microsoft Windows marketplace is looking at Network Computers (or

5. Volatile data are data that may not be recreated from operating system installation media, application installation media, or other single points of storage such as network software depots.

NCs), which share many characteristics with Unix diskless workstations. The evolution of Unix clients is shown in Figure 6-2.

Peer-to-peer workstation configurations are extremely difficult to manage for reasons that we have already discussed. This was something, however, that most Unix system administrators had to learn by experiencing it.

Diskless workstations are easier to manage because all volatile data is on the server, but they suffer performance penalties because all resources except CPU and RAM are remote (remote paging files are a notorious performance issue.) It is probable that thin client systems will suffer from similar performance issues. It remains to be seen if improvements in networking technology have become cheap enough to justify high-speed connections to all clients.

Diskfull workstations moved the diskless workstation's remote paging file to a disk located local to the client system. This configuration solved one of the major performance issues involved with diskless workstations, but the local disk became a "slippery slope". If a local paging file can improve performance if it is local, what about files needed to boot the system or other system files? What about application files? What about the user's data files? And soon we are back to a peer-to-peer configuration if we are not careful.

Dataless workstations combine the positive aspects of diskless workstations with the performance improvements of diskfull workstations, while potentially maintaining the system administration gains over the peer-to-peer configuration. One of the areas where a dataless client makes a huge difference in the amount of administrative work is in the process of performing operating system upgrades. If there is volatile data on each client, then the upgrade process for every system becomes:

- Identify what volatile data is important
- Back up the volatile data
- Upgrade the operating system
- Restore the volatile data

For even a moderate number of systems this becomes prohibitively expensive in terms of system administration effort, potential for lost data, and extra hardware involved (detachable disk drives, tape units, or other devices used for system installation or backup activities).

With a dataless client, a system administrator knows from the start that a system may be upgraded or completely replaced without impacting the user's data. This approach also enables "cloning" or "image installation" of the client system from a "golden image" that is created, qualified against the necessary applications, and then installed on all client systems of a particular class. Every major Unix vendor has a mechanism for performing system image installations, and there are general-purpose tools available for Microsoft Windows and other PC software environments as well.

In a properly configured network environment, with local installation servers hooked directly to the workgroup's network, it is possible to completely install a system in as little as ten to fifteen minutes. The installation time, if short enough, can actually be shorter than the time that could be spent determining the reason for system problems. At some customer sites, the word is "don't troubleshoot, just reboot", where a special version of the boot command actually performs an image reinstallation of the system[6].

With this approach, initial installation of systems, operating system upgrades, and replacement due to failure can become routine operations that even nonsystem-administration personnel may perform. Most of the work involved is early in the process where the image configuration is determined, applications are qualified, and the images are made available to distribution servers. Additional support in the workgroup environment, such as DHCP servers, image installation servers, and remote boot (BOOTP) capabilities are needed in the workgroup. We will discuss this more at a later time.

6.5 The Client System as Extra Compute Power

If you recall the client-server virtual computer first introduced in Figure 1-6, we saw that the client system provided the user's GUI and the workgroup compute server was the virtual computer's primary CPU. But the client system also has CPU resources that may not be in use if no user is present. These "spare" CPU cycles may be used for tasks such as software builds, graphics rendering, or other small-scale parallel operations.

In working environments where the client systems are not used twenty-four hours (a full three shifts) a day, or where they are not fully occupied by users, there may be a substantial amount of idle CPU cycles available within the workgroup. If these CPU cycles can be harnessed, the result may be increased workgroup productivity, reduced time to completion for applicable tasks, and increased return on workgroup hardware investment.

Just what is the key to utilizing this extra resource? The answer lies with the workgroup load-balancing facility. If the load-balancing facility has the ability to detect idle client systems and add them to the available compute pool and to parcel out tasks to them, then the individual client CPUs may be used for tasks that can run independently. Obviously, not all task types are suited to running on individual isolated CPUs such as those provided by the client systems. The client system must also be capable of supporting both the load balancing facility and the potential tasks.

It is also important to have accurate control over when, and if, the client systems are used for task execution. It is not a good situation if a client system's user goes off to lunch, leaving the appearance of an idle client, only to return to a hopelessly loaded system. The load balancing facility must be configurable to prevent this scenario, or *reduced* productivity may result.

6. If a problem is encountered with a standardized image, then troubleshooting may involve reloading the system and testing for the same problem to rule out local software problems.

6.6 Workgroup Client Summary

The client system is the most visible portion of the workgroup from the user's perspective. Picking the proper client system hardware configuration is frequently both a technical and a political exercise, because users may treat ownership of the latest, most powerful client as a status symbol. Providing the user with the proper time-to-completion for their tasks can help alleviate the political aspects of choosing the correct client hardware configuration.

A client system's hardware should have a mixture of CPU, RAM, disk, and graphics resources that is determined by its user's expected tasks. The need for high-performance graphics and floating-point performance may drive the need for a "thick" client where otherwise a NC, X-terminal, or other "thin" configuration would suffice. When a task is too large or compute intensive to run on the client system, there must be workgroup resources available to run the job on behalf of the client.

Choosing a "dataless" client configuration can yield benefits in terms of system administration effort. By not having volatile data on the client system, system installation, replacement, and upgrades can take less time and effort. Cloning, or system image installation, of the client is a good way to ensure common configurations on machines belonging to the same client system classes.

The client system CPUs may represent an additional compute resource if some of the client systems are unused. The burden of detecting and properly exploiting the added resources lies with the workgroup load-balancing facility. Providing accurate detection of active users is an important feature of the load-balancing facility if client CPU resources are to be used.

The evolution of Unix client system configurations has taught us some lessons about today's proposed "thin" clients. It remains to be seen if the current developments with NCs and other low-cost, minimalist client technologies will provide the cost savings, additional system-administration control, and performance levels that they promise. Full featured, low-cost PCs, for under $1000, have already negated some of the advantages of the thin client approach. The "thin" versus "thick" client arguments promise to rage on for some time to come

Our job is to rationally evaluate the user's needs and to provide properly configured client systems. We must do this within the context of the remaining two hardware tiers of the 3TCS workgroup hardware architecture. The following chapters will examine the remaining 3TCS hardware tiers.

CHAPTER 7

Stable Storage: The Workgroup File Server

This chapter discusses some of the more important aspects of configuring the workgroup file server resources. Because data sharing provided by the file server is one of the central reasons for the workgroup, there are quite a few details associated with this hardware component. We will discuss the file server hardware configuration, a generalized model of network data sharing, as well as some of the available data-sharing mechanisms.

7.1 The File Server

If the primary design center for the workgroup client is data sharing, then the file server is the center of the 3TCS workgroup. The file server's job is the distribution of data to client systems via one or more types of networked data-sharing mechanisms. It contains the bulk of the user's data and applications—all of the volatile data if the client systems in the workgroup are dataless. There are a number of resource and configuration choices to be made regarding the file server, some of which are shown in Figure 7-1.

In today's Unix networks, the primary data-sharing facility is the network file system (NFS) from Sun Microsystems, while Microsoft Windows networks use an entirely different file-sharing facility, based on Server Message Block (SMB) protocols. Making the two environments cooperate is a topic we will tackle when we discuss workgroup interoperability issues.

7.2 A General Model of Networked Data-Sharing Mechanisms

The file server provides data to the clients via one or more networked distribution mechanisms. An understanding of the data-sharing facility's characteristics will help us make specific configuration choices for the file server based on the workgroup's needs. Before introducing

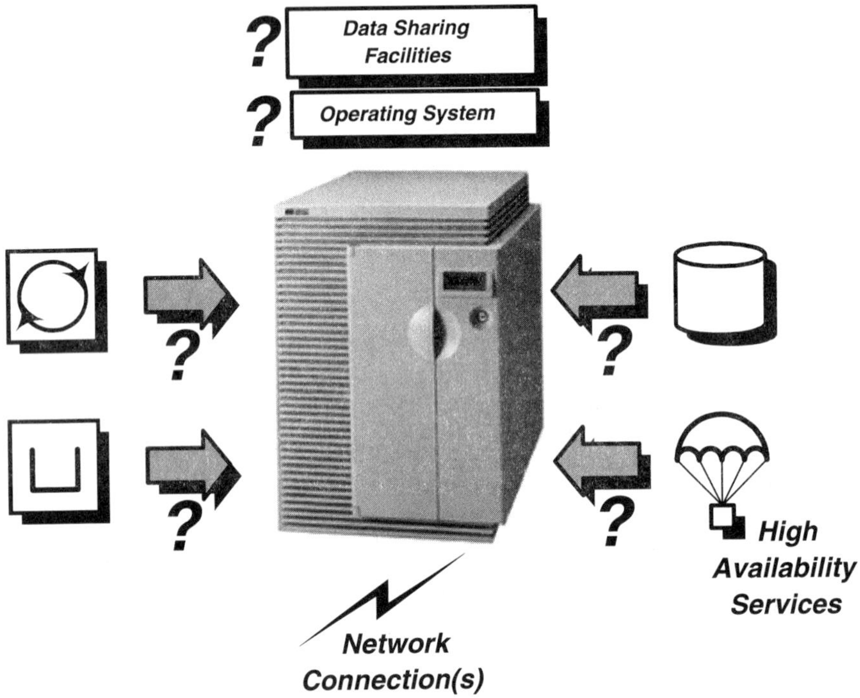

Figure 7-1 File Server Analysis and Configuration Choices

some of the specific facilities that are available for network data sharing, we will examine a general model for a network data-sharing facility that will help us with the components of more specific mechanisms. That generalized model is depicted in Figure 7-2.

The client-side portion of the data-sharing mechanism is usually hidden behind a translation layer that may be inside the operating system or the client-side application. The client systems access the remote data as if they were a local resource, using a procedure that is familiar to the user: Unix systems mount a remote file system, Windows machines map a network drive, and database applications make connections to a remote database.

Requests from the client side of the partnership are sent via a network transport mechanism, usually some form of RPC call. The RPC mechanism used varies from formal, industry standard services like ONC[1] or NCS[2] to proprietary transports implemented on top of network services like sockets. The entire concept of an RPC was generalized from interactions between

1. Open Network Computing from Sun Microsystems.

2. Network Computing System, originally from Apollo Computer, chosen by the Open Software Foundation as the RPC mechanism for the Distributed Computing Environment (DCE).

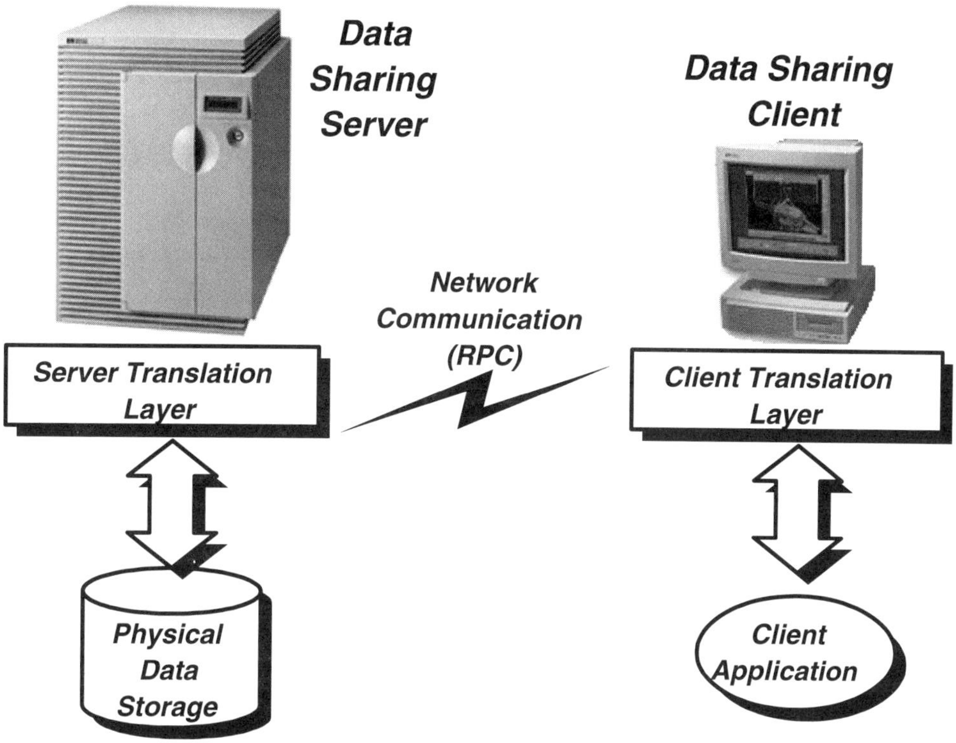

Figure 7-2 A Generalized Model of Network Data Sharing

clients and servers in early network file systems like NFS and the DOMAIN/OS file system. In addition to the RPC mechanism itself, additional infrastructure services, such as directory services and remote file locking, are needed to support the communication between client and server.

Because the server actually contains the data for all of the workgroup clients, its internal workings require more system administration effort. The extra effort administering the server is traded for a simpler interface from the client system's perspective, and the effort is more than made up by the system administration savings on the individual clients. The physical data storage on the server may be a normal physical file system (like the HFS for Unix or the FAT file system for Windows systems) or a more specialized storage repository with its own data management characteristics, like the "raw"[3] disk partitions used by a database.

3. A term indicating that the operating system provides direct, unadulterated access to the disk storage. The opposite of "raw" access, of course, is "cooked" access, in which processing of the data takes place.

Each underlying physical storage service has its own system administration and maintenance requirements. As we have discussed previously, the server exports a well-defined interface to the client system software to support the remote access of server data. The server is responsible for implementing security and access policies for the data as well as servicing the access requests from the client systems.

7.3 Data-Sharing Functional Hierarchy

In addition to the components for network data-sharing outlined in Figure 7-2, a complete file or data sharing mechanism may include one or several layers of additional functionality on the file server. Let us take a brief look at some of the interrelationships in this area.

7.3.1 Physical Storage Management

Local high-speed storage on the file server consists of local physical disk devices either in stand-alone configurations or contained in storage arrays. One of the most basic functions to be performed is carving up the physical disks into logical devices, shares, or partitions to contain data. These logical divisions of the disk storage may then contain the data structures associated with local physical file systems or other data repositories.

Management of the physical storage, how the data is distributed across the physical devices, is the job of the file server's physical storage-management software. The system manager usually decides where the data is located, whether it is striped or mirrored, and it may alter other important access parameters depending upon the expected usage patterns. The arrangement of the data across physical disks and I/O channels has a potentially large influence on overall file server performance.

7.3.2 Local Physical File Systems

The next level in the functional storage hierarchy belongs to the local physical file system, which is resident on a "partition", or reserved area, on the server's disk. Along with the user data files, the physical file system contains uniquely structured data: directory information used to locate the file's data, and "meta-data" that describes the attributes of the file, such as its ownership, size, and protection information. Specific support in the local file system is sometimes required for the file system to be exported by a network file system.

Other functionality provided by the local physical file system may improve required system administration effort or aid in error recovery. An example of this type of functionality is that provided by "journaled" file systems[4] that keep log information about intended changes to file system meta-data. In the event of a server crash or power outage, the file system may be

4. Two examples of journaled file systems are the local file system (LFS) from Transarc (*WWW.Transarc.com*) and VxFS from Veritas Software Corporation (*WWW.Veritas.com*). LFS is the physical file system used by DFS, and VxFS is available on a number of Unix operating systems, including HP-UX (where it is called JFS) from Hewlett-Packard.

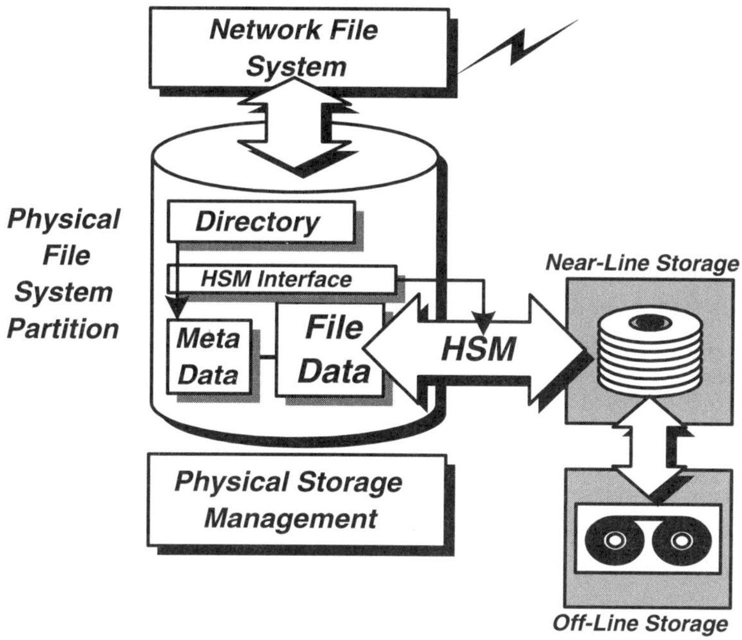

Figure 7-3 Internal Components of a Networked File System Storage Hierarchy

returned to a known state much quicker than would be possible with a scan and analysis of the entire file system structure.

7.3.3 Hierarchical Storage Management

hierarchical storage management (HSM) may be viewed as a layer over the top of a physical file system that allows applications to access data that is resident on less expensive, slower storage media than disks. Frequently an access to a HSM file's data will result in it being restored, or "migrated", from "near-line" or "off-line" storage media before the access is allowed to continue. The data restoration is triggered by an access to the file's meta-data.

To maintain application transparency, the actions required to make the file available are hidden by the HSM layer while the application waits for the data access to be granted. In some cases this might actually include a message to a computer operator to obtain a particular tape from an off-line library and mount it. Similarly, the data may be restored automatically from a near-line optical storage jukebox.

HSM is particularly good for reducing local high-speed storage costs for environments that contain many infrequently accessed files. The infrequently used files may be migrated to slower, less expensive storage media, like magneto-optical cartridges, after some definable period of inactivity. The hierarchy of access is much like that used for CPU cache to main memory relationships.

Issues may arise if the HSM system cannot restore the off-line or near-line file's data within the period imposed by application or other system time-out values. This may be particularly thorny in situations where HSM data is exported by a network file system, like NFS. In this case, the "keep-alive" or retry traffic for file access requests may saturate the network while the data is being restored.

7.3.4 Networked File Systems

The network file system portion of the hierarchy behaves as previously described. The important point to make is that the complexity of the HSM system and any internal specifics of the physical file system are hidden within the file server object, behind the network file system's translation layer. The interface presented to the client is that of a "normal" physical file system, local to the client.

7.3.5 Translator or Bridge File Systems

A translator or bridge file system imports the file system data of one type of file system and exports that data according to another protocol interface. This behavior allows client systems who only understand one protocol or network file system type to interface transparently to other types of network file systems. The price of this transparency may be a lower level of performance or other side effects, like reduced security.

7.4 Specific Examples of Server Data-Sharing Mechanisms

After examining some of the general characteristics of a server data-sharing mechanism and some of the functionality involve with server data sharing, we are now ready to look at some specific examples of ways that a server shares data with its clients. While some of these data-sharing facilities may not be considered file systems, we will continue to call the computer system that shares data a "file" server. This helps avoid confusion by preserving a useful mental model, which includes the basic unit of data sharing between computer systems: a file.

7.4.1 The Network File System

The network file system (NFS) is the defacto standard data-sharing mechanism in the Unix environment, as a matter of fact, you would be hard-pressed to find a Unix environment that does not use NFS if it requires remote file sharing in a LAN environment. NFS provides basic file access support between client and server machines, with the ability to control the behavior of exported file systems. Every Unix vendor has an NFS implementation, and there are many NFS client implementations available for Microsoft Windows systems.

When used with other tools, such as NIS and automounter, NFS provides remote file services in conjunction with automatic client-side mounting of remote file systems on access (automounter) and single-point administration of user login and mount information (NIS.) While NIS is a separate infrastructure service, NFS, automount, and NIS are intimately intertwined.

There are currently two NFS protocol versions available: PV2, which has been available for a number of years, and PV3, which is a relative newcomer on the NFS scene. Both NFS protocols are supported over UDP[5] network transport, which limits their reliable operation to LAN environments, but NFS PV3 also supports the protocol over TCP/IP connections. Along with other improvements, NFS PV3 has added a more efficient protocol, client-side caching of read-only data with CacheFS, support for secure RPC calls, and an improved automounting facility with AutoFS.

Both NFS protocol versions implement a "stateless" interface between the client and server. Each write transaction is posted and acknowledged by the server before the client system may continue processing. In the event of a server failure, the client system will retry the request until the server acknowledges the transaction, and then will continue on. Client systems reading data will cache directory and file information on the data being accessed, but only for a short period of time before rechecking the information with the server.

The NFS services export a physical file system to the clients. On Unix systems this physical file system is likely to be the high-speed file system (HFS), originally introduced with the University of California at Berkeley, Berkeley Software Distribution (BSD) Unix. Other physical file systems are present on several variants of Unix. One example is the previously mentioned VxFS file system. Because NFS is a fairly general transport mechanism, other operating system types are free to export their own physical file system types to client systems, as long as they meet the requirements of the NFS semantics.

7.4.2 The Distributed File System

The Distributed Computing Environment (DCE) was designed by the Open Software Foundation (OSF[6]) as a secure, distributed set of services for implementing widely distributed, secure client server applications over a variety of network protocols. The DCE environment comprises time synchronization, security, remote procedure call, scalable distributed authentication services, and multithreaded application facilities. Its goal was to provide a multivendor, open framework for distributed applications[7].

The distributed file system (DFS) is a fully functional DCE application in the sense that it utilizes all of the basic services provided by the DCE environment. DFS provides secure access to services and file information, replication of file sets, client caching of server data, efficient access over a WAN, and many other desirable features. For efficiently and securely sharing data over a WAN, it is hard to beat DFS. More on this topic later.

5. This stands for Unreliable Datagram Protocol, which I joking call "U Drop Packets" because of its lack of error-recovery mechanisms.

6. The Open Software Foundation is now part of the Open Group.

7. The complexity of DCE, coupled with the entrenched use of NFS, has helped to prevent widespread adoption of DCE in the industry except where special needs outweigh the extra effort required.

One of the interesting implementation details of DFS is that it uses a "statefull" protocol, contrasting to the NFS "stateless" implementation. DFS servers keep track of which clients have particular sets of data cached, and will invalidate the cached information if a client requests exclusive access for writing. This is much more efficient than the alternative—checking back with the server on a regular basis to see if the file has been modified.

For full support of ACLs, replication, and other DFS functionality, the physical file system must provide the ability to store and access DFS-specific meta-data. It is common to find DFS implementations using the local file system (LFS) that was specifically designed to provide the necessary functionality required by the DFS software. Other file system types, like HFS, may be exported by a DFS server, but they may not support the full range of DFS functionality.

7.4.3 Microsoft Windows SMB and CIFS

Microsoft Windows file servers may export their data via the Server Message Block (SMB) protocol, making the data available to Windows clients in the network that access it via the NetBIOS API. The major disadvantage of this particular protocol is the amount of broadcasting that Windows clients do to locate network resources. Care must be taken to limit or contain the broadcasting to avoid impacting network performance for other systems.

Another Windows-based protocol, the Common Internet File System protocol, is a superset of SMB, intended to provide a more efficient alternative that can operate in a WAN environment over reliable, connection-oriented transports. The CIFS protocol provides improved file naming, improved security, and client file caching (with opportunistic locking) when compared to earlier dialects of SMB.

There are numerous physical file systems available on Microsoft Windows clients, including FAT, FAT32, and ntfs. Each of these supports different functionality such as ACLs (ntfs), more efficient allocation unit sizing (FAT32.) The more contemporary file systems support more complex file names, as opposed to the familiar 8.3 format[8] supported by MS-DOS and early variants of Windows.

7.4.4 Software Configuration Management

Software configuration management is rarely thought of as a data sharing mechanism. In its simplest form, configuration management information that is stored by facilities like the Unix revision control system (RCS) may be directory and file information exported by a network file system such as NFS. Interpreting the data and using it requires only the proper commands on the client system.

8. The 8.3 file naming convention consists of an eight-character file name, an implied "." as a separator, and a three-character file extension or type.

A more complex example is Rational Software's ClearCase[9] configuration management package, which has its own physical file system, the multiversion file system (MVFS), but uses NFS (along with additional client-server software and RPC calls) to export the data from the server system's physical file system to client systems. The proper interpretation of the file system data is left to the client's operating system, which contains MVFS components, and the ClearCase client software.

7.4.5 Relational Database Management Systems

There are many relational database systems available in today's market. Each one of these may be viewed as a data repository that enables data sharing via remote procedure calls from client systems. In this way, the contents of the database may be updated or queried by client system applications performing data entry or reporting functions.

Exactly how the data is stored on the server system depends on the individual database system. Some relational database management systems (RDBMSs) use raw disk partitions as data containers, in which case the database software is responsible for managing its own internal data structures and I/O to the disk devices. Other database systems use the physical file system and structured I/O operations provided by the operating system to access the data containers, which are individual files.

In either situation, the complexity of the database and its management tasks is hidden behind the interface provided to the client systems. There are usually fourth-generation languages (4GL) provided for user interface design and query languages, such as SQL, available to search the database for data matching a set of specified criteria. With these tools and others, it is possible to create client-server applications that utilize the RDBMS.

7.4.6 File System Translators or Bridges

In addition to the physical file system and network file system classifications, there is another type of file system that we will call a bridge or translator. The job of this type of component is to take an existing file system type, such as HFS or NFS, and to export it with a different set of semantics. Along with a change in network file system protocol, a translator may also map or alter the security or ownership information to that expected by the client system.

An example of such a translator is the NFS-to-DFS secure gateway available with the DFS. This component takes DFS semantics and exports them to systems that are only able to access data via NFS. It does this job while preserving the inherent security of the DCE and DFS environment.

Other examples of this type of file system translators are the "Samba" file system and the "Advanced Server for HP-UX". The former is a widely available public domain package that allows exporting Unix file systems to Microsoft Windows SMB clients, and the latter is a simi-

9. Information on the ClearCase configuration management system may be found at *WWW.Rational.com*.

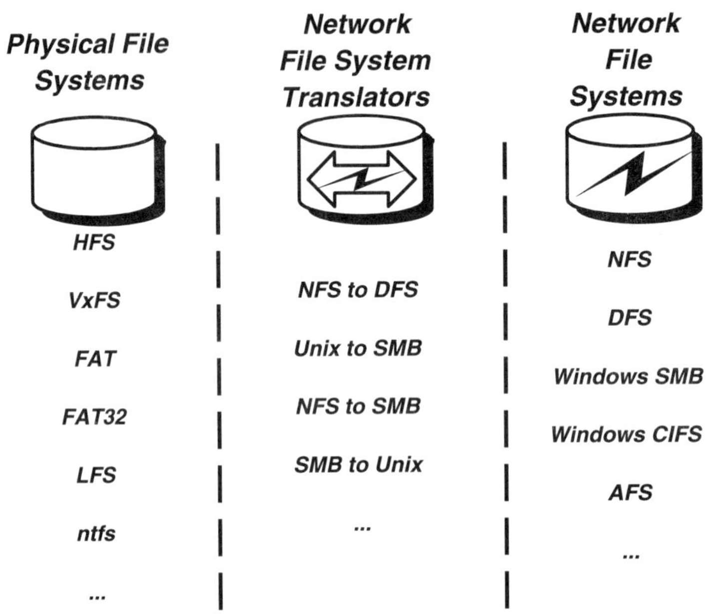

Figure 7-4 Examples of Physical, Network, and Translator File Systems

lar package (with better scaling, print server support, PDC and BDC functionality, and high-availability features), available from Hewlett-Packard for its HP9000 computer systems running HP-UX. Each has its strengths and weaknesses, but both are able to allow Microsoft Windows clients to access Unix file systems, while preserving the file's ownership and security information. Many vendors can provide SMB translation for their Unix systems.

This type of file server component is valuable in homogeneous networks where different client types must share the same file server data. Many times these systems were not originally designed to cooperate in this manner. We will discuss the use of these translator components, along with dedicated server resources, when we cover workgroup interoperability issues in a later chapter

7.4.7 Summary

There are many different choices for physical file systems, network data sharing, and file system translators, based on the clients' and servers' operating systems and the data sharing requirements in the workgroup. Some of the commonly encountered data sharing building blocks are shown in Figure 7-4. Which of these mechanism we choose depends on the design goals for our 3TCS workgroup.

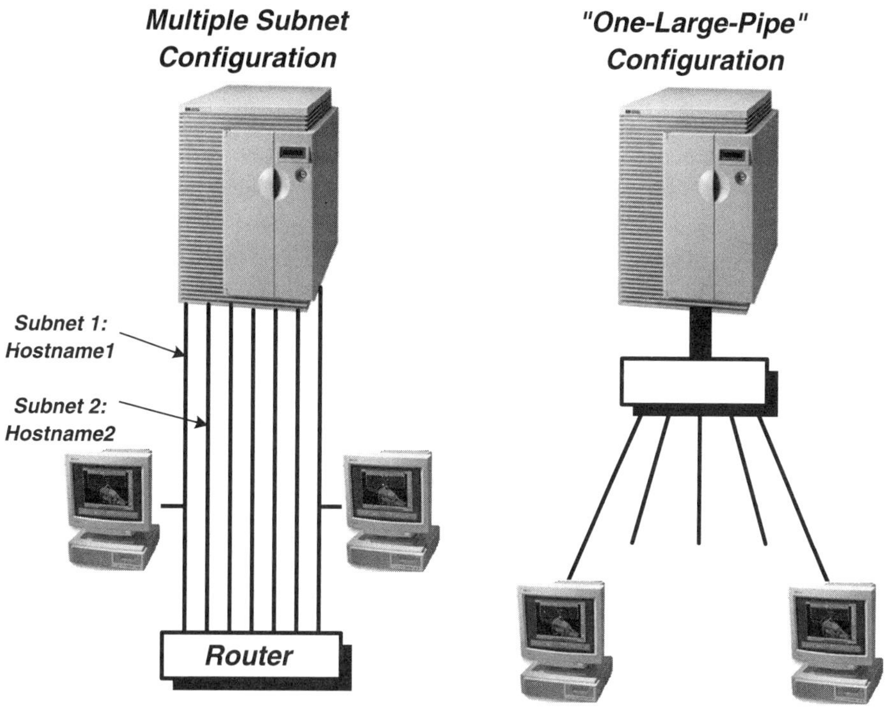

Figure 7-5 One Large Network "Pipe" for the File Server

7.5 The "One-Large-Pipe" Problem

One of the issues involved with administration of file servers is the number of network interfaces present. If each network interface is a separate network subnet, then the management of the server and its associated clients becomes more complex than if there was a single network connection. Multiple subnets usually entail multiple host names (one per subnet), requiring the clients on a particular subnet to mount the proper host name to gain efficient access to the server's data.

This network topology was driven by several factors, including the limited bandwidth of the available network technology and limited numbers of connections per subnet[10]. This particular network architecture is shown in Figure 7-5. One major problem with this architecture is that moving a client physically from one subnet to another requires reconfiguration of the network information and the host name used to access the server's data. There are several other

10. This problem could be exacerbated by the type of TCP/IP network address at use in a particular site. Some network address types allow a limited number of clients per segment.

problems with this architecture, including the fact that the server machine must act as a router for communications between the individual subnets (unless a router is added as shown.)

What is really needed is "one large network pipe" that connects the server to the rest of the network. Happily, we have several developments that have provided large server pipes for networks that use modern technology: higher bandwidth network connections and network switching technology. The additional ability to group multiple high-bandwidth network connections into a single logical link, via aggregation, promises to eliminate the multiple hostname issue.

The single large pipe connection may be one high-speed network link or an aggregated set of links. The network switch pictured in Figure 7-5 may provide a flat network, with no routing. This simplifies administration, eliminating the issues we have already mentioned. We will discuss more about these technologies, including link aggregation, in Chapter 9.

7.6 The File Server and High Availability

Adopting a dataless client model in the workgroup environment can eliminate a lot of effort in backing up important data. The amount of data does not change with dataless clients and a centralized server, but the number of separate systems that must be backed up physically, or over the network, is drastically reduced. This reduction of system administration effort comes at a cost, however: the file server becomes a single point of failure in the network and must be properly protected from outages.

The first potential failure is the loss of important data due to disk mechanism (or other types of hardware) failure. A cold, hard fact of computer life is this: disk mechanisms and interfaces fail, and when they fail data on them are lost. We will examine some of the potential ways to guard against this type of data loss in the next section, on page 104.

The second potential risk associated with a centralized file server is the unavailability of the server and its data-sharing capabilities, with the associated loss of user productivity. Another cold, hard fact of computer life is that hardware components fail—whether it is networking interfaces, RAM, CPU, I/O interfaces, power supplies, or any of the myriad other hardware components that make up the server system. Guarding against loss of data-sharing services is an important consideration when configuring a centralized file server.

7.6.1 Eliminating Single Points of File Server Failure

Designing a server system in such a way as to eliminate single points of failure within the server itself is both a scientific and an artistic endeavor. Scientifically, an understanding of the failure rates and failure modes of all components is necessary to identify potential areas for redundancy. Artistically, a complete understanding of the possible configurations of a particular system's hardware and software components, coupled with the failure rates, is needed to craft a complete solution.

Most vendors can provide specialists in the area of high availability who can design a server configuration with no single point of failure. Because predicted failure rates depend on the original component design, each vendor's solution is likely to be slightly different from the

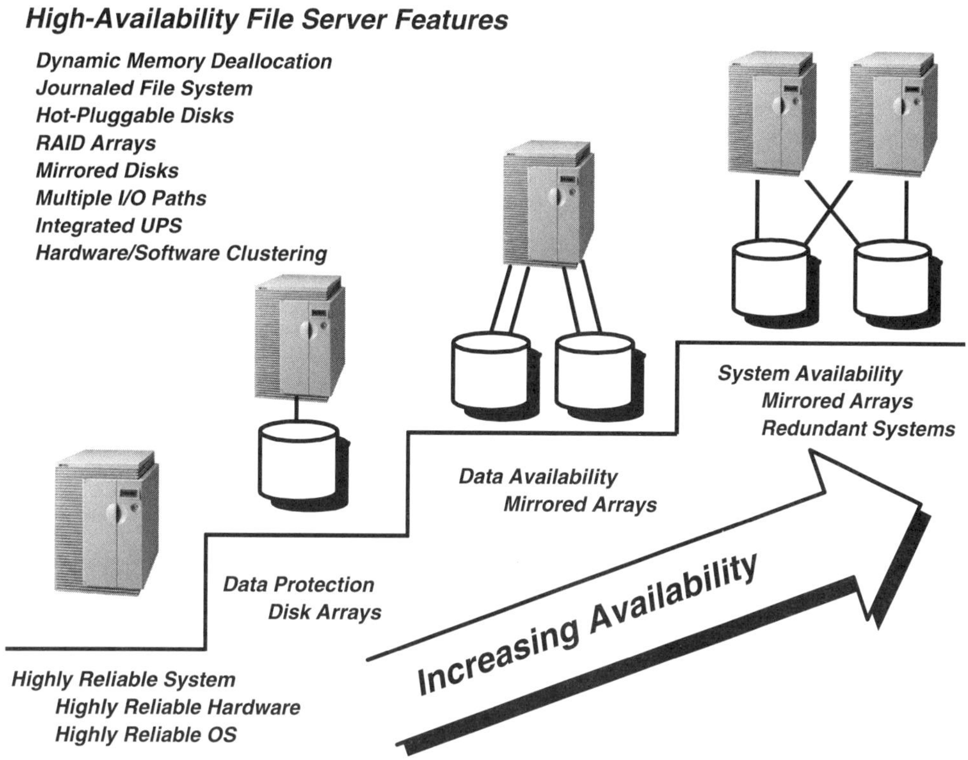

Figure 7-6 File Server High Availability Configurations

other's. There are, however, a common set of hardware features that can make designing a highly reliable server an easier task. Some of these features are listed in Figure 7-6.

7.6.2 Highly Reliable Hardware

Starting with a highly reliable hardware design for the server system is important to minimizing the possibility of failure. Features like dynamic memory deallocation, which allows a system to stop using a bad page of RAM instead of causing a system fault, must be designed into the file server hardware from the beginning. With features like this, the total reliability of the system design is only partially represented in the failure statistics for the hardware, because even though the failure occurs, the system is able to continue operating.

The file server's hardware design can also impact the time to repair a given hardware failure. Certain types of hardware features like hot-pluggable disks can reduce the time a system is kept unavailable for repairs. With the proper operating system support for hot-pluggable devices, many repairs may even be made without turning off the power to the system or rebooting.

Another matter that requires attention lies in the area of uninterruptable power. Many areas of the country experience frequent interruptions of power due to inclement weather, older power distribution systems, or for other unknown reasons. To protect against power interruptions and associated hardware failure or data loss, it is important to have uninterruptable power system (UPS) support for server and network equipment.

A UPS allows the protected system to continue processing for some period of time after a power outage occurs. If the power outage is momentary, then the supported system may continue operation after the outage is over, with only a short pause. If the outage continues longer than the UPS support period, the system is gracefully shut down until power is restored. It is important to ensure that the peripheral storage devices, such as disks, are supported by the UPS so that I/O operations are completed before the system shuts down.

Because the level of hardware service coverage can affect the total time to repair, and therefore the total downtime, it is important to make sure that your server vendor can provide the proper hardware service. The level of service required depends on many factors, including the complexity of the hardware and the potential business losses if a failure occurs.

7.6.3 A Highly Reliable Operating System

A piece of file server hardware is not very useful without the operating system software that makes it work. The operating system software selected for the file server must be robust enough to avoid causing system failures and yet provide the features, like networking protocols, physical file systems, and I/O capabilities necessary to support the server's clients. This seems like an obvious statement, but the selection of a highly reliable system does not always appear to take into account the stability of the OS that will be running on the hardware.

A wholly new operating system, or a new version that has not been thoroughly "wrung out", needs careful examination before committing it to a mission critical position in the environment. If the reliability of a particular OS is in question, one good approach is to try it in a pilot project, testing its capabilities in a noncritical area of the workgroup before installing it elsewhere. Where user data and productivity are at stake, a conservative approach is usually the best approach.

7.6.4 Service Clustering for High Availability

Even with highly reliable hardware and operating system components, failures occur that result in a particular system component or an associated set of services becoming unavailable. When this happens, it is desirable to activate a duplicate set of services that take the place of the originals and to have client systems use the newly "cloned" service without interruption. This service fail-over behavior must also be transparent to client systems that are using the services[11].

11. An example of high-availability software like this is Hewlett-Packard's MC/ServiceGuard product. The "MC" in the product name stands for multicomputer, indicating the clustered nature of the solution.

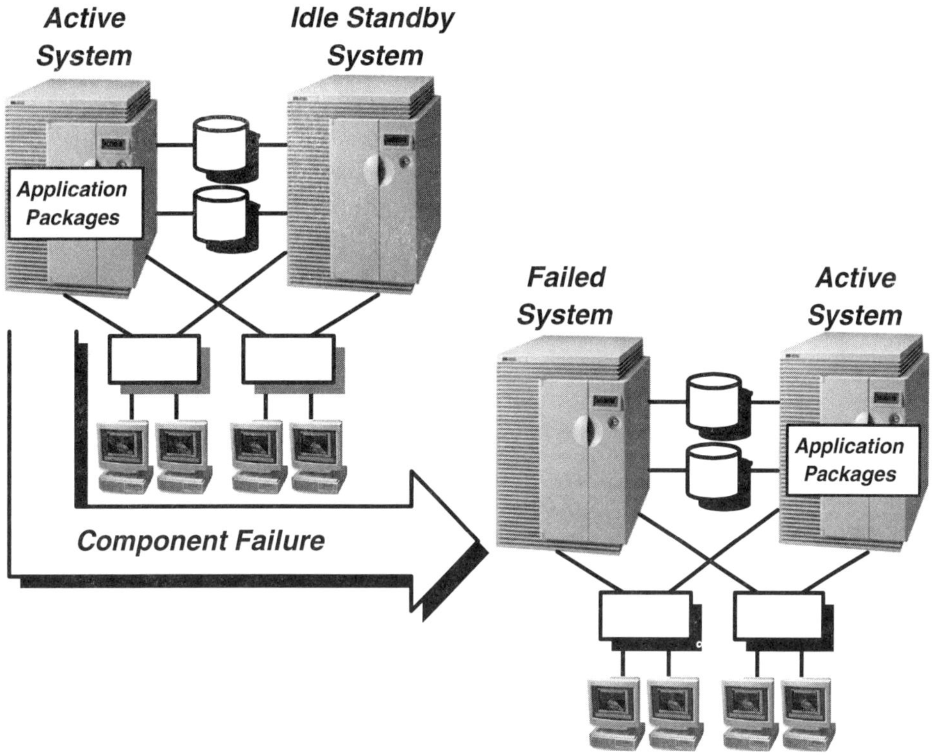

Figure 7-7 Active/Passive Cluster Example

A highly available cluster may take one of two general configurations: an active/passive configuration or an active/active configuration. In the former configuration, there is a completely redundant system standing by idle to be used in the event of a failure. In the latter configuration, a second system is available to provide services in the event of a failure, but that second system is actively running other application software.

The active/passive and active/active configurations each have their own strengths and weaknesses. In the active/passive case, there is a complete copy of the server hardware standing by idle. This results in additional cost for the total configuration, with no corresponding increase in processing ability for the cluster, but guarantees the application packages an identical set of resources when a failure occurs. This configuration is shown in Figure 7-7.

The active/active configuration, on the other hand, allows application packages and services to migrate to other machines, potentially resulting in a resource conflict. This requires that the recipient machines have enough excess capacity to execute the newly acquired packages without adverse effects. This configuration is shown in Figure 7-8.

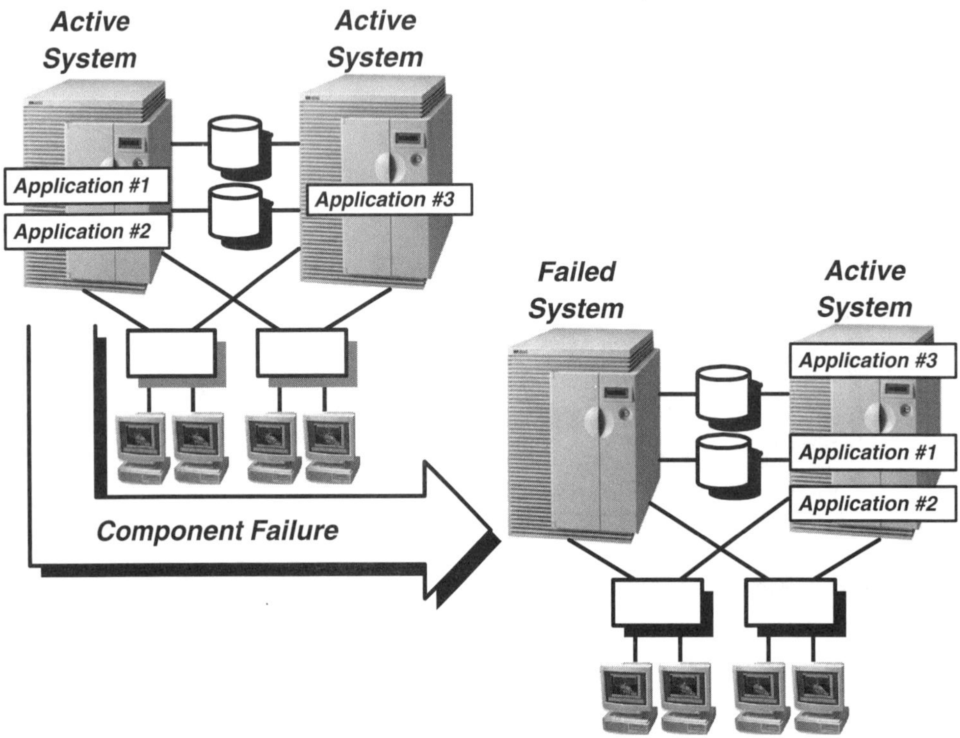

Figure 7-8 Active/Active Cluster Example

Another resource allocation approach is to partition the system resources into preset ratios or specific allotments, between the application packages. One way to do this is to run a so-called fair share scheduler on the cluster's machines to guarantee specific levels of resources for the migrating and resident application packages.[12] The fair-share scheduler will remain inactive until one or more of the system resources reaches one hundred percent utilization, at which point the predetermined allocations are enforced to ensure that no package "starves" the rest for resources.

In addition to the two machine configurations detailed in Figure 7-7 and Figure 7-8, it is possible to have even more machines participate in a high-availability cluster. This opens up the possibility for package migration to be spread over several alternate machines in the cluster, providing some elementary load balancing in the process. This is shown in Figure 7-9.

As you can see from Figure 7-9, the number of connections necessary to eliminate single points of failure tends to grow as the number of machines in the cluster increases. One of the

12. Hewlett Packard's Process Resource Manager (PRM) product is such a resource allocation tool. It allows dividing RAM and CPU resources between multiple competing packages in a predetermined manner.

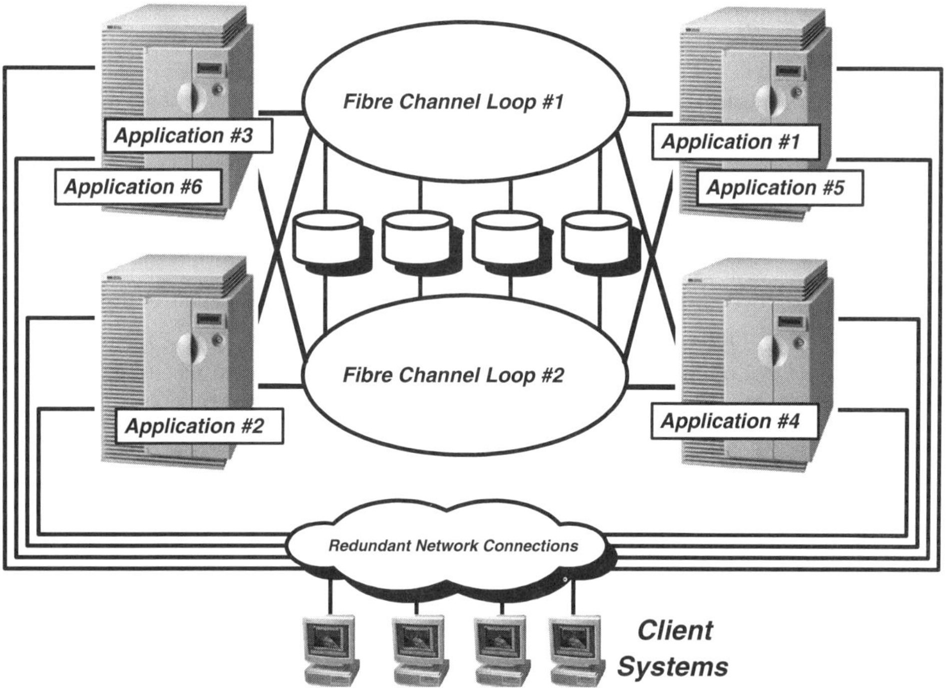

Figure 7-9 A Multiple Machine High-Availability Cluster

areas of connectivity limitation is in the shared storage devices, since most general purpose storage arrays seem to have only two I/O connections available. To increase the number of machines sharing the storage devices, it is necessary to utilize more specialized storage arrays, such as the Symmetrix family from EMC Corporation, which allow multiple parallel system connections per storage device.

All of this service or package fail-over relies on the concept of "locational transparency" that we have previously discussed. To a client system, the migration of a service or application package can be seamless, provided there is no reliance on a specific network location for accessing the service. Thus, locational transparency is the cornerstone of high-availability clustering. Surprisingly, software that was not originally designed for this type of environment may successfully be made highly available with a little informed "rearrangement."

7.6.5 The Planning and Process Aspect of High Availability

Concentrating on just the hardware or software aspects of reliability leaves out another source of unplanned downtime: people and associated processes. People make mistakes, and mistakes can cause unplanned system downtime. It is all but impossible to prevent failures and human mistakes, and so it is extremely important to have disaster recovery processes in place to efficiently deal with system downtime.

In addition to unplanned outages, it is important to realize that planned outages are also a source of system downtime. Examples of planned downtime might be data backups, operating system upgrades, hardware upgrades, and preventative maintenance. To reduce the duration of both planned and unplanned system outages, it is essential to have plans and written processes in place.

Quantifying potential losses and creating a disaster recovery plan for each important system is a highly detailed exercise. As with many other areas of the computer industry, there are specialists that do nothing but analyze customer environments and create disaster recovery plans. We will not explore further details of disaster recovery planning in this book[13].

7.7 File Server Storage Options

The data access characteristics of a file server's clients will determine the I/O access patterns required of the data storage devices. Often, a file server's storage access pattern is random, similar to many database applications. Often the I/O and storage configuration options chosen for large database servers also work well for file servers.

Understanding the storage access patterns for a particular file server can help us choose the proper storage devices for the data. Many times these "patterns" are indeterminate, varying from day to day and hour to hour as client access characteristics vary. In cases like this, we must choose the best storage options, install the file server system, and tune the system's performance to the best of our abilities.

There are a number of storage technologies available for use on today's file server. Each one of those technologies has performance and configuration aspects that make it more, or less, suitable for a file server's mass storage. Understanding the different technologies can help us make good decisions about file server configuration. In this section we will look at some of the more commonly available configurations and detail the pluses and minuses of each.

7.7.1 Just a Bunch of Disks

Just a bunch of disks, or JBOD", refers to a configuration comprising many independently operating disk mechanisms. Each of these disks appears as a separate hardware device to the file server's operating system. Depending on the operating system and its file system size limita-

13. A good primer on high-availability cluster design is *Clusters for High Availability*, by Peter S. Weygant, [9]. While mainly from a Hewlett-Packard viewpoint, the suggestions and approach are generally applicable.

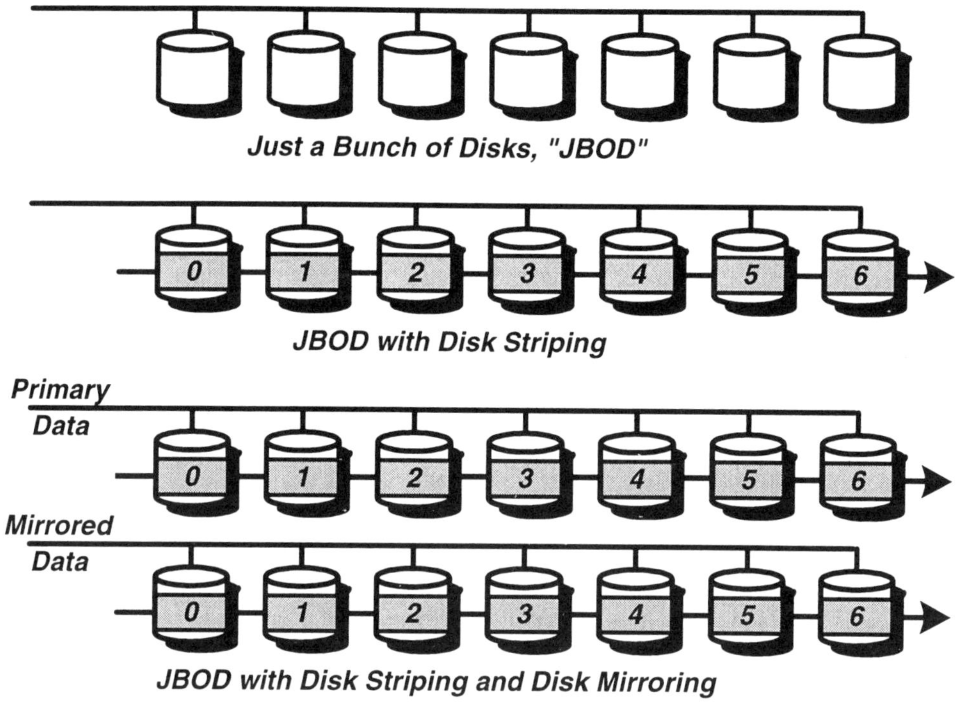

Figure 7-10 Just a Bunch of Disks, Disk Mirroring, and Disk Striping

tions, each of these independent disks may be one or more file systems[14]. A JBOD storage configuration with seven physical disks on a single I/O channel is shown at the top of Figure 7-10.

There are two major negative issues that revolve around the management of many independent file systems. The first involves the amount of system administration effort to create and manage many independent storage areas. The second issue arises when a file or group of files exceeds the storage ability of a single file system: Just how does a system administrator manage the distribution of the data without confusing the user?

Most modern operating systems address the storage-management issues by allowing large physical volume sizes along with large data files. As we saw in Figure 7-3, there may also be a layer of physical storage management above the physical devices, which allows consolidation of physical devices into logical devices or volumes, thus decreasing the system administration

14. For a 32-bit operating system with 32-bit file system functionality, it is common to find either 2 GB or 4GB as the maximum size of an individual file system (or file.) It is usually necessary to provide 64-bit (or larger) addressing capabilities to access larger file systems.

burden[15]. This storage-management layer may also provide other useful functionality, as we shall see.

With many independent heads, all capable of simultaneous movement, properly configured JBOD storage can provide very high-performance access to the files it contains. This is provided, of course, that neither the disk I/O channel nor the disks themselves become "saturated" with more requests than can be handled. Even with large, contiguously allocated file systems provided by the logical storage management software, issues of data locality can arise if multiple clients are accessing the same file.

7.7.2 Disk Striping

One way to deal with potential data access "hot spots"[16], is to spread or "stripe" a logical device containing a file system across multiple physical devices. The storage management layer places each piece of the logical file system, equal to the "stripe size", on a physical disk device in a round-robin fashion and handles mapping access requests to the proper location. With this approach, sequential access to large data files is equally spread across multiple physical devices, potentially preventing any single device from saturating. This configuration is shown in the middle of Figure 7-10.

A JBOD storage configuration provides no inherent protection for the information it contains. As a matter of fact, the larger a JBOD configuration becomes, the more likely a disk mechanism failure becomes[17]. Striping data can actually increase the potential for data loss because the loss of a single disk can damage the stripe for many files, where only the local files on a nonstriped disk would be lost.

7.7.3 Disk Mirroring

A solution for the data loss problem outlined in the previous discussion on data striping is called "data mirroring" or just "mirroring." This method duplicates all data and I/O operations to one or more copies of the original data. In the event of a disk failure, one of the mirrors may be used to rebuild the lost data once the failed disk is replaced. A mirrored and striped JBOD configuration, with a single mirror, is shown at the bottom of Figure 7-10. Note that both mirrors are on separate I/O channels to prevent an interface failure from disabling both mirrors.

Disk mirroring usually is implemented in conjunction with the logical storage management layer of the operating system, where all I/O activity is properly duplicated and mapped to

15. With Hewlett-Packard's HP-UX operating system, this functionality is provided by "Logical Volume Manager" or LVM.

16. Hot spots are caused by shared files that are frequently accessed by numerous client systems simultaneously. Hot spots can lead to disk or channel saturation if data are not properly distributed.

17. Reliability for multiple devices of the same type is equal to MTBF for a single device divided by the number of individual devices involved.

multiple physical devices. Because there is duplicate I/O activity, additional system resources are used for write activities, including updates to the meta-data that is used to track changes in the physical extents, or pieces, of the logical volume. Read activities may actually benefit from mirroring because the mirroring software can choose the least busy mirror to satisfy the read request.

The overwhelming negative aspect of data mirroring is the expense per unit of storage. A mirrored configuration requires one hundred percent (per additional mirror) storage overhead for data protection. For small configurations this may be acceptable, but as the storage requirements for a particular file server grow beyond a certain point, mirroring becomes very expensive. There are cases, like remote mirroring of data, where the additional protection is worth the added expense.

An additional constraint for JBOD and mirroring configurations alike is the total number of I/O channels available per server. Limitations on the number of devices per I/O channel, coupled with the available I/O channels in the server chassis, can limit the total amount of JBOD storage that may be configured. Mirroring and its associated storage overhead will further limit the server's capacity to fifty percent of that without mirroring.

7.7.4 Redundant Arrays of Inexpensive Disks

The acronym RAID" stands for "redundant array of inexpensive disks", although a cursory look at today's RAID arrays can make you wonder where the "inexpensive" portion of the acronym went. Upon closer examination, RAID arrays do offer hardware and system administration cost savings over alternatives like JBOD mirroring and striping, even though they may use similar techniques internally. The administration savings comes from the encapsulation of details inside of the array device.

A RAID array is designed to provide data protection by using both hardware redundancy and special internal methods to store data. Common redundancy features found in RAID array hardware are multiple I/O controllers, multiple I/O paths per I/O controller, nonvolatile cache memory, integrated battery backup, multiple power supplies, and multiple fan units. Nonvolatile write cache allows the RAID array to acknowledge write requests before the data is actually committed to disk, without risking data loss.

Many arrays allow creation of logical file systems, internal to the disk array, with different associated RAID modes. These "pieces of a RAID array" are distinguished from one another within an array by a logical unit number, or LUN, associated with each separate piece or volume. To the file server's operating system, a RAID array LUN appears as a single physical disk mechanisms, even though it is internally made up of other physical devices.

One could view the disk array as hiding the system-management details of the physical storage management internal to the array enclosure. This would be true if the array required no configuration, but alas, most arrays require system-management decisions about how big to make the LUNs, what RAID mode (or level) to use, which of multiple controllers "owns" the LUN, and other potential choices. Still, letting the array management software handle the striping, mirroring, and data-distribution decisions can relieve some of the system-administration burden.

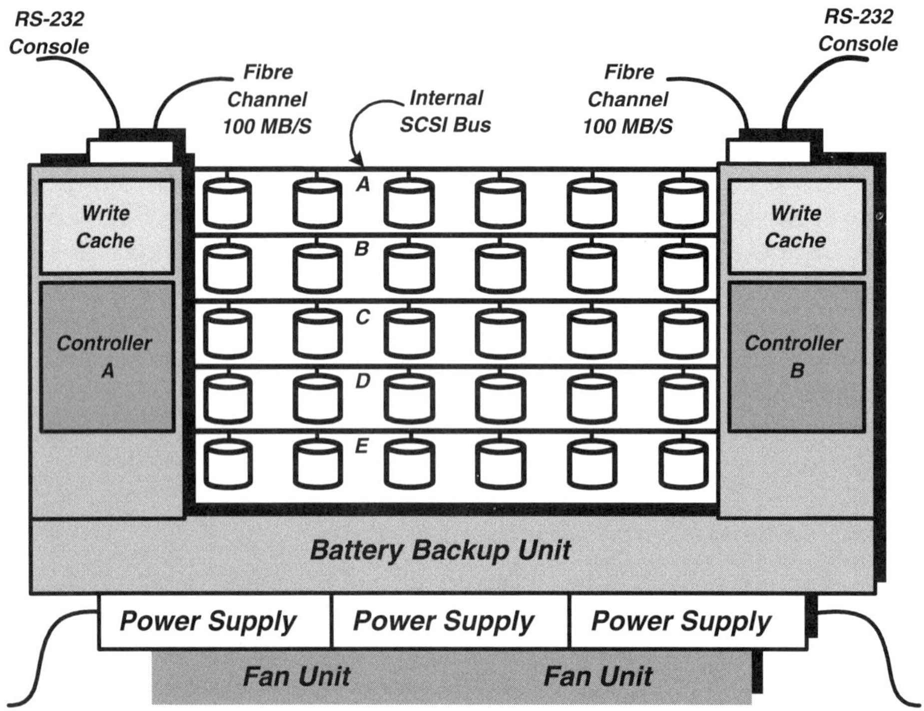

Figure 7-11 Block Diagram of a RAID Array

The I/O and data protection behavior of a RAID array LUN may be described by the RAID "mode" it is operating in. Commonly encountered RAID modes[18] are described in the following sections.

Independent Mode Some RAID arrays can allow access to the internal disk drives as independent mechanisms. This configuration can provide the benefits of the hardware redundancy designed into the RAID array, along with other features like hot-pluggable disks. The striping, mirroring, and other data-protection tasks are left to the physical storage-management facility of the file server's operating system, instead of being internally handled by the array itself. Because this operating mode converts an expensive RAID array into JBOD with hardware redundancy, support for this array configuration is not as prevalent as it once was.

RAID Mode 1 RAID mode 1 consists of data mirroring, with individual disk drives operating asynchronously. Data redundancy exacts a one hundred percent storage overhead due

18. It seems like every week that I read about some new, proprietary RAID mode; one would guess that there is considerable room for improvement over the existing modes.

to data mirroring. Due to lack of striping, this configuration is still open to performance issues involving data "hot" spots.

RAID Mode 0/1 This mode consists of data striping and mirroring and provides the best performance of any RAID mode for random access I/O. Data redundancy requires (at least) a one hundred percent storage overhead for mirroring of data.

RAID Mode 3 RAID mode 3 stripes data across four disk drives with a dedicated parity drive for data recovery; all five drives act as a single virtual disk drive. Data redundancy requires a twenty-five percent overhead for the parity drive. This configuration provides good performance for large, sequential transfers, but provides poor performance for any multiuser random access activity.

RAID Mode 5 Mode 5 provides data striping with parity information distributed across all disk drives[19] and independent I/O paths to each drive. RAID mode 5 supports three to sixteen disk drives, but five is the most typical configuration. Mode 5 provides data redundancy but poor write performance. This RAID mode is best used for read-only or read-mostly data storage where parity is not being recalculated due to writes.

Summary

As you can see from the preceding discussion of RAID modes, there are only two that are most applicable to the type of random access I/O that is commonly encountered on file servers: RAID 0/1 and RAID 5. The ability of a RAID array to simultaneously provide both RAID 5 LUNs and RAID 0/1 LUNs can decrease the amount of system administration effort and increase the flexibility of the storage subsystem over JBOD configurations. At the same time, because RAID arrays hide the internal details of multiple physical disks, a file server's overall storage capacity can be greater than with solutions based on JBOD storage.

7.7.5 Hybrid RAID Array Types

In addition to the "standard" RAID modes, there are many vendors that offer proprietary or hybrid modes that make up for the shortcomings of the individual standard RAID modes. Ideally, we would like a RAID array that would provide the minimal storage overhead of RAID 5 with the performance offered by RAID 0/1. This is not just an unanswered wish; Hewlett-Packard[20] offers just such a device, called AutoRAID.

The AutoRAID array provides RAID mode 0/1 and RAID mode 5 storage areas internal to the array, just like other RAID arrays. The major difference, however, is that an AutoRAID array provides dynamic data migration between the two areas, based on host system access patterns. Thus, this array type can be called an "adaptive" RAID array.

19. Parity information for a given disk drive is stored on a separate drive or drives.

20. Hewlett-Packard can be found at *WWW.hp.com.*

Frequently accessed data is kept in the RAID 0/1 area and migrated to the RAID 5 area only when access patterns allow. Likewise, infrequently accessed data is kept in the RAID 5 area and migrated to RAID 0/1 only when necessary. The system administrator has control over the ratio of RAID 0/1 to RAID 5 space allocated in the AutoRAID array.

Tests have shown that this hybrid RAID configuration provides very good performance for many types of workloads, including the random access activity associated with database servers and file servers. Additionally, because the array is adaptive, the amount of system management effort necessary to configure it is minimal.

7.7.6 Physical File System Type

We have previously touched on the importance of the physical file system used "on top of" the underlying disk storage. Why is the choice of physical file system important to the file server? It is important because choosing the proper physical file system can vastly reduce the amount of time needed to recover file system information in the event of a system failure, and make the server's services available sooner.

In the event of a system failure, repairs to the file system data structures (meta-data), which were under change at the point of the failure, must be made before the system can continue operating. Older file systems, like the high-speed file system[21] (HFS) or the file allocation table (FAT or FAT32) file system, must check the entire meta-data structure for errors before the system boot process can continue. As long as the file systems are small in size and numbers, this time can be tolerable, but the larger the file system involved, the more time this process can take.

Sometimes several hours are needed for utilities like *fsck* and *chkdsk* to finish this analysis and repair process, which must examine the complete set of file system meta-data. This is especially true for the HFS on Unix, because it allows much bigger file systems than its FAT brethren. Because the file server can have hundreds of Gigabytes to Terabytes of data scattered across multiple file systems, a better solution is needed.

This solution is provided by modern "journaled" file systems. The file system keeps a disk-resident "intent log", which contains information about intended changes to the file system meta-data and structure. In the event of a system failure, the log is "replayed" at the next system start-up, limiting the repair activities to only the meta-data that was being modified at the time of the failure.

This can have profound influence on the server's availability. Instead of spending hours repairing a *potentially* damaged file system, the operating system can repair only the portions of the file system that were actually left in an incomplete or damaged state. Wherever possible we should use the journaled file system(s) on our file servers—anyone who depends on the file server will appreciate it.

21. Developed circa 1983 by the University of California at Berkeley for the Berkeley Software Distribution (BSD) version of Unix.

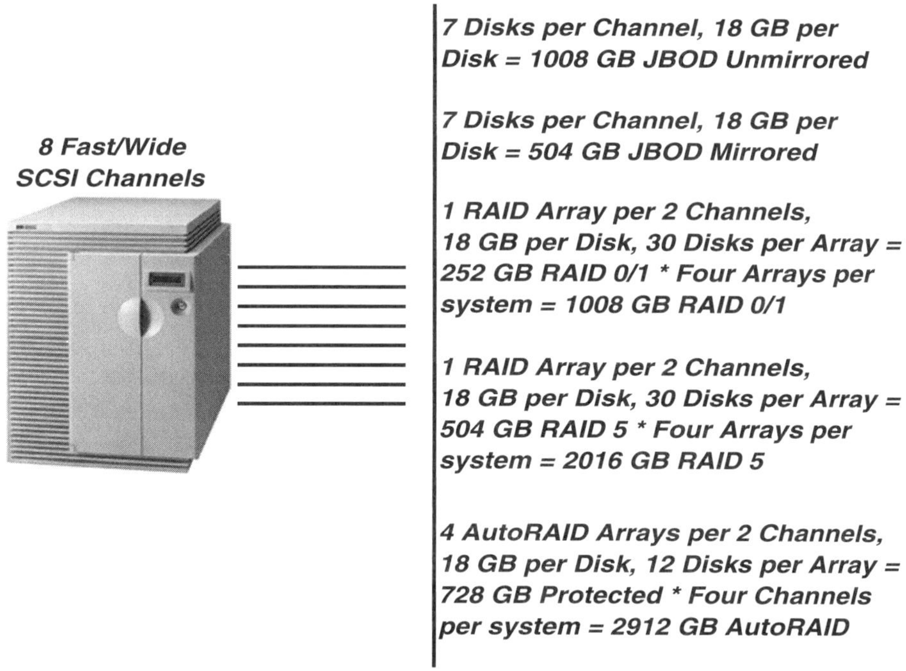

Figure 7-12 File Server Maximum Storage Capacity Examples

7.8 Selecting the Proper File Server Hardware

At this point we will examine some of the specific configuration decisions to be made when configuring a file server's hardware. The configuration process will be somewhat different for each specific vendor's hardware, but the general approach and constraints are the same. Our examples will use a fictitious set of hardware products to illustrate our points.

7.8.1 File Server Storage Capacity

One of the primary design parameters for the file server hardware configuration is the amount of required disk storage. The amount of storage that can be attached to a file server depends on the number of available I/O channels, the number of possible physical or logical devices that are allowed per I/O channel, and the maximum size allowed per file system created on the devices. As previously discussed, a JBOD configuration with data mirroring (a single mirror) can cut the available storage in half.

The selection of file server hardware configuration for this scalable building block must consider the required capacity and the cost associated with the server chassis and the storage technologies used. We need to pick price/performance/capacity points for each possible class of file servers (i.e., workcenter server, workgroup server, or other divisions) that exist in our target environment. Once either the storage or performance capacity of a single server chassis is exceeded, we have no choice but to move up to a more capable chassis or to "split" the server into two separate units.

As the examples in Figure 7-12 show, a file server chassis that provides eight independent high-speed I/O channels has numerous possible storage configurations. Given this number of channels (and ignoring the need for network connections, backup units, and other devices), the examples show several possible disk-storage configurations that push the configuration to its maximum. Why there are specific limitations on the number of devices per channel will be covered in the next section.

This particular configuration might make a good workgroup or workcenter file server, provided that the disk capacity meets the needs of the client systems. Because the examples in Figure 7-12 cover maximum storage configurations, we may always configure the file server with less than the maximum storage if the situation is not as demanding. It is important to characterize data growth trends to ensure that enough free storage is available to cover added clients and the tendency for increased data storage requirements[22].

The examples shown in Figure 7-12 use fairly conservative performance requirements, for example, it is possible to connect more than one RAID array per F/W SCSI channel, although providing multiple paths to the devices for redundancy can make the cabling complicated. If the server is to participate in a high-availability cluster, however, the redundant I/O interfaces can cut the number of total available I/O channels and devices in half unless I/O technologies like fibre channel are used to provide higher channel bandwidth and greater connectivity. There is an associated higher cost with moving to such technologies, which must be traded off against the configuration issues that they solve.

At this point in the configuration, it is also appropriate to consider how much on-line storage may be saved by the addition of hierarchical storage management (HSM) functionality. There are some environments where the requirements for on-line storage might exceed the available server resources, but the usage patterns permit migration of infrequently used data to and from less expensive, slower storage media. In such a cases, augmenting on-line storage with HSM might be a reasonable consideration if the budget permits.

7.8.2 File Server I/O Characteristics

As we have seen, the total number of I/O channels available can constrain the maximum total storage capabilities of a file server chassis. Another set of constraints are the bandwidth of the system bus, the I/O interfaces, and the associated bus converters. It would do us no good to allow massive amounts of file server storage, but then be unable to provide the data to client systems under peak demand conditions.

22. It is always easier to add more data to a computer system's storage than to decide what data may be safely removed.

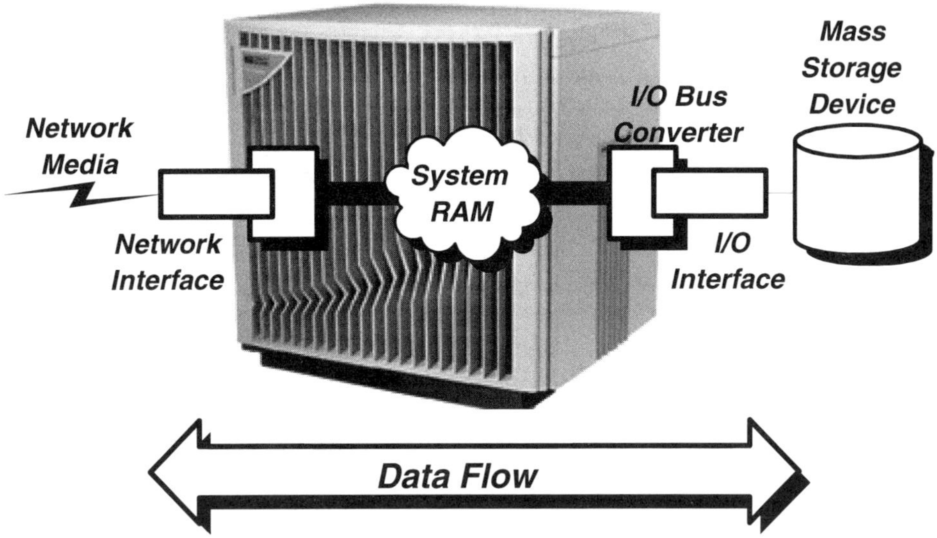

Figure 7-13 Server Architecture Data Flow Analysis

One technique that can be used to look for potential bottlenecks in the file server system is an end-to-end data flow analysis performed on the server's internal I/O and bus architecture. The generalized components along the data path from storage, through the file server, and to the network are shown in Figure 7-13. Data travels from the storage device to the I/O card, through a bus converter onto the system bus, into system RAM, and from there out a similar path to the network. Think of the file server as a large data pump, moving data from the mass storage devices to the client systems via the network.

The key to performing this analysis is to understand the number of client file operations required per second and an average data transfer size per operation. We can then utilize the two values to obtain the total data transmission rate through the server to the storage devices. We will extend this data flow analysis approach to the workgroup environment. See Appendix B for an example of data flow analysis applied to sizing an NFS file server.

Things to watch for in the file server configuration are limited bandwidth in I/O cards, multiple levels of I/O bus converters in the data path, oversubscribed system bus throughput, low CPU to memory bandwidth, or other warning signs of a potential constriction in the data flow. Another potential performance inhibitor is too many devices per I/O channel. An example calculation using Fast/Wide SCSI (20 MB/S) and disk mechanisms capable of 1.2 to 2.9 MB/S data transfer yields only seven allowed devices per F/W SCSI interface.

Storage Technology Interfaces Some of the currently available interface technologies for storage devices are shown in the following table:

Table 7-1 Storage Technology Interfaces

Storage Interface Type	Maximum Data Rate	Maximum Distance	Maximum Devices
Single-Ended (S/E) SCSI	5-10 MB/S	6 meters	8 per bus
Fast-Wide (F/W) SCSI	20 MB/S	3 meters	16 per bus
Wide-Ultra (U/W) SCSI	40 MB/S	25 meters	16 per bus
Ultra2 SCSI	40 MB/S	3 meters	4 per bus
Wide Ultra2 SCSI	80 MB/S	25 meters	16 per bus
Half-Duplex Fibre Channel	100 MB/S	2 kilometers	126 per loop
Full-Duplex Fibre Channel	200 MB/S	2 kilometers	126 per loop

We should note that there are a number of different terminologies in use for SCSI interface types. The exact terminology used and the associated speeds and allowed bus lengths for SCSI devices will vary from vendor to vendor[23]. The common bus length for differential SCSI implementations is 25 meters, so we can suspect a differential interface whenever we see that "magic" number.

The SCSI interface is a point-to-point connection between the host computer and the devices on the bus. There are additional technologies, like fibre-channel, that provide other connection topologies besides point to point. Fibre channel provides point-to-point connections, arbitrated loop, and switched fabric connections to storage devices in both full and half-duplex modes. These configurations are shown in Figure 7-14.

The Storage Area Network With the addition of a fibre channel switched fabric, there are several new and exciting developments in the storage-management area. First, equal access to all storage devices by all attached host systems is possible[24]. Second, there is a new

23. All of the terminology complications involved with the Small Computer System Interface (SCSI) stem from the fact that there are two SCSI bus widths (8 and 16 bits), three signal level specifications (single-ended, differential, and low voltage differential), and multiple clock rates.

24. I have even seen backups occurring between tape devices and disk storage without the involvement of a host system!

term to deal with: the storage area network, or SAN. Third, network attached storage (NAS), such as NFS file systems, may be replaced by access to storage over the SAN.

This set of developments promises to change the way we design and implement access to storage devices in a very fundamental way. With the point-to-point storage interfaces we have today, the easiest way to make storage devices available to other systems is to export the data and mount it on the system that needs access. This is the NAS access mentioned above, and takes place via high-level protocols over the LAN.

A SAN promises to allow access to storage devices without an intermediary server system (unless some type of data translation or cross-SAN access is needed.) The promise is that this type of access will take place at much higher channel rates than those provided by the LAN. It is too early to tell exactly what impact these new developments will have on our file server configuration, but some of the prospects look very exciting.

7.8.3 File Server Networking Characteristics

Referring to Figure 7-13, you can see that the network technology used to interface the file server to its clients is in the direct data flow path. The number and type of network interfaces present in the file server directly determine how much data can flow out of the file server into the network. This is a frequently overlooked fact.

It is important to ensure that the file server can deliver all of its file-serving "potential energy" through the network interface or interfaces. The phrase "potential energy" refers to the maximum number of network file system operations that the server can deliver, which is one of the key design parameters. If the network connection is unable to sustain this level of network file system operations, then the file server is not able to deal with peak loads[25].

Estimate of the required data flow through a network interface can be useful in evaluating the system's ability to service client system requests. If any portion of the data flow path is unable to sustain the required data flow, the file server's performance may suffer, which will result in longer service times to the client systems. Of course, this is only part of the workgroup data flow picture; the intervening network equipment will also affect latency, throughput, and ultimately the client system's view of overall workgroup performance.

Fortunately, the commonly encountered network technologies lend themselves to data flow analysis, provided we know what particular configuration is in place. A data flow–oriented survey of the commonly encountered network types and associated media is listed in Table 7-2 on page 117.

We will cover more networking technology information in Chapter 9, but we need the information in the table to determine data flow rates for network interfaces and the I/O channels that contain the interfaces. We need to make several distinctions about the implementation of the network technology:

25. This is a little like having a Ferrari sports car in your garage up on blocks, with its tires not touching the ground. It is possible to rev the engine, turn the wheels, and not get any results—a fairly expensive noisemaker.

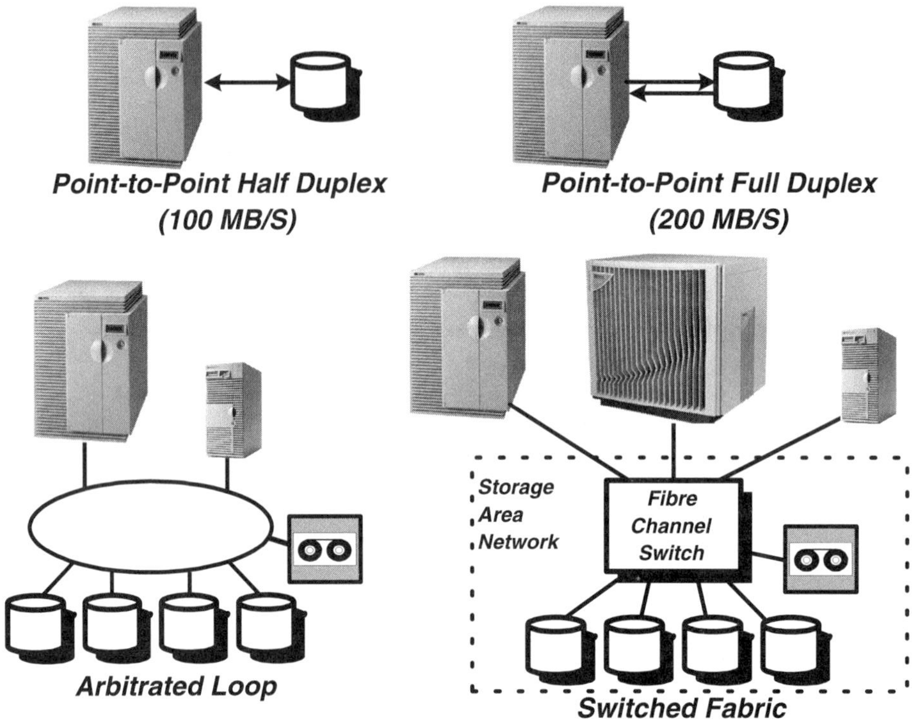

Figure 7-14 Fibre Channel Topologies

Shared Versus Dedicated Ethernet Links Shared LAN technologies, like Ethernet, suffer from collisions caused by multiple devices trying to use the shared media at the same time. These collisions reduce the possible throughput in shared configurations. A commonly encountered figure for the maximum load factor of a shared network media is roughly thirty percent.

Dedicated LAN connections are point-to-point connections that eliminate the possibility of collisions except between the two devices that use the link. This is the case when the host system has a dedicated link with a network device such as an Ethernet switch. These types of links may be driven to as high as ninety percent of the theoretical maximum.

Other types of dedicated LAN interfaces include token ring implementations like FDDI. FDDI rings do not suffer from collisions and so may carry heavier loads than shared media LAN connections. Studies indicate that FDDI can be loaded to roughly eighty percent of its theoretical maximum before performance degrades significantly. Other nice features of FDDI include a 4500 byte MTU size and automatic detection and correction of failed network links.

Table 7-2 Networking Technology Data Rates

Networking Technology	Theoretical Data Rate (Mb/S)	Maximum Usable Data Rate (MB/S)
10baseT Shared	10 Mb/S	0.38 MB/S @ 30%
10baseT Dedicated	10 Mb/S	1.13 MB/S @ 90%
FDDI	100 Mb/S	10 MB/S @ 80%
100baseT Shared	100 Mb/S	3.75 MB/S @ 30%
100baseT Dedicated	100 Mb/S	11.25 MB/S @ 90%
100baseT Full Duplex	200 Mb/S	22.50 MB/S @ 90%
1000baseFX Full Duplex	2000 Mb/S	225.00 MB/S @ 90%
1000baseFX Trunked	6000 Mb/S	675.00 MB/S @ 90%

Full-Duplex versus Half-Duplex Links A half-duplex LAN implementation uses the same physical medium for transmitting and receiving data. In a single medium, point-to-point connection, both parties must agree on the direction data are to flow. A full-duplex connection has both a transmit and a receive medium and is theoretically capable of twice the throughput of a half-duplex connection because sending and receiving can occur in parallel.

Another factor to consider when evaluating the data throughput capabilities for a given network I/O card is the maximum transmission unit (MTU) provided by the technology. A larger MTU size can make a particular technology more efficient at moving data because there are fewer network frames to send (there is usually a fixed overhead associated with sending a frame over the network). As an example, the MTU size for Ethernet is approximately 1500 bytes, while the MTU size for FDDI is approximately 4500 bytes, indicating that FDDI might be better at bulk data transfers.

In reality it is difficult to sustain the maximum theoretical data throughput for I/O cards, because there is software overhead associated with processing the request, formatting the data, and sending the data to the card. The closer to theoretical maximum the channel and the I/O card can operate, the better. With this type of analysis, we are looking for obvious mismatches in capabilities between I/O bus converters, interface cards, and network technologies.

7.8.4 File Server RAM

There are three primary reasons for RAM in most file servers: to contain the operating system code and tables, to run file–server-specific nonkernel applications, and to cache the file system data and meta-data read from the storage devices. To properly configure the RAM in the file server, we must take stock of needs in each of these three areas.

The operating system code, or kernel, is frequently locked into physical memory to prevent paging, which may adversely affect OS performance. The space occupied is used by both operating system code and the data used by the operating system for such things as memory allocation, I/O buffers, or important tables. This RAM, once allocated, is not available for other purposes.

Along with the operating system, there are other system-specific processes that must have available RAM to execute. The number and nature of these processes depends on the operating system, but one example might be system performance–monitoring software that collects data for capacity planning. This type of application requires RAM in addition to that allocated for the kernel and its data structures.

Finally, and most importantly, most operating systems cache file system data and meta-data in system RAM as it is accessed to avoid the need for physical I/O operations to and from the disk storage. In the case of Unix systems, the I/O buffer cache contains physical file system blocks from the disk, and the inode cache (a kernel table) contains file system meta-data. Without the buffering of this data, many additional physical I/O operations would be necessary to support file accesses.

7.8.5 File Server CPU Configuration

Among other things, the file server's CPUs are needed to execute the operating system code used in servicing the network file system requests. Many times the network file system's code is multithreaded, meaning that each request may run independently on a separate CPU. The speed of each CPU and the number of available CPUs affect both the amount of time needed to satisfy the individual requests and the total simultaneous throughput available.

For file servers that can contain multiple CPUs in an SMP configuration, it is important to understand the performance increase that each CPU can provide along with the scaling factor as additional CPUs are added. It is unlikely that adding a second CPU will result in a one hundred percent increase in performance because multiple CPU scaling is not perfectly linear. One of the easiest ways to scale a file server, however, remains the addition of more CPUs as the workgroup requirements grow. Remember that it is possible to suffer from the law of diminishing returns if too many CPUs are added.

Vendors usually have several choices of CPU types available for a given file server chassis. Variations in CPU configuration will include clock rate, instruction and data cache size, as well as processor technology. How all of these factors influence overall performance is difficult to quantify individually. To choose the proper CPU configuration it is best to rely on industry performance benchmarks, which measure the overall performance of a given configuration.

7.9 File Server Operating System Tuning

Once the hardware and software configuration of a file server is complete, we are often tempted to think that our work is finished. Experienced system administrators know otherwise. Most file server systems can benefit from specific tuning to support the services they provide. Some possible areas of file-server tuning include data buffer caching, system table size, network file-system tuning, network tuning, and file-system tuning.

Tuning is not a one-time, static procedure. As the needs of the workgroup change, so do the demands placed on the file server. It is imperative to measure the performance of the server and to adjust the data placement, I/O channel allocation, or other necessary parameters to meet the new requirements.

Often the amount of tuning necessary on the file server is minimal, provided that it is *only* a file server and does not attempt to run other services. The type and amount of tuning activities will depend on what data-sharing mechanism is being provided by the server. We must agree here to defer to other authorities on system performance tuning, because we do not have anything approaching enough space to address the topic here.

7.10 File Server Backup

Because the client systems' volatile data are located on the file server, the file-server storage must be periodically saved to protect the data from potential loss. Backing up the file server's data from a single location takes the place of backing up multiple client systems, which can be a logistical nightmare. Because of the large concentration of data on the file server, however, planning a backup strategy becomes more difficult.

High-speed, high-capacity backup devices are required to deal with the sheer volume of data that must be backed up. These devices tend to cost more and demand precious I/O channels to support the backup devices. Performing the backup operation without making the file server unavailable for long periods of time becomes one of the primary goals.

Careful thought and design must go into file server backup configurations and strategies. The larger the file server's capacity, the more data throughput is required to complete the backup operation. The following sections discuss some approaches to file server static data recovery and backing up the user's volatile data.

7.10.1 Identifying Data to Back Up

As with the client system, it is possible to divide the data on the file server into two basic classes: static unchanging data and volatile data. In the case of the client system we moved the volatile data off of the system and kept only the static data on the local storage. This, of course, is not possible on the file server.

We can, however, do an infrequent backup of the file server system configuration and static data and save that in a safe spot for system-recovery purposes[26]. Frequently the same image installation mechanism used for client systems may be employed to recover the file server's base configuration[27]. Once the base configuration is recovered, the volatile data may be restored.

Once the volatile data have been identified, we can again perform data flow analysis to determine the number and type of backup devices required and the number and type of I/O channels required to perform the backup. The file server must be designed to have the amount of resources available to support the backup tasks. Some times this necessity is overlooked, resulting in performance issues.

7.10.2 Broken Mirror Backups

The software layer that performs physical storage management and data mirroring often allows a mirrored data set to be "broken" or separated from the primary data source. This mirrored information is then available as a complete copy of the data in the primary file system at the time of the separation. To guarantee data consistency, user access to the mirrored data must be prevented for the period of time necessary to separate the mirrors.

To continue providing data redundancy, the mirrored data set should have at least three copies: the primary and two mirrors. One of the mirrors will remain in synchronization with the primary data while the other mirror is being backed up as a read-only resource. With shared data configurations, it is possible to have a dedicated system for backing up the broken mirror. This configuration is shown in Figure 7-15.

Once the backup operation is complete, the broken mirror may be merged back into the mirrored data set. This operation will cause all data blocks in the broken mirror to be synchronized with any modifications that might have occurred in the primary data and its active mirror. Because of this synchronization activity, there will be a period of decreased system performance.

7.10.3 Snapshot Backups

Modern file systems like VxFS and LFS allow the creation of "snapshot" file systems for the purpose of on-line backup. These snapshots are storage areas that contain an exact representation of the original file system meta-data at the time the snapshot was created. The snapshot is a read-only version of the original file system.

Users can continue to access files in the snapped file system at the same time that a backup is being performed on the snapshot, without the two operations interfering with each other. When changes are made to the snapped file system, the old data and meta-data are copied to the

26. This "safe spot" had better be somewhere other than on top of the file server cabinet in the computer room. What would happen if the computer room burned? I frequently encounter backups that are kept in the same location as the system, unprotected from fires, sprinkler systems, etc. Somewhere a disaster-recovery consultant is cringing.

27. The HP-UX image installation facility, Ignite-UX, allows a system administrator to create a bootable system recovery image that can be kept on DAT tape or CD-ROM.

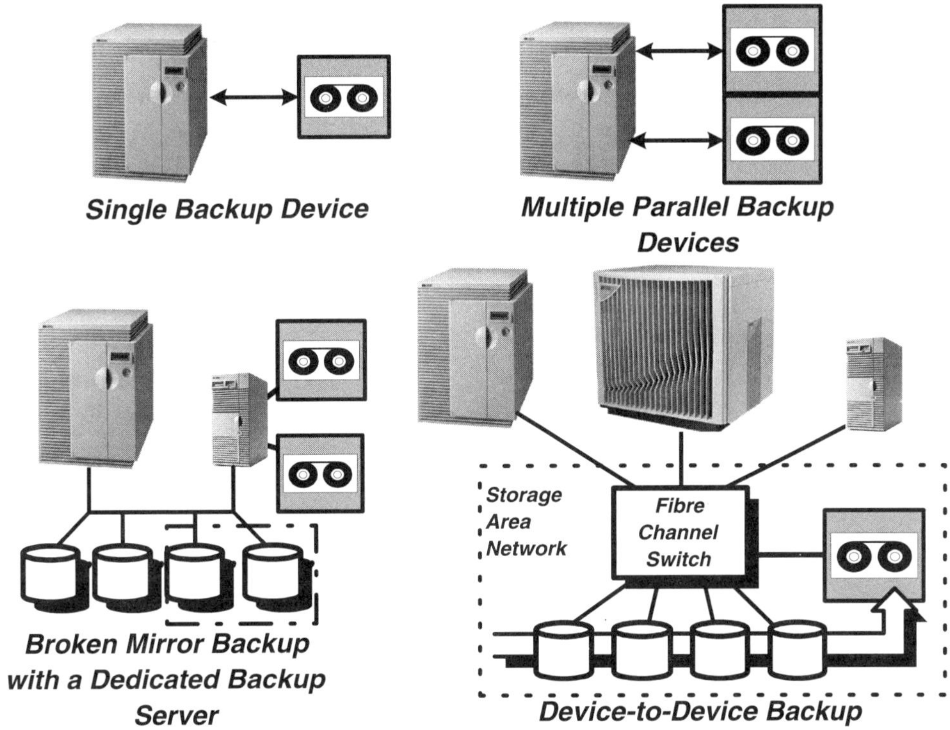

Figure 7-15 File Server Backup Configurations

snapshot file system before the update is performed. There is an additional system overhead for these data-copy operations.

Once the backup operation is completed, the snapshot data may be unmounted and the space reclaimed. In addition to the extra I/O overhead required for file system snapshots, there must be enough free disk space available to contain the snapshot file system. The more active a file system is, the larger the required snapshot file system must be to contain the modifications.

7.10.4 Device-to-Device Backups

As mentioned earlier, the appearance of SAN solutions holds promise for a more flexible data-storage strategy. This also holds true for backup procedures. Because of the independent nature of fibre channel storage devices and the speed of the SAN access, it is possible to back up storage device to tape device, independent of a host computer.

This is the rough equivalent of the "broken mirror" backup shown in Figure 7-15, but without the need for the dedicated backup server hardware. The configuration I saw required a backup tool to configure and start the process, which then proceeded without host involvement. This type of backup is depicted in Figure 7-15.

7.11 Dedicate Your File Server Resources

We cannot finish this section without addressing one of my pet peeves regarding the configuration and usage of a file server: the misguided attempts to use the file server resources for purposes other than delivering data to the client systems. In many, many customer environments I have run into performance complaints with regards to the file server. Usually the complaints involve the response time of the server or the number of client-side time-outs that are seen when accessing remote data.

In most of these situations we have managed to track the problems to application programs, either compute-intensive or disk-intensive tasks running on the file server, that are interfering with the its ability to service clients. There is no quicker way to affect the performance seen by *every* user in the workgroup than to allow this behavior. Thermal-analysis programs, crash simulations, software compiles, and other demanding tasks belong on the compute server!

Almost every specialized application can benefit from system performance tuning. If you run specialized applications on a file server, then tuning the file server functionality detunes the application performance and vice versa. The best way to avoid this paradox and to provide the best performance to the file server's users is to:

<u>Dedicate your file server resources!</u>

7.12 File Server Summary

Whew! This chapter has described some of the important issues associated with the workgroup file server resource. It is possible to write an entire book on just this one topic alone. The amount of information here is representative of the relative importance of the file server in the workgroup environment.

We have discussed several different data-sharing mechanisms that might be considered "file serving" in our workgroup. Those included network file systems, database systems, and software configuration–management systems. A workgroup with several of these data-sharing mechanisms might well require one or more file servers for each different method employed.

Because the file server, in conjunction with dataless clients, creates a single point of failure in the network, our discussion turned to high availability issues. Various configurations which provided data protection, highly available data, and highly available systems were presented. We deferred a complete discussion on disaster-recovery processes to industry experts that specialize in disaster-recovery analysis and assessments.

An examination of the storage options available for file servers led to discussions on JBOD, disk striping, disk mirroring, RAID arrays, and hybrid RAID devices. Our conclusion was that the only RAID modes worth consideration were RAID 0/1 (striping and mirroring) and RAID 5 (striping with parity). The performance and cost constraints of both "standard" RAID modes led us to consider hybrid RAID array types as a potential solution. JBOD can be a good choice if the configuration is small.

The file server's storage capacity, I/O capabilities, networking characteristics, RAM and CPU configuration, and tuning issues were covered in the next section. A performance analysis method using data flow analysis was introduced that we will expand out to the workgroup level. This method will be a regularly used tool in our workgroup design and analysis tool kit.

We looked at the issue of backing up the volatile data on the file server and recommended including the requirements in the file server design from the beginning. Several approaches to backups were detailed, each with the ability to shorten the length of time that the file server was unavailable for the backup process. We noted that the difficulty of providing backup services increases with the amount of data stored on the file server.

Finally we saw a piece of advice that bears repeating here: *dedicate your file server resources*! Avoid running compute-intensive or file system intensive tasks on the file server or suffer a plague of user complaints. Heeding this advice can be one of the simplest ways to improve overall workgroup performance, not to mention that it might provoke a workgroup-wide riot.

CHAPTER 8

Getting the Jobs Done: The Workgroup Compute Server

Although the workgroup compute server can be considered an optional component, its functionality is present in the form of client system compute resources, even though a distinctly separate physical machine might not be. In this chapter we will examine some of the factors that affect compute server performance and some of the specialized compute server configurations that we can apply to our workgroup design efforts.

8.1 The Compute Server

The compute server is an important part of the 3TCS workgroup architecture. The phrase "the compute server" is the answer to the question, "Where do application components run when they require more resources than the client systems can provide?" In this respect the compute server may be considered a set of auxiliary CPUs that are available to the client systems, just as the file server may be viewed as extra disk storage.

The type of applications that the compute server runs will determine how much other resources, like RAM and networking bandwidth, are needed. The number of users in the workgroup and the type of applications that they are running will determine how many and what type of compute servers are present. Because specialized types of compute servers may be a relatively expensive item to purchase, they may end up as workcenter resources shared by multiple workgroups.

There are situations where a dedicated set of compute resources do not exist in the workgroup. This is usually the case where the applications being executed can find sufficient resources to run on the client systems. Many times the workgroup may begin without a dedicated compute server, only to find that the size of the software compilation, the EDA models, or other workgroup tasks outstrip the ability of the client systems.

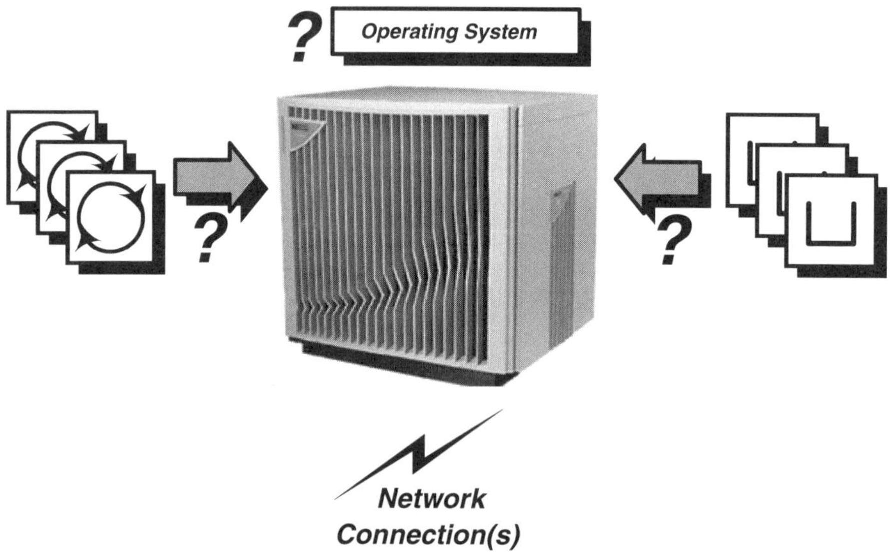

Figure 8-1 Compute Server Configuration Considerations

Trying to retrofit a compute server, load balancing services, and other required elements into an existing workgroup architecture can be a disruptive and involved endeavor. It is far easier to plan on the eventual addition of the compute server and associated services from the start, This can be done by implementing the workgroup so that the load balancing layer and the compute server plug into existing architectural "sockets".

This is the software development equivalent of "stubbing out" missing functionality so that it may be added later. How this is done involves creating "actions" and menus on the user's desktop that act as indirect links to the actual tasks or applications. By later plugging the load balancing checks into the actions, the user may be insulated from the impact of remote scheduling and execution. This approach is covered in Chapter 13.

8.2 Understanding Compute Server Needs

The hardware chosen for the compute server is primarily determined by the application types that it must execute. Floating-point intensive applications require one set of compute server characteristics, parallel applications require another type, and database transaction processing requires yet another[1]. These application types require differing mixtures of hardware

1. Usually, this means lots of CPUs, RAM, and I/O capability. Computer systems in Figure 8-2 were selected for their technical capabilities. The same systems, if used for transaction processing may have many more CPUs and would exceed the bus capability if the computer were to be used for compute-intensive tasks.

resources like integer performance, floating-point performance, I/O capabilities, RAM availability, bus throughput, and differing numbers of CPUs.

We should also differentiate between compute servers that are intended to provide time-to-completion (parallel application) support and those that are intended provide multiple application throughput. In the former case, a single parallel application may run across many CPUs in the same computer[2] or group of machines, decreasing the total amount of time for a single task. In the latter case, a group of independent applications run on the same computer at the same time, completing many tasks at the same time.

Benchmarks like SPECint_rate95 and SPECfp_rate95 can help characterize the integer and floating-point performance of compute server hardware for compute-intensive tasks. For other types of application loads, like transaction processing, different benchmarks and techniques are available[3]. Many times, benchmarks are artificial measures that may not reflect real world results. There is no substitute for actually running your applications and data sets to determine actual performance characteristics.

The *number* of servers required for a particular workgroup also depends upon the number of users and the application type being run. For computationally intensive tasks, an individual server may run out of bus bandwidth before it runs out of the other resources, such as RAM, that are necessary to sustain multiple tasks at the same time. There are general-purpose ways of predicting compute server system bus saturation for such compute intensive situations (see the next section for a general approach based on "Amdahl's law").

While general approaches such as Amdahl's law can help "keep us in the ball park", differences in application data set characteristics may cause wide performance variations even with the same program. With a general approach, we can guess at the compute server requirements and can rule out obviously inadequate hardware configurations, but the end result may be over- or underconfiguration of the compute server. There simply is no substitute for thoroughly understanding the compute characteristics of all workgroup applications and testing each candidate compute server's performance against real applications.

There are a number of everyday design principles that may not have rigorous scientific verification to support their use, but nonetheless are useful. We tend to call these principles "rules of thumb" because of the association with using a thumb as a rough unit of measurement. Imagine that we are artists, standing back from our canvas, arm outstretched, using our thumb to test for the proper perspective. Several common rules of thumb that we will encounter in our compute server–related design and analysis activities are presented here.

2. Message-passing parallel environments like parallel virtual machine (PVM) or message passing interface (MPI) allow compute components from the same parallel application to spread across multiple computer systems linked with networking or shared memory if several components are running on the same machine. Specialized programming is required to make use of this type of environment.

3. For transaction processing, benchmarks like tpmC and TPC.

8.3 Amdahl's Law for System Bus Requirements

A number of computer-related laws are attributed to Gene Amdahl[4]. One of these laws was originally stated:

> **Every 1 MIPS[5] of processor power requires 1 Megabyte per second of throughput on the system bus.**

To fit today's terminology, processor architectures, and performance benchmarks, this may be restated as:

> **Every 1 MFLOP[6] of processor power requires 1.33 Megabytes per second of throughput on the system bus for single precision FLOPs and 2.67 Megabytes per second for double precision FLOPs.**

The numbers used in the second statement of the rule are derived from the amount of data that must be moved to do floating-point operations on today's processors, in addition to the floating-point operations themselves. Today's processors allow multiple floating point operations per instruction[7], but the total number of operations performed for a given unit of data movement is valid, counting the load and floating-point operations together. For double-precision floating-point operations:

$$\frac{8 \text{ Bytes}}{3 \text{ Operations}} \times \frac{1{,}048{,}576 \text{ Operations}}{1 \text{ MegaFLOP}} \times \frac{1 \text{ MegaFLOP}}{\text{S}} = \frac{2.67 \text{ Megabytes}}{\text{S}}$$

We will round this number downwards to 2 MB/S = 1 MFLOP with little effect; see Figure 8-2. An equivalent calculation yields the required data movement for single precision floating-point

4. Early computer pioneer and founder of the Amdahl Corporation. It is difficult to find direct reference to the laws used here, everyone just seems to know them and attribute them to Mr. Amdahl.

5. Million instructions per second, an early measure of computer performance, now commonly replaced by Standard Performance Evaluation Committee (or SPEC) benchmarks like SPECint95 and SPECfp95. SPEC benchmark information is available at *WWW.SPEC.org*.

6. This is millions of, or "mega", floating point operations per second (FLOPS). A sales representative for a well-known computer company once asked me, "What's the difference between a Megabyte, a MegaFLOP, and a one Megabyte floppy?" Maybe we have too many "Mega" things in our vocabulary.

7. Two in operations like the MULTIPLY_ADD instruction, which performs a multiply and an add on values that are already resident in the proper registers.

operations, which was valid at the time the law originated:

$$\frac{4 \text{ Bytes}}{3 \text{ Operations}} \times \frac{1{,}048{,}576 \text{ Operations}}{1 \text{ MegaFLOP}} \times \frac{1 \text{ MegaFLOP}}{\text{S}} = \frac{1.33 \text{ Megabytes}}{\text{S}}$$

For convenience sake, we will round this number downward to 1 Megabyte/S for every MFLOP; see Figure 8-2 for a graph of several currently available high-performance machines.

Using this law appropriately can help us evaluate a particular hardware configuration to see if it matches our performance needs or if it may be "saturated" by system bus activity. We will usually apply this rule to systems that are to provide compute-intensive services, since they are most likely to use floating-point operations and to have high amounts of CPU to memory traffic.

Let's take a quick look at some real-world data to see if the rule holds true. Figure 8-2 plots a number of computer systems, from various vendors, versus their respective system bus capabilities. Wherever a multiprocessor system is shown, the floating point performance is additive across the number of CPUs in the machine[8].

There are several interesting things to note about the diagram:

- Almost every system design in the figure, including that of multiprocessor systems, lies below the 1 MB/S = 1 MFLOP line that represents Amdahl's law. These systems were selected from a list of systems that are intended for compute-intensive tasks.
- The double-precision version of Amdahl's law restricts the number of CPUs per enclosure, and rounding the value to 2 MB/S per MFLOP has only a slight effect on the number of "allowed" processors.
- Those machines and multiple-CPU configurations that lie under the lines representing the Amdahl relationship are more "balanced" for compute intensive tasks than those above the lines.
- Because we are discussing compute-intensive operations, transaction-oriented machines with large numbers of CPUs are exempted from the law.

It is unlikely that hardware designers consciously apply only Amdahl's law when they design hardware systems. What is more likely is that a form of "grand averaging" is at work between hardware design principles, intended usage, implementation cost reduction, or other parameters. With the advent of crossbar-oriented computer systems, the basic requirements per processor may not change, but the available bandwidth per crossbar connection (port) is greater.

8. Actually, the performance will not scale linearly across multiple processors, but we will pretend that it does. This is one reason that the SPEC organization invented the SPECint_rate95 and SPECfp_rate95 benchmarks–to measure the true multiprocessor scaling.

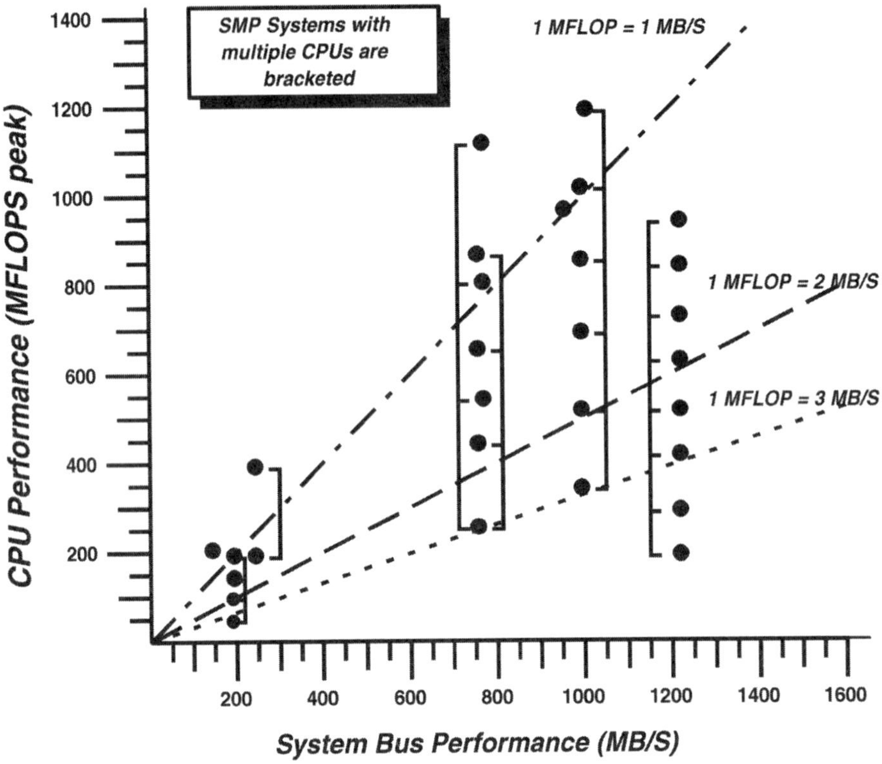

Figure 8-2 CPU Mega-FLOPS Versus System Bus Throughput

Crossbar-oriented[9] machines may not run into bandwidth problems until either the maximum aggregate throughput or the maximum number of connections for the crossbar are exceeded.

8.4 Amdahl's Law of Parallelism

Another one of Amdahl's laws states that the execution time for a parallel program is equal to the percentage of serial or scalar code (including synchronization overhead) plus the

9. A crossbar is essentially a hardware switch that allows multiple simultaneous (nonblocking) connections between ports. Each connection is dedicated, allowing transparent access between CPUs and memory or I/O, up to the maximum number of connections and the maximum rated throughput for the crossbar.

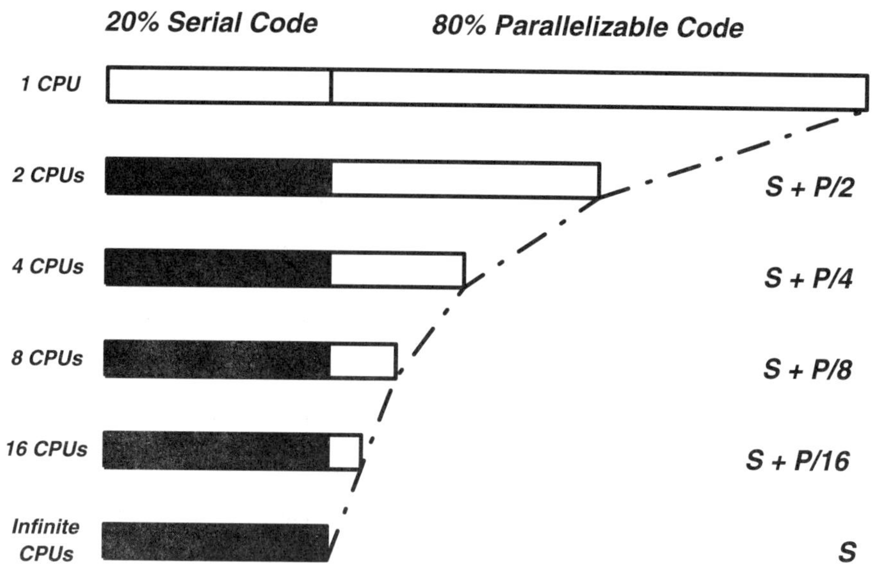

Figure 8-3 The Implications of Amdahl's Law of Parallelism: An Example

percentage of parallelizable code divided by the number of processors available. The following equation represents this relationship:

$$T = S + \left(\frac{P}{np}\right)$$

In this equation, the total time to execute the application is represented by *T*, the scalar or serial percentage of the application (including synchronization overhead) is represented by *S*, the percentage of the application that is parallelizable is represented by *P*, and the number of processors in use is represented by *np*. Additionally, the relationship between the serial and parallel portions of the application is:

$$S + P = 1$$

which indicates that the sum of the serial percentage and the parallel percentage must add up to one hundred percent.

With an infinite amount of processing available, the total time to execute the entire application reduces to just the scalar or serial component of the equation, *S*. Figure 8-3 shows the relationship between the serial code percentage, the parallelizable code percentage, and the maximum theoretical application speed-up for an application that is 80% parallelizable.

Many parallel applications reach the point of diminishing returns by the time four to eight processors are involved with the application components. As you can see from Figure 8-3, the performance will never be better than the limitation imposed by the scalar portion of the code. In reality, an application that has eighty percent parallelizable code is a rarity.

8.5 Summary of Amdahl's Laws

As we have seen, there are two of Amdahl's laws that we can use as rules of thumb when evaluating potential performance of compute server hardware and parallel applications. These two rules can help us from making incorrect decisions about the expected performance of the compute resources in our workgroup. How should we apply both rules in our design or analysis activities?

First, it is important to choose underlying compute server hardware that is capable of executing the types of applications that the users will utilize. If the expected application is floating-point intensive thermal simulation, then the underlying hardware had better support the level of performance required to provide adequate time to completion for the user. Using Amdahl's law of performance can help identify system configurations that may be unsuited for this type of activity. If, on the other hand, the application is database transaction oriented or office automation, then the requirements are not as stringent and the first of our rules may not apply.

The law of parallelism addresses what may be unrealistic expectations about parallel (or multithreaded) applications and the required compute server configuration, that is, that they will necessarily perform better than a monolithic version of the same application. Often the expectation is "All I have to do is add 27 CPUs and it will speed up my application incredibly". Amdahl's law of parallelism should help set realistic expectations for a given application.

8.6 Selecting the Proper Compute Server Hardware

With a thorough understanding of your workgroup's applications, an examination of the available hardware to run them is the next step. Along with the different types of applications, there are several popular hardware architectures to consider when choosing and configuring compute server hardware. Several of these are shown in Figure 8-4 and discussed in the next sections.

8.6.1 Symmetrical Multiprocessor

This type of hardware architecture consists of multiple CPUs, all sharing a common memory and system bus structure. Even though each CPU is considered equal to the others in an SMP machine, the contention for resources like the system bus and the memory may be the limiting factor for some types of compute-intensive applications.

SMP systems cannot contain an unlimited number of processors. Amdahl's law defines some upper limits to the number of CPUs that can inhabit the same SMP chassis. As processor performance increases, the number of processors in a given machine must decrease to keep memory and bus contention from affecting performance. Amdahl's law applies to compute-intensive tasks, so many transaction-processing servers do not suffer from the same limitations[10].

CPU to memory crossbars are beginning to find their way into lower-cost SMP systems, replacing the shared bus, which can help eliminate some of the CPU to memory contention. Other issues, like bus traffic from maintaining cache coherency across many CPUs, may also become a limiting factor as the number of CPUs increases in an SMP machine. Eventually, a given SMP configuration will reach a point where it cannot be scaled further in terms of power supply, cooling, CPU, I/O, RAM, or other resources.

SMP machines are capable of running both parallel and throughput types of tasks. Some implementations of parallel programming environments, like PVM, are designed to use local shared memory for message passing between local parallel components, if possible, instead of network based communications. In a way, we may view an SMP machine as a network of single CPU machines collapsed into a single box.

One of the major differences between an SMP machine and a network of single CPU servers, however, is that within the SMP machine all CPU instruction and data caches are kept synchronized with the shared RAM. This synchronization is needed to prevent destructive interference between multiple CPUs operating on the same data. Maintaining cache coherency can be a major source of system bus traffic for compute-intensive jobs that migrate between CPUs in an SMP machine.

8.6.2 SMP Clusters

Once a single SMP machine has "run out of gas", the obvious solution is to add a similarly configured machine to double the compute-serving capacity. The difficulty with this approach involves the sharing of data between processes running on the now-separate hardware. If cluster-wide communication is needed between components of the same application, a message-passing mechanism is used instead of the "normal" facilities provided for communication between local processes (like shared memory, pipes, and FIFO files.)

In many cases, interprocess communication is not needed, and a shared set of data resources between the machines can allow a dispatcher or "master" process on one of the machines to send tasks to other application components in the cluster. For throughput applications, the SMP cluster is a good way to scale the available resources and get more jobs completed per unit of time. Cluster-wide parallel transaction processing with a shared database resource is a good example of this type of SMP cluster application.

In addition to throughput types of jobs, an SMP cluster may run some kinds of parallel applications, using a set of specialized, message-passing programming environments like parallel virtual machine (PVM) or message passing interface (MPI). Within each SMP compute

10. Many times a transaction-processing server is the same hardware configuration, in terms of RAM and bus structure, as a compute-intensive server but will contain many more CPUs. This is because the processor to memory bus loading per CPU in a transaction-processing environment tends to be lower than in a compute-intensive one.

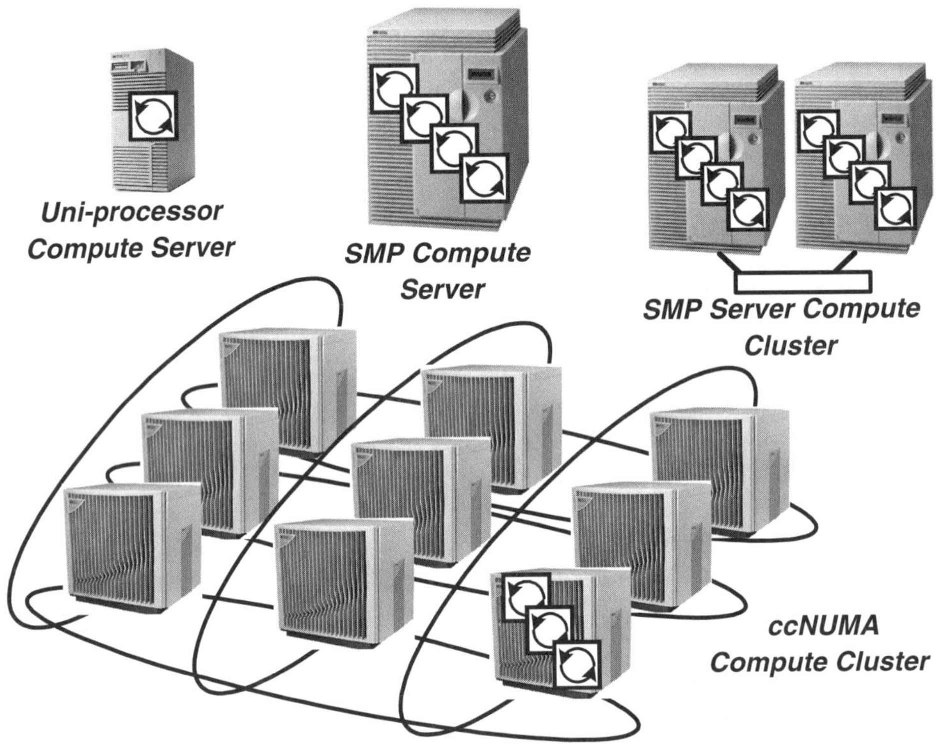

Figure 8-4 Compute Server Physical Hardware Architectures

server, data are shared by passing messages through local mechanisms such as shared memory. For external message passing, either a network connection or a specialized high-speed system interconnect may be used.

Because cache coherency is not maintained across a multiserver SMP compute cluster, specialized programming techniques like MPI and PVM must be used for sharing data between parallel application components. Applications that use these interfaces must be specially designed and implemented to use the message passing features of the virtual machine. Parallelizing an existing application to use message passing often means a complete redesign of the application architecture.

8.6.3 Carpet Clusters

The term "carpet cluster" describes a group of single CPU workstations, often sitting in a corner on the floor (on the carpet), that can serve as a low-cost workgroup compute resource. This compute resource comprises "leftover" workstation hardware that may no longer be suitable for workgroup client systems and might have already been fully depreciated or paid for. This type of system is still potentially useful as a resource for increasing workgroup throughput, depending on the application.

Another similar class of potential compute resources are the individual client workstations that are idle for one reason or another. We discussed the use of this resource on page 84. Both of these types of "informal" compute servers require the use of load-balancing software to properly detect, allocate, and schedule the resources.

8.6.4 Scalable SMP Cluster

Once the compute requirements placed on an individual compute server have exceeded its performance capabilities, there are two approaches: get a larger, more powerful hardware configuration or add another set of resources. Obtaining larger and larger compute servers will eventually reach the point of diminishing returns, as the costs grow ever larger, and the consequences of Amdahl's law set in. Eventually, the second option must be faced, as we saw in the discussion of SMP clusters.

A scalable SMP cluster resembles an SMP cluster, with one major difference: CPU cache coherency is maintained across some or all of the CPUs in the cluster. This group of cache-coherent CPUs is called a coherency domain. Cache coherency across multiple SMP chassis in a scalable SMP cluster allows expanding the amount resources in the computer system, adding RAM and CPUs beyond the capabilities of a single chassis, but maintains the appearance of a "normal" but very powerful computer. This architecture is also called "cache-coherent non-uniform memory access", or ccNUMA.

The advantage of ccNUMA is that applications do not need to go to superhuman efforts to make use of the additional cluster resources. "Normal" applications run with no changes, whether they are parallel or nonparallel. Automatic parallelizing compilers can recompile existing application sources to take advantage of the ccNUMA features, yielding parallelization with minimal effort for some applications.

The major overhead of ccNUMA is the division of system RAM into two classes: local and nonlocal. Accessing nonlocal memory incurs an additional time penalty over local memory, as would be expected. This time penalty is kept to a reasonable value by high-speed interconnections between the nodes of the cluster and hiding the extra memory latency behind normal processor cache-fetching operations.

An interesting side benefit of the ccNUMA machine is that it can run a single copy of the operating system, distributed across all nodes in a coherency domain. This can dramatically reduce system administration overhead on a per CPU basis. A ccNUMA machine can sometimes be partitioned into virtual computers, or subcomplexes, that can be managed by the operating system and allocated to special applications, groups of people, or other special resource users.

An example of the new breed of scalable SMP machine is the Hewlett-Packard Exemplar V2500 server. A basic building block for the V2500 is a "hypernode" containing between two and thirty-two CPUs, a multiport, nonblocking crossbar switch (HP HyperPlane), and up to thirty-two GB of local RAM. Each hypernode is connected to up to four other hypernodes via a 30 GB/S toroidal interconnect, with multiple ring connections in two directions (both x and y.) The entire one hundred and twenty-eight CPUs are a single cache coherency domain, running a single copy of the HP-UX operating system[11].

Up to sixteen of these four-hypernode configurations may be clustered together using HP's HyperFabric switch to form a supercomputing cluster with up to two thousand and forty-eight processors. Because of its hierarchical switched interconnect, I propose that we call this type of scalable compute complex a compute area network, or CAN. This type of configuration is distributed, resilient, scalable, and may be made highly available.

The inherent scalability and flexibility of a ccNUMA machine make it a good resource for workgroups with parallel applications that require specialized compute resources. The expense and size of a computer system like this means that it would more than likely to end up as a work-center resource.

8.6.5 Specialized Parallel Hardware

Workgroups that perform specialized compute operations, like parallel programming research or scientific visualization, may require highly specialized compute hardware. Some of the specialized compute hardware that might be needed are Single instruction multiple data (SIMD), multiple instruction multiple data (MIMD), or vector processors. We will not delve into these hardware types here.

8.7 The Compute Server and Load Balancing

If the compute server is to run applications that exceed the client system capabilities, a transparent mechanism is necessary for identifying the type of task to be run, quantifying the needed resources, determining that the task is too big to run on the client, and locating any available resources within the workgroup to use. In the case of compute intensive tasks, the primary resource of interest is CPU power.

Finding available CPU cycles is usually the task of an infrastructure service which we will call "load balancing"[12]. We have briefly mentioned this service before; see Figure 1-7 for a simplified diagram of the service in operation. This initial introduction to load-balancing and locational transparency was much too simplified, however. We will now delve into the subject a little bit deeper.

11. This system delivers over fifty GFLOPS peak in its 32 CPU configuration and over 200 GFLOPS peak in its 128 CPU configuration.

12. We could make a very strong argument for including load balancing functionality as a standard part of any operating system that participates in a client server environment.

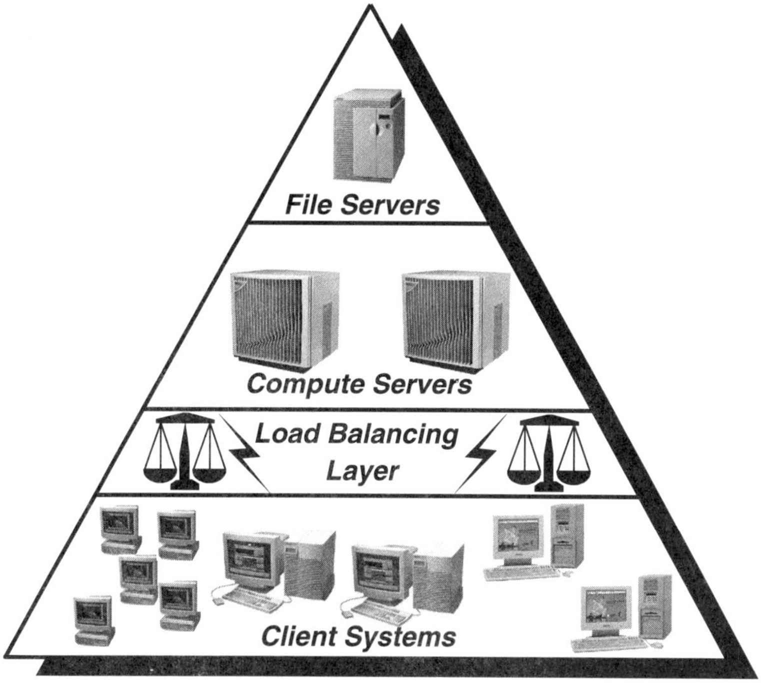

Figure 8-5 Client, Compute, and File Server Tiers with Load Balancing

In addition to finding necessary resources to run specialized tasks, the load-balancing service must be able to queue tasks that cannot run due to short-term resource shortages, rescheduling them when the resources become available. In essence, the load-balancing facility acts as if it were the workgroup equivalent of the operating system component called the system scheduler or dispatcher, locating resources for the user's applications that run on the workgroup client-server virtual computer. Figure 8-5 shows the three hardware tiers of 3TCS with a load-balancing layer added between the client systems and the compute servers.

Let's enumerate some of the desirable characteristics of the load balancing facility. To meet our needs, the load-balancing facility must:

- Run on multiple platform types to support the different client and server hardware and operating system types in the workgroup
- Be highly available and resilient to avoid denial of services to the user
- Provide task scheduling and queuing services to allow for flexible task execution
- Have a priority scheme to allow fair allocation of workgroup resources
- Support transparent access to the user's data and desktop environment settings
- Be easy to manage

In addition to these features, we strongly desire the ability to allow class-based management of the tasks that the load-balancing facility schedules. Just as identifying the system classes is part of the workgroup design effort, we must identify the application or batch job classes, quantify their resource needs, and properly configure the load balancing facility to support our efforts.

One of the most important features that the proper load-balancing facility allows is scaling of the compute server resources. In the previous section we discussed the hardware alternatives available for scaling a compute server. The second, and frequently the most cost-effective, approach requires the ability to transparently dispatch user tasks to multiple machines where once there was only one. This is one of the load-balancing facility's functions.

When capacity planning dictates, we should be able to wheel up a new server, plug it in, and configure it into the resource pool that the load balancing facility manages. Likewise, if the need for a particular compute resource decreases, we should be able to decommission a server and move it to wherever it is needed. All of this may be done transparently, with no visible effect on the user.

8.8 The Compute Server and File Server Access

Because we have moved the user's data and applications to the file server, we now have an additional workgroup design issue to deal with. What happens when the compute server must access the user's data and applications to perform the requested computations? Of course, it must access the data on, and return the results to, the file server, just as if it were the client system that requested the task to be run with local data. To do otherwise would violate our rules about locational transparency and would require the user's data to be on the client system.

Care must be taken to properly size the file server in environments that contain compute servers, since a given client may be capable of running more simultaneous tasks than when the task runs only on the client[13]. This may result in more file system accesses than expected from a previously existing configuration. If running multiple simultaneous tasks increases user productivity, then the goal should be prepared to enable and support this behavior, rather than to discourage it.

Along with properly sizing the file server, it is important to look at the potential traffic between the file server and the compute server. A dedicated high-speed network between the two workgroup components is one solution used by customers of mine. Usually there is an attempt to segregate the client system network traffic from the compute server to file server traffic in order to avoid impacting the client system performance with heavy network loading.

Another issue to deal with is data access by the tasks running on the compute server. The data sets must be either permanently mounted from the file server, or automatically mounted on access. The former approach creates direct dependencies between the compute server and the

13. Software development is one area where compilation servers can drastically increase the peak number of file server accesses during a software "build".

file servers, which are undesirable. The latter solution is preferred over the permanent mounts, especially if multiple file servers are involved.

8.9 Compute Server Summary

In this chapter we have discussed some of the essential characteristics of a compute server, how to integrate its functionality into the workgroup, and some of the hardware options that are available. We started with two of Amdahl's laws, the first providing a rule of thumb for recognizing potentially oversubscribed system bus resources, the second giving us a realistic approach for estimating performance gains realized by parallelization.

We mentioned the need to completely understand the compute needs of the candidate applications that run on the compute server. Additionally, we differentiated between parallelized (time-to-completion) job types and throughput type jobs. There are also specialized programming environments and specialized hardware to support massively parallel applications.

The different configurations of computer servers were discussed, from single CPU, to SMP, to SMP clusters, carpet clusters, and scalable SMP (ccNUMA) machines. As workgroup designers, we have many different scalable choices for compute server hardware. Location of the compute server resource depends on the requirements of users, but many times the larger, more expensive systems are used as workcenter resources, shared by multiple workgroups.

The load-balancing service plays an important role in utilizing the compute server resources. Additions and subtractions of compute resources, based on capacity planning, can be hidden from the client systems by the load-balancing layer. In cases where the client systems represent an underutilized resource, the load-balancing facility may be used to allocate compute cycles from the pool of available clients.

Because the compute server is often executing jobs that must access data on one or more file servers, we noted that there must be a high-speed connection between the compute server and the workgroup file servers. It is also desirable to provide this connection in such a way that the other workgroup elements are not impacted by this potentially high traffic rate. We should note that the data from the file servers must be available to the compute server, so mounting services like AutoFS are useful to provide access without the direct dependencies caused by permanent mounts.

In the coming chapters we will put our study of compute server characteristics to work in our design and analysis activities. The load-balancing facility and its usage will also play key roles.

CHAPTER 9

Network Infrastructure: The Workgroup Foundation

No other portion of the workgroup structure is more important — or seemingly more neglected — than the interconnections provided by the network infrastructure. If data sharing is the primary focus of the client systems and their ability to communicate with the servers in the environment are of paramount importance, one would think[1] that continuously improving network infrastructure would be a primary focus for companies that are interested in the highest productivity possible. Without the properly designed network infrastructure, each individual computer system becomes an isolated island of resources and the sharing of those resources becomes impossible.

Let's examine this critical portion of our workgroup environment in some detail. We will discuss the rapid pace of change in LAN technologies, the evolution of LAN topology over time, and some of the technologies that are important to us, like switched Ethernet, layer three[2] switching, and link aggregation or trunking. Finally we will examine some of the design goals and present an analysis technique for spotting potential network bottlenecks.

Let us also agree that this is not a complete tutorial on networking technologies. There are many excellent books that concentrate on this subject alone. Like many other technologies, there is enough information available that specialists in the field spend a good portion of their time just keeping current on the new developments. We don't necessarily need to be electricians to know how to plug things into the proper outlets.

1. I have heard it said that any statement that begins with the phrase "one would think" is automatically false.

2. We are referring to the layers of the OSI model: Physical, Data Link, Network, Transport, Session, Presentation, and Application. Layer 3 is the Network layer.

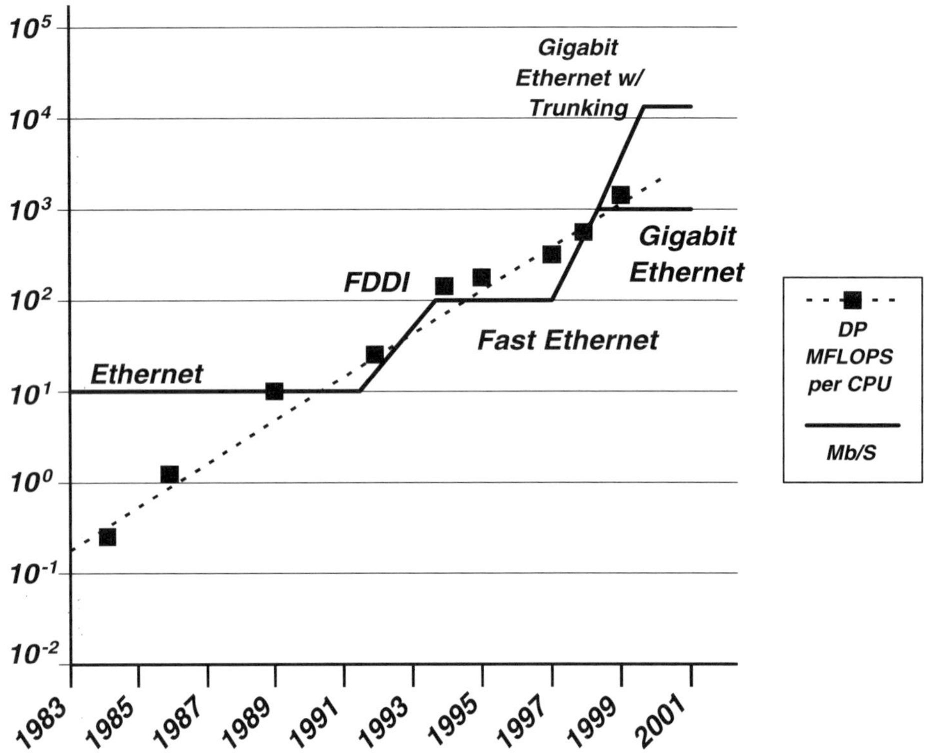

Figure 9-1 Compute Power Versus Network Throughput

9.1 Examining the Pace of LAN Technology Advances

Part of the reason for the apparent lack of attention to networking infrastructure is that the technology for networking is currently changing as rapidly as the increase in performance of the computer systems that use it. This has not always been the case; historically there have been periods of several years (eons as far as technology goes[3]) where the throughput of the available network technologies have been relatively constant and the power of the computing equipment increased rapidly. Ethernet throughput remained "stuck" at 10 Mb/S for almost nine years from its initial acceptance into the marketplace. Recently, however, the rate of change in Ethernet and other networking technologies has accelerated.

3. A comparison was made by Lew Platt, the CEO of Hewlett-Packard, between "dog years" and "technology years", where the often quoted seven dog years per human year were surpassed by the number of technology years per human year.

The changes in technology have also meant changes in the physical media that is used to carry the network traffic between the client systems, the "wiring closet", and the hubs, switches, and routers that direct the traffic flow. The Ethernet thick coaxial cable was replaced by thin coaxial cable, which was replaced by two pairs of a Category 5 UTP[4] cable, which was superseded by four pairs of Category five, which will be replaced by fiber, and so on and so on, ad infinitum.

So, in addition to the expense of upgrading the networking equipment, there may be an additional need to upgrade the physical wiring between the clients and that equipment. And the physical medium that you install today may not be guaranteed to support tomorrow's technologies. It is important to do our homework and pay attention to trends that may affect our ability to upgrade the network infrastructure that is so important to us.

To get an idea of how compute power and network capability have been tracking one another, examine Figure 9-1. The graph compares the increase in CPU power over time, as measured by double precision MFLOPS, against the bandwidth increase of LAN technology in Megabits per second. Note that the scale for MFLOPS and bandwidth is logarithmic!

The available compute power from a single CPU grew at an exponential rate over the last two decades or so (and is still maintaining that trend), while the maximum bandwidth of the LAN technologies remained constant for relatively long periods of time, then grew in discreet jumps that matched the introduction of new technologies. Prior to 1989 the CPU power curve was below the network bandwidth curve, from 1989 to 1998 the CPU power curve was above that of the network, and today we appear to be entering a period where networking bandwidth will again outstrip the CPU power curve.

It is important not to read too much into this representation, it is only one way to examine the given data. A pessimist might say that there is no relationship whatsoever between the two sets of data, a realist might say that the behavior of networked systems indeed *seemed* to follow the trends indicated, and an optimist might look at the right-hand portion of the graph and say, "Hey, the network is finally faster than the computer again!"

9.2 The Evolution of LAN Topology

One of the very important components of our workgroup design is the network "backplane" between the components of the client-server virtual computer (described in Figure 1-6 on page 12). Many existing network installations are stuck back in the "dark ages" of networking technology. To fully understand the current LAN capabilities and how to evolve to them, we must take a look at how the topology of the LAN has changed over the last decade.

We will concentrate mainly on Ethernet technology, since it is the most pervasive and easily understood. Other networking technologies like FDDI and various forms of token ring are

4. UTP is an acronym for unshielded twisted pair.

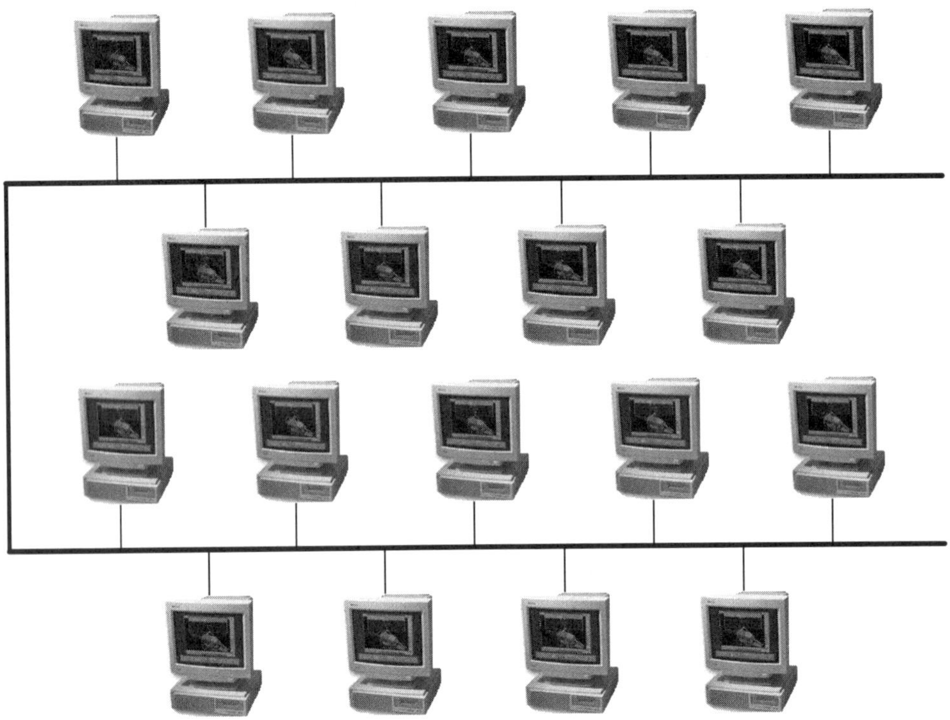

Figure 9-2 A Shared-Media Ethernet LAN

still encountered, but they are rarely the proper choice for new installations. As with many other technologies we will examined, the networking evolution has created a hierarchy of device types to solve the overall networking problem.

9.2.1 A Shared Media LAN

As originally designed and captured in the IEEE[5] 802.3 standard, Ethernet is a shared medium network that interconnects attached systems or nodes. Communication is performed by broadcasting a frame from one node to all other attached nodes. Each individual node examines the frame and determines whether to receive or discard it. The maximum transmission unit (MTU) for Ethernet data frames is approximately 1500 bytes.

When two or more nodes attempt to broadcast at the same time, a collision occurs. The mechanism used is termed a carrier sense multiple access collision detect (or CSMA/CD[6])

5. The Institute of Electrical and Electronics Engineers, located at *WWW.IEEE.org*.

6. Much of the terminology was inherited from the ancestor of Ethernet, Aloha Net, which was a packet radio-based networking scheme originally used in the Hawaiian Islands.

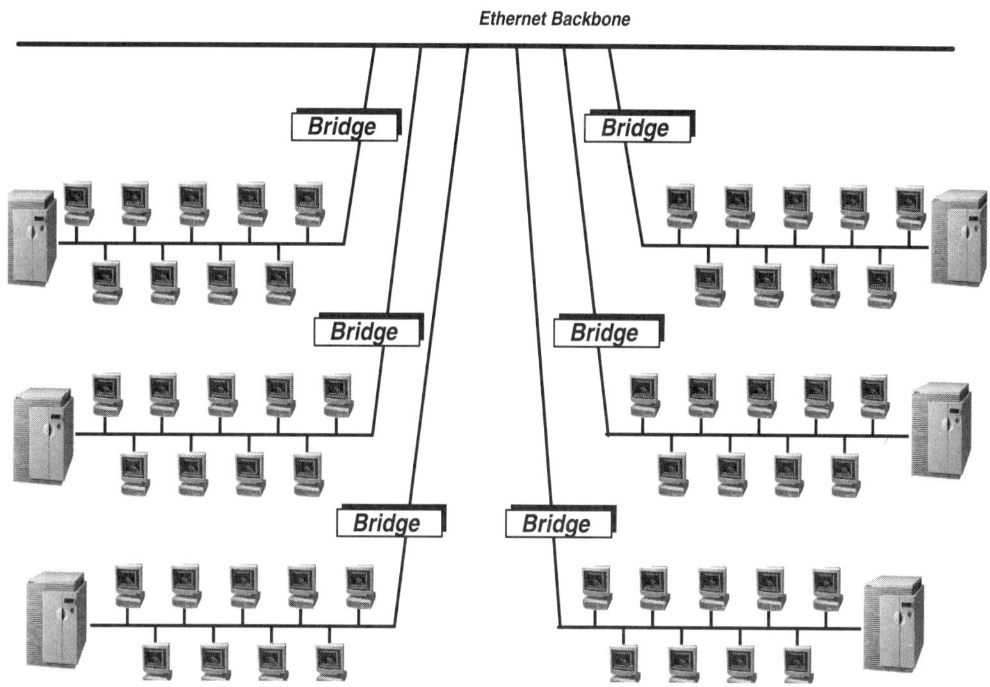

Figure 9-3 A Bridged, Shared-Media Ethernet LAN

medium. Each physical LAN segment is a single "collision domain", and its bandwidth is shared by all attached nodes. Because of the shared medium and the possibility of collisions, a shared Ethernet LAN segment is rarely able to achieve more than thirty to forty percent of the maximum theoretical bandwidth.

There are three basic types of Ethernet frames: unicast, broadcast, and multicast. Unicast frames are intended for a specific destination and are discarded by all but the destination node. Broadcast frames are intended for all nodes attached to the LAN segment. Multicast frames are a relatively new development and are intended for nodes that belong to a multicast group (seemingly halfway between a unicast frame and a broadcast frame).

9.2.2 A Bridged, Shared Media LAN

The shared medium also had an interconnection limitation: only 127 physical nodes could be connected to a single Ethernet segment. Much of this limitation had to do with electrical noise and reflections introduced by the physical connections themselves. Multiple direct connections to the Ethernet medium were replaced with connections to dumb hubs, or concentrators, that provided multiple ports with only a single physical connection to the physical cable.

Once the number of connections per physical segment was able to increase to the maximum possible, the next step was to connect multiple segments via Ethernet repeaters or bridges.

These devices blindly forwarded all signals received at the physical level to all attached segments, increasing the number of interconnected systems, but also increasing the number of broadcast frames being received by each system. Bridges reduced the size of the collision domains, but did not block broadcast or multicast packets. The topology resulting from the addition of bridges is shown in Figure 9-3.

The more systems that were added to the network, the more broadcast frames were generated. In response to this new development, network managers coined the term "broadcast storm". A "broadcast storm" describes the situation where large numbers of broadcasts are propagated to all attached systems in the network, resulting in little or no productive work being done. If the situation becomes bad enough that each time a node attempts to send a frame it encounters a collision, a total network collapse is possible.

Additional functionality was added to "smart" bridges to filter out broadcast packets and other types of Ethernet "noise". This effectively isolated each physical LAN segment and reduced the total size of the collision domain. Unfortunately, this arrangement did not scale well unless the 80/20 rule applied (i.e., when eighty percent of all traffic was local to the LAN segment and only twenty percent was external).

One of the major problems with the bridged solution is the fact that the backbone can very easily be saturated with the traffic between nodes. One way to think of this problem is to visualize the connection of each LAN segment to the backbone as a pipe, through which a fluid (or ether, if you like) can flow. If each of the pipes can theoretically contribute a flow of 10 Mbps, it is not hard to see that a 10 Mbps backbone cannot handle the flow from more than one connection at a time unless the flows are small.

A larger pipe is needed to enable the backbone to pass the traffic without becoming a bottleneck. We will run into this type of "big pipe" problem again and again in our design and analysis efforts, particularly in the connection of servers to the network. It is important to recognize the problem and properly deal with it, whether we are examining the network, disk I/O channels, or other connection types that can suffer from it.

9.2.3 A Routed LAN

The next step in the LAN evolution was the introduction of the router in the late 1980s. A router is an intelligent, manageable[7] network device that allows flexible forwarding, filtering, and translation of multiple network packet types. With the functionality provided by routers, individual LAN segments may be isolated from each other's broadcast traffic, while sharing the types of packets that are desirable.

A router's software implements filtering by examining the content of each packet it receives. Decisions may then be made by the router's software about what to do with the packet, based on its protocol content, packet type, and final destination. There is a cost for the generality

7. "Manageable" in this sense means that the configuration may be changed interactively from a remote location. Information about the router's performance is also available through a software interface.

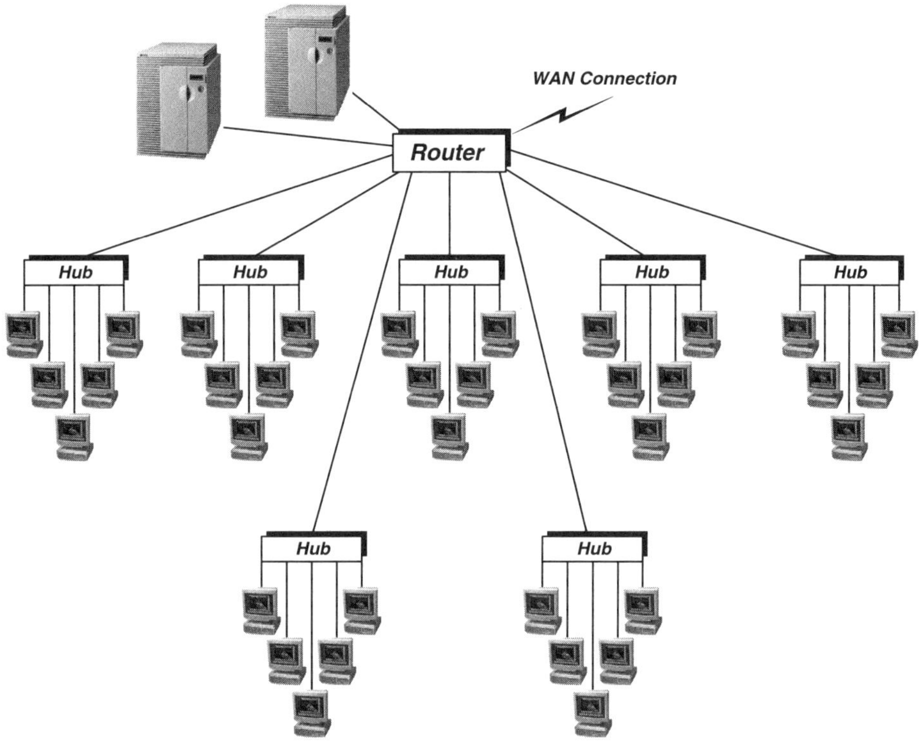

Figure 9-4 A Routed Ethernet LAN

available with a router: they tend to be complex, expensive, and slow, introducing a considerable amount of latency into the path of the packets that they forward. Because of their flexibility and its associated complexity, routers can be difficult to configure and manage.

On the positive side, routers provide a good way to control traffic between LAN segments, they provide excellent security because they can filter out specific packet types, they do not propagate erroneous physical frames, and they make a good interface to WAN connections.

9.2.4 Introducing the Network Switch

A newer development on the network front, arriving in the early 1990s, is the network switch. A network switch (or just "a switch") is essentially a low-latency, high-bandwidth, smart "learning" bridge that interconnects nodes at the media access control (MAC) layer (layer two of the OSI model). A switch allows multiple connections between its ports to be active at the same time, and because the connections are made at the MAC level, they are protocol independent.

Each port on the switch is also an independent collision domain. A network switch "learns" which hardware MAC addresses are attached to each port and forwards traffic to the

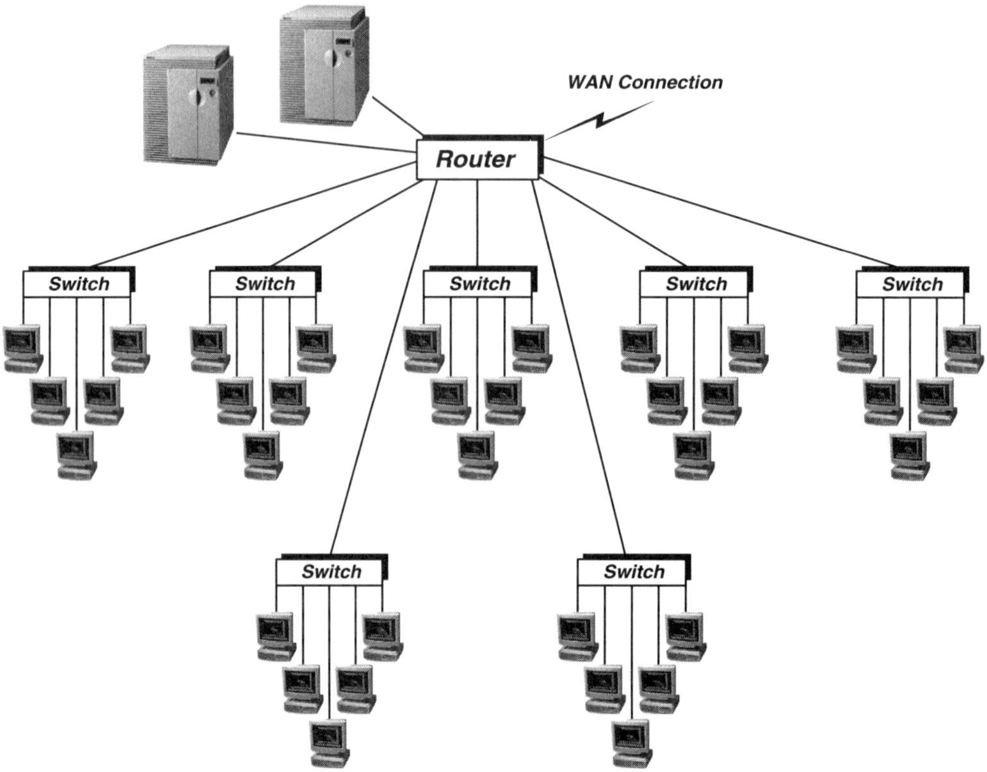

Figure 9-5 A Switched, Routed Ethernet LAN

appropriate port. If the destination is not in the local switch's port-to-MAC translation table, the packet is forwarded to the switch's backbone port. Packets arriving from the backbone port are checked against the local switch's tables and forwarded to the correct port, if appropriate.

To allow multiple simultaneous connections, a switch operates internally at very high rates of speed (backplanes are typically rated in terms of tens to hundreds of Gigabits per second.) To handle packet switching, MTU conversion, flow control, and other necessary features, a switch usually involves an intelligent switching matrix and a shared memory architecture.

A switch has its packet handling functionality implemented in hardware to maintain its high-speed and associated high throughput. A typical comparison between the per packet latency of a switch and that of a router shows a difference of an order of magnitude (tens of microseconds versus tens of milliseconds.) There is a trade-off for the improvement in performance: the switch usually has less functionality than a router (less protocol-handling capabilities, for instance.)

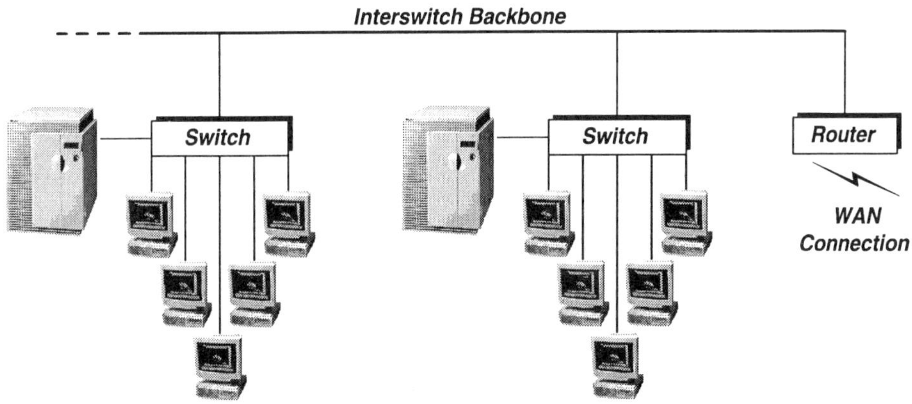

Figure 9-6 A Fully Switched Network

Switches may also perform packet filtering and will forward packets with "unknown" destinations to a "backbone" port. This functionality allows interconnection of switches to increase the size of the switching domain.

9.2.5 Replacing Hubs with Switches

After the first generation of switches appeared, they were frequently used to replace the hubs in the previously described topology. The topology shown in Figure 9-5 has the backbone port of each switch connected to a router that is responsible for forwarding and filtering packets between the different subnets supported by switches.

This arrangement is useful from an evolutionary standpoint, because it eliminates the hubs and associated collision domains, speeding the communications between clients on the same switch. When packets must be forwarded between switches, however, the router still exacts its performance penalty as packets are forwarded between subnets (individual switching domains.)

9.2.6 A Fully Switched LAN

The switch backbone allows interconnecting multiple switches into a single, unified network and eliminates the router as a bottleneck in the forwarding of packets between switches. Furthermore, it is possible to make all nodes connected to the switches share the same network address or subnet. Figure 9-6 depicts a fully switched network.

There are several interesting things to note about this arrangement:

- By default, all ports on the interconnected switches will receive all broadcasts and multicasts.
- Because all nodes share the same network address, the network can be "flat" with no routing.

- Since switches can handle multiple networking technologies like FDDI, Fast Ethernet, and Gigabit Ethernet, links to shared resources like compute and file servers may be scaled to avoid the "concentration effect." (See "Link Aggregation" on page 151.)
- There is now a difference between a network segment (a physical network medium) and a network subnet (a network address). There may now be multiple network segments with the same network address.
- For services that are located by broadcasting, there may no longer be a need to have a server per segment, reducing system administration overhead.
- Systems may now move around in the network without needing to be reconfigured with new TCP/IP address, routing tables, and host names.
- The issue is how to contain broadcast and multicast traffic to the appropriate switch ports.

A fully switched LAN allows the removal of the router to the "edges" of the network, eliminating the potential bottleneck from direct communication paths between the three hardware tiers within the workgroup. Local resources may be attached to each switch, making access by systems on the same switch more efficient. As designers and implementors, a fully switched LAN gives us a lot more flexibility about the location resources in the network.

We now may deploy a switch in the network closet, in place of a router or hub, and attach local file or compute resources as the physical layout of our network demands. Each floor in a building may share a switch and local resources, or the resources may be located in a centralized computer room, interconnected by a high-speed switch "downlink" or backbone. "Collapsed backbone" switches even may be used as if the major external components of the network were contained within a single chassis.

The conclusion you should be reaching is that a fully switched LAN is the ideal backplane for our client-server virtual computer and the 3TCS workgroup. As a matter of fact, if you revisit the chapters leading up to this discussion and examine the empty box in the middle of the figures depicting network environments, you will see that this was the intent all along. Let's continue to examine some of the important network technologies that are available in today's network design tool box.

9.3 Important LAN Technologies and Functionality

A number of new network technologies are becoming widely available, and many of the technologies and protocol improvements are being added to the functionality provided by the network switch. The additional functionality increases the flexibility to configure and control the behavior of the switched local-area network. Other developments, like layer three switching,

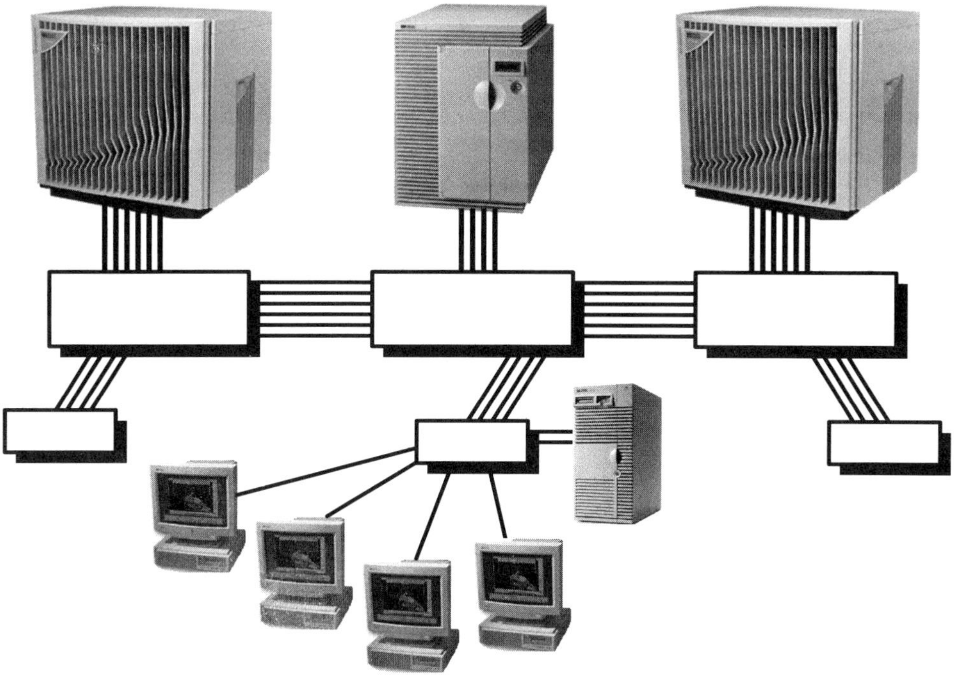

Figure 9-7 Link Aggregation Example

are adding new network building blocks to our workgroup design tool kit. The following are some of the more exciting and useful additions.

9.3.1 Link Aggregation

Link aggregation, or link trunking, is a feature that groups multiple physical point-to-point network links into a single logical network link. The primary applications for this type of connection are switch-to-switch backbone connections, switch-to-server "large pipe" connections, and other point-to-point network connections that require scaling and resiliency.

There are two configuration types to examine for link aggregation: switch-to-switch and server-to-switch. In the switch-to-switch configuration, one of the major network vendors, 3Com, allows six parallel network links per trunk and up to four trunks per individual Ethernet Switch! Hewlett-Packard's "Auto Port Aggregation" for server systems allows up to four 10 Mb/S or 100 Mb/S links to be combined into an aggregate, with as many as five trunks per server system. In both cases, full and half duplex links are supported.

Configuration of an aggregate networking link is currently done with proprietary methods from each of the major networking vendors, but there is promise of a standard from IEEE (802.3AD). The configuration issues involve disabling the "spanning tree" algorithm that is used by network equipment to detect and shut down duplicate network paths. Because the aggregate link consists of multiple network segments in parallel, the spanning tree algorithm would normally shut all but one of the links down to prevent network loops. Link aggregation gives us several very desirable design features:

Large Network "Pipes" Based on data-flow analysis of server network traffic, a designer may place the proper number of parallel Ethernet links between the server and the network switch. Prior to the availability of link aggregation, when a server exceeded the throughput of a single existing network link, it was necessary to add a second network link with a different network address (and MAC address) and host name.

The additional addresses and host names resulted in a more complicated interface between the server and the client systems, increasing the amount of system administration effort needed to manage both the clients *and* the server. Some customers actually preferred to grow a file server to the point that the required network throughput was exceeded, then split the server into two separate physical machines. This was done rather than to deal with the complications of adding a second, third, or *N*th network interface and the associated administrative overhead.

Scalable Point-to-Point Connections With aggregate links, the connection from point to point becomes scalable: run out of throughput, add another parallel link, and reconfigure the aggregate. This type of scalability yields a lot of flexibility in adding extra network bandwidth wherever it is needed, without necessarily causing an upgrade of the networking equipment. The major design requirement is to have additional physical media and interface connections available for increasing the size of the aggregate.

Additional Network Resiliency In addition to the increased throughput gained by multiple aggregate links, there is also a measure of added network resiliency. Because the network traffic is load balanced across the number of configured physical links in the aggregate, the loss of one or more links does not necessarily imply a network failure. As long as there is at least one functional network link available, the aggregate continues to operate.

Figure 9-7 shows an example of link aggregation being used for server-to-switch and switch-to-switch interconnections. Because link aggregation supports both fast Ethernet and Gigabit Ethernet links, we can construct a scalable bandwidth hierarchy all the way down to the client system. This is a very flexible, high-performance approach to workgroup networking.

9.3.2 Virtual LANs

As we previously mentioned, a network switch will forward, or "flood", all multicast and broadcast traffic to every port. As the size of networks grow, the amount of multicast and broadcast traffic may grow to the point that individual systems are no longer able to get productive work done, because they spend most of their time receiving, examining, and discarding packets that are not useful to them.

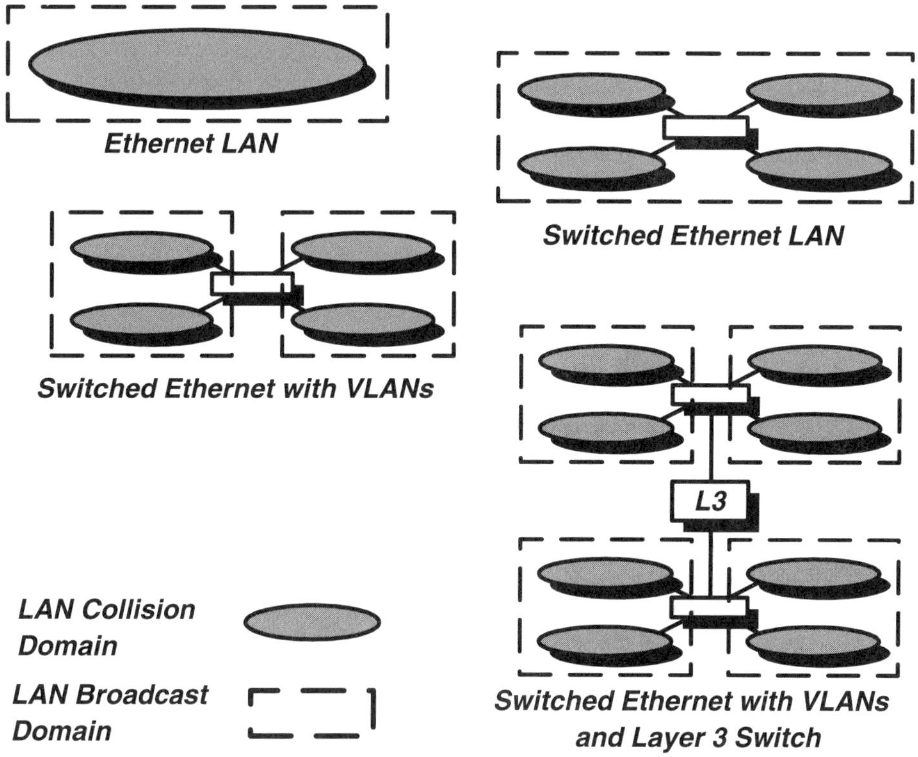

Figure 9-8 LAN Broadcast and Collision Domains with Switching

The type of systems in the workgroup, along with the broadcast and multicast traffic levels that each type generates, will eventually limit the number of systems that may participate in the broadcast domain. A common view of the maximum number of allowed systems in a broadcast domain is that at most one thousand TCP/IP based Unix workstations, or five hundred Windows SMB–based systems, or two hundred Apple Talk–based systems may share a broadcast domain.

These numbers may be great "ball park" figures for homogeneous workgroups, but what happens when different system types coexist in the same workgroup? How do we keep the really "chatty" system types from generating levels of network traffic that affect the performance of the other types of systems? One way to do this is through the use of feature called Virtual LANs, or VLANs.

Using network management software, a network manager may decide which switch ports are to receive broadcast packets from other systems in the workgroup. This is roughly equivalent to the decision about which physical LAN segment a client was to belong to prior to Ethernet switching. Most Ethernet switches allow a port to belong to multiple VLANs at the same time, giving the network administrator even more control over which broadcasts are seen by whom.

We can also think of a VLAN as a class of systems that share common broadcast packets, much in the same way as we identified physical or usage characteristics that separated client systems in classes for system administration purposes. Referring to Figure 9-8, you can see that a switch can make collision domains smaller, but without VLANs, all systems attached to the switch will share each others broadcast packets. Using VLANs can further constrain the broadcast domain to only the ports that belong to a specified VLAN.

The implementation of a VLAN is based on a tag that is placed in the Ethernet frame by the networking hardware. Ethernet switches and other equipment that implement VLANs will recognize the tag and behave accordingly. The VLAN tagging standard from IEEE is designated 802.1Q.

9.3.3 Layer Three Switching

Another important networking technology development is called "layer three switching", in which "layer three" refers to layer three of the OSI model which contains network addresses. Previously using information at this level to route packets would be the exclusive domain of a router, however; the performance and latency requirements of a switched network demand another solution.

A layer three switch is optimized for LAN forwarding of packets, performing the routing at wire speed (in the millions of packets per second.) A layer three switch forwards intersubnet packets based on network layer (layer three) addresses and intrasubnet packets based on MAC addresses (layer two.) Because a layer three switch's functionality is implemented in hardware, much like in an Ethernet switch, it is very fast, but also more limited than that available in a "traditional" router.

Another function provided by a layer three switch is the containment of broadcast packet flooding. We can now increase the size of a network, using switches to reduce the size of a collision domain, VLANs to shrink broadcast domains, and interconnect networks with different network addresses via a layer three switch. See Figure 9-8 for examples of network topologies using a layer three switch.

9.3.4 Ethernet, Fast Ethernet, and Gigabit Ethernet

Now would be a good time to review Figure 9-1; what started with 3 Mb/S Ethernet became 10 Mb/S Ethernet, and has continued through 100 Mb/S, right to 1000 Mb/S, or Gigabit Ethernet. We now have a complete hierarchy of network bandwidths to work with. In fact, if we include the bandwidths available because of link aggregation, we have an even larger selection to choose from.

Not only do we have a number of different bandwidths, we have several different configurations. A dedicated Ethernet switch port can be driven to approximately ninety percent of the theoretical bandwidth of the associated technology. This is in stark contrast to the recommended thirty percent maximum that is available with shared media (with collisions.)

For client system connections, a dedicated Ethernet switch port can result in a large increase in available bandwidth over shared media, since virtually no collisions occur[8]. If the physical wiring between the client and the wiring closet is properly configured, dedicated Ethernet switch ports may replace the shared media hubs that are probably in place. The table below details the difference in bandwidth between shared and dedicated network connections.

Table 9-1 Dedicated Versus Shared Media Bandwidth

Network Technology	*Bandwidth at 30%*	*Bandwidth at 90%*
10 Mb/S Ethernet	375 KB/S	1.125 MB/S
100 Mb/S Ethernet	3.75 MB/S	11.25 MB/S

In a lot of situations, the automatic design assumption is that 100 Mb/S Ethernet should replace 10 Mb/S Ethernet client connections. Actually, moving the client systems to dedicated 10 Mb/S Ethernet is sufficient to handle many situations. A careful analysis will show whether the additional expense of 100 Mb/S ports is necessary.

9.3.5 ATM

Asynchronous transfer mode (ATM) was predicted to take over the networking world in the early 1990s. Several developments, such as the introduction of Gigabit Ethernet, low-cost 100 Mb/S Ethernet interface cards, and low-cost Ethernet switch ports have preempted ATM's predicted takeover. Adding to this, the ability of fast and Gigabit Ethernet to preserve training investments, because the new "flavors" of Ethernet behave just like the older technology, has frequently caused organizations to stick with what they know.

One of the large issues has to do with a fundamental difference between ATM and Ethernet LANs. ATM is a connection-oriented technology, whereas Ethernet LAN is not. Making ATM behave as if it were an Ethernet LAN requires an emulation layer (LAN Emulation, or LANE) that hides the connection-oriented nature of ATM from systems and software that are designed to use a traditional LAN environment. The LANE software, and additional routing hardware required, add cost, complexity, and latency to ATM networking solutions.

ATM still holds a large advantage in environments where a single networking technology is needed to carry data, video, and voice streams, but its complexity and expense have slowed its adoption. ATM is flexible, scalable, and still very useful at the edges of networks, where inter-

8. The only time a collision can occur in a configuration like this is when both the Ethernet switch and the client system attempt to send data at the same time.

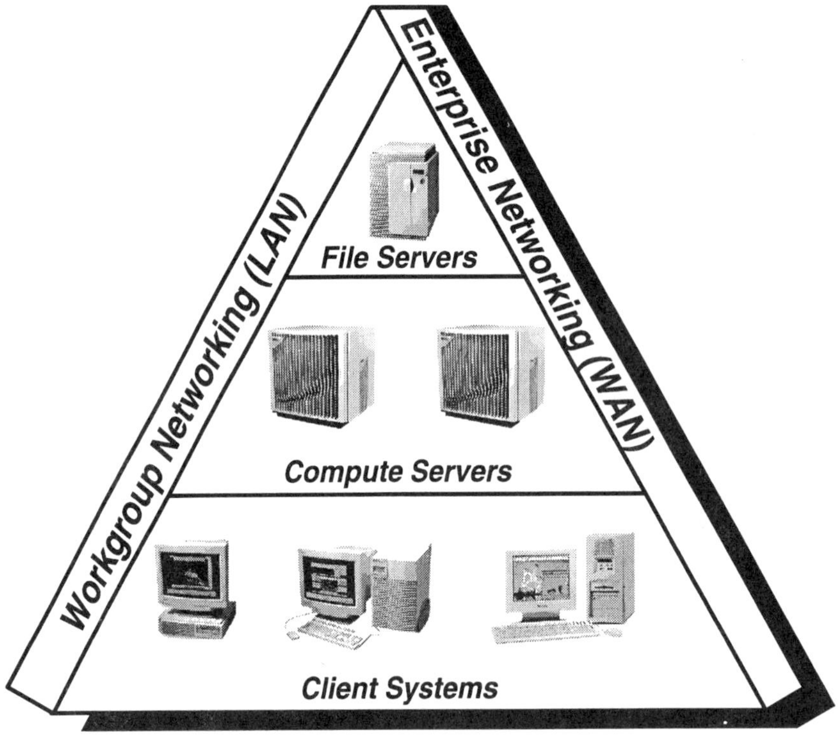

Figure 9-9 Workgroup Hardware and Network Components

faces to telephone company circuits are needed for WAN data transmission. We will discuss the aspects of WAN in the next section.

9.3.6 LAN Technology and Functionality Summary

This section has covered some of the current developments in networking technology that we should be aware of in our design and analysis efforts. Each of the technologies and the associated functionality allow us to craft high-level designs of our workgroup environments or plans for evolving the existing environment towards newer, faster technology. Paying close attention to data flow analysis and expected network usage can help us to select the proper technology from the hierarchies presented here.

Finally, we do not have to be networking specialists to understand the importance of proper partitioning of the network environment. We should, however, rely on the specialists that are available to us for help in managing the intricate details of the network design. It is our responsibility to help translate the network requirements for our workgroup into specifications that will result in a network that supports our higher-level goals.

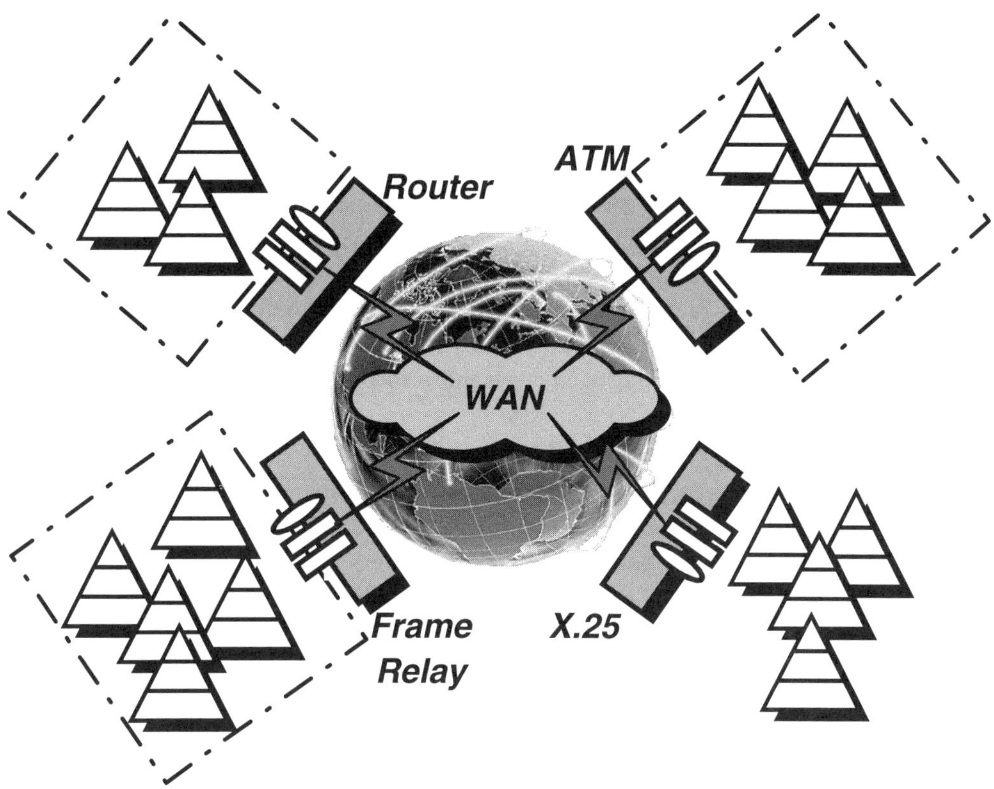

Figure 9-10 Workgroup and Workcenter Interfaces to the WAN

9.4 The WAN Component of Workgroup Networking

The design and management of WAN connections is a very complex, constantly changing topic. For that reason, let's agree that designing WAN connections is beyond the scope of this book. In a workgroup, however, we are required to understand some of the high-level issues involved with WAN connections, their interfaces, and sharing of data and services across a WAN.

A WAN connection between workgroups or workcenters introduces several new areas of consideration *within* the interconnected workgroups. For that reason, we will briefly touch upon some of the issues involved[9]. We may view the WAN as an object, with its own interface characteristics, as described below:

9. For a good treatise on estimating WAN performance, see *Practical Planning for Network Growth*, by John Blommers [4].

9.4.1 The WAN Link Type

The visibility of the WAN link type is usually limited because it is "hidden" from the members of the workgroup behind a network device like a router or an ATM switch. The common link types (router, ATM, frame relay, X.25) are depicted in Figure 9-10 being used to link workcenters together across a wide-area network. Routed, cell-switched, frame relay, and packet-switched networks each has its own characteristic behaviors with regard to error correction, information processing speed, and quality of service features.

These services can be connection oriented (ATM, X.25, frame relay) or connectionless (routers). The distinction between the switches and routers that connect your LAN to the WAN has blurred, with each class of device incorporating protocols and useful features from the other class. Which is used for your WAN, and the performance you can expect, depends on a number of factors, including the cost, existing equipment, and available WAN transport mechanisms.

9.4.2 The WAN Link Speed and Capacity

Familiar transport mechanisms used for wide-area communication are based on T-1 (first-level carrier digital trunk) and T-3 (third-level carrier digital trunk) links, with transfer rates of 56 Kb/S to 1.544 Mb/S (twenty-four 56 Kb/S channels) and 45 Mb/S (44.736 Mb/S), respectively. In contrast to LAN technologies, which only generate frames when necessary, wide-area data transports synchronously generate frames one after the other. If data is available to "ride" in the frame, then it is sent, otherwise an "idle" frame is sent to keep the remote receiver awake and synchronized.

Another common set of transports are based on synchronous optical network (SONET), an all digital, framed[10] transport used in the United States. Most modern transports are designed to allow the older T-1 and T-3 standards to fit comfortably "inside" of the new transmission rates. SONET operates at speed increments of 51.84 Mb/S and above, with several well-defined data rates above that.

Table 9-2 on page 159 shows some of the possible data rates in the SONET hierarchy; currently there are levels defined up to OC-256 (13271.040 Mb/S)! The STS acronym stands for synchronous transport signal level, and is the electrical specification for input devices. The OC stands for optical carrier level and refers to fiber-optic networks. Every SONET level is a multiple of the base OC-1 data rate of 51.84 Mb/S.

We mention this information because you may have encountered some of these "magic" numbers in conversations about ATM, which is designed to ride on top of SONET. You are more and more likely to come into contact with this technology if your environment contains ATM switching equipment providing WAN links to a telephone company. SONET data rates are the "speeds and feeds" for the external WAN carrier technology in the United States, and similar speeds are available in the rest of the world.

10. Overhead, such as routing and virtual channel information is added to the data to make up a complete "frame", much as an Ethernet frame comprises a packet header and data sections.

Table 9-2 SONET Data Rates and Terminology

SONET Description	*Speed (Mb/S)*
Full Duplex STS-1 or OC1	51.84
SONET STS-3 or OC-3	155.52
SONET STS-12 or OC-12	622.08
SONET STS-24 or OC-24	1244.16
SONET STS-48 or OC-48	2488.32
...	...
SONET STS-256 or OC-256	13271.04

The point to be made, and the thing to keep in mind when doing design work, is the difference in speed and capacity between the LAN technology and the WAN technology used to link multiple LANs together. Even though the SONET channel rates listed above are impressive, you need to remember that those channels are shared by many users. To have access to a dedicated, high-speed channel, you must be willing to spend a lot of money, and there must be a local drop point for the service (quite often a telephone switching facility) within reach.

9.4.3 The WAN Link Latency

A WAN link between two LAN environments adds latency to the transmission of packets. How much latency is added depends on the LAN-to-WAN-to-LAN translation equipment, the distance the packets must travel (in whatever altered form), and the speed of the intervening link—among other possible parameters. Our job is to minimize or eliminate as much latency in our environment as we can or to place resources in such a way that latency is minimized.

Too much latency can have some interesting effects on time-dependent services and protocols. If a service provider is located across a WAN link and the client system expects a response within a period of time that is close to the transit time across the link, then the client can end up "missing" the server's response. Situations like this can cause client retransmissions even though the server's response may already be on its way.

Some protocols like the Network Time Protocol (NTP) actually account for the possible latency in the link between client and server. Other protocols, like the one used by NFS (PV2),

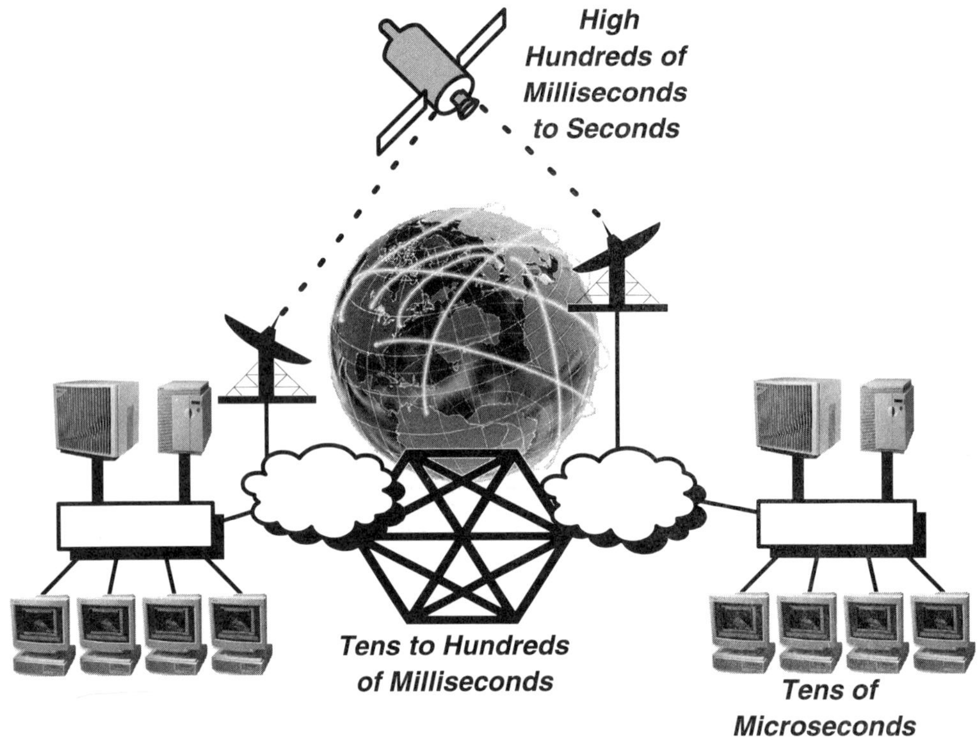

Figure 9-11 WAN to LAN Pathway Latencies

built on top of UDP, were not originally designed to run across a WAN[11]. Trying to "force fit" a LAN-based service into a WAN situation is a recipe for disappointment.

Take one of the pathways in Figure 9-11, for example. Assuming the satellite is in geosynchronous orbit (approximately 22,300 miles) above the earth's surface, the pathway latency between the two LAN segments for a request-response pair becomes 480 milliseconds *best case*[12]. The land-based segment, if it were three thousand miles across the United States, is on the order of thirty-two milliseconds.

11. I have seen this done in several environments by increasing the NFS time-outs and decreasing the size of an NFS read and write request. This amounts to tuning the LAN environment "down to" the WAN performance level, resulting in performance losses in the LAN environment. This is NOT recommended.

12. Here we are ignoring the delays inserted by all intervening transmission equipment and the land-based connection latency between the LAN segments and the satellite transceivers. We are also assuming the speed of light in the calculations, which travels at 186,000 miles per second in a vacuum, slower in other media.

9.4.4 WAN Link Security

Whenever we start sending data across a network link that leaves our sphere of control, we need to worry about whether or not someone else will have access to that data. Whether that data is clear-text passwords being typed into a terminal emulator or design data being transported by a network file system, some form of protection is needed. What we need here is "industrial strength" encryption of the data moving over the WAN to prevent interception by prying eyes.

Secure services and applications for the WAN may be built on top of secure RPC mechanisms like DCE/RPC. This transport provides encryption for WAN operation if the service's designer desires. The encryption and decryption of the RPC data is handled transparently by the underlying software when the packets are sent and received. The DFS file system uses this method to protect file data in transit between client and server systems.

One other potential technological solution is the virtual private network, or VPN. A network of this type may use a public network, like the Internet, as its transport instead of dedicated private circuits. Packets entering the public portion of the network are encrypted and encapsulated in the transport of the public network, possibly by the WAN interface hardware. When the packets reach their final destination, they are unpacked, decrypted, and passed on to the destination systems.

9.4.5 Reliability of the WAN Link

One final WAN link characteristic to examine is total reliability. Under this umbrella, we can consider both total availability and the inherent error rate for a particular link type. Both link characteristics have potential impacts on reliability in the LAN environment, but in different ways.

There are a number of different WAN transport technologies available, including satellite links, microwave links, and fiber connections. Each WAN technology has its own associated bit error rate—only a certain number of bits can pass through the media before one or more are altered or dropped. Data-transmission errors in a portion of a packet's data can cause a retransmission by the sender when the errors are discovered. Retransmissions can cause additional load on the network and the systems involved.

If a link frequently becomes unavailable, then the services and data across the link from a particular workgroup become unavailable also. Tightly coupled dependencies between the systems and services in workgroups separated by a WAN can result in "remote control" outages when the link drops. It is best to replicate services or design loosely coupled relationships with resources across the WAN; we can never know when a careless worker with a back-hoe is in our network link's future.

Some technologies, for example, ATM, are allowed to drop cells (or packets) in the event that the network becomes congested at some point in the circuit. Dropping even a single 53 byte cell can cause an entire frame to be retransmitted. While this is not strictly a media transmission error, the end results are the same—a retransmission of the original data and a reduction in throughput.

9.5 Network Performance Monitoring

Network performance monitoring is a crucial aspect of the network infrastructure. Many pieces of network hardware provide statistics on throughput, utilization levels, and error conditions. This information is your best source for finding network bottlenecks, eliminating errors, or confirming that the network is operating properly.

In addition to the performance information, most network vendors also provide remote access to configuration parameters and system administration features. Network management frameworks, like Hewlett-Packard's OpenView, allow discovery of network topology and integration of network management functions. Without such tools, both network managers and workgroup designers are "flying blind", reduced to guesswork about dynamic network behavior.

Network monitoring is an essential part of the infrastructure, because it provides the data needed to make decisions about adjusting network capacity, workgroup and workcenter hardware distribution, and other higher-level workgroup management decisions. This is an important point—you cannot separate the network performance from the performance of the applications and hardware that use it. There must be a way to share performance data between the network management staff and the workgroup system managers[13].

9.6 Workgroup Network Design Suggestions

Our study of networking in this chapter should point out some major design goals when we are analyzing or designing a workgroup environment. Some of those goals follow.

"Switch the LAN, Route the WAN" For additional performance, using switched Ethernet technology should be the basis for our workgroup. Routers still have their valid place in the network hierarchy, but that is at the edge of the network, where they provide security and interfaces to the WAN and Internet environments.

Dedicated Switch Ports Dedicating Ethernet switch ports to single client systems can dramatically improve performance over shared collision domain configurations, particularly in demanding environments. Dedicated Ethernet switch ports can also speed system installation where image installation techniques are used to roll out multiple client systems simultaneously.

Flat Workgroups Removing routers from the workgroup environment is the first step toward a flat network with little or no routing. Not only does the lack of routing improve performance, it can also simplify system administration efforts by making physical moves easier, eliminating routing related configuration tasks, and minimizing the number of servers needed for services like NIS that are located by broadcasting.

13. While this seems like an obvious point, there are many environments where this does not occur. There may be organizational "disconnects" between the network managers and other system managers because of political divisions, outsourcing, personality conflicts, or other barriers.

Be Wary of the Concentration Effect I like to think of the workgroups in a network as a set of funnels, with client systems at the bottom, which concentrate network traffic towards the "top" of the network hierarchy. Pay close attention to possible peak data rates, and look for and avoid network equipment that has oversubscribed backplanes because they will tend to be choke points during peak usage.

Find and Eliminate Network Bottlenecks It is impossible to completely divorce the network portion of the environment from the applications and services that use it. Many locations suffer from network bottlenecks and performance issues that stem from a lack of understanding of what the network is capable of and how it is being used. See Appendix B for a technique for locating possible network bottlenecks by analyzing NFS data flows.

This is the place to repeat the old adage, "You cannot manage what you do not measure", with respect to installing network management tools. Because of the nature of client-server environments and their dependence on the network, constant vigilance and readjustment of resources is necessary. Without the proper network measurement and management tools, this task is very difficult or impossible.

Use the Available Bandwidth Hierarchy We are blessed with a large number of bandwidth choices for our network hierarchy—be sure to select the proper one for the proper job and traffic rate. Use shared 10 Mb/S or 100 Mb/S technology where appropriate, but do not shy away from trunked versions of ten, one hundred, or Gigabit Ethernet links.

"Single Large Pipe" to Servers When configuring server machines, use single, "large-pipe" configurations for the network link. This can be single, physical one hundred or Gigabit Ethernet links or logical links that are composed of aggregate collections.

Include Legacy Technologies Because our network environments are constantly evolving, there are legacy technologies, interfaces, and associated networking equipment that must be dealt with. Many of the switches that exist today can deal with technologies that are considered legacy (or borderline legacy), like FDDI or token ring.

Use Loosely Coupled Dependencies Across the WAN Loosely coupled client-server relationships can help insulate client systems from the loss of a WAN link. Instead of an immediate failure, a loosely coupled relationship may help hide the short-term loss of a WAN link, much like a UPS can protect a computer system from the temporary loss of power. Some services are easier to deploy in this fashion than others.

Services like the Domain Name Service (DNS) are essential to the proper functioning of the workgroup. DNS is inherently distributed and hierarchical in nature, so accessing it means that sooner or later a WAN link must be crossed to obtain required information from a server. There are several possible configurations for a DNS server, and it is possible to create a "caching only" server in a workgroup that will take all local requests from clients, forward them to external servers, and cache the replies locally. In the event of a WAN failure, the local DNS caching server will continue servicing local clients with information from previous requests.

9.7 Network Infrastructure Summary

The network infrastructure is one of the most important members of the workgroup hierarchy. Without it, every computer in the environment becomes an island of information. The pace of network technology evolution makes it difficult to keep the system performance matched with the available network technology.

Along with network technology progression, the topology of the LAN and the WAN have evolved at each change in available technology. The LAN, in particular, has evolved from shared collision domains to shared media hub, routed networks, and fully switched LAN environments. Understanding this progression, and where your environment is, can help in the design of new environments and the migration of old ones.

As workgroup designers, we now have many more tools at our disposal than our predecessors did. We have ATM, Ethernet, Fast Ethernet, Gigabit Ethernet, and Ethernet link aggregation to help us craft a network bandwidth hierarchy. We have hubs, layer 2 switches, layer 3 switches, and routers to create LAN and WAN connections and to interface to legacy technologies like FDDI and token ring. Our tool box runneth over, but this is a *good* thing!

With these tools we can control the size of our collision domains and broadcast domains. We can choose the proper bandwidth for client, server, and backbone connections. We can control and filter the streams of data running along the backplane of the virtual computers that we provide to our users.

With the available technologies, we can connect the virtual computers in our workgroups together with other virtual computers across WAN links. Even though those links are slower than the interconnections in the LAN, the data sharing that is the primary focus of the workgroup environment dictates no boundaries. We divide the networking components of our workgroup environment into a hierarchy consisting of WAN and LAN components—applying different design techniques and technologies to each member.

We have touched upon enough technology in this chapter to write several books. At this point, we must stop and move on to the other layers of the workgroup model. The more you can learn about the network and associated technology, however, the better foundation you can build for your workgroup environments.

CHAPTER 10

Hardware Architecture: Determining Resource Distribution

This chapter discusses the importance of having a regularly defined hardware architecture for our workgroup environment and recommends some approaches to achieve it. A regular hardware architecture serves as the basis for replicated structure and repeatable designs. It can also help implement enterprise-wide design, management, and implementation processes. As we will see in later chapters, the regular hardware architecture will help simplify the upper layers of the workgroup.

While our major focus is on the hardware architecture layer of the five-layer workgroup model, it is impossible to completely divorce this layer from the network infrastructure below it or the operating environment above it. Some of the discussion in this chapter will build upon the information in the previous chapter and will set the stage for information in the coming chapters. This follows the basic nature of workgroup dependencies.

To start this chapter, we will again examine the hardware tiers of the three-tier client-server architecture and the application components that map onto them. We will begin to show how the workgroup services (software) and their mapping to hardware components can help us determine the resource distribution necessary in the workgroup. We will present some of the more common services and move on to designing scalable workgroup building blocks based on the service-to-hardware pairings.

10.1 Client-Server Components and Hardware Mappings

As we mentioned back in Chapter 5, the three-tier client-server architecture is the fundamental structure that we will use for our workgroup designs. The general mapping of the three client-server application components onto the three hardware tiers are shown in Figure 10-1.

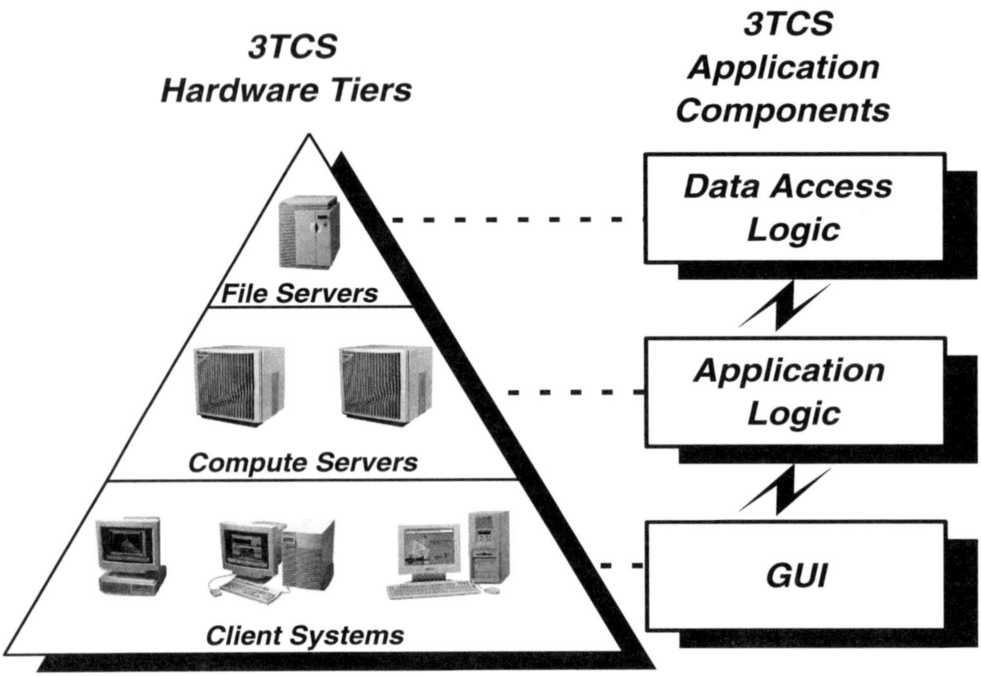

Figure 10-1 Three-Tier Client-Server Application Component Mapping

This arrangement allows us to add specialized servers to the environment to provide service support for client systems and to treat legacy systems as a class of specialized service.

To get more specific when talking about three-tier "application components" and the necessary hardware, we need to re-open the discussion about other workgroup software components (See page 7). Distribution services and support services within the workgroup infrastructure are the glue that make it possible to distribute components of the client-server applications across the workgroup (and enterprise) environment. The distribution services, support services, and the application components all need underlying hardware resources for execution.

Those hardware resources might be located in the workgroup, workcenter, or "out there" in the enterprise, but we will concentrate on the local resources first. Without the proper partitioning of the underlying hardware resources, the application components and the distribution services could end up competing with each other for workgroup resources. Without the proper location and performance of the services, the application components may not perform properly or may even fall apart.

10.2 Scalable Workgroup Building Blocks

We have mentioned scalable workgroup building blocks for the three hardware tiers and their support and distribution services. These building blocks may be the basis for scaling the

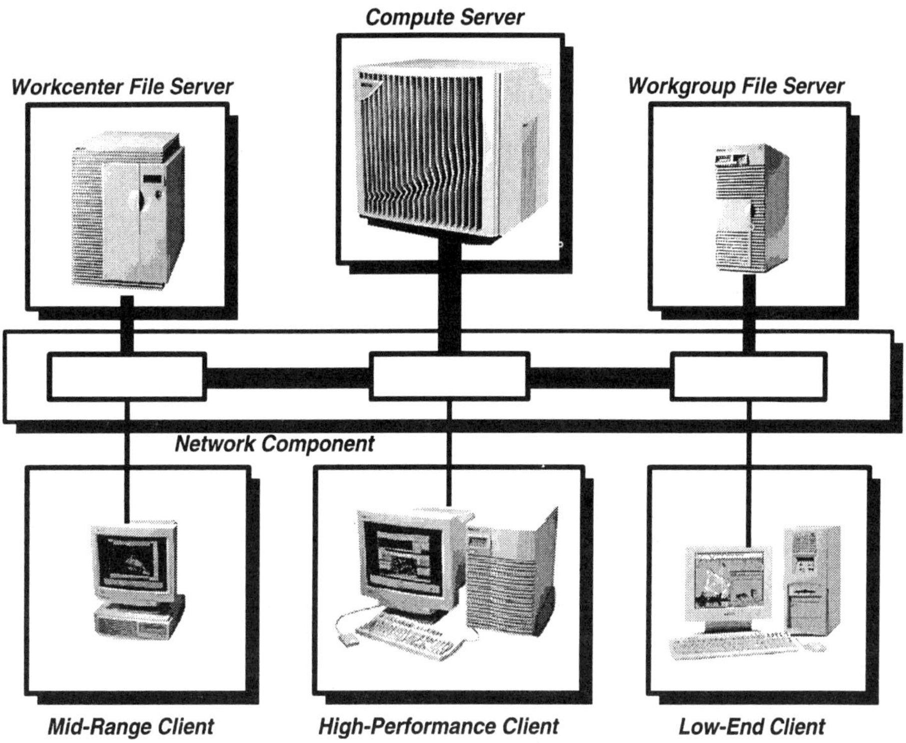

Figure 10-2 Common 3TCS Workgroup Building Blocks

associated functionality and providing replication of the same services within multiple workgroups and workcenters. In other words, when we put the effort into configuring a service and its associated hardware, we want to make sure that they are scalable and reusable across all workgroups that require it.

Using a set of commonly encountered building blocks, we can determine ahead of time what scalable hardware resources are required and the amount of system administration effort needed to support the workgroup. With this approach, instead of hand-crafting each workgroup environment, we may begin to build on past experience and save implementation time and effort. This is not to say that our set of building blocks will cover all situations—when a new and distinct need appears, we may need to design a new building block[1].

Those of you who are familiar with software development will again realize that I am attempting to apply principles from that discipline to workgroup design. All of the arguments for regularity of structure (objects), simple interfaces, reduced complexity, and minimal dependen-

1. I can hear the more creative system administrators in the audience breathing a sigh of relief.

cies arise from lessons learned in software-development projects. We would like to choose a pre-existing design element, scale it to our environment, and predict its behavior, reliability, and administration cost—all based on past experience with the particular building block.

There may be multiple types of file servers and compute servers in the workgroup structure, along with the client systems. To account for differences in configuration and performance scaling, we will define a set of scalable building blocks for our workgroup that include some of the more common workgroup components. Several of the common building blocks are shown in Figure 10-2, including a workgroup file server, a workcenter file server, and several different configurations of client systems.

There are many other examples of the building blocks used to implement different workgroup environments, such as a compilation server and a configuration management server for a software development workgroup. Discovering the individual building blocks in your environment is part of the design or analysis task work, much like determining the client system classes present. We need to apply the same object-oriented analysis process to the workgroup building block environment that we applied to finding client system classes.

It is important to note that the workgroup network is also a building block and must be evaluated based on the scaling needs of the individual workgroup components. Many times the network hardware and the physical wiring configuration is overlooked, resulting in performance issues. The network component itself comprises of individual building blocks, such as ethernet switches, that we discussed in Chapter 9.

In addition to the separately identifiable hardware resources (individual computer systems) that support corresponding software services, there are services that require resources and may not have their own dedicated hardware entities. These are services and associated resources that may be combined or superimposed onto existing computer systems that are part of the standard building blocks. Care must be taken to ensure that there are enough resources for these services and that they do not interfere with one another or the services whose machines they share[2].

10.3 Commonly Encountered Workgroup Components

The first step in determining the resource distributions is to identify as many of the services and application components used in the environment as possible. From this list, we may identify special services or components that require dedicated hardware resources. The remaining services may be collapsed or consolidated onto existing machines, creating shared resources.

10.3.1 "Hidden" or Integrated Client-Server Distribution Services

Distribution services are required for support of the client-server applications in the workgroup environment. If services of this type must share hardware resources with other services, or

2. We must differentiate between making a conscious choice for service location and simply using the "default" approach. One approach attempts to find optimal placement and the other merely preserves status quo.

are running on systems with compute intensive tasks, then clients of the service may suffer from degraded performance. Cataloging some of the common services and how they are implemented can help us avoid this "destructive interference" between two or more services.

Some of the services are integrated into the operating system of the server and client systems that use them. Because of this integration, they will not require dedicated hardware resources. We mention them because they do require system administration effort and they do need to be present to support important workgroup functionality.

Service Name	Description	Dedicated Server Resources?
TCP/IP	Transport allowing common internetworking of client and server systems	No, integrated into each system
Dial-up networking	Transport allowing remote access to workgroup resources (PPP, PTP, SLIP, or other dial-up protocols)	Recommended[a]
Remote login/ execution facilities[b]	Allow user authentication and execution of applications on remote systems	No, integrated into each system
X-Windows System	Sharing of application displays across the network	Yes, on Unix client system[c]
Open Network Computing RPC (ONC)	RPC mechanism used by NFS, NIS, and other distributed services and applications	No, integrated into OS if NIS and NFS are used
DCE RPC	RPC mechanism used by DCE and DFS	No, integrated into OS if DCE or DFS are used

a. Support for dial-up networking implies special server resources like banks of modems and additional security measures, but is placed here for "proximity" to TCP/IP.

b. Examples of this type of service are the Unix Telnet, REXEC, RSH, and RLOGIN services.

c. The X-Windows system is an integral part of all major Unix systems, but must be added to Microsoft operating systems.

Network Transport Services and Remote Access The network transport used within the workgroup needs to be robust and support interoperability between multiple vendors' platforms. That job is filled by the de facto industry standard, Internet Protocol (IP), which provides both unreliable datagram (UDP/IP) and reliable (TCP/IP) data stream transport mechanisms. Virtually all of the services that we will use are based on one of the two services that are integrated into most modern operating systems.

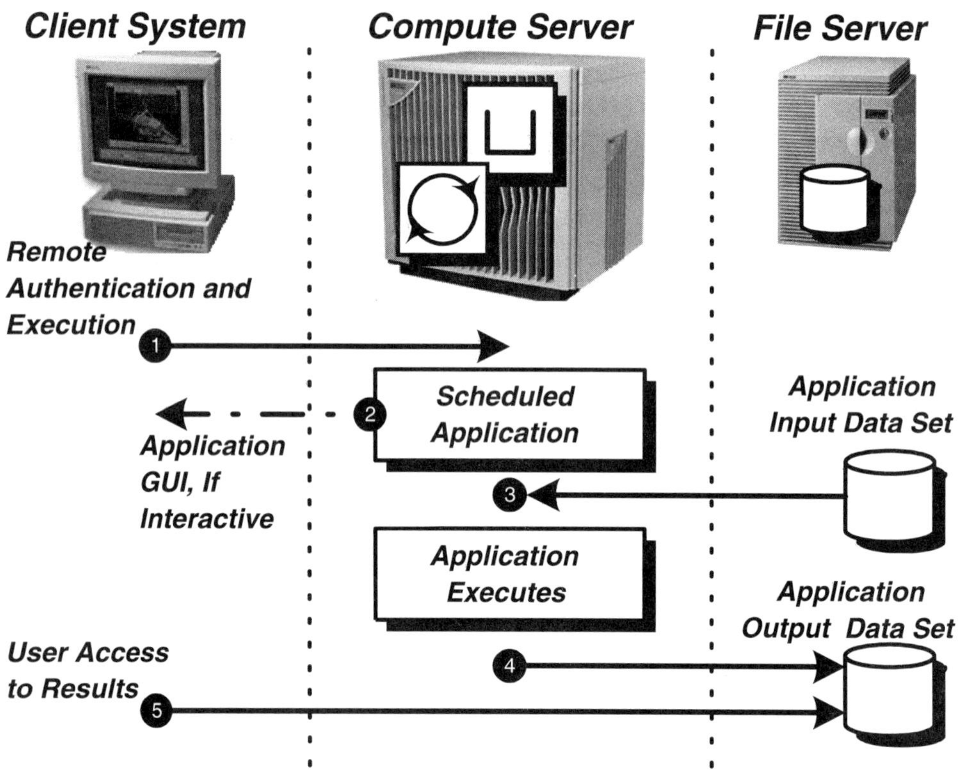

Figure 10-3 Components of Remote Application Execution

The ability to extend TCP/IP protocol services to remote clients via a dial-up (phone or ISDN) link is becoming important as more and more workgroup users need to participate in the network from locations outside the physical workgroup LAN. Protocols like SLIP and PPP, along with services like the Microsoft Windows remote access server (RAS) provide this type of access. It is desirable for security and performance reasons to dedicate hardware resources to this type of service.

The close integration between the IP protocols and the higher-level services that use them creates a set of direct dependencies in all workgroup systems. If the network topology and the individual system's configuration are not properly designed and managed, all of the higher-level services, and eventually the client-server applications relying on them, will suffer. The higher-level services depend on configuration, security, and system administration decisions that are covered in the next chapter.

Remote Authentication, Execution, and GUI Projection Several of the high-level services provided by the operating system are absolutely essential to implementing a 3TCS workgroup. Those services involve the ability to perform remote authentication (login) to remote systems, execute a remote application, project the remote application's GUI to the client system, and transparently access data sets representing the application's input and resultant output. Without these basic services, it is impossible to make use of the second-tier (compute server) portion of the 3TCS workgroup.

This process is depicted in Figure 10-3, with time running from top to bottom in the picture. Because the job is too "large" in terms of computational resources, the client system is free to perform other tasks while the task executes. In this example, all three tiers of the workgroup participate in obtaining the final result for the user.

One could make an argument that the load-balancing service could handle the remote authentication and services in place of the operating facilities. This solution, however, has to consider the extra cost of the load-balancing software against the existing, "free" services provide by the operating system. Even assuming that a load-balancing service handles the authentication and remote execution on behalf of the user, interactive jobs require the ability to project an interactive application's GUI over the network.

On Unix systems, we take the remote execution facilities for granted. We also make great use of the fact that they are available to both programmatic access and access from scripting languages. The flexibility and accessibility of these services means that they are frequently used, along with the X-Windows system to make use of specialized compute resources in our client-server workgroups.

Some systems do not provide these services at all or provide only minimal client functionality. Windows NT 4.0 falls into the latter category, providing minimal Telnet, RSH, REXEC, and RCP *client* support with the standard operating system. There are no standardized mechanisms to project remote GUIs either, although there are some promises for this functionality future releases.

10.3.2 Flexible Client-Server Distribution Services

We will now examine a second set of available client-server distribution services that may require dedicated hardware resources or specialized system configurations. These services may be configured with their own dedicated hardware resource if needed, or can share resources with other services if cost savings are necessary. Table 10-1 on page 172 lists some of this type of services.

Name Resolution Services Computer systems in a network communicate by means of hardware addresses like MAC addresses and TCP/IP address and a set of well-defined protocols. This communication is done very efficiently by means of binary sequences that are less

Table 10-1 Common Client-Server Distribution Services

Distribution Service Name	Service Description	Dedicated Server Resources?
Domain Name Service (DNS)	Distributed lookup of hostname and TCP/IP address associations	Not a requirement
Windows Internet Name Service (WINS)	Resolves NetBIOS names to TCP/IP addresses. Runs on Windows systems only.	Not a requirement
Windows NT Domain Controller	Provides distributed user authentication and licensing services for Windows systems	Not a requirement[a]
DCE Registry	Distributed, replicated user authentication service designed for WAN use	Not required
Kerberos	Authentication service used by DCE and other secure services (secure FTP, Telnet)	Not required, but server should be physically secure
Network Information Service (NIS)	Single point distribution of login, networking, and data access information	Not a requirement
Load Balancing	Provides location and scheduling of resources for specialized applications	No, shares location with resource
Distributed Component Object Model (DCOM)	Windows DCOM allows location and scheduling and communication with distributed objects	No, shares location with resource
Common Object Request Broker Architecture (CORBA)	Common Object Request Broker allows location and scheduling and communication with distributed objects	No, shares location with resources
Dynamic Host Configuration Protocol (DHCP)	Dynamically assigns TCP/IP address and default workgroup information like time server, NIS server, and netmask	Not required
Software Licensing	Enables use of software requiring network licensing	Not required
DCE Cell Directory Service (CDS)	Distributed, replicated directory service used by DCE applications	Not required
Time Synchronization	Required by services like DCE to ensure replication and security	Not required[b]

a. These services are available with Windows NT Server and from translator file systems like Samba. For scaling, dedicated resources are recommended.

b. Time synchronization requires either a network time source or an accurate local time source.

than, shall we say, human readable[3]. The translation between these less-than-friendly network addresses and human readable names is performed by name services like the Domain Name Service (DNS) or the Windows Internet Name Service (WINS).

Name-to-network address translation may also be done by NIS, which can be configured to use DNS as a backup, and by files on the computer system doing the lookup (/etc/hosts on Unix and "*systemroot*\system32\drivers\etc\Hosts" on Windows NT). WINS runs on Windows NT servers and resolves NetBIOS names to IP addresses, and DNS runs on a wide range of operating systems to translate internet names to IP addresses. Fortunately, Windows clients may also use DNS to resolve IP addresses[4].

We will deal more with the configuration of these basic services in Chapter 15.

User Authentication and Security Services Some of the authentication services, like Unix NIS or Windows primary or backup domain controllers (PDC or BDC), may be frequently accessed by systems that are looking up user authentication or licensing information. If the service is heavily used we can "convert" an otherwise general-purpose system being shared by several systems into a resource that provides only the desired service. An example of this would be dedicating a Windows NT system to provide only print services, even though it could be a domain controller, remote access server, or file server.

Both NIS servers and the Windows domain controllers provide user authentication and other essential information to client systems in the workgroup. Each of these services may be replicated to provide scalability and immunity to service loss. Also, both of these services are found by broadcast requests from the client systems, and so must be located such that they are within the broadcast domain of the clients that will use them.

In routed workgroup environments, where each segment is also a subnet, location by broadcast can mean that a large amount of system administration effort is needed to support the service. This is because one slave (or backup) server per subnet (broadcast domain) is required. Flat, switched environments eliminate this additional overhead. In a switched environment, only a primary and a one or two backup servers are needed unless loading or network topology dictates otherwise.

The DCE registry is a user authentication service which obtains DCE credentials for a user. It interacts with the Kerberos authentication server to perform the authorization. The Kerberos version 5 key distribution center server is an integral part of the DCE authentication scheme. The DCE registry is designed to be highly available and distributed.

Load-Balancing Service The load-balancing service may require some dedicated workgroup resources for proper operation. These resources can be as specialized as a "master" scheduling node, dedicated queue directories, and memory and CPU resources for performing

3. Okay, I admit it. There are those of us who can read and understand the darned things.

4. First, the NetBIOS and the internet host name can be configured to be the same. Second, a DNS server running on a Windows NT server may query a WINS server for the NetBIOS translation.

management and scheduling tasks. What the actual requirements are will depend on the load-balancing service chosen for the job.

To submit requests for remote resources, the load-balancing client interface must be available. To accept scheduling requests a server must have the load-balancing server software installed or allow access via remote authentication and execution services. What software is required where depends on the configuration requirements of the load-balancing software itself.

Object Request Brokers and Interprocess Communication Several object-oriented services like the Windows Distributed Component Object Model (DCOM) and the Common Object Request Broker Architecture[5] (CORBA) are frameworks defining interaction between application objects in the workgroup environment. Each of these frameworks has components that are responsible for the location, activation, and communication with remote objects.

In the CORBA framework, the Object Request Broker (ORB) handles the object actions, described above, on behalf of the client. While neither of these services requires dedicated hardware resources, they must be highly available. Unfortunately, neither service interoperates with the other.

Dynamic Host Configuration Protocol Service Dynamic Host Configuration Protocol (DHCP) runs on Unix and Windows NT Server, allowing a client system to obtain an IP address from a centrally managed location. In addition to the IP address, a client system may obtain other default configuration information, such as netmask, default gateway, default routes, NIS server, time synchronization server, and several other parameters. DHCP can save a lot of system configuration effort if used properly.

The DHCP server runs on both Unix and Windows NT Server, and both operating system types have DHCP client software. One of the useful features provided by DHCP is the ability to define DHCP "pool groups" that are serviced by a single DHCP server. Client systems that request DHCP information specify their pool group in the request and are answered only by the server that "owns" the pool group.

Unfortunately, the Windows NT DHCP server does not fully implement this functionality, meaning that the Windows NT DHCP server answers all DHCP requests whether or not they were intended for it. To work around this situation, the DHCP client software may be configured to ignore any response not from the pool group specified in its original request. It would be nice to have the flexibility to run both the Unix and Windows version of the server in the same workgroup, if needed.

Software-Licensing Service There are several-software licensing services available today, all of which involve one or more server processes that maintain a database of vendor-generated license keys. When a user wants to execute a licensed application, the application requests a license from the license server. If a free license is available execution is granted, but if

5. See the Object Management Group's web page at *WWW.OMG.org* for more information on CORBA.

there are no free licenses available the application terminates or waits for a license to be released.

There are several design issues that involve the licensing service and its location. First, the license server must be accessible to every machine in the workgroup that requires run-time licensing. A license server may be located by broadcast or by "hard-coding" a particular license server machine into a client's configuration. If a client is unable to locate an active license server, then applications may terminate or enter a holding pattern, waiting for a license.

Second, the license server must be highly available. Most licensing schemes incorporate "keep-alive" or "call-back" operations to ensure that an application crash will not keep a license tied up indefinitely. If the license server or its system become unavailable, not only will new application users be unable to obtain licenses, but executing applications may fail or spend time waiting for call backs to time out.

The last issue involves perceived application performance. If there are many users, many licensed applications, or high levels of licensing activity, then a dedicated set of resources for licensing is needed. If the proper license server resources are not provided, then users will be unable to use the desired applications or will have to wait for licensing activities to complete. Hidden difficulties like this can help to contribute to negative perceptions of workgroup performance and stability.

DCE and DFS Specific Services The DCE environment comprises many different services and associated server processes. Some of those are the Cell Directory Service (CDS), the Global Directory Service (GDS), the Distributed Time Service (DTS), and the DCE Security Service (DSS or GSS). Each of the DCE services is a client-server configuration and is highly configurable as to location within the DCE cell[6].

DFS is a client-server DCE application that takes full advantage of all of the underlying DCE services. DFS also adds fileset location services, backup services, and application update services to the DCE environment. Many of the services run on the DFS server machine and can share hardware resources with the other DFS components.

Time-Synchronization Service There are many services within the workgroup that depend on accurate time values for their operation. As machines begin to share information in a workgroup, the synchronization of time across the workgroup becomes more important. There are several time-synchronization services available, including DTS (for DCE) environments and the Network Time Protocol (NTP). Both DTS and NTP will interoperate with each other.

A software development workgroup provides a very good example of the importance of time synchronization. In a complex software development environment, build tools like the Unix "make" command are used to rebuild elements of the software system being constructed. There are other similar tools that automate the production of complex software components by

6. A DCE cell is a group of systems that is centered around a common set of purposes and DCE services. This definition is very close to the one we are using for the term "workgroup".

examining dependencies between the low-level software units to decide if recompilation is needed.

To determine whether or not a particular component needs recompiling, the make tool looks at the time stamp for the component's source file and compares it to the time stamp of the derived object (result) from the last compilation. If the derived object is "out of date" with the source file, then a compilation is initiated.

It is not difficult to imagine a software development workgroup with multiple client systems sharing a central repository for their software source and derived objects. If the times on each of the clients is sufficiently different from the others, the time stamps of files on the server system will reflect the time variations on the client systems. If the time variations are large enough, a software build may cause some source files not to be recompiled and others to be erroneously compiled, resulting in indeterminate component versions in the final product.

It is a good idea to synchronize times across all members of the workgroup, and as a matter of fact, the DCE security service and several of the DCE replication mechanisms require time synchronization within a certain minimum window or they will not function.

10.4 Data Access Services

Data access services are required to enable the sharing of data between systems in the workgroup or workcenter environment. Table 10-2 on page 177 lists some of the common data access services.

The Network File System As we have previously discussed, a dedicated file server, while not an absolute requirement, is necessary for adequate data access performance via NFS. For this reason, the NFS file server and its associated services will always be represented as a separate hardware resource in the workgroup.

We also have a choice as to whether to implement servers with NFS PV2 or PV3. Protocol version two is the older of the two NFS protocols and is less efficient than the newer version three. Even though the NFS PV3 server is capable of speaking the PV2 dialect, there may be reasons for maintaining servers or clients that speak only the older dialect.

Automatic Data Mount on Access Whenever we describe a task running on a compute server resource accessing data on the file server, we must recognize that there is an implicit assumption involved. That implicit assumption is that the compute server has visibility to the task's data sets on the file server. Somehow the network attached data must be made transparently available to the task, wherever it executes.

In addition to making the data consistently available, our goal is to provide consistent paths to the data, no matter where the user or process is located in the workgroup. Without this consistent naming, the compute server would be required to access the data via paths that depended upon where the job was actually executed—a situation that is impossible to manage. We will discuss more about this path consistency in Chapter 12.

Table 10-2 Common Client-Server Data Access Services

Distribution Service Name	Service Description	Dedicated Server Resources?
Network File System (NFS)	Allows sharing of data between client and server systems in a LAN	Dedicated server recommended
Automatic file system mount on access	Service provided by NFS AutoFS[a] but implicit in DFS and Dfs	Client system (AutoFS)
Server Message Block (SMB)	Microsoft Windows-based protocol that provides LAN data sharing	Dedicated server recommended[b]
Microsoft Distributed file system (Dfs)	Microsoft data sharing based on Common Internet File System (CIFS) protocol[c]	Dedicated servers recommended
DCE Distributed File System (DFS)	Allows secure, replicated access of data across LAN and WAN environments	Dedicated servers recommended[d]
NFS/DFS Secure Gateway	Allows NFS clients to mount a DFS file system, while preserving DFS security	Dedicated DFS client recommended
Web Server	Application and data access via web browser	Dedicated servers recommended
Proxy Server	Provides secure access to resources outside the workgroup via FTP or HTTP	Dedicated server recommended

a. AutoFS mounts the correct file system from a server based on "maps" that may be distributed via NIS.

b. Microsoft Windows NT is packaged in Windows NT Workstation and Windows NT Server forms. Clients may share data between themselves, but features desirable for large shares are available only in the Server configuration.

c. The CIFS protocol is based on the Windows SMB protocol.

d. The DFS namespace is a collection of filesets that may be located on multiple servers and are position independent (name does not imply location), allowing replication.

Server Message Block Services and Microsoft Dfs The remote resource access protocol used by Windows systems is Server Message Block (SMB.) There are several dialects of this protocol in existence, and the CIFS protocol used in Microsoft's Dfs implements a superset of it, designed to execute in WAN environments. Client and servers that use different dialects of SMB are capable of negotiating a common version of the protocol to use.

In addition to the Windows systems that speak "native" SMB, there are a number of translator packages that make SMB available on a wide range of platforms. So, as workgroup designers, we have a choice as to whether to implement Windows NT Server systems, Unix systems with SMB translators, or both. We must use factors like performance, high availability, interoperability, and administrative cost to decide which approach is best.

DCE DFS and the Secure NFS/DFS Gateway Like NFS, it is best to dedicate a DFS server to the single task of running DFS. This is especially true since DFS is a more complicated file system, with more individual components than NFS. Tests have shown that DFS performs similarly to NFS if the DFS caching features are disabled and has superior performance if the caching features are used.

DFS provides us with a number of features that are very desirable. Among those are high availability (from replication and caching), uniform file access, scalability (high client-to-server ratio), and strong security features. DFS may also interoperate with NFS clients via the NFS/DFS secure gateway.

The NFS/DFS gateway provides NFS client systems with a method of interoperating with DFS. Users with DCE accounts may have fully authenticated access into the DFS data. NFS users without DCE accounts are given unauthenticated access, preserving the security of the DCE environment. System administrator have full control over the extent of the access granted to unauthenticated users via DFS ACLs.

HTTP or "Web" Services An HTTP or web server is a familiar fixture in every network. It can provide data and JAVA-based applications to any client with a web browser. It is likely that there will be several web servers in any workgroup, dedicated to different purposes: project information, administrative applications, or a number of other purposes.

Dedicated resources are recommended for any web server that will maintain a high "hit" rate. A dedicated web server may be tuned for efficiently providing web-based resources to its clients. A shared resource may be suitable for personal web sites or web sites with low hit rates.

Proxy Services A proxy server may be considered a security service, but it really provides controlled access to data outside the workgroup environment. Proxy servers are normally found as workcenter resources, and are used to interface to services in the Internet like remote web or FTP sites, where internal security is an issue. Proxy servers may also provide caching of HTTP data for client systems, attempting to reduce Internet traffic by satisfying as many requests from the common cache as possible.

10.5 Client-Server Support Services

This class of services is not essential to the primary functionality of a client-server application, but it is necessary for a complete solution in the workgroup environment. Many of these services may require dedicated workgroup resources if the workgroup is large enough or can share resources if performance requirements allow.

Electronic Mail Electronic mail is now a service that most of us cannot do without. The mail service may be divided into the client and server (transport) portions. The transport mechanism, whether it is Unix sendmail or some other component, needs to be robust, scalable, and highly available—users will not stand for lost mail or the inability to send e-mail messages.

Table 10-3 Common Client-Server Support Services

Service Name	Description	Dedicated Resources?
Electronic Mail	Communication between users	Recommended
Print Services[a]	Provides users the ability to create hard-copy	Recommended
System Management Console	Provides GUI-based configuration processes for workgroup systems	May be centralized or on every system
System Performance Monitoring	Collects and analyzes workgroup system performance information	May be centralized
Network Management Console	Provides GUI-based configuration processes for network equipment	May be centralized
Network Performance Monitoring	Collects and analyzes workgroup network performance information	May be centralized
Software Distribution	Distributes software packages to workgroup clients and servers	Recommended
System Image Installation	Provides class-based system cloning for clients and servers	Recommended
System Backup Service	Provides data backup services for workgroup servers	Recommended

a. For network enabled printers, the print server may provide boot-time configuration information in addition to spooling services for the printer.

Like many of the support services, whether or not dedicated hardware resources are allocated depends on the usage level. Large numbers of users in the workgroup or high e-mail volumes might dictate one or more dedicated servers for this purpose. Lower volumes of e-mail, or smaller workgroups might dictate shared resources.

Printer Services The decision about dedicated resources for print servers depends on the amount and nature of the printing that occurs in the workgroup. If there is light usage of the print services, then shared resources might suffice. Heavy printing because of a large number of users, project documentation work, electronic FAXing, drafting output requiring raster conversion, or other special needs may dictate dedicated resources.

An additional consideration is the dispersion of the workgroup. If the workgroup is fairly concentrated physically, then a centralized print solution may be best. If the workgroup is geographically dispersed, then a distributed approach is needed.

System-Management Console Most vendor's operating systems provide a GUI-based system administration tool to perform routine system-administration tasks on stand-alone systems. On Hewlett-Packard's HP-UX operating system, this tool is the System Administration Manager (SAM). While this type of tool can help administer local resources, most are not intended for managing the resources for a whole workgroup.

There are system-administration tools intended for managing workgroup sized clusters of computer systems as a cohesive whole. This type of tool may be database driven and may require dedicated resources, depending on the size of the workgroup. The major problem with tools in this classification is scaling[7].

System Performance Monitoring and Analysis Essential for client server environments are tools that allow collection and analysis of system performance parameters over time. In the case of HP-UX, the operating system kernel is instrumented, and over three hundred performance metrics are collected, exported, and made available to performance tools through a well-defined interface. A system manager may choose between real-time graphical display, disk-based logging, and network visible performance data.

When configuring systems that are to run performance-analysis tools, it is important to ensure that enough CPU and RAM resources exist to keep the monitoring software from interfering with the server's primary tasks. The average CPU load for the HP-UX tools is in the two to five percent range, and the associated disk activity depends on the amount of data being collected and the logging frequency. In most cases the minimal load on the system is well worth the ability to locate problems, adjust system resources, and do accurate capacity planning.

Network Management and Performance Monitoring The network management and performance monitoring is just as important to the well-being of the workgroup as the monitoring of the server resource performance. A product like Hewlett-Packard's OpenView network-management platform provides this kind of functionality. If the workgroup is large and contains many systems and manageable devices, a dedicated hardware resource may be needed to support the network-management tools.

Software Distribution Much of the functionality that we are discussing is configured as optional software packages that must be installed, configured, and updated on the target machines. It is desirable to have a common service that can handle the software-distribution function on multiple vendor's platforms. Today there are multiple solutions to the software dis-

7. An example of scaling problems: just how *do* you display icons for a thousand systems on a twenty-inch monitor? Graphical class browsers for software development run into this type of limitation as well when they try to display all class relationships in complicated hierarchies.

tribution challenge, many running on a single platform or offering only minimal support for secondary operating system types.

Each software-distribution service needs dedicated storage for the packages that it makes available for distribution. During the installation process, the CPU and disk resources of the software depot may be heavily loaded, depending on the number of simultaneous installations being performed. A dedicated hardware resource may be needed for each type of installation service (i.e., different Unix variants and Microsoft Windows-based systems).

System Image Installation Aside from the installation of individual software packages, there is the issue of how to deploy the operating system to several hundred client systems in the workgroup. Hand-crafting each client is one solution, but it is extremely labor-intensive, becoming difficult or impossible to manage as the number of client systems grows. A better solution is "image" installation (or cloning) of client systems from a "golden" system image.

Most major Unix vendors support image installation of their operating system. The client system boots over the network from an image installation server, configures the local disks, copies a golden image to the disk, and reboots to the new operating system. This process can save tremendous amounts of system administration time but can also make heavy demands on the image installation server and the network infrastructure.

Because of the huge advantage this approach provides, we should strongly consider designing the network infrastructure and the workgroup services to support it. If multiple client systems are to be installed at once, a dedicated image installation server is strongly recommended, as are dedicated switch ports for clients. In most cases, the faster the network, the faster the image installation proceeds.

It should be noted that this method may also be used to deploy server systems and can form the basis for a very flexible disaster recovery process. We will discuss this more in Chapter 11.

System Backup Services If you have been following our client-server design suggestions, then you will realize that the only data to be backed up in our workgroup design will exist on file servers. These single points of backup in the workgroup can make the backup process much easier than backing up data from hundreds of client systems but can also present unique challenges if the amount of data on the servers is quite large.

We discussed backup hardware possibilities in "File Server Backup" on page 119, so we will defer to that analysis in terms of the hardware configuration required. But we need more than just hardware to support our backup activities. We also need a backup service that can manage multiple parallel backup devices, manage pools of backup media, perform backups over the network if desired, work with hierarchical storage management services if they exist, and support remote control of the backup process in case we wish to utilize centralized management.

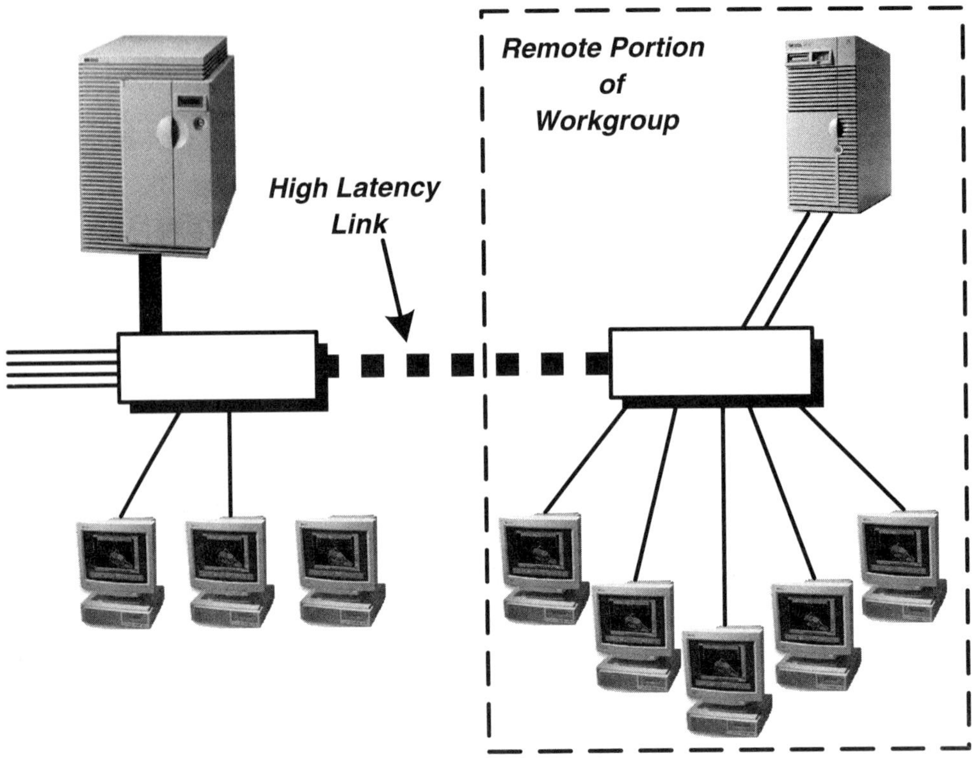

Figure 10-4 Physical or Network Proximity Placement of Resources

10.6 Workgroup Resource Location Strategies

In the previous three sections, we presented an exhausting, but not exhaustive, list of some common services that we might need included in our workgroup environment to support our client-server applications. This set of services was chosen not only because they are a representative set of those commonly encountered in workgroups, but also because they will give us a good "working set" from which to construct example workgroups.

Each of those services is a set of one or more software components that require underlying combinations of network, storage, or computational resources to function. We will now present some general ways of identifying the proper workgroup locations for classes of those resources.

10.6.1 Proximity to Usage

One of the first general strategies that we can use for locating workgroup resources is to place them as close as practically possible to their users. In this way we can minimize the repeated delay that a user experiences when accessing frequently used remote resources. Often

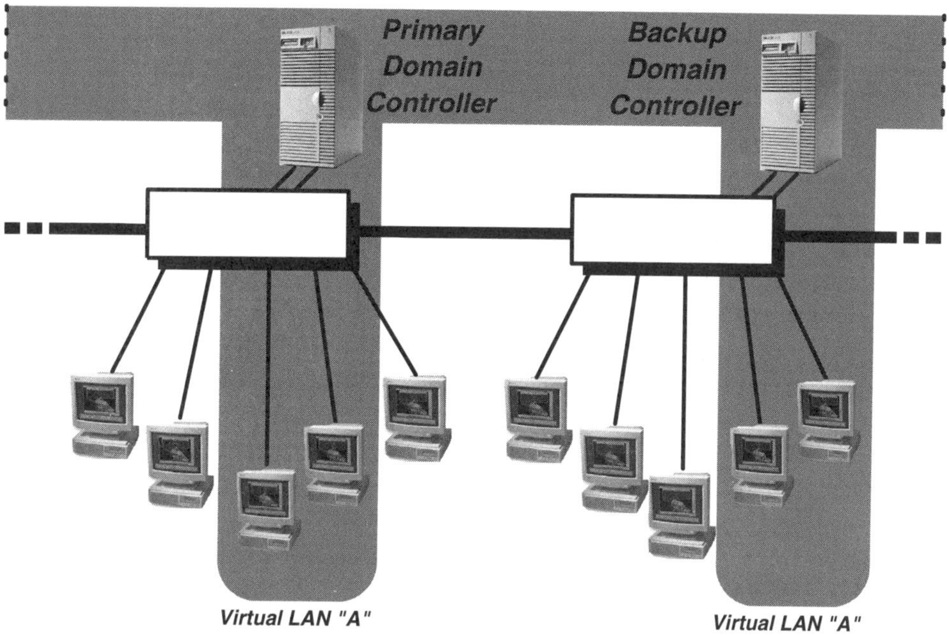

Figure 10-5 Placing Resources to Localize Behavior

both the network proximity and the physical proximity to the resource may be taken into account when placing the resources.

An example of a "physical proximity" configuration might be a remote portion of the workgroup that is located across a slow LAN link like a 56 Kbps T1 leased line or a microwave link between buildings. Local system administration, backups, and software installation might be the requirement because of the low link speed. In this case, locating server resources at the remote site can vastly increase the user's productivity when compared to attempting the access over a slow link, but the requirement for localized system management may be considered a negative aspect of this configuration.

One alternative to this particular configuration is to scale the remote clients back to X-terminals or thin clients, thus reducing the network traffic required to support the remote activities. This approach limits the type of activities that may take place in the remote portion of the workgroup, particularly in the area of high-performance graphics, to applications that are supported by the scaled down client capabilities. This choice may not be acceptable, depending on the tasks performed by the remote users.

There are similar situations, where a slow link is not involved, where this type of resource allocation may improve performance and productivity. Partitioning resources and distributing them so that they are as close as possible to their primary users is one of our design goals. The performance improvement must be traded off against the extra cost associated with providing localized resources, however.

10.6.2 Localization of Behavior

There are a number of workgroup resources that may need to be localized, or reserved, for a particular set of users. This may be because the associated resource usage will interfere with the normal operation of other users in the workgroup, or that the resources themselves need isolation from potential interference by other users in the workgroup. There may be other reasons that a particular set of resources must be set apart from "normal" usage in the workgroup.

For example, we have discussed so-called "chatty" protocols that may create an excessive number of broadcast packets in the network. As we discussed in Chapter 9, networking technology provides us with a way to segregate chatty systems from others in the network. We can control the broadcast traffic from this type of systems by placing them in their own VLAN. This is shown in Figure 10-5.

The diagram depicts several network switches that are connected by a high-speed backbone. The network manager has created a VLAN to isolate Windows-based systems and their primary and backup domain controllers from other systems attached to the switches. This allows the Windows system to broadcast without causing other switch ports to receive the broadcast packets, cutting down on unnecessary broadcast processing by non-Windows nodes.

Another place where this strategy might be used is in dedicated communication links for special uses. A high-availability cluster may need to monitor "heartbeat" packets from each member of the cluster in order to detect system failures. Sometimes dedicated LAN connections are used for system-management purposes and only system administration personnel have access to the dedicated LAN. Yet another example is separating different classes, say interactive versus noninteractive, of LAN traffic from one another to avoid interference.

In the first example, dedicated resources prevent unwanted fail-overs due to heavy LAN traffic. The second example uses a dedicated LAN to provide additional security for system administration services, with only system administration-related systems having access to the separate LAN. Finally, interactive traffic suffers when sharing bandwidth on highly utilized segments, so separating interactive traffic, like X-windows, from other traffic may improve the user's perception of interactive performance.

10.6.3 Hierarchical Placement for Resource Sharing

In Figure 4-5 on page 59, we detailed a hierarchy for network objects that can help us decide where to locate shared resources. That hierarchy details system, workgroup, workcenter, and enterprise classes of resources. But what criteria do we use to place objects and associated resources in one of the levels of this hierarchy? Three reasons might be shared cost, increased utilization, or increased visibility of services.

The compute resource showed in Figure 10-6, at the workcenter level of the hierarchy, is shared by two workgroups. The sharing of this particular resource may be dictated by its pur-

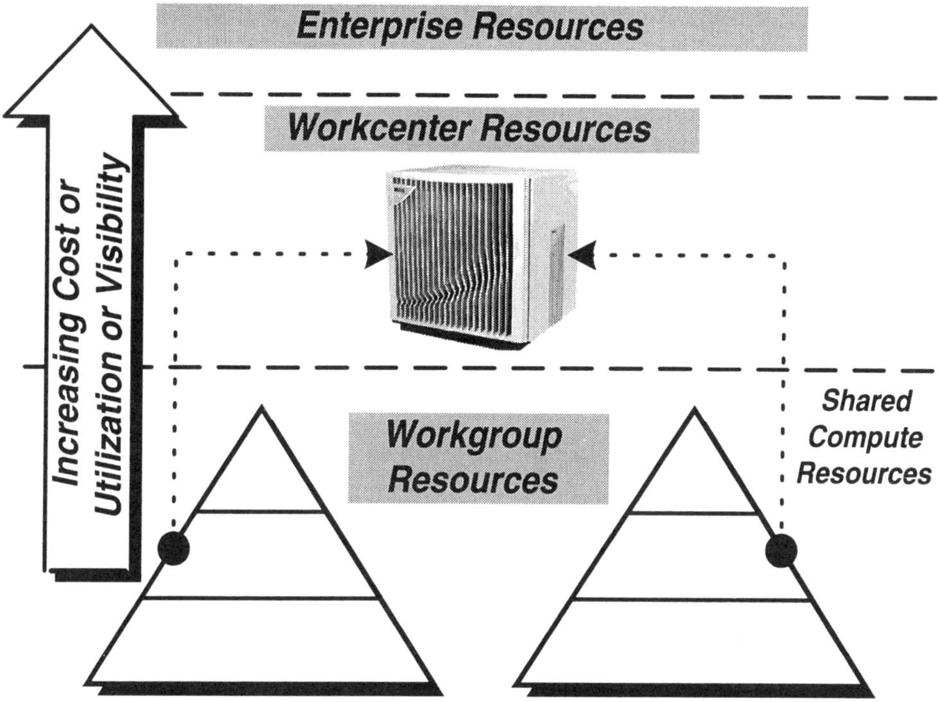

Figure 10-6 Hierarchical Placement of Shared Resources

chase price—a high-performance compute cluster may be too expensive to place in every workgroup. It seems that a lot of reasons for sharing a resource may be traced back to cost savings: full utilization of the resource and reduction in the number of separate resources to manage are two.

Another reason for placing resources at higher levels of the network hierarchy, besides cost, is to match them with the higher performance levels available in the network technology hierarchy. As we move up in the workgroup or workcenter hierarchy, higher throughput networking technology is necessary to avoid the concentration effect. Some services, like image installation, benefit from larger network pipes to their clients.

10.6.4 Dependency-Based Resource Placement

An obvious type of resource location requirement are those resources that have strong dependencies on particular types of hardware. Locating a parallelized compute-intensive application on a single-CPU compute server does not make best use of either resource. While this example illustrates a highly visible dependency, there are others that are not so glaringly obvious.

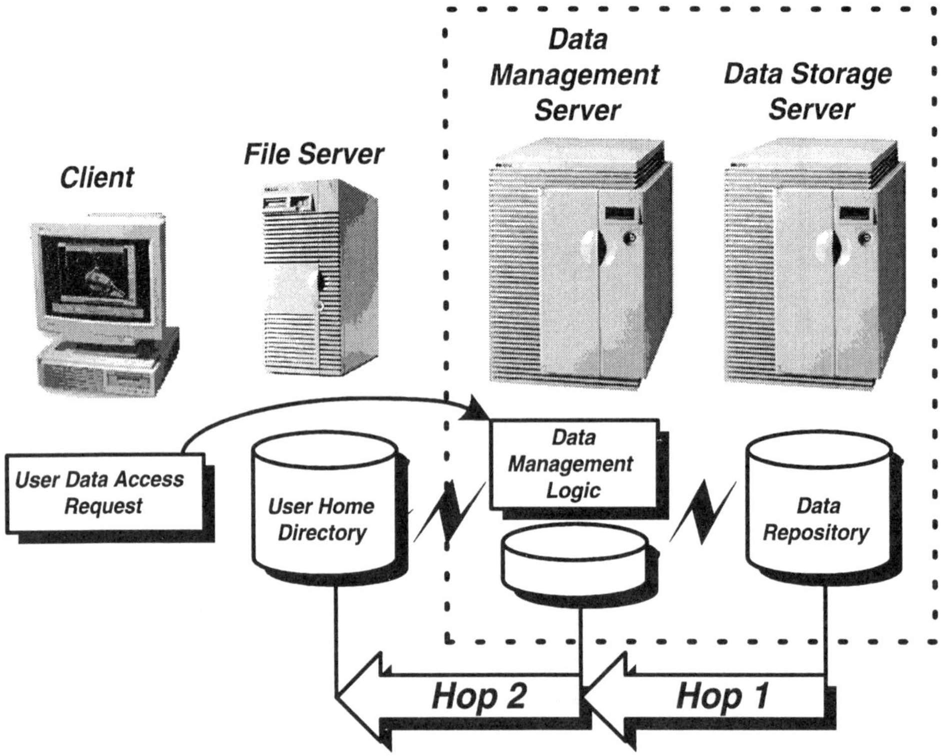

Figure 10-7 Dependency-Based Resource Placement Example

There are a number of workgroup resources that "ride on top of" or depend on other resources and services for their operation. Sometimes locating the dependent portions of the client-server application on the same system as the resources they depend on can improve performance and reduce network traffic. An example in Figure 10-7 shows a dependency between data-storage services and a separate data access management portion of an application.

In the figure, a user request to "check out" a particular set of data is sent to the data management logic running on the data management server. The data management logic's purpose is to control access to the data in the storage management server's repository and to maintain the current state of data in the repository. The data management service accesses the requested data on the storage management server for the client system, and copies it to the user's home directory.

In this relationship, the data-management logic is the client and the data storage server provides the service. The data-management server and the network attached storage management server appear as a single service to the client system even though they have been imple-

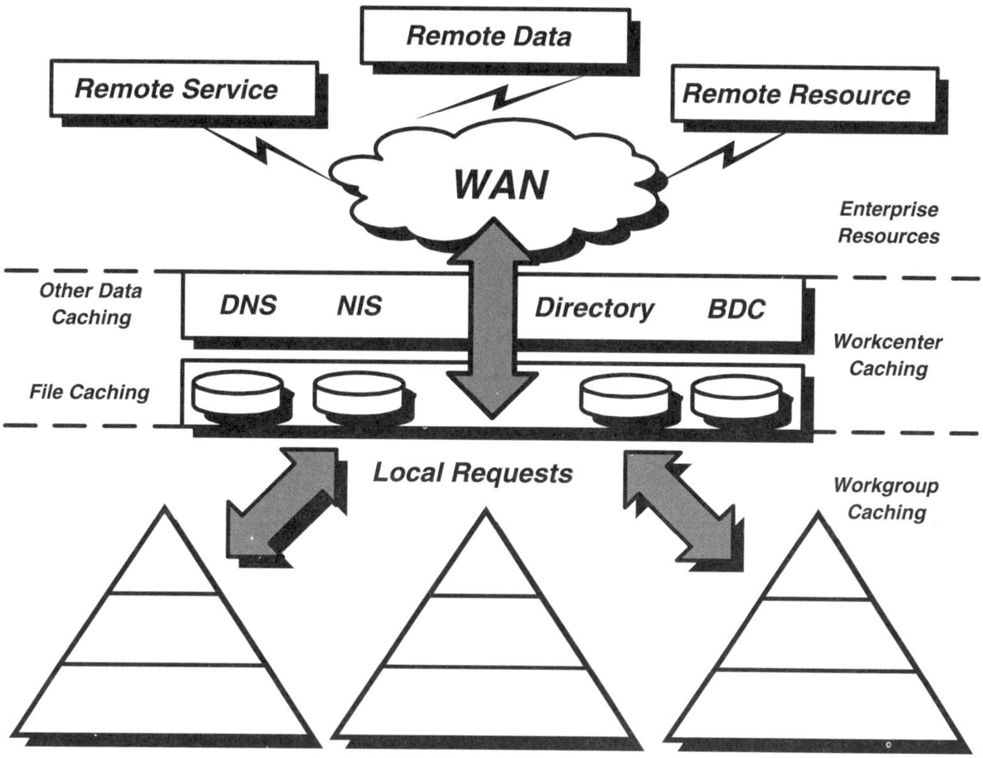

Figure 10-8 Resource Placement with Information Caching

mented as distinct software services on distinct systems. This is the "chained servers" model depicted in Figure 1-4.

The data-management service "hides" the original location of the requested data, preventing unauthorized access and maintaining state information about the data. Once the user is finished using or modifying data, a similar "check-in" process works in reverse. This type of behavior is common in software configuration management and product data-management (PDM) services.

The important thing to notice in this example is that the current configuration of the services and underlying server systems causes the data to traverse the network twice: once from the data storage server to the data management server and once from the data management server to the user's home directory on the file server. This happens whether the data access is performed via a network file system (as in the first hop) or via a special protocol as may be the case in the second hop.

So how do we "fix" this situation? If network bandwidth is not an issue, then we may not have to worry, but this is rarely the case. If the data-management system allowed it, we could configure the hardware relationships so that the data management software ran on the storage management server. This would eliminate one of the network "hops"[8] and reduce the network traffic.

There are other examples of this type of relationship: service-to-storage dependencies and service to service dependencies. Whenever we investigate the components of a client-server application, we should keep this example in mind. Where we place the application components can influence the overall performance of the whole service and may take more total network resources if not done efficiently.

Understanding the client-server application component relationships and communication mechanisms is the key to proper resource placement. The general approach is to hide the details of the relationship inside of a "container" system, reducing the number of interfaces, nonlocal dependencies, and external communication paths. In this way we are repackaging the application components into a more resource-efficient object.

10.6.5 Caching of Nonlocal Resources

One way that we can speed up performance *and* protect services in the workgroup from outages is through caching. With caching, we can convert direct, nonlocal dependencies to loosely coupled, local dependencies. All new requests are funneled through a cache manager that makes the request to the remote service, saves the replies, and satisfies the local request.

A good example of a service that can be configured like this is DNS, which allows a server to be designated as a "caching-only" server. All look-ups are deferred to remote "forwarders" that actually perform the lookup and return the results. Any repeated requests are satisfied out of the cache (if they have not exceeded the cache's "time-to-live" timer and timed out), thus reducing network traffic, speeding the reply, and providing some immunity from unavailable WAN links. A generalized diagram of a caching service is shown in Figure 10-8.

There are also other caching mechanisms available for different types of services. A number of file systems allow client-side caching of data to reduce network traffic and improve local application performance. Some of the file systems will cache data over a LAN, WAN, or both. depending on the underlying protocol and the network transport that is supported. An NFS-to-DFS gateway system may be used to cache DFS data and export it to the workgroup[9].

10.7 Location and Use of Hierarchical Resources

Hierarchical services, such as DNS, often have multiple "entry points" into the service hierarchy for client machines. This means that there are multiple servers available with the same

8. This multiple hop scenario may also happen when network attached storage hardware is used in place of a general purpose file server. The unfortunate thing about specialized NAS devices is that the proposed solution is not possible, since NAS hardware systems are dedicated to one function and cannot run other functions.

9. This will be covered in more detail in Chapter 14.

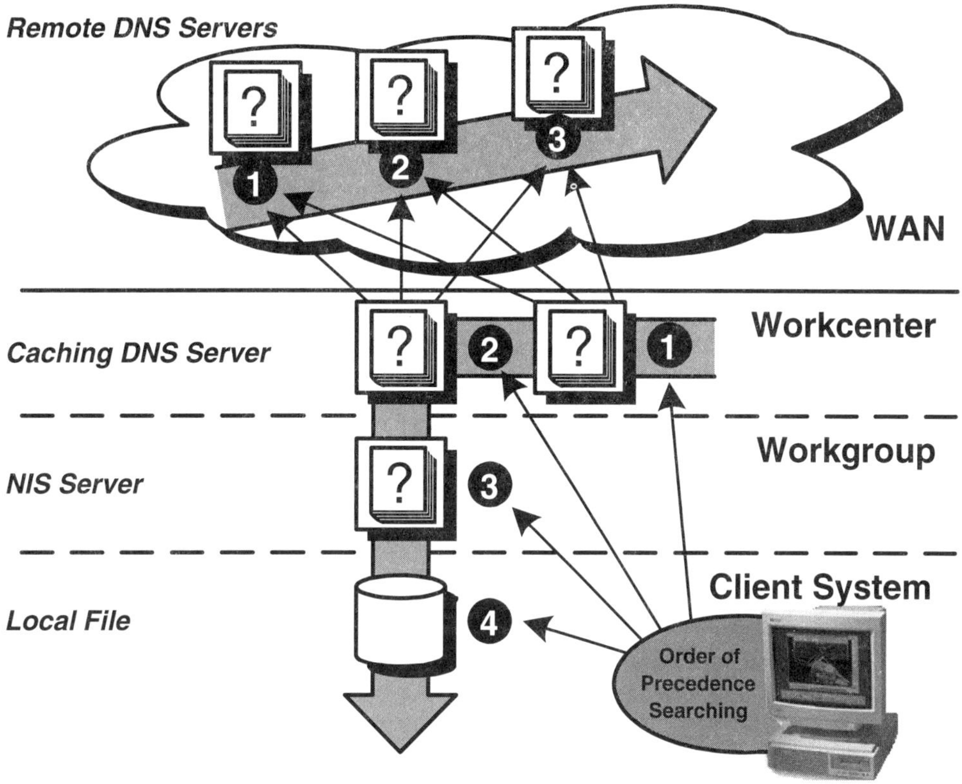

Figure 10-9 Hierarchical Services and Search Precedence

information set. The server resource may also replicated at multiple points at the same levels in the hierarchy.

One of our design decisions involves which server resource to initially attach a client system to and how to fail-over to an alternate service if the primary one becomes unavailable. How do we determine the order of precedence for using such multipoint services? Fortunately, most enterprise class services have mechanisms that help with the sequencing.

In the case of NIS, the client system can either use a specific server (with the *ypset* command) or locate a server by broadcasting. In a routed environment, the broadcast behavior ensures that a client must locate a server on the same LAN segment, since broadcasts are not propagated. If there are multiple servers on the LAN, then the client uses the first one to answer, providing a sort of rudimetary form of load balancing[10].

10. Busy or slow servers will be slower to answer. At least that is the theory.

If the NIS server that the client is attached to becomes unavailable, the client will time-out and again broadcast to locate an available server. The next one to answer is chosen. This is one good reason to have multiple slave servers in the LAN environment, whether it is switched or not.

The client portion of DNS allows the specification of multiple servers and an order of precedence of use. On Unix systems, this information is contained in the */etc/resolv.conf* file. On Windows NT systems, this information is set in the Control Panel's *Network* icon, in the *Protocols→TCP/IP→Properties→DNS* form. If the DNS server at the top of the list does not answer within a time-out period, then the DNS client attempts the next one in the progression.

Some systems also make it possible to switch between multiple services that provide the same information in the event of time-outs. An example of this is the set of services controlled by the Unix */etc/nsswitch.conf* file. This file configures the order of precedence used for searching for several important sets of information.

For example, the source for host name to IP address translations may be specified as one of several services in a particular search order. An example line from this file is:

hostname: DNS NIS files

This specifies that hostname lookups will first try DNS, progress to NIS, then finally fall back to a local configuration file, */etc/hosts*[11]. This particular behavior is called hostname fall-back on Unix systems.

It is important to understand the fail-over mechanisms used by the client portion of the services for two reasons. First, the server resources need to be placed in the network hierarchy to support the natural behavior of the clients. Second, configuring the order of precedence for the search on the client, if allowed, can help us to "bullet-proof" the workgroup against external failure.

An example of using both features will be instructive. If a workgroup depends on a remote DNS server for hostname to IP address translations, the loss of that service can "hang" the entire workgroup. Likewise, the loss of the WAN connection from the workgroup to the rest of the enterprise can cause the local systems to fail. To minimize the effects of the service loss, the workgroup designer can:

- Place one or more caching DNS servers in the local workgroup
- Configure the caching DNS servers to use multiple remote DNS servers
- Configure the DNS clients to use only the caching server
- Place essential host name information, like workgroup servers, in local files like */etc/hosts* and *\winnt\system32\drivers\etc\hosts*

11. Each of the sources may also be configured for specific actions if the service is unavailable, not configured, responds "try again", or the requested value is not found.

- Place all workgroup host names into the NIS host map
- Configure the DNS clients to use hostname fall-back

In the event of a failure in one of the remote DNS servers, the local workgroup caching server will use one or more of the other remote servers. In the event of a WAN failure, the local caching server will continue to supply host name addresses[12]. In the event of a failure of the local caching server, the client will try an alternate server, then fall back on the NIS service, which will supply only the names in its host name database. And finally, if the NIS service is unavailable, the client will use the information in its local file. This process is shown in Figure 10-9.

The ability to configure this type of behavior is one of the fundamental differences between systems that are designed for enterprise use and those that are not. The ability to use hierarchical resource placement, in conjunction with an order-of-precedence search, is essential to hiding failures in the environment. Without both, we cannot provide stable behavior in the face of service failures.

10.8 Mapping Workgroup Hardware Resources

There are two major phases to the allocation of workgroup resources: both a logical and a physical allocation. A survey of the new or existing environment produces the logical requirements for resources, determining the different system and service classes, along with the class memberships. These logical requirements must then be superimposed on a set of physical requirements for the workgroup, including actual workgroup hardware and the location of that hardware. This is shown schematically in Figure 10-10.

Our job as designers is to take the total service needs for our users and map them onto discrete hardware systems that fit the client, compute server, and file server tiers of the 3TCS model. The logical view of the resource distribution is the one that is visible to our users and their applications; both the logical and physical views are what we use to properly allocate and manage workgroup resources. How we eventually place the resources can affect perception, performance, and reliability of the workgroup environment.

We should note that each environment will have its own unique application mixture, existing investments, organizational structure and budgetary constraints—all of which affect the final disposition of the workgroup design. The differences in requirements should not deter us from looking for commonality of structure. It is surprising how overtly different environments actually tend to share internal functionality. Most of the time, all we have to do is look.

We have previously detailed lists of specific services that are commonly encountered in workgroup environments. There was a method to this madness. Not only do we need a set of

12. If the IP addresses are to local systems, then the client may continue to function, otherwise the lookup will succeed but the dependent service will be unable to contact the remote host and will time-out or fail.

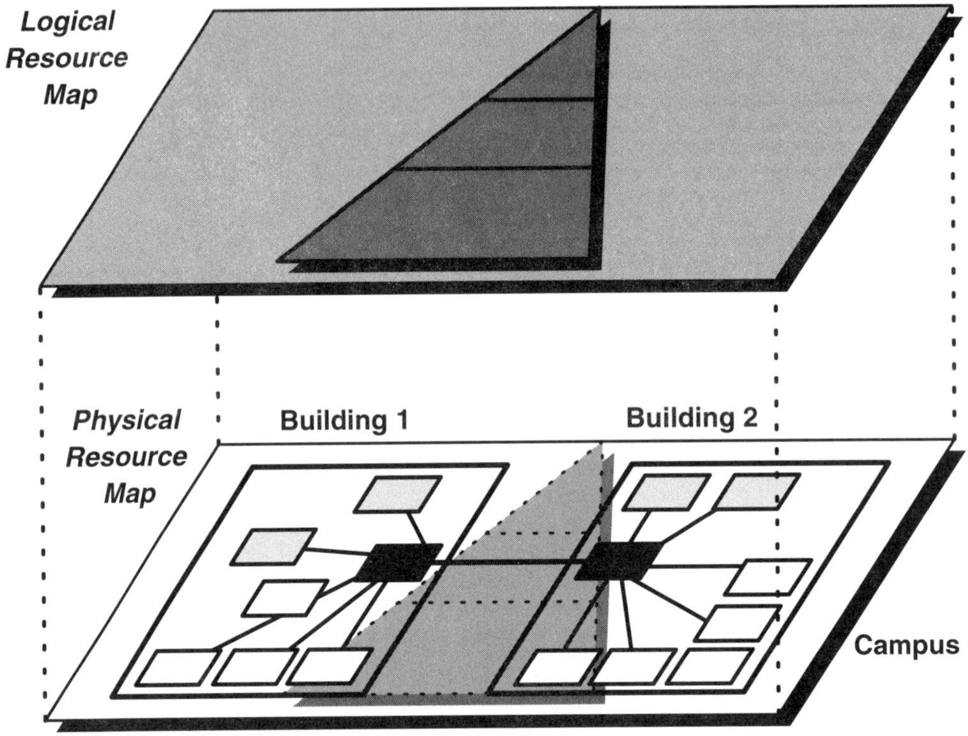

Figure 10-10 Logical and Physical Mapping of Workgroup Resources

example services for the purpose of demonstrating the technique, but we can learn some of the major components and their characteristics as we go along.

10.8.1 A Brief Philosophical Diversion on Structure

Before we start, let's explore a little philosophical advice. A wise man, speaking about imposing rigid structure too early in the learning process, once said,

> "Premature structure stifles creativity. It requires the creation of the final product in the first attempt, with no room for experimentation or failure" [13].

The message here is: don't expect to come up with the final architecture, structure, or solution right away. The entire process will take several tries, many data-gathering missions, and many calls or trips to your software vendor's web pages to start getting the correct picture. The more application documentation you have available, the better.

13. Herbert Kohl, "The Creation of Hope in Public Education", Alternative Radio.

Also, if you are in a hurry to superimpose a structure on your design, you may miss important structural patterns. The more common patterns you can find, the more possibilities exist for consolidation and reuse. If a structural element is rigidly designed into a particular configuration, it is difficult to reuse in others. Don't hurry towards the final solution[14] if you can help it.

10.8.2 Logical Workgroup Resource Allocation

We will now cover some investigative steps that are useful determining the logical resource partitioning. They are also some of the questions to ask during an assessment process. We should not be too surprised by this fact.

We will break the logical partitioning process into several discrete steps, and after each step we will stop and look for common components and patterns. We would like to find all of the puzzle pieces, line them up side by side, and look for ways to fit them together into the "whole picture". We are warned ahead of time that this particular puzzle has duplicate pieces.

Don't worry if you haven't done this before, gaining the experience is the important part. The more experience you have at this process, the easier it is to find the commonality and the areas that need extra attention. Some of the starting analysis steps are listed below, but you will undoubtedly come up with additional steps of your own throughout the process.

- Determine the unique classes of users in the workgroup environment—for example, documentation services, software development, or electrical design automation.
- For each class of users, list the tools and applications required.
- List the individual components of each application along with special data, graphics, and compute needs.
- Note any special communication requirements for application components.
- Determine the required operating system for each of the user's tools, making note of any specialized network transport needs or behavior.
- Where different operating systems are in use, list all versions of any applications that run on multiple platforms, investigate potential data incompatibilities.
- Examine the volume of data expected for each application type.
- Pay attention to expected data lifetimes and production rates for each application.

After this portion of the analysis, we can nail down the many of the client system attributes for the different user classes, based on the operating system, graphics, and other hardware requirements for the applications local to the client systems. We can also infer a required set of 3TCS resources to support the client functionality: compute services, network bandwidth, and file-storage services.

14. That is, unless your boss or the users are breathing down your neck. This section is a philosophical diversion, not necessarily rooted in today's business reality.

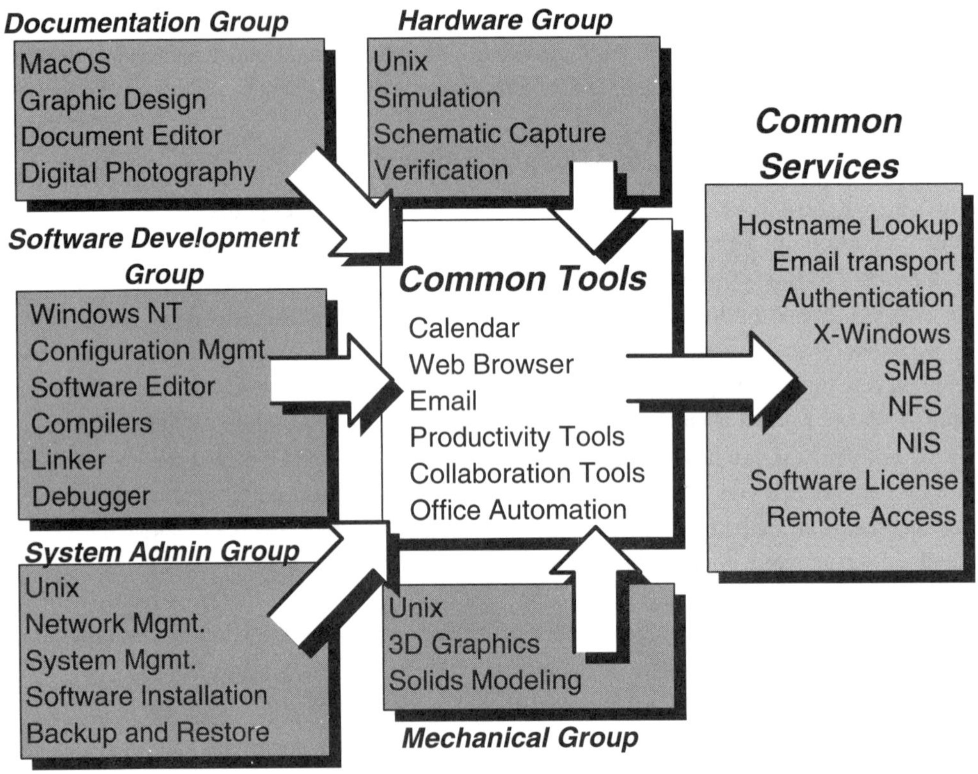

Figure 10-11 Coalescing Workgroup Client Class Information

We can next add user authentication, e-mail, host name lookup, and other infrastructure services to the list of required resources, without too much extra thought. If we are not sure exactly what infrastructure or distribution services are necessary, we can examine existing environments, use software vendor's recommendations, or do research into other designer's solutions. Once we have some idea of the individual client requirements, we can:

- Note the number of expected clients of each class
- Determine the number of required service classes and their membership
- Calculate the expected network loading per client system
- Provide for any existing "legacy" system networking types
- Begin sketching out any VLANs or special network groupings that might be needed
- Determine the number and type of required network devices, along with the number and types of ports per device

At this point in the process, we can choose new networking hardware or examine the capabilities of existing hardware. We also may know if any rewiring is necessary between the client systems and the distribution points (wiring closets) or computer room. The LAN or VLAN groupings of the client systems should start to gel. Knowing the number and type of clients, along with their physical location, allows us to start physically placing services.

10.8.3 Physical Workgroup Resource Mapping

At this point in the resource partitioning, we may know that we need a service, like e-mail, but do not have it specifically located in the workgroup hierarchy. To make intelligent decisions about placing resources, we now need to have information about the physical distribution of the workgroup. Remember that networking features like VLANs allow members of a particular workgroup to be widely distributed physically, no matter what our logical picture might be. See Figure 10-10 for a simplified example of this situation.

One procedure to use is to locate the lowest common denominator in the network hierarchy, usually a switch or hub. Locate all devices at the lowest level in the network hierarchy and, for each such device, examine all of the client systems that are attached. Note the class membership of the client systems.

Refer back to the list of services specifically associated with the client class, and begin by assuming that the service is attached to the network at the same level as the client systems. Ask the following questions:

- Are there adjacent devices at the same level in the network that share this service?
- Is there a large amount of duplicate system administration required to support this service at this level of the network?
- Can the client systems find the service if it is located at the current network level?
- Will the environment be more resilient if the resource is located here?
- Will the client system perform better if the service is located here?
- Is there an existing physical system that can run this service at this level?
- If the resource is moved one level up, will it be located across a slow link or outside of available security?

These questions are designed to help choose initial placement of the resource being examined. Repeat the process for each resource, moving from low to high in the network hierarchy. When you reach a campus-wide backbone, or a common switch "uplink" or backbone, stop. This process is represented in Figure 10-12 for the NIS slave service.

You should realize that this is just an abbreviated example of how to locate the proper place for network resources. The placement results will depend on the characteristics of the individual service and the structure of the network. Going through the exercise for pieces of the network and different services can produce results that can be reused on similar network structures.

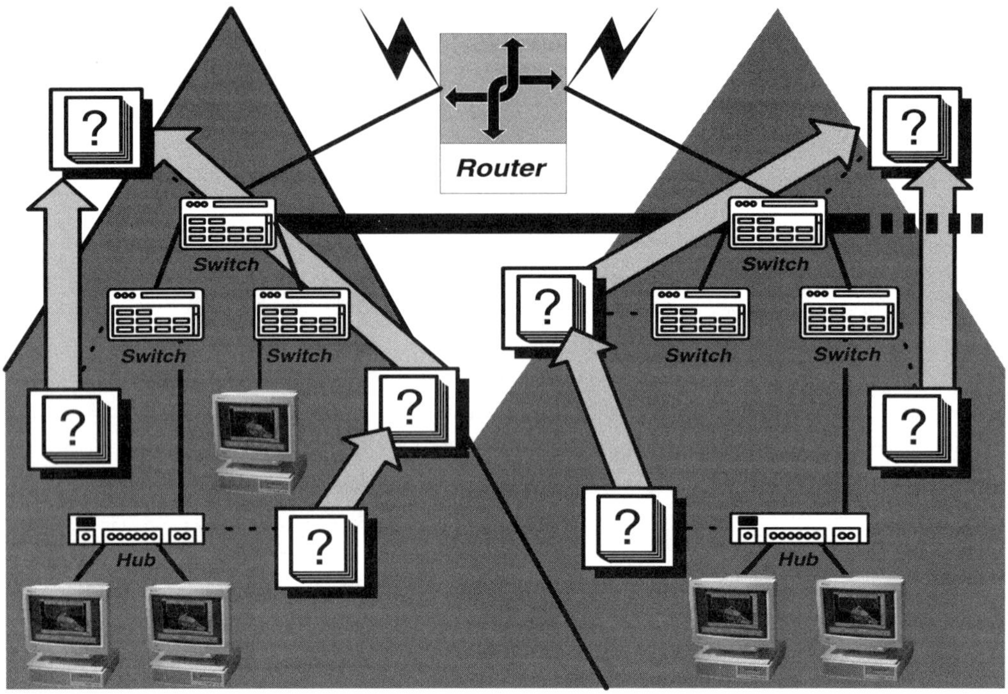

Figure 10-12 Physical Partitioning of Workgroup Resources

Now would be a good time to review the figures in this chapter, with an eye towards the concepts in this section.

With the list of common services in hand, we now need to know which ones can peacefully coexist with each other on shared hardware and how much RAM and CPU resources are required for each. On a physical diagram of the network, there should be little clusters of service icons, representing what we think is the best placement for the required resources. With the total number of clients, load factors, and knowledge about the service behaviors, we can now start allocating hardware.

One of the first rules is: "Use a dedicated hardware resource wherever possible". This is especially true if you have no idea whether two services will interact or what the service behavior is. This may be a temporary allocation until you can "collapse" the service onto an existing machine, moving the temporary resource elsewhere.

Look for common structure that can be turned into scalable building blocks. The hardware structure should start taking shape out of the clusters of services. Remember that it may take several iterations of this process as you discover services that you forgot or discover new building blocks. There may also be adjustments needed to account for services that are added to manage the workgroup resources (see the next chapter).

10.9 Hardware Architecture Summary

Because of the direct relationships between client-server application components and underlying hardware resources, one of the first design activities to undertake is a complete assessment of the application set and necessary distribution and support services for the target workgroup. In an existing workgroup the assessment will uncover the current state of the environment and its usage before any potential loss or disruption of server takes place. In a new workgroup design, we may rely on our previous experience or assessments from similar configurations to catalogue the application needs and determine the hardware resource distribution.

Once all applications and services are determined, we must match them with the proper hardware resources and partition the hardware requirements into individual systems. As the hardware partitioning unfolds, we can determine the necessary network connections between the various systems in the workgroup. During this process, we can look for patterns and "natural" divisions that can become the object boundaries for the design, using the network resource hierarchy as a placement guide.

Because the logical design of the network does not always map to the physical realities, we will need to adjust the resource distribution accordingly. We can use the resource-allocation models described earlier in the chapter to determine if replication or sharing of resources is needed. Some of the specific hardware architecture design suggestions are:

Eliminate or Reduce Dependencies Direct dependencies, especially over a low-speed link, can lead to performance and reliability issues. Placing resources closest to their user is the best approach, even if it entails duplication of data or hardware.

Use Dedicated Hardware Resources for Specific Services Dedicated hardware resources are easier to tune for a specific service than shared resources. It is also easier to measure the usage of a particular service or application component if it is the only resident of a particular system. Budget constraints do not always allow this approach, but it may also be used to temporarily isolate a service for performance measurements. Where potentially conflicting services cannot be given dedicated hardware, a "fair share" scheduler may control usage of RAM and CPU usage.

Repackage 3TCS Components to Eliminate Excessive Network Traffic The example used in this chapter of placing data storage and data access logic on the same computer system to reduce network traffic may be useful for similar services. An understanding of the application or service components and their communication methods is needed for finding and eliminating this type of potential problem.

Isolate Antisocial Network Behavior System transport types whose "chatty" broadcast behavior can affect the performance of other systems may be isolated using VLANs, separate subnets, or other network "filtering" functionality. This allows such systems to function in their native modes but can protect other systems from the impact. It is important to specify and buy network components and management tools that enable these options.

Use Local Caching for WAN Resources Using data or service components that allow local caching of data can convert nonlocal, tightly coupled dependencies to loosely coupled local ones. This not only improves performance, but may increase availability of the service if the nonlocal portion of it becomes unavailable. Caching in this sense can behave similarly to a UPS during a temporary power outage. Investigate the availability of caching in hardware and software components for your workgroup.

Place Shared Resources in the Workcenter Resources that must be shared by multiple workgroups should be placed at the workcenter level of the workgroup hierarchy. Normally this level of network "visibility" would require the resource to be on the building or campus network "backbone". Ensure that visible resources like this have adequate hardware and networking resources to support the workload from multiple workgroups. High availability or redundancy is essential for workcenter resources that service multiple workgroups.

Closer Is Better The closer a resource can be located to its user, the better. Using the network resource hierarchy as a guide, we should place the resources where they are closest to the greatest number of users. Reducing network latency will speed access for the client systems. We need to offset the performance gains, however, with the manageability of the solution, otherwise we would be back to a peer-to-peer configuration.

Use Hierarchical Placement and Order of Precedence Searching Carefully place the server resources in a hierarchy that matches the client's needs. Pay attention to points in the intervening network hierarchy that may cause failures if they become unavailable. Insulate the client systems from the details of the higher levels of the service hierarchy. Where client systems allow it, configure them to use an order-of-precedence search that matches the local service hierarchy.

Once we have some idea of how the resources map into the LAN and physical system environment, we may begin dealing with issues surrounding the installation, configuration, and maintenance of the software components in the environment. That is the subject of the next chapter.

CHAPTER 11

Operating Environment: Management, Measurement, and Methods

The operating environment is the brain center for the systems and services that compose the workgroup. It is the management glue that holds the systems and services together and enables them to support the client-server applications that use them. Without the components of the operating environment, a stable workgroup can progressively degenerate into utter chaos.

This chapter will cover a general set of principles which if applied to selecting or creating tools to manage a workgroup, can make the administrative tasks easier. Unfortunately, there is currently no system administration "silver bullet" for workgroup environments available commercially. There are many reasons for this, including the complexity and "infinite" configurability provided by modern operating systems and network components.

All is not lost! The partial skeletons of tools and some commercially available frameworks do exist to help in the system management of complex environments. The major issue with centralized management tools is scalability. Sometimes information about the best solutions can be found from other system mangers with similar problems to solve. If we can select the proper foundations for our efforts and adopt as much ready-to-use components as possible, our job *may* be easier.

11.1 Workgroup System Management

To visualize the responsibilities of this workgroup layer, picture an endless circle of measurement, evaluation of the measurements against desired values, and corresponding management process actions to adjust performance. It is the job of the processes and tools in this layer to keep the workgroup hardware, network connections, operating systems, and services functioning harmoniously. It is at this level that the prepackaged, canned tools most often fail us as sys-

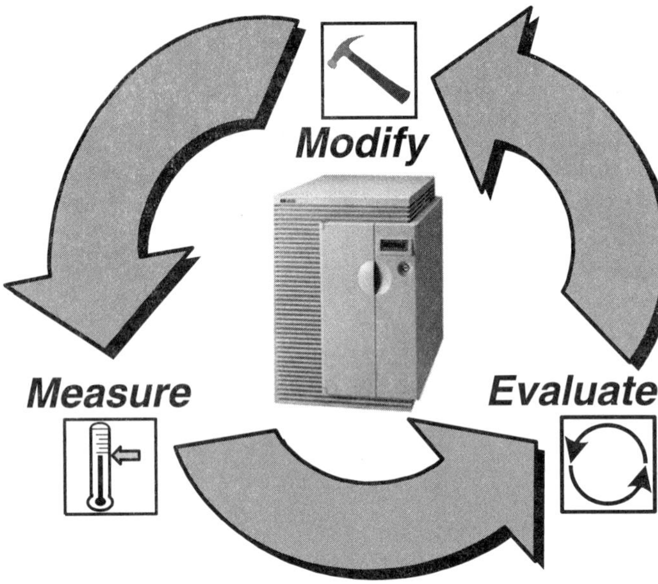

Figure 11-1 Elements of System-Administration Processes

tem managers—forcing customization or outright creation of the necessary scripts, programs, and processes.

Ideally, each managed system in the network, whether it is a client or a server system, would have a well-defined network interface for operations like querying[1] the current system administration state and performing system configuration modifications. The internal details of the system management actions should be hidden behind this interface, allowing us to issue high-level commands like "configure a two Gigabyte JFS partition striped across five physical devices" without needing to know the details of how this is accomplished.

We are not quite there yet. Tools do exist that use the simple network management protocol (SNMP) or the PC DMI (desktop management interface) to query the hardware and software state of a particular system and modify some system parameters. What is really needed is a fully functional two-way street: the ability to query and dynamically set both the low- and high-level parameters of each system.

The operating system needs to incorporate algorithms that dynamically adjust their behavior when controlling parameters are changed (on most systems this requires a reboot of the system) to support the full measure, evaluate, and change cycle. Dynamic, remote tuning of

1. Apollo Computer's DOMAIN/OS had a facility called "AskNode" for this purpose, which was a remote interface to system parameters.

workgroup systems could save rebuild and reboot cycles necessary on today's systems and reduce system administration efforts. This is only a dream today.

11.2 Dataless Clients

We have already discussed the advantages of dataless clients in terms of recovery from failure, and simplifying backup processes, see Chapter 6. In addition to saving effort for backup and providing quick recovery from client system failure, dataless clients have other benefits related to system management effort. Dataless clients can help us get around the system administration crunch and the limited scaling of centralized management tools.

How do we do this, you ask? One of the simplest ways to avoid managing all of the systems in the environment is to not manage the client systems, which usually represent the largest percentage of systems in the workgroup. What this means is that rather than attempting to manage all client and server systems from a central point, a better approach is to centrally manage the server systems and use class-based system cloning to ensure uniform behavior for client system classes.

11.2.1 System Cloning

System cloning performs system installation, over the network or from removable media, using a set of "golden" system images, one for each unique system configuration. Each image is the complete set of operating system commands, local user applications, and system configuration files required to make a functional system instance. The image is a snapshot of a single system that has been properly configured, *once*, and turned into a compressed archive, with hardware and system-specific information removed.

The cloning process consists of a utility that formats the client system's disk and installs the image from the selected media onto the newly created file system structure. Because of the reformatting of the local disks, the cloning process can be thought of as an extremely efficient cold installation. During the install process, the most flexible cloning packages allow configuration scripts to run at multiple points to tweak system parameters. Once the image is installed, the system is rebooted.

We should note that the cloning process also works great for server systems, not just clients. The system image can be a tremendous boon to disaster recovery plans and can make distribution of standardized server systems a lot less tedious. Some locations create bootable CD-ROM images for installation of both client and server systems. For a server recovery, the backup software may be included in the system images, meaning that a system can be cloned and begin restoring backup data right away.

Benefits of System Cloning A cloned installation takes much less time than the sum of the installation operations that created the original golden system. This is because a lot of installation time is spent moving files into place, adjusting access permissions, and performing

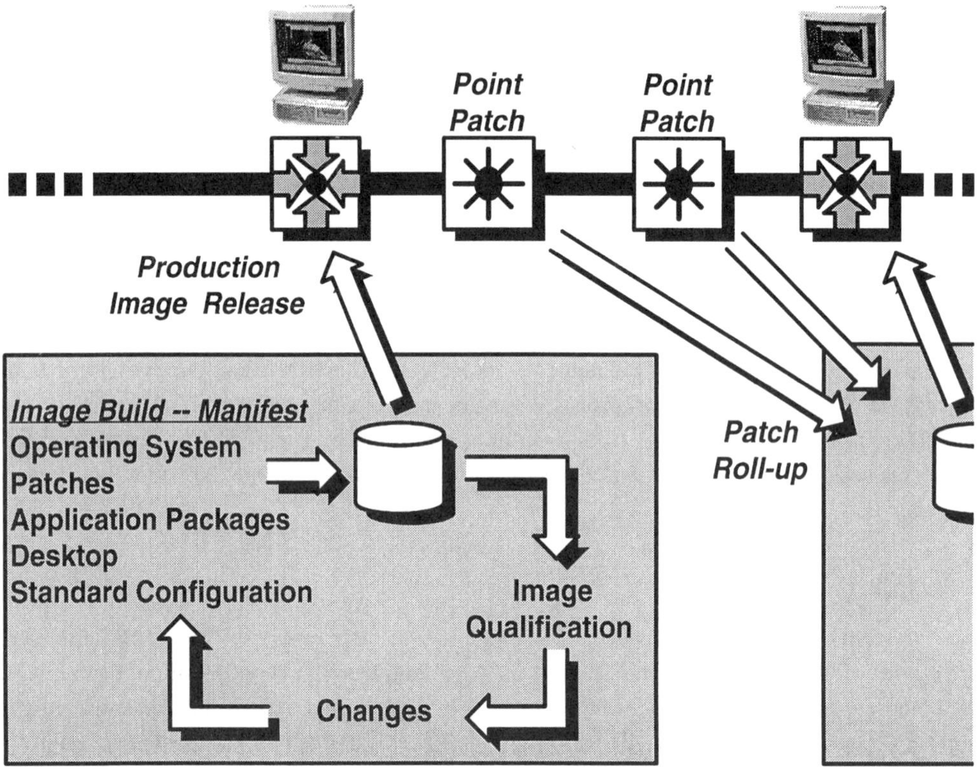

Figure 11-2 A Simple Golden Image Management Process

other repetitive actions. Installation of a cloned system, in a fully switched, high-bandwidth network, can take as little as ten to fifteen minutes. Most cloning software allows fully automated unattended system installation, controlled from either the system itself or the cloning server.

Of course, the smaller the system image, the faster the cloning process. Moving all volatile data, help files, application packages, and infrequently used system commands to central file servers can shrink the golden image appreciably. This approximates a "thin" client, but without the potential performance penalties of having *everything* on a remote server[2].

System cloning can save time, effort, and make the environment much more resilient to hardware failures. If a client system (or a server) fails, the hardware may be swapped for a spare, a new image installed, and the system placed back on the network faster than most troubleshoot-

2. There can be two types of thin client: one type approximates the X-terminal, with only local graphics presentation services, the other type is similar to a diskless system, with memory-based caching of resources. I am referring to the latter type here.

ing processes could find the problem. Some sites that use extensive system cloning have coined the phrase, "Don't troubleshoot, just reboot".

Creating and Managing Golden Images Before pushing a system image out to hundreds of client systems, it behooves us to ensure that the system functions properly, otherwise we are just being very efficient at creating work for ourselves. The phrase "functions properly" includes ensuring proper system tuning for expected applications, freedom from known application bugs or operating system problems, and the presence of all required utilities. Most sites that use system cloning have put a formal qualification process in place for each of the golden images. A simple example of such a process is shown in Figure 11-2.

Qualification of the golden system image includes testing of operating system software configuration and verification of proper application operation in the total environment. For this to work in a consistent way, standardized application data sets and performance information must be available and used to create repeatable tests. Application behavior, performance, and final results are compared against expected values. Any problems trigger an investigation process that could result in changes to the golden image's contents.

Golden Images and Class-Based Administration A frequently asked question is, "Just how many golden images do I need in my environment?" The simple answer is, "One for every different system class". As a matter of fact, we can use unique configuration characteristics requiring a different golden image as a defining characteristic of a system class. A good approach is to encapsulate as many differences in customization scripts as possible and keep the total number of images to a bare minimum.

System image installation software, like the Hewlett-Packard Ignite-UX utility, can often install software from a number of different sources during the cloning process. This flexibility allows us to "derive" new system types, from a standard "base" image by layering functionality on top of it. This process, which is a good way to reduce the number of golden images to manage, is shown in Figure 3-11.

11.2.2 System "Personality" and Structure

The author divides the information that makes up a system into two pieces: "personality" and system structure. The system structure is the ninety to ninety-nine percent of the image information that is the same for all clones of the same system class. The personality is the small amount of configuration information like IP address, host name, DNS domain, and local device drivers that make the system unique. This is depicted in Figure 11-3.

The personality information may be set by postconfiguration scripts that check centralized database information or automatically via services like NIS and DHCP. The DHCP server represents a great opportunity for single-point management of personality information for

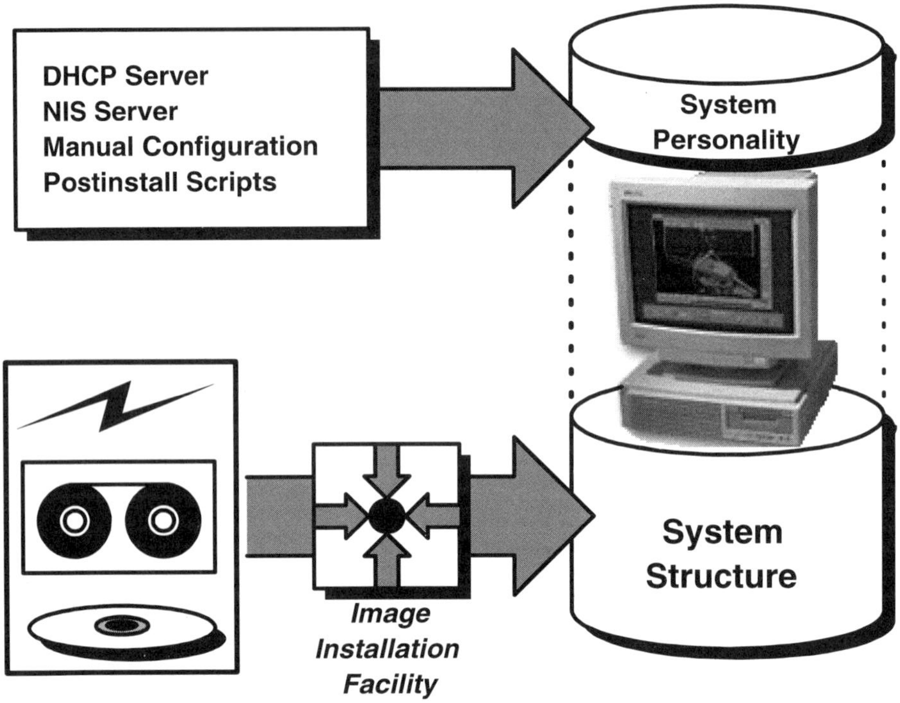

Figure 11-3 Components of a Cloned System

cloned systems[3]. The information from DHCP is usually turned into local configuration information by the DHCP client software when the system is booted.

11.3 Software Package Distribution and Installation

Software installation is one of the primary system administration tasks in a workgroup environment. You might say that everything starts with the software installation process. The classes of software that are routinely installed include the operating system, application software, and updates (or patches) to existing operating system or application software.

With system image installation, the distribution of software may be much simpler—the software is pushed out in images instead of individual packages. There is still a need for soft-

3. The immediate objection voiced about DHCP is that the IP address-to-hostname relationship is dynamic, which is guaranteed to drive network management staff crazy. This does not have to be the case—it is possible to "lock" the two pieces of information together by specifying an "infinite" lease period for the IP address. This loses the dynamic nature of DHCP, but for fixed clients this configuration is very useful.

ware distribution facilities to handle "point" patches to clients[4], installing shared packages on servers, and building the initial client software images. A requirement to maintain software distributions from operating system and software vendors still exists, but the software distributions do not have to be as complex or widespread.

Having a flexible and powerful software installation and distribution facility is a prerequisite for managing a large number of systems. We also require the ability to do the installation over the network. Physically visiting every system with physical media is a time-consuming process, not to mention the logistical problem of providing access to a tape drive or other removable media device on every client. The next sections will cover some of the desirable aspects of a software installation facility.

11.3.1 "Push" Versus "Pull" Installation

There are three basic labels that we can apply to the software installation process, depending on where the control software, or "brains", of the installation software runs and where the software repository is located. Those labels, or models, are "local", "pull", and "push" installations. Each approach has its own characteristics.

The first case is a "local" installation, where the software is read from a local repository, on a locally mounted disk, CD-ROM, or tape drive. A local installation is the least complicated type of installation, because all of the software and control intelligence is on the local system. This eliminates the need for network installation support, and removes dependencies on external resources. Installing large numbers of systems with the local installation model is a very labor-intensive job. Local installation involves lots of media, frequent media swaps, manual interaction, and almost guarantees a non-standard, hand-crafted system configuration.

The second type of installation, the "pull" installation, runs the control software on the target system, accessing a remote software repository over the network. This method removes the need for local media, and many times the installation software may be run with a remote display, so that the system manager does not have to be at the client's console. This process saves time over the local installation but still requires a system-by-system process.

Finally, there is the "push" installation. With this method, a smart installation controller does a simultaneous installation of software to multiple remote systems. The installation control software may use multicasting to save network traffic between the controller and the systems under installation. The push installation saves time and effort over the previous two methods, because a system manager may install multiple systems at the same time from a remote location.

Class-based installation of software is a desirable feature for software installation processes. In the case of pull installations, a system can perform an automated installation by looking up its class information and selecting the proper software packages for installation. The installation process need only worry about one set of system class memberships for this type of operation, reducing the complexity of the install but multiplying the number of operations.

4. A point patch is one that takes a minimal amount of time and may not even require a system reboot. We would not completely reinstall a client system, taking up to thirty minutes, for a simple update that might take one to two minutes.

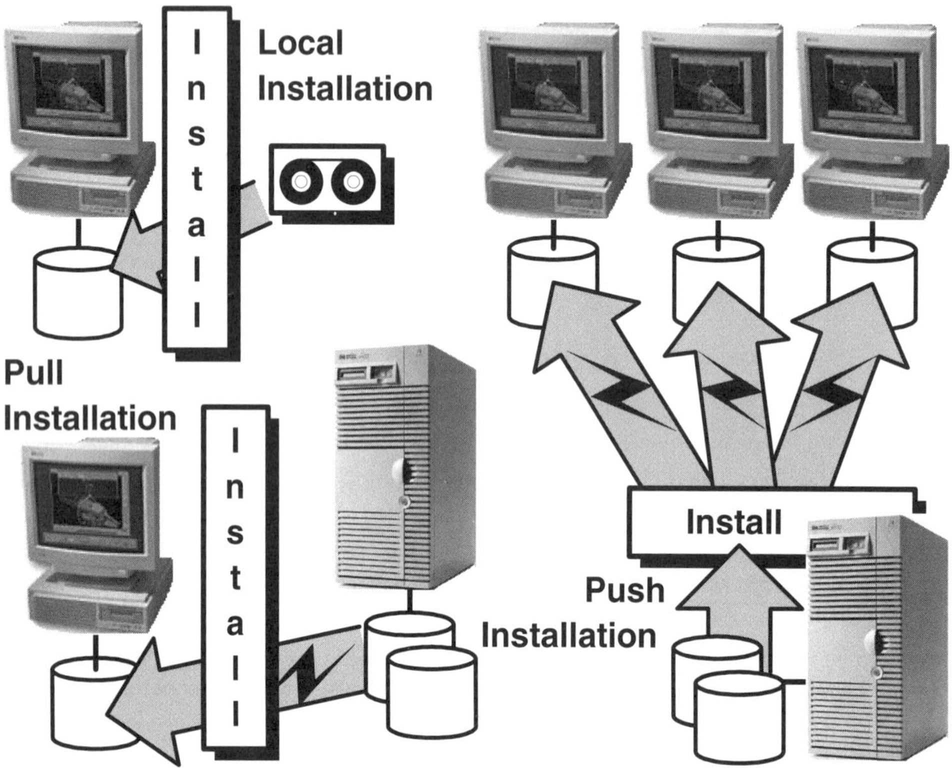

Figure 11-4 Software Installation Models: Local, Pull, and Push

For a push installation, the controlling system requires implicit knowledge about the software state of every target to ensure proper installation. If the system state is checked serially on the software controller, the installation process can take longer than for a pull installation, where the individual systems do the checking. The multisystem push operation canincrease install complexity, especially if multiple system classes are involved, but the total number of manual operations is reduced.

11.3.2 Software Packaging Characteristics

Just installing software components willy-nilly on a system may appear to get the job done, but the final client configuration of the installed data and command components is important to the administrative tasks and use to follow. Packages that scatter data and code together can create backup nightmares and prevent sharing of package sets across the network. There are other issues regarding the structure of software packages that we will explore in the following sections.

Code and Data Separation Keeping application configuration information and data separate from the commands and libraries associated with an application package can make it easier (or possible) to share the package with other systems. We would like to avoid uninten-

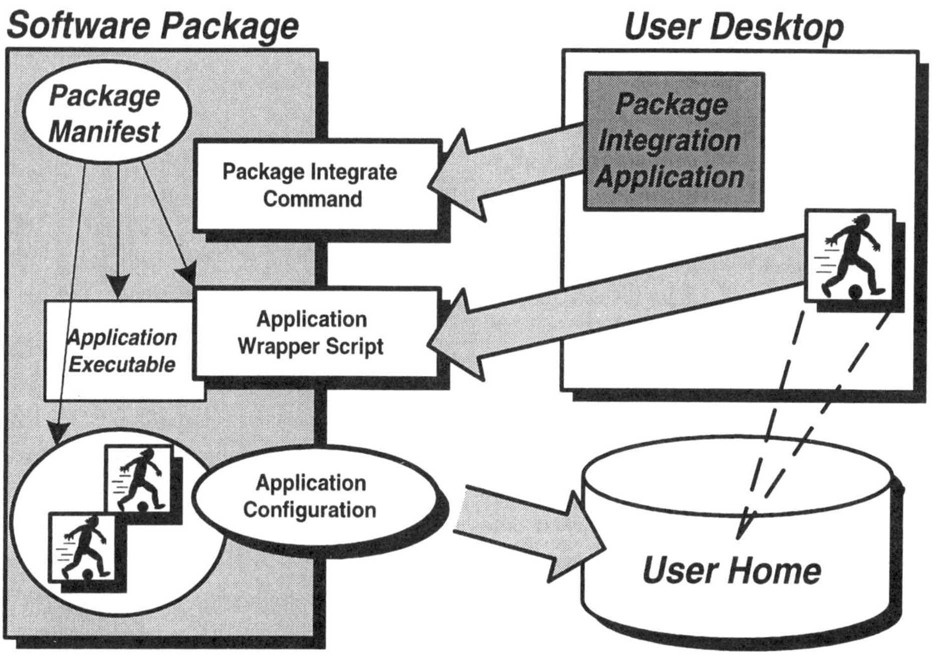

Figure 11-5 Package Integration Interface

tional modification of package contents, and frequently the package is exported to the clients in read-only mode. If an application attempts to write to this shared package, it will fail. The separation of code and data components is often an application packaging issue and may be addressed by manual repackaging of the application to meet local configuration requirements.

The Unix SVR4 standard defines a file system layout that supports the code and data separation goal. Other systems, like Microsoft Windows, may have no such set of recommendations. Code and data separation is an essential part of saving system administration effort for shared packages. We need code and data separation support to enable the use of dataless clients.

Server and Client Package Configurations Many application packages have components that need to be installed on the client system for the application to work properly. This can be information, such as X-Windows configuration defaults, desktop icons and actions, registry information, or environment variables that point to resources like license servers.

As a first-order approach to package installation, we would like to install an application package into a shared directory on a file server (i.e., */opt* on a Unix system), make that shared directory available to the client system (via NFS), and perform a secondary installation that copies the proper configuration information onto the client system. This approach, however, requires that the package be installed on every client system a particular user may touch.

In a dynamic environment, this "one application—every system" requirement cannot always be met. Additionally, the requirement to load the configuration information on multiple clients circumvents the dataless client approach and can dramatically increase the amount of client installation activity. This is not the most desirable way to deal with package integration on the client systems.

One component of solving this problem is to use the hierarchical search patterns of the desktop, placing the configuration information into the user's home directory or other common configuration location that follows the user from client to client. But this is only part of the total solution, because the user's configuration information will grow linearly with the number of applications that he runs from his environment. We will make more suggestions in the next section.

Package Integration Interface The integration requirements vary from package to package. To avoid statically building the information into the user's home configuration, one approach is to provide wrapper scripts that dynamically create the application environment at execution time. The desktop portion of the integration may need to be permanently embedded in the user's home configuration to make it available, depending upon the ability of the desktop to deal with dynamic configuration.

The static menu items in the user's desktop point to the application wrapper scripts in the shared packages, as if they were the application executable. When the wrapper script is executed, it will define environment variables, check for required configuration information, and finally execute the real application. A standard "skeleton" wrapper script may provide a consistent framework for error reporting, debugging, and licensing, logging of the application's actions.

A consistent package integration interface can enable users to view, install, and uninstall the required packages in their environments via a standardized tool. A schematic representation of a package interface is shown in Figure 11-5. This can alleviate a large system administration load associated with configuration of user applications. Support for simultaneous installation of multiple application versions is possible with the proper naming conventions and wrapper script behavior.

Local or Remote Package Installation There are some applications that, because of their size, initialization behavior, or other performance issues, should have portions of their packages installed on client systems. This type of installation may be necessary but should be the exception rather than the rule. Any package installation model should allow for this possibility.

A wrapper script that builds the application environment at execution time can dynamically check for the local components and modify the application configuration to match. Of course, the dynamic building of the environment needs to be moderated to prevent adverse impact on application start-up time. It is usually impractical to perform the local installation at run time, so client systems must be preloaded with the local components.

11.3.3 Maintaining Software Package State

If every software package on the system was completely independent, our software-installation job would be much easier. We will have no such luck—software packages have dependencies on other software packages. Sometimes the dependencies are a complex network that would be difficult to maintain manually.

Our software-installation tools need to deal with the software dependencies for us. It is the software developer and the software packagers that understand the relationships between the packages and the corresponding installation order. The software packaging and distribution tools should automatically detect the encapsulated dependencies and perform the installations in the proper sequence to maintain the software's integrity.

The software-installation facility should also maintain the current software "state" of a system in a system software database that allows query operations. As system managers, we need to know the exact software content of the system to determine information like its patch level and the versions of the installed software units.

11.4 SDU: A Network Software Distribution Model

We have already stated the need for network-based software installation, along with the "normal" installation from local media. The Hewlett-Packard Software Distribution Utilities (SDU) provide a good example of a flexible software installation tool that handles both network and local installation of software packages. The SDU tools create, install, distribute, and manage software objects (described below.)

These tools are based on the POSIX 1387.2, version 1, Software Administration standard and are available on a variety of different platforms, including Unix and Microsoft Windows. The SDU tool set may serve as a model against which we can compare other software-distribution and installation facilities.

11.4.1 SDU Basic Software Installation Units

The SDU tools operate on logical software entities that are packaged and configured by a tool called *swpackage*[5]. The basic units are:

- **Product** —An object that may be installed containing one or more filesets and zero or more optional subproducts.
- **Fileset**—A group of one or more files contained in a product or subproduct. A fileset may also contain control scripts.
- **Subproduct**—An optional subset or partitioning of a software product, which contains one or more filesets.

5. Most of the SDU commands start with the characters "sw". The *swpackage* command is pronounced "swuh-package" by convention.

- **Bundle**—Encapsulates products, subproducts, and filesets into a single software object. A bundle captures a particular configuration or grouping of underlying software objects.

The *swpackage* command takes as its input a specification file and places its output into a directory location that contains software products or bundles that are available for installation. This directory structure is called a depot.

Each software unit has a number of attributes, including the required architecture, the package version, and the required operating system. SDU support a wide range of attribute information. The attribute information is checked against that of the target system and other installation units to ensure proper software installation. Attributes for the product, subproduct, fileset, or bundle are set in the product specification file that creates them.

11.4.2 SDU Software Depots

A software depot may exist in a disk-based directory, or it can also be resident on a distribution medium like a CD-ROM or a tape. The *swcopy* command can move products from depot to depot, including between remote network depots and a local depot. The *swpackage* command is used to create tape depots from a disk-based depot. These tape or CD-ROM depots are used to transport and distribute software depots when using a network is not practical.

11.4.3 SDU Software Tools

The SDU tools enable the installation, configuration, and manipulation of software units. Most of the tools have both a command-line and a graphical user interface. The major SDU tools are:

- **swacl**—Modifies the access control lists which protect software products
- **swconfig**—Configures, unconfigures, or reconfigures installed software
- **swinstall**—Installs and configures software products
- **swlist**—Displays information about software products
- **swmodify**—Modifies software product information in a target or depot
- **swpackage**—Packages software products into a depot or other medium
- **swreg**—Registers or unregisters software depots
- **swremove**—Unconfigures and removes software products
- **swverify**—Verifies the installation of software products

In addition to the tool set, there is a daemon process[6], *swagentd*, that manages SDU requests and creates *swagent* processes to carry out the action. Some of the tool interactions are shown in Figure 11-6. The SDU daemon processes manage a software installation database on the target system that contains complete information about all installed software, the installed

6. A Unix daemon is a special process that is noninteractive and is therefore not attached to input or output devices.

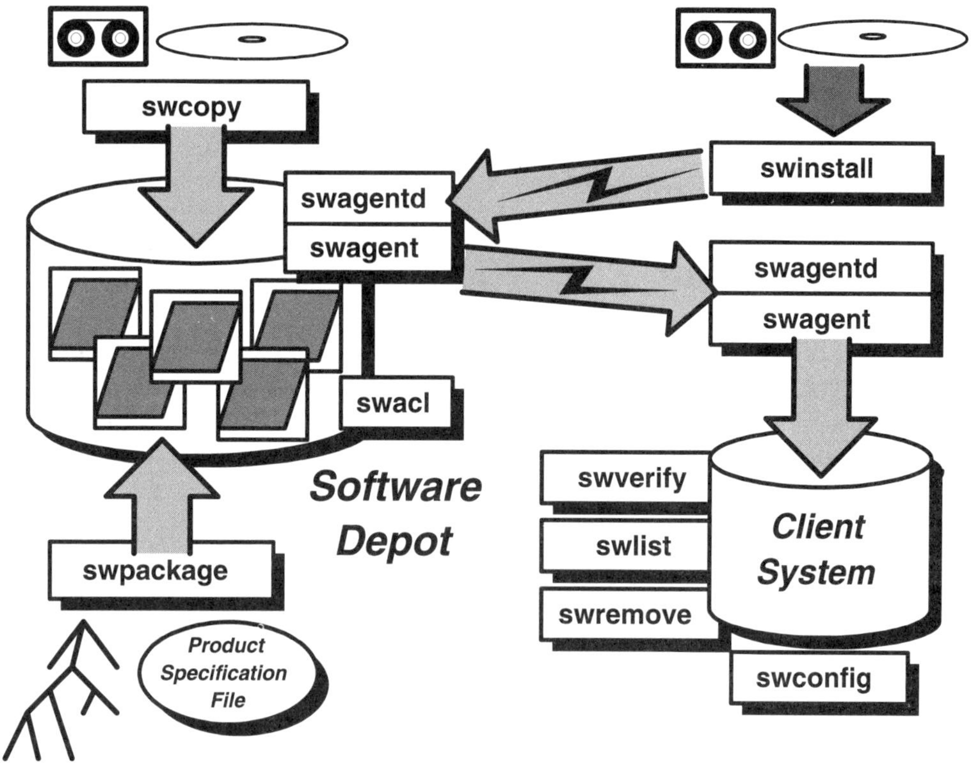

Figure 11-6 Components of the Software-Distribution Utility Facility

versions, the dependencies, and other critical information. This database may be queried locally or remotely with the *swlist* command.

11.4.4 The SDU-Installation Process

A software-installation session starts with the user running the *swinstall* command and selecting a source for the software depot—network, local, or local-media based. The *swinstall* tool then lists the contents of the depot. The user may select the appropriate software for installation and start the installation process. Software in the depot is protected by a group of ACLs that determines who may install the software.

Once the software is selected, it is copied to a work area on the target system, where the internal configuration scripts that finalize the installation are run. SDU provides for a number of software configuration scripts that are run at well-defined points during the installation process: four may be executed during the normal course of software installation and two may execute in the event of an installation failure. The *swinstall* command supports the following scripts:

- **checkinstall**—Executed during analysis of a target selection, checks that the installation can be attempted. Failure of this script prevents installation of the product.
- **preinstall**—Executed immediately before the software's files are installed.
- **postinstall**—Executed immediately after the software's files are installed.
- **configure**—Executed during the configuration of the target, configuring the target for the software and the software for the target.
- **unpreinstall**—Executed immediately after the software's actual files are restored if the install will fail. This script undoes the steps performed by the postinstall script.
- **unpostinstall**—Executed immediately before the software's actual files are restored if the install fails. This script undoes the work performed by the unpostinstall script.

Software being installed will transition through the following states: nonexistent, TRANSIENT, INSTALLED, and CONFIGURED. Software being removed from a system will transition through states in the reverse order. Any portion of the TRANSIENT installation process that fails will result in the software state being set to CORRUPT.

11.4.5 SDU Installation Dependencies

The SDU installation tools manage two types of dependencies between filesets and products: prerequisites and co-requisites. A fileset's prerequisite dependency must be installed and configured prior to the installation of the fileset with the dependency. A co-requisite dependency indicates that the fileset with the dependency and the dependent fileset must be installed and configured at the same time before the dependent is usable.

11.4.6 SDU Network Depots

Local depot directories become available over the network when they are registered with the *swreg* command. The registration occurs automatically when a depot is created on the local system. The path to a remote depot is specified to the SDU tools in the following format:

hostname:/path/depot_directory

A depot may also be unregistered with the *swreg* command, which renders it invisible to network installations.

Software in the depot is locked while being placed into the depot. The software will transition through three states while being added: nonexistent, TRANSIENT, and AVAILABLE. For software being removed from the depot, the state transition is in the opposite order. If part of the placement or removal of the software fails, then the software state is set to CORRUPT.

11.4.7 SDU Summary

The SDU tool set implements a very flexible and powerful software-installation facility. The default installation mode is a pull installation, where the installation control software runs on the target system. With the optional OpenView Software Distributor product from HP, SDU provides the ability to do push installation.

11.5 Class-Based Software Installation

The concept of class-based software installation is a very useful tool in our workgroup environment. We may segregate the software packages required on systems into common groups associated with the system's class. A class-based installation tool should use class information to detect and install software required by the system's class memberships.

While there are several powerful software-installation utilities like SDU, none of them appear to support class-based software management. To manage information in this way, a central database is required that contains a system's class membership and a mapping between the class membership and required software packages. The author has since implemented a class-based software-installation facility as a Unix POSIX shell wrapper script that can execute underlying software installation commands. After implementing the facility, the author has run across several similar tools implemented by other system managers in a variety of environments[7].

The facility was originally implemented over the top of the SDU utilities to provide class-based installation of individual SDU products, bundles, and filesets. Later incarnations of the facility were written such that other installation products could be added to the wrapper script, including the SVR4 package command and simple *tar* archive installation. This class-based tool is in use at several large Hewlett-Packard customers. An overview of its design and operation follows.

11.5.1 Origin of the *load_filesets* Tool

The origin of the was rooted in the necessity to deal with large numbers of operating system patches. The author was performing consulting work at a large technical manufacturing company and was responsible for the system management and roll-out of over seven hundred Unix workstations and associated servers to five separate sites in three countries. Each system, because it was running a complex combination of software development and integrated circuit design tools, required a large number of individual software patches.

Early testing of the installation process indicated that it took approximately three hours to perform the patch installation, which required multiple reboots of the system. Because of the reboots, the installation process required constant manual attention. A quick calculation showed that there were not enough hours in the remainder of the year[8] to meet the requirements of a completely manual installation.

7. Often the first clue that there is a common problem to be solved is when everyone comes up with roughly the same solution in a completely independent manner.

8. Or in the system administration team's lifetimes.

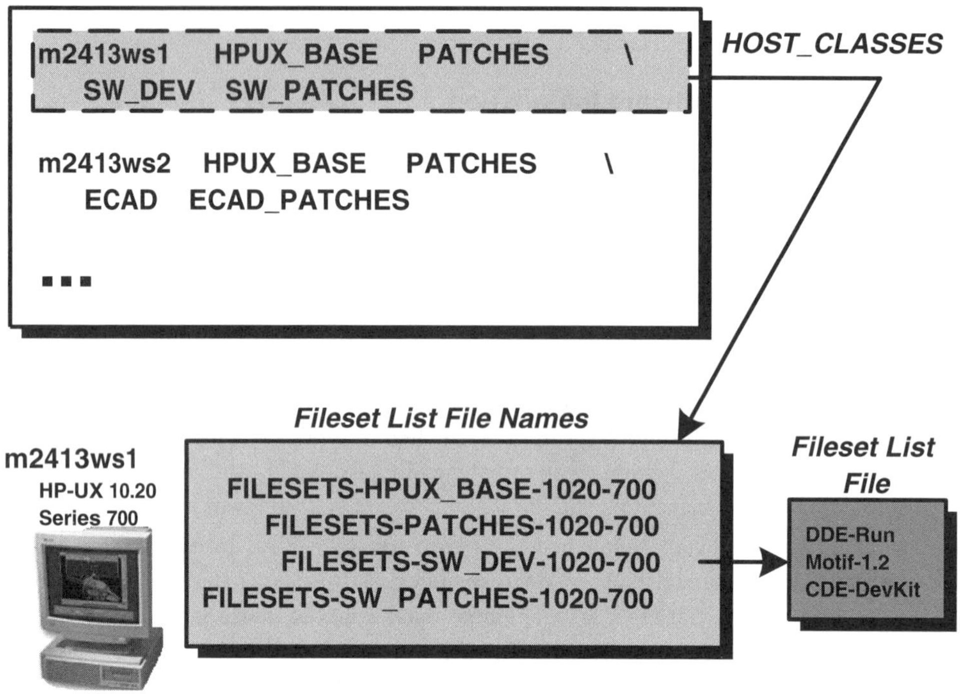

Figure 11-7 Class Database and Fileset List File Relationships for load_filesets

11.5.2 The Class Membership Database

Because the systems all had slightly unique hardware characteristics, software content, and operating system configurations, a class-based scheme was chosen. Because of the commonality involved, a base class with four or five derived system classes was sufficient to deal with the software configurations. Using the standard Unix command set, we developed a simple database scheme.

A central, flat text file would contain the hostname of the client system, followed by white-space delimited class names to which the system belonged. This flat database was stored in a file called *HOST_CLASSES*. An example of a database entry is:

hpupora   HPUX_BASE   OS_PATCHES   APP_PATCHES

A simple *grep* for the client system's host name in the file would yield the complete line. Converting the line to tokens within the shell script and discarding the hostname provided a list of classes that the client system belonged to.

11.5.3 The Fileset List File

The class names from the class database entry were then used to generate a file name for a fileset list file that would contain the ordered list of filesets to install on the client system. The file name for the fileset list file also needed to account for differences in architecture and operating system version. The final format for a fileset list file name was:

FILESETS-<Class_Name>-<OS_Revision>-<Architecture>

The operating system revision and the system architecture are easily generated from the Unix *uname* command, which returns this type of information.

The process followed by the script was to locate the *HOST_CLASSES* database in a well-known location, extract the line containing its host name, and produce a list of member classes. The classes, in turn, were used to generate the fileset list files for the class. Using the previous example on an HP-UX 10.20 operating system and an HP 9000 Series 700 workstation yields:

FILESETS-HPUX_BASE-1020-700
FILESETS-OS_PATCHES-1020-700
FILESETS-APP_PATCHES-1020-700

Each of the fileset list files was located in a well-known location, opened, and used to generate the proper sequence of installation tool commands for the associated class. In the case where there were no dependencies between the individual filesets, the installation tool could configure them in one operation. Where dependencies between filesets existed, or reboots were required, individual sequential installations were called for. The dependencies themselves were handled by the underlying installation tool.

11.5.4 Using a Client-Based Pull Installation

We used a pull installation model to implement the class-based installation process, because it allowed the individual client systems to make their own decisions about what software to install from central depots. The fileset list file contains information about the location of the network depots to use for software installation. In that way, the client system could locate the depot and pull the software to the local disk.

The *HOST_CLASSES* database, the filesets list files, and the installation tool itself were all distributed via an automounter indirect map. By default, the complete package was located under */Admin/filesets*. This allowed single-point administration of the software installation process on the client systems from an administration server.

11.5.5 Executing the Installation Process

To handle the proper installation behavior across system reboots, the installation script is placed in the system start-up process. The script is activated after the NFS and NIS subsystems are started, but before the system is released to the user log-in process. If software installation is

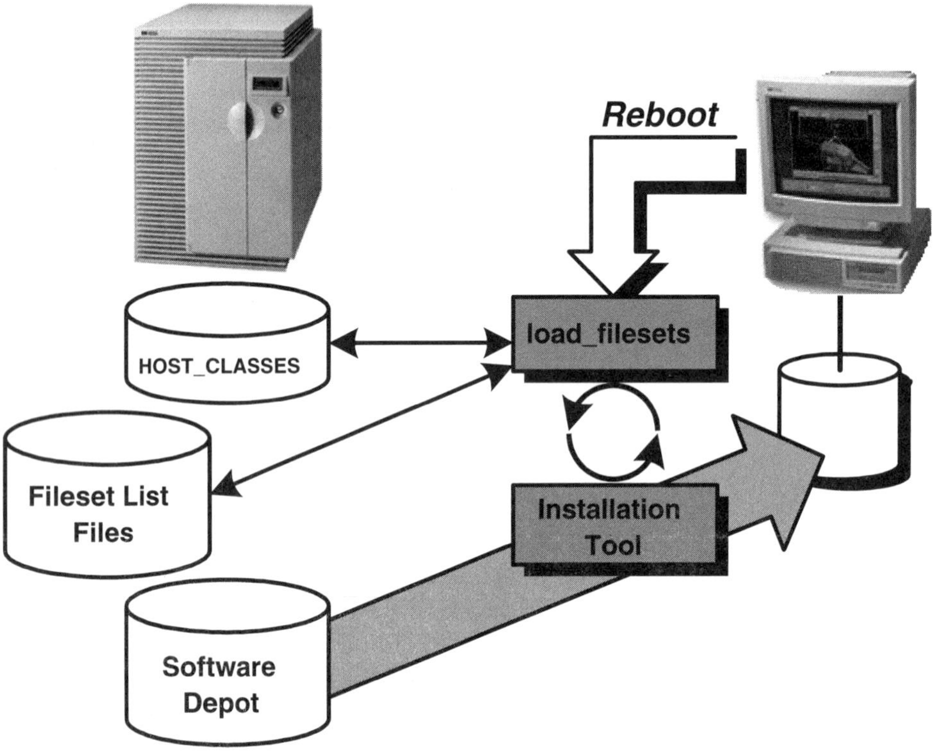

Figure 11-8 The *load_filesets* Tool Operation

necessary, the script will check to see if the software is already installed and will skip to the next entry in the fileset list file if the current entry is present.

The fact that the installation facility maintains a database of the system's software state ensures that software will not be reinstalled (unless a specific override is applied.) The class installation script will install a software unit that reboots the system, run again during the system start-up, detect the previous installation, and install the next software unit. For underlying facilities that are not capable of installing multiple filesets with only a single reboot, this behavior preserves the proper sequencing and allows for noninteractive installation of all required software.

Placing the installation test in the system start-up process allows remote rebooting to trigger the software update process. Any fileset list file that has not been modified within a specified period of time will be ignored, to prevent impacting nonscheduled system reboots. Once a modification is made to the fileset list file, however, the next reboot will trigger the class-based installation process.

A number of override features are used to control the class-based installation behavior:

- Filesets may be reinstalled with an override to the underlying installation tool.
- Installation may be switched off completely by the presence of a lock file, to prevent power failures from accidentally triggering reboot installation.
- Global installation may be disallowed except during certain time windows.
- Individual software packages may be set to install only after a certain date and time.

These overrides are either specified in a global lock file or set as attributes on the fileset list file lines that specify the software unit for installation.

11.5.6 *load_filesets* Summary

The *load_filesets* tool is an example of applying class-based system administration techniques to an automated software-installation process. The management of the class information and the mapping to specific sets of software filesets is a simpler approach than hand-crafting the contents of each system. Now that image installation is a primary client system software management technique, the *load_filesets* tool is mainly applied to point patching of server and client systems.

This tool and its implementation also provide an example of abstraction of lower-level details. Instead of dealing with the installation of single filesets, the system administrator is freed to deal with class relationships. The savings of time and effort multiply as more and more systems are managed, but the system-management overhead remains relatively constant.

11.6 System-Administration Techniques

System administration consists of ensuring the proper hardware and software configuration and operation of the workgroup systems. It involves tasks such as moving resources from place to place, backing up and restoring data, calming frantic users, and performing the day-to-day tasks that hold the environment together. Frequently the system administrator is more interrupt driven than strategic in nature, due to a chaotic environment. But system management should be a more strategic activity—measuring the state of the environment, evaluating the measurements against desired results, and making the necessary changes to meet the expectations of the users, not constantly fighting fires.

But more than performing the individual management tasks, a good system administrator is always looking for the combination of operations that can accomplish the job with a minimum amount of time investment, a high level of quality, and a maximum level of confidence that the proper steps were taken. As we have stated, system administrators are the masters of complexity. If given enough development time, a good system administrator can automate frequently performed procedures and use the time saved for other activities.

The key is not to let things get out of control in the first place. This, of course, is easier said than done in many environments. The rapid pace of technology, the evolution of the environment, and the initial lack of architectural design all can take their toll, and the system administrator usually is the direct recipient of the results. Let's examine how things could work in an ideal system manager's world.

11.6.1 Manual Processes

Everything seems to start with manual processes. We all sit down to perform new administrative tasks, not sure where they will lead us. We study the manuals, ask our peers for suggestions, and dive in. About the third or fourth time we perform the operation, we are already trying to streamline it to save time and effort.

This is the beginning of a manual process. We may even make notes about the proper sequence of operations, the commands to use, and the proper command options. If things stop at this point, we are missing an opportunity. To fine-tune a manual process, it needs to be shared and used by multiple people in a variety of situations—a different process in everyone's notebook does nothing to help consistency.

A central clearinghouse for procedures is one way around the pigeon holing of administration procedures. Sharing manual procedures helps improve them and provides a way to train new system administrators. It is also the basis for the next step in the system administration process "food chain"—automated processes.

11.6.2 Automating Manual Processes

Having a general model for the development of automated administration processes can help with making manual processes automatic. We should realize that system administration operations consist of configuration data and operations that create or modify it. This combination of behavior and persistent data strongly resembles an object. It is no accident that we may apply object-oriented principles to the automation of system administration procedures.

Another general principle we can use in our model is class-based layering of administration objects. There may be a corporate IT department that requires specific configurations for global services like DNS or NTP. Division, workcenter, and workgroup policies may also exist, each with its own set of requirements that must be encapsulated in the process.

This layering can be viewed as deriving system administration objects, allowing each level in the hierarchy to override, or substitute, their own specific set of system-administration objects while retaining the required characteristics of the higher levels of the hierarchy. The end result of the derivation is the final configuration of the system or service that determines its operational behavior or configuration.

For our automation candidates, we should select well-defined, "tried and true" manual processes from the previously discussed pool. If there are multiple system types in the environment, then we should try to automate the same operation across all of them at the same time. A common interface to the operation on all systems is a precursor to enabling higher-level administration operations.

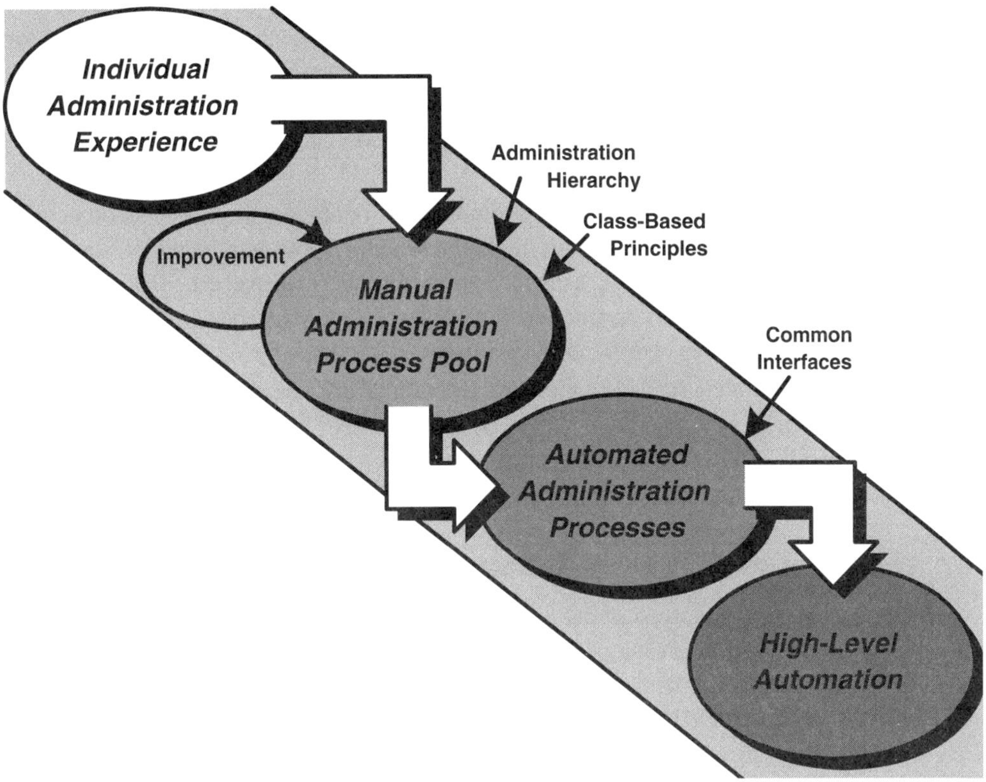

Figure 11-9 The System Administration "Food Chain"

11.6.3 Automated System Administration and Stability

Automation is only practical where enough stability is present in the system interfaces and commands to allow a return on the investment, otherwise it becomes a game of constant catch-up. To break the cycle takes a dedicated investment like that described in Chapter 17. The hardware, operating system, and application turnover rates can affect the overall stability of the system configurations and associated system-administration procedures.

Stability in the workgroup system administration environment is also important. If there is not enough time for the system administration staff to devote to moving processes up the system administration food chain, then the environment may never progress beyond the individual scribbled notes and disconnected scripts stage. The less stable the environment is, the more interrupt driven the system administration staff will be. We can easily become involved in a "catch-22" situation, since stability may only be possible where consistent (automated) processes are applied.

11.6.4 High-Level System-Management Automation

As system-administration procedures move up the food chain, they typically abstract low-level operations into higher-level objects. Each of these management objects contains a set of internal operations and configuration data and presents a control interface that can be used by other higher-level objects. A master script or control platform can call these objects to perform system-administration operations.

Most system vendors have their own system-administration tools, and we should note that these tools differ from what we are describing here. Vendors' tools assume the presence of an administrator, sitting at a console or using a remote display, to drive the management process.What we really would like is an automated, high-level tool to interface to the common system management interfaces on each vendor's platforms.

The ability to remotely manage hundreds to thousands of systems in both LAN and WAN environments is high on our wish list. Unfortunately, we are not there yet. Most tools that have some of the capabilities we are describing suffer from scalability issues and attempt to manage the environment as a monolithic whole—something that we are trying to avoid.

11.7 The Depot Tool: Automated Data Configuration

A good example of the type of automation that is possible, given the need and development time, is the "depot" tool, developed by Wallace Colyer and Walter Wong[9] at Carnegie-Mellon University[10]. The environment at CMU relies heavily on the Andrew File System (AFS)—a predecessor to the current DCE DFS—for its underlying distribution of data. The depot tool is responsible for automating the process of what we might call "secondary" software package installation on client systems, that is, the mapping of globally available package contents to local disk structure on the client system.

The depot tool is a software release–management package, implementing a model based on the need for distribution, installation, customization, testing, and removal and restoration of software packages in a complex software environment. The management environment comprises discrete objects that may be assembled to create the structure presented to the user. This is an automated, operational embodiment of the model described on page 227.

The originators of the depot tool employed four key concepts in its construction: independence, integration, mobility, and simplicity. Independence involves packaging the related software components into self-contained "collections". The process of integration makes the software collections available in a unified directory hierarchy which is presented to the user.

9. *Depot: A Tool for Managing Software Environments*, Wallace Colyer and Walter Wong, Computing Sciences, Carnegie-Mellon University. Proceedings of the 1993 Usenix Large Installation System Administration (LISA) VII Conference.

10. Information on the depot tool may be found under *WWW.CMU.edu*. The path "http://andrew2.andrew.cmu.edu/depot" is where the author eventually wound up.

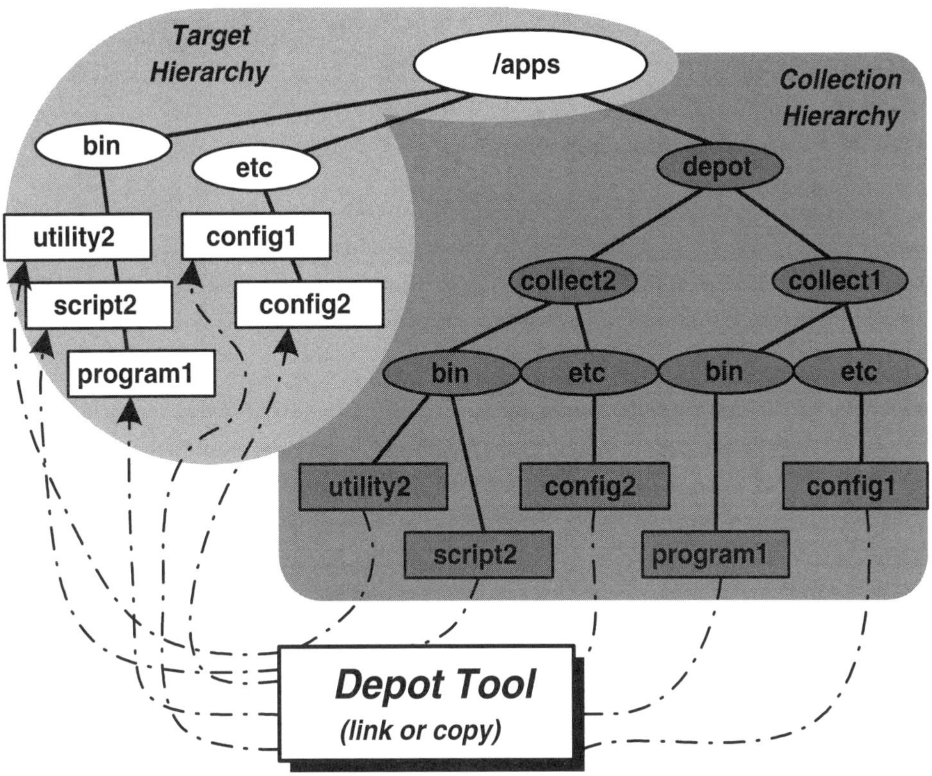

Figure 11-10 The Depot Tool in Action

Mobility allows collections to be added to and removed from the environment as requirements change. Simplicity applies to the mapping process used to make collection components appear in the final structure in a location consistent with the collection's internal hierarchy.

The depot tool, when invoked, maps the collection hierarchy to the final structure below a target directory. The collections are integrated into the hierarchy below this target directory. Collections to be integrated are located with several mechanisms, including a search path. If multiple revisions of a collection are available, then the latest revision is integrated. Components of the collections may be integrated with one of two procedures: copying or linking.

The integration process may occur on the client system, using collections from a shared file system. When collections change on the shared file system, the client must run the depot tool to select the most recent collections for integration. Integration may also occur on the shared file system itself. The target hierarchy is a union of all selected collections and their hierarchies. An example of an integration is shown in Figure 11-10.

Depot is the most flexible example of an automated data-mapping process the author has run across. It is like a Unix *make* command that builds directory hierarchies, instead of application structure[11]. Most experienced large-scale system administrators come to the conclusion that automated data mapping is an essential system administrative tool, but end up with less general solutions—for a variety of reasons.

11.8 Performance Monitoring

We may create the initial conditions of our workgroup, carefully planning the amount and location of the resources it contains. With the passage of time and changes in the organizations that use it, however, the actual state of the workgroup's systems and services is subject to "environmental drift". The workgroup is an evolving entity, and we must constantly adjust its configuration to meet the changes in its user's needs.

System-performance monitoring is the feedback that validates the resource adjustments and system administration actions that we take. It also provides information about the scale and magnitude of the changes that we need to undertake for a given system. It is truly surprising how many environments run "open loop", without the benefit of performance measurements as feedback. Historical performance monitoring data is invaluable for troubleshooting and system tuning.

11.8.1 Monitoring Client Systems and Applications

We might be tempted to ignore the client systems when we design the performance collection and monitoring services for our workgroup, but the client system's performance is important to ensuring proper application performance for its user. By monitoring the client systems with resource thresholds and a set of alarms, system managers can head off problems and capture error conditions as they occur.

Furthermore, information collected from representative client systems can provide the information necessary to make adjustments to the network and associated server sizes, as well as client operating system parameters and client hardware configuration. We should not overlook the importance of the client systems, because they are what drives the remainder of the environment for the user.

Monitoring client application performance can help us determine when it is necessary to move a particular application "through" the load-balancing service and to a compute server. The transparency of resource allocation can sometimes hide the fact that a particular application component might be running on the user's client system. If the user's system is bogging down

11. Given this book's theme of applying software development to system administration, you can probably see the appeal.

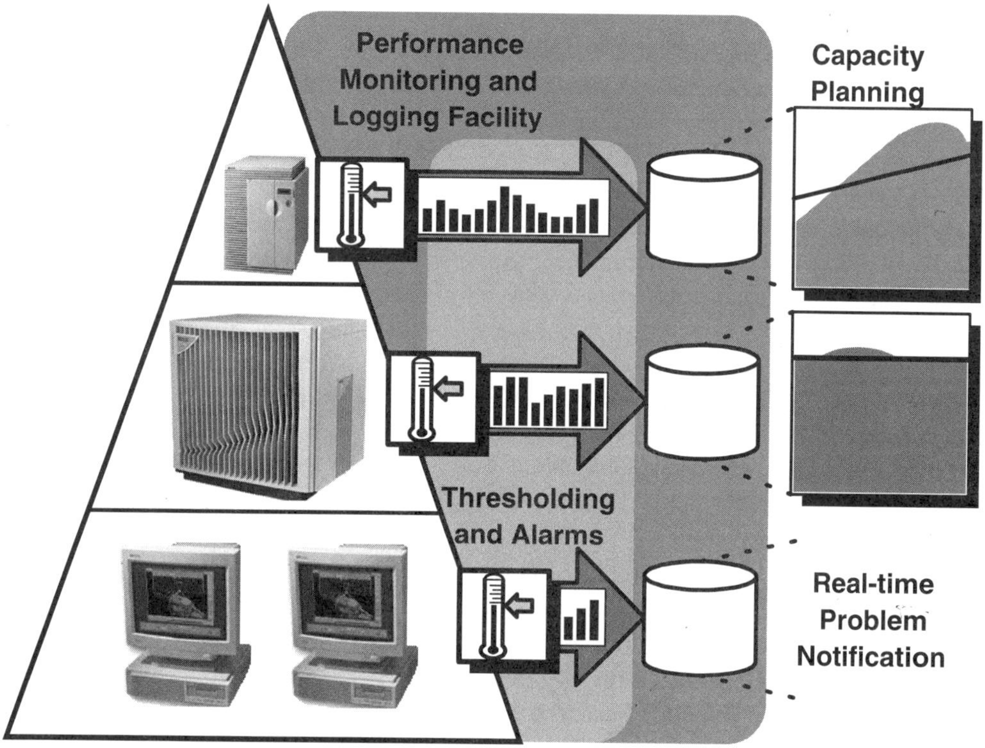

Figure 11-11 Workgroup Monitoring and Capacity Planning

with activity, we should know right away, so that we don't allow problems to become entrenched[12].

11.8.2 Monitoring Compute and File Servers

Because servers, both compute and file, are central to the operation of the workgroup, their performance is critical. We must balance high-utilization factors, to have a good return on our server investment, and utilization rates that are so high as to cause performance degradation. There is a fine line separating high utilization from overutilization.

The way to prevent overutilization of hardware resources is to continuously collect server performance information and subject it to analysis. Only long-term analysis can differentiate between a temporary situation and a trend that will eventually swamp the server's resources. We

12. System managers have to fight what the author calls the "they says", those nagging little misconceptions that get started when a user observes puzzling behavior. A user's explanation of such a problem frequently resembles the prototype sentence: "*They say* that the <insert object here> has problems".

must stay ahead of the user's resource requirements to maintain the virtual computer's illusion of compute power on demand.

One of the primary external file server parameters to measure is response time to client requests. From the client's point of view, that is frequently the single most important factor other than availability. File server performance benchmarks often include not only the maximum number of operations per second the server can perform, but also information about the matching request response time.

Internal to the file server object, there is more measurement complexity to deal with. To minimize the server's response time to client requests, we must be aware of the operating system parameters that affect overall performance and collect data to use for decision making. Based on that data, we can make tuning decisions and hardware configuration decisions and decide when to split the server into multiple resources. It may be useful to have a simulation or model for the particular service that can predict response time based on the parameter values.

A compute server's resources must also be monitored to provide adequate resources to the workgroup users. The primary compute server resource is raw CPU power and secondarily system RAM. A shortage of either resource can impact the performance of the compute server and cause requests for compute resources to queue up, impacting time to completion for the users. We must be able to tell when the workgroup virtual computer needs more CPU power.

The monitoring of system resource usage over time and the utilization of the collected data to predict future resource needs is frequently called "capacity planning". The idea, of course, is to detect trends and patterns in system usage and add resources to the environment before shortages occur. We should note that we can also use capacity planning to detect available resources that may be decommissioned and moved elsewhere.

11.8.3 Network Devices and Segments

We need to monitor the performance of network devices, such as routers, switches, and hubs. Along with the monitoring function, most network devices allow remote network management operations, given the proper interface to their software. With dedicated switch ports for each client, the network performance monitoring can focus on the backbones and switch uplinks.

A network management tool like Hewlett-Packard's OpenView Network Node Manager (NNM) can help provide a common interface to network devices. NNM will "discover" each device in the network and provide a network topology map with icons representing different equipment. Network administrators can click on the icon and remotely access the performance statistics and management consoles for the device.

Occasionally there are areas that need specific measurements. Network monitoring tools like Hewlett-Packard's NetMetrix[13] product provide special "probes" that can be attached to individual LAN segments. The probes may be remotely queried for the results of the monitoring.

13. See *WWW.HP.com* for more information on OpenView Network Node Manager and the NetMetrix products.

It is possible to determine the network traffic makeup in terms of protocol type and other very useful statistics.

11.9 Operating Environment Summary

The operating environment is one of the most complex and important portions of the workgroup. The system administration efforts are frequently divided up between two or more organizations: an enterprise service provider and the local administration staff. Sometimes there are even more groups with their fingers in the pie. This organizational complexity often exceeds the underlying functional complexity. System-administration procedures need to take the requirements of organizations in the administrative hierarchy into account.

Aside from simplifying the organization, we can concentrate on continuous improvement of manual system-administration processes, aiming for their eventual automation. We have touched on some of the methods, like class-based administration, that can help us design or choose tools for managing complexity. Several examples of such tools, like depot and load_filesets, were given to illustrate useful principles.

More than anything, it is important to have automation, centralized management, and simplicity as goals for your system-administration environment. The operating environment layer is essential for supporting the next layer in the workgroup functional model—the data-sharing layer. If we are successful at managing the resources and reducing complexity, we will be rewarded in the layers that lie above.

CHAPTER 12

Data Sharing: Local Access and Global Visibility

The primary focus of a workgroup is sharing data between its users, indeed, the reason for a network connection is to enable the sharing of data. The discussion in Chapter 7, "Stable Storage: The Workgroup File Server" on page 87, showed some of the possible physical storage mechanisms that may be used to hold user data, and the previous chapter discusses hardware resource allocation to support the services required by the workgroup. But the workgroup may use many different physical locations and services to store data: file servers, multiple physical file systems, network drives, and the like. How do we give the workgroup users a consistent, manageable view of physically disjoint data stores?

This chapter discusses the presentation of the data to the client systems and the client-server applications that use it. We will study some of the different data presentation mechanisms, their positive and negative aspects, available security, and their effect on system-management practices and user perceptions of the workgroup environment. Finally, we will recommend methods of data presentation that make the client's view of the stored data consistent and understandable from the user's point of view.

12.1 Presenting a Consistent Data Access Interface

The problem with data is that users access it. The paths to discrete pieces of data end up getting saved in all kinds of locations: start-up files, program "last-file-accessed" menus, user scripts, and other less frequently used places. This creates direct dependencies, and user expectations, on the data and its location.

If, for whatever reason, the data moves, the direct dependencies are broken and applications fail. The movement of data can also confuse the user and result in loss of productivity. For these reasons, we must insulate the user from any changes that occur in the location of the data

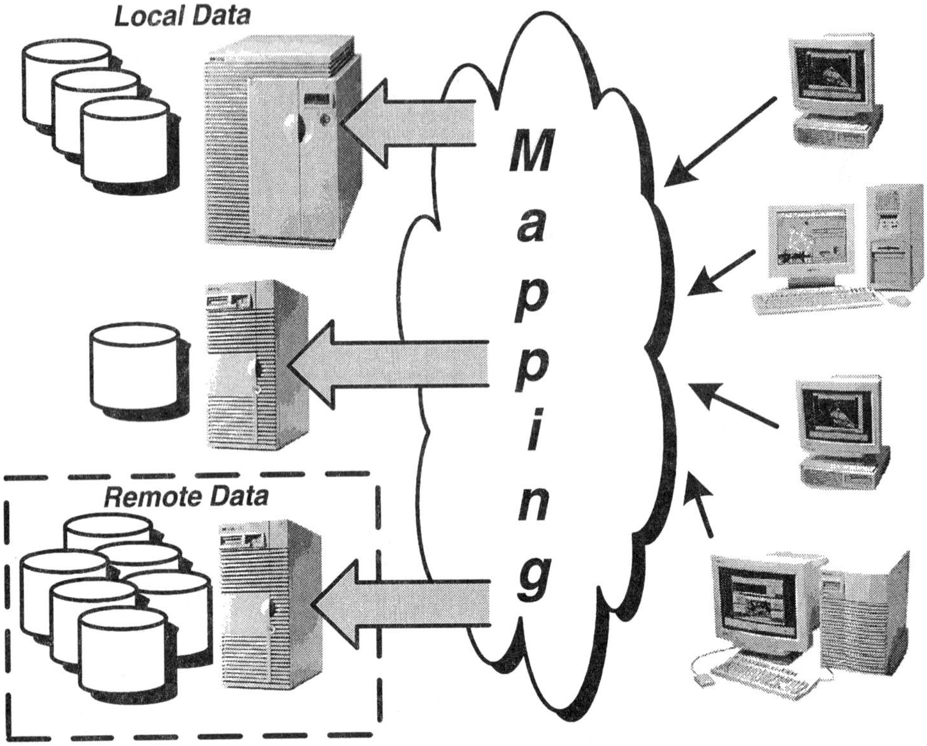

Figure 12-1 Mapping Client Access to Server Data

that he or she accesses. The way that a user gets to his or her data sets should not change from day to day or from location to location in the network.

There are different techniques for providing insulation from changing data location. Some data access methods provide this useful feature as an integral part of their operation. Still others require that we, as workgroup designers, create and implement a consistent scheme for our users. Let's examine some of the important aspects of data presentation and some methods for implementing it in our environments.

12.1.1 Consistent File Paths and Naming Conventions

Consistently locating the right data for a given task involves the two components of the file or data set name: the path to the data and the specific file name. There may be multiple routes to the same file, but whether or not there are multiple paths to the data, we want them to remain the same every time the data is accessed. To provide this type of data access consistency while still allowing system administrators to adjust the data's location requires careful design, organization, and presentation of the data.

File-Naming Conventions Available formats for naming data files vary from system to system, based on the limitations imposed by the operating system's file systems. Unix systems generally allow between 128 and 256 characters in a file name, with both upper and lower case characters being significant and no limitations on how the characters are distributed in the name (i.e., no explicit file extension.)

Microsoft Windows systems still rely heavily on the old 8.3 convention (eight characters plus a three-character file extension) but provide new "long" file names; both formats are case insensitive. The long file name format is case preserving, but still case insensitive, with the restrictions of the 8.3 format removed. Many applications still understand only the old MS-DOS names.

Having a consistent set of file extensions and conventions for data files can be difficult in environments that have to interoperate between two schemes like those we just described. Higher-level workgroup facilities, like the user's desktop actions (See Chapter 13), rely on being able to properly identify the type of file being operated on. The more consistent the file-naming scheme, the more intuitive working with the files will be for the user.

Consistent naming provides additional advantages, too. With a consistent, well-defined set of file-naming conventions in place, task automation becomes easier. Tools, scripts, and other environmental "glue" can more easily make decisions about actions to take with the data files they are passed.

File Paths: Local and Remote File path names provide a way of specifying the location of physical data to applications that users want to operate on. It is a little like following someone's directions to the local grocery store: "First you go down the street to the right, take the first left, and it's two blocks up on the right". In all probability, it is possible to find multiple routes to the same location—some longer and some shorter.

Path components are directories, that can contain information about other directories and files. The convention in a hierarchical file system (there are other models) is to separate path components with a slash character ("/" on Unix, and "\" on Microsoft Windows systems), starting with the highest level, or root, of the file system. To access the component at the end of the path, the operating system "walks" the directory tree, following the specified path.

There are two classes of directory tree: those that are local to the system doing the accessing, and those that are remote. Most modern operating systems make both types available in the local file system hierarchy, helping to make remote access transparent to the user. How the data is accessed actually depends on the path conventions followed by the operating system in question.

Microsoft Windows systems have an additional set of conventions that determine the starting point for walking the file's path. In the first variation, all access is relative to a local "drive letter" between "A" and "Z". There is a "current drive letter" that specifies the starting point for any accesses that do not explicitly specify a drive. An example path in this convention is "*C:\Windows\system32\drivers\etc\hosts*", to get to the host to IP address lookup file.

Another convention for accessing resources in a Microsoft Windows environment is the UNC, which follows the "*server_name**share_name**file_name*" convention. The UNC specification may be used to directly access a resource but more commonly is used to map a network resource to a local drive letter or port. The first component in a UNC specification is the NetBIOS name, which must be resolved to a network address for access. Once the drive is mapped, the remote file system appears to be local to the user.

In the Unix world, system managers can mount network resources, via NFS, into the local file system hierarchy. The mount information for a remote file system resembles "*hostname:/path*", where the hostname portion is a name that must be resolved to a TCP/IP address. Once the mount is performed, the remote file system is locally visible to the user. Notice the similarity in function, if not form, of the two specifications.

12.1.2 Consistent Client Views of Data

Even if all of the data files in the workgroup environment are consistently named, we need to provide client systems with a consistent way of locating them in a potential sea of data. How the client system "views" the workgroup data can make this either simple and intuitive or difficult and incomprehensible. The implementation of the mapping process is frequently left up to us as workgroup designers and system managers.

The generalized data-presentation model we will adopt is shown in Figure 12-1. The client system views all server data, whether local or remote (outside the current workgroup), through a "mapping" function. The mapping function provides consistent path names and access abilities, no matter where the data is in the network hierarchy or at which workgroup client the user is located.

In chaotic environments, the data-access mapping has broken down or was never thought out in the first place. The users have to follow thought processes like, "I'm on system X, so the data I used yesterday on system Y is located over there instead of over here, or was it ...?" They may also have to "know" that all data of a particular type is located on a particular server, in a particular directory, which opens the door to creation of direct dependencies in their scripts and menus.

To provide a consistent interface to the workgroup data, we need to provide consistent routes to the data via the paths available to, and specified by, the user. The path to a particular file needs to be consistent not only in time, but also with regards to where the user is located in the workgroup or enterprise. Simply put, we can state this as "Same file, same path, all of the time".

There are a number of ways to implement the consistent presentation of data in our workgroup environment, depending upon what types of data-access mechanisms are in use. Some facilities, as we shall see, inherently provide consistent data access independent of client system position in the network, multiple data sources, or similar issues. We will cover this information in the next sections.

12.1.3 Code and Data Separation

The Unix System V Release 4 (SVR4) specification details a file system layout that separates writable data from read-only data for Unix system commands, configuration files, and for user applications. There are designated directories for statically and dynamically linked system utilities (*/sbin* and */bin*), variable data (*/var*), system configuration information (*/etc*), and optional software packages (*/opt*).

One of the most important aspects of this file system layout is that it separates writable system data from static configuration data. One of the primary reasons for this is to support a read-only system partition. Another is to allow the exporting of read-only application software packages, contained in */opt*, to remote systems via NFS.

We can view the SVR4 layout as creating a separation of code and the configuration data that it uses, much in the same way that compilers create applications that have separate code and data segments. The compiled applications are created this way to allow the code, which does not change, to be shared by multiple users at runtime. It is the separate data that is unique to each instance of the application.

This principle is important to us as system administrators and designers. One copy of an application package, exported with read-only access via a network file system, may be shared by multiple clients without the fear of modification. As a matter of fact, modification of most system packages takes "root" (superuser) level access, and the default behavior of NFS is to deny remote file access to any superuser.

If the application package contained configuration information or data files, the package would need to be writable by every system that mounted it, potentially allowing destructive interference. With code and data separation, the configuration data that determines the local behavior of the application may be located anywhere, including local to the client, so that it may be freely modified without fear of corrupting shared package data[1].

12.2 Consistent Data Access with Automounter and AutoFS

This section is not intended to be a complete tutorial on the automounter or AutoFS. There are quite a few good books on the topic that fill that need. For more information on these tools, see *Managing NFS and NIS* by Hal Stern, [8]. We need here to cover only some of the high-level essentials.

1. This is something that Microsoft Windows systems are terrible at. Windows software developers routinely place programs, icons, configuration files, and data files in the same directory, often under a subdirectory of "Program Files". This creates a backup nightmare, along with the inability to share application packages between systems. Most savvy system administrators try their best to separate application from data, but it is often a losing battle.

There is no inherently consistent data-access mapping provided by NFS. The tools AutoFS, automounter[2], and NIS, which are a standard part of the NFS environment, are intended to enable (not provide) that functionality. With these tools we have the flexibility to create our own data-access scheme, rather than relying on someone else's model. The up-front investment of time to create a consistent scheme is the disadvantage to the "build-it-yourself" approach with NFS.

The automount daemon process passes itself off as a remote NFS server. Whenever the user touches an NFS mount point controlled by the automounter, the Unix kernel passes the access to the automounter. The automounter will consult a set of maps, which determine how, and where, the automounter will make a remote file system magically appear. Once the file system is no longer accessed, the automounter will automatically become the autodismounter, unmounting the remote file system.

12.2.1 The Automounter Master Map

There is a top-level "master" map, that specifies mounting information or one or more submaps. The master map may be specified on the automounter command line, with an optional switch that causes the NIS map information to be ignored. This allows automounter map information to come from three locations: the command line, a local file, or the NIS master map.

There are three basic types of automounter mounts that may appear in the automounter master map: direct, indirect, and special. The general format for all master map entries is:

```
Mount_Directory   Map_Name        [-NFS_Mount_Options]
```

Note the position of the options; it is different from the position of the options in the submaps. Any options specified in the submap will override options specified in the master map. An example master map follows:

```
/net        -hosts            #Special map entry
/tools      auto_tools        #Indirect mount sub-map
/-          auto_direct       #Direct mount sub-map
```

12.2.2 Special Automounter Map Entries

A special map entry may be the "-hosts" entry, which allows access to host's exported file systems, or the "-null" entry, which cancels the effect of a previously specified mount. The format for the host map is:

2. The functionality called automounting used to be provided by the "automount" application. With the advent of AutoFS, automount has become a communication tool that talks to the automount daemon, "automountd". We will use the term automounter to describe the combined functionality of the tool set.

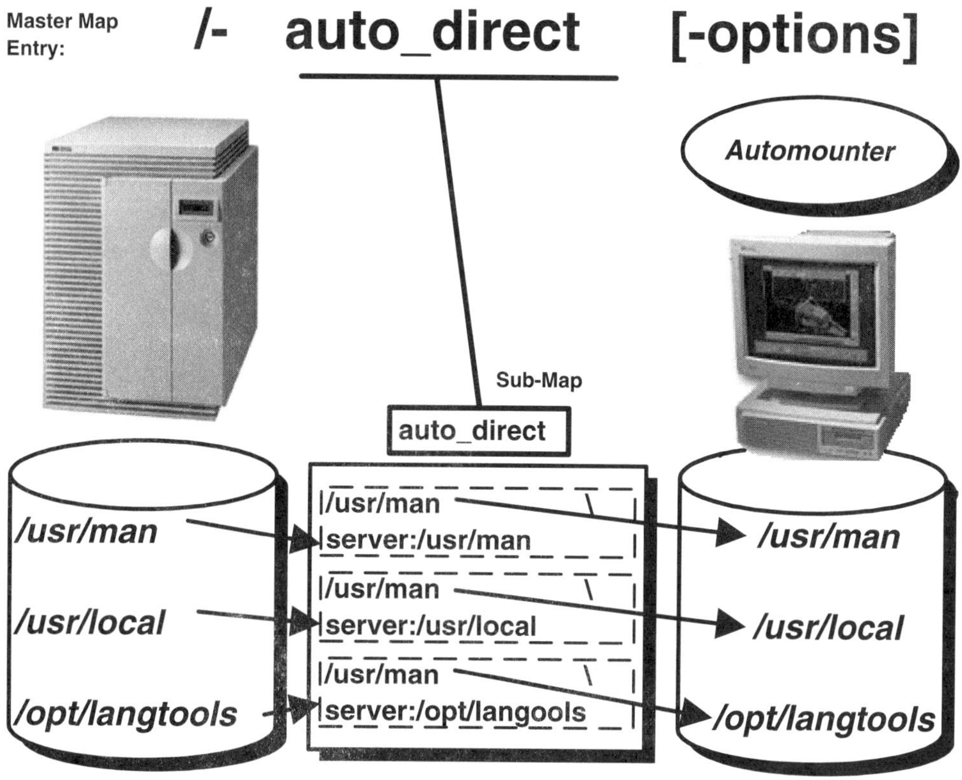

Figure 12-2 Automounter Direct Mount Points

```
/net        -hosts
```

This entry allows access to a host's exported NFS file systems by specifying a path of the form "*/net/<hostname>*". This allows functionality similar to that provided by the Windows UNC specification format, "*\\server\share_name*". While this access is convenient, it also means that each server must export the world—an action that invites unwanted dependencies.

12.2.3 Direct Automounter Map Entries

Direct automounter mounts will overlay any directory structure on the local disk. In this respect, they are identical to local mount points. Unix system managers have often placed minimal functionality into the local directory that is "hidden" by the automounter mount point, just in case the mount fails. This practice is guaranteed to cause no end of confusion to users.

Direct mount points are installed as links by automounter when it starts and thus are always visible. This means that browsing a directory that contains direct mounts will cause all of

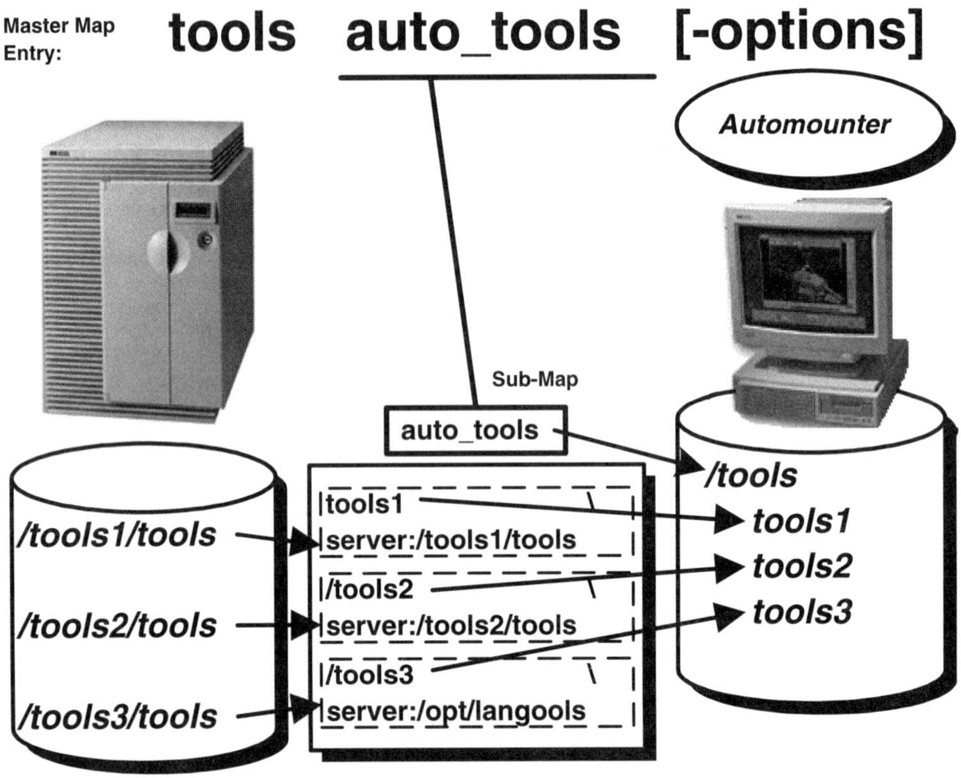

Figure 12-3 Automount Indirect Mount Points

them to be mounted. Touching many direct mount points all at once can cause a "mount storm" that can degrade server performance.

Direct automounter map entries in the master map have the format:

```
/-                    Map_Name          [-NFS_Mount_Options]
```

Submap entries for direct maps have this format:

```
/Directory_Path    [-Options]        server:/Directory_Path
```

Direct mounts are less confusing to users because the expected directories are there (in the form of links) and do not need to be touched to magically appear. A direct map may be viewed as providing one-to-one mapping between a remote directory and the local file system. This is shown in Figure 12-2.

12.2.4 Indirect Automounter Map Entries

Indirect maps allow us to mount several directories or file systems from different sources under a single, common directory. Indirect mount points are not visible until they are accessed, which prevents mount storms caused by recursive directory operations. This behavior can be confusing to users who expect directories to be constantly available.

Indirect mount points may be viewed as a many-to-one mapping of the file systems in the map to the mount point on the client system. The format of an automounter indirect entry in the master map is:

```
/Directory          Map_Name          [-NFS_Mount_Options]
```

Submap entries for indirect mount points have the format:

```
Sub-directory       [-Options]        server:/Directory_Path
```

The subdirectory field is the name to user for the directory when it is mounted underneath the automounter-managed directory. An example of an indirect map and mount points is shown in Figure 12-3.

12.2.5 Hybrid Automounter Mount Points

We discussed the pluses and minuses of direct and indirect mount points in the previous two sections. There is another configuration called a hybrid mount point that is not directly supported by the automounter, but can provide the positive aspects of direct and indirect mount points, without the negatives. This type of mount point involves creating a Unix soft link that points to an automounter managed directory. The link is always visible, avoiding the potential user confusion caused by indirect mount points. Listing the contents of a directory containing the links will not cause a mount storm, because the automounter will not mount the directory until the link is followed.

12.2.6 Load Balancing with Automounter Maps

Entries in automounter submaps for direct and indirect mounts may specify multiple servers for rudimentary load balancing. The first server in the list that answers is used to satisfy the request. The format for this type of entry is:

```
Directory_name     server1:server2:/Directory_Path
```

The theory is that a busy server or a server that is farther away in the network will answer more slowly than a faster or closer server.

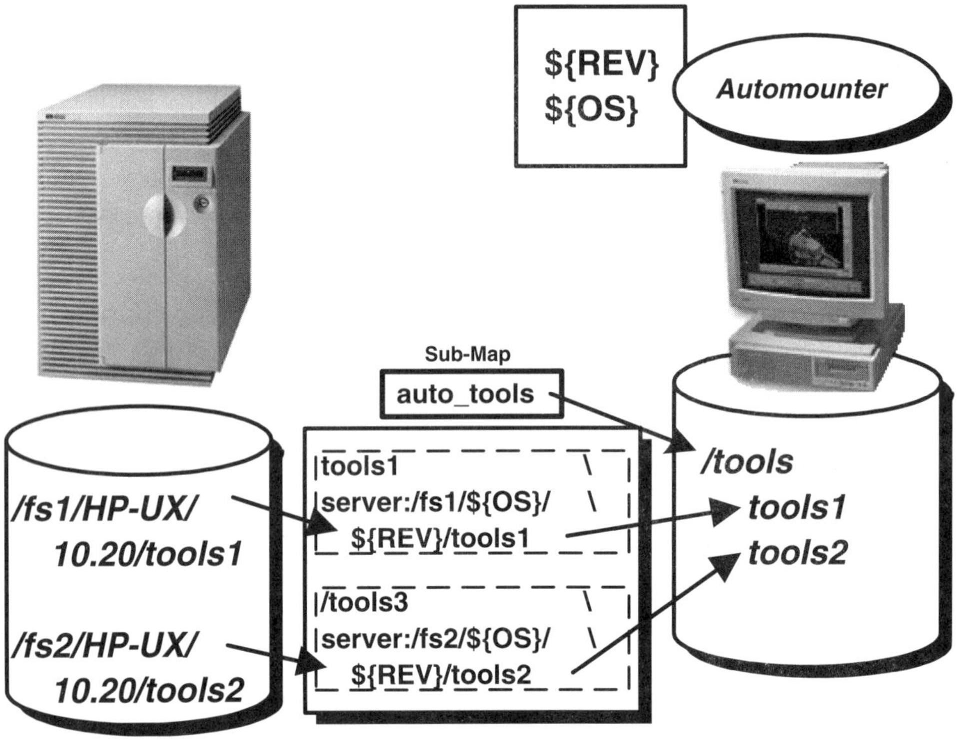

Figure 12-4 Automounter Map Interpolation

12.2.7 Interpolated Automounter Maps

If Unix environment variables are encountered in automounter maps, then the automounter will attempt to interpolate (replace or expand) those variables with the associated variable values. The automounter allows specification of environment variables on the command line with the "-D" switch. An example automounter command line follows:

```
/usr/etc/automount -D REV=10.20 -D OS=HP-UX
```

This little "trick" allows a system manager to segregate data on the NFS server, based on a set of client parameters, like the operating system type and revision. An example of this process is shown in Figure 12-4. A similar function is built into the DCE DFS cache manager in the form of the *@host* and *@sys* variables, described in a later section.

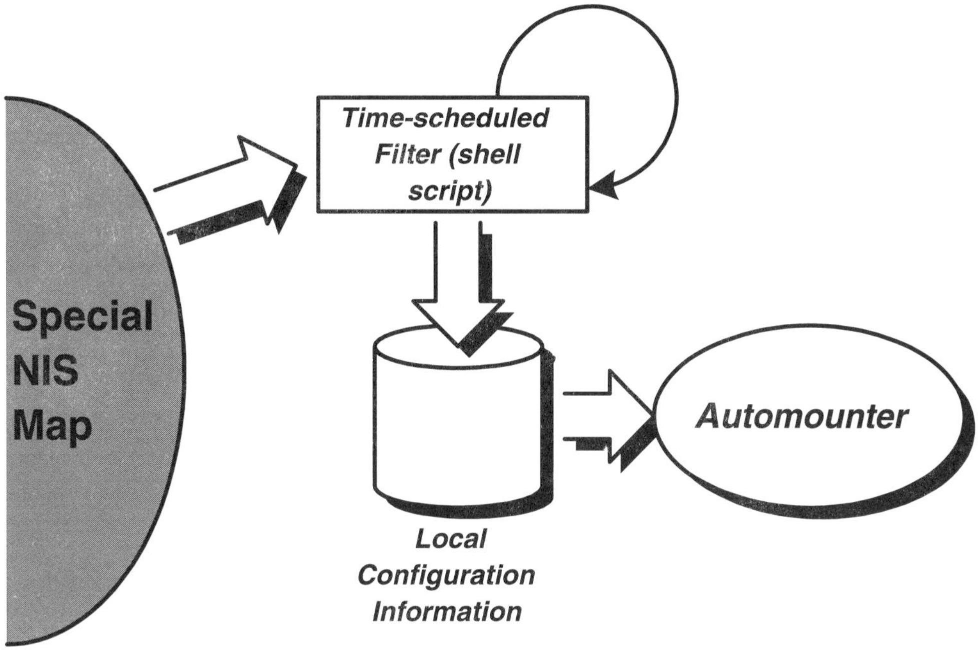

Figure 12-5 Creating Customized Mounts from NIS Data

12.2.8 Maps and Mounts from NIS

Another technique that is extremely useful is the dynamic creation of automounter maps or hybrid links from NIS maps. The central distribution of the map information via NIS enables the client system to read the map, dynamically alter it, and then invoke the automounter with a disk-based version of the master and submaps.

This approach can also be used for creating local configuration files fcr things like print server and e-mail server directories, based on network "closeness" or other factors. The possibilities are endless. See "RAPTOR Data-Sharing Implementation" on page 369, for an example of this type of configuration process in a real environment. The general process used is shown in Figure 12-5.

12.2.9 Common Maps and Map Naming Conventions

There are a core set of maps that seem to turn up frequently in customer environments. An indirect map for user home directories, direct maps for frequently used and infrequently changed system resources, indirect maps for project data, system management tools, special data, and user applications. That amounts to *auto_users*, *auto_direct*, *auto_project*, *auto_tools*, *auto_data*, and *auto_apps*. Also encountered are *auto_vob* for Rational ClearCase data and *auto_shares* for Windows NT shared directory access via NFS.

The recommended convention for indirect maps is to user the name of the automounter managed directory as the "*<name>*" portion of "*auto_<name>*". The author also uses *auto_direct* for all direct mounts and *auto_link* for the indirect map used for hybrid links. These conventions make it easy to connect the managed directory name with the map that defines it, but are only recommendations.

The many-to-one mapping provided by indirect maps affords us with a great way to collect information from a number of servers and present it to the users in a single, logical place on the client system. The indirection provided by the automounter maps allows system administrators to move the server location for a data set without affecting the path that users access it with. We will discuss this more a little later in this chapter.

12.2.10 Automounter Summary

The NFS automounter provides us with a facility for controlling how NFS data is presented to client systems using NFS as the data access mechanism. We may select from one-to-one mappings with direct mounts, one-to-many mappings with indirect mounts, or may increase visibility and reduce mount storms with hybrid mounts. The information that drives the automounter may be distributed from a central location with NIS, which saves modification of configuration files on every client system.

12.3 Consistent Data Access with Microsoft Windows

To maintain consistent access for drive letters, the drive letter to network share mapping needs to be recreated every time the user logs into the system. This can be set up in the Windows file manager, but details like changing passwords on the share or an unavailable share can break the mapping. For consistency, some environments use a utility that is run at user login, which reads local configuration file information and recreates the drive letter and printer port mappings.

This is the technique used by the Hewlett-Packard PC common operating environment (PC-COE). In addition to allowing the user to map his own set of network resources (drives and printers), the PC-COE drive mounting utility also maps a consistent range of drives ("*I*" through "*N*") to standard network locations. Once applications, user data, and utilities are known to be in the same location from session to session, an environment may be built that consistently presents the data and applications.

One of the shortcomings of Microsoft Windows is the requirement to map network drives, and the apparent lack of an automated, single-point administration method for presenting common sets of data to users[3]. The number of available drives is also an issue, since local drives

3. The Microsoft Dfs server component promises to allow system managers to present a logical view of multiple physical shares and servers, mapping larger "clumps" of data to a single drive letter (we still won't be rid of the darned things.) As of this writing, this functionality is slated for release in Windows 2000.

(floppies, CD-ROMs, and hard disks) must share the maximum of twenty-six drives with network drives. This "drive letter" model is a severe limitation in enterprise environments[4].

With two Gigabyte limitations on the size of a Windows physical file system partition (FAT), the number of drive letters also restricts the total amount of storage the client system has direct access to. In a best-case scenario, the client could access a maximum of 52 Gigabytes simultaneously without manually unmapping and remapping network drives. This sounds like a lot of data, but in some technical environments a single data file may approach, or exceed, a Gigabyte of data. The two Gigabyte partition limits are problematic here as well.

The size limitations on the file system partitions stem from the 32 bit nature of the file system code, since 32 bits only allows access to a total of 4 gigabytes worth of data. We should fully expect these size issues to stay with us until a 64 bit version of the Windows NT operating system is available (or at least of the file system code.) Unix systems suffered from similar limitations until the file system code was converted to 64 bit data structures.

12.4 Consistent Data Access with DCE DFS

We have detailed two environments that both require system-management effort to provide a consistent data-access mechanism. Unix systems using NFS require mounting and unmounting of remote data to prevent client system hangs, and we must build the data mapping by hand. Microsoft Windows systems suffer from the same data mapping problems and are a little behind in providing automated tools to address the issues.

There is one network file system that was designed from the start to provide secure, consistent, WAN-based access to data: DCE DFS. There is no DFS equivalent of automounter and no need to create a consistent view of the distributed data in the environment. This is because a client system has access to the entire DFS name space—all exported filesets and their replicas, within a consistent set of naming conventions. Let's examine what DCE DFS has to offer.

12.4.1 The DCE Cell

The basic structural unit within DCE (and DFS) is called a cell. A cell comprises a set of users, computers, and other resources. The cell is the basis for common services and system administration policy and may consist of multiple machines across multiple LANs or WANs. A particular user and a particular machine may only belong to one DCE cell.

Cells may be connected together, and trust relationships can be established by mutual agreement of the system administrators. A cell to which a user or system belongs is called the "local" cell, and all other cells are "foreign" cells. A diagram of this relationship is shown in Figure 12-6.

4. I have been to some Unix customers that routinely make hundreds of mount points available to their users through automounter maps.

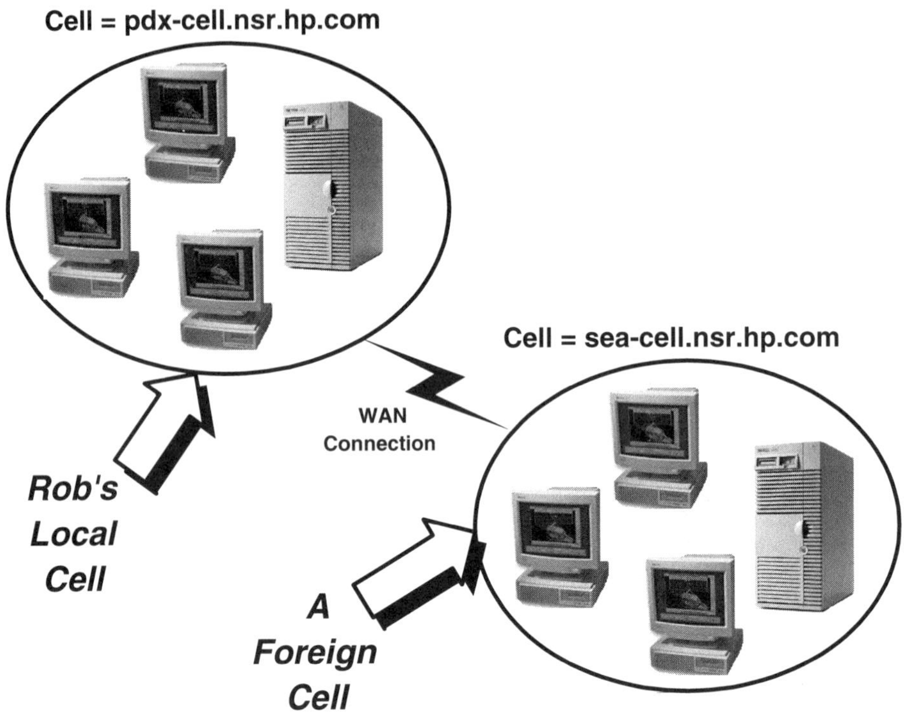

Figure 12-6 DCE Cell Structure

12.4.2 DCE Secure Core Components

DCE, from its very beginning was designed to provide a secure, scalable, distributed environment for building heterogeneous applications. The core components of DCE comprise multithreaded program support, an RPC call facility, a Distributed Time Service (DTS), a security service, and a directory service. DFS is a DCE application, taking full advantage of all of the core components.

The security service provides a registry service, which contains information about DCE principals, users, and associated accounts. The registry service provides users, groups, and organizations, which are the basic units used by the authentication service to allow a principal to authenticate themselves. The authentication service in DCE is based on Kerberos version five.

Security in DCE is based on mutual authentication—this means that both principals and machines must prove their identity to each other. When a user supplies the correct password, he or she is given a set of credentials to use in accessing data and services. A set of credentials is called a ticket.

The security service also provides a way to determine the principal's privileges, based on identity and group membership. A server within the DCE environment uses the privilege service

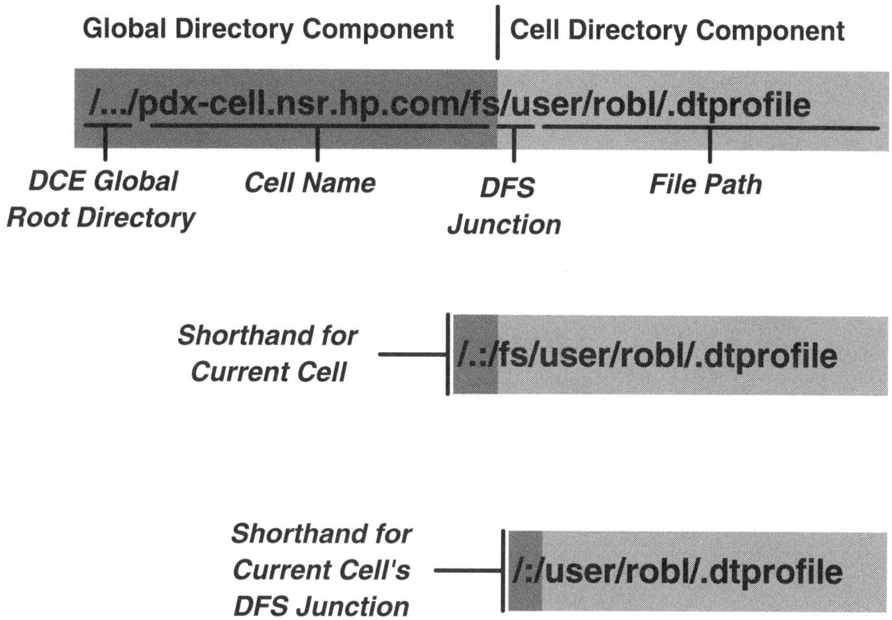

Figure 12-7 DFS File Path Formats

to determine the user's rights to use the service. Every object, services included, may have an access control list (ACL) that determines who may access the object and what operations they are allowed on the object.

The directory service allows clients to find objects in the DCE environment. The directory can hold information about files, directories, services, and machines, to name a few items. There are two components to the directory service: the cell directory service (CDS) and the global directory service (GDS). The CDS handles locating objects within a cell, and the GDS (which is X.500) handles location of global objects, like cells. The GDS may be replaced by DNS.

The minimal DCE cell requires a CDS server, a security (SEC) server, and a computer to run them. This cell would not perform or scale very well, so you will never encounter such a simplistic configuration. A cell may range from several to thousands of individual computer systems.

12.4.3 The DCE Distributed File System

DFS is a true client-server application. DFS client systems run a cache manager which is responsible for communicating with the DFS server processes to access DFS files. The cache manager saves a copy of the file being accessed on the local disk and will refresh that file on access if it changes on the server. A DFS client can also be a DFS server.

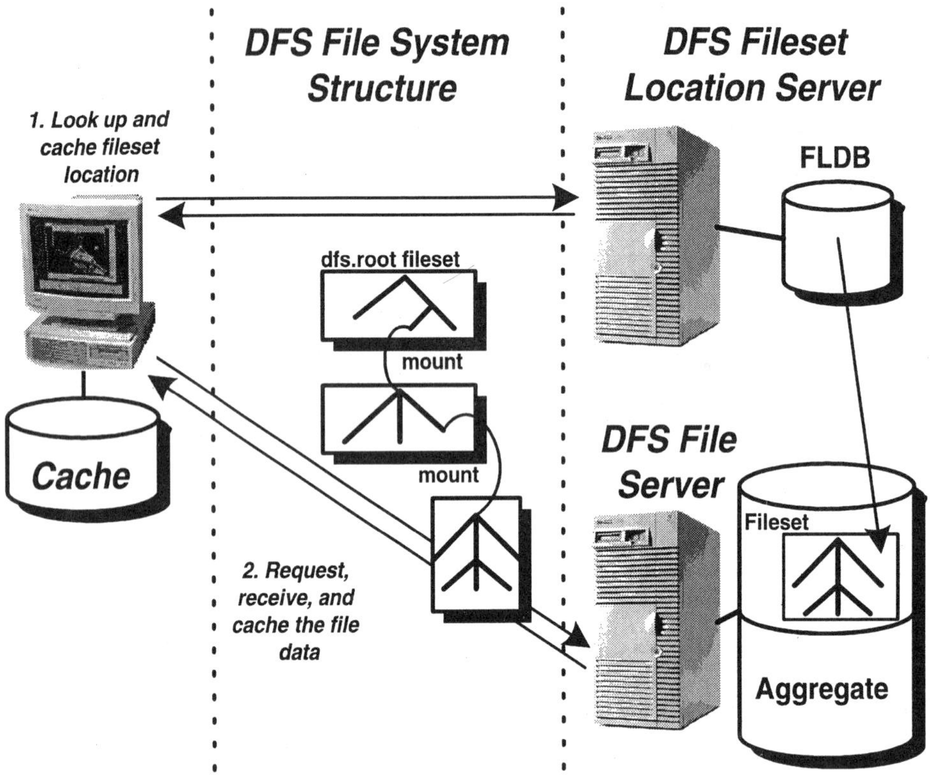

Figure 12-8 DCE DFS File Location and Access

There are a number of DFS server functions: file servers, fileset location servers, backup servers, system control machines (which distribute security information to other servers), and binary distribution servers (which distribute binary files to other systems of the same type.) A DFS server may perform any combination of these varied roles, yielding a lot of flexibility in how the services are distributed.

DFS files are organized into a hierarchical tree, just like Unix files. All DFS files are stored in units called filesets[5], which contain a subtree of related information. The fileset is also the basic unit of DFS administration for backups, replication, and space quotas. DFS filesets are stored in physical partitions called aggregates, and multiple filesets may be stored in a single aggregate.

5. This is true if the DFS local file system (LFS) is used. Files may also be exported from the Unix UFS.

12.4.4 DFS File Access

First of all, users do not need to know where the files they are accessing are physically located. The DFS path guides the client's cache manager to the proper data in the DFS namespace. The DFS namespace is a subset of the whole DCE namespace, and we do not have room to describe the entire DCE structure. An interesting aspect of the DCE directory structure is that processes, systems, users, and services show up in it, not just file system information[6].

The DFS portion of the namespace starts under a DCE "junction" in the cell directory called "fs", for file system. Paths in DFS may have a global component that locates the specific DCE cell the DFS data resides in, and a local component that "homes in" on the actual data. There are also two shorthand notations for specifying DFS paths. Examples of the three formats are shown in Figure 12-7.

Each DFS fileset contains related files and directories, arranged in a tree. The fileset is attached to the DFS global file system structure at a mount point. The information in the mount point provides the fileset name, but not the physical location of the fileset. The cache manager must consult the fileset location database (FLDB) to find the fileset associated with the mount point.

The FLDB contains information about the fileset, including its name, a unique ID number, replication information, and the physical location of the fileset on a server and in a particular aggregate. To speed access, the DFS client will cache FLDB information once it is looked up. Every fileset has a read-write version, but a fileset may also have up to sixteen read-only replicas. The access to a DFS fileset is shown in Figure 12-8.

The DFS cache manager also provides two special variables, *@sys* and *@host*, that can be used in DFS paths. If these variables are encountered in a DFS path, then the cache manager replaces them with predetermined values before resolving the path component. The *@sys* value is replaced with a value, derived from the *uname* command, which describes the machine's architecture and operating system type. The *@host* value is replaced with the name of the client system, as returned by the ***gethostname()*** system call.

These variables allow us to create links whose target data varies depending on host name and operating system type. This is similar to the functionality provided by automounter map interpolation, although it does not provide as many different possible variable substitutions. We may still make good use of these variables in creating consistent views of DFS data for heterogeneous clients.

12.4.5 DFS Access Control Lists

DFS files and directories are protected by access control lists (ACLs), which are backwards compatible with Unix file and directory access mode bits. The Unix user, group, and other mode bits map to *user_obj*, *group_obj*, and *other_obj* ACL entries. The user or group specified

6. This seems counterintuitive at first. This is why we will conveniently ignore all but the DFS portion of the directory namespace.

in an ACL is assumed to be from the default cell, unless another cell is explicitly used. This allows objects to reside in other than the default cell, yet remain protected.

There are six access rights used in a DFS object's ACL. For files and directories, the rights are: **r** - read; **w** - write; **x** - execute; and **c** - control the ACL. For directories, two rights are added: **i** - insert an object into the directory; and **d** - delete an object from the directory. In order for a user to perform an action on an object, he or she must have **x** access to all directories above the object.

The exact usage of DFS ACLs is beyond the scope of this discussion. The control is fine-grained enough for even the most exacting of security experts. We could probably write a chapter just on DFS ACLs, but in the interest of keeping our sanity we won't.

12.4.6 DCE DFS Summary

DCE DFS provides features, as part of its natural behavior, that we have to design and implement in both NFS and SMB network file systems. There is built-in path consistency, potentially across the entire world of data. There is no need to mount or map remote file systems or filesets; that is handled as part of the access process. There is built-in caching and replication for improved performance and resiliency.

The entire system is designed to allow replication of data and services to provide immunity from failure. If one fileset location database is not available, a client system will automatically switch to another one. If a particular fileset server is not available, clients will use the next available server to access data.

The DFS behavior is implemented with a stateful protocol. The DFS server remembers which clients have what files cached and will automatically notify them when the server data changes. This guarantees consistency without the check-back behavior exhibited by NFS clients. Clients may write to cached data, if given permission by the server, without fear of destructive interference from other clients. Distributed, byte-level locking is supported for full POSIX file system compliance.

The client independence from data location, scalability, WAN support, and extra security are all features that are needed to implement enterprise-wide sharing of data with a minimum of effort. To implement this behavior from the other file system and data-sharing mechanisms would be tremendously difficult, if it were even possible. DFS is at least a file system for us to compare all others against functionally, and we should keep it in our bag of design tricks.

One feature of DCE DFS that is often overlooked is the level of interoperability that it provides. DFS is available on a wide range of system types, from Unix to Windows NT. Studies have shown that without caching it performs as well as NFS, with caching enabled, it can be much faster. Because of caching and statefullness, DFS provides functionality over the WAN, which other network file systems can't (at the moment, anyway.)

The unfortunate side of DCE and DFS is that they are substantially different from what we are all used to, in terms of both functionality and system administration procedure. The author likes to say "It took me three months to figure out that I could set DFS up in a day." This is a

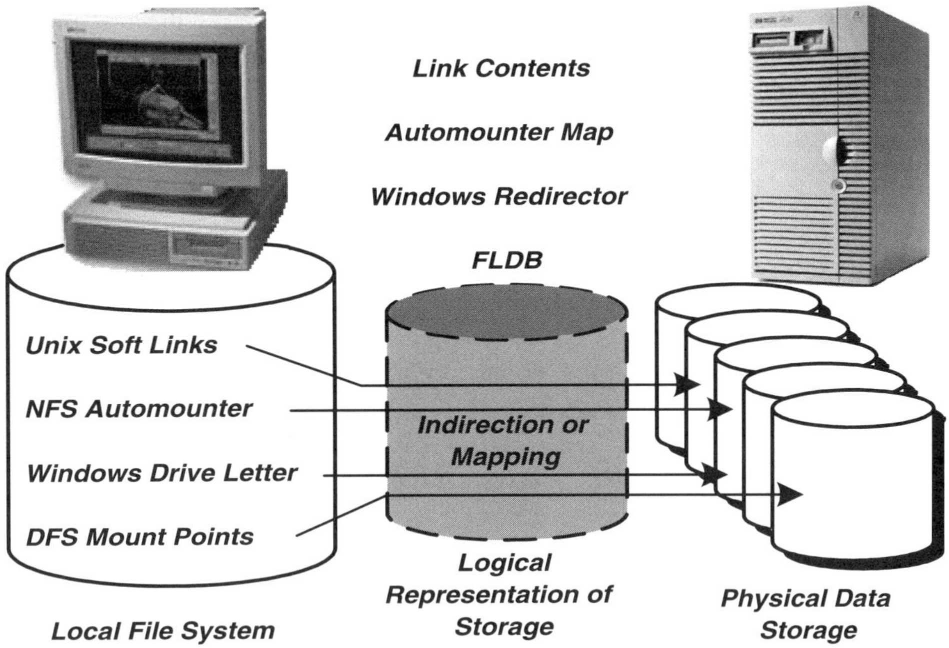

Figure 12-9 Indirection as a Data-Mapping Tool

small indication of the learning curve involved with this technology. We can justify adopting it only where the needed functionality outweighs the additional effort required, but we should not dismiss it out of hand.

12.5 Moving Data Without Rewriting the World

On a local system, direct access to data or application packages is done with path names that follow the directory hierarchy from the file system root to the data being accessed. If the files being accessed are moved, then a new path must be specified. Paths that are specified in scripts and application configuration files will "break", unless they are updated. A time honored tradition in the Unix system administration world is to use Unix symbolic links to provide insulation from data movement.

A hard link is a duplicate directory entry that points to the same meta-data for the file. This type of Unix link may only be used if the two entities are within the same physical file system partition. A symbolic link contains a text string that is read and substituted into the file path in place of the symbolic link's name. This type of link may cross partition (or system) boundaries, because the text may "point" anywhere in the namespace, as long as the target is mounted in the local file system hierarchy.

But what a symbolic link really does is introduce a level of indirection between the data access and the data. The data access refers to the link, which determines the final destination. Altering the contents of the link, but not the link's name, will change the final destination of the access without changing the path the user specified to perform the access[7].

If you look closely at the schemes used by Microsoft Windows, the NFS automounter, and the DCE DFS, you will notice the use of indirection in all of them. With the NFS automounter, the indirection is supplied by the contents of the automounter map, creating a set of stable paths for data access, yet allowing the system manager to alter the data location by changing the server and path specification in the map. The Windows scheme allows accessing data through a local drive letter, and as long as the path to the data remains the same, the drive letter may be mapped to a different location[8]. A lookup of a fileset in the FLDB by DFS determines the physical location for data access, allowing the data to be moved without affecting the user access.

Indirection is a very important concept to us; it allows us to use "smoke and mirrors" to insulate client systems from direct dependencies on data location. While indirection does exact a performance price over direct access, it saves a tremendous amount of system administration time and improves overall reliability. I think you'll agree that the trade-off is worth it.

12.6 Mapping Different File System Types

A client system may access many different data sets on behalf of its user. The data sets may reside on several different network file system types, depending upon the workgroup's heterogeneous population. There are several gateway mechanisms that we can use to present "foreign" data sets in the client's native file system language.

Data access is not the only process that needs to be translated by a gateway or file system translator. User authentication and access policy must be translated by the gateway system to account for differences between the two differing environments. Other issues include mapping upper and lower case character differences, the ubiquitous slash character, and other format differences. The gateway system may also be able to authenticate the user against both the native service and the "foreign" service.

12.6.1 DFS-to-NFS Secure Gateway

The DFS-to-NFS secure gateway provides a means for granting authenticated access to the DFS namespace from NFS workgroup clients. A gateway server machine is a DFS client in

7. Apollo Computer's DOMAIN/OS allowed the substitution of Unix environment variables into the link text. The final path was resolved using the user's environment variable values. These "variant links" were extremely valuable for supporting the three operating system environments and file system structures that were simultaneously supported on an Apollo node: Apollo's Aegis, BSD Unix, and SYSV Unix.

8. The drive letter scheme and the lack of symbolic link functionality can severely hamper our efforts at creating the necessary indirection on a Windows system.

the DCE cell to which access is provided. The gateway machine exports the DCE global root, "/ …" via NFS.

Each NFS client that wishes to access the DFS namespace can then mount the DCE global root. All users of the NFS client have *unauthenticated* access to DFS data. Users may authenticate themselves to DCE on the gateway server or may have versions of the DCE authentication service installed on their NFS clients.

The gateway server locally caches DFS data being accessed by the NFS clients it supports. It can be used to convert what would otherwise be a WAN dependency over NFS to a local dependency within the workgroup. If the file is cached, the client can continue to access the file from the cache, even in the event of a failure of the WAN link.

If we want to avoid confusing the avid NFS user, we have to do a little work. We can hide the DCE global root or other DFS specific path names behind the NFS automounter. Another approach is to create the proper symbolic links on the client systems to provide a level of indirection.

12.6.2 DFS to Windows NT "Network Drive"

DFS client software is available on Windows NT systems, allowing access to the DFS namespace behind a Windows NT drive letter. This presents DFS data to the client system in a format that applications are used to.

12.6.3 NFS to "Network Drive"

NFS client software is available from several sources on Windows NT, allowing access to NFS data in the workgroup. Again, the file systems are presented to the Windows client system as local Windows drives.

12.6.4 NFS to SMB Gateways

Another approach to presenting NFS file systems to Windows-based clients is through an NFS-to-SMB (or CIFS) gateway. The gateway system mounts the appropriate NFS file systems and presents them in the native protocol for Windows clients.

12.7 User Profile Data and "Home" Environment

The user needs a place to call home, a familiar place to return to time and time again—an environment that is customized for his or her working habits. That is the "home" environment, the default location and set of configuration settings presented to the user at login time. There is a difference in behavior between Windows systems and Unix that must be accounted for in the client system environment. We will cover the high-level details of both Unix and Windows user "home" environments.

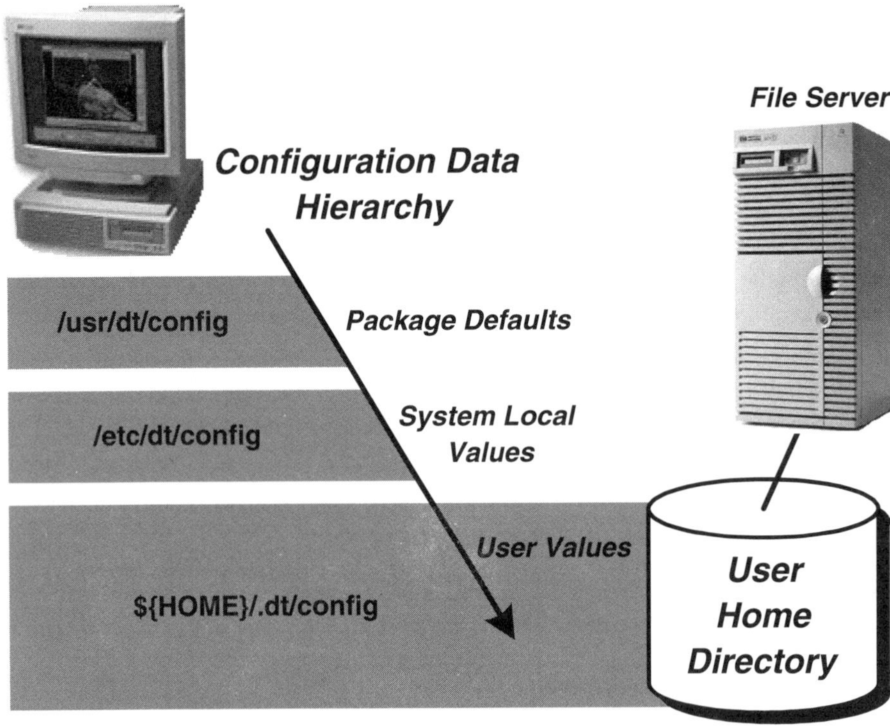

Figure 12-10 Sample Unix Configuration Data Hierarchy

12.7.1 Unix Home Directory and User Profile

The user authentication information (so-called "GECOS" information) in the Unix */etc/passwd* file specifies a directory for the user to begin his or her session in the "home" directory. The user's home directory is the logical place to put any data that need to follow the user around from client to client. That is, of course, provided that the user has only a single home directory. In our workgroups, this is a strong design recommendation—not providing a single home directory will result in added complexity, additional system administration effort, and potential user confusion.

Application configuration information that is specific to each Unix user is stored in configuration files (or directories) in the user's home directory. By convention[9], many of these files

9. You know, one of the things that I really like about Unix is the available set of what can be called conventions, paradigms, or idioms. The apparent absence of these conventions, or the presence of multiple conflicting paradigms, is one of the things that bugs me about Microsoft Windows. I guess I need to be a little more patient—common need breeds common features.

begin with a ".", rendering them invisible to casual observation. There is usually a readily discernible searching hierarchy for configuration information, ending in the user's home directory.

Because of this particular Unix idiom, it is important for a user to have only one home directory. This should be located on a file server and mounted on client systems when the user logs in. Multiple user directories breed configuration discrepancies, confusion, and data duplication.

Most Unix applications follow the user home directory convention for locating configuration information. Because the command shells allow flexible configuration (one file for login, one for logout, and one file for new subshells), it is possible to thoroughly customize their behavior. There is also a system-wide profile script that is executed when a user logs in.

The shell configuration scripts in the user's home directory can make behavioral decisions based on the operating system type the user is logged into. It is a simple matter to make a Unix "*uname*" command call to determine the operating system type and version. The ability to dynamically load and execute blocks of shell interpreter code can help encapsulate system differences in standard start-up scripting.

12.7.2 Microsoft Windows User Data and Profile Information

Microsoft Windows systems also provide the ability for a user to have individual profile information that controls the behavior of their desktop. A new profile is created from the default profile for each user on a machine when he or she first logs in. The system manager can use the system policy editor tool to set values into the default profile that cannot be overridden by the user.

The system manager may also set profile values that apply to all users of a particular system. The user's profile information, including start-up menus, is a combination of the "all users" profile and the current user's profile. Profile information is stored in *\Windows\Profiles* on the current system.

There is a provision made for "roving" profiles that follow the user from client system to client system. These appear to be implemented as a download of the user's profile information from the domain controller at login time. The author's profile information, which is fairly basic, is approximately 1.3 Megabytes of data. If the profile cannot be loaded from the domain controller, the user may operate using previously cached profile information.

You can view the current user profiles, and their size, on your Windows NT client in the *My Computer→Properties→User Profiles* tab. The roving profile behavior may also be enabled with the *Change Type* button on this tab. The roving profile will maintain the settings from the last client system that logs off.

Each user may have a logon script associated with his or her account that gets executed when the login occurs. The logon script is kept on the domain controller that validates the user's logon request. The logon script may be used to configure aspects of the user's environment in conjunction with the settings maintained in the user's profile.

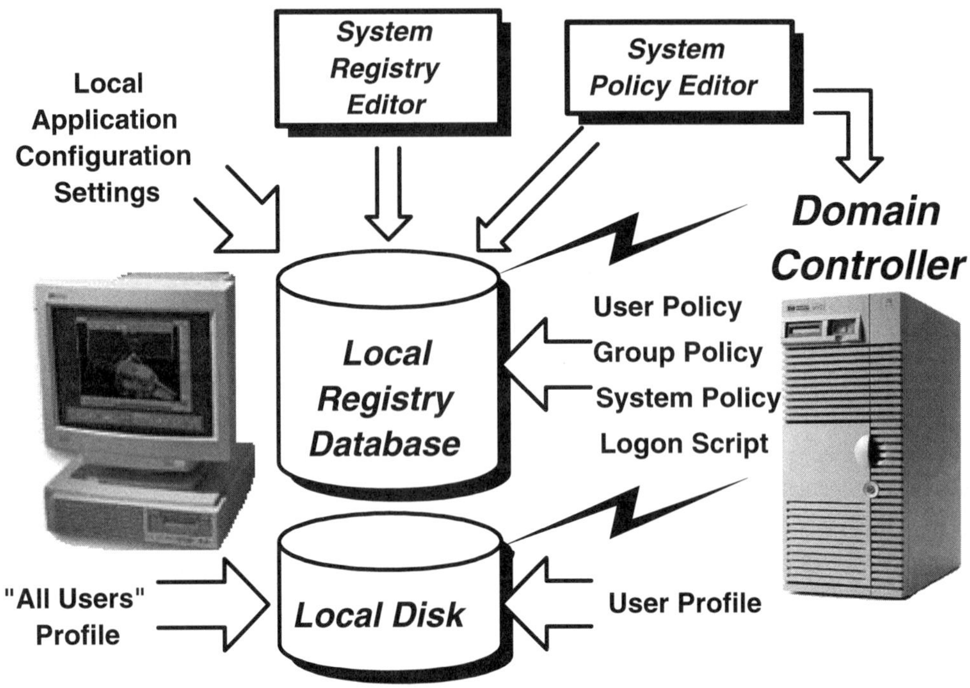

Figure 12-11 Microsoft Windows Logon Configuration Hierarchy

The concept of application configuration information in a user's home directory is foreign to Microsoft Windows systems. Most application configuration information is kept in the Windows registry, which is a memory-resident database containing all manner of operating system hardware, application, and user configuration information[10].

In addition to the logon script and the user profile, policy information for the user may be merged into the client system's registry at logon time. After the user's profile is loaded, if a specific policy exists on the domain controller for the user, then it is merged into the client registry. If any group membership policies exist, the highest priority group policy is merged into the client registry.

If no user or group policies exist, the default user policy settings are merged into the client's registry. Finally, a policy may be applied to the specific client system that the user is logging into. All of these policies may affect the aspects of the user's environment such as disabling the ability to run system commands (like the registry editor), disabling access services in the

10. Anyone who has had a registry problem knows that the registry is a massive single point of failure. Loss of even a small portion of the registry information can mean reloading the entire system. Whereas Unix configuration problems can usually be traced to a single configuration file, diagnosed, and corrected with your favorite text editor, registry problems are much more difficult to deal with.

control panel, and providing customized icons, applications, and start-up menu entries on the desktop.

12.7.3 Home Environment Summary

The Microsoft Windows and Unix operating systems take two fundamentally different approaches to maintaining user configuration settings and providing a standardized login environment. Unix stores desktop and application configurations in a hierarchical precedence on the client system that ends with the user's home directory as the final authority. Microsoft Windows systems use a combination of information that comes from system-wide and specific user profiles and the local system's registry database. The information in the registry may come from user, group, or system policy information that is stored on the domain controller that processes the user's logon request.

Both environments allow configuration of the desktop environment by the user but offer protections against execution of "dangerous" tools. The Unix environment primarily restricts access via user account and group membership in conjunction with file and directory permissions, while specific Microsoft Windows system commands may also be disabled by applying policy information to the local registry database. Both desktops allow the creation of restricted environments that may be focused on user application activities.

Both environments can operate in a peer-to-peer mode, with the equivalent of a home storage location on a local client. Unix may be configured to place all user login information and user-specific application options into a central storage location that exists on a file server. This information container, or home directory, follows the user to any client system that he or she logs into. Machine-specific login, application, and desktop behavior may be implemented with a hierarchy of local configuration files.

The concept of a default home directory appears to be foreign to the Microsoft Windows environment, however. The Windows remote logon scripts, remote policies, and remote "roving" profiles, may be viewed as the equivalent of a remote repository for user login configuration, existing on the domain controller. The local registry settings are the equivalent of the local hierarchy of configuration information described for Unix systems.

What we have are two different environments trying to solve the same problem: providing functionality and familiarity on the desktop, without sacrificing security or ease of administration. Since both operating systems have come from a fundamentally different background, it should not surprise us to find major differences in approach. Both of these environments are candidates for system cloning, which can remove the need for much of the system administration burden associated with configuring client desktop environments.

12.8 Workgroup Authentication Services

Different environments have different ways of authenticating users. Distributing user authentication and system-management information to client systems is one of the basic prerequisites for allowing users to logon and access data in the environment. The authentication services may themselves be viewed as data-distribution mechanisms. We will cover the high points of the most frequently encountered models.

12.8.1 Windows NT Domains

The Windows NT environment provides two management models: the workgroup and the domain. A workgroup, by Microsoft standards, consists of no more than ten workstations, each with its own management information. A domain is a collection of computers that share a common directory services database.

Each Windows domain contains a primary domain controller (PDC) that contains the master directory services database. The PDC authenticates user logon requests and also distributes software licensing information, policy information, and user profile information. To maintain availability and allow for load balancing, the domain can contain a number of backup domain controller (BDC) machines. In the event of a PDC failure, a BDC can be promoted to the PDC function.

A Windows NT user is associated with a unique security ID (SID). A group also has a unique SID. A Windows NT user can belong to one or more groups. Access to resources in the Windows NT environment may be based on ACLs which grant specific rights to users and groups. Trust relationships may be established between Windows NT domains that allow a user with an account in a trusted domain to be validated by a trusting domain. This is called pass-through authentication.

12.8.2 The Unix *Passwd* and *Group* Files

By default the Unix operating system maintains a local database of authentication on each system. This database is contained in two files: */etc/passwd* and */etc/group*. The */etc/passwd* file contains lines of ASCII user names, matched to numerical values for both the account's UID and GID, which are the basis for Unix authentication and access control.

The */etc/group* file contains an ASCII group name, matched to a numerical group ID (GID), and a list of ASCII user names that belong to the group. These two files are searched by a set of system library routines like *getgrent()* and *getpwent()*, which look linearly through the files for information matching the passed key.

One major complaint about this implementation is that there is no consistency checking between the two files; there may be disconnected or duplicate entries in either or both files. Another complaint is that the files must be readable by all users on the system, although they should be protected against modification by anyone but the root (super) user. Although the passwords in the file are encrypted, the world access opens the door to password-guessing attacks. The DCE registry import command, discussed later, is one of the few tools that performs a rigorous check on the information.

The linear nature of the password search algorithm means that if two users have duplicate user ID (UID) values and a conversion from UID to ASCII user name is needed, then only the first entry with a matching UID will be located. This configuration mistake can make it appear that user "angela" owns the files that really belong to "bob". The linear nature of the search is important to enabling NIS as part of the Unix authentication scheme, as we shall see.

This linear search behavior also enables a system administrator's "cute trick", which allows configuring local superuser capability without giving away a globally used root password. Two entries are placed in the */etc/passwd* file. First comes "root" with a UID value of zero[11] and its own account password. Next comes another entry, say for user "owner", also with a UID value of zero, but its own unique password. When a user logs on as "owner" with the separate password, he or she is given a UID value of zero which is superuser capability, without needing the "root" password[12].

12.8.3 The Network Information Service

NIS is a simple client-server database system, providing a number of very useful workgroup functions for Unix systems. First, information in the NIS database is distributed to all NIS client systems, augmenting or replacing system configuration files. Some of the files that may be centrally administered are */etc/passwd, /etc/group, /etc/hosts, /etc/netgroup, /etc/networks, /etc/protocols, /etc/rpc,* and */etc/services.*

An NIS map is really a simple, hashed database which is created using the *dbm(3x)* database utility. The *makedbm(1M)* utility takes an ASCII file and creates the hashed database by interpreting the first white-space delimited field on each line as the look-up key. A look-up operation with this database takes at most two file system accesses.

As one would expect, there are server entities involved with NIS operation. In fact, NIS has two types of servers: a master server and a slave server. The master server creates the maps and distributes them to any slave servers that are registered with it. Slave servers provide redundancy and load balancing and are located by client system broadcasts.

The basis for distributing is an NIS domain, which comprises a master server, slave servers, and client systems—all sharing a common set of databases or "maps". An NIS domain name is similar to a DNS domain name but is *not* the same. An NIS domain such as *pdx.nsr.hp.com* is simply a way of identifying a set of maps for client systems to bind to. The map databases are contained in a directory on the master server that has the same name as the domain. A client accesses the map information for a particular NIS domain by calling the *domainname* routine with the desired domain value.

For the files that NIS augments, special markers are inserted into the */etc/passwd* and */etc/group* at the point that the look-up process is to "escape" from the normal linear search of the file and use the domain-wide NIS information. If the information is not found in the NIS

11. The root account by convention (or necessity) is usually the first entry in the */etc/passwd* file.

12. Of course, this arrangement relies on the good will of the "owner" users, because with superuser capability, they can change the "root" account's password or edit the */etc/passwd* file. There are small programs that allow a user temporary root capabilities without the need for a password. Typically, the program will allow anyone in its database to become root for a single command, logging the access.

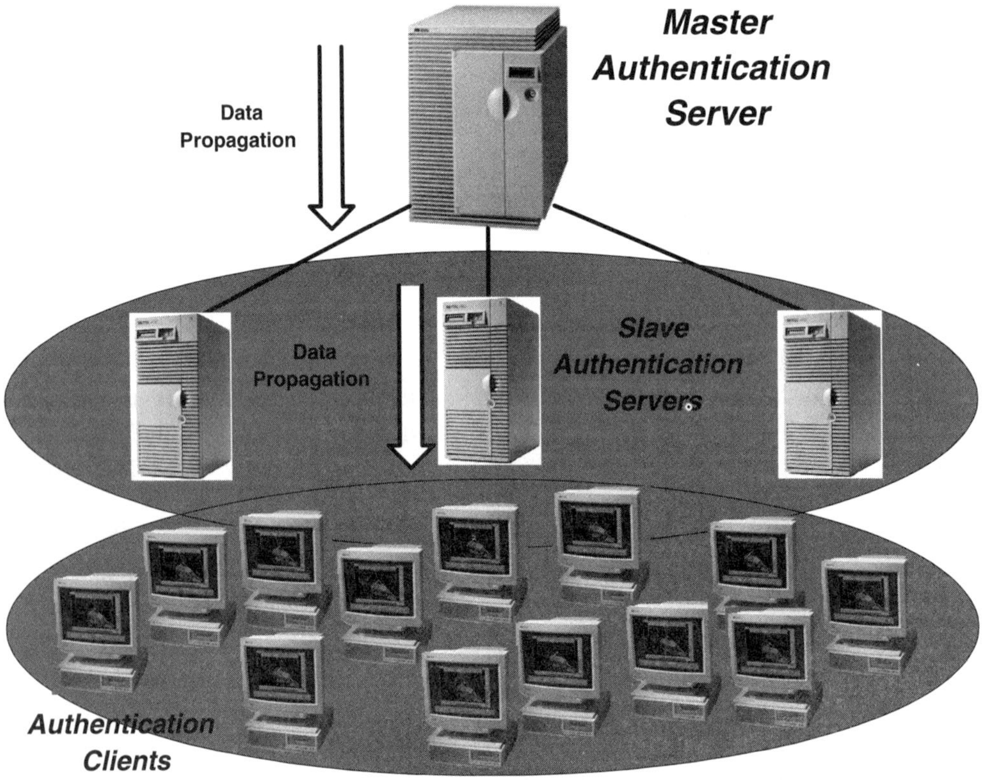

Figure 12-12 Generalized Distributed Authentication Service Model

database or if the NIS service is not available, the search continue to the end of the local file. Both the */etc/passwd* and the */etc/group* files may be augmented with NIS information. An example of a very simple (nonfunctional) */etc/passwd* file and the special NIS marker follows:

```
root::0:0:Local root account:/root_home:/sbin/sh
+::0:0:::
fred::1000:20:Just in case no NIS:/home/fred:/usr/sbin/sh
```

One of the most useful features of NIS is the fact that it allows us to add new maps to the standard set. NIS does not know or care what the map contents are, it just distributes the data and performs the keyed lookups. It is a simple matter to use commands on the client system to access and filter the map contents, providing us with a general purpose distribution mechanism for single-point administration data.

12.8.4 The DCE Registry Service

The DCE registry is a replicated service that manages a DCE cell's security database. The database contains entries for DCE principals—any entity that needs to be authenticated. The registry service allows DCE administrators to access and modify the database of DCE users: groups, organizations, and accounts. Changes to registry information are propagated from the master registry daemon to the replicated sites to maintain consistency across the DCE cell.

The DCE registry is compatible with Unix login information contained in */etc/passwd*. As a matter of fact, there are tools that will import passwd file information (except the actual passwords themselves) into the registry and export registry information to the password file. The synchronization of information between the DCE registry and the Unix password file is essential for maintaining a common view of file and directory permissions from the Unix client. This compatibility, however, is one of the major criticisms of the DCE registry—that it is too Unix oriented.

12.8.5 User Authentication Summary

There are a number of prevalent user authentication services in use in workgroup environments. The model for each of these is based on propagation of information from a single master server, to slave servers, and eventually to client systems within the workgroup (or cell, or domain.) Some services like NIS are more flexible than others, and we can bend them to our own purposes if the client systems speak the required protocols.

If we have separate but equal environments, where the authentication service supports only homogeneous client systems, we do not have to worry about interfacing the disparate services. But such an environment is only a fantasy. We need to face the prospects of providing common user names, common accounts, and common access rights to users in the workgroup. We will delay more discussion on this topic until Chapter 15.

12.9 Controlling Access to Data

Okay, we have data in the workgroup environment, and we have methods of authenticating users and granting access rights to data and services in the workgroup or even the enterprise environment. How do we protect data from unwanted access, or even accidental deletion? We will tackle the subject of access rights and data security in the next sections.

As we have previously mentioned, there are many good books on computer security[13], so we will not even attempt a complete survey of the possible topics. Instead, we will concentrate on the access-control methods that are employed, in conjunction with user authentication, to grant or deny access to resources.

13. See Glen Bruce and Rob Dempsey, *Security in Distributed Computing* [13], for good coverage of security in environments similar to the ones we are discussing.

12.9.1 User Access Models

All of the authentication schemes we have discussed up to this point have special values that uniquely identify users, groups, or principles within the system environment. After the users has authenticated themselves with the system, they are given a set of identifiers that are used to determine their access to system objects.

Unix Access Model We have mentioned the Unix UIDs and GIDs several times in this book. These values are stored in the meta-data for a file or directory and are used to control the user's access to that object. The three sets of Unix permission bits—owner, group, and other—are tested against the user's (or a process's) authenticated UID and GID values, and a set of access rights are granted base on those permissions.

There are other issues that may depend on the version of the Unix operating system being used. The UID and GID values were originally represented by 16 unsigned integers. In large environments, the 32768 possible values were not enough; in one particular environment, there was a need for at least forty thousand individual users.

To expand the values possible for the UIDs and GIDs, the HP-UX operating system, and others have increased the size of the integer values to 32 bits. Because there are implicit assumptions in application code regarding, this can create interoperability issues[14] and, worse yet, security holes. If the new "large" UIDs and GIDs are to be implemented, they must be implemented consistently across the environment. The new functionality opens the door to using unique values, like an employee identification number, for his or her UID value.

Windows NT Access Model When a Windows NT user logs in, they are issued an access token, which is used to determine whether or not access to an object will be granted by the system. The access token contains a user ID, the user's group memberships, and the set of privileges the user has been granted. Every process run by the user receives a copy of the user's access token.

System administrators may place access control on a wide variety of Windows NT system resources. The security information for an object is stored in a security identifier (SID) that contains information about the object's owner and an access control list that specifies who may access the object and how they may access it. The information in the user's access token is compared against the SID to determine if access will be allowed. If the information in the access token is compatible with the requirements of the SID, then access is granted.

This access-control process is much more flexible than that provided by the Unix operating system, even though the approach is similar, with the access token replacing the user's UID and GID values, and the SID replacing the directory or file ownership information and access rights. The Windows NT access rights offer more granularity than the Unix **rwx** rights.

14. It needs to be said that using the system-defined types, like UID_t or GID_t, to declare variables holding UID and GID values prevents the changes from affecting application code. Not all programmers use the proper types in their code.

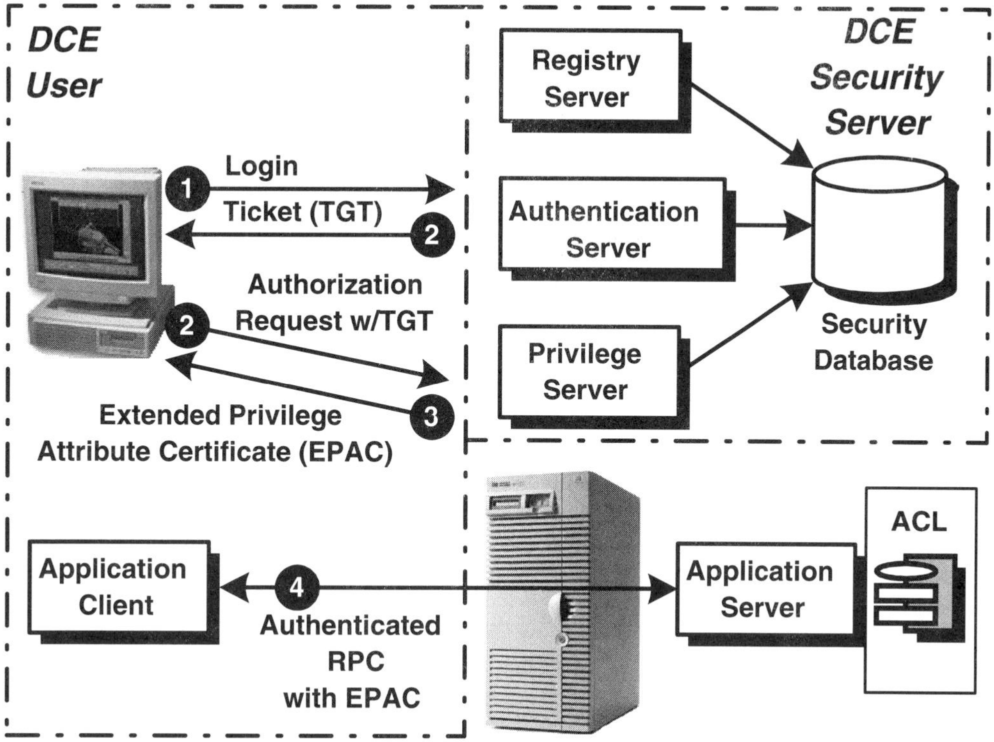

Figure 12-13 DCE Security Access Model

DCE DFS Access Model The authentication mechanisms of DCE incorporate Kerberos[15] Network Authentication Service, version 5, which was developed at the Massachusetts Institute of Technology (MIT) as part of the Project Athena. Kerberos uses a combination of secret key technologies to allow mutual authentication of both principals involved in a transaction. The fundamental assumption is that the network cannot be trusted.

The three components of the DCE security system, the registry service, the authentication service and the privilege service work together to authenticate the user and provide a certification called the Ticket Granting Ticket, or TGT. A DCE user consists of a principal plus a DCE account. Once granted, the TGT allows the user to make additional requests for tickets from application servers, but has a limited lifetime.

When a DCE client wants to use a DCE server, the server is located in the DCE directory service. The client communicates its request to the server, which inspects the user's authoriza-

15. In Greek mythology, Kerberos was the three-headed dog that guarded the gates of hell. What a great name for a security service!

tion credentials and the ACL associated with the resource the user wishes to access. The server may grant or deny access.

The authentication and authorization information passed between client and server is encrypted so that only the intended recipients may decrypt them. If desired, the application data may also be encrypted. We may prevent the unwanted examination of information that might be intercepted by third parties.

DCE uses a data structure called a Universal Unique Identifier (UUID) to identify objects in the environment. A UUID is an immutable 128 bit entity guaranteed to be unique across all space and time. UUIDs are used to uniquely identify users, groups, interfaces, cells, and other objects in the DCE environment. The UUIDs for principals play the same role in access control that Unix UIDs and Windows NT SIDs play; they uniquely identify ownership of directories, files, and objects.

12.9.2 Control of Data Access

Control of user operations on file and directory objects form the basis for data access security. The different access-control schemes must be synchronized to allow client systems to access data in a uniform manner. This is not always an easy task.

Unix File and Directory Access Control Unix file and directory permissions have three fields: one for the owner, one for the group, and one for all others. This scheme works fine for single systems or small groups of systems, but it may not be flexible enough in complex environments.

The downfall is the inability to more accurately specify access by users outside of the object's owner and group. If, for example, a user wanted to grant read and write access to one of his files to another user by specifying "**rw-**" access in the "others" field—the file is readable and writable by everyone else, not just the intended user. This is why some Unix systems extend the normal access-control mechanism with ACLs.

The access permissions are interpreted differently, depending upon whether the Unix object being protected is a file or a directory. See Table 12-2for a list of access permissions and the allowed operations.

Even with the limitations of the Unix permission scheme, it is still possible to design flexible access schemes using the group permissions and the Unix UMASK filter to implement group-based security. See "RAPTOR Data-Sharing Security" on page 369 for an example of a workgroup data security implementation using Unix permissions.

Microsoft Windows NT Access Control Lists Microsoft Windows NT provides a very flexible method of specifying a list of users or groups that can access a resource. The access-control lists, or ACLs, can associate a user or group of users with a specific set of permissions. An ACL consists of individual access control entries (ACE) that make this association. The Windows NT ntfs physical file system is required to support file and directory ACLs.

In addition to the permissions that are listed in Table 12-2, Windows NT provides a standard set of permissions that make setting access permissions easier for the system administrator. The Windows NT permission possibilities for a file or directory are “Read”, “Write”, “Delete”, “Change Permission”, “Execute”, “Take Ownership”, or any combination of these permissions. Standard file combinations are “No Access”, “Read”, “Change”, or “Full Control”. A directory may have “No Access”, “List”, “Add”, “Read”, “Add and Read”, “Change”, and “Full Control” (all of the above) permission combinations. Custom combinations are also permitted. Table 12-2 maps the mnemonics to the combination of access permissions.

Table 12-1 Windows NT File and Directory Access Combinations

Permission Mnemonic	***User Permissions***	***Group Permissions***
No Access[a]	(None)	(None)
List	(RX)	(Not specified)
Read[a]	(RX)	(RX)
Add	(WX)	(Not specified)
Add & Read	(RWX)	(RX)
Change[a]	(RWXD)	(RWXD)
Full Control[a]	(All)	(All)

a. Permission combination available for both files and directories.

You can see the possible permissions by selecting an ntfs file or directory and using the *File Manager➔File➔Properties➔Permissions* button. The access-control list entries and the possible permission combinations are visible in the “File Permissions” list box.

12.9.3 DCE DFS Access-Control Lists

DCE DFS access-control lists are used to enhance Unix permission mode bits, not replace them. As a matter of fact, the DFS supports POSIX access control and POSIX supports backwards compatibility with Unix access control. The evaluation of a DCE or DFS ACL is a complicated process to which we cannot do justice in our limited space. We will only touch the surface in this section.

Each ACL has a default cell, and a user or group is assumed to be from that cell unless a specific cell is stated. The default cell may differ from the cell where the object, which is protected by the ACL, is located. A DFS ACL requires three entries: the *user_obj* entry, the *group_obj* entry, and the *other_obj* entry.

The *user_obj* is the authenticated DCE user whose UID matches the UID stored in the object's owner field. The *group_obj* is the DCE group whose DCE GID matches the GID stored in the objects group field. The *other_obj* represents any other user from the default cell. Files and directories are created with the creator's DCE UID and the creators primary DCE GID. If any entry other than the three required entries exists, then another object, called *mask_obj* must exist.

The *mask_obj* is the union of permissions for entries other than *user_obj* and *other_obj*. Permissions granted to these other entries are filtered through the *mask_obj* values. Only the intersection of permissions between the entry and the *mask_obj* are granted. If this all sounds a little complicated, it is because it is.

ACL entries are evaluated in a set sequence to determine a user's access rights. The evaluation proceeds through the different ACL entry types, including the three required entries. The evaluation stops after the first ACL entry is matched. If an applicable user entry exists, then the evaluation process does not examine any group membership information.

It is important to realize that the flexibility available in the DFS ACL facility also has associated complexity. To provide secure data access across an enterprise or multiple enterprises requires "industrial-strength" measures. DCE and DFS certainly provide such a facility.

12.9.4 Service Access Control

Both Windows NT and DCE environments allow a system manager to control access to services in the same manner that they control access to disk-based resources: through the user of ACLs. Unix allows controlling the access to system services with a variety of approaches but does not count ACLs among them. Access-control lists are not the only way to protect services, Unix can disable services, make use of external network filtering equipment, only reply to specific network addresses, or implement security in the client-server protocol.

There are two major areas of workgroup security concerns: internal security and external security. One area of external security is remote access services, such as dial-up lines that may open the workgroup up for external attacks. Additionally, direct external connections to the Internet also may open the workgroup up for intrusion. We can hope that the internal security concerns are primarily focused on providing services, rather than preventing inappropriate access[16].

These concerns may be addressed by call-back units, firewalls, filtering routers, proxy servers, or a number of other security solutions. We should rely on experts in the security field to help us make the correct decisions about securing outside access to services in the workgroup. We will focus on making the proper services available to the systems that need them within the

16. We still have to be careful not to allow inexperienced or malicious users to subvert or damage the availability of workgroup services, but the level of security may not need to be as intense as when dealing with external interfaces. There are, of course, environments that require intense internal security levels.

workgroup and will not cover the in-depth security issues associated with interfacing the workgroup to the outside world.

12.9.5 A Comparison of Access Permission Schemes

Table 12-2 lists the various "raw" access permissions available in the Unix, Windows NT, and DCE DFS environments. As you can see, DCE DFS and Windows NT are similar in func-

Table 12-2 A Comparison of Access Permissions

Environment	***Rights Mnemonic***	***Privileges***
Unix Files	r	Can open and read the file contents
	w	Can modify contents of the file
	x	Can execute the file (as a script or application)
Unix Directories	r	Can list file names in the directory
	w	Can add, remove, or rename files in directory
	x	Can list file attributes and "cd" to the directory
Windows NT Files or Directories (ntfs)	r	Can read the file or directory
	w	Can write to the file or directory
	x	Can execute the file
	d	Can delete the file
	p	Can change the permissions on the object
	o	Can take ownership of the file
DCE DFS Files[a,b]	r	Can open, read, and lock the file
	w	Can write to or lock the file
	x	Can execute the file (also requires r rights)
	c	Can change the file's ACL
DCE DFS Directories[b]	r	Can list the contents of a directory
	w	Can rename, create, or delete a directory object
	x	Can list information about the objects in a directory
	c	Can change the directory's ACLs
	i	Can insert an object into the directory
	d	Can delete an object from the directory

a. These operations may require other rights in addition to the basic rights.

b. Most of these operations require x rights on all directories leading to the directory in question.

tionality, and both are supersets of the "standard" Unix permission scheme. The more stringent protection in these environments can be "opened up" and mapped to the Unix scheme where necessary. This may be done in a number of ways, including with special groups and ACL entries.

12.9.6 Data and Service Access Summary

We are faced with a number of different ways to control the user's access to data and services in the workgroup. Both requirements present unique challenges to workgroup designers. An understanding of the tools we have to work with can help us choose common ground for the workgroup environment. We will cover more of this topic in Chapter 15.

The limitations of the Unix permission scheme may be offset by lower complexity than methods using access-control lists. The difficulty of managing access-control lists on every object in the environment can be staggering. One technique for reducing this management overhead is to use a small set of groups in the ACL entries. It is far easier to add users to a group than to add user entries to all affected ACLs. In this respect, all three approaches are similar.

The need for up-front design effort cannot be overstated. Implementing security policies affects all levels of the workgroup functional model. The authentication mechanisms and access models are a central fixture of this design effort.

12.10 The Client System's View of the Data World

Now that we have surveyed the authentication services and the service and data-access methods, we need to examine the various classes of data that we will present to the client system and the user's desktop environment. The desktop is really where the entire workgroup data-sharing model is presented to the user. What we present to the user and how we protect it is part of the overall design of the workgroup data-sharing model. The general model presented in Figure 12-1 is shown in Figure 12-14 with access control added.

If the client system is a "thin" client, then there must be an intermediate system to provide desktop access to the workgroup data. For X-stations, for example, there must be a host system to provide the compute power that drives the presentation capabilities of the client. For a network computer (NC), there must be a server system that provides the desktop applets and mediates access to the workgroup data share.

12.10.1 Application Packages

The application packages used by the client system must be available for installation or configuration into the client desktop. Distribution of these packages is best handled in the same way as application data—by a file server. Users must be able to view, access, and install the packages from the distribution points in the workgroup.

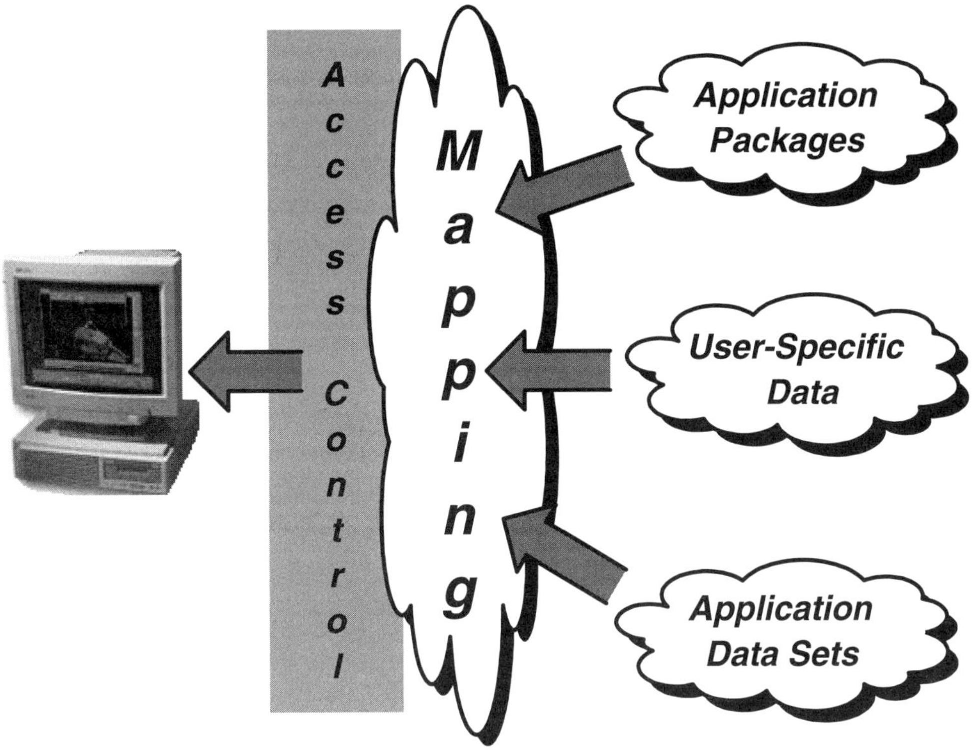

Figure 12-14 The Client System's Window on the Workgroup

12.10.2 User-Specific Configuration

Every user has a particular set of application packages and associated configuration information that must be available during every session. Additionally, the desktop configuration settings that create the user's custom working environment must be recalled at login time. There is a strong argument for using the same data-distribution mechanism for this information that is already in place for the remainder of the data classes.

12.10.3 Application Data

One very important class of data that must be available to the user is the data sets operated on by his or her applications. This data, like the previous two classes is located on a file server. The application data must be transparently accessible by client systems and compute servers that may run applications on behalf of the user. The actual location of the data should be hidden from the user.

12.11 Data Sharing Summary

Both Unix and Windows systems have the concept of mounting or mapping a physically attached or network file system onto the client system. For compute tasks that can run anywhere in the workgroup on multiple compute servers accessing data sets on multiple file servers, it is not practical to maintain all possible mounts. Cross-mounting all file systems creates a set of direct dependencies, with $O(n^2)$, that can be a nightmare to administer.

For NFS-based data access, there is AutoFS to handle automatic mounting and dismounting of remote file systems. AutoFS will automatically mount an NFS file system into a predetermined location on the client system when it is first accessed and will dismount it after it is no longer used. The mounting actions are controlled by automount "maps" that may be distributed via NIS, providing a single point of administration for common map information.

For Windows-based systems, there are two possible ways to access data. First, access to data sets on NFS or SMB servers may be configured as a network "drive letter", with letters running from A to Z. This yields a maximum possible twenty-six mounts at one time. Additionally, the mapping process is largely a manual one, so this method is most useful if the same drives are always remounted from session to session.

Windows also provides the ability to specify a path to a resource in Universal Naming Convention (UNC) format. This UNC format resembles the format used by the Apollo Computer DOMAIN/OS to provide a consistent path name to all file system resources, independent of the user's position in the network. The Windows format is *\\server_name\share_name\subfolder\file_name*[17], which provides the OS with enough information to access the remote resource, provided the proper services and redirectors are installed.

Last, and certainly not least, we have the DCE DFS approach to consistent resource access. Because the POSIX standard requires multiple slashes in a path name to be collapsed to a single slash, the *//hostname/path/file* was disallowed with DFS. Instead, another naming convention was invented that would be POSIX compliant but would still provide consistent access.

For DFS, files (and services) may be accessed from anywhere in the global DCE name space with a path format like */.../pdx-cell/fs/usr/robl/document*. The string "/..." signifies the root of the DCE name space, *pdx-cell* specifies the name of the cell in which the resource is located, *fs* specifies that the resource is within a DFS fileset[18], and the *usr/robl/documen*t portion specifies a path to the resource.

In addition to the "*/.../cell_name/fs/path/file*" convention, there are other short-cuts. The */.../cell_name/fs* portion of the specification may be replaced by */:./fs/path/file* if the resource is in the same cell as the user, or by */:/path/file* if the resource is in the current cell's DFS storage.

17. Only the slashes have been changed to confuse the innocent.

18. Other services and resources can actually show up in the DCE namespace, which is maintained by the two directory services, the Global Directory Service (GDS) for access to cells, and the Cell Directory Service (CDS) for access to resources in the DCE cell.

It is always recommended to use the long form, fully-qualified version of the path in programs or scripts to prevent problems if they are run outside of their "home" cell.

The goal of all of these approaches is to provide the user with consistent naming conventions to access data and resources from anywhere in the network. AutoFS can provide consistent naming, but because it is a configurable layer over the top of NFS file sets, it is still possible for inconsistencies to creep in.

The Windows "drive letter" scheme is a constant source of potential inconsistency. If I hear one more person say, "All you have to do is go out to the Z drive to get the file", I'll scream. A drive letter is merely a reference to a network share that requires a "\\server\share" type UNC and a password to complete the mapping. There is no magic attachment between the "Z" drive and any particular file server resource.

There are a number of user authentication services in use, each of which may be viewed as another type of data-distribution mechanism. All of these services use a similar model, and one would hope that the industry could eventually agree on a common authentication service that all operating systems could share. This would be logical, practical, and would save tremendous effort in the integration of dissimilar operating systems[19].

The client system must present a logical view of data and services to the user. The data portion of this equation consists of classes such as user configuration and customization information, application data, application packages, application configuration information, and access to services like printing. How we map the physical storage onto the user's desktop and control access to it will ultimately affect the user's ability to use the data in an effective and productive way. The next chapter will cover the user's desktop and the environment we will provide to empower the user to use the available data.

19. The cynical observer would comment that since this is logical, practical, and a smart thing to do is a virtual guarantee that it will never happen. We can always hope otherwise.

CHAPTER 13

The Application Environment: Enabling the User

We have finally reached the very highest level in the five-layer workgroup functional model. This is the part of the workgroup that is the most visible to the user; it is used for the entire time that he or she is doing their job. But aside from its overtly visible aspects like menus and icons, the application environment presented by the user's desktop provides applications with a set of integration services, like interprocess messaging, audio and video services, remote execution, and user session management.

All of these facilities, when coupled with the look and feel of the desktop, can increase the apparent intelligence of individual applications, molding them into a cohesive solution. The goal is a unified, intuitive, easy to use environment that increases user productivity. This chapter will cover some of the aspects of creating such an environment.

13.1 The User Desktop as an Integration Vehicle

The data-sharing layer makes data sets and application packages available to the client system desktop and the application environment. Each user, or class of users, has a particular collection of tools and data that he or she uses on a regular basis. We may make the total collection of data and application packages visible to the client systems and use the desktop environment as a filter to reduce the available tools and data to the user's "working set".

If the desktop and the client system are the user's window into the workgroup's data and applications, we can open that window to any extent we wish. With desktop-integration services, we have the ability to create unique views of the workgroup data and application packages based on the user's class membership and experience level. The contents of the desktop menus and toolboxes determine what the user can or cannot do, and the access allowed by the file management facilities determines which data can be seen and which is invisible.

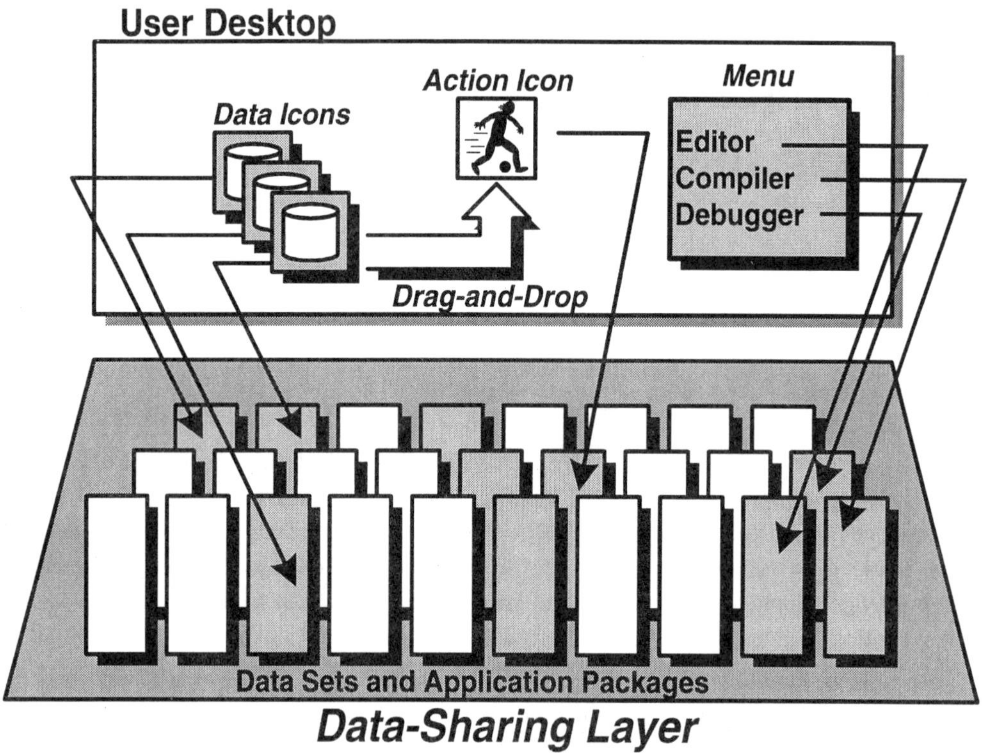

Figure 13-1 The Desktop as a Presentation and Integration Service

Desktop behavior allows the user to manipulate the data at a high level by moving icons or groups of icons representing the data to the icons that represent an action to perform on the data. The allocation of client-server resources, scheduling of application components, and passing of data and command options are done automatically to save effort and reduce the possibility of errors. This is a good example of using object-oriented principles to simplify complex user tasks.

13.2 The Desktop Look and Feel

The "look and feel" of a desktop is the sum total of the visual characteristics of the windows and the behavior of operations from pointing devices and the keyboard. Each window on the screen represents a communication path between the user and an application component "behind" it. The windowing system maps input from the pointing devices and the keyboard to the appropriate code behind the window.

The window borders and other "decorations" allow the user to manipulate the windows by moving, resizing, closing, maximizing, or minimizing them. Input that is not mapped or "focused" on a particular screen element either flies off into the bit-bucket[1] and is ignored or is caught by the window manager. Everything else may or may not produce a response from the appropriate application.

From an application's point of view, if it is aware of the desktop environment, the look-and-feel characteristics are provided in a standard set of APIs and window system components. There are several different levels of integration into the desktop, including no active participation, partial participation, and full participation. An application that has no knowledge of the desktop services may still be integrated using the standard action interface "application builders" or wrapper components.

The windows on a display are related in a hierarchical structure, much like the tree structure in a hierarchical file system. Each window has multiple attributes associated with it that tell the window-management portion of the desktop how to control its behavior and appearance. These attributes may be user configurable, accessible directly through configuration files or through programmatic interfaces. Windowing applications will provide a default set of window attributes that will allow the user interface to function properly.

13.2.1 The Desktop Messaging Service

In addition to the direct actions invoked by the user, the desktop messaging facility may schedule and pass data to other applications in the environment that were not directly activated by the user action. This chaining of processing events allows otherwise separate, manual actions to be connected and automated. The richness of the desktop integration facilities determines the extent to which processes may be automated.

The messaging system also plays a part in managing the user's session configuration. When the user logs out of the desktop, the messaging system will send a "save state" message to each application that is actively integrated into the desktop. It is then up to the application to save information like window position or color configuration and to terminate gracefully.

Aside from the programmatic interface to the messaging system provided by the messaging API, the file type and action database system may be used to make "dumb" programs appear to be integrated and desktop aware. A user drag and drop of a file icon onto an action icon, or the selection of a standard operation on an object, may trigger the execution of one or more programs. If a scripting language and command-level interfaces to the desktop message system available, then wrappers may be created around otherwise nonparticipative applications.

The desktop messaging system may also allow the remote execution of applications on behalf of the user. If this facility is available, the messaging service must handle user authentication on the remote machine, passing local configuration (environment) information to the remote machine and remote scheduling of the application. The ability to consistently access the user's data sets is necessary for the success of the remote action. This feature of the messaging

1. That legendary entity that catches all of the unwanted or unused bits from system I/O operations.

service may be used to implement "poor man's" load balancing or to localize the execution of specialized applications to specific compute servers.

13.2.2 Icons

Icons are graphical representations of underlying objects. In the desktop environment, an icon may represent a file, an application, or some other abstract object like an action with a small graphics image. An icon encapsulates the details of the underlying object and should present the user with an intuitive picture of what the object being represented is.

An icon is an important part of the desktop paradigm, because it allows a user to manipulate underlying objects with simple operations like selection, drag and drop, or mouse clicking. An icon is immediately recognizable as a particular type (or class) of object or "thing", without needing to scroll through long lists of commands or file names. By hiding the underlying details iconic representation of objects allows novice users to be more productive sooner, yet still allows experienced users to perform complex manipulations at a high level.

13.2.3 File Type and Action Databases

As we have previously discussed, file objects in the desktop environment are associated with icons and a standard set of actions. Likewise, a desktop action has an icon and an application associated with it. How are these associations created?

The desktop has a database that contains the set of defined file types and actions. Each of the definitions contains other attributes that help the desktop services perform the correct operations when the object is used. These database definitions may be extended or customized to provide new behavior for the desktop objects.

13.2.4 Graphical File and Application Management

Along with all of the other window-based tools, there is one that is responsible for access to graphical representations of data and applications. This tool is behind the "file manager" or "application manager" window. It provides the graphical, object-oriented representations for data, actions, by mapping underlying objects to the proper icon and positionally presenting them to the user.

Files are differentiated from one another in the file manager based on the file extension (the portion of the file following the ".") information contained in the file type and action database. The file type information maps the file extension to an icon and a standard set of actions that may be performed on the file. Selecting the file icon by clicking on it (one, two, three times, left, right, middle…) properly with the mouse buttons will perform the default action on the object type.

The file manager, working with the object definitions in the file type and action database, allows whole text commands, or sequences of commands, to be executed on an object with a

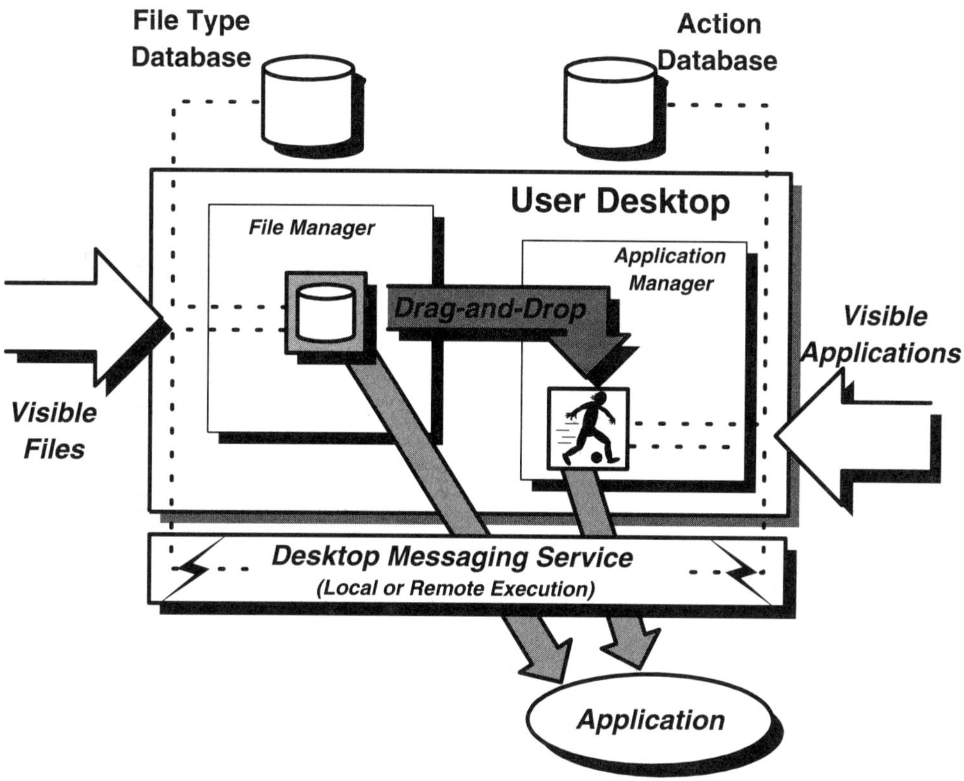

Figure 13-2 File Types, Actions, and Desktop Messaging

single click. A click can generate a local or remote sequence of events that automatically produces the desired results, as if by magic[2]. Now that's abstraction.

The file manager, masquerading as the application manager, can also display sets of icons that represent actions. This trick of using one tool to do two things can sometimes be confusing, but it does create some powerful options. Essentially, an empty file, in a special location, is mapped to an entry in the action database. The action database entry contains information about the associated icon, application, and permitted file types.

To activate the action, a user selects a file icon in the file manager window, holds down a mouse button, and drags the data icon over an action icon in the application manager window. When the user releases the mouse button, the application associated with the action is scheduled.

2. A famous science fiction writer, Arthur C. Clarke, said "Any technology when sufficiently advanced appears as magic."

The scheduled application is also passed the file represented by the file icon as a parameter on its command line. The application processes the file, returning the results to the user either graphically or in the form of data files.

13.2.5 User Session Management

The desktop session manager is a component of the desktop environment in charge of managing attributes of user sessions. This session management consists of login (authentication), restoration of the user's desktop customizations, recreating the last set of applications that were running, saving the size and state of the desktop windows prior to logout, issuing shutdown messages to executing applications at logout time, and performing the logout operation.

13.2.6 User Desktop Customizations

Only the individual user can determine what set of customizations can make his or her desktop environment "home". The ability to customize aesthetic as well as functional aspects of the desktop is very important for fine-tuning it to the user's working style. The customizations need to "follow" the user from client system to client system as he or she moves so that the same configuration is presented during each session.

Part of the customization of the environment is the addition of frequently accessed tools into the desktop menus. The desktop software usually allows dividing the menu items into standard, nonconfigurable items and user-configurable entries. By restricting the user's ability to customize menu items, we can design an environment and control its contents.

13.3 Common Windowing Systems

In our workgroup environments, there are two prevalent windowing systems to deal with the X-Windows system and the Microsoft Windows desktop. Both systems support a bit-mapped graphics display, pointing devices like a mouse or track-ball, and consistent window management behavior. The major difference at this time is that the X-Windows system allows applications to project window-based GUIs over the network to remote X-Windows servers[3].

13.3.1 The X-Windows System

X-Windows is based on a standardized network protocol, an X-Windows server that manages the client display resource, and a set of standard component libraries that allow application developers to create X-Windows clients. The X-Windows protocol allows display updates and user input to be sent transparently over the network to remote X-Windows client applications or to client applications running on the same system as the X-Windows server.

3. There are third-party packages that allow Windows systems to duplicate this behavior, and we have the promise of integrated functionality in the next version of Windows NT.

The X-Windows system provides for a window manager that is separated functionally from the X-Windows display server. Because of this, there is a wide range of window managers available to X-Windows users. One of the most common look-and-feel application toolkits is OSF Motif, which provides application developers with a standardized set of preconfigured "widgets"[4] for constructing X-windows applications.

X-Windows is available on a wide range of operating systems, not just Unix. Several versions of the X-Windows server are available for Windows NT. A common feature of Windows X-servers is the ability to create and manipulate X-windows client GUIs directly with the Microsoft Windows window manager, rather than maintaining a separate workspace or desktop for X-windows clients. This helps hide the fact that there are two windowing paradigms in use.

13.3.2 The Windows NT Desktop

A Windows NT application designer uses component toolkits that provide standard "controls" that implement the look and feel of the Windows NT desktop. This windowing API is part of the standard services provided by the Windows NT operating system. The Windows NT windowing services are very similar to those provided by other similar systems. Unlike the X-Windows system, however, it is hard to separate the window manager and display manager functionality from the total desktop.

The Windows NT window management functionality and the configuration of its window attributes is largely hidden from the user, except for the visible interface provided by the "Appearance" tab in the control panel's "Display" icon. Sets of standardized window attributes (like border width and color) may be packaged into "schemes", saved, and restored through this interface. This behavior is consistent with the general Windows philosophy of hiding overly complex details from the user, no matter how experienced.

13.4 Desktop Environments on Top of Windowing Systems

The basic windowing functionality provided by X-Windows and the Windows NT windowing system are the basis for complete desktop environments. To the basic ability to handle window functions, a complete environment adds a variety of tools and application integration facilities. Several of these environments are covered next.

13.4.1 Web Browsers, HTML, and JAVA

The web browser is becoming the most popular user interface technology in the industry. It may be viewed as "riding" on top of the client system's native windowing system. On Unix, the web browser is an X-Windows client—on Microsoft Windows systems, the browser uses the standard (local) window facilities. A combination of HTML features, browser-specific scripting

4. A widget, or control, is a standard interface component, like a text input box or a "yes/no" query, that is prepackaged for application software developers.

languages, multi-media plug-in extensions, and active programming languages like JAVA can provide a very rich user interface environment[5].

More and more complete applications are being developed using the facilities described above. The system and display-independent nature of the HTML can allow very flexible development: the active part of the application may run either on the client system or on servers in the background, and the GUI portion of the application may be projected to any system that supports the browser.

We should mention that this environment is not a desktop in the purest sense of the term. Several efforts are underway to provide desktop environments based on browser technology. To date, these are fairly immature and suffer from slow performance, but continue to promise hardware-independent desktops, thin client support, and other tangible benefits.

13.4.2 The Windows Active Desktop

In addition to the "classic" Windows desktop described above, Windows 98 supplies an "active" desktop that closely integrates web browser functionality with "traditional" desktop behavior. The user can choose which of the two desktop paradigms he wants to use. As of this writing, the jury is still out on whether or not this environment is more intuitive and productive.

There is another twist to web browser and active desktop integration. In addition to the active desktop, many Microsoft products are now using the Microsoft web browser as their user interface. If the Microsoft web browser were an X-Windows client, then that would allow browser-based Microsoft application GUIs to be remotely displayed on other system types. Unfortunately, this is not the case.

13.4.3 The Common Desktop Environment

The Common Desktop Environment (CDE) was born of an effort by multiple Unix vendors to produce a standardized desktop environment for Unix platforms. The original initiative, called COSE (Common Open Software Environment) has apparently faded into oblivion, but CDE and the companion Unix95 standard live on. They have since become an industry-wide standard, available from the Open Group.

CDE comprises the X-Windows system server, the OSF Motif look and feel, session management, messaging services from ToolTalk®, a window manager that provides multiple workspaces, help facilities, a database facility that provides an object-oriented mapping of file types to application actions, and much more. Fortunately, for all of the flexibility and associated com-

5. There is still much room for misdesign and overuse of interface features. Sometimes web pages make my eyes hurt, they are so busy with flashing, dancing, blinking applets. This is a little like the programmer who discovered a character-based terminal's inverse, half-bright, underlined, flashing character attributes and decided to use them all at once in his application's screen.

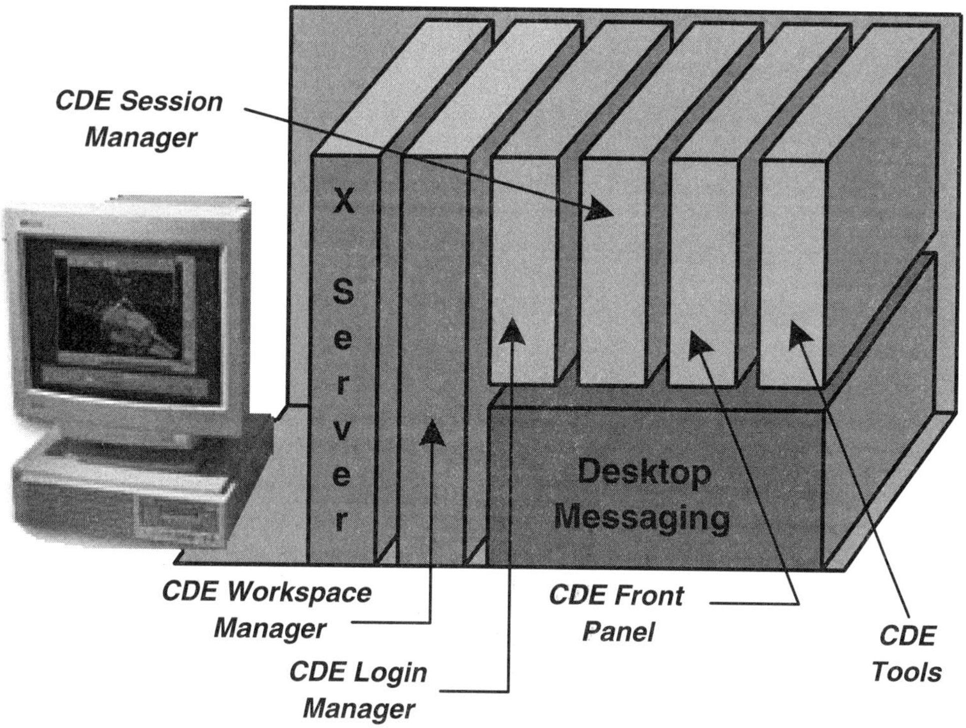

Figure 13-3 CDE Desktop Components and Structure

plexity, the CDE environment is easy to configure. We can take a minimalist approach, or dive into all of the gory details[6].

Example CDE File Type Definition An example of a CDE file type for HTML files is presented to demonstrate the flexibility available:

```
DATA_ATTRIBUTE                  HTML
{
        ACTIONS                 Open, Print, HtmlEdit
        ICON                    HtmlData
        IS_TEXT                 true
        NAME_TEMPLATE           %s.html
        MIME_TYPE               text/html
        DESCRIPTION             This file contains Hyper-Text Markup \
                                Language for display by web browsers.
        PROPERTIES              visible
}
```

6. For more information on configuring CDE, see *Configuring CDE: The Common Desktop Environment*, by Charles Fernandez [12].

This definition contains attributes that are attached to the data type: the file type is not hidden (PROPERTIES) and can be viewed by end users (IS_TEXT). New files of this type should be created with ".html" as the extension (NAME_TEMPLATE). The file type has its own icon (ICON), has an associated MIME (multipurpose Internet message extension) type (MIME_TYPE), and has three actions associated with it (ACTIONS). To get CDE to use the definition, it is placed into a file in one of the standard places that CDE searches.

Sample CDE Action Definition Action definitions provide more functionality than data definitions and so are potentially more complicated to define. In the previous definition for the HTML data type, we specified three associated actions: Open, Print, and HtmlEdit. This example will define the HtmlEdit action.

```
ACTION                      HtmlEdit
{
          LABEL             Activate an HTML editor
          ICON              HtmlEdit
          TYPE              COMMAND
          WINDOW_TYPE       NO_STDIO
          EXEC_STRING       /usr/local/bin/html_edit -file \
                            %(File)Arg_1"Enter file to edit: "%
          EXEC_HOST         %DisplayHost%
          DESCRIPTION       This action runs an HTML editor. If\
                            a file is dropped on the action icon, it\
                            will be passed to the application. If no\
                            file is specified, the user will be asked\
                            for one.
          ARG_TYPE          HTML
          ARG_CLASS         FILE
}
```

This action definition associates an icon with a command (COMMAND), does not create a terminal emulator window (WINDOW_TYPE), will accept only the proper data type (ARG_TYPE) and only files (ARG_CLASS). Finally, the action will execute on the system that the display server is running on (EXEC_HOST) and will accept a drag and drop file or will prompt the user for a file if the action icon is clicked.

13.4.4 CDE Configuration

CDE was designed to allow easy configuration and integration of application packages and related information like actions and icons. The configuration files in CDE are designed to provide system-wide values, which may be overridden by the user with local values. The system-wide values may be shared by all client systems in the workgroup, with the global values being modified on a local basis for each user's environment.

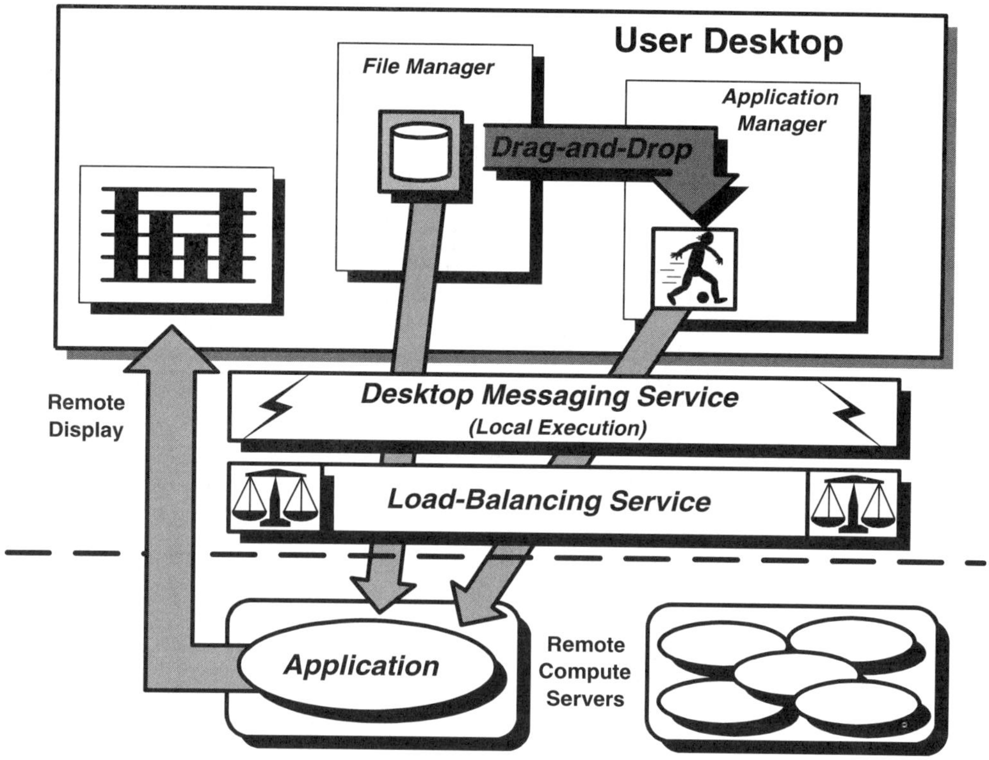

Figure 13-4 Integrating Load Balancing with the Desktop

The location of the configuration files determines the order that they are read by CDE. We can affect the final behavior of the environment by placing the proper configuration information in the correct location. Because information later in the search path overrides earlier information, we have an easy way to provide global defaults or user-specific values to control the desktop. This is exactly the sort of behavior we want if we are to use class-based administration and invest a minimum amount of effort.

13.4.5 CDE Availability

CDE is available on every major Unix vendor's platform. Also, the CDE components, including the messaging service, have been ported to the Windows NT environment. This allows us to use the CDE environment on all of the client systems in the workgroup, both Unix and Windows NT. Additionally, all client types are able to participate in the action and remote messaging activities.

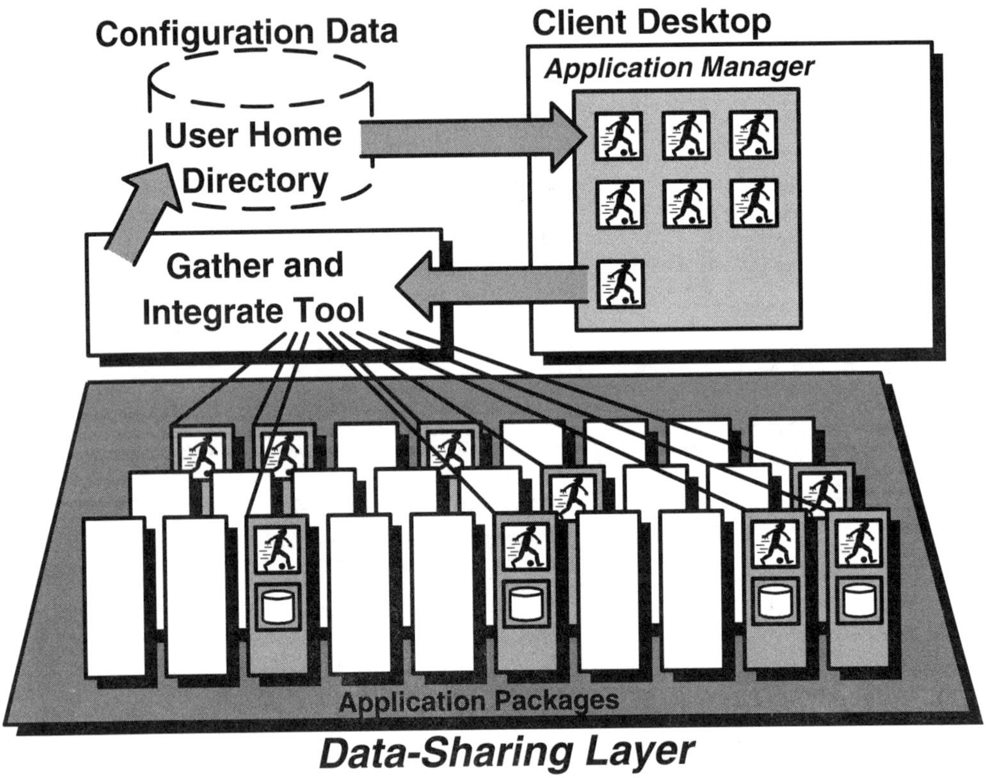

Figure 13-5 Package Integration with the Desktop

13.5 Using a Load-Balancing Service with the Desktop

We have mentioned a load-balancing service several times in previous chapters. Actually integrating the load-balancing facility into the user's environment can be done in several ways. One flexible and transparent way to add the load-balancing functionality to the environment is to plug it into the desktop action definitions.

Instead of directly executing the application with the action definition, a wrapper script is called. The wrapper script can make decisions about the size and type of the job, then choose local execution or remote execution through the load-balancing service. To the user, the details of where the job is actually executed should be immaterial, as long as the expected results are produced in the expected amount of time.

As we have mentioned before, the ability to project the interactive application's GUI over the network is an important part of this approach. For batch jobs, the display projection is not essential. Other issues to be dealt with are consistent paths to data and applications and user authentication on any remote server machines.

13.6 Integrating Application Packages with the Desktop

The underlying data-sharing layer of the workgroup can "present" application packages to the user's client system. The availability of packages "underneath" the client desktop is only the first step in allowing the user to make use of them. Each package should contain configuration information, like icons, actions, and wrapper scripts that must be integrated into the desktop environment menus, file manager, and application manager, to make them visible to the user.

One approach to package integration is to provide an application that displays the available packages, allowing the user to choose the proper versions for installation. Once selected, the package-integration data (the package interface) are added to the appropriate location to make it visible. Each client system has its own method of integration, but adding information to the client system itself is counterproductive—either the user moves to another client and the information will not be there, or the continual install-remove-install action becomes a performance issue.

The user's package configuration information must be located in a place that follows him or her around from client to client. On a Unix system, that is the user's home directory. For Microsoft Windows systems, the information needs to be placed in a "roving" profile.

13.7 Collaborative Tools on the Desktop

In addition to the "local" tools that run on the desktop for the user, there are a class of tools, which we will call "collaborative tools", that run *between* two or more desktops. These collaborative applications enable sharing a combination of video, audio, or graphical information between two or more users. This real-time sharing can increase communication and group productivity, particularly between widely separated users.

There is a wide range of available applications that run across the network: video conferencing, shared "white" boards, shared three-dimensional model viewers, internet phones, and a whole host of others. To add these tools, which are usually time-sensitive and network bandwidth "hogs", to a user environment, we must first take note of where we are in the workgroup model—the very highest level. For the user's desktop to support demanding collaborative tools requires the proper design and cooperation of all of the lower levels in the workgroup model—a frequently overlooked fact.

The network design may need to take collaborative tools into consideration, not only in terms of bandwidth[7], but in terms of hardware functionality. Collaborative tools may make use of special protocols or network features like multicast packets. Some networking hardware allows the real-time creation of VLANs or multicast groups to isolate other nodes from the direct effects of this type of traffic. Without these features, the whole workgroup's performance is likely to suffer.

7. An MPEG encoded video and audio stream can take 1 Megabit per second or more, depending on quality level.

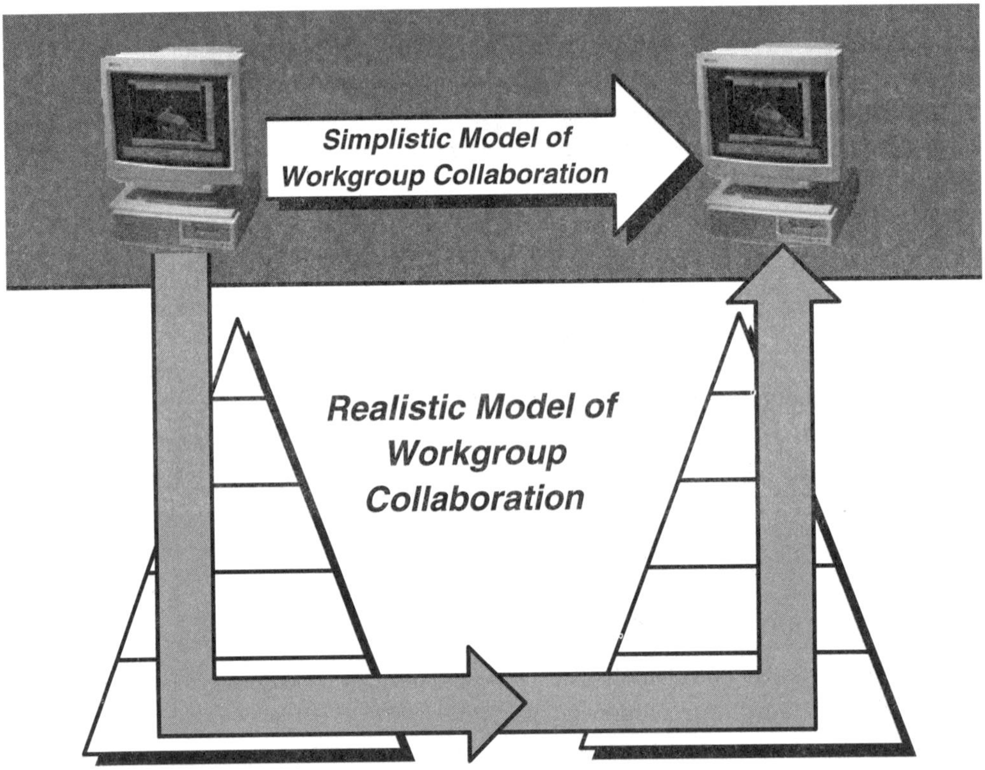

Figure 13-6 Collaboration Uses the Whole Environment

In Chapter 10, we discussed procedures for picking network and computer hardware distribution in the workgroup. Part of that process was a survey of applications that are expected to run in the environment. The addition of collaborative tools, because of their performance and network bandwidth requirements, must not be an afterthought or the careful design and layout of the workgroup will need reworking.

Another requirement for the proper operation of collaborative tools is the ability to access both local and remote data in the network. There are performance, consistency, and security issues involved in providing this ability to the users. We discussed components of this portion of the workgroup design in Chapter 12.

13.8 Application Environment Summary

The application environment is the pinnacle of visibility in the workgroup environment. As workgroup designers, we have a number of desktop features that can help us create a cohesive and easy to use environment for our users. The choices we have for desktop environments include the Microsoft Windows desktop, the CDE, and browser-based technologies.

It is surprising how often we overlook the part that the client system's desktop plays in the integration of workgroup applications and data. Even where the rich environment of CDE is available, the customizations are frequently limited to adding user menu items. The remote execution facilities alone can aid us greatly in creating a client-server environment, particularly in small workgroups where the extra-strength solution of load balancing is not needed.

By studying the common features in the available desktops, we can help make our user's environments more consistent from system to system. We will discuss this topic in greater detail in Chapter 15.

Finally, the use of collaborative tools is becoming more and more common as organizations are distributed across buildings, whole sites, or even world-wide. These tools will provide productivity improvements only if the underlying workgroup structures, including the network and data distribution mechanisms, are designed to support them. Adding performance hungry collaborative tools to a workgroup as an afterthought is a recipe for poor performance.

If the user's desktop is the pinnacle of visibility in the workgroup[8] environment, it is also the point at which all of the environmental problems are brought into sharp focus. This is because the user's desktop is also the starting point for the workgroup environment's dependency tree. If you close your eyes and visualize the object dependency tree that fans out from the user's desktop, it is hard to keep from screaming in terror.

8. See Chapter 5 and Figure 5-10 for discussion of desktop visibility issues.

CHAPTER 14

Enterprise Access: Gluing Workgroups Together

Most of our focus in this book has been on the LAN, or internal, portion of the workgroup environment. But our hierarchical resource model does include enterprise-wide resources. Some of these remote resources may be located in workgroups "at corporate" or in an external supplier's environment, still others may be located in workgroups within the local workcenter managed by other organizations. Each of these locations presents a unique set of requirements for data sharing.

This chapter will cover some of the methods we have at our disposal for enabling wide-area sharing of resources between workgroups. We will concentrate mainly on the interface between internal workgroup mechanisms and the external services and data.

14.1 Requirements for WAN Resource Sharing

As we discussed in Chapter 9, the WAN component of the network has different characteristics than the internal workgroup networking, which is based on LAN technology. The primary differences are speed and latency, however, there is also a different reliability component[1]. Along with different performance characteristics, there are a different set of requirements for sharing WAN-based resources.

Our 3TCS workgroups will certainly need to use remote services and share remote data. Before the workgroup is established, remote access to data and services needs to be a major design consideration—not everything will be local to the workgroup or workcenter hierarchies. As more and more companies start sharing resources with remote divisions or suppliers, WAN

1. It is fairly difficult for someone to dig up your LAN connection with a backhoe without your knowledge.

access is becoming a bigger and bigger issue. Some of the design issues and choices are addressed in the coming sections.

14.1.1 Loosely Coupled Access

We discussed dependencies between network objects in Chapter 3. To prevent remote failures from causing "remote-control" outages in our local workgroup, we would like any remote object located across a WAN link to be a recognized, managed, loosely coupled, nonlocal dependency[2]. In other words, if a remote failure occurs, we would like the local user of the resource to be as unaware of that failure as possible until it can be repaired.

We qualified that last statement because it is not always possible to have full functionality when a remote resource decides to take an unexpected vacation; a secondary DNS server may be "further away" in terms of network hops and exact a performance penalty. Sometimes we need to limp along or even stop working temporarily. What is most important, however, is that we do not have *local* system failures or, worse yet, loss of data because of a remote failure.

14.1.2 Service and Data Replication

Replication of server resources allows a client system to fail over to another copy of the service if the primary source fails. There are two components to this: the server replication mechanism and the client search algorithm. Services like the Windows NT domain controller, the DCE DFS fileset location database, DNS, and the DCE registry all use replication as a means of load balancing and providing immunity from failure.

The client system that is using the replicated service needs a starting or "entry" point for its initial use of the service. If a failure of that starting point occurs, the client will utilize the search mechanism defined by the client portion of the service to locate a new server. Some of the client search behavior is configurable, and some is not, depending upon the service involved.

The server portion of the service, if it provides replicated data, has a conundrum to deal with: how to guarantee that all replicas of the data are synchronized. The most common method of tackling this problem is to designate a "master" site for the data which is writable and a set of read-only replicas. This is the approach used by NIS, DCE DFS filesets, and the Windows NT domain controllers. Many times when we hear the terms "primary" and "backup" or "master" and "slave", we can substitute the phrases "writable" and "read-only", respectively.

Replication provides a level of indirect access between client systems and the primary source of the information, which is "behind" the replicas. This level of indirection can insulate clients from an inability to access the primary site. When the resource is a remote one, across the WAN, the insulation from failure can help workgroup reliability. The multiple levels of indirection are shown in Figure 14-1.

2. This is a real mouthful; maybe we should substitute RMLCNLD?

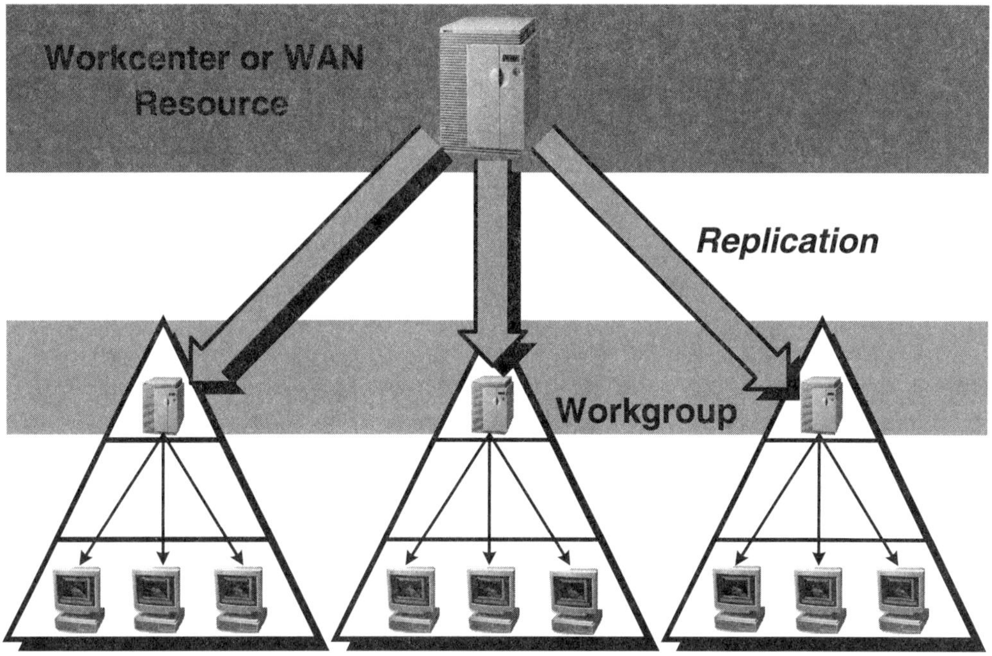

Figure 14-1 Loosely Coupled Access to Replicated WAN Resources

Replication Data-Transfer Methods How the information from the primary site is updated at each of the replicas differs from service to service. There are two general approaches: immediate updates and background updates. Immediate propagation of the information changes can keep replicas up to date within very tight limits. This type of update process, however, can have a high network overhead, especially if the changes are large and the modifications are frequent. If a replica is not available for some reason, there must be a mechanism for getting it updated at a later time.

Background updates (DCE CDS terminology calls this "skulking") may be the fall-back mechanism for replicas that are unavailable. This update method may also be the method of choice if complete synchronization of the replicas within strict time limits is not needed. This brings up another point: often replication services have a dependency with regards to the system clocks—replication depends on accurate synchronization of time between the primary and secondary service providers.

The Microsoft Windows NT Replication Service Microsoft Windows NT allows replication of information from an "export server" to multiple client "import servers". This behavior is offered by the Directory Replicator service, and importing may occur on either a Windows NT Server or Windows NT Workstation system, but exporting is limited to Windows NT Server systems.

This service is primarily intended to replicate logon scripts, user profiles, and system policy information to import multiple systems. Another thing to note is that the service is not necessarily intended to operate over a WAN link. There is nothing to prevent replication of other information with this service. Subdirectories of the *\winnt\System32\Repl\Export* directory are exported to the identified import systems, and placed in the *\winnt\System32\Repl\Import* directory.

How the client systems in the workgroup locate and use the replicated files is an exercise apparently left up to the system manager. Any load balancing that might occur appears to be the result of manual client configuration. There is no fail-over mechanism for information that is not associated with information maintained on a domain controller[3].

DCE Replication Because of its intended use as a WAN-based, secure environment for applications, a number of services in DCE are replicated. Those services include the registry service, the Cell Directory Service (CDS), the Distributed Time Service (DTS), and the DFS Fileset Location Database (FLDB). Because of its distributed nature, we can use the DCE environment to provide WAN-based services to our workgroups.

DCE DFS is a good example of how data replication and insulation from actual data location can improve performance and availability. The cache manager on DFS clients assigns ranking to file servers and FLDB servers, based on comparing the client and the server's IP addresses for adjacency and connectivity information.

This ranking information is used to determine which replica to use when accessing a replicated fileset and which FLDB server to use when there are more than one. The ranking information may also be manually set by the system administrator. The preferences for both the DFS file server and FLDB servers are handled this way.

DCE DFS Replication DCE DFS fileset replicas are read-only copies of a writable fileset on one DFS server machine. A fileset may be replicated on up to sixteen other DFS servers. Changes made to the read-write fileset must be propagated to the read-only replicas.

There are two DCE DFS propagation methods: release replication and scheduled replication. With release replication a system administrator must manually "release" or propagate the fileset with a command. Scheduled propagation occurs automatically according to a set of parameters set by the system administrator.

14.1.3 Using Replication in the Workgroup and Workcenter

How widely a particular server or data set is replicated depends primarily on the physical locations of the workgroups that use it. If there is no commonality across workgroups in the enterprise, then it is impossible to identify shared sets of data that may be replicated in local

3. If a failure of a domain controller occurs, the client system will attempt to locate an alternate domain controller. If the logon and system policy information is replicated on every domain controller, then the client system will have access to identical information. But what about other, "normal" files?

workcenters or workgroups, even if there is a central IT department that maintains enterprise-wide services. For sharing, the resource must be commonly agreed upon and "pushed up" to the enterprise level of the hierarchy for management and distribution to the lower levels.

If a single workgroup is split across multiple sites, then the workgroup system administrators for that workgroup may control the replicated information, even if the remote sites are connected by a globally administered WAN link. The complexities of administering services like DCE DFS may be beyond the personnel capabilities of the smaller workgroup administration group, teaming up with other workgroups can help with the allocation of dedicated system administration resources. There are frequently economies of scale when talking about use of widely distributed resources.

Aside from who designs, implements, and administers the replicated services, the use of replication in the workgroup involves several key decisions. Two primary questions are: "How many local replicas do we need?", and "How do we interface the LAN-based workgroup data access mechanisms to the WAN-based ones?" We will discuss these questions next.

How Many Local Replicas? The answer to this question is "start with at least two". Having two replicas in the environment avoids creating a single point of failure (SPOF) for clients that use the resource. This means at least two NIS servers (a master and a slave), two Windows NT domain controllers (a PDC and a BDC), two DNS servers, and two of everything else that clients require to be highly available.

Load balancing between servers may occur automatically as part of the client portion of the service (as in DCE DFS), or we may need to explicitly configure different classes of clients to use different replicas. If we are really tricky, we can distribute the initial replica use among the different classes and reverse the order of use in case of a failure. As an example, with two DNS caching servers, we could configure half of the clients to use server one as the primary and server two as the next server to try, and the other half of the clients to use server two as the primary and server one as the fail-over resource.

Having two of everything may not be possible in your environment[4], so we can bend the rule if the availability of the service or data is adequate for the client's needs. But availability is only part of the picture—the other part is performance. Sometimes the load on a particular service requires that we have more than two replicas available to handle the load from the clients. In that situation, we desperately need load balancing built into the client portion of the server, or the system administration will overwhelm us.

One solution frequently encountered is to distribute specialized NIS maps containing client system to server mappings for a particular service like e-mail. The client system's start-up process reads the map and creates the proper local configuration information to use the service. For NIS this might be *ypset* options, for e-mail directories—automounter information, for DNS clients—resolver entries, and so on.

4. This "Noah's ark" configuration can be a burden on small workgroups.

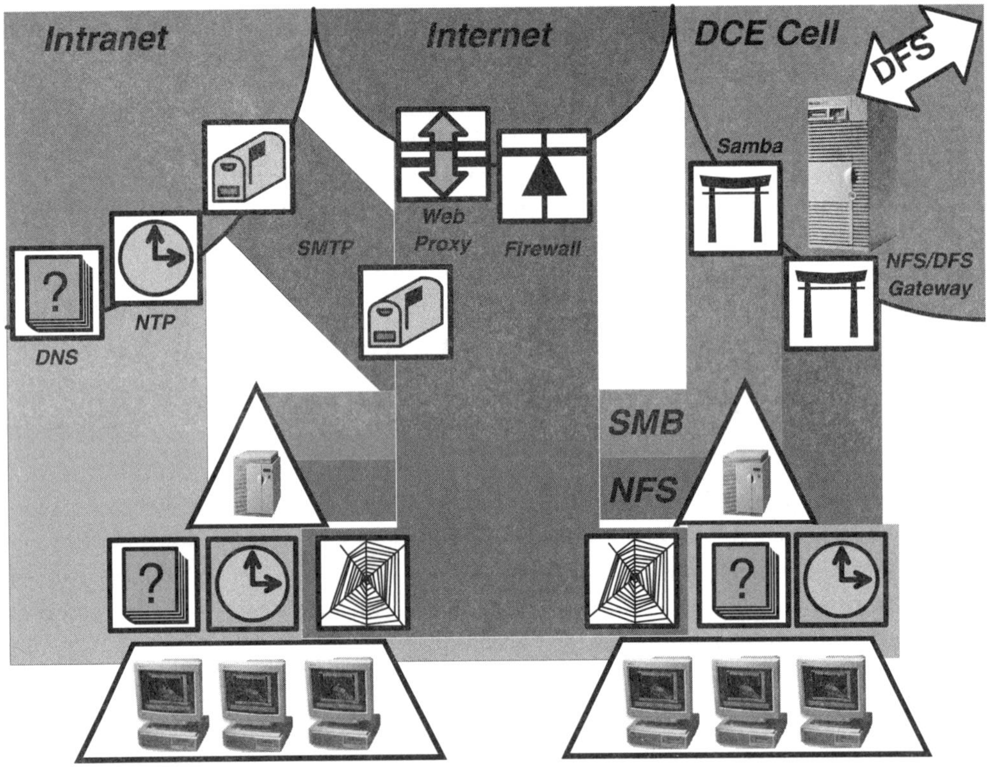

Figure 14-2 Gateways to the WAN

This method allows distribution of configuration meta-data from a single location. Instead of requiring manual configuration operations on all client systems, the client system automatically performs the proper conversion of the configuration meta-data to the actual local configuration data. This is single-point administration of manual load balancing, managed from a central location.

Wide-Area Data and Service Gateways In our earlier discussions of gateway machines, we mentioned their ability to translate semantics from one file system or service protocol to another. Most of the examples we used were for translating to or from SMB and NFS, the two LAN-based workgroup data-sharing mechanisms. We also mentioned the DFS-to-NFS secure gateway as a way to export the DCE root to the NFS client systems in the workgroup.

Because of its security and design, DCE DFS makes an ideal mechanism for sharing data over WAN connections. If we cannot or will not use DCE DFS as the primary workgroup data mechanism, then we should strongly consider using it as the WAN mechanism, especially since the LAN-based solutions do not work well in WAN environments. If the workgroup clients already use DCE DFS, then our job of adding the WAN component is relatively easy.

It is also possible to provide DCE DFS to SMB gateways by using Samba or other Unix facilities that can authenticate the user to DCE. With this combination, a DCE DFS client running a Samba server can export both local Unix file systems and remote DCE DFS filesets to local SMB clients. The issue becomes coordinating the user authentication information across the three environments: DCE DFS, Unix NFS, and Microsoft Windows SMB. If Unix vendors and Microsoft would allow a neutral authentication service, say Kerberos, to perform the operations for their systems, our jobs would certainly be a lot easier[5].

Figure 14-2 shows workcenter interfaces to a set of intranet and Internet resources. We have separated the DCE cell from the intranet and Internet portions of the WAN because of its special characteristics. Another way of visualizing the structure is to imagine the DCE cell superimposed on *both* the Internet and the intranet.

14.1.4 Wide-Area Data Caching

The DFS-to-NFS secure gateway system described in the previous section is configured as a DCE DFS client system and can therefore cache remote DFS files that are accessed by the NFS clients it services. This caching means that once the file is accessed, it will be cached on the gateway's disk in the DFS cache. Access from that point will occur as if the file was really local to the DFS to NFS gateway.

The DFS client cache manager does not necessarily cache the entire file; instead it caches "chunks" that are between 8 kilobytes and 256 kilobytes when kept in a disk cache and 8 kilobytes if in a memory cache. Disk cached information persists across system reboots, so unless the file changes or the cache fills, accessed files will remain cached. When data on the DFS server changes, the server notifies all client cache managers that they must obtain a new version of the data on the next read.

There are other examples of caching that can help us with WAN resources. We have already shown how a caching-only DNS server can insulate the local systems from failure of remote DNS servers. The caching increases performance for requests that refer to already cached data. Other examples of services that use caching are web proxy servers, DCE CDS, and many of the other DCE service clients.

14.2 Trust and Authentication Between Groups

To share data and services between two groups that do not completely trust each other requires establishing a mutually agreed-upon authentication and access relationship. Both Windows NT and DCE allow users that are foreign to a cell or domain to be authenticated, providing the proper trust relationship has been established between the entity requiring the authentication and the "home" cell or domain for the user.

5. There is hope. Several Unix vendors have secure versions of services like FTP and Telnet that use Kerberos for authentication. Rumor has it that Windows 2000 will also use Kerberos for authentication. If by some chance occurrence, we end up with a common (or interoperable) service we can all rejoice.

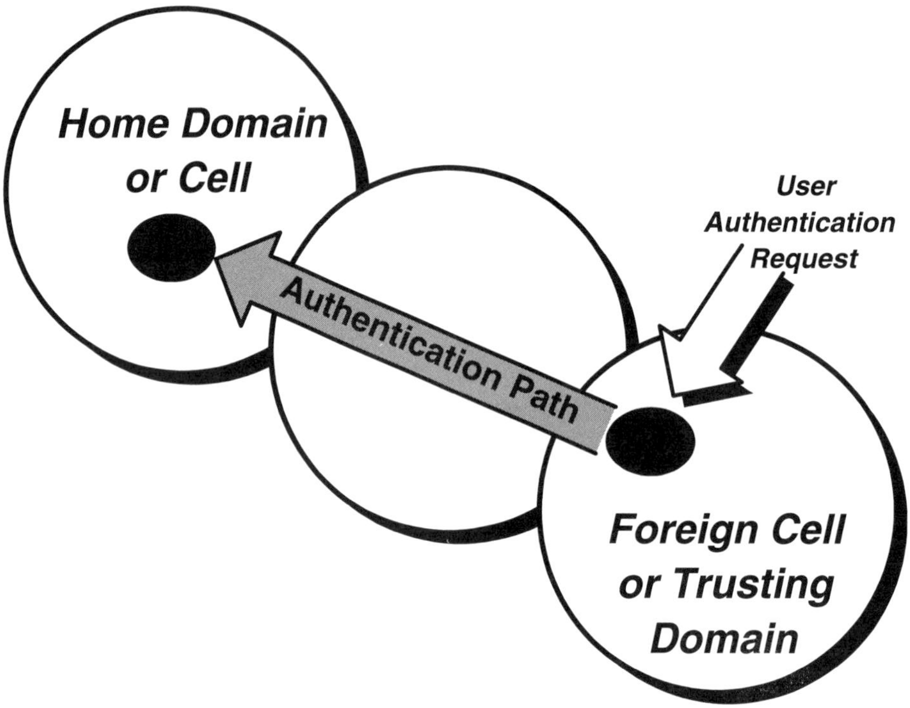

Figure 14-3 Trust Relationships

Windows NT allows "pass-through" authentication between a trusting domain and a trusted domain. The trusting domain honors the user authentication performed by the trusted domain. When one domain trusts another, user accounts and global groups[6] in the trusted domain may be given access rights to resources and services in the trusting domain.

DCE, too, allows trust relationships between separate cells. Each cell must have a special foreign cell surrogate entry in its registry for the other cell's principal. The two authentication services convey information about their principals to each other, allowing one cell to obtain a ticket to a principal in the other cell. The two cells are termed "trust peers" and the sequence of other cells that must be traversed when a principal in one cell communicates with another is called an "authentication path."

DCE DFS ACLs have features that support access control for principals in other cells. First of all, a cell other than the default cell may be specified in the ACL for an object. A user from a foreign cell may create an object in another cell, and the object's default ACL will spec-

6. A Windows NT global group is valid in its own domain, on servers and client systems in its own domain, and in trusting domains.

ify the foreign cell. Users may thus create objects in foreign cells that are protected from unwanted access.

In addition to the required user_obj, group_obj, and other_obj entries, DCE DFS ACLs have entries for foreign_user, foreign_group, and foreign_other. This set of ACL entries can specify permissions for principals from a specific foreign cell. These special entries are part of the standard ACL evaluation sequence, so a foreign user can be given rights to local resources.

14.2.1 Consistent Enterprise Security

Whatever data or resources we wish to share across the enterprise, we must design a way of providing consistent authentication and access across all connected workgroups. We may be hampered because the LAN-based authentication services may not perform in a WAN environment. We also may run into issues with a local system's ability to support the number of unique user identifiers required for an enterprise. For example, 16 bit Unix UIDs are sufficient for only 32,768 individual accounts[7].

Of course an enterprise-wide authentication and single logon system are only necessary if data can be shared across the whole enterprise. But given the business needs for distributed activities, it is an eventuality that must be taken into account[8]. To maintain consistent authentication and access policies, we may need to interface a WAN authentication mechanism with whatever LAN-based systems are in use.

Another approach might be to make each independent workgroup or workcenter environment a DCE cell and to enable intercell authentication. Authentication interfaces exist for every major vendor's environment, including Windows NT. It is possible to use the WAN capabilities of DCE to transport common authentication information, which may be translated or downloaded into the "native" authentication system. See "Using External Sources to Update a Windows NT PDC" on page 329 for an example of this type of interface.

14.3 WAN Data Encryption

Encryption is an essential part of any WAN data-sharing scheme. We do not have space to cover the subject of encryption in any depth here. (See *Security in Distributed Computing* [13] for a good coverage of the technologies in use.) Suffice it to say that any time data appears "in

7. Unix systems, like HP-UX, may allow 32-bit UIDs, which increase the number of potential users to over 4 billion.

8. No pun intended.

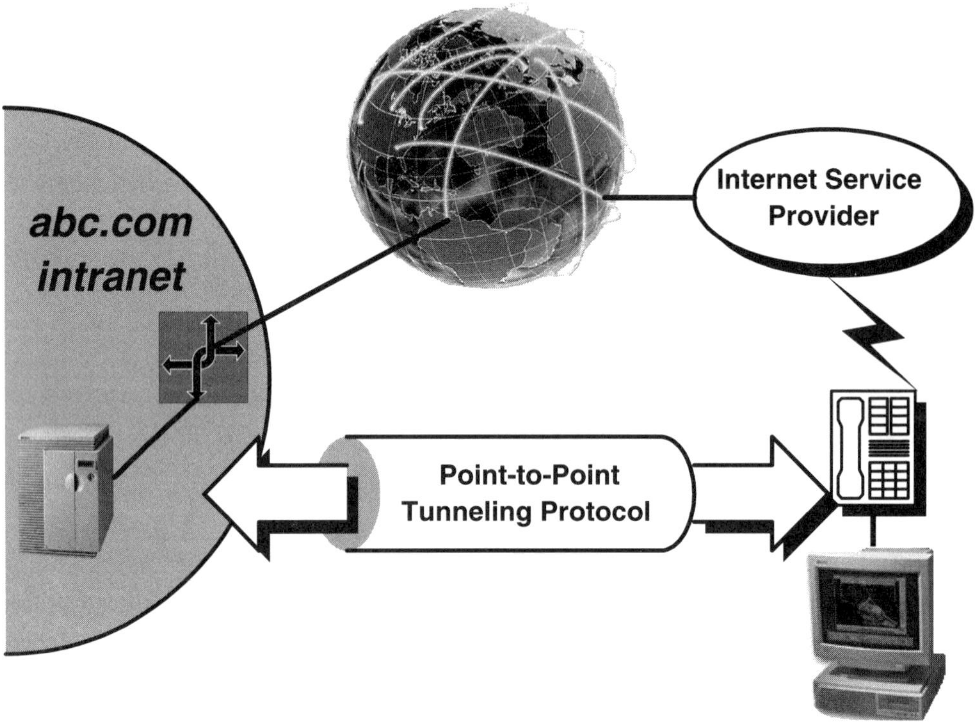

Figure 14-4 Point-to-Point Tunneling Protocol Connections

the clear", it is subject to interception and misuse. This applies not only to passwords, but to RPC call contents and network packets containing file system information[9].

Systems like DCE and Microsoft Windows NT go to great lengths to prevent "clear text" passwords from traveling across the network, where they might be intercepted. Any authentication information is accepted from the user and encrypted before it leaves the local system. Windows NT's Remote Access Service (RAS) also supports encryption of authentication and logon data and may be further configured to encrypt all data that passes between a client and the RAS server.

DCE client-server communications are protected by multiple possible levels of encryption. DCE supports six different levels of encryption—from none to full encryption (DES)—of all data transferred. The application developer may choose what level is appropriate. The level of encryption can be negotiated by the DCE client but must meet or exceed the requirements of the server application. DCE can encrypt the RPC information, but not the data portion, of all com-

9. Running a nonencrypted file system over a public WAN? Ever wonder why your competitor's product closely resembles yours?

munication between the client and server. Additionally, an encrypted checksum may be added to each packet to detect tampering.

Another area where encryption is finding extensive application is in Virtual Private Networks (VPNs). Network hardware encrypts and routes network frames over the Internet using Point-to-Point Tunneling Protocol (PPTP), where the frames are decrypted and passed on to their final destination. Client systems using PPTP can access corporate intranets via dial-up lines from an Internet service provider (ISP), or through other direct connections to the Internet. All current predictions point to a rapid rise in the use of VPNs.

14.4 Check-In, Check-Out Containers

Let's take a look at a practical use of WAN data sharing. One of the features of Product Data Management (PDM) systems is the ability to manage large amounts of design data associated with product development efforts. A check-in and check-out model is used to mediate access to design data under the PDM system's control. In addition to collecting all design data in one place and protecting the data from unauthorized access, the hope is that consistent control and visibility of the data can allow reuse of design components.

But reusing a design component means that other groups, divisions, or organizations need access to the component information in the PDM repository. The information may be in a centralized "corporate" PDM repository or in another remote workgroup's PDM repository. How do we provide enterprise access to this information?

The PDM check-out operation may involve propagating the design information to the user's work area via a specialized protocol. We briefly discussed some aspects of specialized PDM data management in Chapter 10, where we noted that running the data-management component of the PDM system on the same physical server as the data repository could eliminate one network hop for data being checked out. Even with the extra hop eliminated, the movement of the data over a WAN link may represent a performance bottleneck.

A specialized approach, which we will call "check-in, check-out containers", can address the WAN aspects of exporting the data and also provide additional security. The general sequence of operations is:

- User's client system sends a check-out request to the repository software.
- The repository manager checks out the data and places it in a well-known DCE DFS location.
- ACLs on the data are set to permit access by the remote user only.
- The user accesses the information via DFS, and it is cached locally on the client system or intermediate gateway server.
- The user completes examination or modification of the data with local applications.
- The client system sends a request to the repository manager to check in the data.
- The data-management software moves data back to the repository.

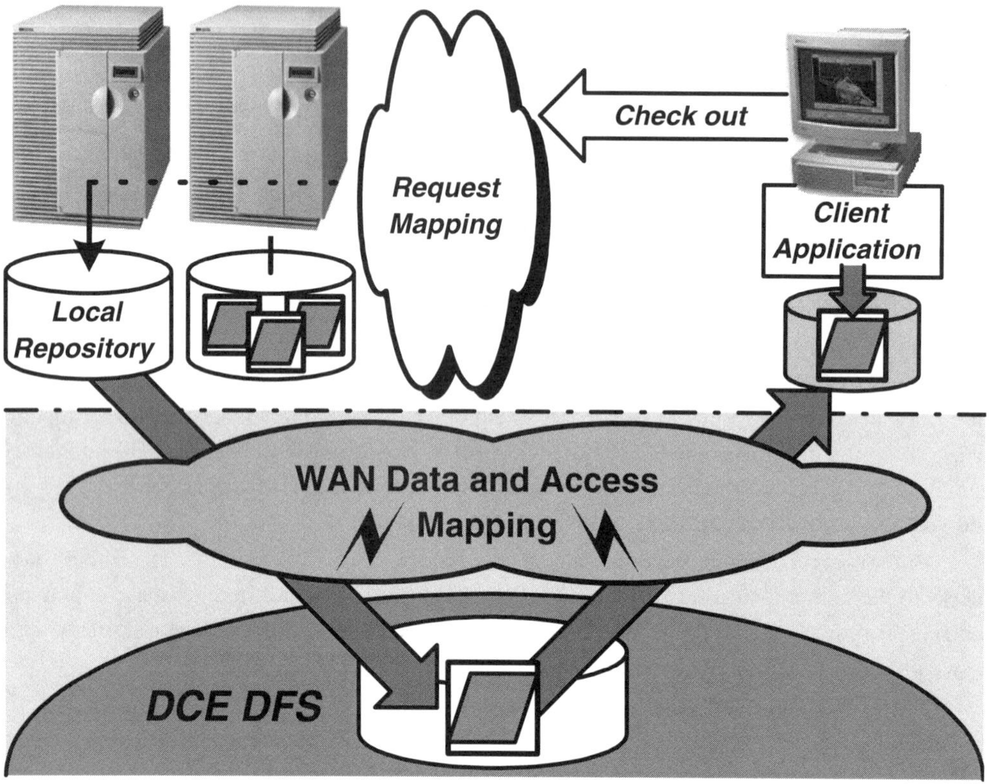

Figure 14-5 Using a WAN Check-in, Check-out Container

Because neither the PDM software nor the user's client system may know about DCE DFS, this method may require "creative data mapping" underneath the server and the client system. Additionally, the user's request for a specific piece of information may be mapped to a particular PDM server, providing an illusion of a single, very large repository. A diagram of this is shown in Figure 14-5.

14.5 WAN and Workgroup Summary

The sharing of data and services across a WAN involves several major components: WAN authentication services that enable trust, data access controls, and encryption to protect data in transit. We can implement workgroups using WAN-capable environments like DCE, but the added complexity of that environment may be more than we need for local functionality. One way around the extra local complexity is to implement the WAN portion of the environment separately from the workgroups and use well-defined interfaces between the two components.

The software systems that implement WAN access utilize two mechanisms to improve performance and reliability: caching and replication. Replication allows access to multiple copies of the same data, most often in a read-only access mode. Caching keeps local copies of data closer to its users, often reading ahead to ensure that sequential accesses can be satisfied from the cache. The proper configuration of these two attributes, or the rearrangement of software structure to provide them, can improve the workgroup user's performance and reliability.

Finally, there are custom configurations of local workgroup software components that can provide flexibility for WAN data sharing. One example of this can be called a "check-in, check-out container", because a WAN-based file system provides a globally visible location to contain information checked out of data-management software, such as PDM. Proper mapping of access rights and file system locations can make the data appear to the client system as if it came from a local repository.

If you get the sense that the WAN component of our design hierarchy is limited in its available choices, you are correct. There are not many compute environments that were designed for WAN operation, the notable exception being DCE. What this means is that most of our technology choices involve LAN workgroup components that have somehow been extended in the hopes of dealing with WAN operation. As the available bandwidth in WAN technologies increases, and as more and more companies express the need to share data across their enterprises, look for this situation to change.

CHAPTER 15

Interoperability: Cooperation Within the Workgroup

As much as any computer vendor would like to completely own a customer's environment, this rarely happens. Heterogeneous environments are a fact of life for those of us that design and implement computer workgroups. With the wide variety of computer vendors and operating system variants, making everybody's equipment interoperate can present some challenges[1]. Because they are the most commonly encountered, we will concentrate on studying two system types: Unix and Windows NT. The following table is a brief outline of the level of difficulty encountered when integrating combinations of these two environments.

Table 15-1 Interoperability Challenge Levels with Unix and Windows NT

System Types	*Unix Variant*	*Windows NT*
Unix Variant	Minimal difficulty[a]	N/A
Windows NT	Difficult[b]	Minimal difficulty[c]

a. Systems interoperate at the standards level, system administration procedures and commands are different from variant to variant. No difficulty between the same variant.

b. A number of major differences make interoperability with existing Unix systems difficult.

c. Adding combinations of DOS, Windows 3.1, or Windows 9X, or Windows NT 3.51 into the mixture makes interoperability more difficult. Not all applications support new Windows NT functionality.

1. Anyone care to nominate this as the understatement of the year?

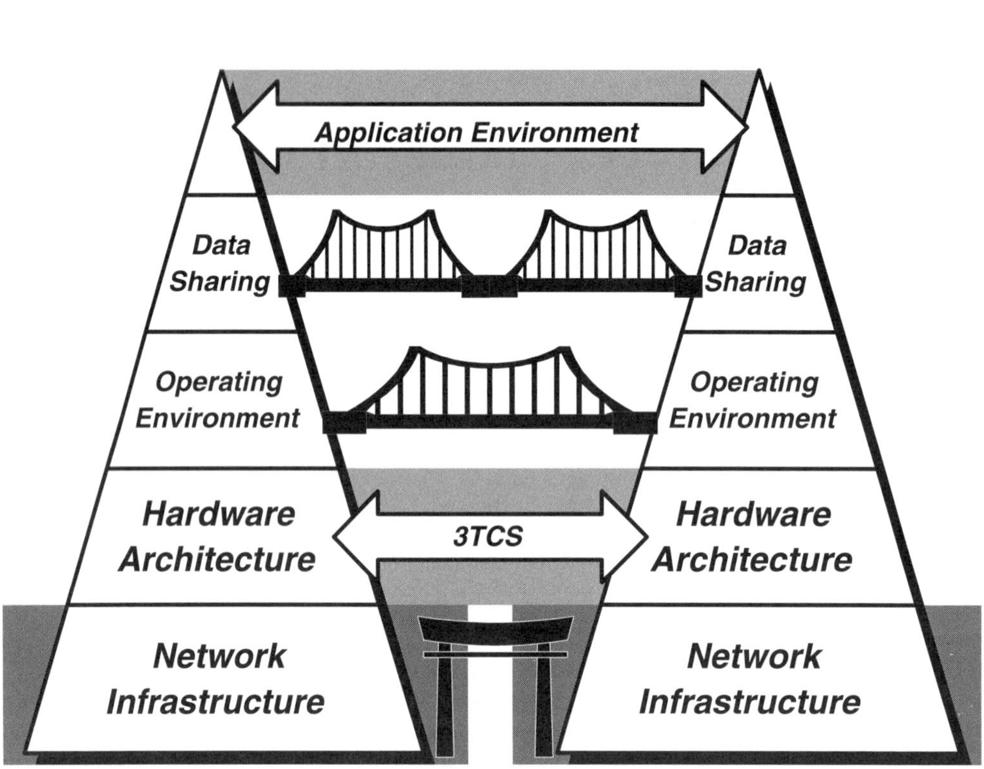

Figure 15-1 Interoperability Between Workgroup Functional Layers

You need to have realistic expectations: interoperability does not happen just because a new type of machine is dropped into the workgroup. Interoperability requires design effort and planning for optimum success. In this chapter, we will cover some of the general aspects of interoperability and then apply them to making different system types "talk together." As a base model, we will use the five-layer workgroup functional model to examine the areas of required interoperability.

15.1 Client-Server Architectural Interoperability

At the most abstract level, interoperability is required to allow client-server application components and data to be distributed across different system types. We would like at least the illusion of a seamlessly integrated environment, no matter what the underlying hardware or operating system strata might be. We will define interoperability as:

> **Interoperability is the transparent sharing of data, compute, application resources, and system administration techniques between dissimilar system types in the 3TCS workgroup.**

Unfortunately, we often have to create the required illusion of transparency. While we are filling in the functionality holes in two dissimilar environments to make them interoperate, we may not think we have time to sit back and philosophize about *why* the integration is difficult. But this is precisely what we should do if we want to succeed at recognizing architectural mismatches ahead of time. The starting point for an interoperability design is a comparison between the client-server architectures offered by the two operating systems and the environments they create.

In the situation where unequal functionality is intentional, say in an operating system that specializes only in a singular task like massively parallel computing, we may choose specialized client-server components to run only on that system, providing an interface to the workgroup that "hides" the internal differences. If the client server model used by two operating systems is the same or similar, then we can expect that making them cooperate will be easier. Having similar environments means we have the flexibility to delegate the location of components and data as we desire.

15.2 Interoperability Within the Workgroup Functional Model

To really make two or more operating systems interoperate takes a concerted systems engineering effort. The larger the operational "distance" between the environments, the larger the required effort to make them meet on common ground. The approach the author likes to use in tackling interoperability projects is summarized by a pseudo-equation:

$$\text{Interoperate} = \text{Investigate} + \text{Originate} + \text{Automate}$$

This little mnemonic details the high-level steps necessary to make environments interoperate. First, thoroughly investigate the capabilities of both environments. Next, design and implement a solution (e.g,. a manual process, a software package, or a particular set of system or subsystem configuration values). Finally, once the solution is verified, automate it—on one or both systems in scripts or other tools. Be prepared—continued refinement and adjustment to changes in the environments are usually necessary with any form of automated interoperability tools.

15.3 Levels of Workgroup Interoperability

It is at this functional level that we have a design choice to make: Just how interoperable do we need the different environments within the workgroup to be? We may choose between one of several possible interoperability models, each with different levels of interoperability at each of the five functional layers. Explanations for three possible general models follow.

15.3.1 Loosely Coupled Interoperability—Separate but Equal

Loosely coupled interoperability may be a starting point for interoperability between existing workgroup systems and a system type that is a newcomer to the environment. Interoper-

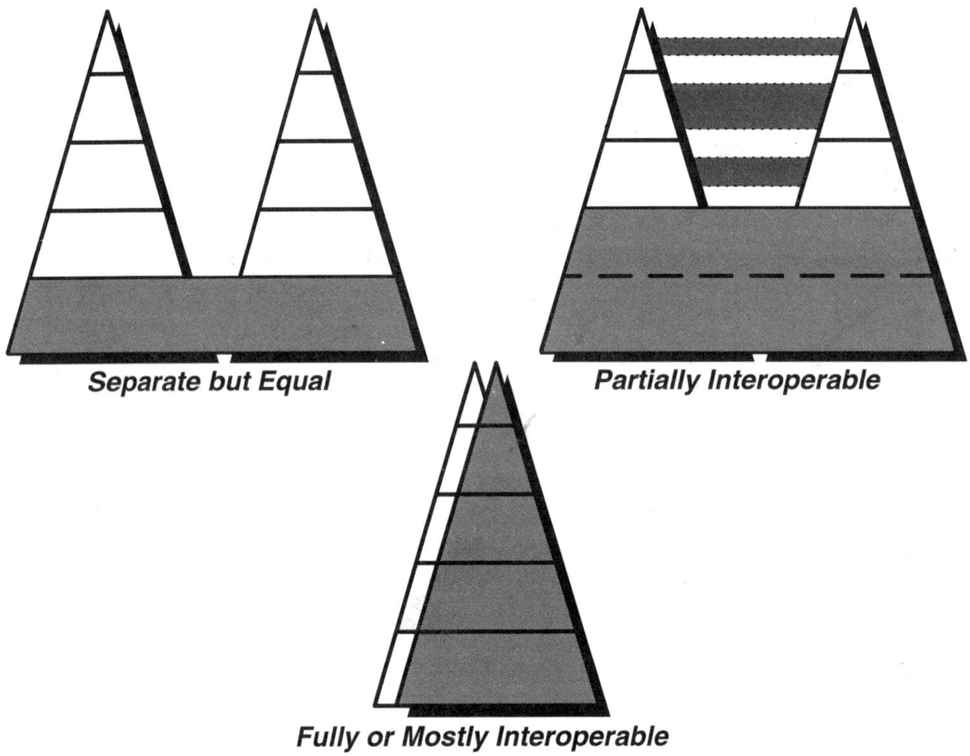

Figure 15-2 Different Levels of Workgroup Interoperability

ability may exist at the network infrastructure level, but any commonality above that may be the result of chance, not design. Data sharing and common system administration processes may be limited or impossible with this model of interoperability.

If this configuration is chosen as a starting point for further integration, goals for the final environment should be set and progress measured against them—just like any other migration. The workgroup architecture may evolve through the next two models as experience is gained with the details of making common subsystems and services work together.

To begin evolving an environment, it is essential to apply good project management and change management procedures. See Appendix A, for a simple change process to follow. Also, see Chapter 17 for an excellent example of managing evolution in a complex workgroup environment.

15.3.2 Partially Interoperable—Some Shared Services

An investigation into the capabilities of two (or more) system types usually yields at least some potential commonality in their services. The "out of the box" configuration of the two systems, however, may not lend itself to interoperability without adjusting some of the default system parameter values to enable interoperation. There are other possibilities: gateways, or bridges, between the services in the two environments.

Investigation is a key activity here. Without being aware of all possible configurations for both (or multiple) system types, it is difficult or impossible to locate common ground for interoperability. An assessment process is extremely useful in determining needs, especially if an existing environment must evolve to accept new system types. If this is the starting point for the workgroup design, then the advice in the previous section still applies.

15.3.3 Fully Interoperable— Completely Shared Environment

Interoperability at all visible workgroup levels does not happen by accident[2]. A definition of complete interoperability entails transparent sharing of data, services, and applications across multiple platforms at all levels of the functional model. Ideally, the system administrators and users should not be aware of differences between platforms in terms of performance, look-and-feel, system administration processes, or application availability.

In practice, our ideal definition of complete interoperability is difficult if not impossible to attain unless we have unlimited time and money at our disposal. This is not pessimism at work—it is a consideration of the sheer cost of creating a "perfect" environment. Platforms exhibit functional differences for a reason: their designers chose a particular set of implementations as a way of better meeting projected user needs. We may need to be satisfied with sweeping minor mismatches and functional "blemishes" under the workgroup carpet.

This does not mean that we should give up on attaining interoperability "nirvana". Continual adaptation, adoption, and improvement of interoperability methods can move an environment closer and closer to the desired state. There is also an important part to be played by continued feedback to *both* or *all* system vendors involved in the workgroup environment about your interoperability needs[3].

Next we will take a survey of the general interoperability issues that arise in the 3TCS workgroup environment. To keep these issues in a logical arrangement, we will group them into the five layers of the workgroup functional model. Once we have enumerated some of the challenges, we will look at specific solutions.

15.4 The Network Infrastructure and Interoperation

If two environments cannot share a common network infrastructure, then simple interoperability is out the window from the very start. Fortunately, most systems today share a common

2. If it does, then chances are you are not working with a heterogeneous environment.

3. Many times funding of products, projects, and services that you need for interoperability is in the hands of marketing people who may not understand the importance of a particular building block. There is hardly a worse feeling than that caused by a vendor's cancellation of an essential portion of your environment.

method of physical network connection: Ethernet. High-performance workstations and servers come standard with auto-sensing 10/100 Mbps Ethernet interfaces; even low-end clients frequently have Ethernet interfaces built in or available as add-in interfaces.

Because we have a lot of networking building blocks in our tool kit, connecting even dissimilar networks together is fairly easy. Figure 15-1 shows two different networking infrastructures being connected by a gateway. If MTU size or protocol translations are needed, today's network hardware can usually[4] handle it.

15.5 Hardware Architecture and Interoperation

It should be obvious by now that our hardware architecture of choice is 3TCS[5]. With client-server application components, services, and operating systems that are flexible, we can arrange the hardware into a 3TCS workgroup structure as we have discussed in previous chapters. For less nimble environments, we may have to add 3TCS functionality or live with limited flexibility. We can bend the rules, but 3TCS is the architectural basis for the rest of the functional workgroup layers.

Another possible way to adhere to 3TCS architecture even if the application components are rigidly fixed in place is to encapsulate them within higher-level objects in the workgroup. An example of this might be a legacy database server running an operating system that does not play well with a 3TCS environment. Placing a more capable server "in front of" the legacy server using a chained server configuration can hide the inherent inflexibility and make the data available to client-server applications[6].

Our task is to choose hardware-application combinations that enable us to utilize the 3TCS architecture. Wherever possible, we will adapt nonconforming architectures into this configuration. If modification or reconfiguration of a particular component is not possible, then we will hide it behind an object "veneer" that makes it appear to be a 3TCS "team player". The risk of this approach is that the encapsulated component may change its behavior due to software upgrades or other modifications, necessitating a new version of the veneer.

15.6 The Operating Environment and Interoperation

The operating environment layer is where much of the interoperability issues reside when integrating or connecting dissimilar environments. Even systems with a common set of services

4. I say "usually" because there is still some hardware out there that has inadequate flow control, buffer management, or performance levels, all of which can cause problems with MTU conversion.

5. If not, go back to Chapter 1 and start over.

6. This can sometimes be as simple as providing the proper terminal emulation software on the 3TCS client system, which is equivalent to moving the GUI component to a remote client.

and commands, like the various Unix "flavors", have different options for performing similar operations. This can lead to process differences unless the details are hidden.

There are a number of industry operating system standards that can help ensure that systems can interoperate. Examples of these types of standards in the Unix community are POSIX[7], Unix95, and SVR4. Several of the standards-based environments are also available on other operating systems, like Windows NT.

Differences in other management tools and processes, like those related to software distribution, operating system installation, data backup, and performance monitoring increase workgroup complexity. The associated increase in system administration complexity tends to be hidden by the organizations performing the tasks, but one sign of an overcomplex environment is increasingly narrow system administration specialization[8]. We should adopt tools and system administration processes that work across as many platforms as possible, even though this takes global development effort.

15.7 Data Sharing and Interoperation

Data sharing, as we have often repeated, is the primary focus of the workgroup environment. When there are different types of systems in the workgroup, a common data-sharing mechanism must be chosen. There are several possible approaches to doing this. We will discuss each of the possibilities, which are diagrammed in Figure 15-3.

15.7.1 The Native Mechanism from One Client Type

An example of this would be to choose either SMB or NFS as the data-access mechanism for a Unix and Windows NT workgroup. Since the mechanism is native to one of the client types, the other clients will need to have the service added.

There are disadvantages to this choice. First, there is the added expense and system management overhead of adding a service to the client types that are lacking the chosen mechanism. Second, unless the software added to the client system is properly tuned, there may be a performance disadvantage.

15.7.2 A Common Mechanism for All Client Types

Choosing this option means adding the client software for the data-sharing mechanism to all system types in the workgroup. An example of this approach would be the choice of DFS as the data-sharing mechanism for the workgroup.

7. POSIX is an acronym for the Portable Operating System Interface standard from the IEEE.

8. Other signs of overly complex environments are high system administration personnel turnover, excessive working hours, and low system reliability. Another sign of potential problems in a chaotic environment is a high system-to-administrator ratio—a high ratio is desirable from a cost standpoint, but only reasonable when the amount of work required matches the number of available administrators.

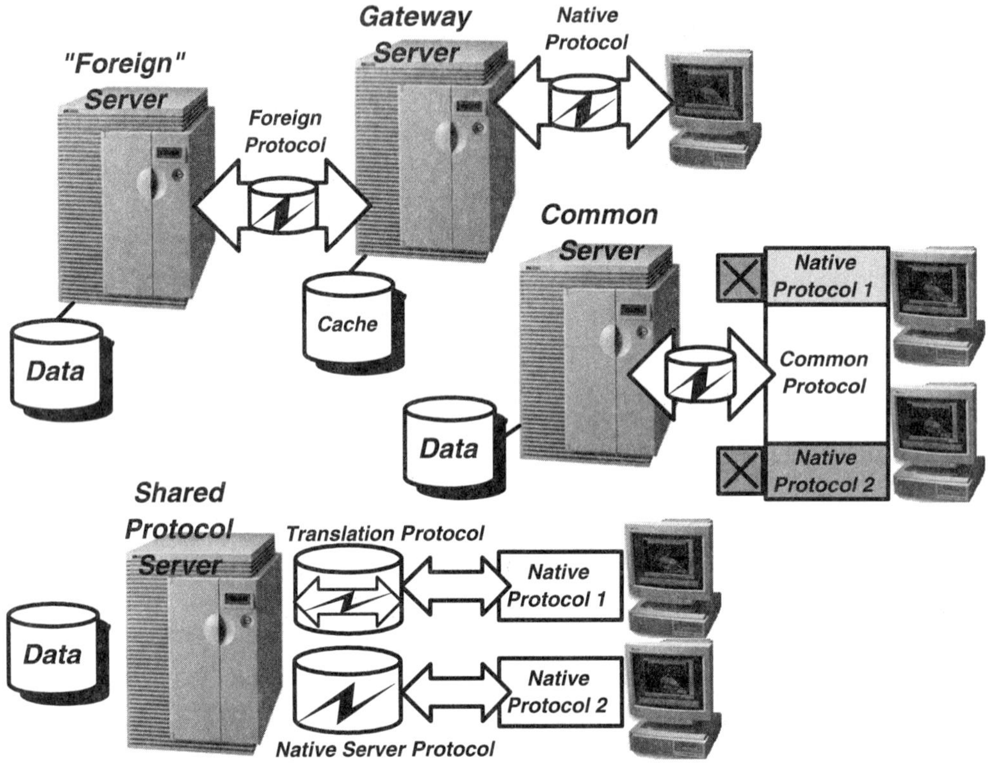

Figure 15-3 Data-Sharing Interoperability Architectures

Disadvantages of this option include those mentioned above, plus the possibility that the client software may not be available for all system types in the workgroup. Sometimes additional functionality or security benefits might outweigh other disadvantages.

15.7.3 Data-Sharing Gateways

Of the three general solutions, this one usually requires the least amount of modification to the client systems. This is because the "foreign" data-sharing semantics are mapped to the client's native access method.

Disadvantages of this approach include extra workgroup hardware, extra system administration effort, and potential performance impacts due to increased data access "paths" through multiple servers. Several different gateway products are available that map between popular data-access mechanisms, including DFS to NFS and NFS to SMB. We will refer to this type of file server as a "gateway server".

15.7.4 A Translation Layer on a Native File Server

This method is similar to providing a data-access gateway, but does not necessarily require extra hardware. One or more translation file systems are run “over the top” of the native file server’s file system, essentially providing two or more different sets of network file access semantics from one hardware platform and a common data store. Care must be taken to properly size the file server hardware to support multiple sets of file services.

This is an extremely attractive option, particularly where a second client type is being added to an existing workgroup. Examples of this type of software are the public domain Samba server and the Advanced Server for Unix[9], both of which export Unix file systems via SMB. We will refer to this type of server as a “shared protocol” file server.

15.7.5 Common Data Presentation

In addition to different data-sharing services a client system may have different data-presentation models. After making sure the data is consistently *available* to the client systems, we must ensure that it is available to the users and their applications in a form that is consistent with their client system’s presentation model. Differences in data-presentation models can make this a difficult task, particularly between Unix systems and Windows NT.

On Unix systems, file hierarchies (local or remote) are mounted into the directory structure under the file system root directory “/”. Paths to files are specified starting at the root directory and proceeding through each intervening directory until the file is reached. Thus, a path like */projects/project1/Software/source/module1.c* may be a local file, or it may exist on a remote file server, depending on how the system administrator decides to present the data.

On Windows NT systems, file hierarchies are made available under “drive letters” that run from A to Z. A file path starts at a drive letter and proceeds through succeeding directories to the file. A Windows NT path resembles *C:\Data\rob\Source\module1.c.* Another Windows NT resource access method uses Universal Naming Convention UNC semantics. The UNC format for access to files is *\\server_name\shared_resource\directory\file.*

As you can see, and probably already know, some basic differences between the two methods leave room for user confusion. The use of different slashes, the existence (or lack) of a drive letter, and the UNC are all possible sources of confusion. Additionally, there are differences in the handling of upper-case and lower-case characters—Unix is case sensitive, and Windows systems are not.

We must find ways of consistently presenting data from different sources to the client systems and applications in the workgroup. The preceding analysis is only a high-level look at some of the issues. We may have our work cut out for us.

9. This is SMB protocol code ported to Unix by AT&T, then licensed to other Unix vendors. Hewlett-Packard’s version of this software for the HP-UX operating system is called Advanced Server/UX, or ASU.

15.8 The Application Environment and Interoperation

Users should be able to concentrate on doing their daily jobs without needing to consciously switch gears when they change from one client system type to another. Each client system in the workgroup needs to provide a familiar, consistent environment to support the user's activities. There are some areas of interoperation that can help meet this goal.

15.8.1 Common "Look and Feel"

Choosing a consistent client desktop paradigm involves examining several aspects of the desktop. These include menu mechanisms, common window management (operations like maximize, minimize, close, resize, and move) behavior, visual file management, and desktop tools like calendars and calculators. A user should not have to be retrained to move from one client type to another.

The desktop paradigm provides the integration facilities for the user's applications. It is responsible for presenting data and application options to the user, as well as scheduling the application and managing its GUI. All of this functionality falls under the general phrase "look and feel".

Behind many of the desktop behaviors, there usually lurks a messaging facility. This facility schedules applications, maps drag-and-drop actions to the proper applications, and can allow the desktop to perform an action on a remote system, if authorized to do so. Interoperation of the messaging facility may be necessary to provide full desktop functionality.

15.8.2 Common Application Set

Having the same set of applications available on each type of client system helps maximize user familiarity and productivity. Every application need not run on all types of client system, they only need to be available somewhere in the workgroup, along with the ability to project the application GUI over the network to the client system[10]. Each user's desktop environment must provide access to the base tools for accomplishing his or her job, along with auxiliary tools like office automation applications, web browsing, and Email.

15.8.3 Application Interoperability

In situations where different client systems are to run the same application, it is absolutely essential to find out which versions of the application are available for which operating system and platform combination and *exactly* what differences exist between the versions. To ignore this advice is to run into data conversion issues, functionality differences, unfixed bugs, performance issues, and a whole host of other potential application interoperability issues—all of which will directly affect the workgroup users.

10. This, of course, presents difficulties for applications running on Microsoft Windows systems.

Common Application Functionality We all tend to view an application as a single entity, but experienced system administrators know the answer to the question, "When is the same application not the same application?" The answer to this question is, "When the application software versions are different[11]". Strangely, something as simple as incrementing the version number of an application can involve a tremendous amount of work on the part of a software vendor—they do not do it unless there is a darned good reason.

This also holds true for operating system revisions. An increment in the version number of an operating system can trigger a complete "qualification" cycle by every independent software vendor (ISV) that releases their product on the hardware and operating system platform[12]. To make matters even more interesting, sometimes the version of application that you need to run is tied to a particular version of the operating system, potentially one that is older or newer than the version you are supporting in the majority of your environment.

One way to isolate the need for special operating system or application versions is to create compute resources that execute only the specialized version. This becomes a dedicated compute resource available to the client systems and users with the special need, localizing the version exception to a single class of compute server. The flexibility of 3TCS lets us handle this type of requirement with relative ease, while we hope all the way that it is temporary in nature.

Word Size Issues A workgroup environment has a considerable investment in application software, and being able to preserve that investment while making the transition to new versions of application software (and operating systems) is important. This functionality is the domain of the underlying hardware and operating system, and the native size of the computer "word" compiled into applications is specified by the total number of available binary bits used in the native data types. The ability of the combined hardware and operating system components to run software compiled for both the old and new word sizes is key to preserving application software investment.

While the Windows world has mostly finished a transition from 16 bit to 32 bit applications, the Unix world is embarking on a transition from 32 bits to 64 bits. The underlying RISC CPU chips used in Unix vendor's systems may have been capable of running 64 bit software for some time, but full utilization of the 64 bit features requires a 64 bit enabled operating system and recompilation[13] of the applications that wish to use the new features.

What is the driving force that causes customers to migrate to new operating system versions and transition to completely new versions of critical applications? The answer, quite sim-

11. Or when it has patches or "service packs" applied to it.

12. This is because changes to the operating system application programming interfaces (APIs) or in the operating system's behavior may cause applications to malfunction.

13. Making the transition to a new programming model may require rewriting portions of the application to fix bugs caused by data size assumptions. Recompilation may be the final step in the process, but for most applications it is not the only one.

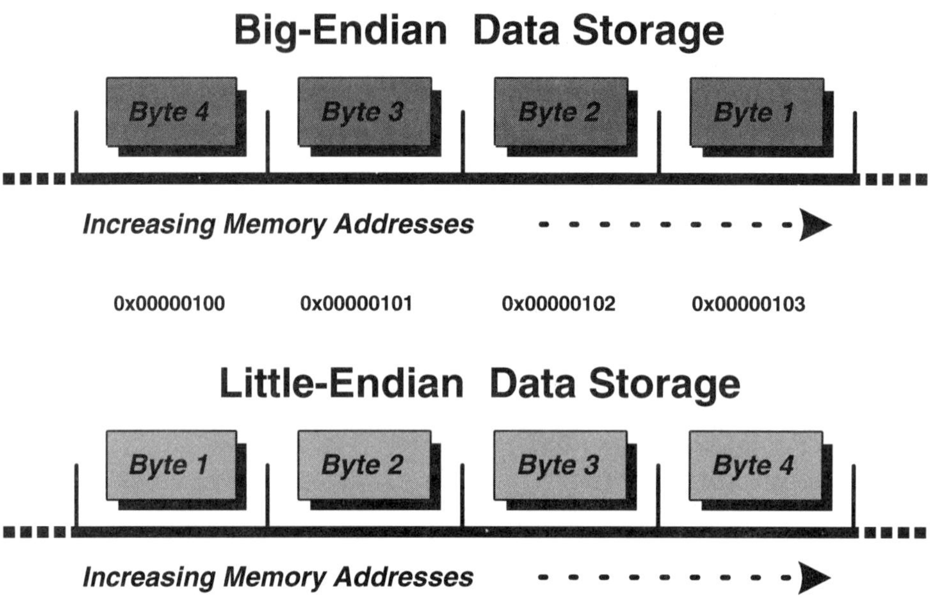

Figure 15-4 Big-Endian and Little-Endian Memory Representations

ply, is "data". The native word size used by the operating system is an indicator or how much data may be addressed by the virtual address system, and 32 bits is no longer enough.

Because of the ever-increasing size of simulations, chip designs, and other data sets, technical customers in the Unix world are beginning to run out of virtual address space in their applications. A 32 bit word can address up to 4 Gigabytes of virtual address space, and while that seems like a lot, some of today's programs have filled it up. Sixty-four bit address spaces, the next step, can contain many terabytes of data, solving the data space crunch[14].

There are issues, aside from operating system and hardware capability, that surround 64 bit programs. First of all, not every application needs the increase in address space, for some 32 bits is just fine. Second, there is a price to pay for 64 "bitness"—increased size of application files, more memory usage, and potentially slower execution. This is why most 64 bit operating systems will continue to run both 32 and 64 bit applications.

This extra set of choices, of course, complicates our decisions about selecting application components for our workgroup. We may have to choose between 32 and 64 bit versions of the operating system *and* 32 or 64 bit versions of some applications. To make the proper choice, we must thoroughly understand our workgroup users, the tools they use, and their data requirements.

14. But for how long? A program, like a gas, will expand to fill all of available memory.

Common Data Formats When an application program is asked to save the state of internal data, the easiest thing for it to do is just copy the appropriate data regions out of memory to a disk file. To restore the program state (i.e., bring back a drawing, document, or other data set), the program merely reverses the process. Sounds easy, doesn't it?

Now imagine that the same application runs on two different client hardware configurations and writes data to a common file server. Next, imagine that each of the hardware configurations, transparent to the application software, stores memory-resident data in a different order from the other. Can you see that even though the application behavior is identical on both hardware platforms, there is a data interoperability issue if the two platforms want to share the common data?

This is precisely the problem presented by what the industry calls "big-endian" and "little-endian" hardware implementations. A big-endian CPU stores the most significant byte of a multiple byte quantity at the highest memory address. A little-endian CPU stores the most significant byte at the lowest memory address. See Figure 15-4 for a comparison of big-endian and little-endian data storage.

The RISC CPUs used by most Unix vendors are big-endian in their memory implementation. The Intel processors used in most Windows NT clients are little-endian in their memory implementation. Unless application software takes special steps to ensure consistent data across big-endian and little-endian platforms, we will be forced to deal with data interoperability issues.

So, when integrating Unix and Windows NT or other similar systems, we need to take care when selecting applications that can run on both platforms. While most software vendors have discovered and dealt with the big-endian and little-endian issues, there are some applications that do not. We need to know about this up front, so we can avoid sentencing our users to a professional lifetime of using data converters before they can run an application.

15.9 Unix-to-Unix Interoperability

The Unix operating system has existed in one form or another since 1965. In over thirty years of evolution, it has steadily gained in functionality and industry acceptance. Every major computer vendor had its own version of the Unix operating system. The number of vendors supplying Unix, coupled with the inherent flexibility of the Unix operating system, created substantial differences between the versions. To say that this is unfortunate would be a tremendous understatement.

The number of Unix versions, and their functional differences, present challenges to customers who want to integrate more than one version into their "Open Systems" computing environments. Over time, market pressure and competition has forced Unix vendors to adhere to groups of common standards[15]. This has improved the interoperability of Unix systems, but has not removed all of the barriers.

15. Some of these standards were produced by formal standards bodies, and some by winning total market share—so-called de facto standards. Other standards may be initiated by informal processes like Request for Comment (RFC) communication among the user and vendor community.

The number of available Unix standards is truly amazing; there are standards for many of the aspects. Some of these are SVID (System V Interface Definition, multiple versions), FIPS (Federal Information Processing Standard), AES (OSF Application Environment Specification), Unix95 (formerly a Common Open Software Environment, or COSE standard, now owned by the Open Group, defines the requirements for applying the "Unix" brand to an operating system), and XPG2-XPG4 (the X/Open Portability Guide, versions two through four).

15.10 Levels of Unix-to-Unix Interoperability

Making Unix systems of different "flavors" interoperate is not nearly as difficult as it used to be. The major differences between the Unix variants now lie mainly in system-administration procedures and application availability. This is not to say that interoperability is always easy.

15.10.1 Unix Network Infrastructure

The standard physical interconnection between Unix systems is Ethernet. Every vendor's systems come with, at a minimum, 10baseT connections built in and more than likely autosensing 10/100baseT. There are, of course, options available for other physical networking technologies, like X.25, FDDI, or ATM. Ethernet is by far the most ubiquitous.

The networking protocol standard used by Unix for interoperation is TCP. Every Unix system supports this protocol, and most other high-level system protocols (NTP, SMTP, NNTP, SNMP, …) are based on either UDP or TCP/IP. Network communication frequently takes place over "sockets", a high-level interface to the network pioneered by the University of California at Berkeley in BSD Unix.

15.10.2 Unix Hardware Architecture

Unix systems have no required hardware architecture, but all components exist to support 3TCS operation. These include X-Windows, remote execution facilities (rsh, rexec, and other BSD facilities), and remote user authentication for commands like rlogin, telnet, and ftp. While many Unix environments may be configured in a peer-to-peer architecture, at least some aspects of such environments (NFS, NIS, and X-Windows) require a client-server configuration.

15.10.3 Unix Operating Environment

The major differences in the Unix world start at the operating environment level in the workgroup functional model. Every major Unix vendor has differences in commands and system-administration procedures, partly because of hardware differences and partly because of their unique Unix implementation. Even standards like the System V Release 4 (SVR4) layout, which sets forth a consistent policy for system directories and file placement, are interpreted differently by different implementors.

Different versions of system utilities like scripting languages, while interoperable, still create minor differences that must be accounted for. Addition of public domain software, which may have different functionality depending on who ported it to the platform[16], can also create extra issues. There are a number of tools, particularly those from the Free Software Foundation (FSF), that are widely ported, stable, and consistently functional across many platform types.

The shell interpreter is an important part of the Unix operating environment, not only as an interactive interface to the operating system commands, but as a custom tool-development facility for shell "scripts". The ability to rapidly capture Unix commands in an interpreted language is an essential part of system administration-automation, application development, and customization of user processes. Some Unix applications are as much as eighty percent shell scripts[17].

Windowing versions of the shell scripts are available that allow development of X-Windows applications entirely in shell scripts. An example is the dtksh (the desktop Korn shell), provided by CDE. Another example of the windowing script approach is found in the Tcl/Tk scripting language and window components. Scripting languages like Perl and Perl/Tk, which are available on a wide variety of platforms, enable the creation of multiplatform scripts and provide powerful interfaces to the operating system features like sockets, remote execution, and interprocess communication.

The discussion of scripting is an important one[18]. This one Unix facility, or set of facilities, enables a lot of interoperability and automation, especially when different Unix variants are involved in the environment. Without the "glue" provided by scripting and common Unix command sets, interoperability would be difficult. Fortunately, both are available to us on most major vendors' Unix systems.

15.10.4 Unix Data Sharing

Interoperability between Unix systems at the data-sharing level is fairly easy to describe: it is primarily based on NFS and NIS. NFS allows sharing of user data between Unix systems from all major vendors. Likewise, NIS allows the single point administration of common user login information and system configuration files involving network configuration, user access, automatic data mounting, and host name to IP address translation.

Changing an NIS managed file on the NIS master server, a system administrator is able to push those changes to all slave servers and to all NIS clients. Within seconds, the changes are

16. This frequently happens because the creator or person porting the software is more familiar with one system variant than another, resulting in features that may be difficult to implement or port to other systems.

17. Of course this percentage varies tremendously. The ability to quickly capture behavior in scripts, then transform portions into compiled code for added speed was a common approach. This is one reason why the C shell scripts resemble the C programming language, along with leveraging experience.

18. This will also be important when we discuss Unix and Windows NT interoperability later in this chapter.

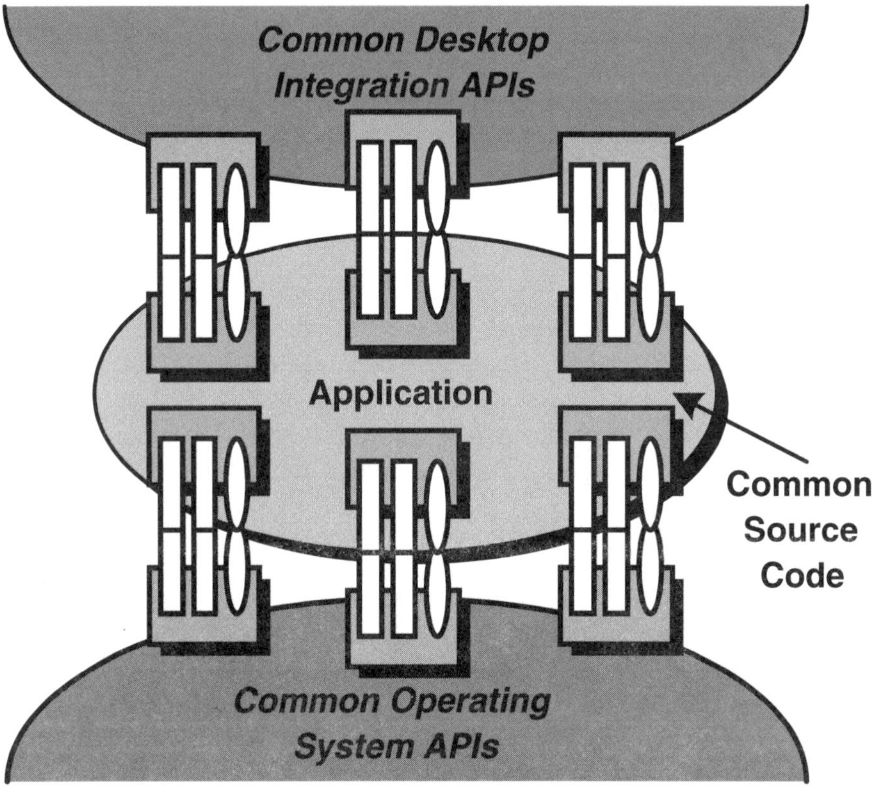

Figure 15-5 The COSE Environment

propagated without the need to log onto the remote clients or servers. This is a tremendous time-saving device that can be used for any system that has NIS client software.

NIS basically implements a simple keyed lookup of data and maintains databases on the server machines for that purpose. The client system passes the key and the database (or map) that should be used for the lookup, and the server returns the value. Exactly what is in the databases does not matter to NIS, so the number of standard maps is frequently extended by system administrators for use in other single-point administration applications.

15.10.5 Unix Application Environment

Prior to the arrival of CDE, most Unix systems had their own user desktop environments. Most but not all of these desktops were based upon X-Windows, with differing widget sets. The result of the "look-and-feel wars" of the late 1980s was that the Motif look and feel won. This does not mean that the proprietary look-and-feel environments disappeared, only that they were relegated to secondary status on each vendor's Unix platform.

CDE and the standard now called Unix95 (or just Unix branding) both originated in the mid 1990s as part of the Common Open Software Environment (COSE) initiative. The promise at the time was an environment that would provide a common set of operating system and desktop integration APIs, allowing application developers to target a single Unix environment. The big benefit was to be a common set of source code on all Unix vendor's platforms that supported the initiative[19]. Many of the promised benefits have not materialized in spite of the existence of the standards.

CDE, however, represents a standard way to provide desktop integration for Unix applications. Many of the CDE features are ahead of the corresponding functionality available in the Microsoft Windows environment. CDE enables us to hide many system differences behind a wall of common look and feel. The COSE environment, including CDE, is shown in Figure 15-5.

15.11 Windows-to-Windows Interoperability

The issues of interoperability between different versions of Microsoft Windows are similar to the issues seen when integrating different dialects of Unix, although the solutions may not be as hard to find. The fact that one company controls the content and behavior of the Windows operating system means that there is not as much divergence from the original "standard" as we have seen with Unix. This is not to say that supporting the multiple versions of the Windows operating system is easy.

An environment that contains only versions of Microsoft Windows is often referred to as if it were homogeneous. The name is the same, but the details have been changed to torment the innocent. Just the sheer number of versions of the operating system (and required patch levels) can create issues if all users cannot be migrated to the latest version all at once. The current versions are Windows 3.11, Windows 95, Windows 98, Windows NT 3.51 (workstation and server), Windows NT 4.0 (workstation and server), and the soon-to-be-released Windows 2000 (the operating system previously known as Windows NT 5.0[20]). We will ignore MS-DOS here.

The variety of physical file systems (FAT16, FAT32, ntfs), differences in support for long file names (the old 8.3 format versus the new), device driver differences, different display and desktop paradigms, and application support all conspire to create interoperability issues, even inside of the "homogeneous" Windows world. It just shows that nobody is immune to the effects of increasing complexity. Even with these issues (and more), the environment still enables its users to be extremely productive.

19. This "shrink-wrapped", common source environment for software developers is something that the Microsoft Windows platforms are very good at.

20. No relation to the artist previously known as Prince.

15.12 Levels of Unix to Windows NT Interoperability

By far the most difficult design problem to tackle is to make the Unix portion of the workgroup interoperate with the Windows NT portion of the environment. There are major areas of the two environments that need major engineering effort to interoperate. There are signs that the level of disagreement between the two environments may be slowly abating.

First, Microsoft has released a Unix interoperability pack, at extra cost, that provides some minimal Unix commands and services, including an NFS client interface. Second, the Unix world and third-party software vendors are increasingly adopting (or rewriting) Windows NT functionality to run on the Unix platforms, and vice versa, to provide the needed interoperability[21]. We are already into second and third generations of these interoperability solutions from software vendors other than Microsoft and the Unix system houses.

In the coming sections, we will survey the interoperability issues, and some of the potential solutions, between Unix systems and Windows NT. Again, we will group the issues according to the five layer workgroup model. By now you should be comfortable with this approach.

Because many of the interoperability solutions are available from third-party software vendors, we may need to mention particular solutions and their *current* features. When we do this, realize that the feature set is subject to change and that there may be other packages that provide similar functionality. Mentioning a particular package here is for example purposes only and does not constitute an endorsement of the package for a particular situation—for best results, perform your own research and reach your own conclusions.

15.13 Unix and Windows NT Network Infrastructure

Client systems from major Unix and Windows NT hardware vendors either come with or will support network interface cards (NICs) for the familiar 10/100 Mb/S Ethernet connections, so the physical connections to the network hardware are the same. The same UTP wiring and RJ-45 plugs work with both system types. This gets us from system to wiring closet with relative ease.

Fortunately for us, the lowest level of network protocol interoperability is also a common standard: TCP/IP. We can reuse our network design knowledge to a large extent in both Unix and Windows NT environments. The TCP/IP setup for both systems is familiar enough that a system manager can configure a system to interoperate at the network level with relative ease. There may be other protocols encountered, but their use is waning, at least in heterogeneous workgroups.

Both Unix and Windows NT allow dial-up access to the TCP/IP network, providing protocols like Serial Line Internet Protocol (SLIP) and Point-to-Point Protocol (PPP) to remote clients. This enables remote clients to easily connect to the workgroup LAN from external

21. If I were to make a prediction, I would say that in a few years we will end up with "UntIX", which is Unix with a lot of Windows NT functionality, and "NTix", which is Windows NT with a lot of Unix functionality.

locations. There are hardware solutions that provide dial-in connection and authentication, and they may be used to provide access for both types of workgroup systems.

It All Adds Up to Zeroes There are some trouble areas in terms of network notations that can cause system administration issues at this level. An example of this is the Microsoft Windows habit of inserting or allowing leading zeroes into the TCP/IP address fields in system-administration forms and other graphical input mechanisms. On a Unix system, by convention, any number that begins with a leading zero is interpreted as an octal[22] value.

Octal notation groups binary bits into threes, with values running from 0 to 7. Hexadecimal notation groups binary bits into groups of four, with values running from 0 to 9, A, B, C, D, E, and F (sixteen unique numerals). A decimal value of 4095 is represented in octal by "07777" and hexadecimal by "0xFFF". The leading "0" in the octal value and the leading "0x" in the hexadecimal value are conventions used by Unix and the input conversion routines in the system library.

One system administrator, who prefers to remain anonymous, ran into this difficulty when moving from his native Windows environment to Unix. To enter the TCP/IP address of his brand-new Unix workstation, he entered the value complete with leading zeroes in three of the four octets. Unix happily interpreted the three numbers as octal values, not quite yielding the expected results.

We have mentioned previously that Microsoft Windows systems can be very "chatty" in resolving names to TCP/IP addresses. We mention this situation again, because it has implications when the network is laid out. Depending on how the WINS service is configured, each resolution from a NetBIOS name to a TCP/IP address will cause a broadcast on the LAN that the client attaches to. We will discuss this more in a coming section.

Aside from the small problems of terminology and notation, the two environments interoperate very well at this level if properly configured. Because Ethernet is Ethernet, the networking equipment we have discussed previously (see Chapter 9), and the design principles may be applied to both environments. This just serves to underline the facility of industry-wide standards.

15.14 Unix and Windows NT Hardware Architecture

This level comprises both the underlying hardware and the operating system architecture. Comparing both of these architectures can help us find structural and functional differences that must be handled.

22. I first encountered octal on a Digital Equipment Corporation (DEC) PDP-8 computer. This machine had 12 bit words and a whopping 8 kB of core (real core) memory. Ah, progress.

15.14.1 Unix and Windows NT Hardware Architecture Comparison

One of the fundamental differences between today's Unix systems (except Linux) and Windows NT is the underlying hardware. Most major Unix vendors have their own RISC chip set that is used in their products: Hewlett-Packard's PA-RISC®, Sun Microsystems' SPARC®, and Digital Equipment Corporation's (now Compaq Computer Inc.) Alpha®. Microsoft Windows NT runs primarily on processor chips produced by Intel® Corporation.

This means that binary program files do not interoperate between Windows NT and RISC-based Unix systems. The current Intel architecture, IA-32™, is a 32 bit processor that is slated to be superseded by a new 64 bit architecture, IA-64™. Just as RISC processors represented a major advance over CISC processors in terms of performance, the new IA-64 processor is based on another advance: EPIC[23] technology.

The reason we mention EPIC here is that it promises a common hardware base for the Unix and Windows NT operating systems. Major system vendors have announced support for system hardware that will include the IA-64 processor. At least in the case of HP-UX and Windows NT, both operating systems will run on the same native hardware. In the future, this could offer the ultimate in "reusable", relocatable hardware resources for our workgroups.

15.14.2 Flash! It's The PC BIOS

A major complication in the management of Intel-based PC hardware is the PC's Basic Input-Output System (BIOS). The BIOS provides a level of hardware independence for the Windows operating systems, presenting a standardized interface to the underlying hardware in the PC. This includes providing support for CD-ROMs, floppy disk drives, video devices, and behavior of the system hardware during operation—without the BIOS, the hardware can be nothing more than an expensive boat anchor[24], unable to do something as simple as boot from a floppy.

The BIOS contains functionality that is built into the kernel of most Unix systems, but unlike the Unix kernel, the BIOS code "lives" in either ROM or EEPROM (so-called stable storage.) Like most software, the BIOS can contain bugs that require updates, and herein lies the problem. To update the BIOS code, the system must execute a special tool to "flash", or reprogram, the EEPROM that contains the BIOS. The BIOS may be flashed by booting from a floppy or by network-based tools, like HP's TopTools, that allow remote-control BIOS updates.

The BIOS represents one more component of every PC client machine that must be kept up to date, and flashing the BIOS represents another set of manual system administrative procedures to deal with. It also represents a potential danger to the well-being of the hardware being

23. explicitly parallel instruction computing.

24. The author learned this the hard way when his PC vendor provided the incorrect BIOS for his machine. After placing the errant code into his machine's EEPROM, the machine was dead as a doornail, except for some Morse code beeping. To fix this problem required installing a new system motherboard with a "fresh" BIOS!

flashed. Fortunately, some PC systems have a "recovery mode" that will restore the previous version of the BIOS in the event of a failed flashing operation. This recovery feature is certainly worth purchasing if available, in spite of the extra expense.

15.14.3 Unix and Windows NT OS Architecture Comparisons

In addition to the underlying hardware, we need to consider the fundamental operating system architecture of both Unix and Windows NT. Differences in the architectures mean more design work for us to make them interoperate. There are some fundamental architectural differences between Unix and the Windows NT 4.0 operating systems that we must be aware of.

Architectural Flexibility Unix makes no formal distinction between a client system and other configurations, whereas Windows NT is formally divided into Windows NT Server and Windows NT Workstation products. The Unix approach gives us more flexibility than Windows NT to partition the resources in our workgroup. For Windows NT systems, services like DNS may only run on a Windows NT Server system, unless they come from a third party.

Unix provides both client and server portions of many services like telnet, rsh, and rexec, along with full multiuser capabilities, and the ability to project bit-mapped application GUIs over the network via X-Windows. These services are essential to the compute server tier of the 3TCS model, as we have previously discussed.

Windows NT lacks a good portion of this functionality[25], including the multiuser capability[26] that is necessary for a compute server to execute multiple interactive jobs for multiple users simultaneously. Front-ending users with either file server or database server clients allows the appearance of multiuser activities but is not as functional or flexible as we would like. The conclusion that the author has reached is that the current version of Windows NT, and in fact all Windows operating systems, is essentially a two-tier client-server architecture. We diagram this type of mismatch in Figure 15-6.

I know what I am saying here may be controversial, and I don't want you to misunderstand. Windows NT is fully capable of supporting most of the necessary additional functionality (the lack of simultaneous multiuser support is most problematic), but it is not present in the base operating system. Because of this, there is extra effort in terms of finding, qualifying, installing,

25. The client portions of rcp, rexec, and telnet are present in rudimentary form (telnet only supports a very simplistic terminal model), but not the server functionality. There is also no native ability to project application GUIs across the network—adding an X-Windows server helps, but is not the native windowing facility.

26. I have heard the term "sequential multi-user" used to describe Windows NT's user login model. What this really means is that the Windows NT 4.0 user model is multiple users per workstation, but only one at a time— or "sequentially." Great marketing spin, but it doesn't help us much as architects if we require *simultaneous multi-user* services or what most of us would call simply multi-user.

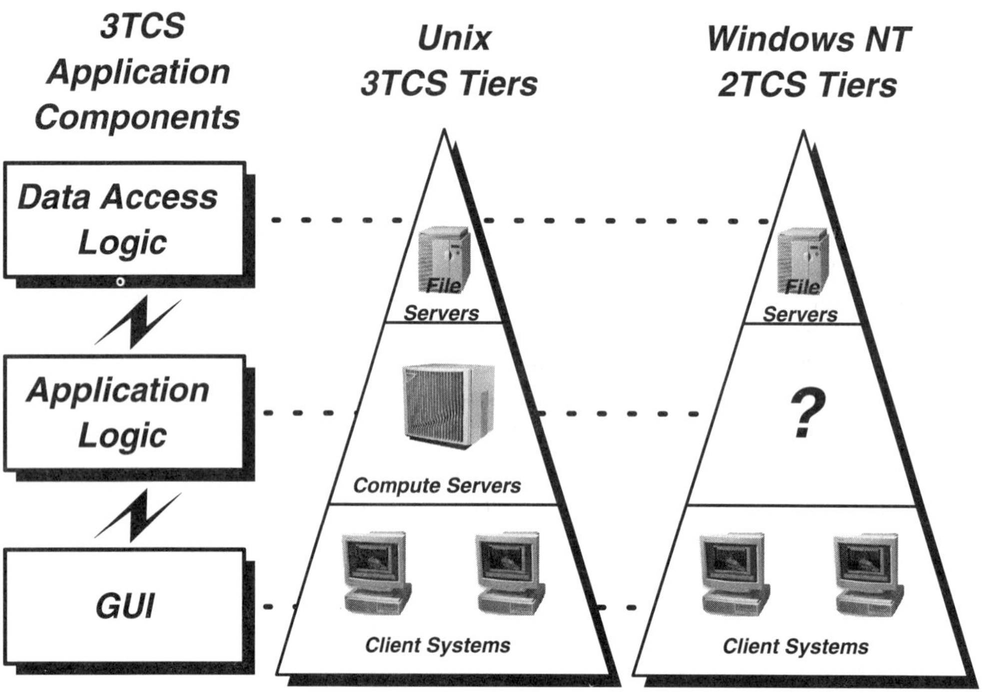

Figure 15-6 A Comparison of Two Client-Server Architectures

and maintaining third-party packages on every client system. This adds to the complexity and expense of the total workgroup solution[27].

Those of you that know about Windows NT, Terminal Server Edition might respond that it provides multiuser capabilities. It is, however, a very special version of the operating system and cannot have the normal service packs applied to it. Microsoft has promised to make this technology part of the release of Windows 2000, but as of this writing we do not know in what form it will be released.

Whether the missing tier was intentional[28] or the result of evolving from a different application base, we cannot guess. Now that we know the "why" of some of the interoperability issues between Unix and Windows NT at this level, we need to concentrate on finding solutions

27. Lest you think that I exaggerate, during a recent benchmark for a large manufacturing company, we had to add third-party software amounting to five-thousand dollars to *each* Windows NT client system to make it support all of the required applications and interoperate with existing Unix systems.

28. The less compute sharing that occurs, the greater the number (and power) of client systems and client operating systems that can be sold.

to them. In the meantime, we can hope that future versions of the Windows NT operating system will address the question, “Where does the application run when it gets too big for the client?”

15.15 Unix and Windows NT Operating Environment

There are a number of very basic services that must interoperate before Unix and Windows NT can co-exist in a meaningful way. This section will touch upon the configuration of some of those services and make suggestions about interoperability approaches.

The Unix world uses the Domain Name System (DNS) for name to TCP/IP address resolution. Windows NT makes a distinction between NetBIOS names and internet names, primarily because NetBIOS was never intended for use beyond a LAN environment but still forms the basis for Microsoft Windows name resolution. The Berkeley Internet Name Daemon (BIND) implements the DNS services on a Unix platform.

The final result for both services is a TCP/IP address, such as “15.24.64.98”, which can then be translated into the system’s media access control (MAC) address by the internet software. Windows NT system names are NetBIOS names and can be up to fifteen characters in length. Each node in a DNS database can be up to sixty-three characters in length. Neither service is case-sensitive.

The DNS database is a hierarchical arrangement called the domain name space. Each domain in the hierarchy has a name and may contain subdomains. The path through the name space comprises the DNS node names separated with a “.” character. The tree is resolved from right to left until a DNS server is found that can return the proper TCP/IP address to the client system resolver.

The DNS database is “static” and at its basic level must be updated manually. The Microsoft training material seems to imply that this is a disadvantage and that WINS is a more powerful service, since it is dynamically updated and used with DHCP to save administrative overhead. This may or may not be true, depending upon how well your network management tools deal with the uncertainty of dynamic name to address mappings.

The service that translates NetBIOS names into TCP/IP addresses is the Windows Internet Name Service, or WINS. A Windows NT client system can operate in one of several NetBIOS name resolution modes. These modes are listed Table 15-2.

It is important to ensure that the Windows NT clients are configured to minimize broadcasting or that they are isolated from systems that may be impacted by the extra broadcast traffic. Another option is to place all Windows NT systems and their WINS servers on a separate set of VLANs.

Only systems running Windows NT Server can be configured as a WINS server or as a DNS server. Most Unix systems include the DNS server, BIND, as a standard part of the operating system release, so any system in the workgroup may be a DNS server. Most Unix sites have automated their DNS database management, and versions of BIND for Unix do exist that allow dynamic interaction with services like DHCP if desired.

Table 15-2 Windows NT Name-Resolution Modes

WINS Mode	Resolution Method	Comments
b-Node	Broadcasts	Performance issues, broadcasts contained by some network equipment
p-Node	Peer-to-peer contact with WINS server	All clients must know the IP address of the server, and will fail if the server is unavailable
m-Node	Mixed use of broadcast and peer-to-peer	By default, behaves as a b-node, uses p-mode if the name cannot be resolved by broad-cast
h-Node	Mixed use of peer-to-peer and broadcast	By default behaves as a p-node, falling back to b-node if the name cannot be resolved by the WINS server
Microsoft enhanced b-Node	Mixed use of broadcast and static local file	The LMHOSTS file may contain entries to be cached at start-up. The cache is checked first, followed by a broadcast, then the LMHOSTS[a] file is searched

a. This file is located at *\winnt\system32\drivers\etc*.

WINS servers can also interoperate with DNS, allowing Windows NT clients to transparently use DNS for all name resolution. One possible approach to the name service dilemma is to make the NetBIOS and DNS names the same and use a single name service. This allows both the Unix clients and Windows NT clients to use DNS for name resolution and provides a static structure that can cover the majority of nodes in the workgroup. For nodes that need dynamic TCP/IP address allocation, such as mobile computing devices, DHCP and WINS can be used.

The goal is to avoid using multiple services where one is sufficient. DNS's ability to search multiple servers and to handle both "local" and internet names without broadcasting is a mark in its favor. Enabling a consistent naming policy across the enterprise, while delegating management responsibility, is also a good reason to use DNS over WINS.

The difficulty we have is that we need to choose a name resolution service that works for both Unix and Windows NT, or be trapped into maintaining two separate services. The extra system administration effort and complexity is a very strong argument for only one service, and since DNS is the only one that works for both system types, it is a logical choice. In environ-

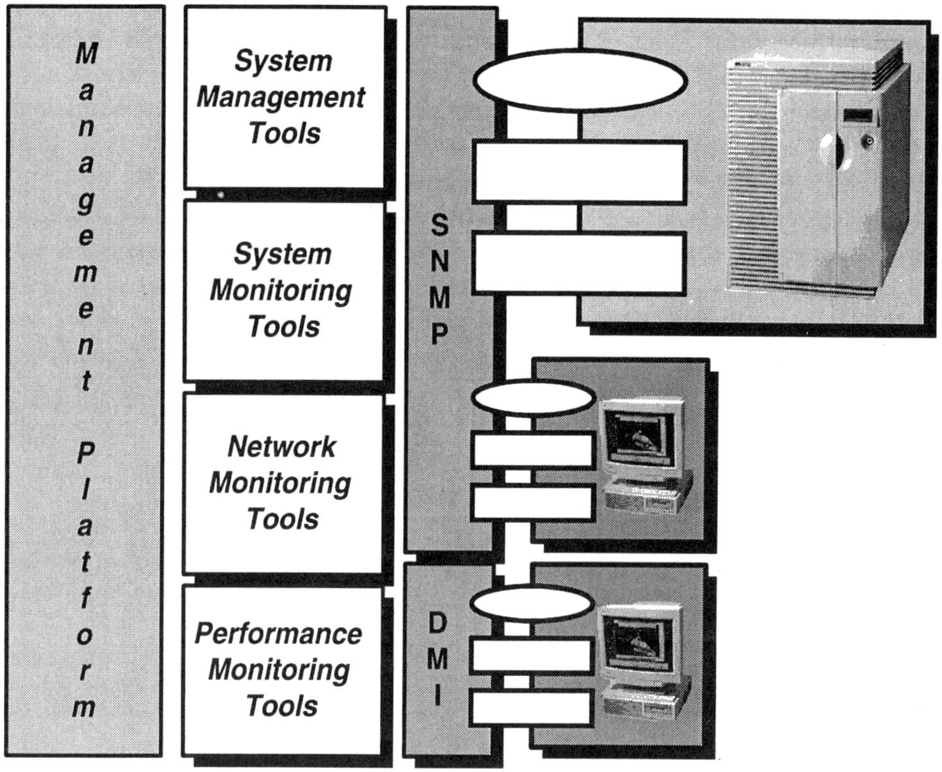

Figure 15-7 System Management Interfaces and Integration Platform

ments where WINS is firmly entrenched and where there is little experience with DNS[29], these arguments (and others) may break down.

15.16 System-Management Services

System management tools are also available that operate with both Unix and Windows NT systems. There are several system management platforms available in the industry, but the author is most familiar with the Hewlett-Packard OpenView platform, which provides a common umbrella for integration of a number of system administration tools. An integration platform like OpenView provides a common interface to underlying tools and management protocols. This is pictured in Figure 15-7.

29. See Paul Albitz and Cricket Liu, *DNS and BIND* [14], for a complete treatise on using DNS in your environment.

Most Unix systems and network equipment may be managed with the Simple Network Management Protocol (SNMP). There is also a system management interface specification from the Desktop Management Forum (DTMF), called the Desktop Management Interface (DMI), that can allow remote management of Windows systems. A version of this interface is also available for the HP-UX operating system, enabling DMI management, but the abilities of DMI do not currently approach those of the SNMP-based tools. To complicate matters, each PC vendor currently implements DMI to varying levels on their platforms.

Microsoft provides a product called Systems Management Server (SMS) that can help manage Windows NT systems, LAN Manager domains, and NetWare servers. Because of its limitations in terms of system support, SMS is of limited use to us in a heterogeneous environment. If SMS is already installed for management of Windows systems, then we should choose an overall system-management platform that can integrate with it to provide a complete solution.

With system image installation, we can wipe most of the management of individual client systems away. This does not eliminate the need to monitor client system performance and to implement minor performance tuning changes without completely reinstalling the client. The management (e.g., backup, resource balancing, data configuration) and monitoring of server resources is still an essential set of activities, even if the server systems themselves are installed with image installation.

15.16.1 Infrastructure Services

There are a number of essential infrastructure services that both Unix and Windows NT need to provide to their users. We must choose services that run on both platforms or services that interoperate or, as a last resort, design our own interoperability solutions.

Our goal is to have as many shared services as possible between the two environments. Figure 15-8 shows a workgroup environment with four categories of services: Windows NT—only services, Unix-only services, common (shared) services, and interface services. Some of these services, and recommendations or examples of providing them, are discussed in the following sections.

Load Balancing We need a load-balancing service that is both "industrial strength" and runs on a variety of platforms, particularly Unix and Windows NT systems. A popular load-balancing service is the Load Sharing Facility, or LSF™, from Platform Computing[30]. LSF provides job queuing, job migration, accounting, and many other desirable load-balancing features.

System Image Installation We have previously trumpeted the virtues of dataless clients and system image installation. We should like to have an image installation facility that works for both Unix and Windows NT, but this does not appear to exist at this time, primarily because the formatting of a system disk is still a very operating system-specific operation. Each

30. See *WWW.platform.com* for details on this product.

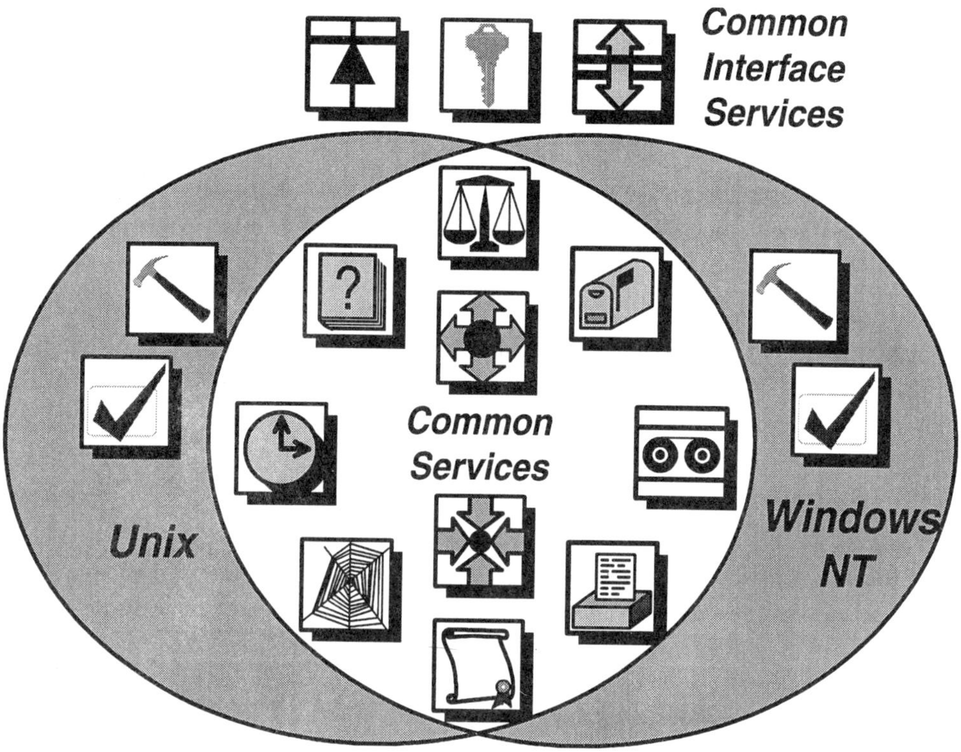

Figure 15-8 Shared Infrastructure Services

Unix vendor has its own facilities, like Hewlett-Packard's *Ignite-UX* or the Sun® Microsystems' *JumpStart* installation technology, but the Microsoft Windows operating system has no innate facility.

There are third-party tools, like *Norton Ghost* from Symatec™ Systems[31] Inc., that will clone any Intel-based operating system's disk (including Linux[32]) from a system image. *Norton Ghost* will perform the operation over the network and can also use multicasting to reduce network traffic. One of the primary requirements for a common cloning facility will be the ability of the Intel-based hardware boot process to deal with network booting via protocols like BOOTP.

31. See *WWW.Symantec.com* for more information on *Ghost*. Symantec Systems Inc. has apparently purchased the makers of both *Ghost* and Quarterdeck's *DriveClone* products.

32. See *WWW.Linux.org* for more information on the Linux operating system and its capabilities.

Network booting, and support for BOOTP, is built into most Unix systems due to the need to support diskless client systems and network system-installation processes. Most of the Unix cloning services also use a common network file system like NFS or a protocol like FTP to enable client access to the system images. Windows cloning services require booting from a special floppy, and therefore physical presence at the client system, to perform a network installation.

Software-Installation Services A common software-installation service for Windows NT, HP-UX, and other Unix variants is available: the SDU tool set. When integrated into the HP OpenView management platform, the Software Distributor allows push installation of software to Unix and Windows client systems.

Backup Services A number of common backup services are available for Unix and Windows systems, one of which is Hewlett-Packard's Omniback-II product. Omniback integrates into the HP OpenView management platform to allow control of the backup process for both types of systems. With dataless clients, we only need to back up the file server systems to ensure user data integrity, but covering both system types with one tool offers big savings in complexity and system administration effort.

Electronic Mail Electronic mail consists of two basic elements: the mail transport and the mail client. The mail transport, or post office, operates on mail servers, receiving, sending, and storing electronic mail on behalf of the user. The mail client allows the user to talk to the post office, composing, sending, reading, and filing e-mail messages. The major issues with e-mail post office software are scaling and interoperability.

Unix uses the Simple Mail Transfer Protocol (SMTP) implemented with the *sendmail*[33] daemon process. A generalized parsing facility and a set of parsing rules, implements a store-and-forward mail transport system. To support Unix e-mail, the DNS system has special entries, called mail exchange (MX) records, that can point to the post offices in a DNS zone, facilitating the delivery of mail. The *sendmail* functionality is available as a standard part of virtually every Unix system and is also available as public-domain (free) software.

There are numerous e-mail clients that can interoperate with either Unix or Windows NT post offices via protocols like Post Office Protocol (POP). These clients, including web browsers like Netscape Communication Corporation's Netscape and Microsoft's Internet Explorer, provide intuitive interfaces to the e-mail post offices while hiding the details of the underlying transport. The web browsers and most e-mail clients are available in both Unix and Windows NT environments. For consistency we should select one that runs on all client system types or provide transparent access to the application on its native platform.

Web Services A variety of web services are available, including proxy servers and web servers, from a number of vendors. Choosing the proper service for our workgroup depends

33. Information on the *sendmail* utility is available from *WWW.Sendmail.com.*

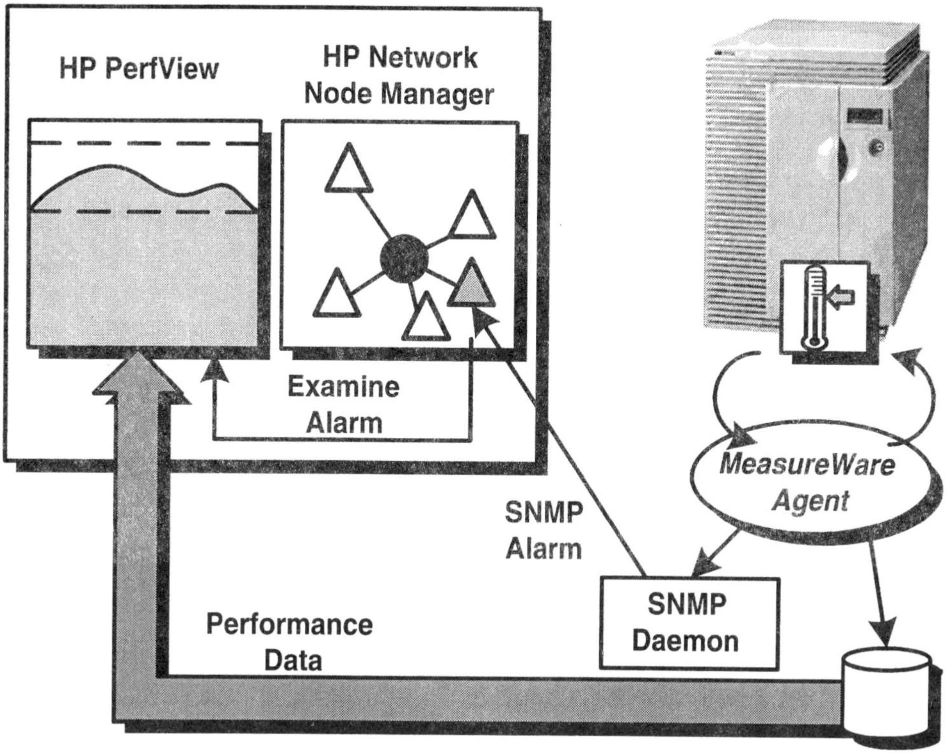

Figure 15-9 System Event Triggering Management Event

on scalability and the ability to seamlessly support both the Unix and Windows NT environments. This is fairly easy to do, since most web browsers will use standard protocols and port values to interface to the servers.

Print Services Sharing of printers between Unix and Windows NT can be easy if the Unix system environment supports the LPD protocol, which is also supported by Windows NT. The Samba and ASU servers also allow Windows NT clients to interface to Unix print services.

15.16.2 System and Network Performance Monitoring

Hewlett Packard offers a product called PerfView that provides system performance monitoring capability over the network. Performance information is collected by the MeasureWare agent, which runs locally on Windows NT and a variety of other platforms, including Unix. The combination of PerfView Management Console, Analyzer, Monitor, and the MeasureWare Agent allow system managers to compare actual application performance against expectations and to perform capacity planning using the collected data.

The HP Network Node Manager (NNM) provides a graphical view of the network in an intuitive graphical format. NNM discovers network devices and provides a multilevel map, which indicates the health of the network. An event correlation engine evaluates error messages and pinpoints the root cause of failures. A network icon that indicates a problem may be expanded until the segment or device causing the alarm is located. NNM collection stations may be located throughout the environment, so that data may be collected locally and forwarded to one or more Windows NT or Unix management stations.

If NNM and PerfView are installed on the same management console, PerfView can pass alarm messages to NNM. NNM can indicate when a MeasureWare alarm has been received by changing the color of the icon on the network map representing the system where the alarm occurred. PerfView can then be activated to display the graph representing the alarm condition. This capability is shown in Figure 15-9.

There are a number of other products that provide additional management and measurement capabilities. There are several points to be made about these tools:

- Issues of scalability that are normally associated with tools of this type are eliminated with the distributed data collection and analysis architecture. This may be called a "manager of managers" architecture.
- Integration of multiple tools under a common management platform may provide a synergy that is not available from the individual tools.
- The manager of managers architecture can allow us to monitor local workgroup conditions, making those available to local system administrators, while forwarding information to higher-level management personnel.

Limited space prevents a complete description of the capabilities of the HP OpenView platform[34]. Investigation of this and other potential monitoring solutions is essential to choosing the proper solution for our workgroup.

15.16.3 Adding Unix Functionality to Windows NT

Windows NT has a POSIX subsystem that provides a POSIX.1 compliant interface to the Windows NT kernel. For POSIX applications, the ntfs file system also provides POSIX.1 compliant behavior with case-sensitive file naming, a "last time accessed" time stamp, and hard links between files. This subsystem provides POSIX functionality for applications written to that standard but does not provide Unix commands.

There are two different approaches to adding Unix command functionality to Windows NT systems. The first is to add commands to the Windows NT environment that behave like Unix, but use the Windows NT system calls. The second approach is to either replace the

34. See *WWW.hp.com* for more information on the OpenView platform and management tools.

POSIX subsystem with another more functional subsystem, or to add an entirely new subsystem.

Adding Unix Tools To Windows NT We will highlight two examples of the first approach: the Microsoft Windows NT Services for Unix Customers Add-On Pack and the MKS Toolkit® from Mortice Kern Systems[35]. The first is an interoperability package offered by Microsoft that includes NFS client software and a set of tools licensed from Mortice Kern Systems. The second approach is to add the entire MKS Toolkit, consisting of approximately two-hundred familiar Unix tools, to the Windows NT environment. Both of these packages include the MKS version of the Korn shell, which can overcome some of the shortcomings of Windows NT scripting.

Adding a Unix Environment to Windows NT One way to get Unix interoperability is to add a complete Unix environment to your Windows NT system. One product like this is Interix™ (formerly OpenNT) from Softway Systems Inc.[36] This environment is Unix branded and provides industry-standard interfaces like command shells and over three hundred commands, daemons, and other utilities. The features include:

- POSIX.1, POSIX.2, and ANSI C interfaces
- BSD sockets implemented over Winsock
- SVID IPC (message queues and semaphores)
- X11R5 Windowing system clients and libraries
- X11R6.3 Windowing system display server
- OSF/Motif® 1.2.4 window manager and libraries

This abbreviated list only scratches the surface. The Interix environment can also supply telnet and rlogin servers and NFS client software. Because of the binary mismatch, the applications will need to be recompiled on, and potentially ported to, the Interix Windows NT environment. There are a number of configurations of this environment, and you should investigate its capabilities.

15.17 Unix and Windows NT Data Sharing

The major issues in sharing data between Unix and Windows NT involve differences in user authentication, file protection, and the native network file systems. There are a number of third-party and public domain solutions that can make sharing data between the two systems easier.

35. See *WWW.Mks.com* for more details on the MKS Toolkit.

36. See *WWW.Interix.com* for more details on the Interix product.

SMB on Unix We have already discussed the Samba server and the Advanced Server product available from several Unix vendors. These software servers enable a Unix system to export its native file system via SMB to Windows clients. They also provide other useful functionality.

Both Samba and ASU are able to function as Windows NT domain controllers, authenticating Unix users and participating in a Windows NT domain. Samba and ASU can map a Windows NT account to a set of Unix UIDs and GIDs, preserving the proper local file protections and exporting the proper semantics to Windows clients. It is possible to maintain a consistent set of accounts for a user, so that he or she can use the same account name and password to log into either system.

Samba can also authenticate a user to the DCE environment, allowing Windows users to access underlying DFS file systems. This can enable a Unix server to provide file storage to Windows NT clients, to Unix systems via NFS, and to share data over wide areas with DCE DFS. A flexible combination, indeed.

The ASU product from Hewlett-Packard scales better than Samba, can provide an interface to Unix print services, and can be a PDC. Additionally, ASU can participate as a package in a Hewlett-Packard MC/ServiceGuard high-availability cluster. The ability to protect the workgroup's Windows file services from failure is an important consideration.

NFS on Windows NT There are quite a few NFS client products available for Windows clients. Adding NFS client software to every Windows client can be quite a system administration burden without the help of an image installation facility. Aside from the system administration issues, there can be performance and compatibility problems unless one of the latest generation of NFS clients is used.

We should also note that providing an NFS client on a Windows NT system without providing automounter capability can present system administration issues. A user should not have to manually provide the proper mapping of NFS data to Windows NT drive letter. In complex environments this is all but impossible and runs counter to our objective of "transparent" mapping of data within the workgroup. If automounter functionality is provided in the NFS client, then NIS access to automounter maps is the next issue to tackle. One source of an NFS client with this functionality is the Reflection® NFS Connection for NT from WRQ[37] Inc., which supports automounting and NFS PV3 connections.

One way of lessening the system administration burden and avoiding the addition of software to every client system is to configure NFS-to-SMB gateway machines in the workgroup. NFS gateway products can handle both NFS PV2 and PV3 connections between the gateway system and the NFS servers. The disadvantage to this approach is the potential performance degradation caused by an NFS intermediary, which has to be weighed against the potential savings

37. See *WWW.WRQ.com* for more information on this product.

in system administration effort. Unless the gateway system also provides automounter and NIS support, we may be back to requiring the user to have knowledge of the data's location.

NIS on Windows NT There is an implementation of NIS that is available for Windows NT from Tektronix®, called WinDD NIS[38]. WinDD NIS can keep passwords synchronized between Windows NT and Unix systems, which is a major advantage to the product.

Using External Sources to Update a Windows NT PDC An interesting technique of keeping DCE and Windows NT accounts synchronized was reported by David E. Grimmer[39], of the University of Iowa. The DCE password strength checking routine, which verifies the "quality" of the clear-text DCE password, was used to export the DCE password to a client application that runs on a Windows NT Primary Domain Controller. This arrangement is shown in Figure 15-10.

The password information is passed to the remote application in an encrypted RPC packet. The remote application on the PDC uses the password information to update the user's password in the Windows NT domain. Success or failure is passed back to the DCE password checking routine, which will update the user's DCE password if the PDC change was successful. This method of communicating with the Windows NT PDC was enhanced to allow secure remote management of the Windows NT account information from remote Unix scripts that automatically add user accounts.

This is a great example of the type of interoperability tool that users are often forced to implement when vendors do not follow common standards. It can be very difficult to implement a connection of this type without modifying or compromising the two services involved, but this solution manages to avoid that. We can only hope that this type of solution eventually becomes available to us, either commercially or in the public domain.

15.17.1 Unix and Windows NT Application Environment

There are several issues to address in making the Unix world interoperate with Windows NT. We must consider the desktop look-and-feel, the melding of X-Windows and the Windows NT application GUIs. A number of solutions are discussed in the next sections.

The Common Desktop Environment There is a version of CDE available for the Windows NT environment from TriTeal® Corporation[40], called WinTed™. This Windows NT version of CDE facilitates running Unix applications alongside native Windows NT applications

38. See *WWW.Tektronix.com* for information on WinDD NIS.

39. *Synchronizing NT and Unix NT Passwords with DCE*, by David E. Grimmer, Proceedings of the 1998 InterWorks Conference and Exhibition, April 25-30, 1998, Santa Clara, CA, p. 847.

40. See *WWW.Triteal.com* for more information.

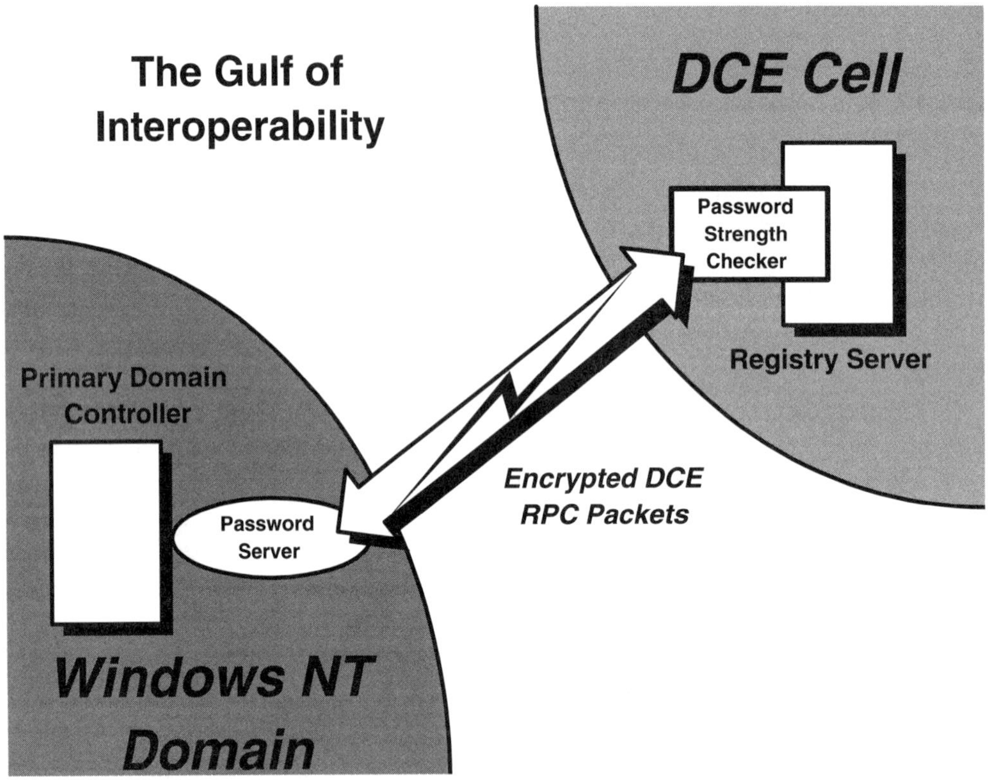

Figure 15-10 Integrating Windows NT Domain Controllers into DCE

on the Windows NT desktop. The WinTed environment provides desktop utilities, central administrative features, along with a multiple workspace PC X-Windows server.

WinTed may gather its desktop actions from multiple Unix CDE server systems, integrating them into the WinTed desktop. This environment includes the CDE messaging system to support remote execution of CDE actions. This product can make the job of providing a consistent desktop between Unix and Windows NT clients much easier.

Sharing Application Windows with Windows NT and Unix Since Unix applications do not run on Windows NT and Windows NT applications do not run on Unix, we need to find a way to bring the two worlds together on the user's desktop. There are two approaches to this: run X-Windows on the Windows NT system or project the Windows NT application GUIs to Unix systems via X-Windows protocols. There are a number of products that provide either solution.

MetaFrame™ from Citrix® Systems, Inc. allows a specially modified Windows NT Server system to project application interfaces to X-Windows displays. MetaFrame may be used to provide access to Windows NT office automation products for Unix workstations and X-stations. The Citrix product will be integrated into the Windows 2000 release.

Working in the opposite direction, it is possible to add an X-Windows server to the Windows NT system. Most products allow a separate X-Windows display, much like turning the Windows NT system into an X-station. Another behavior is to create and display the X-windows GUIs as if they were native Windows NT windows. The latter is the preferred approach, since its behavior is closer to what a Windows NT system user expects.

Providing Unix Commands on Windows NT Windows NT provides a POSIX subsystem that allows POSIX compliant applications to run, once they have been ported to Windows NT. Under the POSIX subsystem, only an ntfs partition provides a POSIX compliant file system, including case-sensitive file names. In addition to the POSIX subsystem, Microsoft offers an extra-cost interoperability package that provides a number of Unix commands, including a version of the Korn shell and an NFS client. This may be a good start, but there are other, more complete solutions available.

Scripting on Windows NT The native scripting language on Windows NT is Visual Basic (VB), whose use is far more extensive than the ".bat" scripting language. VB may be fine for applications that have been developed on Windows systems, but for applications that must be moved to Windows NT from Unix the lack of common scripting presents a porting barrier. Many Unix applications have a large shell-script content, relying on Korn Shell, Borne Shell, C-Shell, or POSIX Shell for glue to hold the executable components together. Porting these applications to Windows NT without support for Unix command script interpreters can be a major chore.

Microsoft is apparently implementing a command-line scripting facility to augment or replace the ".bat" facility. This facility may be extremely useful if it is interoperable with existing script languages and command interpreters from Unix systems. The exact details of this facility and its true utility remain to be seen.

One scripting language that is freely available between both environments is Perl[41]. Perl is a powerful interpretive scripting and text-manipulation language that provides a wide range interface packages to many system features like the Windows registry, sockets, and HTTP. Perl is a good choice for shell scripts that must run in both the Windows and Unix environments.

Perl is readily available on virtually every system because it is the scripting language of choice for Common Gateway Interface (CGI) applications used by web sites for interfacing HTML forms and pages to external processing.

15.18 Interoperability Summary

We have covered some of the issues that revolve around designing an interoperable environment out of dissimilar operating system types. There are varying degrees of interoperability

41. See *WWW.Perl.org* for more information on the Perl language. See also Larry Wall, Tom Christiansen & Randal L. Schwartz,"*Programming in Perl*" [13].

possible, and the specific needs of the workgroup should drive the amount of effort that goes into crafting a perfect solution. It is possible to evolve the workgroup interoperability in stages from "separate but equal" to "partially interoperable" to "completely interoperable" or "mostly interoperable" as you gain experience with the different aspects involved.

Adding a new operating system type to an existing environment or designing a workgroup that is to contain multiple system types both require investigation of capabilities in each separate system type. Application of project management and change management methodologies is strongly recommended. An environmental assessment of an existing workgroup is also recommended before adding a new system type.

Dealing with interoperability issues drains time and effort from other, more important workgroup issues. While industry standards have helped alleviate some of the interoperability issues, the drive by some vendors to grab market share by creating "slightly incompatible" versions of services and application components hurts us all. If experience serves, this behavior will only stop if we all stand up and say "Enough!", and again focus on adopting common standards.

One thing that became readily apparent in doing the research for this chapter is the dynamic nature of the Windows NT application marketplace. Many products that the author knew about disappeared, others were purchased by other companies, and still others changed names and web sites. It is hard to recommend a common set of solutions in such an environment and expect the landscape to remain constant for any period of time. We can end up spending a lot of our time staying abreast of the current developments in interoperability tools.

One final word before we close this chapter. There is a new development on the Unix and Windows NT block: Linux, which promises Unix functionality on the same inexpensive hardware that executes Windows NT today—the processors from Intel. In stark contrast to Windows NT, Linux is an "open source" operating system, which means that its source code is publicly available and widely distributed.

There are thousands of developers working on the Linux environment, and we have just begun to witness application suites being ported to it. The Linux operating system runs a full suite of public domain compilers, debuggers, and commands from the Free Software Foundation (FSF) and other public sources. Additionally, because it is a Unix system, it interoperates very well with its Unix brethren.

One can only hope that a little competition may persuade Microsoft to start thinking about interoperability between Windows NT and other systems a little more seriously. Linux is already making inroads into Internet service providers (ISPs) because it provides good performance and reliability on hardware that has long since been unable to run Microsoft Windows. Only time will tell how the presence of Linux will change the dynamics of the PC industry; we can certainly hope for the best.

CHAPTER 16

Case Study: Workgroup Design for Power Users — AORTA

All of the abstract approaches and principles we have studied up to this point are useful in workgroup design, but a real example of their application can help us use them in a more connected, holistic way in our own endeavors. This chapter will show many of the ideas and approaches applied in a practical manner: a workgroup environment that is the result of teamwork between Philips Research Laboratories, Philips Semiconductors, and Origin B.V. in the Netherlands[1]. This environment is called AORTA[2].

16.1 AORTA Introduction

The AORTA workgroup is one of the best implemented client-server environments in the world, possessing a number of unique features. AORTA should serve as a powerful example of what may be engineered with some of the principles we are studying. The following quotes serve to frame two of the underlying AORTA design precepts:

> **When people are limited to the CPU power on their desks, the entire set of computer hardware must be replaced frequently to keep in step with technology.**
>
> **—*Plan 9 from AT&T Bell Laboratories*, Rob Pike and Ken Thompson, 1988**

1. Information about Origin B.V. may be found on their web site, located at *WWW.Origin-IT.com.*

2. Architecture of ORigin Technical Automation.

We will soon come to a situation in which it is economically feasible to have 20 or 50 or even 100 computers per person. Clearly the current model of giving each person a personal computer or workstation breaks down under these conditions.

—*Amoeba,* A.S. Tanenbaum and S.J. Mullender, 1990

16.2 The AORTA Workgroup Environment

The AORTA environment had its beginnings at Philips Research in The Netherlands, where it was implemented by the CAD Support department. This group was responsible for the support of the electrical CAD environment used by the Philips Research IC Design Center. In 1992, this environment was approximately four hundred Apollo Computer, Inc., workstations, supporting analog electronics, digital VLSI design, test and analysis, software development, and the CAD support group itself.

16.2.1 Motivation for a New Computing Architecture

The 1989 purchase of Apollo Computer by Hewlett-Packard necessitated a migration to the HP-UX operating system, and the newly introduced HP 9000 Series 700 workstations. To quote a paper delivered by the principal architects:

Faced with an inescapable transition, it seemed an ideal opportunity to reconsider the suitability of the 'one person—one workstation" model of computing in the light of experience.

...

More effective computing paradigms have already been proposed by two influential research projects: Plan 9 from AT&T Bell Laboratories, and Prof. Tanenbaum's Amoeba development. It's in the spirit of these projects that we decided to design a new computing infrastructure[3].

Additionally, experience with "traditional" technical computing environments—those constructed with Unix workstations, a few servers, and a local-area network—exposed some fundamental weaknesses:

- Keeping desktop technology up to date with the latest developments is expensive.
- There can be huge amounts of idle computing resources.
- Resources are fragmented across many desktop machines.
- A desktop-centric environment is administration intensive.
- It is difficult to adjust a desktop system to meet widely varying compute needs of individual users.

3. Ronald van Driel and Daan Reuhman, *The X Station: A High-end Workstation in Disguise*, Proceedings of the International Hewlett-Packard Users Conference, Maastricht, The Netherlands, April 1994.

To address these issues, the decision was made to implement a new computing architecture, which was called NXA, for NatLab X-terminal Architecture. By 1994, NXA was in use at several other sites within Philips.

The NXA architecture has been commercialized by Origin and is now called AORTA. In the last several years, NXA/AORTA has been adapted to the newest technologies and standards in a close cooperation between Origin and Philips Research (NatLab). For convenience, in the remainder of this chapter we will refer to the NXA/AORTA environment simply as "AORTA."

An assessment of the existing Apollo environment's resource usage, prior to the migration, produced the following interesting statistics[4]:

- Vastly varying user needs: ten percent of users consume sixty-five percent of CPU time.
- Low CPU load level: 1–1.5 CPU hours per day per user (fifteen to twenty-five percent).
- Actual users were less than potential users: only seventy percent of stations concurrently in use.

The architects believed that there must be a better way to allocate the compute resources in a workgroup and decided to reimplement their compute environment. This was the beginning of what is now called AORTA.

16.2.2 A Global Overview of AORTA

Having an idea of what the goals of the original environment were can help us understand the design choices that were made. Let's summarize the AORTA objectives, from a paper written by Ronald van Driel at Origin B.V. The objectives of AORTA are to:

- Create a virtual computer, based upon dedicated servers and a standard desktop
- Provide a single engineering desktop for each user and a single repository for storage of user data and applications
- Use "thin" clients wherever possible, central resources where feasible, and conform to industry standards where possible

The design goals for the environment were:

- Provide the best performance for the budget
- Create a single-system view of resources
- Accommodate large jobs
- Enable global system and software upgrades
- Reduce overall cost

4. From Ronald van Driel, *Evolution in Computing: from Workstation to X station*, unpublished presentation, March 26, 1996.

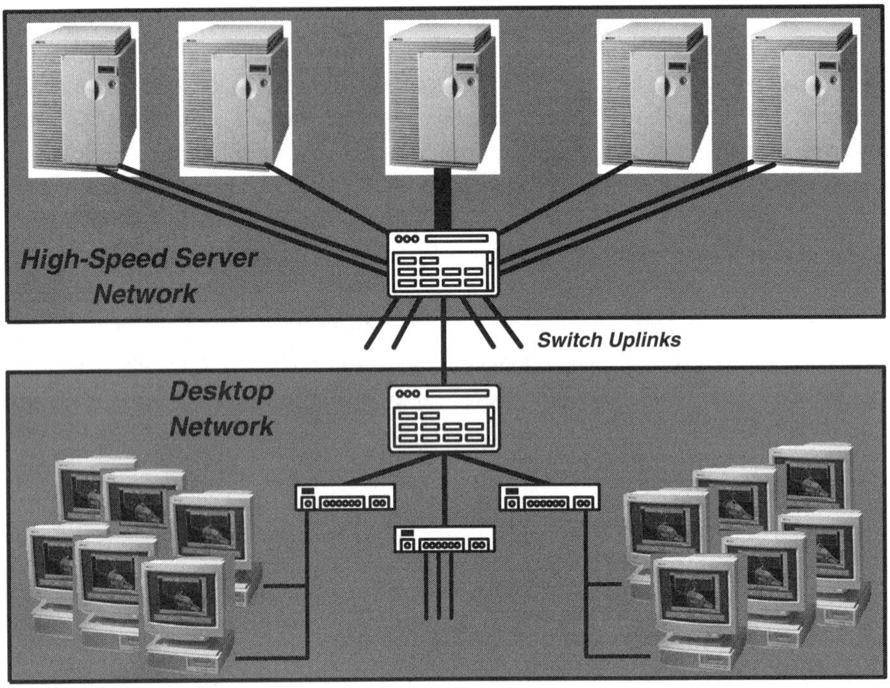

Figure 16-1 AORTA Two-Tier Network Architecture

To meet these goals, AORTA comprises two virtual computing layers. The first is a virtual desktop network that manages user log-in to a session and subsequent user interaction. The second layer is a virtual computer-room network where file services and batch computer services are provided. Load-balancing services take care of distributing the workload between dedicated servers.

To a user, AORTA might look like a traditional technical computing environment, but there is one important difference: a user can access all available resources in the workgroup transparently. Subsequent sections will look at the high-level implementation details, broken into the five layers of the workgroup functional model.

16.3 AORTA Network Infrastructure

The network infrastructure in an AORTA workgroup is divided into a two-tier hierarchy: a desktop network and a high-speed server network. Because the high-bandwidth traffic between servers is isolated to its own network, the client performance is not impacted by bulk data transfers. The desktop network can function adequately with a 10 Mb/S shared Ethernet, but the use of shared 100 Mb/S Ethernet is also permitted to support newer clients with autosensing 10/100 Mb/S interfaces.

Servers are located on dedicated Ethernet switch ports. Connections in the high-speed server network are switched Ethernet—trunked 100 Mb/S Ethernet or even GbE for file servers. The connection between the desktop network and the server network are provided by fast switch-to-switch uplinks. The structure of the network is shown in Figure 16-1.

16.4 AORTA Hardware Architecture

The AORTA workgroup comprises four general classes of clients: X-stations, PCs, Unix workstations, and Windows NT workstations. There are five types or classes of server: login servers, batch servers, compute servers, infra-servers, and file servers.

16.4.1 AORTA Client Systems

The initial design of the AORTA environment (NXA) used only X-stations as the client interface. Because the X-stations are presentation-only devices with no general-purpose local compute power, a Unix system is required to "host" the user's desktop session. This so-called "login server" is discussed further on in this section.

In addition to the original X-stations and Unix workstations, AORTA now supports Windows NT workstations with X-windows server software as clients. A user desktop session is automatically assigned to a login server by load-balancing software. This is a key concept for supporting thin X-station clients.

The decrease in price of PCs equipped with fast graphics cards, coupled with the demand to run office application on a designer's desktop, has made the PC with X-windows server software a serious replacement for the X-station. This type of client system also is hosted by a login server to provide access to the compute server resources. The architects note that a substantial system-management effort is required to add PCs to the environment, since they must maintain a separate infrastructure for supporting the Windows clients.

Unix workstations are used as AORTA clients where special graphics capabilities are required. Workstations, when they are used, are installed as dataless clients—with both application software and user data provided by remote servers. Selecting a Unix workstation as a client implies special needs—the application size or the data access characteristics might require a higher-speed network connection to a Unix workstation.

The price-to-performance ratio offered by Windows NT workstations and the fact that Unix CAD applications are becoming available on them has led to an increasing number of Windows NT workstations in the environment. A Windows NT workstation also allows native execution of the office automation tools. Windows NT workstations are expected to be the desktop of choice for the foreseeable future.

16.4.2 AORTA Server Systems

Servers provide the majority of resources within AORTA, and the designers recommend the following rules to increase the reliability and flexibility of their deployment:

- The server configuration contributes to the relatively high availability of AORTA: batch, compute, infrastructure, and login servers (as well as desktops) are redundantly present, eliminating single points of failure (SPOF).
- Place all servers in a conditioned computer room. This also increases security because fewer people need access to the computer room.
- When looking at pure price performance, realize that server systems have built-in reliability features that are not available in workstations. This will make workstations appear cheaper and should be taken into account.
- One of the easiest ways to increase overall reliability of servers systems is to install a mirrored system disk.
- It is desirable to use UPS, either on a per-machine basis or for the whole compute room. Introducing a UPS creates a new SPOF, therefore, it is of high importance that all file servers share the same UPS.
- The network and each file server are SPOFs.
- Placing the all server and disk hardware in 19-inch racks saves footprint and provides a manageable physical environment in which all cabling is properly placed
- A console switch or terminal server[5] should replace individual server consoles, reducing fire risk and saving both money and space. The use of a terminal server provides remote system-management capabilities.
- Critical servers should be on a high-level maintenance contract.

Most AORTA servers perform a single task, and tuning the system for that task is vital to the overall performance of the workgroup.

Login servers deal mainly with the user's login session and the desktop tool set, including electronic mail, text editors, word processors, calendars, and the user desktop itself (HP VUE[6], CDE, or Open Windows[7]). Login servers must provide good interactive response while simultaneously running many small processes.

Interactive compute servers run resource-intensive interactive applications, such as simulators, that require resources beyond the scope of a login server. Compute servers must provide good interactive response while running a small number of potentially large interactive sessions concurrently. The number of concurrent sessions is limited by both the available CPU power and the amount of available system RAM.

Batch servers run traditional noninteractive CAD applications for analysis, simulation, and verification. Batch servers are limited to a small number of jobs to optimize throughput and

5. A hardware device, with multiple serial ports, that provides access to those ports via a network protocol like telnet

6. Hewlett-Packard's Visual User Environment, a forerunner to much of the functionality in CDE.

7. The windowing environment from Sun Microsystems Inc.

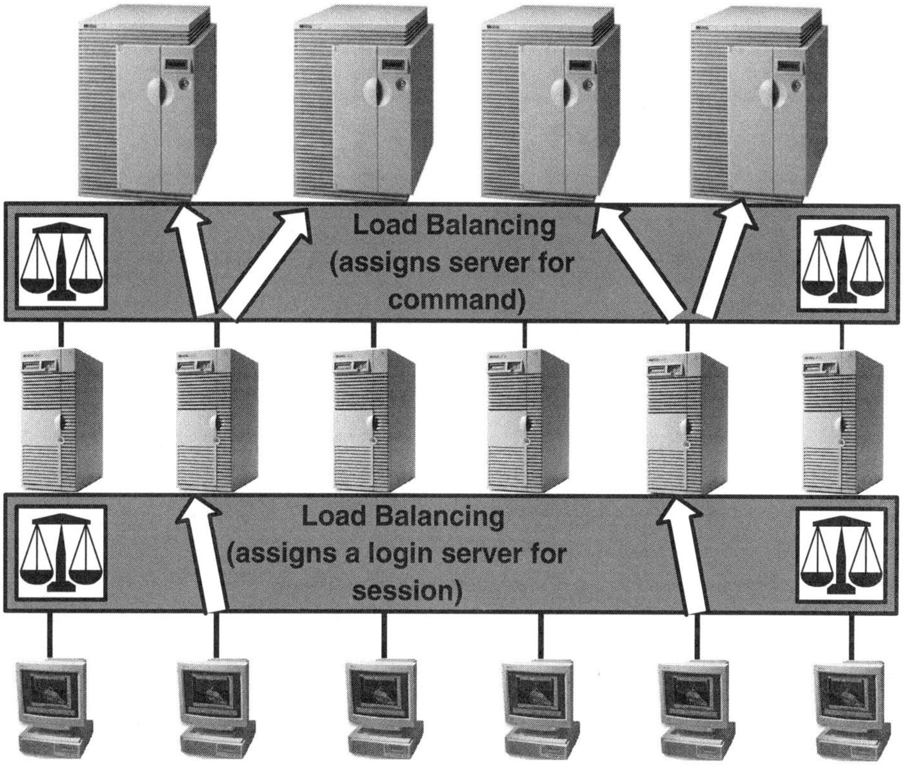

Figure 16-2 AORTA Load-Balancing Layers

provide predictable turn-around time. A batch server runs no more than one to two jobs per CPU at the same time.

Infrastructure or "infra"-servers consolidate infrastructure services like BOOTP, DHCP, TFTP, DNS, SMTP-gateway, license, print, and plot services. The infra-server also runs the thinclient load-balancing software for the desktop tier. Most of these services are also replicated on other infra-servers in the environment, resulting in very good availability.

Because AORTA relies heavily on dynamic resource allocation, it is not known in advance which server will execute a particular task. A fundamental assumption, because of this, is that the task's data is not resident on the server's local disk. In the AORTA workgroup, all user data, project data, and applications are located on one or more dedicated file servers. Therefore, the availability of the file servers strongly determine the overall availability of the computer infrastructure.

It is extremely important to ensure that the file servers are available. AORTA file servers use mirrored system disks and RAID or mirror technology for all other disks. To improve time-

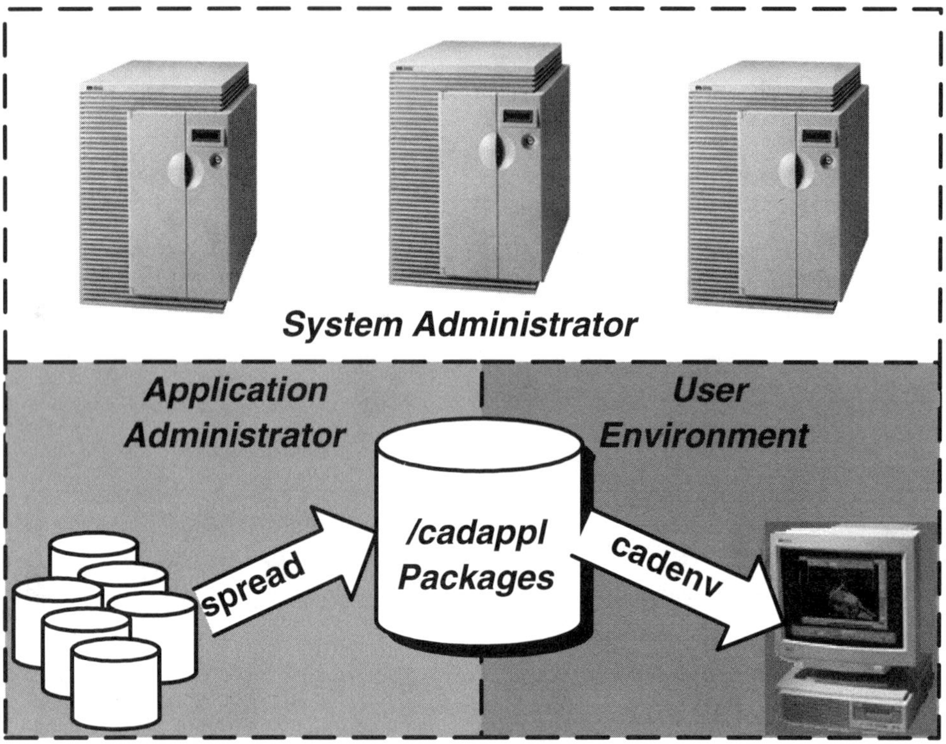

Figure 16-3 Separate Application and System Administration Domains

to-repair, disk mechanisms are hot-swappable. Devices with a high error probability, such as tape devices, are preferably not connected to a file server.

One of the most critical areas of a particular file server configuration is the time needed to reboot the system after it has been stopped abnormally. There are system features that can aid in shortening this time, including journaled file systems. A shorter reboot time translates to greater file server availability to the users.

AORTA file servers are dedicated to the task of providing user data via NFS. To prevent destructive interference between NFS and other processes, the file server should run only processes that are absolutely necessary. This can also reduce the system administration overhead for the file server.

16.5 AORTA Operating Environment

A key concept in the AORTA environment is load balancing; just like there are two tiers to the network infrastructure, there are two levels of load balancing in an AORTA workgroup. One level exists between the desktop client systems and the login servers. The second level is between the login servers and the remaining compute resources in the workgroup. This arrangement is shown in Figure 16-2.

Centralized servers help reduce the system-administration overhead for the AORTA. To manage the servers, the AORTA support staff uses several custom-developed tools. One tool summarizes the Unix accounting information and allows reporting of CPU and memory usage. The long period of time for this report is very useful for capacity planning, an essential system-management process.

Another custom tool provides information about the current administrative state of a server system. The information that system administrators need is summarized and presented on a single screen. System managers may access this information over the network via the SNMP protocol.

The AORTA system administration processes differentiate between system administration and application administration. This separation is supported by a special administrative user ID, and a special access control mechanism in a custom application distribution tool called “spread”. This tool allows application support personnel to manage software without needing the “root” password. This is shown in Figure 16-3.

16.6 AORTA Data Sharing

Applications and data in the AORTA environment are distributed from centralized, dedicated NFS servers via automounter maps. Two indirect NIS maps are employed, one to make user home directories available (*auto.home*) and another that mounts all other directories (*auto.sys*). There are entries in the *auto.sys* map for e-mail server directories, the CAD application packages, and other essential distribution points on the file servers.

The application software is arranged in packages, and distributed under a single logical directory hierarchy that starts with the */cadappl* directory. One of the important provisions of the data-sharing mechanism is the ability to provide multiple versions of the same application package at the same time. The prototype directory hierarchy that supports this is */cadappl/<package_name>/<release>*.

An intermediate directory called */links* insulates the user environment from underlying software location changes in the application packages. This directory is physically present (not under automounter control) and contains symbolic links to information presented by the automounter maps. If we were to examine the */cadappl* directory, we would find that it is a symbolic link, pointing to *../links/cadappl*, which for an HP-UX system is a symbolic link that points to */sys/cadappl_hpux*. Likewise, the */var/mail* directory is a symbolic link to *../links/mail*, which points to */sys/mail*.

The eventual stopping point for the links is the automounter map, which is responsible for correctly mounting the data from the associated server. This scheme implements the hybrid link

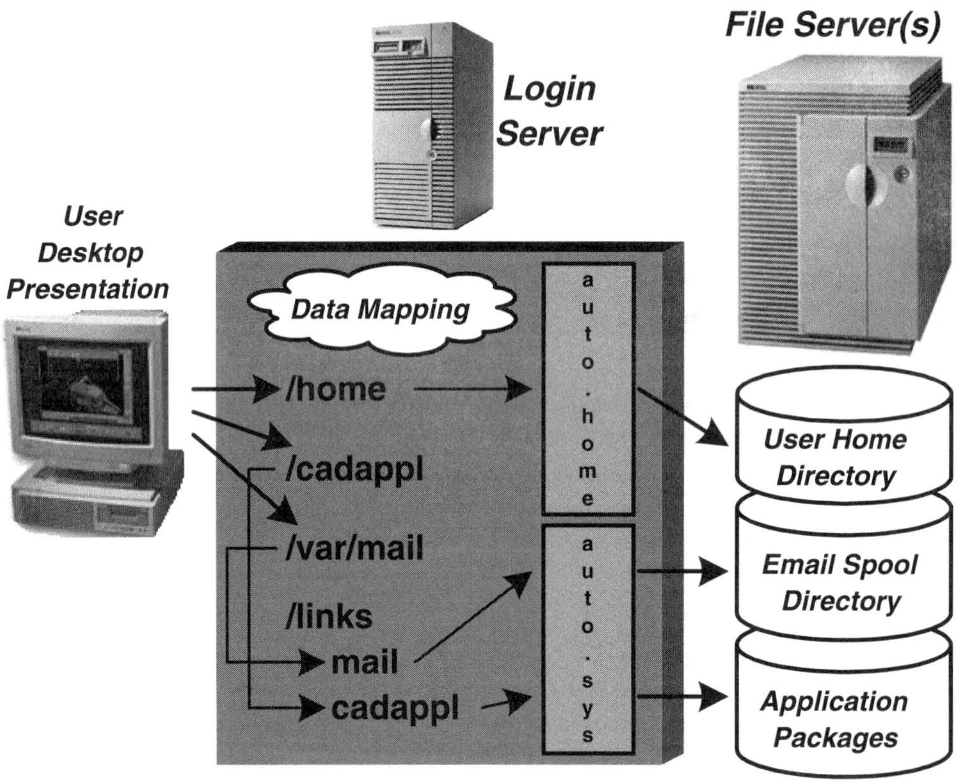

Figure 16-4 AORTA Data Presentation Model

approach previously discussed, but with an added twist. The */links* directory implements a second level of indirection "in front of" the automounter maps.

This indirect data-access arrangement provides the following benefits:

- All systems may be built with the same logical data structure presented to the user.
- All external references are concentrated in a single directory.
- It is possible to switch the data references to another server by modifying the links in the */links* directory[8].

The data-presentation relationships are shown in Figure 16-4, along with several sample links. We should make an important point: the data-presentation model must work for multiple

8. There are multiple entries in the automounter map for replicated packages, one for each server. The links may be altered to point to the entry for an alternate replica.

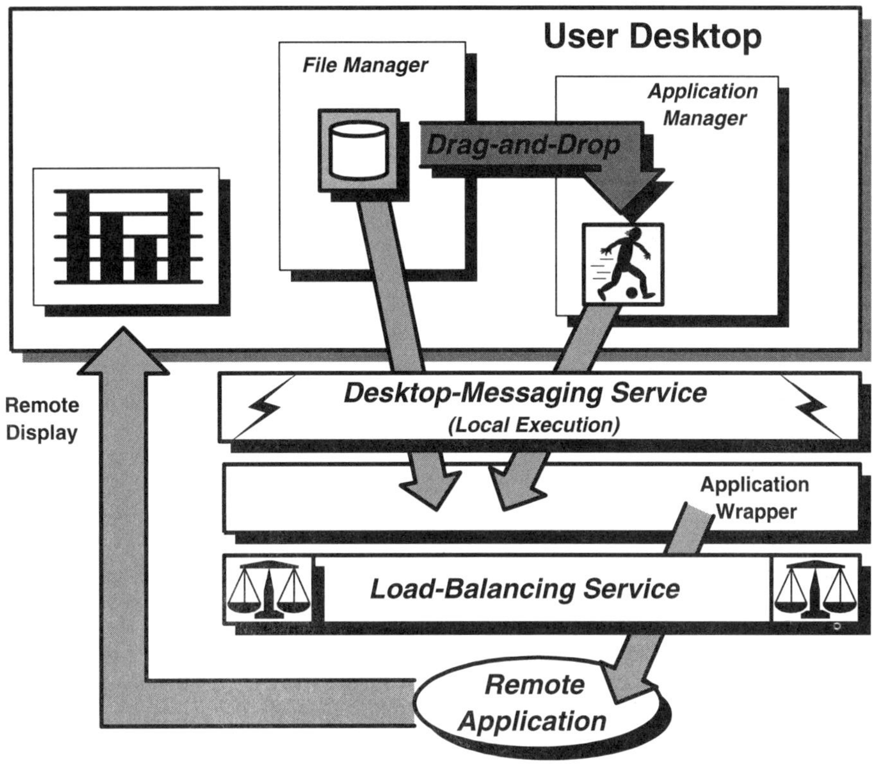

Figure 16-5 AORTA Application Scheduling Process

users on a login server, presenting each with its own unique view of the underlying workgroup data and packages.

Note that the indirection in the data model is only between the user desktop environment and application packages—the user home directories are provided directly. This is not accidental. The user home directories are the top of the data dependency tree: menus, scripts, actions, and other data and application references all begin there.

The levels of indirection present the user with a single consistent view of underlying workgroup data. Changes in the structure or location of the data are hidden in the links and automounter map information. Connecting the user to a different server requires only the modification of the links. This helps maintain the stability of the user desktop, which we will discuss next.

16.7 AORTA Application Environment

The */cadappl* directory, which may be replicated on several servers, distributes the application packages to the user's desktop. The application environment on the user desktop presents the available application packages to the user through a tool called *cadenv*. The *cadenv* tool allows the user to view the available software packages and install the required version into his or her desktop.

The preferred AORTA desktop is based on CDE and the Korn shell, both readily available on Unix systems. The belief is that the user environment should be rich enough that the user does not need to change it for daily work. The default environment, contained in the Korn shell's *.kshrc* initialization file, is installed by an automated system administration script.

The AORTA system administrators divide the user community into three groups, each with different expertise levels:

- The novice user, who will accept whatever they are offered. The novice does not possess enough knowledge to modify the environment.
- The standard user, who will use the default environment if they perceive it as being easy to use and providing enough functionality.
- Power users, who will change everything anyway.

The design goal is to ensure that the desktop environment is configured to place most users in the first two groups. If too many users do not like the default environment, then problems and increased system administration effort result from overmodification.

Applications that are resource intensive are load balanced on a per invocation basis. The actual application invocation occurs in a wrapper script providing two functions. First, the wrapper script makes the application self-contained by providing the proper search paths and environment. Second, the wrapper script starts the application via the load-balancing service. This process is shown in Figure 16-5.

The AORTA desktop environment provides the user with a consistent view on the workgroup resources available for use. Once the user selects the appropriate applications for their daily tasks and adds them to the desktop, the underlying architecture provides the illusion of virtually unlimited compute power—the client-server virtual computer. This is pure client-server at architecture at its finest.

16.8 AORTA Environment Summary

The AORTA workgroup environment provides its users with access to multiple, dynamically configurable virtual computers for completing their daily work. This arrangement gives each user the impression that he or she has unlimited compute power, but hides details, like the location of data and compute resources, beneath the desktop. It is the unique use of multitier load balancing coupled with a strong client-server infrastructure that makes this apparent magic possible.

Some of the key features of AORTA are:

- Three-tier client-server architecture

- Multiple-tier load balancing
- Dedicated server hardware
- Replication of application packages
- Support for thin desktop clients
- Dynamic resource allocation
- Consistent desktop presentation of resources
- Class-based system administration

As you have seen, there are four classes of desktop devices, five classes of servers, and three classes of users in this description of the AORTA environment. Each of these classes is well characterized and supported by features designed by the AORTA architects.

The current high-level description, however, cannot adequately depict the complete flexibility of AORTA. The fact that the AORTA environment is capable of supporting a wide range of demanding technical computing needs with thin clients is the ultimate tribute to its abilities[9]. The design and implementation principles combined here are useful in any workgroup—many of them can be found individually in other environments.

If you compare the system administration (operating environment) of AORTA to that of the RAPTOR project in Chapter 17, you will see marked similarities in several areas: the application wrappers (what RAPTOR calls "invocatables"), the replicated distribution of those packages, and the levels of indirect reference between the user's desktop and the underlying data-sharing mechanism.

These powerful system-management models supply an object-oriented way of managing application packages and dependencies on the user's desktop—it is no accident that similar solutions crop up in multiple places. But it is the combined innovations in AORTA that have yielded tremendous improvements over the "traditional" architecture.

The AORTA architects have tracked the overall savings from their efforts, comparing the cost of operating the new environment that of the old "traditional" architecture. Some of those results are:

- A fifty percent savings in investment and depreciation
- A sixty percent savings in maintenance and repair
- At least a twenty-five percent savings in system-administration costs

9. The fact that the AORTA designers could get engineers to turn in the "latest greatest" workstations on their desks for thin clients is also a tribute to their political skills.

An AORTA workgroup that supports approximately three-hundred and ten simultaneous users contains approximately thirty-eight servers.

Table 16-1 Sample AORTA Hardware Resources

AORTA Resource	Number of Systems	Users or Jobs per System
Log-in Server	13	22–30
Compute Server	14	8–35
Batch Server	6	1–3
File Server	5	62[a]
Client Systems	310	1

a. The number of users per file server depends on the data-access patterns. This number is only an average, assuming even data distribution across the servers.

The utilization of the AORTA hardware resources is high, yielding a good return on compute hardware investment. Recall that measurements of the original environment indicated a fifteen to twenty-five percent overall CPU utilization factor. With only seventy percent of the available seats logged in, the RAM utilization was low as well. For current AORTA resource utilizations, see the following table.

Table 16-2 AORTA Resource-Utilization Statistics

AORTA Resource	Average CPU Utilization	Average RAM Utilization
Log-in Server	35%	95%
Compute Server	65%	75%
Batch Server	70%	25%
File Server	30%	90%
Average for All Servers	45–55%	70–80%

The AORTA concept is a powerful client-server architecture, arguably the best implementation of 3TCS in the technical computing world. The principles used in AORTA are of great value, whether they are applied to new or existing workgroup environments. We can use concepts from AORTA as the basis for our vision of future client-server environments.

CHAPTER 17

Case Study: Design, Redesign, and Evolution — The RAPTOR Project

In late 1996, the Spokane, Washington manufacturing division of Hewlett-Packard's Microwave Communication Group undertook a complete redesign of their computing environment[1]. Early in the process of planning the project, the team visited several sites to investigate state-of-the-art architectures, share best practices, and trade experience. The author of this book was a host to one of these visits.

17.1 The Initial HP SPOKANE Environment

This HP division develops and manufactures test equipment for the wireless communication industry. The computing environment supports electrical, mechanical, and software engineering efforts as well as the divisional manufacturing processes. User development groups from manufacturing, firmware development, information technology, printed circuit board development, ASIC developers, and mechanical engineering use the environment. Members from personnel and marketing organizations also participated in the new project.

The existing compute environment consisted of 600 Unix systems and was behind the evolutionary curve, both in terms of operating system revisions and availability of new high-performance hardware that was tied to a newer version of the HP-UX operating system. The operating system in use was also slated for obsolescence at the end of 1997, and there were no plans for HP to make that version year 2000 (Y2K) compliant.

1. The information in this section was kindly provided by the RAPTOR project team at Hewlett-Packard's Spokane, Washington, division. Much of it comes from the project's web site and a paper published by Daniel Krantz at the InterWorks 1998 Conference and Exhibition in Santa Clara, California.

A description of the overall architecture and IT support climate taken from Dan Krantz's InterWorks paper is at once instructive and familiar:

> Unfortunately, this critical computing infrastructure had never been carefully engineered but rather grew from years of disjoint efforts and locally developed system administration tools. Our internal customers were becoming increasingly dissatisfied with the quality of service they were receiving from their Information Technology staff [2].

17.2 Elements of the RAPTOR Project Organization

Any change in an environment of this size was bound to affect project delivery dates and cause further disruptions. While we have spent little time in this book on project management in favor of technical architecture and details, the importance of approach should never be minimized. How the project is organized is critical to its success.

17.2.1 Project Goals

Based on a poll of the user community, the project team concluded that the project goals should be:

- Increased reliability
- Simplified data sharing
- Improved consistency
- Enhanced system performance
- Reduced overall support cost

Again, quoting from Dan Krantz:

> [The project goals are] a challenging list, but to make the problem more interesting the IT staff had to overcome a credibility problem and re-establish working relationships with key customer groups. The first challenge was not technical; we needed a successful project charter and an innovative project organization in order to accomplish the necessary changes[3].

The RAPTOR[4] project team realized that to be successful they must have strong management sponsorship and a formal project management process. From the author's experiences, this

2. From *Rebuilding a UNIX Infrastructure*, Daniel Krantz, Proceedings of the InterWorks '98 Conference and Exhibition, page 685.

3. Ibid.

4. Rapid advancement of productivity tools, operating systems, and reliability.

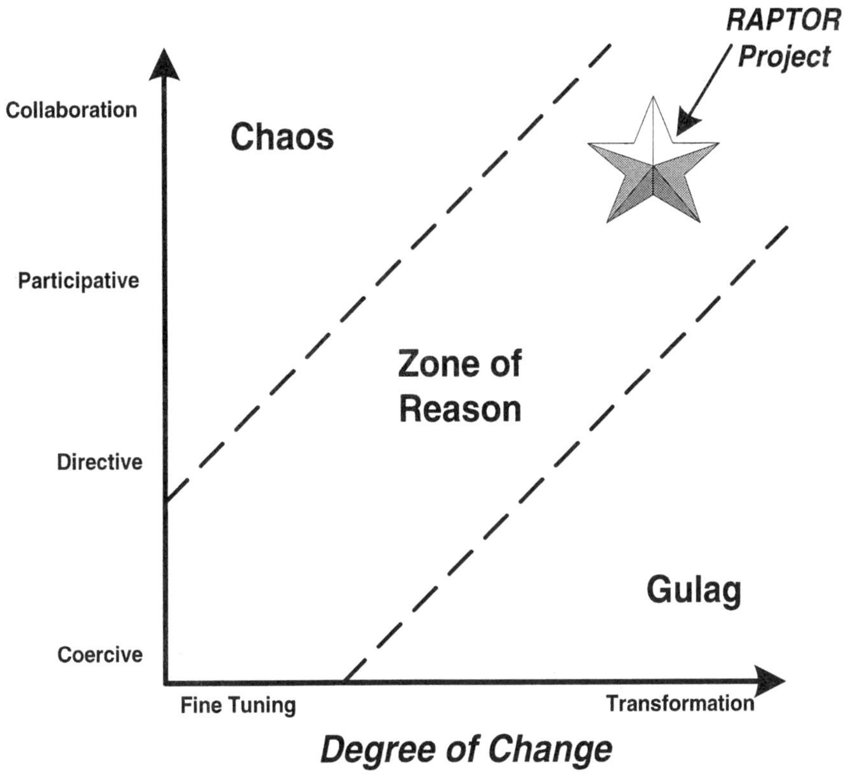

Figure 17-1 Change Magnitude and End-User Involvement

realization, along with their strong focus on meeting their *customer's* needs, puts them into the minority of projects of this nature.

17.2.2 Project Sponsorship

Strong sustaining sponsorship was lined up between divisional management—the IT Unix manager, the research and development manager, and the manufacturing managers. The project's sustaining sponsors also provided the business context and rationale for the change. In addition, the sponsors provided staffing for a cross-discipline project team consisting of IT staff and productivity engineers from R&D and manufacturing groups.

17.2.3 Change Management

Figure 17-1 shows the model used for managing the change in the compute environment. The project team realized that the size of change they were advocating would not occur without collaboration with the end users. Their approach was as follows:

> Even with a collaborative approach, end-user resistance is inevitable. Rather than fight it, successful change projects strive to fully understand the customer's point of view. The key is to **listen for understanding**. Providing end-users with ample, diverse, and creative opportunities for feedback can be the best resistance management approach. Some users may not fully understand the change, its full impact, and the meaning to their daily work life. They may not believe in the need for the radical change that is being proposed. Therefore, communication from the change project to the end-users is also important. Finally, a natural response to change is the attempt to bargain, to minimize the impact. This will be a significant challenge for the change project that is striving to be customer oriented but without compromising the improvements that have been diligently implemented. Tackle end-user resistance compassionately and together with the support of strong sustaining sponsorship, your change project can be a success.[5]

We should note here that the author believes that this approach is one of the secrets to change-management success and has never seen it explained in better terms.

17.2.4 Project Management

The project team adopted a formal project management philosophy, aligned with the Project Management Institute's® Body of Knowledge[6] (PMBOK). This consists of three elements:

Define the Project Establish the vision; the team members need to know why they are doing the project. You will get better results when everyone wants to contribute. Clarify the underlying values to which the project will adhere. Determine the priority of time, scope/quality, and cost.

Plan the Project Generate the task lists and create a work breakdown structure. Determine roles and responsibilities and effort and duration estimates. Define task interdependencies and analyze the critical path. Develop a schedule that can be easily communicated to sponsors and end-users in the form of a Gantt chart. Generate the project budget and finally develop a risk management plan that addresses contingency plans.

Work the Project While monitoring and managing progress, it is important in this phase to communicate with sponsors and end-users. To keep project team spirits high, the project lead should communicate praise. Use a lot of random positive reinforcement, such as mentioning member names in project status reports and direct compliments to individuals.

A formal project plan helped strengthen the credibility with the end-users and also helped avoid the "chaos cloud" (see Appendix A). A project name was chosen—RAPTOR—along with

5. Op. cit., p. 686.

6. See *WWW.pmi.org* for more details on the Project Management Institute.

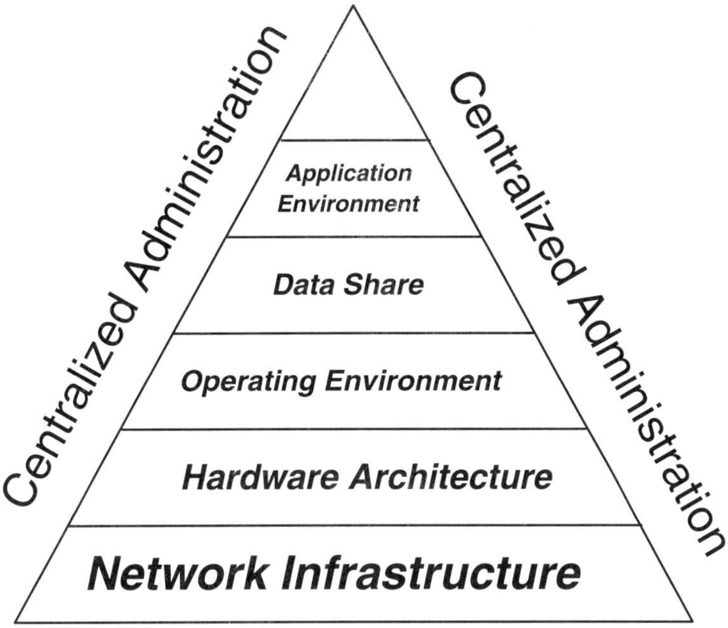

Figure 17-2 RAPTOR Unix Infrastructure Pyramid

a project motto of sorts: "Raptors are birds of prey: possessing keen vision and aggressively pursuing their target". The vision for the project was set:

- Spokane will have a world-class Unix Infrastructure.
- RAPTOR will be known for its reliability.
- RAPTOR's flexibility will allow it to maneuver with the ever-changing customer needs.
- RAPTOR's adherence to a structured architecture will foster consistency and cost-efficient maintenance.
- The project will be noted for its method of proactive partnership.

A quote from the RAPTOR web page summarizes the scope and previews some final results of the project:

> RAPTOR is not just an implementation plan for converting to HP-UX 10.20, RAPTOR is our effort at creating the **best Unix environment** for our customers. We have addressed Y2K issues, increased reliability, simplified data sharing, improved consistency (of applications,

workstations, and [user] accounts), enhanced performance and improved the cost structure through advanced system administration techniques. The architectural changes at Spokane Division are based on quantifiable benefits to our customers.

Let's analyze just how the RAPTOR project accomplished its goals by evolving an existing architecture to an entirely new one. We will break the analysis down into the five layers of the workgroup model, which is how the RAPTOR team chose to break the environment down into more manageable pieces (see Figure 17-2 for the model they used—it should seem familiar).

17.3 RAPTOR Network Infrastructure

Before the improvement project, most clients and servers had shared 10 Mbps LAN connections, with a few servers benefiting from dedicated connections. One select group of developers had a 100 Mbps segment. There were approximately 60 HP-UX stand-alone workstations and 500 HP-UX diskless cluster clients. The cluster servers were primarily workstations, which also performed services like providing applications, file storage, and compute serving.

The site was interfaced to the HP Intranet by an aging Cisco AGS+ router.The router was upgraded to a Cisco 7206 with full duplex 100baseT links to Hewlett-Packard 100baseT Ethernet switches on each major subnet. These switches in turn feed department level 100baseT switches for clients and localized servers via trunked full-duplex 200 Mbps links.

Departmental servers connect into 100baseT switches at lower layers in the network hierarchy. In this way, each shared server is directly "visible", in a network sense, to other workgroups. Each server also connects to a private 100 Mbps network for backup and NIS traffic. All servers are multihomed into the major subnets on 100baseT full-duplex links. Servers with site-wide functionality connect into 100baseT switches at the top of the network.

Within the workcenter level of the RAPTOR network, a number of resources are globally visible or shared between multiple workgroups. These include site file servers, management servers, NIS master servers, installation servers, and Windows NT resources like primary and backup domain controllers.

Figures 17-3 through 17-7 show high-level details of the HP Spokane RAPTOR network; there is not space in this book lfor a more detailed set of pictures. At the WAN level in

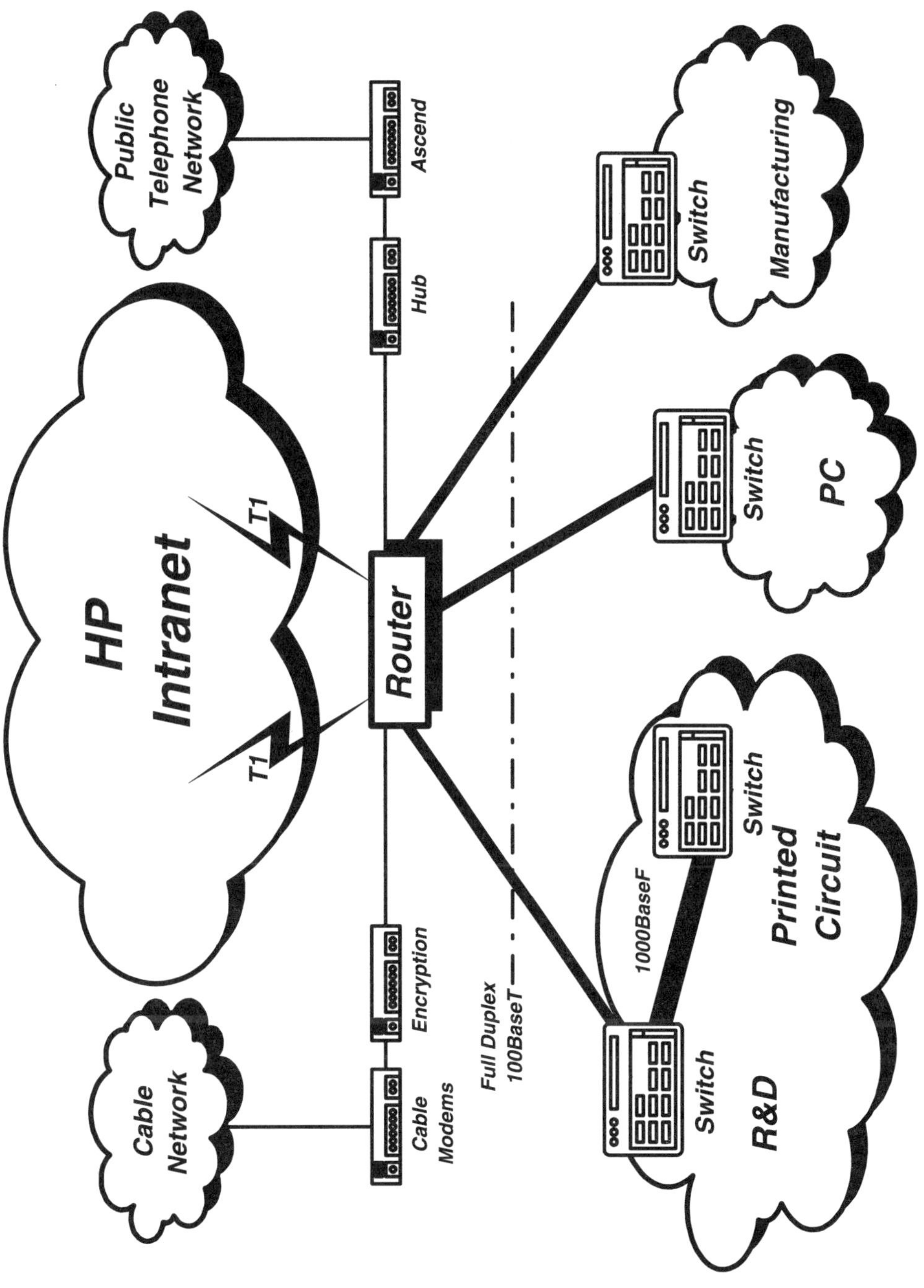

Figure 17-3 Top Level of HP Spokane's RAPTOR Project Network

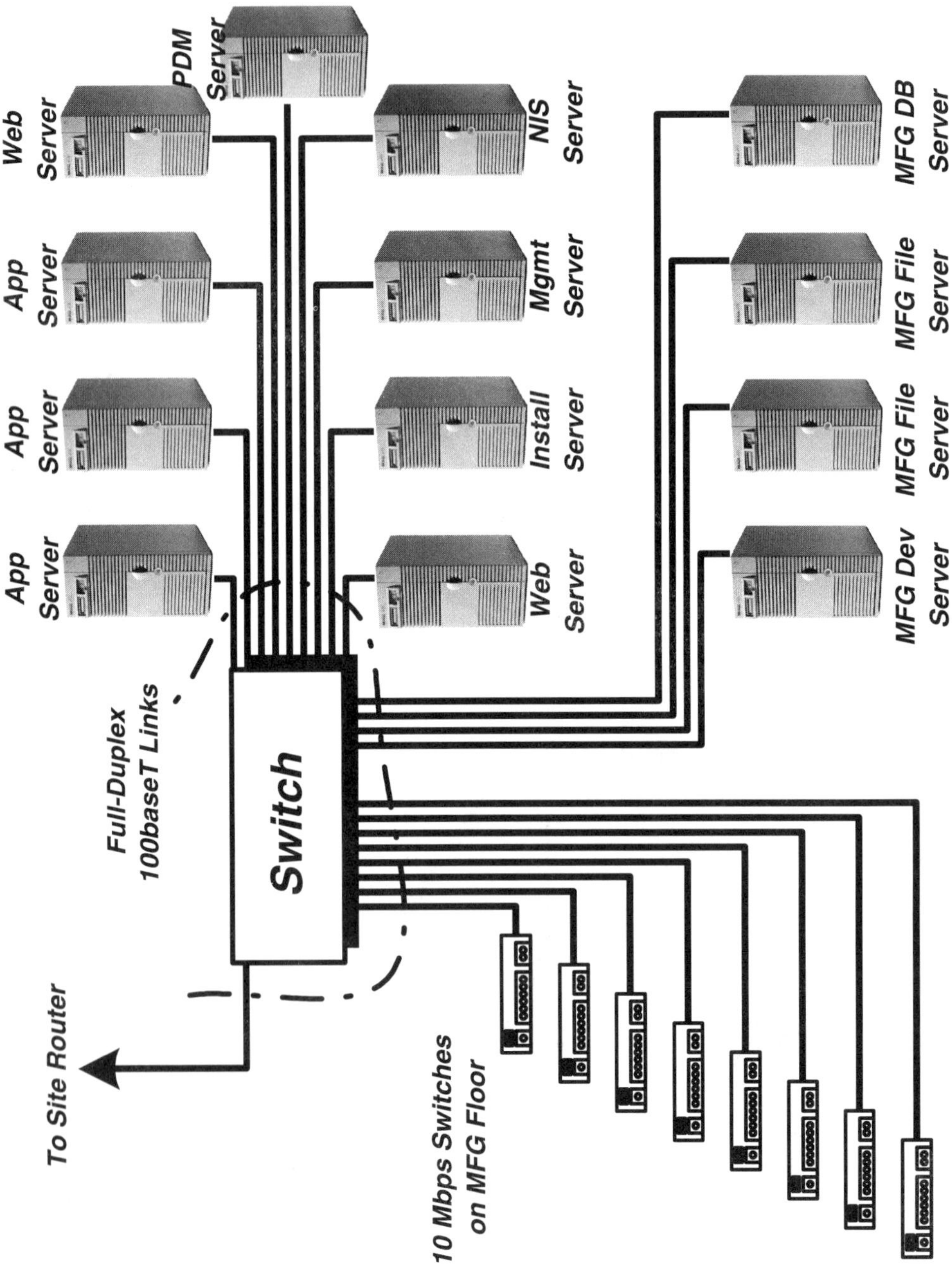

Figure 17-4 HP Spokane's RAPTOR Project Manufacturing Network

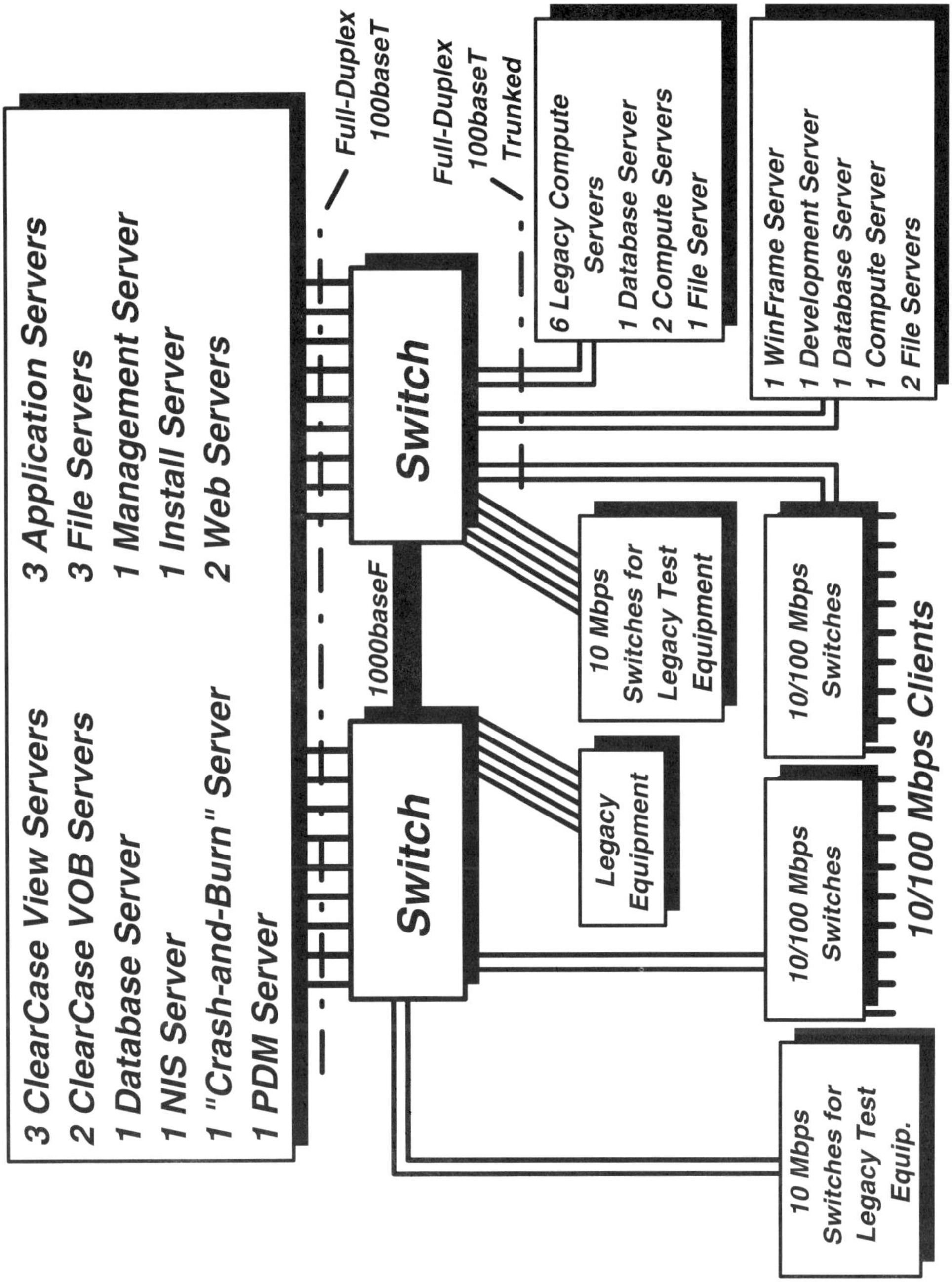

Figure 17-5 HP Spokane's RAPTOR R&D and PCA Subnet

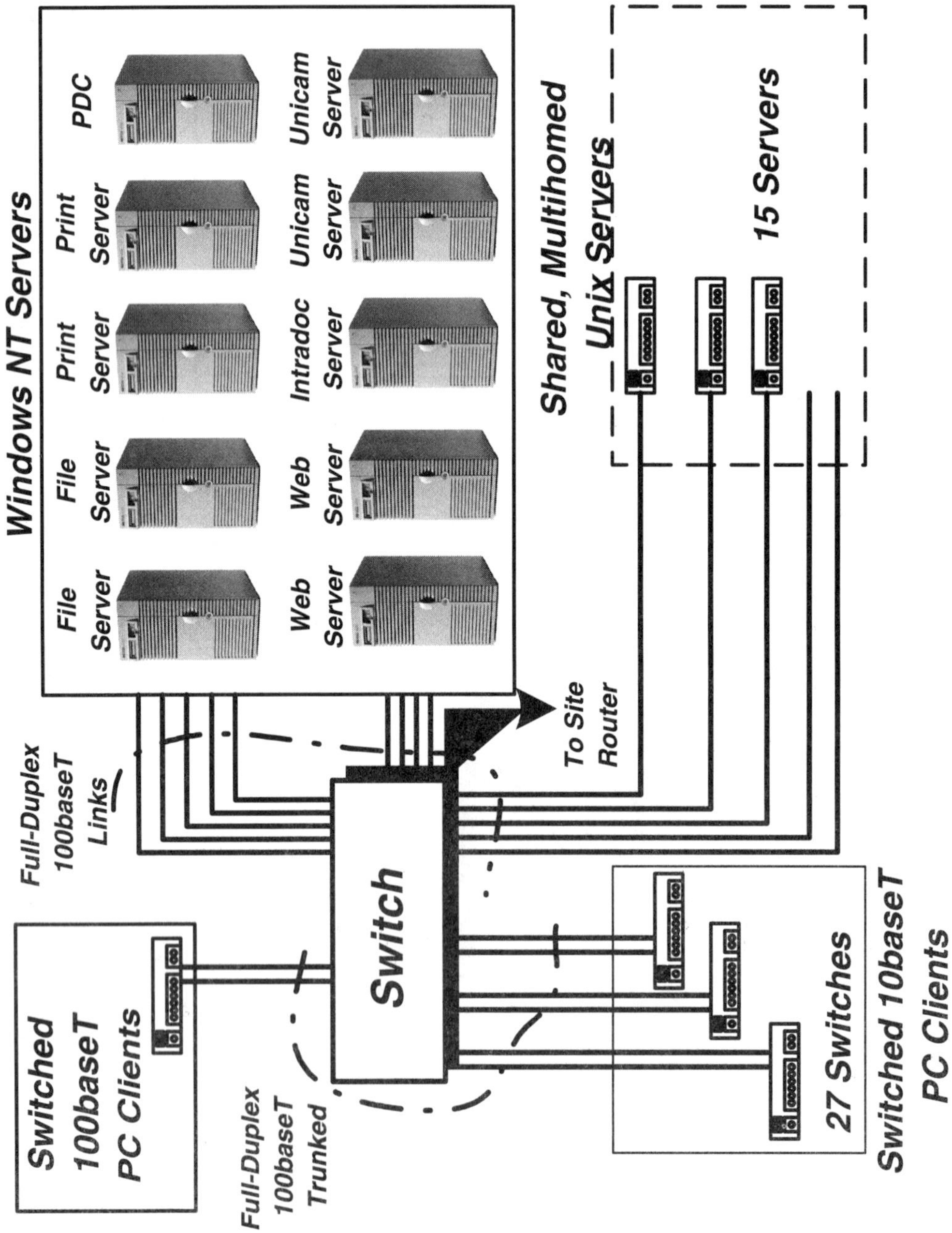

Figure 17-6 The RAPTOR Project's PC Subnet

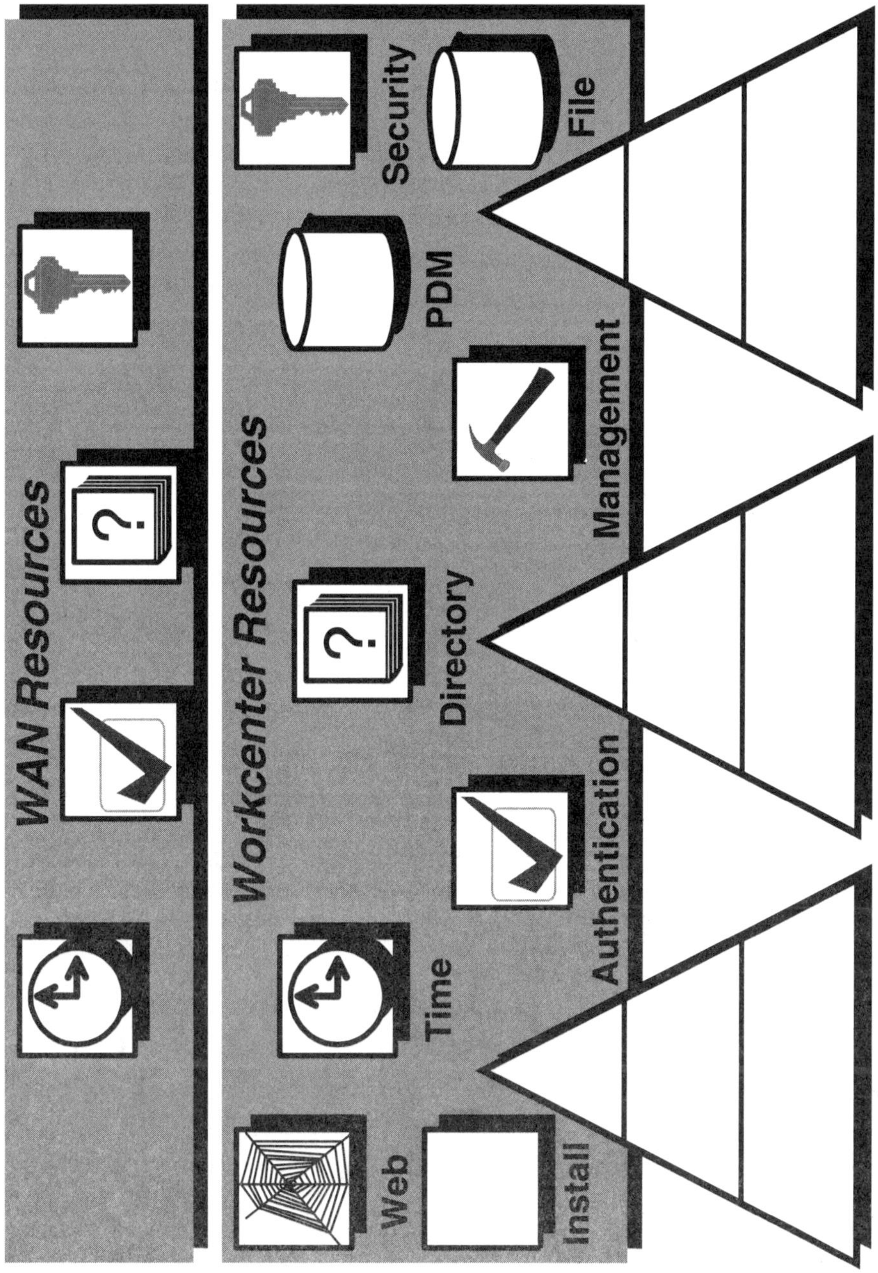

Figure 17-7 Resource Map for HP Spokane's RAPTOR Network

Figure 17-3 is Hewlett-Packard's Intranet, one of the largest in the world. Corporate IT services provides DNS, Windows NT primary domain controllers, Internet security, and other global services that are essential to distributed operation.

The RAPTOR environment uses DNS for IP address to host name resolution. The RAPTOR designers wanted client systems to evenly distribute themselves among the available DNS servers on the site. A weekly job runs on each workstation that randomly selects a DNS server from a set of site-wide server weightings. Thus a client can dynamically tip the odds towards a more responsive name server.

One of the essential shared services in both the WAN and workcenter environment is Network Time Protocol, or NTP, which is used for time synchronization. NTP is a hierarchical arrangement of time servers and clients into layers, or "strata". Stratum one time servers synchronize to atomic clocks; stratum two servers synchronize to stratum one servers and among themselves. The HP Intranet contains a number of stratum three servers that sites may synchronize with. HP sites are expected to establish as many stratum four time servers as they feel are necessary. These time servers poll one or more stratum three servers and use a sophisticated algorithm to average the results, factoring in transit and processing time. Within the Spokane site the stratum four time servers broadcast time packets rather than polling clients individually. Broadcast clients, the majority of systems at the site, use the same sophisticated algorithms to deduce the correct time from information received from stratum four servers. Thus all systems at the Spokane site are synchronized within the limits of the NTP protocol.

17.4 RAPTOR Hardware Architecture

The RAPTOR team replaced the old NFS clusters with stand-alone workstations and dedicated servers. A general server philosophy was adopted with the following points:

> Whenever possible, servers should be dedicated to a single task. A 'combined' server may experience destructive interference, adversely affecting performance to all users of the server resource. Dedicated servers may be tuned to best support the resource they are providing. Failure of a single "combined" server makes multiple resource unavailable to client systems.[7]

Four categories of RAPTOR servers are defined:

- Application servers will be optimized for read-only I/O and storage capacity. They contain and distribute entire applications and utility programs for execution on local clients.
- File servers are optimized for read/write I/O and storage capacity. They contain and distribute user data and project data.
- Compute servers have CPU horsepower with potentially larger bundles of user memory. They will typically be used to perform large computations in batch mode.

7. RAPTOR project web page, "RAPTOR Hardware: Server Philosophy".

- Database servers combine file server and compute server features. They are able to support large amounts of I/O, but also handle random indexing and sorting computations that drain CPU and memory resources.
- Management servers are dedicated to management software, like NIS, DNS, NTP, OpenView network management, Ignite-UX, and software distribution.

Each of these servers is an HP D-Class (currently D390) two-way server system. Characteristics of this system are shown in Table 17-1.

Table 17-1 Basic RAPTOR Server Building Block

HP D390/2	*Description*
CPU (1 or 2)	PA-8200 @ 240 MHz
RAM	At least 1.0 GB
Two internal disks	9.1 GB each, mirrored
Three 100baseT interfaces	R&D subnet, MFG subnet, and server backbone
NFS IOPS	5000 estimated
SPECint_rate95	230 estimated
SPECfp_rate95	300 estimated
TPM	11,000
SPECweb96	4017

Disk storage capacity is added to the server with Hewlett-Packard's AutoRAID disk arrays, a form of adaptive RAID array that moves data between RAID 0/1 and RAID 5 depending on access patterns. Active data is kept in RAID 0/1 for maximum performance, while less active data is kept in RAID 5 for less storage overhead and lower cost.

This array provides hot swappable disk mechanisms, redundant controllers, redundant power supplies and fans, as well as battery backed write cache. Each array chassis holds up to twelve disk mechanisms. The usable storage in the AutoRAID array is scalable to a maximum of 37.8 GB using 4.3 GB disk mechanisms, 82.3 MB using 9.1 GB disk mechanisms, and 166.4 GB using 18.1 GB disk mechanisms. RAPTOR file and application servers use twelve 18.1 GB disks in the AutoRAID array.

The combination of a low-cost, scalable computer system and a scalable storage solution yields a very flexible hardware building block for use in the RAPTOR environment. Having a single hardware solution allows the RAPTOR project to stockpile spare parts and simplify administrative procedures.

17.5 RAPTOR Operating Environment

The RAPTOR system administrators support one thousand user accounts, six hundred client systems, and more than twenty-four servers. This support is provided by six system administrators. The goal in the RAPTOR environment is to centralize as many of the system-management activities as possible: the administrators cannot afford to log into every machine to perform maintenance tasks.

System Installation The old system-installation procedure in which the administrator attempted to consistently customize the systems had grown to an eight-hour manual process. Without automated tools, the results were seldom as consistent as desired. The new installation and configuration process had to meet these requirements:

1. Automated, with minimal input required
2. Controlled from system being installed or from a remote administrative machine
3. Install multiple clients at once
4. Choose from a set of standard configurations
5. Decrease the installation time from eight hours to two

The solution for all of the installation requirements was found in the HP-UX Ignite-UX tool[8]. A small number of workstation clients was developed, which were differentiated by such things as operating system filesets and kernel parameter settings. The administrators specify system "personality" information, such as IP address and workstation class, and Ignite-UX does the rest.

The operating system used in the RAPTOR environment is HP-UX 10.20, which may be made Y2K compliant with the addition of a patch bundle. In upgrading from the old HP-UX 9.X systems, the image installation facility Ignite-UX is used to "cold-install" from scratch, ensuring that each client system is an identical "clone" of a system golden image for its class. There are several points in the installation where custom configuration scripts can run to further automate the customization process.

Server Configuration Each server system class has its own set of kernel parameters tuned for its particular activity set. These parameters affect soft link performance, dynamic buffer cache size, process virtual data space, the maximum number of open files per process, the total number of open files on the system, the number of inodes in the inode cache, and the maximum number of processes allowed per system. Variations in these HP-UX kernel parameters are enough to define performance differences in the five types of RAPTOR servers.

8. The Ignite-UX tool is available for download free from *WWW.Software.hp.com*.

All server systems have a standard system disk configuration, consisting of eight volumes in a logical volume manager group. Each server uses internal hot-swappable disk drives to store the system data, and the entire volume group is mirrored for increased reliability. The file system used is the JFS journaled file system, with the HP on-line-JFS product to allow disk defragmentation, file system resizing, and on-line snapshot backups.

Data on server systems are stored on a separate LVM volume group. This allows shorter system recovery time in the event of failure, because the system data is separated from the larger amount of served data. Because of mirroring and hot-swappable disk mechanisms, root disk failures can be repaired without impacting the server's users.

The workstations are dataless clients, with all volatile data stored on NFS servers. This allows image installation of the client systems without the need to back up user data first. Client systems are cloned with the Ignite-UX utility.

Software Installation Software installation on the HP-UX operating system is handled by a set of tools, collectively called Software Distribution Utilities, or SDU which are based on a POSIX standard. This set of tools allows installation and management of basic units called filesets and more complex collections of multiple filesets called bundles. Installation is performed from a software depot, which may be on hard media—CD-ROM or DAT tape—or from a depot over the network.

HP-UX[9] operating system functionality, products, software updates, and software "patches" are all provided in this common format. A database on each client system contains information about all installed software, both bundles and filesets. The information in this database may be manipulated with tools from the SDU suite and also queried either locally or remotely.

Software Maintenance Besides an automated system-installation process, there was a need for an automated software maintenance process. It is a fact of computer life that software upgrades and problem fixes are continually made available. Manually dealing with these upgrades and fixes on a large number of systems is a never-ending task.

In the predecessor environment, software maintenance ("patching") was done on an ad hoc, reactive basis—only when absolutely necessary. Since the driving force behind the RAPTOR infrastructure was to achieve higher consistency and reliability across the systems, a different approach was needed. To achieve this, the software maintenance process is both proactive and automated.

Backup Process The old backup strategy relied on HP's OmniBack I product and DAT[10] drives distributed throughout the computer room. Whenever a file restore request was made by a user, an administrator had to search through OmniBack log files and hundreds of

9. The SDU tools are also available for other operating systems, such as Windows NT.

10. Digital audio tape.

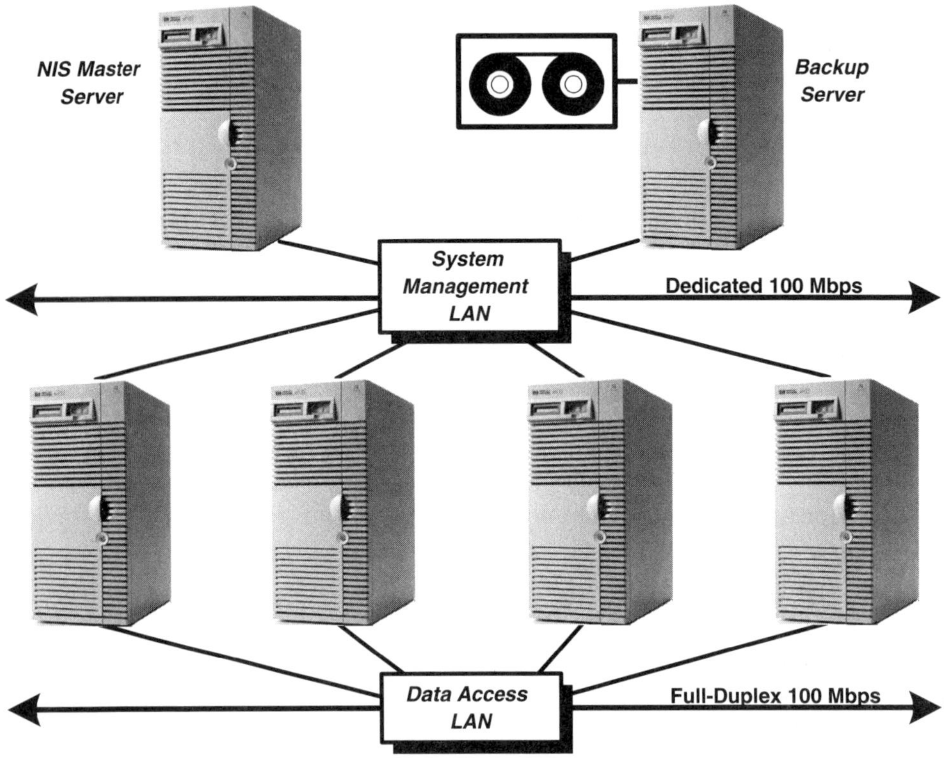

Figure 17-8 Dedicated System Management LAN for Backup and NIS

DAT tapes to find the requested data. Both the backup hardware and software were replaced in the RAPTOR environment to make this process more efficient.

First, the backup hardware now consists of four HP SureStore DLT tape libraries, with 48 slots each. This allows a month of backup data from the RAPTOR environment to be on-line, and up to two years worth off-line.With the dataless client-server model, the backup servers no longer need to reach over the LAN to grab Gigabytes of data from individual workstation clients.

Each backup server has dedicated 100 Mbps connections to the file servers that house the data. This provides sufficient speeds for the DLT library to keep the tape streaming. This arrangement provides backup rates of up to 20 Gigabytes per hour.

The second part of the picture is the new backup software OmniBack II version 2.5, which allows a hierarchical backup structure. A "manager of managers" allows a single application to control all backup servers and tape libraries. This has greatly shortened the amount of time involved in user file restoration requests.

When a request is made, an administrator determines which file server contained the data, then uses an OmniBack tool to determine which backup server has the file. The user's file is restored from the on-line DLT library, again using OmniBack. This has reduced most file restore operations to less than thirty minutes.

User Account Management Prior to the RAPTOR effort, the systems in the environment maintained independent user account information. Each administrator wrote his or her own set of scripts to manipulate the distributed user account files. Consistency was a problem with this approach.

The RAPTOR goal was to provide all users with a single login that was valid across the entire site. The team desired consistent Unix group membership information and the ability for user password changes to be valid across the entire site. The solution chosen for implementing those requirements was the Network Information System, or NIS.

The entire Spokane site is a single NIS domain, and the master server communicates to NIS slave servers over a dedicated 100 Mbps server backbone. The private management network allows the separation of NIS traffic from production data flow. All systems in the RAPTOR network are NIS clients, with most servers taking on NIS slave server responsibilities.

With multiple administrators updating NIS information, the RAPTOR team decided to use configuration management to control the NIS source files. Some of the files that are under configuration management control are automounter maps, */etc/group*, */etc/passwd*, */etc/netgroup*, */etc/services*, and */etc/mail/aliases*. Using NIS to distribute the common system administrative information allows all six hundred to clients see any changes to the files within seconds of the NIS "push" operation.

Performance Monitoring No client-server environment is complete without the ability to track system usage and adjust resources to meet changing needs. The RAPTOR system administrators make extensive use of system monitoring to provide trend analysis and real-time alarm notifications. Every client and server in the environment runs the HP MeasureWare performance data collection agent, which makes information from the instrumented HP-UX kernel available to external performance tools. This arrangement is detailed in Figure 17-9.

The HP PerfView graphical analyzer tool is used for graphical representation of system performance. The trend analysis can also be used to visualize gradual increases in system resource utilization, allowing adjustments that head off potential performance problems. A comparative analysis of two or more systems can reveal which system is experiencing the greatest resource constraint, helping to choose the best candidate for resource upgrades.

The real-time alarm capabilities of MeasureWare warn the administrators of client system performance problems even before the user has asked for support help. Specific MeasureWare "rules" are applied, and any exceptional events will trigger alarms. Automated responses to the alarms send electronic mail to the support team along with a Simple Network Management Protocol (SNMP) packet for the HP OpenView network management software.

System administrators receive the e-mail and use the monitoring information to track down the problem on the system in question. This proactive approach to problem resolution can

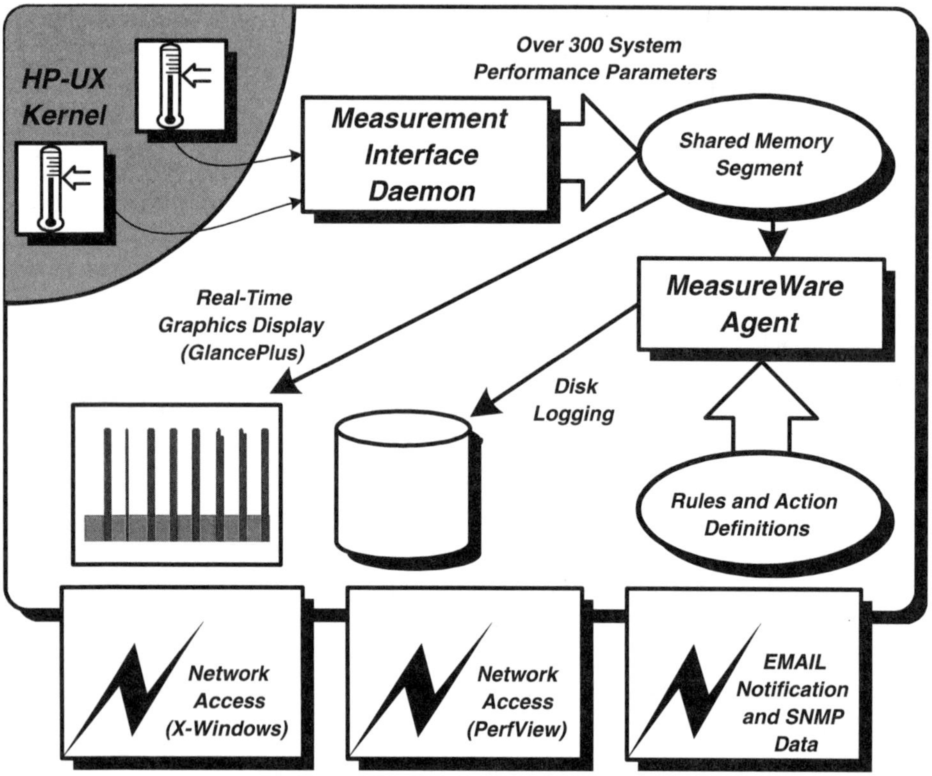

Figure 17-9 RAPTOR System Performance Monitoring

solve many problems before they result in user performance complaints. The user community has responded favorably to this approach to system administration.

In addition to the real-time monitoring of system performance, the RAPTOR environment is monitored by HP OpenView Service Reporter, which provides graphical performance trends and availability information. The information in the report is updated to an internal web page nightly. This information allows the system administrators to target servers that may be impacting user performance and reliability.

RAPTOR System Administration Procedures Much of the information in this chapter was gleaned from the RAPTOR project web site and Daniel Krantz's InterWorks presentation. One striking thing is that there is web-based documentation for system administration tasks like adding a user account to RAPTOR, changing a user name, moving a user's home directory between servers, and many others. These global procedures are well documented using web technology.

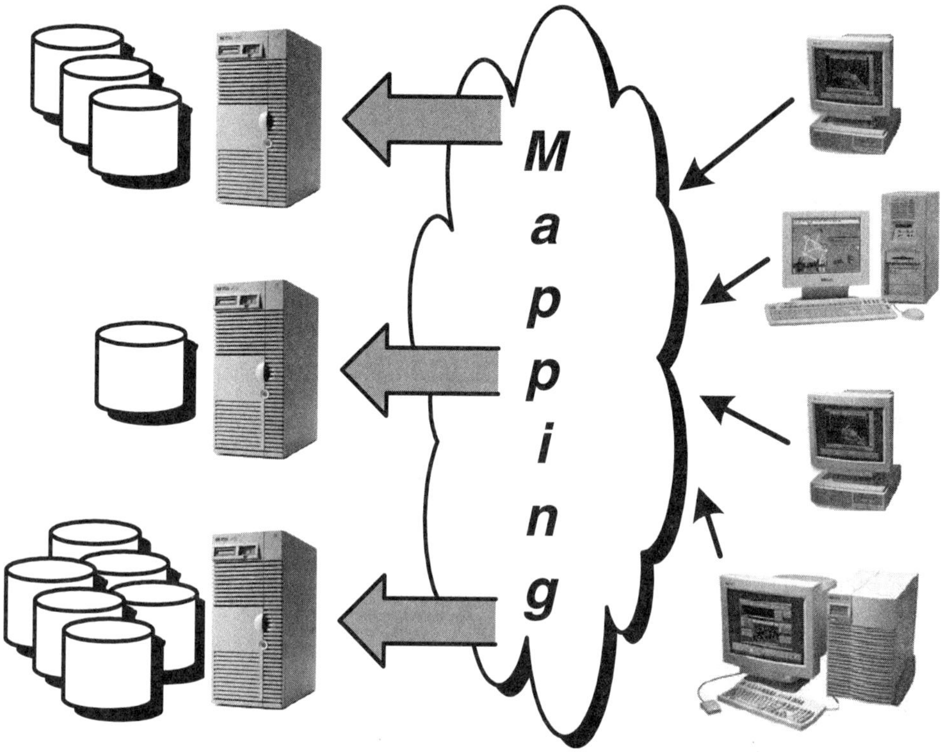

Figure 17-10 RAPTOR Global Accessibility Model Data Mapping

In addition to the system administration documentation, there are training pages for a variety of user types. There is a certain amount of on-line training available on the web pages, but there are also pointers to other training classes and information sources. Both the system administration community and the user community have a wide range of information available for their daily needs.

17.6 RAPTOR Data Sharing

The RAPTOR goal was to adopt a Global Accessibility Model (GAM) in which the same directory structure is presented to the end user, independent of which workstation they are using. Path names to disk-based resources are consistent across all workstations for this purpose. Furthermore, there is no need to know on which machine the data is physically stored.

In the old infrastructure, data was stored on the individual workstations. In order to create the GAM with NFS, multiple mount points would need to exist from every machine to every other machine. This creates dependencies on the order of $O(n^2)$ complexity, where n is the number of machines in the environment.

With six hundred systems, the number of links would approach 360,000—a number much too large to maintain. When machines are added to or removed from this type of environment, all of the machines must reflect the change. Worse yet, if a user powers off their system, all of the links from the other systems would be broken. Reliability suffers tremendously.

In the current RAPTOR environment, all volatile data, such as user home directories, project data, and e-mail are placed on high-availability file servers. The GAM is implemented with just a linear number of mounts, which yields *O(n)* complexity. The data on the file servers is "mapped" to the client systems, presenting a single, logical, consistent view of the data—which is independent of its location. A schematic representation of the mapping process is shown in Figure 17-10.

17.6.1 RAPTOR Benefits from Client-Server Data Storage

The client-server storage of data, coupled with the dataless client systems, helps the RAPTOR environment meet its objectives. According to the RAPTOR environment's designers, the client-server data storage approach helps.

Increase Reliability The internal disks of local workstations contain many single points of failure (SPOF). With file servers, however, most of these SPOF instances are eliminated. The computer room where the servers are housed is on UPS supplies to protect from power surges and outages. This also allows the client systems to mount the NFS file system asynchronously without major fear of data loss.

Improve Consistency Each client workstation presents the same directory structure to the end user. With the order of magnitude reduction in the number of NFS links, the consistency goal is attainable. Directory name changes and workstation changes (name change, addition, and removal) no longer impact the other systems.

Enhance Performance The file servers have multiple network interfaces and direct connection to the high-performance network backbone. Previously data was sprinkled throughout the shared 10 Mbps network. Access to shared data is ten to twenty times faster.

Minimize Productivity Loss If a user's client system should experience a hardware failure, they could just log on to a different workstation and immediately resume work. Had the data been on the failed client, a time-consuming restore operation would be required and any subsequent changes from the time of last backup would be lost forever.

Faster System Backups A central file server is much easier to back up than a distributed client base. The network would be severely impacted during the distributed remote backup of multiple client systems. The length of time required for a nightly backup eats directly into the amount of time available for other nightly batch jobs, such as large-scale compilations.

Simplified Data Sharing The end user does not need to know which machine physically contains the data. The logical mapping is the same on all systems. This abstraction not only eliminates much frustration, but also enables system administrators to relocate data for load balancing purpose, without impacting the user community.

17.6.2 RAPTOR Data-Sharing Implementation

The previously described RAPTOR data-sharing environment uses the NFS automounter and indirect maps for its implementation. Automounter indirect mounting is used because of its flexibility and its friendlier bandwidth. Changes to the contents of an indirect automounter map are recognized immediately by the automounter, whereas with direct mapping, the changes are not recognized until the automounter is restarted.

The network friendliness comes from the fact that client systems only mount those directories that are being accessed and automatically unmount unused directories. The indirect behavior can have a disadvantage—the absence of expected directories can confuse end users. This disadvantage may be addressed by using a hybrid approach: creating soft links in the local file system that point to automounted directories.

The hybrid links are created by an automated system maintenance script called "auto_links", which runs several times a day on each system. The script parses the NIS distributed automounter maps[11] and builds the necessary symbolic links to the mount points controlled by the automounter. If an incorrect link is found, it is fixed. If the link conflicts with a local file or directory, the local instance is granted precedence. This allows both local and remotely located packages to coexist in the same directory.

RAPTOR Data-Sharing Security The Unix operating system identifies users and processes by a combination of User ID (UID) and Group ID (GID) values. These identifiers are also used to protect disk-based resources like files and directories from unwanted access or to enable access for members of the same group. Part of any Unix data-sharing environment must be a scheme to assign UID and GID values to protect user and system data.

The UID value is uniquely associated with an individual user's login account. The RAPTOR project has goals for group security in the environment:

- Enable convenient file access between co-workers rather than restrict data sharing
- Provide write protection for files and directories as needed
- Minimize accidental file deletion or access to sensitive data

In addition to the goals for simplifying data sharing, a group allocation strategy is used, with three elements:

- The user's base group
- Any additional group memberships

11. This is a fairly common technique in Unix-land. A system administrator uses NIS to distribute global data, and the client system determines how to best use the data.

• The Unix UMASK filter

A combination of all three of these elements gives the user the ability to control access based on their team's business model. Unix files and directories have sets of read (**r**), write(**w**), and execute (**x**) permissions for the file's owner, the file's group owner, and "all others" or "other". File access is determined by checking the user's UID against the file's owner permissions field, the user's base group, and other groups that the user belongs to against the file's group permissions field, and finally the file's "others" access field.

The base group is the default group, specified in the NIS database, that the user resides in after logging on. The default base group for the RAPTOR environment is GID twenty, with the name "users". A user account can be granted access to additional groups as defined in the NIS database, but HP-UX 10.X limits the total number of groups for any one user to sixteen. The default base group for a user may be set differently if business needs are met.

The UMASK permissions filter affects the initial value of the file mode (permission) bits for newly created files. Initial file permissions are filtered by the UMASK filter, which turns off any bits in the file permissions that are set in UMASK. The RAPTOR environment sets a default global value for UMASK of 022, resulting in a default file permission of **rwxr-xr-x** for new files. This default value of UMASK may be overridden by the user in his personal Unix shell profiles.

The file permission scheme used by the RAPTOR environment is shown in the following table.

Table 17-2 RAPTOR Group Permission Strategy

Base Group "Users"	*Base Group Not "Users"*
The user creates a file that can be read by anyone. With the default UMASK of 022, new file permissions are **rwxr-xr-x.**	A group who wants to share write access to common data, but the rest of the user community should have read-only access. With a base adjustment and a UMASK of 002, new file permissions are **rwxrwxr-x.**
A user would like to create files that anyone else can modify. With a UMASK of 000, new file permissions are **rwxrwxrwx.**	A group that wants to restrict read access to their data so that only their group can see the files. With a base group adjustment and a UMASK of 027, new file permissions are **rwxr-x---.**

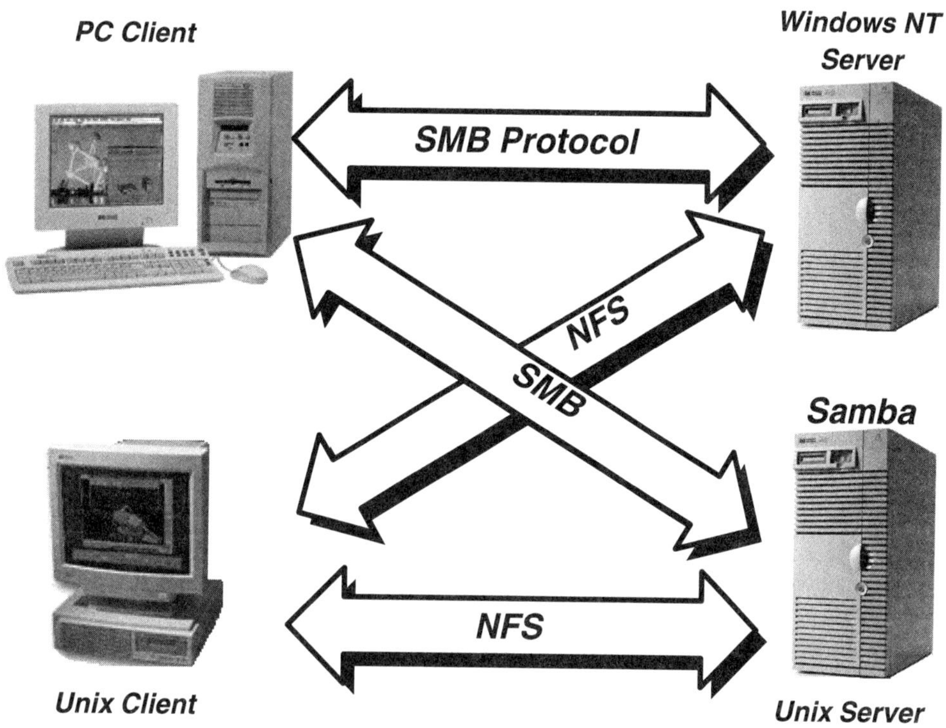

Figure 17-11 RAPTOR Shares Data Between Unix and Windows NT

RAPTOR Data Sharing with Windows NT The primary Windows NT data interoperability tool in the RAPTOR environment is provided by Samba. Samba translates a Unix (or other) file system to SMB semantics for Windows 3.1/95/98/NT clients.

The Samba server validates a user against the remote Windows NT primary domain controller. For PC users who have logged into a valid NT domain, it is not necessary to enter a second logon name or password when connecting to Samba shares. To the user, this provides transparent access to Unix file systems.

After the authentication is completed, the NT account is mapped to a Unix account of the same name. On some shares the user may be forced to connect under a specific group, but by default the user will be mapped to the group specified for them in the Unix NIS database. If the user does not have a user account, they will be mapped to a limited-access account.

The RAPTOR environment Samba servers are configured to not force a Windows NT browser election and to not be WINS servers, presumably to limit broadcast activity. One of the issues that must be dealt with is the difference between Unix and Windows NT file naming case. The SAMBA servers in the RAPTOR environment are configured to properly map character case between Unix and Windows NT.

A user wishing to access his Unix home directory from a Windows NT PC need only map a network drive to *samba**login*, where *login* is the combined Unix/NT login account name. This is automatically enabled for every user who has a RAPTOR Unix account and a Windows NT domain account. The data-sharing environment is shown in Figure 17-11.

Along with the standard user shares, a number of restricted shares are available globally. The access to those shares might be restricted on a group or even a user basis, depending on the share contents.

17.7 RAPTOR Application Environment

The RAPTOR application environment provides user access to the tools required for their daily jobs. The basis for the application desktop environment on the Unix client systems is the Common Desktop Environment, or CDE, which is a standard part of HP-UX 10.20. In addition to the CDE desktop's common services, access is provided to a set of RAPTOR "invocatables", which are specially encapsulated applications.

17.7.1 RAPTOR Invocatables

Applications in the RAPTOR environment are "wrapped" into a standardized package called an "invocatable". Invocatables were developed to ensure consistent application behavior from user machine to machine, dynamically generate the required application environment without the need for massive user profiles, and be transparent to the end user. Invocatables provide the following benefits:

- Centralized logging of all application behavior on site
- Automatic error notification to support staff
- Filtering of confusing warning messages
- Simple license management if not provided by application vendor
- Verification of hardware and OS compatibility
- Verification of software dependencies
- Verification of colormap availability
- Checking for other running instances
- Limitation of core dump size
- User-controlled multiple versions
- User-controlled color usage

An invocatable is a wrapper around the application that provides the above-listed benefits. There are automated tools to deal with RAPTOR invocatables, including a "decision maker", to help decide whether or not to use the invocatable facility for a given application, and an automated invocatable builder, in the form of a JAVA enabled web-based application.

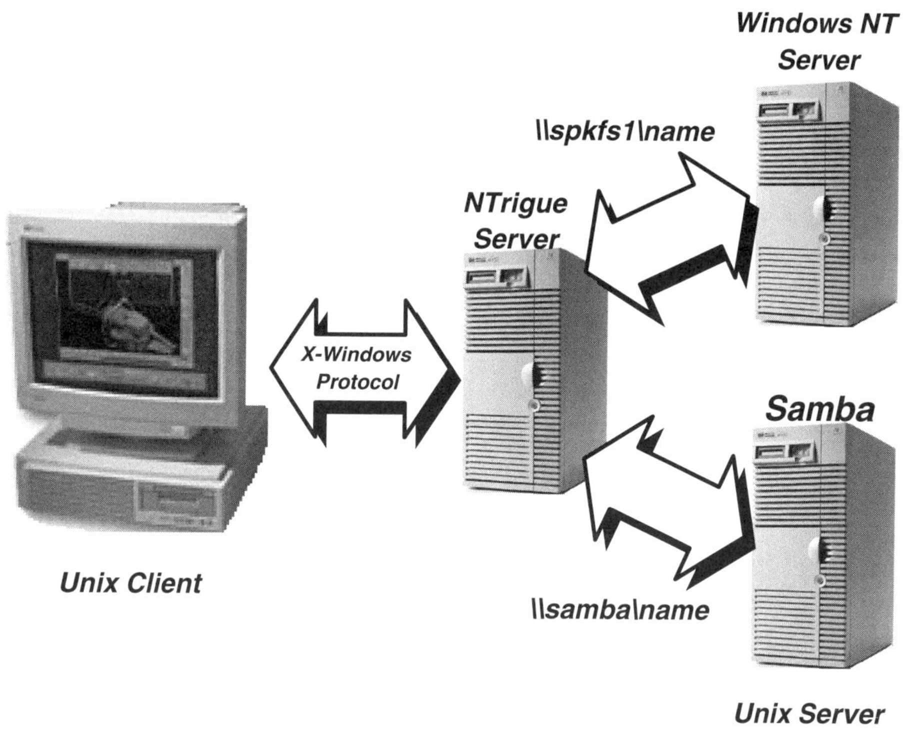

Figure 17-12 RAPTOR Application Sharing with NTrigue

RAPTOR Application Sharing with Windows NT Application interoperability between Unix and PC clients in the RAPTOR environment is provided by NTrigue[12], from Insignia Systems. NTrigue translates between Windows NT application windows and the Unix X-Windows system. In the RAPTOR network, NTrigue supplies access to standard sets of office applications like Microsoft Project, Microsoft Office 97, the Lotus SmartSuite, and ViSiO Professional.

The NTrigue applications run on a native Intel platform and access user data on either Unix file servers running Samba or on a Windows NT file server via a standardized set of paths. This data sharing is shown in Figure 17-12. Administration of NTrigue may be handled via NIS. The product may also authenticate Windows NT users via NIS and provide NIS to primary domain controller synchronization.

12. The NTrigue product technology has been sold to Citrix Systems Inc., which produces a product called "MetaFrame". See *WWW.Citrix.com* for details of the MetaFrame product.

17.7.2 The RAPTOR CDE Desktop

Part of the application environment is a set of standard configuration files that are placed in the user's home directory. These files include the user's shell profiles and the configuration files for the behavior of CDE. The standard RAPTOR system administration procedures list settings for these files, and tools exist to generate skeleton configurations with default values in place.

CDE provides application integration services, including messaging, file types, user menus, drag-and-drop actions, and a set of multiple workspaces to help the user manage the desktop. The RAPTOR CDE desktop provides the user with access to standardized tool sets like e-mail, SharedX (allows X-Windows to be displayed on multiple clients simultaneously), Netscape Navigator for web-based activities, and NTrigue. The users may configure their desktops to meet the needs of their daily jobs, choosing from the sets of invocatables and standard tools provided by the RAPTOR Common Operating Environment (COE).

17.8 RAPTOR Project Results

There is no better way to evaluate the success of the RAPTOR project than to compare its results with the original goals, which were to:

- **Increase reliability**—There has been a sixty-nine percent decrease in end-user downtime.
- **Simplify data sharing**—Data has been consolidated from six hundred separate locations to five, a two order of magnitude reduction in complexity.
- **Improve consistency**—In the previous environment, users had an average of ten accounts, with some individuals having as many as eighty. Each user now has one sitewide account, a one to two order of magnitude reduction in complexity. The site has gone from over five hundred different workstation configurations to five strictly defined classes (General, General+, ClearCase, ClearCase+, and Manufacturing), a two order of magnitude reduction.
- **Enhance system performance**—The ability to easily adopt new technology into the RAPTOR environment has provided an order of magnitude increase in performance. The network infrastructure went from shared 10baseT to full-duplex, trunked 100baseT and some Gigabit Ethernet, a ten to twenty-fold improvement.
- **Reduce overall support cost**—The RAPTOR project resulted in a ten percent cut in the cost of services provided to its users.

By anyone's measure, particularly in the eyes of the RAPTOR users, the original project goals have been met and benefits continue to accrue.

> "RAPTOR is an HP-UX 10.X roll-out that offers a 10X improvement across the entire infrastructure, with a 0.10X price cut."

To summarize, let's once again quote Daniel Krantz:

> "A chaotic computing infrastructure can be re-engineered into a first-class productivity vehicle for its user community. We combined credibility-building project management fundamentals with a divide and conquer approach to the technical problems. We have positioned Unix systems for the next evolution in computing technology. With renewed faith in their Information Technology group, our engineers can now focus on the innovative product development and manufacturing that will propel us into the next millennium[13]."

13. From *Rebuilding a UNIX Infrastructure*, Daniel Krantz, Proceedings of the InterWorks '98 Conference and Exhibition, page 685

CHAPTER 18

Afterword: What Is Next in Workgroup Architecture?

There is much debate today about what technology is going to "take over" the world of computing. Anyone who has been around the computer industry for long enough has seen the latest and greatest claims for the new technologies come and go several times. Once the hype surrounding a new technology has worn off, reality sets in, and we all must find ways to implement real solutions from the surviving technologies.

Each time this cycle begins, we are told that there will be a clear winner, the one remaining technology, reigning supreme. So far, this has not happened with anything near the frequency that is predicted—let us hope it does not. The computer industry has seen intense competition between tools and technologies on any number of occasions: CISC versus RISC, Pascal and Modula-II versus COBOL and FORTRAN, the Unix GUI wars, object-oriented languages versus nonobject implementations, token ring versus Ethernet, the web browser wars, thick versus thin clients, and on and on.

What we have to do as solution designers is evaluate each new technology, adopt it when it meets the needs of our users in terms of cost and functionality, plan the implementation, implement the plan, and then start the process all over again. In this sense, solutions based on older technology give way to solutions built from newer technology, and we hope they are built on a stable foundation of experience. This is the nature of change and adaptation (adoption) of new technological tools.

Our charter as systems engineers is to choose the right tool for the right job, in spite of hype and the newest marketechture[1] in the industry. The good news is that today's competition

1. This is an artificial architectural creation, born of marketing hype, high-level slideware, with very little practical content. Greg Astfalk of Convex Computer likes to say, "The content value of a slide is inversely proportional to the number of colors used", which is a concise summary of the problem, as facetious as it sounds.

and today's new technologies help to drive us all forward in our understanding and methodologies—the hype keeps us interested and motivated. But instead of one clear technological winner, we adapt and blend multiple technologies into available tools for our solutions "bag of tricks".

In the final analysis, if we do this in the right way, with the right amount of feedback to our technology vendors and the right amount of input from our users, there is one clear winner—the computer industry as a whole. As a result of this whole process, we get to keep our jobs, learn new things, and continue on.

18.1 Workgroups Trends for the Future

The rapid change in the computer industry is legendary. Where else can you buy a hardware product that is superseded by one that is twice as fast and costs less—all in the span of less than eighteen months, er, a year, oops, nine months? If only the software quality portion of the equation would balance.

Predicting where we will be in the future as workgroup designers is a dangerous thing for credibility's sake, but I don't tend to shy away from risk. So, here we go.

18.1.1 Networking Infrastructure

Networking bandwidth will continue to escalate, right up to the limitations of a single fiber. When that is reached, trunking (or new approaches) will continue to increase the parallel bandwidth between switches and computer systems. The network will continue to keep pace with the compute capabilities of the CPU.

As client system performance increases, the desktop connection must follow. Shared physical media for networks has given way to dedicated segments and increases in bandwidth are outstripping the capabilities of copper media to run reasonable distances. We may very soon end up with fiber to every desk, just to keep up with the increase in available client compute power.

With both WAN and LAN speeds increasing and the physical breadth of a LAN growing, the traditional lines between those two portions of the network hierarchy are starting to blur. I expect that trend to continue with the next generation of satellite communication poised to extend dial-up workgroup connectivity to any point on the earth. Maybe we will eventually end up with a wide local-area network (WLAN) or a whole earth area network (WEAN).

18.1.2 Hardware Architecture

The next-generation processor from Intel, IA-64, is based on Explicitly Parallel Instruction Computing (EPIC) technology, which is the next step in the progression that has led from CISC to RISC. It promises to continue the exponential growth of compute power beyond today's RISC processors. This means more powerful clients and servers for our workgroup environments and increasing demands on bus architectures and the network infrastructure.

We now have ccNUMA compute clusters, which can maintain cache coherency across hundreds of CPUs with a single copy of an operating system running the show. This solves, in part, the dilemma posed by Amdahl's law for bus requirements—what can you do when a bus will only support one or two CPUs? Look for the crossbar switch interconnect to be even more prevalent in future high-performance computer designs.

18.1.3 Operating Environment

Will there be a clear winner in the operating system arena? I don't believe so; Unix will continue to meet high-end needs with its stability, flexibility and functionality—Windows-based systems will continue to make inroads into traditional Unix markets and be the system of choice for IT professionals. But I have noticed a trend: both Unix and Windows NT are adopting interoperable services (or third parties are producing them), as customers demand a solution instead of a competition.

Although the crystal ball is murky in this regard, we can all hope for improvements in system administration tools for heterogeneous environments. The ability to manage complex client-server environments is still fertile ground for automated tools that can handle the tasks that are manual, repetitive, and less productive in nature. We can all keep our fingers crossed.

18.1.4 Data Sharing

Data sharing is still the primary focus of our workgroup, indeed enterprise, activities. As more and more companies become distributed or multinational, the need for secure, robust wide-area data sharing increases in importance. Because all monolithic organizations end up subdividing themselves into smaller units, outsourcing core incompetencies, and working with other distributed groups, the need for secure data sharing between different organizations will also continue to grow. Secure environments similar to DCE will be the rule, rather than the exception.

We cannot continue predictions without including JAVA, web browsers, and the Internet. This set of new technological tools has not yet hit its stride as a solution. The promise exists of a very powerful, flexible approach to sharing data across multiple platforms, a new set of tools for creating widely distributed client-server applications, and a new object-oriented paradigm for application development. What are we to make of all of the hype?

Of course the pundits would have us believe that everything will be completely different when we wake up tomorrow. My own belief is that this new approach will not displace the existing technologies for some time—there will certainly be a long transition period, if it is to happen at all. It is more likely that we will end up with a melding of technology once again.

18.1.5 Application Environment

This is probably the most difficult portion of the environment to predict, because it is the most flexible. As the capabilities of the compute environment grow, so too do the capabilities of the applications. Today we are solving problems that ten years ago nobody dreamed we could tackle. Look for this trend to continue, placing more demands on client systems and compute servers.

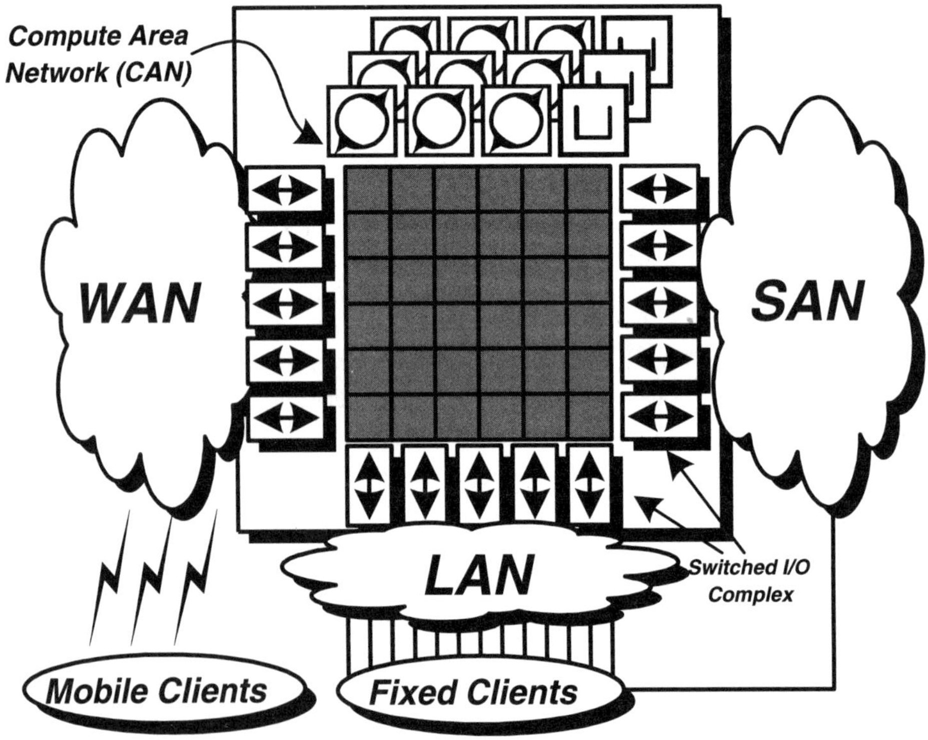

Figure 18-1 A Possible Future Workgroup Architecture

What new desktop paradigms can we expect? The jury is still out on the "active desktop" that melds web browsing interfaces with the more familiar icons, file managers, and local resources. One thing is certain, the client-server architecture, in its various forms will live on in tomorrow's applications.

18.2 A Future Workgroup Picture

Combining some of the technology mentioned in the previous predictions, a good dose of what is available today, and a little imagination, we can take a look at one possible architecture for a future workgroup. That vision is presented in Figure 18-1. Let's take a closer look.

First of all, we have noted Ethernet switches, fibre channel switches, crossbar switches, and compute-cluster interconnects (switched.) One thing that all of these components have in common is that they use switching to move data from point to point in a mesh of connections. While we currently have a range of transports, hardware, and bandwidths in use, it is not too far-fetched to imagine a common data-switching mechanism that can handle moving data between

CPUs, RAM, and I/O interfaces in the compute area network (CAN), as well as through the other networked components.

Another feature of our futuristic architecture is that network attached storage has been replaced by direct access, within the workgroup, to storage technologies in the storage area network (SAN.) This removes the intermediate file or data server from the data access chain except where translation or some other form of mapping is needed. Where clients need file serving capabilities, CPU and RAM resources may be reserved for the purpose.

The load-balancing service for the environment is charged with allocation of resources much like today's services. There, the similarity ends—what we really have is a dynamic resource allocation service (DRAS), which is capable of reserving one or more virtual computers on behalf of the client system's user and associated applications. The resources managed include operating system type, I/O devices, storage connections, data-translation services, application services, or other essential components from the workgroup resource pool.

The major difference between the LAN connections and WAN connections for clients is the use of different technologies to deal with the mobile versus the fixed nature of the client connections. The same resource allocation services are available to the mobile client as to the fixed client, allowing either fixed or remote clients to be presentation services (GUI) only or a fatter design if desired. Mobile clients will require slightly more resources than the fixed workgroup clients but will still have full capabilities through the DRAS layer.

The extra flexibility and dynamic configurability is not too different from what we have today, with a few extensions and improvements. And here our vision must end. Only time will tell if any of our predictions will come true.

APPENDIX A

A Simple Model for Managing Change in Your Environment

Very few people seem to realize it, but making changes to an operational environment is a very difficult thing to do without the proper planning. What will follow is an admittedly simplistic model of the change process, and some recommendations about managing the process of change. The intention is to introduce some useful mental models that can help with formulating or choosing more robust methodologies, and not to present an all-encompassing change-management system.

A.1 Observations About Change and the Migration Process

Experience in applying migration methodologies in real customer environments has yielded several important, but not surprising lessons:

- Planning is the most important part of any migration process.
- Solving environmental problems involves more that changing to new technologies.
- There will *always* be a transition period.
- Change is a continuous process.

While the first point would seem to be self-evident, it is truly astounding the number of projects that are underway and in trouble before any detailed planning is started. This is usually the point where I am called in. Once the wings are unbolted from the plane in midair, it is a difficult undertaking to reattach them.

The second point is also frequently overlooked. In addition to technology implementation, the plan must focus on organizational learning (skills and processes) and gaining "buyin" from the end-user community. The informal organization (Joe and Fred out in the parking lot) has negatively impacted the success of many a transition.

If attempts at planning have been made, one element that is invariably omitted is a period of transition from the old environment to the new. The planners seem to have a magical, mystical belief that one day they will come in to work and everything will have spontaneously transformed itself into the new order. In reality, there is almost always a period of time where at least parts of both environments must exist simultaneously.

The final point to make is that change is a continuous process. Technology and business needs are continually evolving at ever-increasing rates. While the technology adoption rate for different industries varies, any environment that remains static will quickly fall behind. Planning for continuous change in your environment is essential to success.

A.2 A Five-Step Migration Methodology

Our simple migration methodology consists of five steps:

- Develop a vision of the future
- Inventory the existing environment
- Build the transition plan
- Implement the transition plan
- Continue enhancing the environment

The first step in the methodology is to develop a vision of the future. Our group has established reference models, guidelines, and an interviewing process, which provide a framework for describing the future environment, processes, and necessary skill sets from a number of perspectives. Because each environment is unique, custom work is performed within the established framework for every separate environment.

Inventorying the existing environment is used to form a clear understanding of the current business processes and technologies before any changes are made. During this step, the organizations within the environment and the interviewers work together to assess the current state of the environment. Based on experience, the very act of assessing today's environment uncovers previously unknown information about the people, processes, and technologies involved, which are critical to the transition process.

Next comes crafting the transition plan. A complete transition plan may only be crafted when the differences between the current reality and the future vision are well understood. Some of the elements contained in a good transition plan are:

- A statement of objectives
- Technology, infrastructure, and organizational impacts
- Current and projected resource allocations
- The transition task list
- A task responsibility list
- A return on investment analysis

Implementing the transition plan involve crafting a schedule, charting the relationships between tasks, assigning responsibilities, and other necessary project-management activities. The time division between planning and implementation depends upon the complexity of the actions, the current state of the environment, available transition resources, and a number of other factors. In one migration example, the customer planned for one year to completely upgrade an eight hundred workstation software-development environment, taking only a single weekend to make the final change-over.

Once the set of changes is implemented, it is important to realize that the five-step process needs to begin again. The period of time between environmental migrations varies from industry to industry and customer to customer but may be viewed as a relatively constant process.

A.3 Mental Models of Change

In any complex situation, the tendency is to adopt a simple model of the situation and attempt to put it to use. Many organizations adopt a very simplistic model of the change process and drastically underestimate the complexity of their environment. The simplistic approach to change is "You just go from point A to point B". This is shown in Figure A-1. This simplistic approach to a complex problem has resulted in many failed migration attempts.

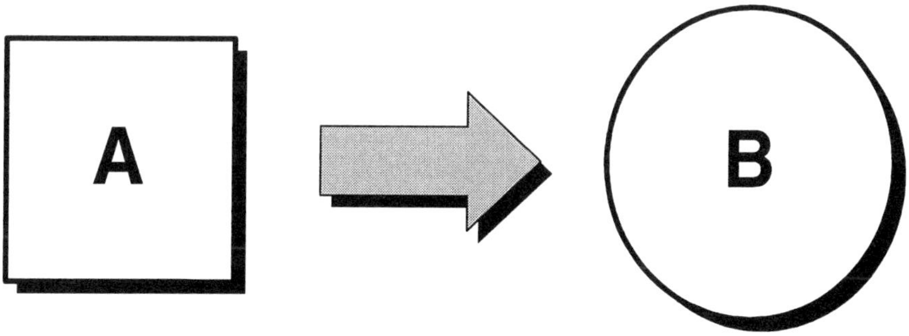

Figure A-1 An Overly Simplistic Model of Change

In the simplistic model of a change or transition, the current environment just magically gives way to the new order. A more realistic model involves the deconstruction of the current environment, a period of uncertainty (or chaos), followed by a reconstruction of the elements into the new environment. This is depicted in Figure A-2. Without careful attention to objectives, responsibilities, and timing, it is possible to disappear into the chaos cloud and never return. Using a better model can help in the visualization of what lies ahead.

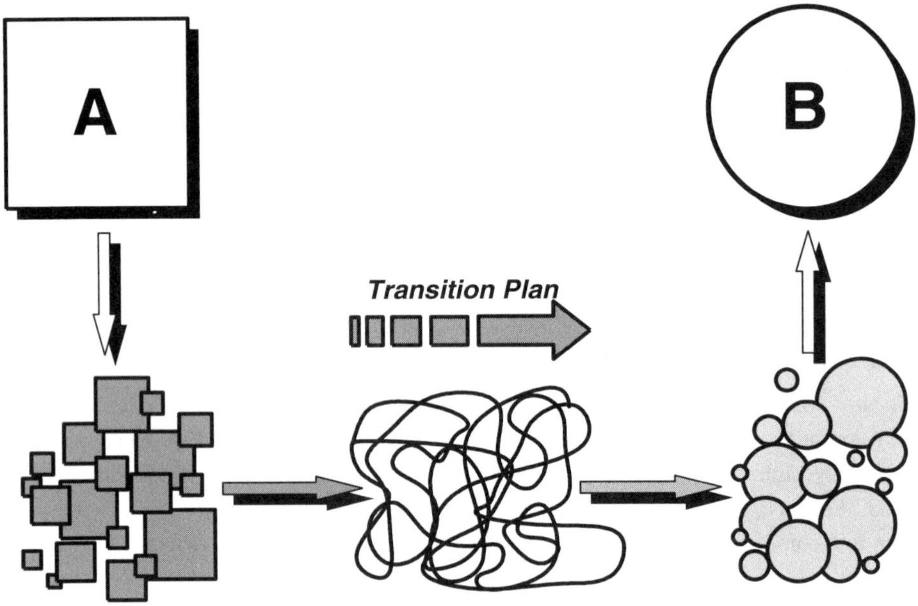

Figure A-2 A More Realistic Model of Change

The transition plan plays an important role in shortening or eliminating the period of chaos between the deconstruction of the old environment and the construction of the new environment. It provides a means to measure the success of the migration, to recognize new issues as they arise during the implementation, and to know when the migration is finished.

From a workflow process point of view, the transition plan will identify and schedule changes to current processes. The transition plan should also address the organizational needs of each constituency impacted by the migration. Different groups in the organization will have different concerns when migrating to a new environment. These needs are typically addressed by activities like individual meetings, classroom education, technology workshops, and change-management seminars.

An improved model of the transition process, then, contains the vision setting, the assessment of the current environment, the transition plan, and the periods of deconstruction and reconstruction. During the transition-planning process, it is important to realize that any environment undergoes constant change.

Planning for continuous change and adjusting activities and choices accordingly can make an organization more adaptable to new technologies as they become available. Linking today's migration activities to potential future changes can save effort and expense later on. This continuous process is shown in Figure A-3.

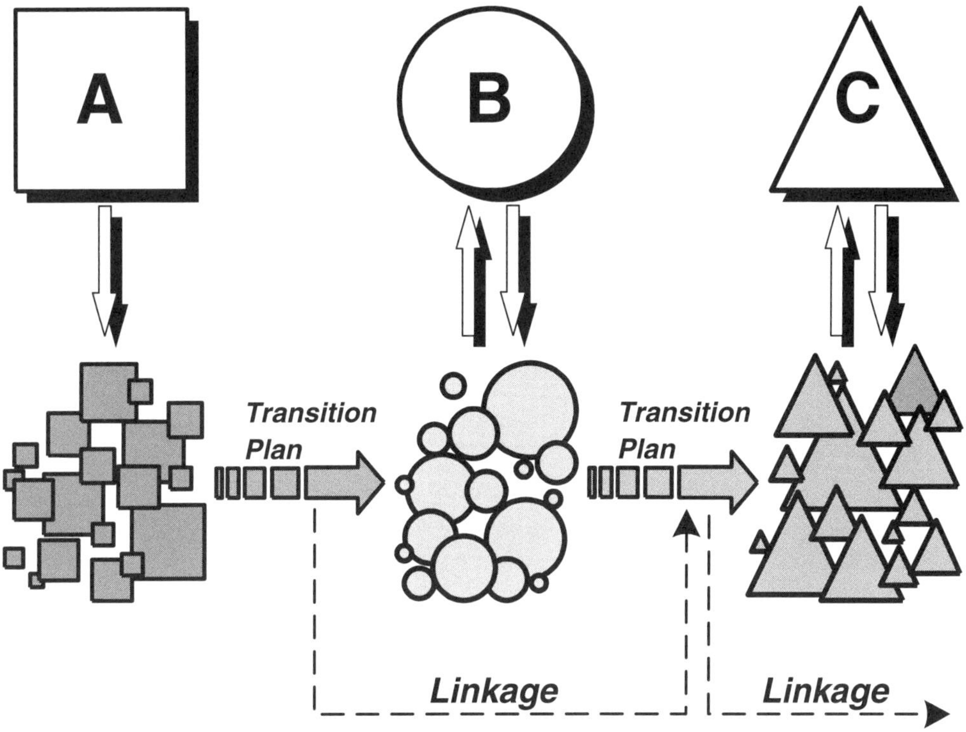

Figure A-3 A Model for Continuous Change

An example of this type of continuous approach applied to a real customer's networking technology migration is:

- Realizing that 10baseT networking over shielded twisted pair is inadequate for today's engineering server needs and a migration is needed
- Surveying the industry, seeing that several new networking technologies like ATM are becoming available on fiber-based transport, but are potentially too immature for extensive implementation
- Installing the more mature FDDI technology over fiber-optic cable as an interim approach
- Waiting for ATM to mature, but in the meantime Gigabit Ethernet technology becomes available at less cost, with less complexity and learning curve
- Moving to GbE when it becomes a pervasive technology, with no additional media changes to the physical medium

In this particular example, the customer's willingness to look ahead and link the current migration to future plans worked extremely well. Because the proper type (and correct number) of fiber-optic cables were installed, the transition to future technology was done at less expense by extending the life of the physical networking medium.

A.4 Managing Change in Your Environment Summary

We have just examined some of the issues involved with migrating from one environment to another and have presented a simple high-level model for visualizing and managing this migration. This simplistic model of change management and migration is not applicable in all environments. Certainly in extremely complex situations and "industrial strength" approach is necessary, but the hope is that the mental model and methodology may serve as a basis for more involved migration projects.

APPENDIX B

Network Data Flow Analysis for NFS Workgroups

Data flow analysis is a useful technique for locating potential network bottlenecks or design deficiencies. The technique presented here was developed by members of the Hewlett-Packard Technical Solutions Consulting group for performing environmental assessments in existing Unix workgroups or for designing new workgroup environments for our customers. While it should be considered a rule of thumb, the method has been validated on numerous occasions, in real-world customer environments.

Because of our team's focus on engineering environments and the current prevalence of Unix in those environments, the data flow analysis focuses on NFS behavior. The focus on NFS as the primary network data-sharing mechanism does not prevent a similar analysis from being done for other data-sharing methods. The information used for the analysis for NFS is readily available from both client and server systems, without resorting to network monitoring or network analyzers (sniffers.) Other data-sharing mechanisms might require initial data gathering on network traffic types and flow rates, using either a sniffer or higher-level monitors like RMON2 to identify the associated data flows.

B.1 NFS and the SPEC_SFS Benchmarks

NFS performance reporting is done officially with the SPEC System File Server (SFS) benchmark. There are currently two SFS benchmarks available: SPEC_SFS1 (SPECsfs93) and SPEC_SFS2. The SPEC_SFS1 benchmark is designed to test the throughput of file servers that run the NFS protocol version two (PV2) over UDP services. The SPEC_SFS2 benchmark is intended to test either NFS PV2 or the newest protocol, PV3, running over either UDP or TCP/IP connections.

Table B-1 NFS SPEC_SFS1 Operation Mixture

NFS PV2 Operation	SFS Mixture	Operation Description
Null	0%	No Operation
GetAttr	13%	Get File Attributes
SetAttr	1%	Set File Attributes
Root	0%	Find the Root of a File System
Lookup	34%	Get a File Handle
Readlink	6%	Get the Value of a Symbolic Link
Read	22%	Read Data from a File
Wrcache	0%	Not Used
Write	15%	Write Data to a File
Create	2%	Create a New File
Remove	0%	Delete a File
Rename	0%	Rename an Existing File
Link	0%	Create a New Hard Link to a File
Symlink	0%	Create a New Symbolic Link to a File
Mkdir	0%	Create a New Directory
Rmdir	0%	Remove an Existing Directory
Readdir	3%	Read a Directory Entry
Statfs	1%	Get File System Statistics

The SPEC_SFS1 benchmark, which is the one we will concentrate on, measures NFS performance in terms of NFS I/O operations per second (IOPS) and response time. The NFS server is subjected to higher and higher levels of client requests, until the file server can no longer keep up. At this point the server's response time will begin to increase, and throughput may decrease, as it attempts to satisfy the client requests. The test procedure is continued until the server's response time reaches the "unacceptable" level at fifty milliseconds.

Reporting an NFS server's performance entails a formal report format mandated by the SPEC committee. Not only are the server's IOPS rating and response time reported, but also the server's hardware configuration, the server's software configuration, and any special tuning done to the server to obtain the reported results. The official reports are available from the SPEC web site at *WWW.SPEC.org*.

B.2 The SPEC_SFS Benchmark Details

The SPEC_SFS1 benchmark attempts to simulate a client server environment using NFS by sending an artificial mixture of NFS requests to the NFS file server. Each one of the requests is an RPC call that causes remote action on the NFS server on behalf of the client making the request. The standard mixture of NFS (RPC) requests for the SPEC_SFS1 benchmark is shown in Table B-1.

The SPEC_SFS2 benchmark uses an RPC request mixture that is based on a survey of approximately one thousand NFS servers in different environments. This mixture promises to be a bit more realistic than the one used in SPEC_SFS1. Details on both benchmarks are available at the SPEC web site.

B.3 The SPEC_SFS1 Benchmark and NFS IOPS

The SPEC_SFS1 benchmark defines one thousand NFS IOPS to be one thousand RPC calls of the standard mixture. Each read and write request defaults to an 8 KB transfer, and the other RPC calls average 192 bytes. With the defined mixture, the average NFS IOP is 3.2 KB, which we will round to 4 kB to account for packet headers, variable length data, and other overhead.

Using this NFS "magic number", we can now calculate flow rates in terms of NFS IOPS through the workgroup and its components. We can also evaluate networking technology choices on the basis of the ability to carry NFS IOPS. The maximum possible number of NFS IOPS that a particular networking technology can handle is easily calculated by the following formula:

$$\text{Maximum theoretical NFS IOPS} = \frac{\text{N megabits}}{S} \times \frac{\text{1 byte}}{\text{8 bits}} \times \frac{\text{1 NFS IOP}}{\text{4096 bytes}}$$

This theoretical maximum value is often instructive, especially where there are improper performance expectations set about a particular networking technology and its NFS capacity. See some of the NFS design examples later in this appendix for real-world performance bottlenecks that have been found in customer workgroups.

An example calculation of this type, for 10 Mb/S Ethernet would yield:

$$\text{Maximum NFS IOPS} = \frac{10 \text{ megabits}}{S} \times \frac{1 \text{ byte}}{8 \text{ bits}} \times \frac{1 \text{ NFS IOP}}{4096 \text{ bytes}} \cong 300 \text{ NFS IOPS}$$

This calculation has interesting implications for anyone who might think that their five thousand NFS IOP server was going to perform with only a single 10baseT network interface. It is truly surprising how many times this type of situation is encountered.

You should notice that this calculation yields the *absolute maximum value*, since shared 10baseT Ethernet cannot reasonably be expected to deliver one hundred percent of the theoretically available bandwidth. Studies have shown that shared Ethernet can only be loaded to roughly thirty percent of capacity before interactive performance of X-windows clients begins to suffer. Keeping below the thirty percent loading factor yields an absolute maximum of one hundred NFS IOPS per shared 10baseT segment.

Before we go too far with this concept, let's pause for a reality check. The figures that we are calculating are rough, ballpark estimates that are useful for determining if there are gross design problems or mismatches in the workgroup environment. We adopt this method of calculating data flow because it is easily done without taking actual measurements of network traffic. In real environments, there are many variables, such as different RPC mixes that may skew results from our "magic number" approach.

Table B-2 shows calculations for the networking technologies first presented in Table 7-2. This type of data analysis can show us "where to look" in a complex environment for likely trouble points. In the final analysis, there really is no substitute for taking actual measurements with network probes, performance monitoring software, or other, more accurate means as verification.

B.4 Data Flow Analysis Methodology

To make a process or methodology useful, it must be reduced to repeatable, documented steps. Four basic steps have been identified over the course of many environmental assessments. A discussion of those steps follows.

B.4.1 Gather Network Configuration Information

The first step in data flow analysis is to draw an accurate picture of the current network topology, placing all network equipment like switches and routers, all computer systems, and all interconnection technologies on the drawing. Notes involving the speed, number, and configuration (trunked, half-duplex, or full-duplex) of each network segment are essential.

The diagram of the network can cover as much or as little of the network as is necessary to describe the area being analyzed. The pictures and information cover the bottom two layers

Table B-2 Networking Technology Data Rates

Networking Technology	*Theoretical Data Rate (Mb/S)*	*Maximum Usable Data Rate (MB/S)*	*NFS IOPS*[a]
10baseT Shared	10 Mb/S	0.38 MB/S @ 30%	93
10baseT Dedicated	10 Mb/S	1.13 MB/S @ 90%	276
100baseT Shared	100 Mb/S	3.75 MB/S @ 30%	916
FDDI	100 Mb/S	10 MB/S @ 80%	2441
100baseT Dedicated	100 Mb/S	11.25 MB/S @ 90%	2746
ATM OC-3[b]	155.52 Mb/S	19.44 MB/S	4594
100baseT Full Duplex	200 Mb/S	22.50 MB/S @ 90%	5493
ATM OC-12[c]	622 Mb/S	83.53 MB/S	18373
1000baseFX Full Duplex	2000 Mb/S	225.00 MB/S @ 90%	54,931
1000baseFX Trunked	6000 Mb/S	675.00 MB/S @ 90%	164,794

a. Calculations performed using maximum usable data rate, which takes into account loading factors.

b. Calculations for ATM must take into account that data is broken into 53 byte "cells" comprising 5 bytes of header and 48 bytes of data.

c. See "The WAN Link Speed and Capacity" on page 158 for an explanation of the "OC-NN" terminology.

(Network Infrastructure and Hardware Architecture) shown in Figure 5-11. Once the diagrams are complete, we can move to the next step.

B.4.2 Measure the Client System Needs

It is difficult to properly size an NFS file server or the intervening network infrastructure unless some bounds may be placed on the NFS loads generated by client systems. The NFS IOPS per client system have profound effects on the number of client systems per network segment, the size of the NFS file server's "large network pipe", and the configuration of the server hardware.

Fortunately, there are some simple ways to measure the number of NFS RPC calls and, therefore, the number of NFS IOPS being generated by the client systems. The Unix operating system provides a command, *nfsstat*, that provides the number of client or server NFS RPC calls and the RPC mixtures. This command makes it fairly easy to measure the client NFS activities without resorting to network analyzers.

There are several approaches to using the *nfsstat* command to measure client NFS IOPS:

Running Average The *nfsstat* command can be used to zero the counters containing the RPC counts. To obtain an average number of NFS IOPS per second per client, the counters are zeroed at the beginning of the work week and totals are taken at the end of the work week. Dividing the total number of RPC calls by the number of seconds in the work week yields the average number of NFS IOPS per second for a given client system. The average number should be determined for a wide range of clients to account for usage variations in the environment. You should also realize that the average number is less useful than measurements that yield a peak number of NFS IOPS per second. This is because the peak readings will better represent the maximum demand that a client can place on the network at any one time.

Time Offset Peak Measurements The *nfsstat* command can be run in a script that zeroes the counters, sleeps for a fixed period of time, dumps the counters, calculates an NFS IOP per second value, and then resets the counters. Again, measurements should be taken on a range of client systems. This technique yields more useful information than the previous method in terms of peak NFS IOP per second readings.

Operational Mixture Measurements This method uses *nfsstat* to measure the number of NFS IOPS for a given operation such as reading a drawing or model, saving a document, or other common client system operations. Using the elapsed time for each operation, the peak number of NFS IOPS generated per client can be calculated. This method is best used in relatively simple environments where extended measurements are not required.

Table B-3 contains some of the basic, rule-of-thumb estimates for client system NFS IOPS. Note that these numbers are just rough estimates, there is no substitute for actually measuring the client system activities.

B.4.3 Perform Dataflow Analysis

Once the measurements of client system NFS IOPS is complete, the data flow analysis, can begin. Let's say that we are constructing a workgroup, centered around NFS as the data-sharing mechanism, that is to have two hundred Unix and PC clients. Twenty of those clients are to be documentation workstations, fifty are to be electrical CAD simulation, and the remaining one-hundred and thirty are to be software engineering stations.

If we assume worst-case NFS IOP generation, using our "standard" table, we would need an NFS server and network infrastructure that could sustain four thousand seven hundred and sixty NFS IOPS, or a total of 19.5 MB/S. This figure is valid if everyone in the workgroup generates the "standard" worst-case NFS IOP values and attempts their most demanding tasks all at once. For both existing and new configurations, we should actually measure client NFS IOP activity to verify our numbers.

Table B-3 "Typical" Unix Client NFS IOP Numbers

Description of Environment	*NFS IOPS per Client*
PC and Office Automation	1-3 NFS IOPS
Light Unix (Interactive)	3-8 NFS IOPS
Intense Unix Workstation (CASE, MCAD)	10-20 NFS IOPS
Extremely Heavy Unix Workstation (Simulation)	25-40 NFS IOPS
NFS Abusers (Software Build)	50-125 NFS IOPS

This worst-case scenario is unlikely behavior, but the safety margin for the design (and any room for growth) depends on the accuracy of the per-client NFS IOPS measurements and the NFS operation mixture for the workgroup. If accurate measurements are available, then the data flow analysis may be fine-tuned to match reality. Otherwise, to maintain acceptable performance levels and provide for growth, we must overconfigure the network and server hardware.

B.4.4 Recommend Adjustments to Network and Server Configurations

A diagram of this example is shown in Figure B-1. Note that for the two classes of Unix workstations with heavy NFS IOP traffic, a dedicated 10baseT switch port would suffice or the peak NFS IOP traffic. For the documentation workstations, it may be possible to put several client systems per switch port without noticeable performance impacts. The server-to-switch connection could be a single full-duplex 100baseFX link, unless the redundancy of a second link is desired.

Depending on the necessary storage capacity, the fibre channel disk interface should provide sufficient interface capacity to handle several large disk arrays. In addition to the growth room, the throughput also should be adequate. We will not go any further into the details of this example; hopefully you can see the general approach and will be able to apply it in your efforts.

B.5 Examples of Problem NFS Configurations

In eight years or so of doing environmental assessments and using data flow analysis on NFS based workgroups, I have accumulated quite a few examples of problem configurations. I always try to realize that computer system structure follows the structure and personality of the organization that funds, manages, and dictates their use. So these configurations are seen as evo-

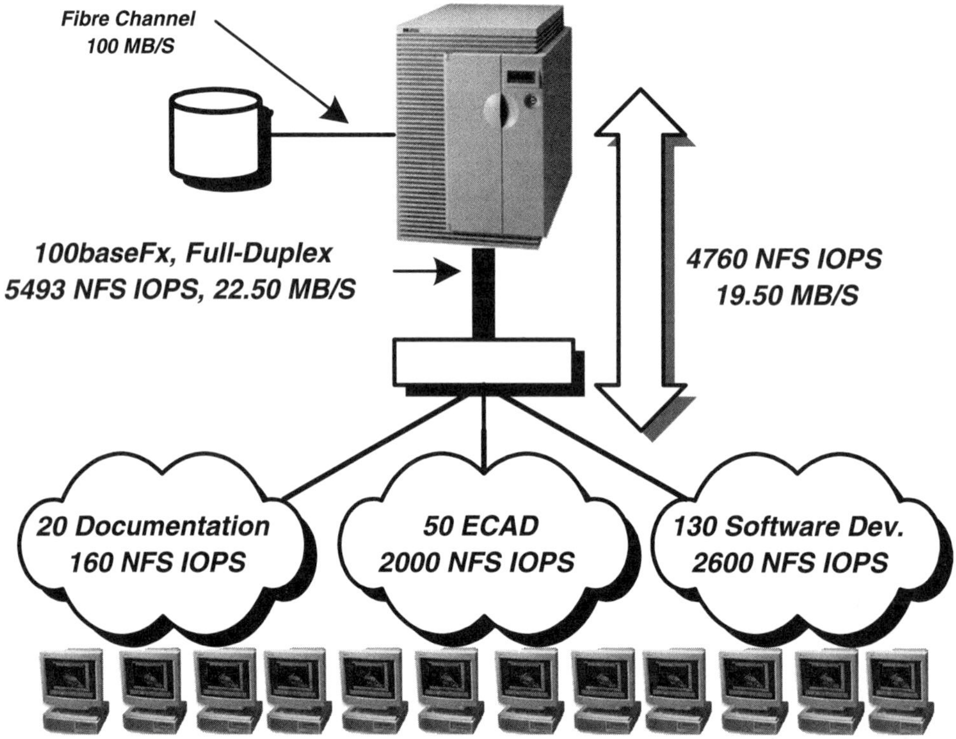

Figure B-1 Workgroup NFS Dataflow Example

lutionary creatures created by imperfect situations and representing opportunities for drastic improvement.

B.6 Why Does My NFS Server Only Support Half of My Clients?

The configuration in this example was encountered at a major manufacturing customer, who was perplexed as to why his NFS server was only handling half of the load that he expected. This situation was mentioned as a side topic during a seminar on NFS performance. I followed the steps previously outlined, asking questions about the client systems, measured NFS IOP rates, network configuration, and finally the server configuration. I drew a picture, similar to Figure B-2, complete with notes.

Let's start at the bottom of the diagram. Six hundred client systems and a measured rate of 10 NFS IOPS per client at peak usage. Dedicated ports for each client on FDDI to Ethernet bridges (10 Mb/S per port, 270 NFS IOPS per port), made by a reputable networking company. No obvious problems yet.

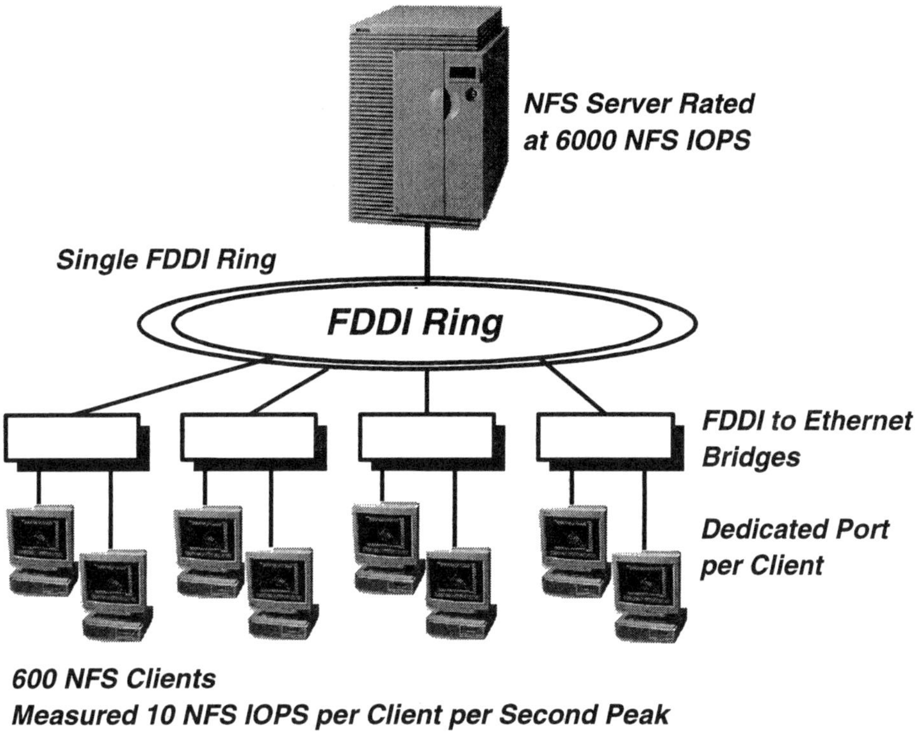

Figure B-2 Why Doesn't My NFS Server Support All of My Clients?

The interconnection between the FDDI to Ethernet bridges and the server is a single FDDI ring. Let's repeat the maximum throughput calculation for FDDI:

$$\text{Maximum NFS IOPS} = \frac{100\text{ Mb}}{S} \times \frac{1\text{ byte}}{8\text{ bits}} \times \frac{1\text{ NFS IOP}}{4096\text{ bytes}} = 3051\text{ NFS IOPS}$$

Theoretically, our calculation shows that the FDDI ring is only capable of handling one half of the expected peak throughput from the client systems. This whole exercise took about fifteen minutes worth of discussion.

The NFS performance issues had been ongoing for about four months when this customer asked his NFS server vendor to help him with the problem[1]. The proposed solution was to add another NFS file server to the FDDI ring. Do I need to tell you that this did not solve the problems?

Let's tally up the costs involved, at least the obvious ones. First of all, is the lost productivity of three hundred engineers. Add to that another (superfluous) NFS server identical to the first. What was really needed was a second FDDI interface in the first server, as our simple calculation shows.

B.7 An Example for a Large Environment

The basic requirements for this NFS server analysis come from a customer question that was received in a request for proposal (RFP) involving a large software development environment. We will use the request as the basis for making some calculations about the required server size. To paraphrase the RFP:

> **What is the largest number of users that can be successfully supported by an NFS server? Assume that ten to twenty percent of the users have workstations and the others are accessing the server from a PC, X-station, or character-based terminal. This question applies to a computing environment that will have approximately five thousand users. We want to minimize the number of servers to reduce system administration costs.**

This may not seem like a lot of information to go on, but it is frequently left up to the hardware vendor to specify a complete solution on sketchy details[2]. We do not have space for a complete response (the original was over three hundred pages), but we can sketch in the details of the analysis process.

B.7.1 Where Do We Start?

All we have to work with from the request is the expected number of clients in the environment and a rough idea that there will be three client classes involved: X-station (or equivalent thin client), PC workstations, and Unix workstations. Initially, we need to determine three things: client load numbers, required LAN capacity, and required server capacity.

An unstated requirement is the need for NFS as the primary data-sharing mechanism. We can infer this from the request for ten to twenty percent Unix workstation clients and the need for file serving and configuration management scalability for up to five thousand users. It is still the case that Unix servers are more stable and scalable and provide more high-availability features than their Windows NT counterparts. Let's start with the client characterization.

1. The server vendor involved in this example exercise will remain nameless, but it was not my employer, Hewlett-Packard.

2. This is why RFP processes should include question-and-answer cycles.

B.7.2 Client NFS Characterization

We should start by determining the current client NFS loads. As a matter of fact, we should perform an environmental assessment on the customer's existing workgroup (see Appendix C). If we cannot measure existing client loads, then we need to fall back on some "standard" values such as those in Table B-3.

Using those numbers for the three classes of client systems yields the values shown in the following table.

Table B-4 Design Values for NFS Traffic

Client Class	*Average NFS IOPS*	*Design Value*
Unix Workstation	15-24	24 IOPS
PC Workstation	0.5-10	10 IOPS
X-station or Thin Client	15-24	24 IOPS

For safety's sake, we will choose the highest values for each class, with the exceptions of software builds. We will need to ensure that we can handle the extra load that a full build can generate. Any numbers that we use in our assumptions need to be stated and later verified against our customer's expectations.

B.7.3 NFS Loading Calculations

The first step is to start by assuming infinite LAN capacity and calculating the total number of required NFS IOPS. For the Unix workstation clients, the calculations are:

$$\text{20\% of 5000 Clients} = \text{1000 Clients} \times \frac{\text{24 NFS IOPS}}{\text{1 Client}} = \text{24,000 NFS IOPS}$$

For the remaining clients, we will assume a fifty percent mixture of each remaining type. The X-stations will require Unix login servers for desktop support and will generate the equivalent load of a Unix workstation for each user. The calculations for the X-station per-seat NFS loading follow:

$$\text{40\% of 5000 Clients} = \text{2000 clients} \times \frac{\text{24 NFS IOPS}}{\text{1 client}} = \text{48,000 NFS IOPS}$$

Finally, the PC workstations will generate the following load:

$$40\% \text{ of } 5000 \text{ Clients } = 2000 \text{ clients} \times \frac{10 \text{ NFS IOPS}}{1 \text{ client}} = 20{,}000 \text{ NFS IOPS}$$

Our calculations give us a grand total of 92,000 NFS IOPS for all five thousand clients. We should realize that this is a peak number of NFS IOPS; the day-to-day average may be less. This is where having realistic measurements of an existing environment can really help. Without realistic measurements, we must overconfigure the network and hardware to make absolutely sure that performance requirements are met.

B.7.4 How Many NFS Servers?

We now have an idea of the magnitude of the requirements for the NFS portion of this environment. Using the NFS IOP "magic number" of 4 kilobytes per NFS IOP, we can arrive at a total figure for the total workgroup data flow. A data flow of 92,000 NFS IOPS represents 359.4 Megabytes per second! Hewlett-Packard's 16-way SMP V-2500, configured as a NFS server[3], can deliver approximately 50,000 NFS IOPS, which means that at least two are required to meet the performance requirements.

But the NFS servers are single points of failure. How are we to deal with the possible failure of one or both NFS servers? To provide complete redundancy, we need a total of four servers. We will configure the four servers in a high-availability cluster, with two performing NFS server activity and the other two being used as compute server resources. In the event of a failure with one of the NFS servers, an NFS service package can migrate from one of the primary servers to one of the backup servers. If we make the assumption that only a single server will fail at one time, we could squeak by with three servers in the cluster[4].

B.7.5 NFS Server Network Data Flow

Both of the active servers must be able to deliver 50,000 NFS IOPS through the network, which is a total of 204.80 Megabytes per second, and the secondary servers must be equally configured. To choose the proper network technology, we can check with the information in Table 7-2 for maximum throughput for a particular network technology.

3. At the release of this book in spring of 1999.

4. Because Hewlett-Packard's MC/ServiceGuard clustering product allows "hot" standby hardware, the secondary server or servers may be used for other purposes until a failure occurs. We would choose to use the compute power as compilation or testing engines for the workgroup clients, or to run combinations of other workgroup services.

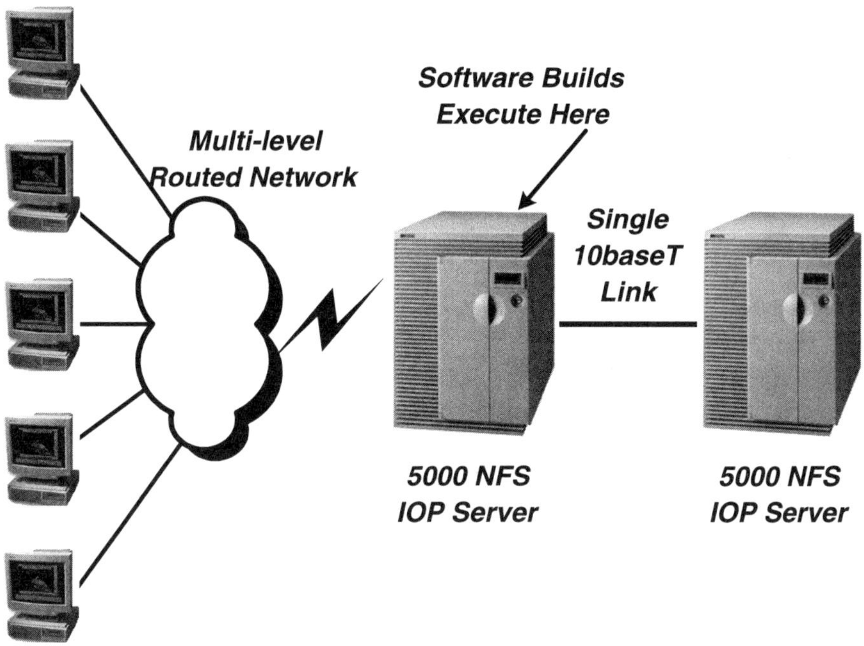

Figure B-3 "Houston, We Have a Problem"

Based on the information in that table, the servers each must have two Gigabit Ethernet interfaces to support the desired data rate. If we add a third interface, we will have additional redundancy. To eliminate single points of failure, we should multihome the servers to a second network switch, which means adding three more interfaces per server, for a total of six. Because each V-2500 has twenty-four I/O slots, we still have plenty of connectivity for storage devices.

B.8 "Houston, We Have a Problem"

Our second example involves a call for help from a customer who had just purchased a new NFS server for use in his software development environment. This NFS server was added in response to an "emergency" situation requiring more storage for the build process, and so was added in a rather hasty manner without our involvement.

Following the previously described procedure, the configuration shown in Figure B-3 came to light. There were a number of obvious problems with this design—you should be able to spot at least two immediate problems. Let's look at them.

First, the single 10baseT link between the first server and the second server is only able to sustain two hundred and seventy NFS IOPS, maximum. The second NFS server's performance will be limited to this value. It took only a cursory glance to notice this problem.

Second, the path to the second file server is through the first, effectively using it as a router. Computer systems performing TCP/IP forwarding are not good substitutes for network

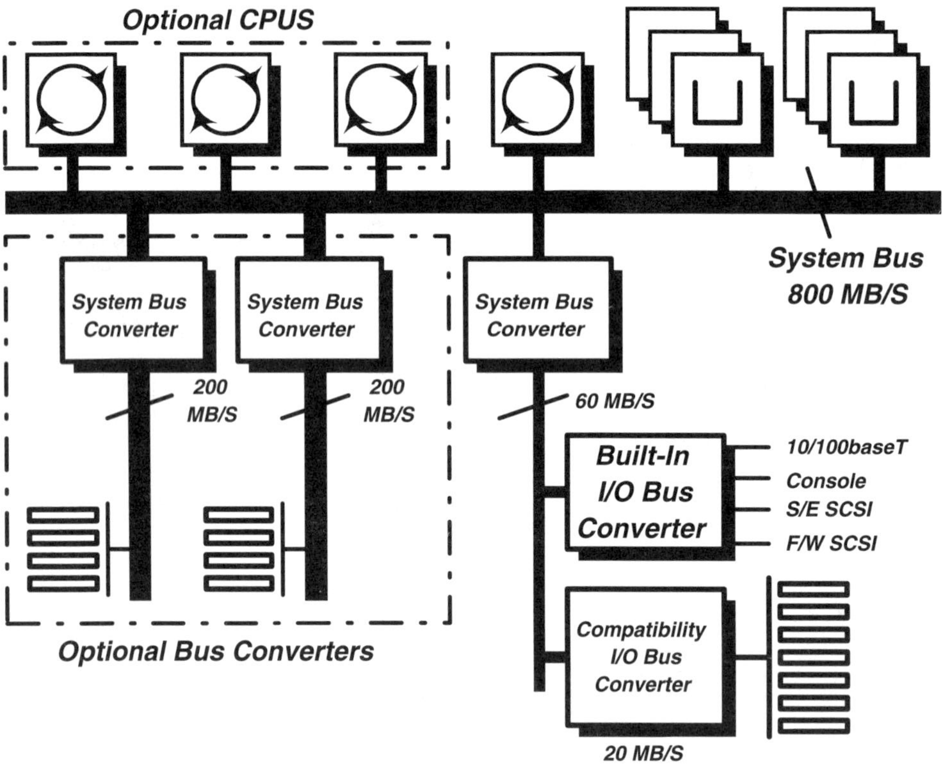

Figure B-4 File Server Block Diagram

equipment like routers and switches that are optimized for the tasks. The software builds taking place on the first server not only slow down its NFS response to its clients, but will also slow down the TCP/IP forwarding to the second server. This is a good example of how a bad situation can be made even worse.

The last recommendation that I would have for this configuration is to replace the network "cloud", which has multiple subnets and routers with an Ethernet switch. This can remove a lot of the latency between the NFS servers and the client systems. The major improvement in performance, however, would come from correcting the first two problems that we noted.

B.9 Think Inside the Box

For our last example, we will use a fictitious file server hardware configuration to apply the data flow analysis technique to the internal bus and I/O structure. It is perfectly possible that everything "on the network side" of the server is properly configured and able to handle the data flow rates required for client NFS demands, but the internal workings of the server or the storage

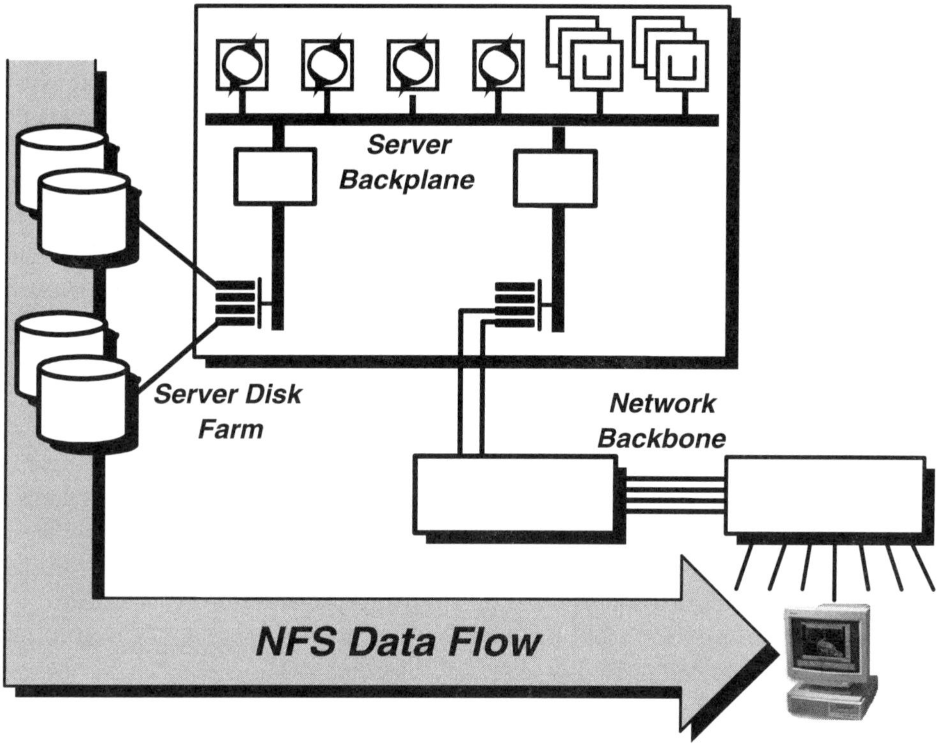

Figure B-5 Components of the NFS Data Flow Chain

configuration is the limiting factor. Situations like this can happen, even if the file server configuration has a high NFS IOP rating in the SPEC benchmarks, if attention is not paid to how the benchmark system was configured[5].

The file server hardware shown in Figure B-4 has several configuration characteristics that are typical of servers from today's hardware vendors. The base configuration, without the optional I/O subsystems and CPUs, has built-in hardware to support the system console, an autosensing 10/100baseT LAN connection, F/W SCSI internal system disk drives, and S/E SCSI for tape backup. Additionally, there are expansion slots for "compatibility" interfaces to legacy hardware. The base system may be intended as a low price/performance point and not the best performing configuration.

The base configuration may be scaled up by adding more CPUs, additional RAM, and optional high-speed I/O converters. The system bus is fast enough to sustain all I/O bus convert-

5. Part of the SPEC benchmark reporting requirements is the complete hardware and software configuration of the server under test. This information is often instructive.

ers as well as CPU to RAM and CPU to CPU (cache coherency) traffic. Some vendors will specify the peak data rates for the bus and I/O converters, so it is important to look at both the peak and the sustained transfer rates for these items.

One of the first tendencies for someone who is buying a new server is to conserve cost by using the compatibility or low-speed expansion slots that come "standard" with the system. In this example, there are two issues with using those slots for disk or network interfaces. First, the total sustained data transfer rate for the compatibility slots is 20 MB/S. Second, there are two bus converters in the data path between the system CPU, RAM, and the I/O card slots.

At best, the compatibility slots could provide approximately four thousand eight hundred and eighty-two NFS IOPS worth of I/O, if they were completely unhindered. In reality, there will be contention for the bus converter data path between the internal disk drives with the OS on them, tape drives during backup, and other traffic destined for the built-in hardware. Arbitration for use of the bus between multiple converters will slow down the overall throughput—how much depends on the characteristics of the bus and the design of the converters themselves.

Also, the total throughput of 20 MB/S must be divided up between as many as seven I/O cards, leaving approximately 3 MB/S for each card. Therefore, the actual number of cards that may be used is limited, since a single F/W SCSI card could use the entire bandwidth of the converter. It is a false sense of economy to use the built-in I/O for file server operation—we should strongly consider adding one or more of the optional bus converters for I/O connections.

The optional bus converters can provide as much as 50 MB/S for each slot, if all four slots are occupied. Remember that some disk interfaces, like fibre channel, can theoretically use as much as 100 to 200 MB/S. At that rate there is bandwidth enough for only two interface cards per bus converter. Networking is also a consideration—now would be a good time for you to review Table B-2 to compare possible network data rates against the available bandwidth for this configuration.

B.10 NFS Data Flow Analysis Summary

As good as the data flow analysis technique is, we must be careful not to extend it too far. Better estimations of data flows based on information collected from network performance and analysis tools will yield more realistic results than our crude NFS "magic number". This is yet another reason to strongly recommend network performance–monitoring tools for your workgroup environments.

One of the things that makes data flow analysis possible for NFS is the existence of standardized industry benchmarks like SPEC_SFS1 and a good understanding of the NFS internal workings. While data flow analysis may be applied to other protocols and data-sharing methodologies, it is made more difficult by closed systems, nonstandard measurement techniques, or new technologies that lack the necessary experience base. In such difficult cases, it is possible to reverse engineer the information needed for data flow analysis from network performance information.

Data flow analysis is a useful technique for locating potential bottlenecks in the complete workgroup data flow chain. While our examples concentrated on NFS as the primary traffic in the network, this type of analysis can be applied to other types of data-sharing traffic as well. The utility of this approach has been proven time and time again in real-world environments.

APPENDIX C

Workgroup Environmental-Assessment Methodology

For existing workgroup environments that are to migrate to new technology or structures, there must be a way to uncover the current operating state to prevent the loss of essential services. The evolutionary nature and complexity of computer environments means that today's workgroup is almost certainly different from its initial designer's intent and that new uses of the functions and services exist that are unknown to even the administrators of the workgroup. An environmental assessment is one possible method of uncovering all aspects of the workgroup environment.

This section covers the process used for environmental assessments, which, when coupled with the five-step model for change described in Appendix A, can help chart a course for implementing desired changes. The environmental-assessment process determines the baseline configuration of the workgroup environment, from which decisions about potential changes and impacts may be made. Without understanding where you are, it may be very difficult to move forward without creating chaos.

C.1 Extending the Workgroup Functional Model

We first introduced the five-layer functional model for a workgroup in Chapter 5. This model is intended to help us place some structure on a complex environment that comprises the physical portions of the workgroup. Because an environmental assessment should include all aspects of the workgroup environment, including people and their processes, we will add information to the original diagram, as shown in Figure C-1.

Within the workgroup pyramid, you will notice the familiar five layers; outside of the pyramid, we have added associations between "People", "Process", and the individual layers of the

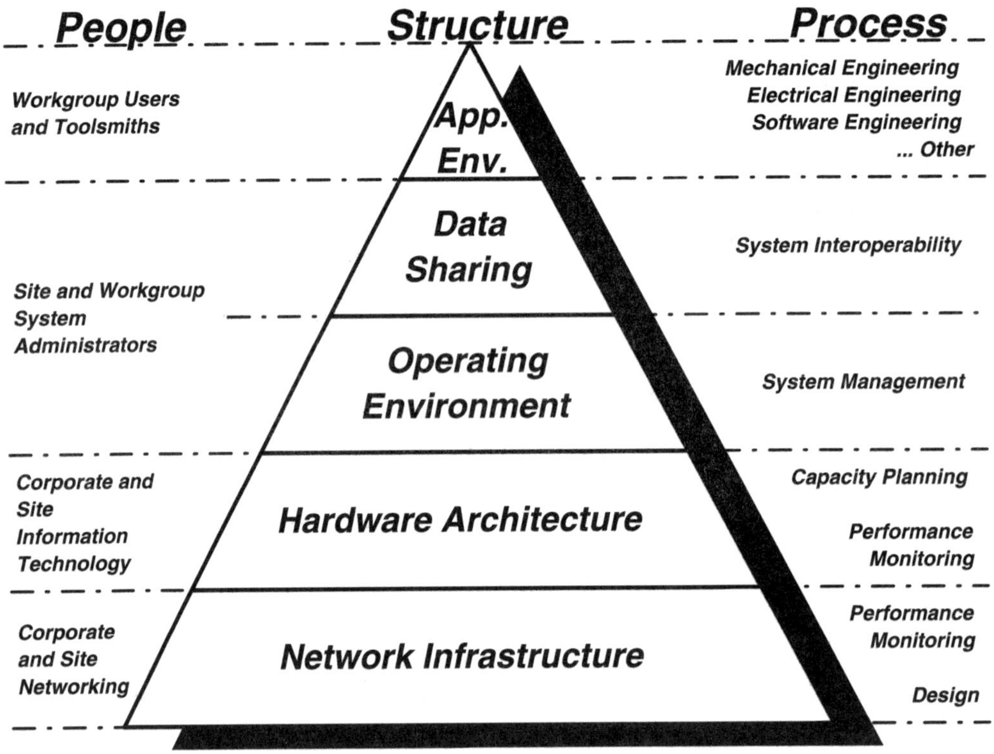

Figure C-1 A Modified Five-Layer Workgroup Model

model. It is important to note that not all locations, sometimes even within the same company, will have the same associations, particularly with regards to the people responsible for portions of the environment. This also holds true for the "Process" side of the pyramid.

C.2 People and Responsibilities

At some companies, there is a corporate-wide responsibility for networking design, installation, and support. Other companies have a global networking strategy but delegate details to each individual division or organization. Still others have an "every man for himself" approach, where it is difficult to locate any overarching goals or strategies. Because every environment is different, hard and fast divisions of responsibility, like those shown in Figure C-1 need to be taken as guidelines.

It is the job of the assessment process to uncover the actual grass-roots approach to the processes and responsibilities in the environment being examined. My experience has been that the reality of the environment almost never matches the formal definitions or expectations of its owners. Often this is because the formal organization, as it is defined, cannot meet the user's needs, so an "informal" organization forms. It is very dangerous to attempt a migration or change in such a circumstance, without totally understanding the adaptations that have taken place.

As with other aspects of the workgroup environment, the networking layer responsibilities may be divided into a hierarchy. It is easiest to understand the structure if the hierarchy is divided into LAN and WAN components. When this is the case we can concentrate mainly on the LAN portion of the workgroup network and only the interfaces to the WAN portion. Where there is a mixture of responsibilities, the assessment process becomes more difficult because there are more people involved.

The responsibility for hardware also varies greatly; sometimes corporate IT is responsible for all hardware. Other times, the organization using the workgroup is responsible for client systems, and there is a site engineering IT group that manages servers and workcenter resources. Frequently, there is an organizational wall between corporate IT and engineering IT groups, with duplication of staff and other resources.

The operating environment can be the most complex portion of the workgroup to assess. It consists of operating system management, release, and upgrade control, software installation, essentially the management of the entire software base that runs on the underlying virtual computer. There is usually a fairly large staff and, if the environment is complex, many specialists in different areas of the environment.

Who controls the system administration resources also varies from company to company and environment to environment. Sometimes the system administrators report to site or corporate IT. Other times they report to the users of the workgroup, and not infrequently a good portion of the system administration staff *are* the users of the workgroup. The more complex the system administration organization is, the more difficult the assessment.

Finally, at the top of the "food chain" is the actual user of the workgroup resources. The ideal situation occurs when the users may focus on their primary job tasks without worrying about system administration, performance issues, or other distractions. In many environments, however, the users are at least partly responsible for managing their own systems, either formally or informally. In this case, the user may be viewed as belonging to both the user community and the system-administration community.

C.3 Process and Action

On the process side of the pyramid in Figure C-1 are some possible sets of processes associated with the people and structure portions of the model. In many respects, identifying processes in the environment is one of the most difficult tasks. This is especially true if the associated organizational structures are intertwined.

A process is the basis for repeatable action, whether the action is manual or automatic. Most analytical types such as engineers, system administrators, and book authors seem to have an ingrained dislike for the "P" word. Possibly this is due to our perception of processes as the embodiment of inflexibility, lack of creativity, and unthinking authority. But this is not how a real process should be.

Without realizing it, we all create processes, write them down in our notebooks (or short-term memory) and implement them to save ourselves time. We modify them, when circumstances warrant, to fit the changes in our approach to problems—to do otherwise would be to propagate erroneous actions. Some organizations have global processes and others rely on the processes that each individual develops for themselves. The more "individualized" an environment is with regard to process, the more difficult it is to uncover the actual processes and services that are being used.

This is not to say that organizations with formal processes are easy to assess, either. What is written down and what is actually implemented and used are often two different things. Frequently the written process is a "dead" document, written only to satisfy a requirement on someone's list.

It is the assessment's job to uncover the reality of the process landscape. There have been a few recipients of the final environmental-assessment report that have seen vastly different results than they expected. More than a few are surprised at the amount of unrecognized activities that take place in their environment.

C.4 The Environmental-Assessment Methodology

Now that we have discussed the additions to the five-layer model and some of the different results that we might encounter, it is time to study the assessment process itself. For each layer of the model, we will:

- Interview a representative cross section of the people associated with the particular layer in the structure
- Sort the raw interview responses into groupings corresponding the five-layer model
- Look for dependencies or common threads between the information from the current level and other layers
- Look for dependencies or common threads between the people, process, and structure portions of the model
- Seek confirming information about the interview data from the environmental measurements
- Draft a the final environment-assessment report

The assessment process is fairly simple, even though it has six steps. The majority of the work, and skill, consists of crafting the proper questions and following them until they are logically exhausted[1]. Performing assessments of this type takes a broad and deep base of knowledge about the components of the environment being assessed.

1. This can often lead the interviewer to *physical* exhaustion, as well.

1. The interviews must be conducted in a professional and nonpolitical way. A key component of this is never divulging the source of the information. The fear of adverse consequences will prevent accurate information if the sources are not kept anonymous. Locating the "representative cross section" of people for the interviews can be one of the more challenging tasks in a complex organization.
2. Sorting the data and locating dependencies can begin immediately after the first interviews are finished. Sometimes the sorting criteria must be modified, or the data must be duplicated in multiple sections associated with the layers. Dependencies or common sets of observations may not begin to appear until after multiple interviews are completed. After each interview, all information must be reexamined, looking for any dependencies between the structural layers or across the three areas of People, Structure, and Process.
3. Seeking confirming information is an important part of the process. Confirmation may come from measurements performed in the environment based on interview information or from additional questions which are added to the interview process based on suspected issues. It is important to have multiple sources of confirmation for information, especially where political motivations for particular answers are suspected.
4. Drafting the final environmental-assessment report is the final step in the process. A good structure for the final assessment report follows the five-layer assessment model. I prefer to have six sections: observations, analysis, conclusions, recommendations, a prioritized task list, and appendix containing the sorted raw data—each of which has a section for one of the five levels in the pyramid model. The raw data, as noted above, should have the names of any sources removed for the final report.

One final question about the assessment process needs to be answered: "What is the basis for comparison for the environment being assessed?" As with the interview step in the process, the experience level of the person or team doing the assessment is the most important aspect. Industry standard solutions, good tricks learned, and best practices all play a role in the comparison. The more experienced the assessors, the better the assessment.

C.5 Environmental-Assessment Summary

The results of an environmental assessment form the baseline for implementing changes in the workgroup being assessed. This is the "Point A" portion of the simple change management model presented in Appendix A. Once the assessment is finished and a vision of the new environment is crafted, we can produce a task list and implementation plan to actually effect the change.

The environmental assessment, if rigorously performed, can help an organization implement the change it desires. Between the beginning of the assessment and the final report, there is a lot of repetitive, challenging work to be done. Based on past results, the rewards from the process are well worth the time and effort expended.

APPENDIX D

Workgroup Design Icons

The complete set of design icons that were used in this book are shown in Table D-1. A brief explanation of their application is given.

Table D-1 Workgroup Design Icons

Icon Description	***Recommended Icon Usage***
Web Service	Web server, web browser
High Availability	Wherever resources are associated with extra reliability
Measurement	Point on a system or network where measurement data is taken
Load Balancing	Identifies systems or applications providing load-balancing resources
Encryption or Security	Represents application or system component that provides high security or encryption
Installation	System image installation server or software install depot
Graphics	High-performance graphics device
Compute	Compute intensive resource, CPU
RAM or Memory	Memory-base storage or cache

(continued)

Table D-1 Workgroup Design Icons *(cont.)*

Icon Description	*Recommended Icon Usage*
Directory or Look-up	Directory service, such as DNS or NIS, that provides data in response to keyed query
Time	Time synchronization server, such as NTP or DTS
Authentication	System providing user authentication services
Network Attached Storage	Network accessible storage, like NFS or SMB
Network Storage Translator	Network accessible storage, translating a physical or NAS storage mechanism to another dialect or protocol
Disk Storage or Database	Physical storage in a local disk, file system, or database
Object	An entity in a network, system, workgroup, or other level of the network heirarchy
Action	User desktop representation of an application
Management	System providing network or system administration services
Backup Services	Long-term off-line storage of workgroup data
Hierarchical Storage Management	Short term near-line storage of workgroup data
Proxy Services	Service intermediaries like web proxy and SOCKS
Firewall Services	Security protection for "open" subnets that connect to the Internet
Print Services	Central locations for share printing resources, including print spools
E-mail Services	Central locations for e-mail resources, including delivery and transport agents

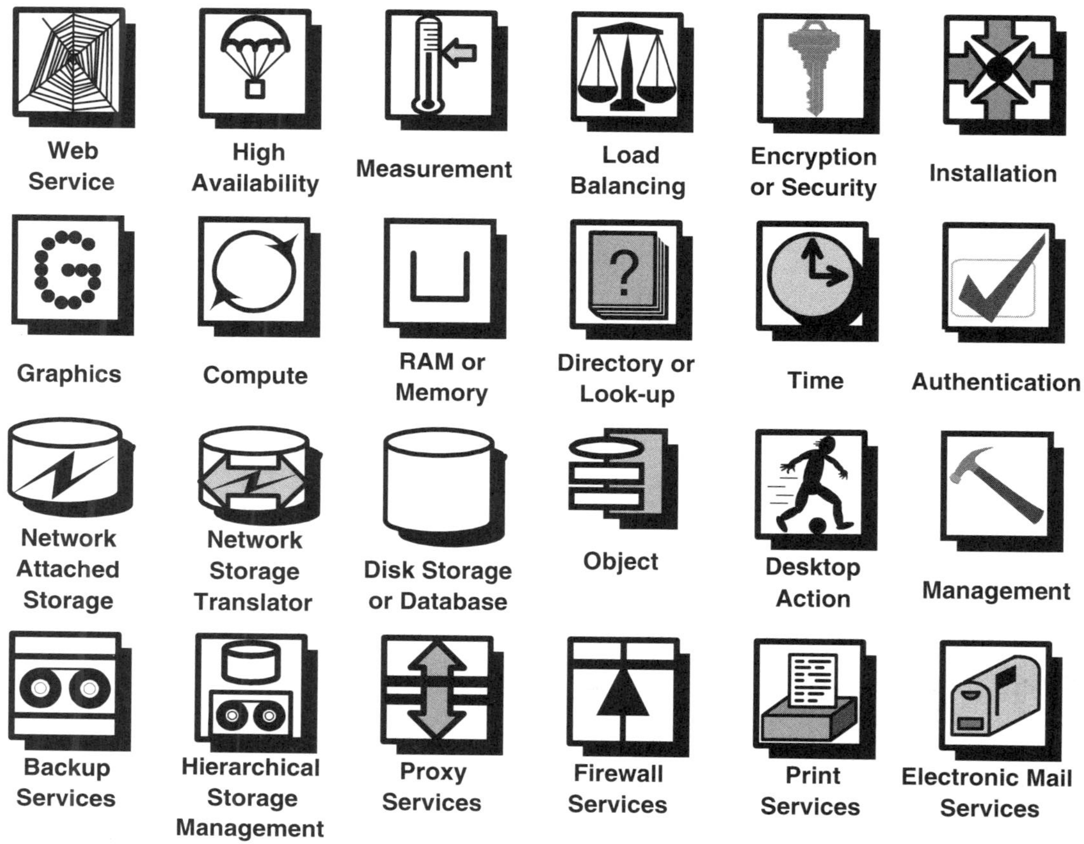

Figure D-1 Workgroup Design Icons

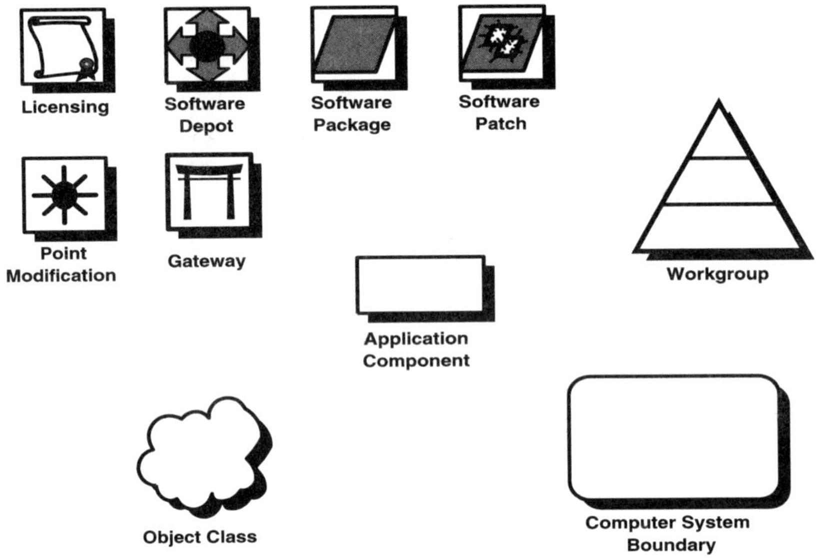

Figure D-2 More Workgroup Design Icons

The icons in Table D-2 are shown in Figure D-2.

Table D-2 High-Level Workgroup Design Icons

Icon Description	***Recommended Icon Usage***
Computer System Boundary	A container for holding other objects or icons, represents a physical system
Application Component	A uniquely identifiable portion of a client-server application
Workgroup	A collection of systems, following the 3TCS model, that share common data, system administration, and security processes
Class	A group or collection of objects that share common traits, a template for actual object characteristics
Licensing	System providing licensing services
Software Depot	Storage for software to be installed
Software Package	A software unit of installation

(continued)

Table D-2 High-Level Workgroup Design Icons *(cont.)*

Icon Description	***Recommended Icon Usage***
Software Patch	An upgrade or emergency modification to a software unit
Point Modification	Identifies modification point in a process
Gateway	Identifies a location where a translation takes place

Acronyms and Abbreviations

3TCS	Three-Tier Client Server
4GL	Fourth-Generation Language
ACL	Access Control List
API	Application Programming Interface
ASCII	American Standard Code for Information Interchange
ASIC	Application Specific Integrated Circuit
ASU	Advanced Server for Unix
ATM	Asynchronous Transfer Mode
BDC	Backup Domain Controller
BIND	Berkeley Internet Name Daemon
BIOS	Basic Input-Output System
BOOTP	Boot Protocol
BSD	Berkeley Software Distribution
ccNUMA	Cache Coherent Nonuniform Memory Access
CAN	Compute Area Network
CDE	Common Desktop Environment
CD-ROM	Compact Disk Read-Only Memory
CDS	Cell Directory Service
CGI	Common Gateway Interface
CIFS	Common Internet File System
CISC	Complex Instruction Set Computer

CORBA	Common Object Request Broker Architecture
COSE	Common Open Software Environment
CPS	Characters per Second
CPU	Central Processing Unit
CSC	Client Server Computing
CSMA/CD	Carrier Sense Multiple Access/Collision Detection
DAT	Digital Audio Tape
DCE	Distributed Computing Environment
DCOM	Distributed Component Object Model
DFS	Distributed File System
DHCP	Dynamic Host Configuration Protocol
DLT	Digital Linear Tape
DMI	Desktop Management Interface
DNS	Domain Name Service
DRAS	Dynamic Resource Allocation Service
DSS	DCE Security Service
DTMF	Desktop Management Forum
DTS	Distributed Time Server
EBCDIC	Extended Binary Coded Decimal Interchange Code
EDA	Electronic Design Automation
EPROM	Erasable Programmable Read-Only Memory
EEPROM	Electrically Erasable Programmable Read-Only Memory
EPIC	Explicitly Parallel Instruction Computer
FAT	File Access Table
FDDI	Fiber Distribution Data Interface
FIFO	First In First Out
FIPS	Federal Information Processing Standard
FLDB	Fileset Location Database
FLOP	Floating-point Operation
FSF	Free Software Foundation
FTP	File Transfer Protocol
GbE	Gigabit Ethernet
GDS	Global Directory Service
GID	Group Identifier
GUI	Graphical User Interface

HDLC	High-level Data Link Control
HFS	High-speed File System
HSM	Hierarchical Storage Management
HTML	Hypertext Markup Language
HTTP	Hypertext Transfer Protocol
IEEE	Institute of Electrical and Electronics Engineers
IOPS	Input/Output Operations per Second
ISP	Internet Service Provider
IT	Information Technology
IP	Internet Protocol
ISDN	Integrated Service Digital Network
JBOD	Just a Bunch of Disks
LAN	Local Area Network
LANE	Local Area Network Emulation
LCD	Liquid Crystal Display
LFS	Local File System
LUN	Logical Unit
MAC	Media Access Control
MDA	Mechanical Design Automation
MIMD	Multiple Instruction Multiple Data
MIPS	Million Instructions Per Second
MPI	Message Passing Interface
MTU	Maximum Transmission Unit
NAS	Network Attached Storage
NC	Network Computer
NCS	Network Computing System
NetBIOS	Network Basic Input-Output System
NFS	Network File System
NIS	Network Information System
NNTP	Net News Transfer Protocol
NTP	Network Time Protocol
ONC	Open Network Computing
OO	Object Oriented
OOA	Object-Oriented Analysis
OOD	Object-Oriented Design

OOP	Object-Oriented Programming
ORB	Object Request Broker
OSF	Open Software Foundation
OSI	Open System Interconnect
PDC	Primary Domain Controller
PDM	Product Data Management
POP	Post Office Protocol -or- Point of Presence
POSIX	Portable Operating System Interface
PPP	Point-to-Point Protocol
PPTP	Point-to-Point Tunneling Protocol
PVM	Parallel Virtual Machine
RAID	Redundant Array of Inexpensive Disks
RAM	Random Access Memory
RAS	Remote Access Service
RDBMS	Relational Database Management System
RISC	Reduced Instruction Set Computer
RPC	Remote Procedure Call
SAN	Storage Area Network
SA/SD	Structured Analysis/Structured Design
SCSI	Small Computer System Interface
SDLC	Synchronous Data Link Control
SID	Security Identifier
SIMD	Single Instruction Multiple Data
SLIP	Serial Line Internet Protocol
SNMP	Simple Network Management Protocol
SMB	Server Message Block
SMP	Symmetric Multiprocessing
SMS	Systems Management Server
SMTP	Simple Mail Transfer Protocol
SONET	Synchronous Optical Network
SPEC	System Performance Evaluation Committee
SPOF	Single Point of Failure
SQL	Structured Query Language
SVID	System Five Interface Definition
SVR4	System Five Release Four

TCP	Transmission Control Protocol
TGT	Ticket Granting Ticket
TTY	Teletype
UDP	User Datagram Protocol
UID	User Identifier
UNC	Universal Naming Convention
UUID	Universal Unique Identifier
UPS	Uninterruptable Power Supply
UTP	Unshielded Twisted Pair
VLAN	Virtual Local-Area Network
WAN	Wide-Area Network
WINS	Windows Internet Naming Service
XPG	X/Open Portability Guide

Bibliography

References

[1.] Booch, Grady. *Object-Oriented Analysis and Design with Applications.*
Menlo Park, CA: Addison-Wesley, 1994, ISBN 0-8053-5340-2.
This is quite probably the best text in existence about object-oriented programming, analysis, and design.

[2.] Graham, Ian. *Migrating to Object Technology.*
Menlo Park, CA: Addison-Wesley, 1994, ISBN 0-201-59389-0.
A good treatise on the elements of object technology in the information technology world.

[3.] Norman, Donald A. *The Psychology of Everyday Things.*
New York, NY: Basic Books, 1988, ISBN 0-465-06709-3.
This book should be required reading for every engineer who is designing human interfaces of any kind.

[4.] Blommers, John. *Practical Planning for Network Growth.*
Englewood Cliffs, NJ: Prentice Hall, 1996, ISBN 0-13-206111-2.
A great treatise on networking technology, measurement, and design.

[5.] Saunders, Stephen. *Gigabit Ethernet Handbook.*
New York, NY: McGraw-Hill, 1998, ISBN 0-07-057971-7.
A complete treatise on the Gigabit Ethernet technology in its many forms.

[6.] Humphrey, Watts S. *Managing the Software Process.*
Reading, MA: Addison-Wesley, 1990, ISBN 0-201-18095-2.
Great coverage of the complexities involved in software design and implementation.

[7.] Gamma, Erich et al. *Design Patterns: Elements of Reusable Object-Oriented Software.*
Reading, MA: Addison-Wesley, 1994, ISBN 0-201-63361-2.
Defines common patterns used to solve specific problems in object-oriented programming.

[8.] Stern, Hal. *Managing NFS and NIS.*
Sebastapol, CA: O'Reilly & Associates, 1992, ISBN 0-937175-75-7.
A great introduction to managing and using NIS and NFS.

[9.] Weygant, Peter S. *Clusters for High Availability.*
Upper Saddle River, NJ: Prentice-Hall PTR, 1996, ISBN 0-13-494758-4.
An introduction to the issues of high availability and design of Hewlett-Packard MC/ServiceGuard clusters.
Hewlett-Packard Part Number B3936-90007

[10.] Goralski, Walter J. *Introduction to ATM Networking.*
New York, NY: McGraw-Hill Inc., 1995, ISBN 0-07-024043-4.
A highly technical discussion of all aspects of ATM. Particularly useful because it describes other networking technologies and compares them to ATM.

[11.] *Microsoft Windows NT Technical Support.*
Redmond, WA: Microsoft Press, 1997, ISBN 1-57231-373-0.
Self-paced training for the Windows NT operating system.

[12.] Fernandez, Charles. *Configuring CDE: The Common Desktop Environment.*
Upper Saddle River, NJ: Prentice Hall PTR, 1996, ISBN 0-13-102724-7.
A complete guide to CDE and its configuration.

[13.] Glen Bruce and Rob Dempsey. *Security in Distributed Computing: Did You Lock The Door?*
Upper Saddle River, NJ: Prentice Hall PTR, 1997, ISBN 0-13-182908-4.
Provides a practical approach to security in distributed computing environments.

[14.] Albitz, Paul and Lui, Cricket. *DNS and BIND.*
Sebastopol, CA: O'Reilly & Associates, 1992, ISBN 1-56592-010-4.
A valuable treatise on the operation of DNS and the BIND daemon.

[15.] Wall, Larry , Christiansen, Tom, and Schwartz, Randal L. *Programming in Perl.*
Sebastapol, CA: O'Reilly and Associates, 1996, ISBN 1-56592-149-6.
A good introduction to the features and programming idioms of the Perl language.

[16.] Garfinkel, Simson and Spafford, Gene. *Practical Unix Security.*
Sebastapol, CA: O'Reilly & Associates, 1994, ISBN 0-937175-72-2.
Good coverage of Unix security issues, along with suggestions for dealing with them.

[17.] Yourdon, Ed. *Classics in Software Engineering,* edited by Ed Yourdon.
New York, NY: Yourdon Press, 1979.
Unfortunately, this book is now out of print. See *WWW.Yourdon.com.*

Index

A

B

C

D

E

L

M

N

O

P

R

S

T

U

V

W

X